Sanctiprize

*Focus beyond
what you can see!*

Dennis

Sanctiprize

DENNIS BANK

CREATION
HOUSE

SANCTIPRIZE by Dennis Bank
Published by Creation House Books
A Charisma Media Company
600 Rinehart Road
Lake Mary, Florida 32746
www.charismamedia.com

All Scripture quotations are from the Authorized King James Version of the Bible.

Hebrew and Greek definitions are from the *Strong's Exhaustive Concordance: Blue Letter Bible*.

Additional definitions are from: *New Webster Encyclopedic Dictionary of the English Language*; *New Oxford Dictionary of English*; *Strong's Exhaustive Concordance*; and *Vine's Concise Dictionary*.

Word study sources include: *The Complete Word Study New Testament, KJV*; *The Complete Word Study Old Testament, KJV*; *Thayer's Lexicon: Blue Letter Bible*; and *Vine's Expository Dictionary of New Testament Words: Blue Letter Bible*.

In some cases, names have been changed to preserve the privacy of the individual described, or the description is a composite character based on multiple individuals.

Design Director: Bill Johnson
Cover design by Nathan Morgan

Visit the author's website: www.sanctiprize.com

Library of Congress Control Number: 2010940909
International Standard Book Number: 978-1-61638-441-8

First Edition

11 12 13 14 15 — 9 8 7 6 5 4 3 2 1
Printed in Canada

ABOUT THE TITLE

Sanctiprize is a composite of two words, *sanctification* and *prize*. *Sanctification* means to be fully restored to the person we were originally created to be by the King of kings. *Prize* is something deemed highly valuable recovered from the enemy by war. *Sanctiprize* therefore is the King of king's mission to recover you from the captivity of the god of this world and restore your heritage as a King's kid of living throughout eternity being holy, without blame, and empowered by the Father's love. This is the essence of the gospel of Christ and His salvation.

Important Notice to Readers of *Sanctiprize*

According to feedback from those who have read this work so far, they all report they experienced considerable resistance from the kingdom of this world as they tried to concentrate on their reading and apply the personal ministry located later in *Sanctiprize*.

So this is what I want you to say or rather command before you even start to read and repeat this as often as you need thereafter. This is not a prayer, as you are speaking directly into the kingdom of this world so no need to close your eyes. What I'm asking you to do now will be explained in full as you proceed through this book. But you need to do this now in order even to get that far.

> *In the name of Jesus Christ of Nazareth I command the spirit of slumber, of confusion, of the wandering mind, of spiritual pride, of rebellion, of distractions, and of enmity to loose me and depart from me now. I am a son/daughter of the most high God and furthermore I get to appropriate the blood Jesus shed on my behalf to overcome you Satan and you must not torment, distract, confuse, or tempt me, so get behind me now. I declare my allegiance only to my Father in heaven and His Son Jesus Christ through the Holy Spirit, amen.*

You may also choose to use the entire chapter of Psalm 91 as your declaration against the devil. I would suggest you rewrite it out in full in your journal and personalizing it and then use the scripture as your prayer.

CONTENTS

DEDICATION

For my thoughts are not your thoughts, neither are your ways my ways, saith the Lord. For as the heavens are higher than the earth, so are my ways higher than your ways, and my thoughts than your thoughts. For as the rain cometh down, and the snow from heaven, and returneth not thither, but watereth the earth, and maketh it bring forth and bud, that it may give seed to the sower, and bread to the eater: So shall my word be that goeth forth out of my mouth: it shall not return unto me void, but it shall accomplish that which I please, and it shall prosper in the thing whereto I sent it. For ye shall go out with joy, and be led forth with peace: the mountains and the hills shall break forth before you into singing, and all the trees of the field shall clap their hands. Instead of the thorn shall come up the fir tree, and instead of the brier shall come up the myrtle tree: and it shall be to the Lord for a name, for an everlasting sign that shall not be cut off.

—Isaiah 55:8–13

PREFACE
The Journey

NAIVE AND TWENTY-THREE years of age, I sat at the table in an interrogation room at the Royal Canadian Mounted Police (RCMP) detachment at my posting in west central Alberta. I was a young constable given the assignment to investigate an incest complaint involving a stepdad and his stepdaughters. The alleged perpetrator sat rigidly with arms crossed at the end of the old table. I was doing my best to recall my training and how to put my feelings and presumptions aside in order to obtain an accurate statement from this guy. A lot was at stake here as we had little evidence to go on. So in order to lay a charge, it was necessary to get an admission in a written statement from the offender himself.

This would be the first of many such investigations over the next few years. The work was as dark as the lid of the pit of hell would be opened up day after day after day. As a Christian I knew the offenders of these serious sex crimes were created by God and loved by Him, and I despaired at the serious situation these families faced. I spoke of the difficulties with my wise pastor. He said, "Dennis you must love the person no matter what he did, no matter how horrific the crime, but it is OK to hate the sin. You must separate the person from the sin so you can still love him."

"Well," I thought, "I don't have much love on my own for these people; but maybe if I pray before each interrogation, God will give me a measure of love. Let's see what happens."

Before long I was back in the small cinder block interrogation room with another suspect regarding a series of sexual offenses against members of his own family. I looked at him across the table and silently asked the Lord to give me His love for this dad so I could separate him from what he had done. Immediately my disdain was gone, and I knew he could sense it. Before long he disclosed the entire string of offenses. I remember him saying, "I can't believe I am telling you all this." I believe once he felt the disdain of the police officer go and felt a genuine concern for him take the place of disdain, the wall of protectionism fell down.

> You must love the person no matter what he did, no matter how horrific the crime, but it is OK to hate the sin.

Then the most difficult of cases would be given to me—the perpetrator was a peace officer as well. The investigation began with the victim and non-offending family members early in the morning. The remainder of the day and early evening was spent conducting the preliminary groundwork. I located the suspect around 11:00 p.m., arrested him, and brought him to the notorious interrogation room. I talked to him for hours and got absolutely nowhere. I was exhausted, having now worked twenty-two hours straight on this intense case. I knew if I didn't get full disclosure from him, he would walk away a free man, as I had no physical evidence to charge him. A few minutes after 5:00 a.m. my bag of tricks was depleted, but I finally remembered to pray. There was a seven-minute silence in the room, which by now had become very smelly and uncomfortable. During that seven-minute "eternity," I prayed that God would give me His love for this man and give me wisdom, as I was spent. My prayer was interrupted by the man's statement: "Everything you have said about me is true!" He went on to give a complete disclosure, and he then pleaded guilty in court to keep his family from having to testify.

Some months later I ran into this fellow and his wife. He grabbed my hand and shook it saying, "Thank you, what you have done for me is the greatest thing anyone has ever done for me." Surprised, I replied, "I think we need to talk." I took them over to a local diner for coffee. I said, "You need to know what happened in that interview room. It isn't me you want to thank but rather the God who loves you intervened and softened your heart." His family was now in the restoration process, and he was relieved of the shame and darkness he had lived with for so many years—all because he was touched by the love of the Father.

Over the next few years many more such cases were conducted with all but one ending in a full written confession followed by a guilty plea in court. Somehow CBC television got wind of what was going on and came to interview me for a film they were producing. It would become a training video on sexual assault and incest for police and probation officers, social workers, mental health practitioners, and lawyers. In the end, the only statement of mine that wasn't edited out from the six-hour camera session said something about a

> It isn't me you want to thank but rather the God who loves you intervened and softened your heart.

policeman needing to learn to love an alleged perpetrator and separate him from his crime so that person might open up and confess his deepest, darkest secrets. I often wondered how my peers in the police force took this love thing.

This brief encounter of seeing the love of God move the mountains of resistance would soon come to an end, dropping me into a wilderness experience lasting over twenty years. Through that I would have to grow up, as I had much to learn. Shortly after the release of the video, a superior officer had me transferred to another posting. He took over my portfolio involving a sexual assault treatment program and the investigative work in the process. Whatever this senior officer's motives in this maneuver were really none of my concern, for I knew that God in His grace closed that door to save me from continued long-term exposure to such depravity and darkness. But what I learned in that interrogation room would become the foundation for the understanding of the love of our heavenly Father, even though it would be many years before I learned how it would apply to other areas of my life.

Shortly after resigning from the RCMP, I followed what I believed to be God's call to be a pastor. I relocated my family to go to seminary, but I soon dropped out as I found the intellectual pursuits of theology to be the lowest spiritual point of my life. The Bible was seldom opened. More heed was given to what others have said about the Bible, along with lengthy discussions on what was wrong with the Word of God or seeking answers to obscure questions that no one was asking. Even from my very limited understanding, I could see that the methods taught for church growth, church ministry, and church administration were often carnal and separated from what I read in my Bible. I got myself in trouble for refusing to take a computer quiz that would determine what my spiritual gifts were. In my rebellion I thought that the best place to find out what spiritual gifts I had would be from the Lord whom I was to be serving. The listing of the spiritual gifts on this computer quiz was abbreviated to reflect the gifts this seminary felt were still in use for today's church.

Now I was confused. What was the purpose of resigning from a good job with the RCMP to go into the work of ministry only to become disillusioned with the place that was to prepare me for my calling? With a family of three children to support, I took up residential painting and continued studying the Word through at least twelve hundred audiocassettes. They were from several Bible teachers who taught the entirety of the Bible—verse by verse and from cover to cover. One day I complained to the Lord, "You know I enjoyed police work a whole lot more; and it certainly was a lot more prestigious than coming home plastered in paint every day." Then the Lord reminded me that because of the repetitive nature of painting, I could listen to the Bible teaching uninterrupted every day while still being able to support my family. I had to repent of my nonsense.

The doors didn't seem to open for a church plant. I felt very strongly that unless I saw an obvious move of God preparing the way, I would wait. I knew that if I were to plant a church as the work of my flesh, I would always be maintaining it as the work of my flesh. So I pursued many business booms and busts, taking my poor beloved wife down a very unpredictable and unstable path. At one point, I thought I had arrived in the business world after receiving a nomination for "Entrepreneur of the Year" in an annual event sponsored by a large international accounting firm. Here is the irony: within one year of the nomination, my business was insolvent due to the loss of a large contract, forcing me into personal bankruptcy. I had always maintained that there was no way a business run on strong Christian principals should ever go bankrupt. I believed right up to the last moment that God would intervene through a miracle and my business would be saved, and I would return to prosperity. That never happened.

Sometime later I was reviewing a journal and found a note I had written about two and a half years earlier. It said, "Lord, if you deliver me from this business, I'll devote the rest of my life in the service to many!" Even with the success attained at the startup of this business, I felt out of place—like a Jonah who was resisting the call of God. I wanted out, but I guess I just hoped the landing would be a little softer. I would later learn that not only was I out of the will of God but I was so driven to succeed because of the fear of failure and poverty that my fear became my faith. So what I most greatly feared came upon me.

Shortly after the bankruptcy, my beloved wife left in a desperate attempt to get my attention. I thought of all things, my marriage was solid, even though we had our brainstorms from time to time. We dated once or twice a week and read every marriage book we could get our hands on. I think part of the problem was we had zeal for a great marriage but not according to godly wisdom. All we learned from the plethora of books was how to more intelligently find offense in each other, but we did not have the proper tools to deal with the root issues. We worked on our marriage, we communicated, we spent time together, and we worked stuff out as we went along the best we knew how; but the relationship was still in trouble.

> Not only was I out of the will of God but I was so driven to succeed because of the fear of failure and poverty that my fear became my faith. So what I most greatly feared came upon me.

Then we attended a weeklong conference where we were set free from many things that held us captive and were pulling us apart. We were soon reunited believing our marriage was restored.

Based on the teaching we received, our experience, and the study of the Word, we put together a four-day seminar on healing and restoration. We saw the hand of God move to heal and restore on many occasions. This was exciting! In more than twenty years of leading many small fellowship groups, I could not recall a single healing or the obvious work at the hand of God.

Then the opportunity came for the ministry work of our dreams. We were asked to run a Canada-wide ministry on behalf of a rapidly expanding international ministry. We did a cross-Canada tour with this ministry and were preparing to relocate to Eastern Canada to set up a ministry center. Then as quickly as it started, it was over. Avoiding the details, we were basically derailed by an e-mail that in one short sentence released us from our new role. We had spent our savings, had taken our boys out of school, and had listed our home to sell. Now that door slammed shut.

This was the final straw for our marriage. Within a month my wife left again for what was to be a one-year separation. The emptiest time in my life happened when my beloved wife loaded up the last of her belongings, and I watched out the window as the taillights of her car disappeared down our half-mile-long driveway. Just a few minutes prior, I had spoken harshly to her. I spoke words through my pent-up anger and swelling pride that hurt her deeply. Somehow when it happened I felt justified; but deep down I knew there was no justification, and I was wrong. Shortly thereafter came another big blow in the form of legal documents petitioning for divorce and citing irreconcilable differences. Now I knew gut-wrenching pain to a level I never even knew existed. The painful irony of it all is that we had a ministry of reconciliation; we could help others but not ourselves.

Since I had shut down my business in preparation to move, I now had to restart a business, but this time with absolutely no funds. I recorded in my journal that except for forty-five dollars, my money had run out. "So this means I'm about to see the salvation of the Lord!" The next morning, I went to my mailbox and in it was a check for one thousand dollars! I was not expecting it. Within a week, I was introduced to a businessman who happened to need a contractor to develop a condominium project. He hired me and agreed to pay a significant portion up front, allowing me to get a truck and materials and hire staff.

Things went very well, on time and on budget, until I submitted the invoice for the final one-third payment. The developers informed me they didn't have the money. The economy had taken a nosedive, and they were in trouble. Wow! Now what do I do? I had worked so many months to finally get a paycheck to pay all the bills that had mounted, but instead, I now had a mountain of creditors to pay and no way to look after them.

Then a ray of hope came. I was contracted to complete the construction of a large custom home with a substantial profit share at completion. Once again, I received a significant portion up front. Things were good until I invoiced for the predetermined draw only to find out the owner had given up on the leveraged project and left the country. My bad financial situation suddenly got much worse.

Days later I was presented with an opportunity to renovate about nine hundred modular homes. We completed the first two and were paid. Everyone was happy and all seemed good—finally! However, at the completion of the third project, not only was a large portion of the profit sliced off, but also the owners decided to cancel the project, providing little by way of explanation. How could this be happening? Not only did I have no money to look after my personal living expenses and pay hungry divorce lawyers, but now I was now liable for outstanding payables on three projects with a lengthy collection process ahead that would require even more legal expenses on the several hundred thousand dollars outstanding.

This all happened within fourteen months of the departure of my beloved, in addition to the turmoil and family difficulties that transpired with the divorce petition. I felt that even my wilderness tests were getting tested.

The interesting thing is that each affliction brought to the surface another area of my life that needed to be cleansed and surrendered. In the midst of it all, God gave me the most unusual peace, so I knew that He was the one who closed the door on the new ministry and on the business ventures, and even permitted the marital separation. It was for what He wanted to teach this servant of His. You see, when I was on the mountaintop, I didn't learn because I wasn't listening. In fact I didn't think I had anything more to really figure out. When I skidded into the valley below, I began to see my wretchedness, and I cried out to the Lord for deliverance and freedom from my calamity.

> I knew that what I had believed and how I had behaved in my Christian life had gotten me into the deep waters where I found myself.

When my beloved departed, I immediately fell into a rapid downward spiral emotionally and spiritually, which lasted for three or four months. I felt so hopeless and such a failure. I knew I had to stand for my marriage no matter how difficult things became. I knew that what I had believed and how I had behaved in my Christian life had gotten me into the deep waters where I found myself. My sister became a rock for me as she also struggled through her own marriage wilderness. My sister Adrianne never once judged me nor would she allow me to speak negatively about my beloved wife. Then a call came from my brother, who informed me that his wife also just left and would be filing for divorce as well.

What developed were the closest of bonds between two brothers and a sister as we sought the Lord together, first to reconcile us individually to become whole and free us from our personal captivities and then to trust our marriages, families, and business to the Lord. We spent hours every week challenging each other in the Word and encouraging each other to grow in the Lord, realizing that this spiritual wilderness was not about our spouses but about us, and God had our attention.

I don't know what got into my sister but she repeatedly pleaded with me to write a book on the work of reconciliation. I protested, saying, "Look at me and the desperate situation I am in. I hardly qualify to write such a book. How could God give me such an assignment at this time?" She didn't listen very well and continued to gently encourage me to write. She was praying for me as I began to feel the Lord directing me to comply and get on with it. I had been recording in my journals the scriptures that the Lord was using to teach me and pull me back out of the daily adversities and set me back upon the solid rock. In order to grasp the scriptures, I was in the habit of writing the verses out, often a full chapter at a time and studying what the Spirit of God was trying to reteach me.

I saw so much truth in the Bible that I was not living out in my own life. In fact I was powerless to change on my own, especially in areas of struggle, like that of pride, anger, striving, lusts, perfectionism, accusation, lying, rejection, unseemly behavior, and the inability to overlook offense.

Then one wintery morning, as I sat in the steam room at the gym, I was asking the Lord to show me what He meant by exhorting us to seek first the kingdom of God and in so doing He would supply all our other needs. "What does it really mean to seek Your Kingdom?" Rather than give me insight to my question, I felt a very strong compulsion in my heart to start writing and through that, He would show me the answer to my cry. As I often did, I began to recite the Lord's Prayer in my heart. When I was done I received a second equally strong compulsion in my heart instructing me that the prayer I just prayed was to be the outline for my book. How could something I so often prayed be the outline to a book? But intrigued, I changed my plans for the day and returned home to take a closer look at the passage. Within a couple of hours I knew why I had received such instruction regarding using the Lord's Prayer as an outline, and I couldn't wait to get started.

> I would often do a "tough love" thing, which is really saying, "If you don't do what I feel is right then I'll do wrong to teach you!"

I also scribbled down a title, *Sanctiprize*, and then proceeded to study what it might mean.

I must admit that I was thinking that this book would be easy. I had already spent almost two years writing a two-hundred-page manual for a seminar, so I would just alter it to fit the format of a book. But that was not to be the case. As I began, each chapter "happened" to relate to a struggle I was personally facing at the time, and I could not write a word until I had received some level of personal freedom in that area of struggle. This was in sharp contrast to when I wrote the first ministry manual, which I just went to work on and completed with very little personal restraint or application.

I confessed to the Lord that if the writing of this book was just so I could recover my household and myself from the snare of the devil, I would be content with that. As I investigated the scriptures in search of answers, I was given the most unusual peace that made the storm happening around me become still. I then knew what Paul meant by saying, "I take pleasure in infirmities, in reproaches, in necessities, in persecutions, in distresses…for when I am weak, then am I strong" (2 Cor. 12:10).

Have you ever felt so disqualified and exhausted that God couldn't possibly use you? I certainly felt that way until I saw the heart of my Lord in Isaiah 48:10: "Behold, I have refined thee, but not with silver; I have chosen thee in the furnace of affliction."

I wept when first impacted by those words, and actually I am so doing now at the recollection of the goodness of my Lord that He chooses me in the furnace of affliction; and He makes no apologies for His reasoning.

Sanctiprize is a step-by-step recovery process that a brother used in the most difficult wilderness experience of his life to find wholeness, purpose, and restoration to become the person he was created to be, from the foundation of the world. Oh, I still stumble and make my messes, but now my recovery and restoration to wholeness and peace is so very quick. I love it when things that used to greatly vex me or distract me reoccur, and rather than become bitter, I can have compassion on those that caused offense and pray for God to bless them.

I always knew I needed to forgive those that I felt wronged me, but I seemed to retain their trespass in my heart. I would often do a "tough love" thing, which is really saying, "If you don't do what I feel is right then I'll do wrong to teach you!"

> Have you ever felt so disqualified and exhausted that God couldn't possibly use you? I certainly felt that way until I saw the heart of my Lord.

I've learned that it is not about the senior officer that moved me out of the way and took credit for my work; it was about how I would respond. Would I forgive, and could I see that God in His grace actually got me out of a bad place? It wasn't about the low point in seminary; it was about trusting the Lord with my ministry and allowing His Spirit to teach me. Would I have the courage to stand and be able to hear the still small voice of the Lord as He led me?

It wasn't about the many years of small things in ministry; it was about my personal walk and sanctification so that I would be prepared for my Master to use me whenever he called. It wasn't about the company that cancelled my business contract, causing me to go bankrupt; it was about where my treasure lay. It wasn't about the ministry that dumped me; it was about realizing that I had embraced pride, of which I needed to repent. And furthermore, it was about trusting that God was redirecting me and that He has another assignment for me, and He needed to get me off the boat. It wasn't about my beloved wife leaving and filing for divorce; it was about whether I would ask the Lord to change me to become the husband He required of me. And of equal importance, would I obey the Word and stand on His commands and hope in Him when there appeared to be no hope? Or would I listen to the counsel of man when they say, "Hath God said?" (Gen. 3:1). It wasn't about the three business deals where I was defrauded; it was about whether I would learn to be patient and allow the Lord to fight for me and to provide my needs without fear and without taking matters into my own hands. It wasn't about my reputation; it was about dying to self, as a dead man is not concerned about what others say and accuse. And finally, it is not about my circumstances; rather it is about submitting to the One who I will one day give account to regarding what I did with what I was entrusted. What if Paul waited for ideal circumstances before commencing his ministry? He would not have accomplished what he did for the kingdom of God. What if Jesus waited?

There is an extraordinary set of principles in the kingdom of God, and I am so very eager to proclaim to you that God indeed has plans for you that are far beyond what you can think or imagine.

Whose report will you believe?

INTRODUCTION
A Note from the Author

I MAKE NO APOLOGY for the volume of scripture in this writing, as I know that the Word of God will accomplish the purpose for which God sent it (Isa. 55:11). My role is only that of a messenger who proclaims the Word of the King of kings and then provides some commentary. The glory is to my beloved Father in heaven.

> When prayer isn't working ask the "discerner of the thoughts and intents of the heart" what is amiss.

Due to the large numbers of scriptures used in this book, I have chosen to provide definition or to expand on concepts by inserting my wording within the verses themselves. Words that were inserted by me are in brackets. The words that I am emphasizing are in italics.

> For the word of God is quick, and powerful, and sharper than any twoedged sword, piercing even to the dividing *asunder* [separating] of *soul* [mind] *and spirit* [heart], and of the *joints and marrow* [body], and is a discerner of the *thoughts* [mind] and intents of the *heart* [spirit].
> —HEBREWS 4:12, EMPHASIS ADDED

Now in this next verse you'll note that parentheses are used around the words added by the original writer of that particular scripture as his own commentary to something he witnessed or was taught of by the Holy Spirit. These are in the King James (Authorized) Version.

> He that believeth on me, as the scripture hath said, out of his belly shall flow rivers of living water. (But this spake he of the Spirit, which they that believe on him should receive: for the Holy Ghost was not yet given; because that Jesus was not yet glorified.)
> —JOHN 7:38–39

If you see three or four dots (….), I omitted a section of a verse or an entire verse(s) that did not relate to the point being made. That does not mean the omitted section is not important or not inspired, it just means it was not relevant to the teaching at hand.

The reader is encouraged not to just accept whatever I say, but to dig into Scripture to see if what is being said is true. Be fully persuaded in your own heart of what the Spirit of God is saying to you for today.

Finally, this writing requires you to make many decisions; choose either to accept or reject—but you must make a decision.

OUR FATHER WHO ART IN HEAVEN

*No man hath seen God at any time; the only begotten Son, which
is in the bosom of the Father, he hath declared him.*
—JOHN 1:18

OUR FATHER DESIRES to have us relate to Him and to worship Him from the vantage point of our spirit. God is a Spirit and they that worship Him must worship Him in spirit and in truth (John 4:24). However there is an occasion in Scripture where our heavenly Father allows us a glimpse of Himself in the following heavenly scene:

> I beheld till the thrones were cast down, and the Ancient of days did sit, whose garment was white as snow, and the hair of his head like the pure wool: his throne was like the fiery flame, and his wheels as burning fire. A fiery stream issued and came forth from before him: thousand thousands ministered unto him, and ten thousand times ten thousand stood before him: the judgment was set, and the books were opened.
> —DANIEL 7:9–10

The Ancient of Days is a being that has a head full of hair, is clothed in a white garment and sits upon a throne. His uncontainable power and glory blazes forth from His majestic person. Your Father, yes, *your* Father thrives in an awesome and a phenomenal ministry control room.

In the next scene you have the Father and the Son, two different God beings, in the same place at the same time.

> I saw in the night visions, and, behold, one like the Son of man came with the clouds of heaven, and came to the Ancient of days, and they brought him near before him. And there was given him dominion, and glory, and a kingdom, that all people, nations, and languages, should serve him: his dominion is an everlasting dominion, which shall not pass away, and his kingdom that which shall not be destroyed.
> —DANIEL 7:13–14

Jesus is given dominion and glory in Daniel's prophetic vision, which is why we call Him *Lord*.

The Ancient of Days is your Father, a living being. This is your first portrait of your Father in heaven.

You have an earthly dad who was given the assignment by our heavenly Father to nurture, govern, and love you until the Master has need of you. Consider what your older brothers, brothers you haven't even met yet, wrestled with. "Have we not all one father? Hath not one God created us?" (Mal. 2:10).

Your earthly father and mother really only participated with your heavenly Father to land you here on earth. It is written that you were the apple of your Father's eye (Ps. 17:6) much before the day known as your birthday.

> Blessed be the God and Father of our Lord Jesus Christ, who hath blessed us with all spiritual blessings in heavenly places in Christ: According as he hath chosen us in him before the foundation of the world, that we should be holy and without blame before him in love.
> —Ephesians 1:3–4

The truest thing about you is that you were created before the earth was formed to be just like your loving heavenly Father.

> But now, O Lord, thou art our father; we are the clay, and thou our potter; and we all are the work of thy hand.
> —Isaiah 64:8

Not only were you designed and created by Him, but you are named after Him. Ephesians 3:14–15 tells us, "For this cause I bow my knees unto the Father of our Lord Jesus Christ, Of whom the whole family in heaven and earth is named." The name that now identifies you is only a temporal name, but your Father in heaven has another, a very special name, a name that will be descriptive of your role throughout eternity.

Isaiah 62:2 confirms this: "And the Gentiles shall see thy righteousness, and all kings thy glory: and thou shalt be called by a new name, which the mouth of the Lord shall name."

I am a messenger with a message to inform you about your true heritage. The concept to grasp here is that the One who thought about you way back, who designed you to the highest of specifications, who then created you accordingly, and then named you after Himself loves you so much He can't take His eyes off of you. That person is God the Father. You were then placed in the home of earthly parents as both you and your parents had a season of learning to go through in preparation for the next stages of eternal life. I know things have been very difficult here for some of you and even more unbearable for others at the hands of your "earthly dads" and "earthly moms," yet just wait until you hear the rest of what I have to tell you about who you are. Movies have yet to be made about this story. But before I tell you about that,

I must have you consider what you get to do. I will tell you about your first, actually your only assignments. You see, God's expectations are no secret; He tells us in advance what He requires of us and then gives us our lifetime to get it right. That is known as grace. What does your Father require of you?

> And now, Israel, what doth the LORD thy God require of thee, but to fear the LORD thy God, to walk in all his ways, and to love him, and to serve the LORD thy God with all thy heart and with all thy soul.
> —DEUTERONOMY 10:12

> Thou shalt not avenge, nor bear any grudge against the children of thy people, but thou shalt love thy neighbour as thyself: I am the LORD.
> —LEVITICUS 19:18

Two basic commands are given for which our Master will evaluate us. The evaluation we receive will govern not only how we enjoy this present life but also the next stages, such as the Millennium and onward throughout eternity. God is consistent yesterday, today, and forever in what is desired of us. These commands are like the "Believer's Charter," with the rest of the Bible providing the interpretation of how those commands are to be carried out. These commands from the Old Testament are bridged into the New Testament.

> He tells us in advance what He requires of us and then gives us our lifetime to get it right. That is known as grace.

> And thou shalt love the Lord thy God with all thy heart, and with all thy soul, and with all thy mind, and with all thy strength: this is the first commandment. And the second is like, namely this, Thou shalt love thy neighbour as thyself. There is none other commandment greater than these.
> —MARK 12:30–31

Those commands sound simple enough, but let me ask some direct questions: How can you truly love God your Father when the mention of the word *father* brings up painful hurts? How can you truly love God your Father when you don't understand why or even blame Him for not being there when you needed Him most? How can you truly love God your Father when you feel He is allowing pain and suffering to destroy people when you feel He could stop it? How can you love your neighbor or somebody else if they did something really nasty to you or said the unpardonable about you?

Further to loving my neighbor, I am to love myself? Yes, you are to love another in the same way you love yourself. This isn't a self-centered, prideful thing; this love is different, really different. But how can you have that love for yourself if you are laden down with guilt, shame, loneliness, rejection, despair, or low self-worth, or if you are given over to stuff that disgusts you or you hate the story the mirror reflects?

God gave three commandments because He knows we are not good with a lot of rules at the same time and knowing what was the very best, he wanted us to experience life as He intended it. The Greek word for love here is *agapeo*. It is necessary to bring into our conversation the original language because there is a mystery to be revealed that remains hidden if we stick only to our limited English language. But how do I have that deep love in my heart, my soul, my mind, and my body? First of all, aren't my soul, mind, and heart the same? Well, they are interrelated but quite different; otherwise, the Word of God could not separate them.

> For the word of God is quick, and powerful, and sharper than any twoedged sword, piercing even to the dividing asunder [separating] of *soul* [mind] *and spirit* [heart], and of the *joints and marrow* [body], and is a discerner of the *thoughts* [mind] and intents of the *heart* [spirit].
> —Hebrews 4:12, emphasis added

This verse uses the word *spirit*, which is interchangeable with the word *heart* in Mark 12:30. We are to love (*agape*) God in our soul, our spirit, our body, and our mind. The Word separates them all to inspect their respective fruit.

As I was contemplating the meaning of the love-commanding verse, I looked up the word *heart* in the *Strong's Concordance*. The *Strong's Concordance* is a valuable reference tool to assist Bible students in their understanding of the Scriptures. The word *fountain* jumped out at me in the definition of *heart*. It is the organ at the center of the blood circulation system, paralleling the center of all spiritual life. It is the fountain of the thoughts, passions, desires, appetites, affections, purposes, endeavors of the understanding, and the seat of the intelligence of the will and character. It is the central or most-intimate part of anything.

That's it! I thought, as the blood raced to my brain. *The heart or spirit is the fountain of our life to which our soul, mind, and body relate.*

Proverbs 13:14 tells us that "the law of the wise is a fountain of life, to depart from the snares of death." The central message of the law of the wise is to "agape" the Lord God with everything within us and secondly to agape everyone else, including our enemies, as ourselves. The law of agape is the fountain of life.

The Fountain

To illustrate, picture in your mind a large, ornate, concrete garden water fountain. The heart or spirit is the invisible water pump of the fountain, the dancing water display is the soul, and the pool, which collects and processes it all, is the mind, and the physical structure would be the body.

The body of the fountain deteriorates depending on the acidity and the minerals present in the water. It is also affected by harsh climates and exposure to the elements and requires much upkeep, as do our bodies. The body simply contains the Temple of the Spirit of God; it is merely the tent.

> Know ye not that ye are the temple of God, and that the Spirit of God dwelleth in you? If any man defile the temple of God, him shall God destroy; for the temple of God is holy, which temple ye are.
> —1 Corinthians 3:16–17

How do we defile the Temple of God? We defile it by bringing into the temple that which is unholy, unchristlike, or of our fleshly, sensuous lower nature.

The caretaker of a fountain needs to know what cleansing agents work best to keep the body of the fountain looking its best. Likewise we need to know how to be good caretakers of our vessels, our bodies.

> How may we defile the temple of God? We defile it by bringing into the temple that which is unholy, unchristlike, or of our fleshly, sensuous lower nature.

> For this is the will of God, even your sanctification, that ye should abstain from fornication: That every one of you should know how to possess his *vessel* [body] in sanctification and honour.
> —1 Thessalonians 4:3–4

None of the parts of the fountain are self-cleaning. They all require the caretaker to recognize the defilement and take steps to remove them. We must thoroughly understand the owner's manual to know how to possess our vessel or body. Most of us don't read the owner's manual, the Bible, because we already think we know what it says. Or perhaps, we are of the understanding that when we became Christians, our vessels were thoroughly cleansed, never to need cleaning again. The following verse is addressed to the "dearly beloved," fellow believers in the church—yes, Christians—and look what they had to do:

> Having therefore these promises, dearly beloved, let us cleanse ourselves from all *filthiness* [defilement] of the flesh and spirit, perfecting holiness in the fear of God.
> —2 Corinthians 7:1

The dearly beloved saints had to cleanse the filthiness out of not only their flesh but their spirit as well. Actually the cleansing of our spirit is a process, not a onetime event.

> And the very God of peace sanctify you wholly; and I pray God your whole spirit and soul and body be preserved blameless unto the coming of our Lord Jesus Christ.
> —1 Thessalonians 5:23

The pump of the fountain

The pump of the fountain, which represents our heart or spirit, is interesting. In the garden fountain, the electric pump receives its power from an outside power source, and it only circulates what it draws through its intake—it can draw on purified or contaminated water. The three prongs of the power cord are connected to the electric power receptacle. The three prongs of the power supply consist of the ground prong, which suggests we are grounded in the Word of Jesus; the second prong, known as the hot side, which represents the power of the Holy Spirit; and the last prong, known as the neutral or return side, which is necessary to complete the circuit, represents the love of the Father. Our spirit is powered by the Godhead, which consists of Father, Son, and Holy Spirit.

The spray of the fountain

The spray of the fountain represents the soul. The inspiring part, or the personality, of the fountain is the ever-changing character of the water spray. The soul displays the personality, which impacts others by the force behind it. It simply puts on display what is being circulated through the pump, the spirit. The soul submits to our spirit and accordingly displays the fruit of our spirit, which is either pleasant or nasty.

> For every tree is known by his own fruit. For of thorns men do not gather figs, nor of a bramble bush gather they grapes. A good man out of the good treasure of his heart bringeth forth that which is good; and an evil man out of the evil treasure of his heart bringeth forth that which is evil: for of the abundance of the heart his mouth speaketh.
>
> —Luke 6:44–45

Whatever the heart treasures, good or evil, is made very obvious as it is put on display through our soul—our personality, and our mouths play the supporting role.

The pool of the fountain

The pool of a fountain can be clear so everyone can enjoy the beauty of the goldfish and plant life. Or, bird droplets, fish by-products, scum, and various uninvited organisms may contaminate it. The pool is open and exposed to not only re-collect the water of the fountain, but also will receive everything that is floating around its environment. Our mind processes what comes from our spirit, and it also deals with everything that it sees, smells, senses, hears, or tastes from our environment.

Our minds are forcibly subjected to many things that defile. Nonetheless, our minds need to work as filters so contaminates aren't collected and further circulated to our spirits. Contaminates build up as sludge and slow the pump down to a trickle of its potential. Contrast that to Jesus' words: "He that believeth on me, as the scripture hath said, out of his belly shall flow rivers of living water" (John 7:38).

Our minds are the faculty by which we articulate the thinking and feeling of the spirit, good or bad. If we are conformed to the world, our minds do little to protect our spirits, as, knowing no restraint, we allow everything inside of us that our environment has to offer. Scripture has already revealed to us that our spirit, soul, and body need to be cleansed or sanctified; and now this passage in Romans informs us to do the same to our minds.

> I beseech you therefore, brethren, by the mercies of God, that ye present your bodies a living sacrifice, holy, acceptable unto God, which is your reasonable service. And be not conformed to this world: but be ye transformed by the renewing of your mind, that ye may *prove* [discern, examine, and approve] what is that good, and acceptable, and perfect, will of God.
> —ROMANS 12:1–2, EMPHASIS ADDED

Satan knows he needs to target our minds in such a way that we actually take pleasure in sin so we'll hide from the light. It is difficult to want to stop participating in the sin we actually are entertained by.

> In whom the god of this world hath blinded the minds of them which believe not, lest the light of the glorious gospel of Christ, who is the image of God, should shine unto them.
> —2 CORINTHIANS 4:4

The filter of a righteous man needs constant discipline and maintenance to remain clean.

> A righteous man falling [to slip up] down before the wicked is as a troubled [fouled] fountain, and a corrupt [perverted] spring.
> —PROVERBS 25:26

If we permit only pure thoughts to enter our spirit, then the fruits of our spirit will be Christlike. The writer of much of the New Testament, Paul, said that the spirit is willing, but the flesh is weak. The flesh is the sensuous nature of the mind—that which runs wild in its imaginations. If the flesh has not been crucified, it gets out of control. Satan manipulates us to make our spirits subject to the flesh (our carnal nature) and to our minds, instead of the other way around.

THE BATTLE IN THE MIND

I believe the Scripture teaches of two different levels of reason within our thought center.

> I thank God through Jesus Christ our Lord. So then with the mind I myself serve the law of God; but with the flesh the law of sin.
> —ROMANS 7:25

The mind is described as originator of the higher part of reason, which is able to judge soberly, calmly, and impartially. The thought process of the mind is distinct from perception by feeling, and it is able to provide forethought rather than acting on impulse. Our wonderful minds are capable of reasoning divine truth, discernment, application, and governing one's own lusts. Now the battlefield: in contrast, the lower part of the thought center is the flesh, being the sensuous or self-gratifying, pleasure-indulgent thinking of man. It is impulsive behavior with cravings to misbehave and oblivious to consequences.

The Bible says that if we try to listen to both sources of reasoning—the mind and the flesh—we are double-minded. Double-mindedness is the wavering between the two, resulting in unstable and unpredictable action.

> Submit yourselves therefore to God. Resist the devil, and he will flee from you. Draw nigh to God, and he will draw nigh to you. Cleanse [confess sin] your hands, ye sinners; and purify [required of saints in divine service] your hearts, ye double minded.
>
> —JAMES 4:7–8

With the discerning mind we choose Christlike behavior and through the flesh we represent the devil. *Double-minded* means we are trying to process the thoughts originating from two opposing kingdoms, and that is insanity!

The following passage is addressed to believers, and they are commanded to purify their hearts (spirits) to become single-minded.

> Unto the pure all things are pure: but unto them that are defiled and unbelieving is nothing pure; but even their mind and conscience is defiled.
>
> —TITUS 1:15

Now if the mind isn't filtering out the unclean, filthy stuff will pass by the filter and enter into the spirit. No matter what you do, you will not be able to purify the water, as you won't be able to keep up with both the new contaminants and the old stuff at the same time. The mind and conscience are defiled when the mind starts to agree with the fleshly impulses at the exclusion of godly thinking.

> And even as they did not like to retain God in their knowledge, God gave them over to a reprobate [unfit, unproved, rejected] mind, to do those things which are not convenient [fit].
>
> —ROMANS 1:28

Our minds are no longer capable of discerning divinely inspired recommendations. James tells believers what happens when our flesh fuels our tongues:

> But the tongue can no man tame; it is an unruly evil, full of deadly poison. Therewith bless we God, even the Father; and therewith curse we men, which are made after the similitude of God. Out of the same mouth proceedeth blessing and cursing. My brethren, these things ought not so to be. Doth a fountain send forth at the same place sweet water and bitter?
>
> —JAMES 3:8–10

The behavior of the unruly tongue isn't tamed by any carnal means; rather the sanctification of the spirit is required to reprogram our minds to change what comes out of our mouths. Our mouths are the read-out of what is fed into our thought processors.

We are double-tongued! We curse with negativity by predicting evil and ruin on others. Perhaps you have felt the call of God on your life and yet felt distant, as though something is blocking your relationship with your Lord and nothing seems to work to change that.

> Therefore judge nothing before the time, until the Lord come, who both will bring to light the hidden things of darkness, and will make manifest the counsels of the hearts: and then shall every man have praise of God.
>
> —1 CORINTHIANS 4:5

The best filter for a water fountain is one that utilizes light. Ultraviolet light is deadly for germs, algae, and viruses of the pond. Likewise our fountain, consisting of body, soul, and spirit requires light to expose our dark side and destroy the evil we have been harboring.

Perhaps you have felt the call of God on your life and yet felt distant, as though something is blocking your relationship with your Lord and nothing seems to work to change that.

We will travel together through the Word to discover what needs to be "purged" in order for us to be suitable for the Master's use.

> If a man therefore purge [cleanse thoroughly or disinfect] himself from these, he shall be a vessel unto honour, sanctified, and meet for the master's use, and prepared unto every good work. Flee also youthful lusts: but follow righteousness, faith, charity [agape], peace, with them that call on the Lord out of a pure [as by fire or like a vine by pruning] heart.
>
> —2 TIMOTHY 2:21–22

Our mind makes the decision to obey the Word as the Holy Spirit inspires it. Sold out, active conformity and submission to the Word will lead to an internal cleansing, enabling us to love with intensity.

> Seeing ye have purified your souls in obeying the truth through the Spirit unto unfeigned love of the brethren, see that ye love [agapeo] one another with a pure heart [spirit] fervently.
>
> —1 PETER 1:22

So what comes out of a purified spirit, soul, and a mind that is obedient to the truth? I don't have to make anything up as the Word presents this colorful fruit in Philippians 4:8:

> Finally, brethren,
> whatsoever things are true [eliminates gossip],
> whatsoever things are honest [reverend, honorable, venerated for character],
> whatsoever things are just [in keeping the commands of God, innocent, faultless],
> whatsoever things are pure [chaste, sacred, immaculate, clean],
> whatsoever things are lovely [acceptable, pleasing],

> whatsoever things are of good report [speaking favorably, conducive
> to success];
> if there be any virtue [particular moral excellence of thought, feeling,
> or action],
> and if there be any praise [commendation],
> think [reason, deliberate, meditate] on these things.

If your thought life has not lined up with this passage, why not renounce all thoughts that are found to be in rebellion and ask the Lord to forgive and to lead you to such purity.

The payback for a cleansed fountain is enormous and eternal.

> And he said unto me, It is done. I am Alpha and Omega, the beginning
> and the end. I will give unto him that is athirst of the fountain of the
> water of life freely. He that overcometh shall inherit all things; and I will
> be his God, and he shall be my son.
> —REVELATION 21:6–7

The famous One, God Himself, can't wait to look on His overcomer kids and say, "You are my son, my daughter, in whom I'm so well pleased."

Overcome? I can't even overcome my habit of chewing with my mouth open. How am I going to overcome all this stuff that defiles my body, soul, and spirit? Friends, stay tuned in to this station.

> As puberty is to our bodies
> And maturity is to our souls
> Agape is to our spirits!

COMPLIANCE TO THE COMMANDS OF AGAPE

I appreciate the honesty of the Scriptures, especially when it shows the weakness of the ones chosen to minister the gospel to the world by Christ. Peter, a typical guy, had trouble grasping the *concept* of the agape love of God, never mind what must be done to have it! Let's take a look at a tender time for Peter when he became very teachable.

> Then saith Jesus unto them, All ye shall be offended because of me this
> night: for it is written, I will smite the shepherd, and the sheep of the flock
> shall be scattered abroad. Peter answered and said unto him, Though all
> men shall be offended because of thee, yet will I never be offended. Jesus
> said unto him, Verily I say unto thee, That this night, before the cock
> crow, thou shalt deny me thrice. Peter said unto him, Though I should
> die with thee, yet will I not deny thee. Likewise also said all the disciples.
> —MATTHEW 26:31–35

Jesus knew that Peter was speaking with good intentions but he was taking confidence in his carnal nature—his flesh—and not of the Spirit. Perhaps there was a hint of self-sufficiency or arrogance or even pride. Another gospel writer noted in the same event that the disciples had an argument amongst themselves as to who would be greatest in the kingdom. So Christ in His discernment needed to put His finger on the doors that Peter had opened that would lead to much difficulty in his life. Soon thereafter Jesus admonished Peter again:

> Watch and pray, that ye enter not into temptation: the spirit indeed is willing, but the flesh is weak.
>
> —MATTHEW 26:41

Another witness to Peter's upcoming adversity, Luke, added further insight into Jesus' knowledge of what Peter was about to face and offer of strength to endure.

> Contrariwise, presuming on the grace of God isn't good, as we are developing the fruit of a hardened or proud heart to compel us to an eternal place of wrath. Grace is a covering by God where He temporarily tolerates our error and holds off on casting judgment to give us room to repent.

> And the Lord said, Simon, Simon, behold, Satan hath desired to have you, that he may sift you as wheat: But I have prayed for thee, that thy faith fail not: and when thou art converted, strengthen thy brethren.
>
> —LUKE 22:31–32

We'll talk more on this later, but we see here that a door was opened, which allowed Satan legal authority to work Peter over. Because Satan had legal right to Peter, we notice that Christ did not stop him (as we know He can stop the works of all evil), but here He didn't but rather prayed that Peter would not fail his next learning experience. Christ also said that following this test Peter would be converted. What needed to be converted in Peter? The scriptures record this same Peter walking out on the water during a storm to meet Jesus. This guy walked on water and needed to be converted? If Peter didn't know how to love after being a disciple of Jesus for three years, chances are that the rest of us have something to learn here as well.

As Jesus predicted, Peter soon denied he was a believer in Jesus on three occasions, and the rooster was only too happy to say, "He told you so." Christ is then crucified, and three days later He is raised from the dead. Meanwhile Satan sifts Peter. The next time Jesus meets Peter, He continues to teach him and puts His finger on the heart problem that resulted in Peter's fall.

> So when they had dined, Jesus saith to Simon Peter, Simon, son of Jonas, lovest [*agapao*] thou me more than these? He saith unto him, Yea, Lord; thou knowest that I love [*phileo*] thee. He saith to him again the second time, Simon, son of Jonas, lovest [*agapao*] thou me? He saith unto him, Yea, Lord; thou knowest that I love [*phileo*] thee. He saith unto him, Feed my sheep. He saith unto him the third time, Simon, son of Jonas, lovest [*phileo*] thou me? Peter was grieved because he said unto him the third time, Lovest

[*phileo*] thou me? And he said unto him, Lord, thou knowest all things; thou knowest that I love [*phileo*] thee. Jesus saith unto him, Feed my sheep.
—JOHN 21:15–17

Jesus asks, "Peter, do you agape Me?" to which Peter replies, "Lord, You know I phileo You." Undeterred, Jesus asks again, "Peter, do you agape Me?" Again Peter replies, "Yes, Lord, You know I phileo You!" Jesus wasn't done; but this time He agrees with Peter and says, "Peter, do you phileo Me?" Now Peter is a little uptight but he knows the light has been shed into his spirit; and he says in exasperation, "Lord, You know all things. Yes, I phileo You!"

> If Peter didn't know how to love after being a disciple of Jesus for three years, chances are that the rest of us have something to learn here as well.

It is interesting that Peter, the tough and weathered fisherman, knew at what level he was able to love. Why is this conversation Jesus had with Peter so very important?

Let's refer again to the greatest commandment:

> And thou shalt love [*agapaō*] the Lord thy God with all thy heart, and with all thy soul, and with all thy mind, and with all thy strength: this is the first commandment. And the second is like, namely this, Thou shalt love [*agapaō*] thy neighbour as thyself. There is none other commandment greater than these.
> —MARK 12:30–31

Jesus was graciously teaching Peter, since He knew that if Peter were to face judgment regarding his obedience to the greatest of commands, he would be found lacking. The greatest commandment requires us to "agape" the Lord our God with all our heart (spirit), soul, mind, and strength (body) and to "agape" our neighbor as ourselves. Peter admits that he indeed did not "agape" his Lord, but rather he was only able to attain to the level of "phileo" love. That is why Peter was so grieved when Christ pursued him with His line of interrogation.

In our English translations there is only one word for *love*, whereas in the original Greek there are many; and they are profoundly important to understand.

What is the difference between *phileo* and *agape*?

1. *Agape*: is shown by what the one who loves deems best for the person loved. "For God so loved the world that He gave" not what He necessarily wanted, but what man needed, as God perceived his need. God's love for man is doing what He knows is best for man and not what man may lust for. When a person "agapes" another, it is impossible for him to stop "agaping," regardless of what the other may do. This kind of love changes not and is not moved by circumstances.

2. *Agapao*: indicates the direction of agape

3. *Phileo*: to have common interests; to have personal affection and to approve of, to like, to be fond of doing; intelligence or higher purpose is not necessarily involved. However "phileo" love is fickle, as it will boast it's loyalty in one moment and then deny the object of his affection the next. It is the kind of love that loves one minute and hates the next. It is unpredictable and usually has expectations attached.

4. *Philadelphia*: brotherly love emanating from a shared spiritual life. It is still a good love but doesn't go far enough.

The Lord asks Peter twice if he has the deep spiritual love, agape, of the Father for Him, to which Peter is only able to respond, "I have 'affection' towards you." This is after Peter denied Jesus three times, but before Peter is filled with the Holy Spirit at Pentecost. The Lord created mankind to love at the agape level. So He provokes Peter to pass the shallowness of phileo. Does Peter eventually get it? Let's take a look at what he writes a few years later:

> Seeing ye have purified your souls in obeying the truth through the Spirit unto unfeigned [sincere] love [*philadelphia*] of the brethren, see that ye love [*agape*] one another with a pure heart fervently.
> —1 PETER 1:22

Peter, no doubt recalling the Lord's admonition, exhorts the church to have brotherly love if that is all you can do. Then it is as if Peter takes a sigh and recalls Jesus' admonishment and goes much deeper, "But go for it, go for the agape love, and do so fervently or intensely."

We are all able to phileo love, which is an affection that we can perform in the level of the soul or mind, even as heathens do. Probably ninety-nine percent of couples fall into "phileo" at best and feel that is the sufficient amount of love they will need to last a lifetime. Affection is shallow and may be temporary as our likes and dislikes are subject to change as the years go by. That is why we can retort, "I don't love you anymore." Actually, we don't fall out of *phileo* love; rather we fall into sin as we saw what happened to Peter. We can phileo our favorite fast-food restaurant, but as soon as we have a bad experience there, we switch our affection to another.

Now I'm about to make some of you squirm uncomfortably. What about *eros* love? Isn't that the third type of love that is required, particularly in marriage?

Eros is a Greek term for *love*, but it is not found in the Bible. The closest I am aware of is what the Bible calls lasciviousness. *Lasciviousness* means to satisfy yourself, knowing no restraint. Falling in love (*eros*) is all about sex and/or control, coupled with unmanageable frowardness. It is temporary and usually lasts until the perpetrator gets what he wants. It is the type of "so-called" love that will participate in "one-night stands." Nonetheless, it is the foundation of all too many marriages and common-law relationships. There is a "deservedness" in *eros*—it is all-consuming, where you may betray your own principles.

Amnon, one of David's sons, lusted after his stepsister Tamar and concocted a plan to get her into his chambers by faking illness and demanding that Tamar serve him privately with a romantic dinner for two. As a king's son, he could have just asked to have her to marry and it would have been done. When she came in, he forced himself on her.

> Howbeit he would not hearken unto her voice: but, being stronger than she, forced her, and lay with her. Then Amnon hated her exceedingly; so that the hatred wherewith he hated her was greater than the love [*ahabah*] wherewith he had loved her. And Amnon said unto her, Arise, be gone. And she said unto him, There is no cause: this evil in sending me away is greater than the other that thou didst unto me. But he would not hearken unto her.
> —2 SAMUEL 13:14–16

The word for *love* here is *ahabah*; human desire for a human object. It is the prostituting of another for selfish pleasure. This pleasure seeker sees their partner as an "object" not as a person, definitely not as a daughter of our Father. *Ahabah* is a Hebrew word that would be similar in meaning to the Greek word *eros*.

You can't stop yourself from entering the danger zone. The force of eros is such that you begin to do things that you are not meant to do.

I know what some of you are thinking, that if eros is gone from the marriage, all the fun goes with it. Come on, God created intimacy in marriage. Could you imagine it in agape where selfish desires take a back seat?

> But the fruit of the Spirit [not the soul or flesh] is love [*agape*], joy, peace, longsuffering, gentleness, goodness, faith, meekness, temperance: against such there is no law. And they that are Christ's have crucified the flesh with the affections and lusts. If we live in the Spirit, let us also walk in the Spirit.
> —GALATIANS 5:22–25

Eros love occurs at the level of our carnal nature or the flesh. Phileo love is what our soul and mind are able to best perform. Agape is the love of the Father that ministers to us at our spirit level.

Could you imagine God's love for us just being a fickle affection such as phileo? That would mean as soon as we tripped up, we would be little more than cosmic dust. God loves us at the deep spirit level because He knows that we'll fall into hopeless fear, anxiety, and despair (hell) if His love doesn't meet us where we need it. God is able to love us even when we behave as His enemy because he sees our authentic spirit. With that kind of love we feel secure in His love for us. That, by the way, is the love with which we are to love our enemies because it is able to detect that very small flicker of the divine image in every man, woman, and child. With agape love for our enemy, we do what our spirit says is best for them. It doesn't mean we are to run up and give them a big bear hug and join their glee club.

God has designed that deep agape love of His to be streamed through Jesus

Christ to the husband and then through the godly husband to his wife and children. I call that the "love stream."

> But I would have you know, that the head of every man is Christ; and the head of the woman is the man; and the head of Christ is God.
>
> —1 CORINTHIANS 11:3

If his wife is separated from that love, she will experience hell in her spirit but may never be able to articulate what is wrong. I know I just caused some of the dear saints to ask, "Should he be using that word *hell* in this book?" Well, hell is a place that is absent of God's love.

Actually, if a man treats his wife poorly, he too, will experience a hell of his own. Let's look at a group of men that were bewildered at all the calamity and evil things they were experiencing as well as an obvious abandonment by God. Could it be that God was allowing them to suffer for their attitudes and behavior toward their little lady? The prophet of the Lord tells these fellows exactly what their problem is:

> Probably 99 percent of couples fall into "phileo" at best and feel that is the sufficient amount of love they will need to last a lifetime.

> Yet ye say, Wherefore? [What?] Because the LORD hath been witness between thee and the wife of thy youth, against whom thou hast dealt treacherously [two-faced, unfaithful, infidelity; to offend or cause to stumble]: yet is she thy companion, and the wife of thy covenant. And did not he make one? Yet had he the residue of the spirit. And wherefore one? That he might seek a godly seed. Therefore take heed to your spirit, and let none deal treacherously against the wife of his youth.
>
> —MALACHI 2:14–15

Infidelity to the marriage covenant occurs when our wives do not receive the full stream of agape love they are entitled to by God.

These men were experiencing the results of a spiritual vacuum in their lives, as God did not accept their offering anymore. Yet they did not make the connection that their difficulties were the result of how they treated their wives. It is clear in verse fifteen that God is holding us accountable to how we treat our wives at the spirit level. He says take heed to your spirit—not your soul, not your body. Not understanding our wives at the spirit level is a block to answered prayer. God is a witness to how his daughters are being offended, and He will not allow the unrepentant to be blessed while they are secretly being a curse in someone else's life.

> There is a "deservedness" in *eros*—it is all-consuming, where you may betray your own principles.

How is man to demonstrate our Father's agape?

Adam dealt with his own sin by exposing Eve's sin to protect himself. Would agape love have done that to his bride? No, of course not.

Men are to love their wives at the same level that Christ expected Peter to love Him and the same level we are commanded to love our neighbor and ourselves—agape.

> That he might present it to himself a glorious church, not having spot, or wrinkle, or any such thing; but that it should be holy and without blemish. So ought men to love their wives as their own bodies. He that loveth his wife loveth himself…This is a great mystery: but I speak concerning Christ and the church. Nevertheless let every one of you in particular so love [*agapao*] his wife even as himself; and the wife see that she reverence her husband.
>
> —EPHESIANS 5:27–33

The household of the married man and woman is the matrimonial church. This matrimonial church is a model of the ecclesiastical church where Jesus is the husband and the members, whether man or woman, are the chaste wife. Sin causes the same problems in either church.

> God has designed that deep agape love of His to be streamed through Jesus Christ to the husband and then through the godly husband to his wife and children. I call that the "love stream."

In both churches the wives are given the command to reverence their husbands. Reverence is also used in Mark 6:20 where Herod feared (reverenced) John, knowing he was a just man and pursued holiness. John the Baptist chased sanctification. Reverence is a feeling of deep respect and esteem, mingled with affection, and portrayed through humble submission.

The command given to the husband to agape his wife is not conditional on her behavior and neither is the command to the wife here to "reverence her husband," conditional on his behavior. These commands cannot be obeyed while we are in eros or phileo love. It is possible for a husband or wife to agape and reverence their partner without reciprocation, as agape empowers us to do what we cannot do on our own. However, it is easier for the husband to agape his wife if she respects him, and at the same time, it is easier for the wife to have reverence for her husband if he agapes her. Both are in obedience to the Word. Some teach that a woman has only to reverence her husband to the degree he submits to God or to the degree he loves her. That suggestion places the woman in an ungodly role of being judge; and when you judge, one elevates himself or herself in superiority, as god over another.

When an offense has occurred, in the mind of the one hurt, it is dealt with differently according to the type of love we are manifesting. If the offended is functioning in agape, the offense is taken to the Lord to ask why we were hurt and then restoration is sought in respectful gentleness with the purpose of bringing both the offended and offendee to holiness. The person that did the wrong, responding in agape, would want to restore the one he hurt and desire to turn away from being an offense to others. If functioning in phileo, still a good love, the offended will confront the offense or stumbling block because they were hurt and they need their pain to go away. They seek to be nurtured and want the other person to pay a price for the wrong. In an eros response, the offense is generally greeted by pride, anxiety, and indifference with the offender saying, "What's her problem?"

> The household of the married man and woman is the matrimonial church. This matrimonial church is a model of the ecclesiastical church where Jesus is the husband and the members, whether man or woman, are the chaste wife.

Men must understand their wives at the spirit level if they want their lifeline to God to be connected—if they want their prayers to be heard.

> Likewise, ye husbands, dwell with them according to knowledge, giving honour unto the wife, as unto the weaker vessel, and as being heirs together of the grace of life; that your prayers be not hindered.
> —1 Peter 3:7

Agape is loving with knowledge of what is best for the recipient. It is ministering to them and covering them with the agape love blanket of our Father.

Do the gals get to agape their husbands?

> Notwithstanding she shall be saved in childbearing, if they continue in faith and charity [*agape*] and holiness with sobriety.
> —1 Timothy 2:15

Really, even if you perceive your mate as your enemy, you are not excused from loving him or her, as we are even to agape our enemies. Peter provides unusual insight in how to conduct ourselves if our mate is struggling.

> Likewise, ye wives, be in subjection to your own husbands; that, if any obey not the word, they also may without the word be won by the conversation [chaste manner of living] of the wives; While they behold your chaste conversation coupled with fear.
> —1 Peter 3:1

If we judge and make decisions regarding a person based on what their flesh does, we are in error. Christ is the only one whose activity of His flesh matched the purity and holiness of His spirit.

> Henceforth know we no man after the flesh: yea, though we have known Christ after the flesh.
> —2 Corinthians 5:16

The fleshly part of man is fabricated, and the love they express is from habit, sheer will, and determination. Christ has a love that oozes out of Him, even to the point of death. No human being is capable of agape love apart from the empowering of the Holy Spirit, which we'll discuss in a later chapter.

> Agape doesn't overlook sin but covers us while we are developing our ability to discern between lust and purity; between right and wrong; between light and darkness and between eros, phileo, and agape.

Agape covers

Agape doesn't overlook sin but covers us while we are developing our ability to discern between lust and purity; between right and wrong; between light and darkness and between eros, phileo, and agape.

Agape is other-centered, as it always seeks to act in such a way to do what is best for another. Our pride would seek to expose and gossip about the sin and misadventures of those God loves.

> And above all things have fervent charity [*agape*] among yourselves: for charity [*agape*] shall cover the multitude of sins.
> —1 PETER 4:8

> Hatred stirreth up strifes: but love covereth all sins.
> —PROVERBS 10:12

Noah fell to a point of personal disgrace. When his youngest son, Ham, saw the drunken state of his father, he took delight in exposing the situation to his brothers. His brothers, however, refused to see the humor in the plight of their beloved dad and took a blanket and went in backwards to cover Noah's exposure. The younger son came from a position of eros love, which is only self-seeking. His two brothers were at a much higher level of agape, which covered and did what was best for the person being loved. As it turns out, Ham's reaction was of greater sin than the sin of the one he was making sport of, and it opened the door for a curse in his life. The fruit of agape to the honor of Shem and Japheth was a blessing. Choose this day blessing or curse: agape or eros.

> Men must understand their wives at the spirit level if they want their lifeline to God to be connected— if they want their prayers to be heard.

> And Noah began to be an husbandman, and he planted a vineyard: And he drank of the wine, and was drunken; and he was uncovered within his tent. And Ham, the father of Canaan, saw the nakedness of his father, and told his two brethren without. And Shem and Japheth took a garment, and laid it upon both their shoulders, and went backward, and covered the nakedness of their father; and their faces were backward, and they saw not their father's nakedness. And Noah awoke from his wine, and knew what his younger son had done unto him. And he said, Cursed be Canaan; a

servant of servants shall he be unto his brethren. And he said, Blessed
be the LORD God of Shem; and Canaan shall
be his servant. God shall enlarge Japheth,
and he shall dwell in the tents of Shem; and
Canaan shall be his servant.
—GENESIS 9:20–27

> Agape gives of itself
> for the benefit of
> the person loved.

How does Christ demonstrate our Father's agape?

What does the agape of the Father look like look like when Jesus wears it?

> And walk in love, as Christ also hath loved [*agapao*] us, and hath given
> himself for us an offering and a sacrifice to God for a sweet smelling savour.
> —EPHESIANS 5:2

Agape *gives* of itself for the benefit of the person loved. Christ redeems us
back from slavery to sin by paying the price in full for our release from the
bondage of sin. By having a greater regard for others, Christ demonstrated
the agape of the Father by sacrificing Himself to redeem our lives for eternity. Christ came not to expose and celebrate our sin but to cover it with His
blood. He did what He knew would be best for us; through agape, Christ
completely died to Himself and His own necessities so that you and I would
have a fighting chance to change the course of our eternity.

> Wherefore, as by one man sin entered into the world, and death by sin;
> and so death passed upon all men, for that all have sinned.
> —ROMANS 5:12

> For the wages of sin is death; but the gift [*charisma*] of God is eternal life
> through Jesus Christ our Lord.
> —ROMANS 6:23

The term *gift* used here is the word *charisma* in Greek, which references the
gift of divine grace, the gift of faith, the gift of knowledge, the gift of holiness,
and the gift of virtue.

But Jesus Christ didn't pay such a high price to parole us so that we could
continue our crime spree. We are placed on parole, a covenant relationship,
while we remain on earth in its present state. We are then entitled to an absolute and full pardon when we are brought before Him in the day of the believer's judgment.

Parole is the release of a prisoner temporarily or permanently before the
expiry of a sentence, on the undertaking of good behavior. I call this grace,
which is the patience of God's agape that covers us while we are working out
our salvation, learning to get it right.

Pardon is to release an offender from the legal consequences of a conviction,
and implicitly from blame.

Paul educates the believers on the facts of sin:

> For sin shall not have dominion over you: for ye are not under the law,
> but under grace. What then? shall we sin, because we are not under the
> law, but under grace? God forbid. Know ye not, that to whom ye yield
> yourselves servants to obey, his servants ye are to whom ye obey; whether
> of sin unto death, or of obedience unto righteousness?
> —Romans 6:14–16

Though we have sinned, we, as believers, are on parole and have agreed to enter into a covenant of obedience. If we commit infidelity and serve sin as believers, what happens?

The most common answer is that we are under grace, so there is no problem. Under grace you can still choose death or righteousness according to verse sixteen. Grace is a covering to give us space to recognize our sin and repent—a covering by God, where He temporarily tolerates our error and holds off on casting judgment to give us room to repent.

The Word always provides the best commentary of its teachings; and in Romans 2:4 it gives us the most complete definition of *grace*:

> Or despisest thou the riches of his goodness and forbearance [toleration]
> and longsuffering [slowness in avenging wrongs]; not knowing that the
> goodness of God leadeth thee to repentance?

Goodness is a synonym of *grace*; the end result of both is repentance. Grace never overlooks sin; it realizes though that we may be slow in grasping the concept, we have erred; so grace does have an element of patience.

> But after thy hardness [stubbornness] and impenitent [unwilling to
> repent] heart treasurest up unto thyself wrath against the day of wrath
> and revelation of the righteous judgment of God...
> —Romans 2:5

And, if we don't repent?

> ...Who will render to every man according to his deeds.
> —Romans 2:6

Is this an accurate understanding of grace? To double-check or to get a second witness, we will review the final judgment of the church by Christ as told in Revelation to see how He interprets the grace we found in Romans. Under grace the church was given space to repent, and for those that still are too stubborn to repent, they will enter judgment.

> And I gave her space [time, either short or long] to repent of her fornica-
> tion; and she repented not. Behold, I will cast her into a bed, and them
> that commit adultery with her into great tribulation, except they repent
> of their deeds.
> —Revelation 2:21–22

It is repentance that will sanctify us—bring us back into favor—so that our pardon is not revoked. That is easy enough, isn't it? Both Romans 2:5 and

Revelation 2:22 appoint the unrepentant to experience the Great Tribulation, which is a severe chastisement here on earth designed to lead people to repentance by considerable calamity.

Grace is also taught in the Old Testament, which provides additional commentary on the doctrine of grace of the New Testament. I'll allow it to speak for itself. God is consistent in grace in both the Old Testament and New Testament alike. What has changed is *how* we are redeemed, which is through the finished work of Jesus on the cross.

> We were created in the image of God as Holy, without blame in agape love and that is where we have fallen from and to which we are commanded to return.

> The LORD, The LORD God, merciful and gracious, longsuffering, and abundant in goodness and truth, Keeping mercy for thousands, forgiving iniquity and transgression and sin, and that will by no means clear [to exempt from punishment] the guilty; visiting the iniquity of the fathers upon the children, and upon the children's children, unto the third and to the fourth generation. And Moses made haste, and bowed his head toward the earth, and worshiped. And he said, If now I have found grace in thy sight, O LORD, let my LORD, I pray thee, go among us; for it is a stiffnecked people; and pardon our iniquity and our sin, and take us for thine inheritance.
>
> —EXODUS 34:6–9

To properly represent the Father, our fountain will need His heart; our software will need to be reprogrammed, as we are unable to represent the Father while walking in our flesh and displaying a carnal love.

> A new heart also will I give you, and a new spirit will I put within you: and I will take away the stony heart. And I will put my spirit within you, and cause you to walk in my statutes, and ye shall keep my judgments, and do them.
>
> —EZEKIEL 36:26–27

Agape love is a gift of the Spirit. We need the Holy Spirit empowering us in order to stream the love of the Father.

> According as he hath chosen us in him before the foundation of the world, that we should be holy and without blame before him in love [*agape*].
>
> —EPHESIANS 1:4

We were created and designed by God with the intent that we would remain holy or sanctified, expressing the completeness of His personality—agape. This is the opportunity Adam was given. Did you know that Adam never repented? Job contends, "If I covered my transgressions as Adam, by hiding mine iniquity in my bosom" (31:33).

Conditions for agape

We cannot receive agape unless we are obeying the commandments of God. Our disobedience not only affects us but everyone we are supposed to love. Disobedience causes a breach in the agape stream.

> As the Father hath loved [*agapeo*] me [Jesus Christ], so have I loved you: continue ye in my love [*agape* streamed]. If ye keep my commandments, ye shall abide in my love [*agape*]; even as I have kept my Father's commandments, and abide in his love [*agape*].
>
> —JOHN 15:9–10

In order for the agape stream from God through Jesus to man to be evident, we must reciprocate agape through obedience and consistency. God's love for us is perfect, consistent, and predictable. It is our carnal return love that is temperamental and unpredictable. Do you feel that God isn't using you or that Christ's witness isn't really evident through your life? Listen up for the excitement of good news! The love block is disobedience and rebellion in your life; and God wants to reveal it to you so that agape can be reseeded and the love stream restored. Once restored, Christ will manifest or make Himself and the Father's agape very evident through you.

> We do not choose to walk the narrow way once and that is good for life; we must choose to walk the narrow way every day for life.

> He that hath my commandments, and keepeth them, he it is that loveth [*agapeo*] me: and he that loveth [*agapeo*] me shall be loved [*agapeo*] of my Father, and I will love [*agapeo*] him, and will manifest myself to him.
>
> —JOHN 14:21

A believer walking in the victory of agape looks at the commands of God as something he gets to do rather than suggestions that must be rebelled against.

> And this is love [*agape*] that we walk after his commandments. This is the commandment, That, as ye have heard from the beginning [origin], ye should walk in it.
>
> —2 JOHN 1:6

The command of agape has been a consistent requirement by God throughout history; obedience is the prerequisite. God changes not.

Within a body of believers, a false charis-matic teacher or prophet may be at work. Even though they are of another kingdom, they can be used by God to prove or to test the character and resolve of a person that He is checking out to expose error and then develop their true leadership potential.

> If there arise among you a prophet, or a dreamer of dreams, and giveth thee a sign or a wonder, And the sign or the wonder come to pass, whereof he spake unto thee, saying, Let us go after other gods, which thou hast not known, and let us serve them; Thou shalt not hearken unto the words

of that prophet, or that dreamer of dreams: for the LORD your God proveth you, to know whether ye love the LORD your God with all your heart and with all your soul. Ye shall walk after the LORD your God, and fear him, and keep his commandments, and obey his voice, and ye shall serve him, and cleave unto

> God tests our love for Him. I tell you this, the walk of a believer is not for part-timers or the uncommitted at heart.

him. And that prophet, or that dreamer of dreams, shall be put to death; because he hath spoken to turn you away from the LORD your God.

—DEUTERONOMY 13:1–5

God tests our love for Him. I tell you this, the walk of a believer is not for part-timers or the uncommitted at heart. If any person failed the test and listened to the false teacher instead of God, he would have committed idolatry. The false teachers and the consequences of their doctrine are God's judgment on the people who are seeking a teacher to say what they want to hear.

In addition to testing our love through discernment of good and evil, God also allows testing through wilderness experiences to test our faith and to break the proud of heart.

> And thou shalt remember all the way which the LORD thy God led thee these forty years in the wilderness, to humble thee, and to prove thee, to know what was in thine heart, whether thou wouldest keep his commandments, or not.
>
> —DEUTERONOMY 8:2

> Who fed thee in the wilderness with manna, which thy fathers knew not, that he might humble thee, and that he might prove thee, to do thee good at thy latter end.
>
> —DEUTERONOMY 8:16

Another fashion of testing is through tribulation and difficulties to show us what is in our heart. God, through His mercy, wants us to see for ourselves what is within our hearts so we can cleanse ourselves ahead of judgment. The Holy Spirit knew some would be trying to invalidate application of the Old Testament as being for today, so He stated that it applied to the latter prophetic days, which includes us today. This promise worked for the early people of God, and it will for us as well.

> But if from thence thou shalt seek the LORD thy God, thou shalt find him, if thou seek him with all thy heart and with all thy soul. When thou art in tribulation, and all these things are come upon thee, even in the latter days, if thou turn to the LORD thy God, and shalt be obedient unto his voice; (For the LORD thy God is a merciful God;) he will not forsake thee, neither destroy thee, nor forget the covenant of thy fathers which he sware unto them.
>
> —DEUTERONOMY 4:29–31

Jesus Christ is scouting planet earth to select who will stand the "agape test" to be on His team throughout the Millennium and beyond for eternity.

> And hast made us unto our God kings and priests: and we shall reign on the earth.
> —REVELATION 5:10

> For the eyes of the LORD run to and fro throughout the whole earth, to shew himself strong in the behalf of them whose heart is perfect [complete] toward him.
> —2 CHRONICLES 16:9

Agape is a most powerful weapon in overcoming oppressions such as fear; agape is an empowering of the quintessence of God.

You can just see God scanning His creation, searching with excitement to find those children of His, whose one desire is to be in a relationship with Him and where the agape is mutual. A person whose heart is perfect toward the Lord means they are no longer searching anywhere else for fulfillment; their eyes are no longer wandering.

Agape, judgment, and obedience

"Repent for the kingdom of heaven is at hand" (Matt. 4:17), Jesus proclaimed. Ready or not here I come!

> Blessed are they that do his commandments, that they may have right to the tree of life, and may enter in through the gates into the city.
> —REVELATION 22:14

Maturity of agape developed through testing is what gives us boldness with assurance in the Day of Judgment. What hopefully has happened through wilderness experiences, the pain of tribulation, and exposure of idolatry and pride is that we are reconciled to become the person we were created to be from the foundation of the world—holy, without blame, with unrestricted access to God through agape love. Agape is the most powerful weapon in overcoming oppressions such as fear; agape is an empowering of the quintessence of God.

> Herein is our love [agape] made perfect, that we may have boldness in the day of judgment: because as he is, so are we in this world. There is no fear in love [agape]; but perfect love [agape] casteth out fear: because fear hath torment. He that feareth is not made perfect in love [agape].
> —1 JOHN 4:17–18

Our boldness is evidence of agape projecting through us. If we are living, walking, and talking agape, we will have confidence and assurance of the outcome at our appointment for judgment; and furthermore, we have put away the torment fear produces in our lives. Actually fear and agape are mutually exclusive of each other.

Agape and knowledge

The overflow of this power love of God is the ability to apply truth through knowledge and judgment. Judgment is discernment of all things spiritual.

> And this I pray, that your love [*agape*] may abound yet more and more in knowledge and in all judgment;
>
> —PHILIPPIANS 1:9

Agape and prayer

How's your prayer life? Are mountains being moved or are you having trouble even stirring up dust? Prayers work when we are found in full compliance to the Word of God. When prayers aren't working, take a diagnostic test through Scripture to find the hindrance. You'll find as you walk in agape, many things in your spiritual walk will change dramatically.

> Many people and the devil included believe in God, but do you believe God?

> And whatsoever we ask, we receive of him, because we keep his commandments, and do those things that are pleasing in his sight. And this is his commandment, That we should believe on the name of his Son Jesus Christ, and love [*agapao*] one another, as he gave us commandment.
>
> —1 JOHN 3:22–23

The first commandment is to agape the Lord your God with all your heart, soul, mind, and strength (Matt. 22:37). I find it intriguing that the word *believe* is substituted for *agape love* in 1 John above. *Believe* means a lot more than to simply accept something as true intellectually. It stands true that one can't agape without believing in that person. Many people and the devil included believe *in* God, but do you believe God?

Whatever we ask we receive because of our agape. Not being in agape would be a block to answered prayer. The following oft-quoted verse has two conditions attached in order for it to be filled:

> And we know that all things work together for good to them that love [*agapeo*] God, to them who are the called according to his purpose
>
> —ROMANS 8:28

There is no guarantee that all things will work together for good to them that phileo God. Furthermore, as we desire that all things in our lives will work together for good, we need to ensure we are called according to His purpose. What's that purpose? Our purpose is to be conformed or brought into likeness and harmony with Jesus Christ.

> For [refers to previous verse] whom he did foreknow, he also did predestinate to be conformed to the image [absolute moral excellence] of his Son.
>
> —ROMANS 8:29

So we have to ask another question to unravel the mystery here. What does this image look like that we are to conform to?

> And have put on the new man, which is renewed in knowledge after the image of him that created him:...Put on therefore, as the elect of God, holy and beloved, bowels of mercies, kindness, humbleness of mind, meekness, longsuffering; Forbearing one another, and forgiving one another, if any man have a quarrel against any: even as Christ forgave you, so also do ye. And above all these things put on charity [*agape*], which is the bond of perfectness.
> —COLOSSIANS 3:10–14

Or more simply put:

> According as he hath chosen us in him before the foundation of the world, that we should be holy and without blame before him in love [*agape*].
> —EPHESIANS 1:4

What is the bottom line? For those who submit to a sanctified walk of agape and holiness, all things work together for good. Why did I say sanctified? To be without blame, you would have to be sanctified. To walk in agape and holiness requires obedience and sanctification; there are no shortcuts. I've tried all the shortcuts, and each time I came up short of the glory of God.

This messenger will show you through Scripture the narrow path to the real thing, where all things work together indeed for good, and prayers are answered.

Faith and agape

The secret of faith is found through agape. Agape is often listed along with other types of love, which weakens it for it is so much more than emotion. Agape is a "divine empowerment or commission."

> For in Jesus Christ neither circumcision availeth any thing, nor uncircumcision; but faith which worketh [is empowered] by love [*agape*].
> —GALATIANS 5:6

Want to see agape faith in its purity?

> No man taketh it from me, but I lay it down of myself. I have power to lay it down, and I have power to take it again. This commandment have I received of my Father.
> —JOHN 10:18

If we were in Jesus' place, we might have said, "God said I would be raised from the dead, and I know that if I have enough faith He will do what He said." That statement is already making provision for failure.

However, when faith has reached its optimal, all the words of the Father are treated as a commandment. That is unwavering faith through agape. Jesus received the promise of the Father, and Jesus regarded it as a commandment. God never gives suggestions.

Benefits of agape

1. God will be manifested and glorified through us (2 Thess. 1:12).
2. We will be covered in our sin until we repent (1 Pet. 4:8).
3. Boldness and assurance at judgment (1 John 4:17).
4. We will be known of God (1 Cor. 8:3).
5. We will benefit more than we can think or imagine (1 Cor. 2:9).
6. Spiritual balance and covering in the household and marriage (1 Pet. 3:7; Eph. 5:33; 1 Tim. 2:15).
7. Able to love our brothers and sisters as well as our enemies (1 John 4:21).
8. Power to overcome and defeat sin. (1 John 4:18).
9. Defeats all fear (1 John 4:18).
10. Able to properly love ourselves (Matt. 22:39; Eph. 5:28).
11. Peace (Ps. 119:165; Gal. 5:22).
12. God will be heard of us (James 1:2–8).
13. Right to the Tree if Life and access to the Holy City of God (Rev. 22:14).
14. Selected to govern with Christ in His one world kingdom—not the one world church that is being set up now where men are positioning themselves as rulers and adherents (Rev. 1:6, 20:6; Rom. 8:17, 30; Dan. 7:18, 27).
15. Faith that moves our mountains (Matt. 17:20).

> Whatever we ask we receive because of our agape. Not being in agape would be a block to answered prayer.

Dine with our Lord

When Jesus says to come and dine with Him, He would offer a three-course meal:

1. Appetizer: Grace is the appetizer, which holds us over until we get to the main course.
2. Main Course: The main course of the gospel is sanctification, leading us to repentance and nourishing us with the power to renew our body, soul, mind, and spirit through Jesus Christ.
3. Desert: We have to eat many things in the main course that we may not really like but they are good for us. Well, desert is the reward; the reward is agape.

This agape teaching sets the destination of our Christianity at the onset. Next we will begin a journey together to align ourselves with the reconstruction necessary for agape to flow out of every part of our body, soul, mind, and spirit. Being filled with the agape love is a process that involves testing; it is not a single event. This process requires our zeal in sanctification, or cleansing, which will be covered in the next several chapters. And then at the end of this writing, we will pray together to appreciate the fullness of this love that the Lord requires us to express.

Breaches in the Love Stream

When there is a breach in the love stream, those that are downstream of the breach will experience a drought or an indescribable emptiness. Isaiah calls this drought an old waste place.

> The LORD shall guide thee continually, and satisfy thy soul in drought, and make fat thy bones: and thou shalt be like a watered garden, and like a spring of water, whose waters fail not. And they that shall be of thee shall build the old waste places: thou shalt raise up the foundations of many generations; and thou shalt be called, The repairer of the breach, The restorer of paths to dwell in.
> —Isaiah 58:11–12

There are three breach locations that will result in a spiritual drought: between me and God, between me and myself, and between me and another person.

Breach with God

A double-minded person is one who is trying to experience all the pleasure of two kingdoms: God's and Satan's. He is divided in interest. We may think this is a good plan; however, it doesn't work that way, as God won't stand next to disobedience and rebellion. God is either in the front seat or He doesn't board your bus.

It is the same as expecting a wife to be excited about the continued unfaithfulness of her husband with an extra lover. The cause of spiritual conflict is you going ahead and doing something, all the while knowing it is wrong.

A double-minded person is one who is trying to experience all the pleasure of two kingdoms; God's and Satan's. He is divided in interest.

Do you feel that something is preventing you from receiving the benefits and protection of a powerful heavenly Father? If we are not able to communicate with the living God, the problem lies on our end. Paul helps us to recognize what sin is standing in the way of communion with God, namely: idolatry, ungodly associations with rebellious people, and personal spiritual defilement. A ruthless house cleaning is required to make ready our temples for divine occupation.

> And what agreement hath the temple of God with idols [a worship or allegiance diversion]? for ye are the temple of the living God; as God hath

said, I will dwell in them, and walk in them; and I will be their God, and they shall be my people. Wherefore come out from among them, and be ye separate [limit exposure to those in rebellion to the gospel], saith the Lord, and touch not the unclean [anything that defiles a holy temple] thing; and I will receive you, And will be a Father unto you, and ye shall be my sons and daughters, saith the Lord Almighty.

—2 Corinthians 6:16–18

There is no such thing as a lukewarm relationship with God. He won't stand for it. You are either *hot* or you are *not*.

I know thy works, that thou art neither cold nor hot: I would thou wert cold or hot. So then because thou art lukewarm, and neither cold nor hot, I will spue thee out of my mouth.

—Revelation 3:15–16

I know that God would consider agape as hot. Take your chances as to whether phileo or eros line up with lukewarm or cold, as I won't be judge as to how God views it. The only acceptable relationship with God is one that is *hot*! The folks that are cold are lost and they know it; whereas the toughest to reach are those that are lukewarm, having their religion and traditions all figured out for God to approve.

Of the million or so people of the nation of Israel that were freed from their captivity in Egypt, only two men overcame fear, doubt, and unbelief and actually saw the promise of God fulfilled. Only Joshua and Caleb were able to enter into the Promised Land. Joshua nailed it when he spoke to those that were lukewarm amongst his large congregation when he said they found it evil to serve the Lord as the Lord commanded.

> The only acceptable relationship with God is one that is *hot*! The folks that are cold are lost and they know it; whereas the toughest to reach are those that are lukewarm having their religion and traditions all figured out for God to approve.

And if it seem evil unto you to serve the LORD, choose you this day whom ye will serve; whether the gods which your fathers served that were on the other side of the flood, or the gods of the Amorites, in whose land ye dwell: but as for me and my house, we will serve the LORD.

—Joshua 24:15

As for you, you must choose which kingdom you believe. Not making a choice does not place you in neutral territory; by not choosing to serve the Lord, we immediately default to dedicate ourselves to the service and sacrifice to the kingdom of this world.

Breach with yourself

Who am I, and what am I doing here? This may be the oldest and perhaps most universal question of humankind—I need to belong.

We know what the image and likeness of God is. We were created by the Maker to be just like Him, our heavenly Father. So any characteristic, emotion, or infirmity that is not in the image and likeness of God is not us, and it is not who and what we were created to be.

> And God said, Let us make man in our image, after our likeness: So God created man in his own image, in the image of God created he him; male and female created he them.
> —Genesis 1:26–27

God reminds us how we were created. The truest thing about you is that you were originally designed with a DNA of righteousness and true holiness. We are to put on the new man, which literally means to "sink into new clothes."

> And that ye put on the new man, which after God is created in righteousness and true holiness.
> —Ephesians 4:24

To accomplish what God needs to do in us, He must renew our knowledge of what it would be like to be in His image in our body, soul, mind, and spirit. The prophet Hosea writes that without knowledge the people perish (4:6).

> The truest thing about you is that you were originally designed with a DNA of righteousness and true holiness.

> And have put on the new man, which is renewed in knowledge after the image of him that created him.
> —Colossians 3:10

I've spent years trying to do things to get God to perform for me. If I didn't see any change, I thought it was because I wasn't doing my devotions often enough or long enough or perhaps I wasn't sacrificing enough to get His attention. But it's not by our works but by His works through the Holy Spirit where we receive the washing of regeneration, the restoration to our pristine state of origin. He intends to do an extreme makeover in us in order to restore us to original created form.

> Not by works of righteousness which we have done, but according to his mercy he saved us, by the washing of regeneration, and renewing of the Holy Ghost.
> —Titus 3:5

It is very important to realize that God not only created you in His image (holy and without blame or sanctified), but He did that before Genesis 1:1, before the foundation of the world. We had to be in His likeness in order to have a meaningful relationship with him.

According as he hath chosen us in him before the foundation of the world, that we should be holy and without blame before him in love.
—Ephesians 1:4

The Father was thinking about you for a long time before you entered the womb. Your earthly father had no idea about anything regarding you before you were born. The best he could do was to count all your fingers and toes and try to burp you; He could just inspect the goods as delivered.

Before I formed thee in the belly I knew thee.
—Jeremiah 1:5

Soon after choosing us, a perfect world was created for mankind to move into and have fellowship with God.

However, shortly after the world was created, Satan fell and corrupted the earth and mankind with everything that is devilish. God was grieved, knowing that all His kids would be born into a corrupted environment and would be exposed to defilement. He couldn't just scrap the whole thing and start over because we were already created and destined to arrive on earth.

> Predestination ought not to be a big mystery. God knew us all before the world began and decided beforehand (predestined) that we would all be in the image of Christ.

For whom he did foreknow, he also did predestinate to be conformed to the image of his Son, that he might be the firstborn among many brethren.
—Romans 8:29

Predestination ought not to be a big mystery. God knew us all before the world began and decided beforehand (predestined) that we would all be in the image of Christ. But even though that was God's will, He still left it up to us to choose our destiny kingdom.

I believe the Bible teaches that God had all of our names written in the Book of Life, which is really the invitation list for us to spend eternity with Him. He only blots our names off if we refuse His lifelong invitation for us to make Jesus complete Lord over everything in our life.

He that overcometh, the same shall be clothed in white raiment; and I will not blot out his name out of the book of life, but I will confess his name before my Father, and before his angels.
—Revelation 3:5

For further insights on the Book of Life and our invitation, check out these verses: Revelation 20:12, 15; Exodus 32:33; Psalms 69:28, 109:13; 2 Peter 3:9; Ezekiel 18:4; and Luke 10:20.

God always has and always will desire everyone to choose to accept His invitation, His destiny, and His purpose.

Who will have all men to be saved, and to come unto the knowledge of the truth.

—1 Timothy 2:4

Can you just see God rubbing His chin as He contemplated your design and how He would make your tent, your body, unique from everyone else? Actually we may think the tent to be important, but God puts most of his creative effort into your spirit and soul, which is much more complex, intriguing, and, no doubt, very entertaining. When God looks at you, He sees and communicates with you at the spirit level. In fact, when God lists His three greatest creative achievements, He lists the heavens and the earth; and He considers the spirit of man as an equal to the vastness of all creation.

> You are to love yourself at the level of your spirit—that is to love yourself from the inside out, not from the outside in.

> The burden of the word of the LORD for Israel, saith the LORD, which stretcheth forth the heavens, and layeth the foundation of the earth, and formeth the spirit of man within him.
>
> —Zechariah, 12:1

Who you are is not reflected in a mirror; that is just your tent. And you know what happens to tents? They deteriorate and fade from exposure. Ask God to tell you how He sees you. Agape love is at the level of the spirit, and the agape you are to have for yourself is much more than skin deep. You are to love yourself at the level of your spirit—that is to love yourself from the inside out, not from the outside in. We may be blessed with a beautiful tent when we are young, and hopefully as we mature the beauty of our spirit becomes so distracting that no one even notices the tent anymore. Stop being in "eros" with the tent, for that is idolatry.

> But now, O LORD, thou art our father; we are the clay, and thou our potter; and we all are the work of thy hand.
>
> —Isaiah 64:8

Prayer of Self-acceptance

Father, I am special. I know You created me before the foundation of the world for Your own special reasons. Thank You, Father, for the spirit, soul, and body that You gave me. I accept them as a gift from You, and I repent for all the wrong attitudes I have toward them.

Forgive me for saying _____ when I look in the mirror. Forgive me for harming my body by _____. I unconditionally forgive _____ for what they said about me. I forgive _____ for what they did to physically, emotionally, or sexually hurt me. I forgive _____ for doing things to me that made me want to reject myself. As I have forgiven them, I release them to You in my forgiveness.

Father, forgive me for not loving myself for the person You, the Potter, created me to be. I dedicate my life and my entire being to You, Father, and I rejoice in Your grace and mercy extended toward me. I pray in the name of Jesus Christ of Nazareth.

I appreciate that Paul, as a past Pharisee (they promote themselves as sinless), was able to pen this famous passage on what it is like to struggle with sin.

> For the good that I would I do not: but the evil which I would not, that I do. Now if I do that I would not, it is no more I that do it, but sin that dwelleth in me.
>
> —ROMANS 7:19–20

Paul reflects, "Hey, I know I struggle with sin but I also know that my sin is not me, this is not my true heart." You are not your sin. Your heart is good. The real you is created in the image of God and it wars against the false self.

You may have a disease, but you are not a disease; ditto for guilt, fear, self-hatred, rage, and anger. I may have an addiction to alcohol, but I am not an alcoholic. To say you are a disease is to make you cohabit with the enemy, whereas the enemy is to be defeated through your salvation and you are to claim victory.

When I am one with a characteristic that is not in the image of Christ, I portray that I am double-minded:

- I'm just shy
- I'm an addict
- That's just my nationality, we are all feisty
- I'm just high-spirited
- My dad was angry and so am I
- I am deathly afraid of speaking in public

To love ourselves, we have to reveal the real enemy and separate from that which is not us.

> As far as the east is from the west, so far hath he removed our transgressions from us.
>
> —PSALM 103:12

The entire Godhead was involved in your creation, and you are told what each part of the Godhead contributed to your compilation of soul and spirit. If God didn't give us fear, where did we get all these countless phobias?

> For God hath not given us the spirit of fear; but of power [Holy Spirit], and of love [God the Father], and of a sound mind [God the Word, Jesus].
>
> —2 TIMOTHY 1:7

Fear and countless other negative attributes were given to us by Satan, who was given legal access just as he gained to Peter or Eve. Satan duplicates the kingdom of God with his own imposters. For faith he gives fear. Faith in God places hope in our future, whereas fear projects despair and calamity into our future. Fear is Satan's faith.

> For the thing which I greatly feared is come upon me, and that which I was afraid of is come unto me.
>
> —Job 3:25

Whatever you meditate on the most will become a permanent part of your soul and spirit.

> As a man thinketh in his heart so is he.
>
> —Proverbs 23:7

> Now faith is the substance of things hoped for, the evidence of things not seen.
>
> —Hebrews 11:1

Fear and faith both produce their respective fruit. One fruit is of Satan, the other of God.

The only one that can reprogram you is God. Consider what He promises to do for you in order to return you to your true heritage, which is in the "image of God." He gives us a new software package.

> A new heart also will I give you, and a new spirit will I put within you: and I will take away the stony heart out of your flesh, and I will give you an heart of flesh. And I will put my spirit within you, and cause you to walk in my statutes, and ye shall keep my judgments, and do them.
>
> —Ezekiel 36:26–27

The stony heart that God promises to remove is a demonized heart. This passage is a prophecy that wouldn't be fulfilled until after Christ's ministry was completed on the Cross. In the Old Testament there were no provisions to do this type of heart transplant.

Breach with others

Although I wouldn't suggest you imitate what Jesus did in this next passage, it illustrates the truth that even though the words may come out your beloved's mouth, the origin is not of them but of Satan. When Peter rebuked Jesus, our Lord discerned who was really talking to Him. He looked right through Peter and rebuked Satan for the words that came out of Peter's mouth. Jesus didn't take offense with Peter nor make him one with his sin.

> And he began to teach them, that the Son of man must suffer many things, and be rejected of the elders, and of the chief priests, and scribes, and be killed, and after three days rise again. And he spake that saying openly. And Peter took him, and began to rebuke him. But when he had turned about and looked on his disciples, he rebuked Peter, saying, Get thee behind me, Satan: for thou savourest not the things that be of God, but the things that be of men.
>
> —Mark 8:31–33

Realizing the sin in others is not them, to see them separate from their sin, is the perspective of one living in the image of Christ and operating at the level of agape.

> Put on therefore, as the elect of God, holy and beloved, bowels of mercies, kindness, humbleness of mind, meekness, longsuffering. Forbearing [to sustain] one another, and forgiving one another, if any man have a quarrel against any: even as Christ forgave you, so also do ye. And above all these things put on charity [*agape*], which is the bond of perfectness.
>
> —Colossians 3:12–14

> The purpose of disciplining children is not for the parent's convenience or out of fear that the child won't turn out right but, to bring them up to holiness and sanctification in agape so they'll be most like their heavenly Father.

If you react to someone in rage and anger, all you are doing is satisfying the evil that dwelleth in them and in you.

The oldest lie in the book began in the garden with Satan suggesting to Eve that she was not fulfilling her destiny in the relationship she had with the Lord and her husband Adam. "Really, Eve, you are being brainwashed and held back," Satan taunted. "God told you what was best for Adam but you have to look after yourself, don't you want to be the one in control and stand up?"

> But of the fruit of the tree which is in the midst of the garden, God hath said, Ye shall not eat of it, neither shall ye touch it, lest ye die. And the serpent said unto the woman, Ye shall not surely die: For God doth know that in the day ye eat thereof, then your eyes shall be opened, and ye shall be as gods, knowing good and evil. And when the woman saw that the tree was good for food, and that it was pleasant to the eyes, and a tree to be desired to make one wise, she took of the fruit thereof, and did eat, and gave also unto her husband with her; and he did eat. And the eyes of them both were opened, and they knew that they were naked; and they sewed fig leaves together, and made themselves aprons.
>
> —Genesis 3:3–7

What level of love was Eve functioning at here? Could Eve say her downfall was because of the family she grew up in?

You may have some characteristics that resemble your parents, but you are most like your heavenly Father. Actually your parents have absolutely no influence regarding what you will look like, what kind of personality you'll have, or what sex you'll be.

Parents are entrusted with the management and nurturing of the affairs of the Father's kids from conception until the Father needs them. The parent's role is that of a governor or tutor.

> Now I say, That the heir, as long as he is a child, differeth nothing from a servant, though he be lord of all; But is under tutors and governors until the time appointed of the father.
>
> —GALATIANS 4:1–2

God made husband and wife one, desiring for them to be inseparable and thus providing a better environment to raise godly children for the Lord.

> Yet ye say, Wherefore? Because the LORD hath been witness between thee and the wife of thy youth, against whom thou hast dealt treacherously: yet is she thy companion, and the wife of thy covenant. And did not he make one? Yet had he the residue of the spirit. And wherefore one? That he might seek a godly seed. Therefore take heed to your spirit, and let none deal treacherously against the wife of his youth.
>
> —MALACHI 2:14–15

Godly seed means a special possession of God or godlike one. The purpose of disciplining children is not for the parent's convenience or out of fear that the child won't turn out right, but to bring them up to holiness and sanctification in agape so they'll be most like their heavenly Father.

What does an environment to raise up godly children look like?

> Furthermore we have had fathers of our flesh which corrected us, and we gave them reverence: shall we not much rather be in subjection unto the Father of spirits, and live? For they [earthly fathers] verily for a few days chastened us after their own pleasure; but he for our profit, that we might be partakers of his holiness.
>
> —HEBREWS 12:9–10

> Sin may have separated you from His presence, but it can't separate you from His love.

All discipline is to be for the profit of the recipient, which is how discipline through agape is designed by God to work.

There are two things to grasp: (1) learn to separate yourself from what is not really you and (2) learn to separate others from the part of them that is not really them. Why? Because you must forgive them, so God, in turn will forgive you, when you seek Him for forgiveness.

THE LOVE STREAM RESTORED

The first place to be reconciled is to God. Sin may have separated you from His presence, but it can't separate you from His love.

> But God commendeth his love toward us, in that, while we were yet sinners, Christ died for us.
>
> —ROMANS 5:8

For some reason I concluded that God was mad at me, and that Jesus, my friend, was busy stopping lightning bolts destined for me. God does hate sin, of course, but He loves you, He knows you are *not* your sin.

But I would have you know, that the head of every man is Christ; and the head of the woman is the man; and the head of Christ is God.

—1 CORINTHIANS 11:3

- The head of Christ is the Father,
- The head of man is Christ,
- The head of the wife is the man.

The intended love stream from the Almighty to creation starts with the Father, flows through Jesus to the man, and from there, flows to the woman and the children.

A self-check here: when you read the above verse, do you find it evil to serve the Lord through such an arrangement?

The person, the love, the speech, the thought, and the action of the only wise God are to be imaged in creation first to a man then to His daughters. God ordained this love stream, not for man's benefit and ego, but that God's daughters would receive this amplified benefit of His love.

Jesus "went about doing good" (Acts 10:38). Doing good is to be perfected in the home, the matrimonial church, before you look elsewhere to minister, just as we see in the criteria for deacons and elders in the Word. (See 1 Timothy 3:1–13.) "Doing good" is not the same as coming home after work and "expecting good."

With respect to you ladies, daughters, and wives, we haven't done a good job of the one thing we were to get right. I've had to repent to my wife and my children many times for failing to properly represent our Father's love to them.

How many of you as children cannot remember your father saying, "I love you"? Perhaps eight out of ten of us have never heard those words from our dads, "Son, I love you," or "Daughter, I love you." The conclusion is that the bulk of Christianity hasn't experienced the love of our God in our family as we were supposed to, and many feel they have been abandoned. But wait, the Word says that God is a Father to the fatherless (Ps. 68:5).

"Doing good" is not the same as coming home after work and "expecting good. You may have had a poor example of an earthly father, and most likely he, in turn, had a poor example of an earthly father; but God the Father loves you. He sent His Holy Spirit to get your attention, and the fact that you are reading this book is not by coincidence. Would you like to make peace with Him?

In many households the father is alive and at home, but the children are still fatherless and the wife is a widow emotionally and spiritually because he does not represent Jesus as husband.

Pure religion and undefiled before God and the Father is this, To visit the fatherless and widows in their affliction, and to keep himself unspotted from the world.

—JAMES 1:27

Do you come from a family that is a little messed up; do you wish you were born into a normal family? You are!

> For this cause I bow my knees unto the Father of our Lord Jesus Christ,
> Of whom the whole family in heaven and earth is named.
> —EPHESIANS 3:14–15

We were all formed directly and personally by Him before the foundation of the earth was laid. God named us after Himself! We're part of His family. (See Isaiah 64:8; Acts 17:24–31.)

The father sets the emotional well being of his daughters and sons. Children of an unloving father will look for eros love simply because they don't know any better.

You may say, "Well, I knew my father loved me." Did he say it? Did he abuse you emotionally, physically, or sexually? Did you have to drive yourself to perform in order to meet his approval? And so we wonder why we don't trust God. If you had an earthly father that didn't properly represent God the Father to you, you may shudder when I say "father."

A greeting card company provided Mother's Day cards to a prison and they found that all the prisoners sent cards to their mothers. This was so successful they thought they should try the same at Father's Day. However, not one prisoner sent a card to his dad. When did their lonely prison sentence start? When they were left fatherless!

Our Father is God. Your husband for eternity is Jesus, whether you are male or female.

> For I am jealous over you with godly jealousy: for I have espoused you to one husband, that I may present you as a chaste virgin to Christ.
> —2 CORINTHIANS 11:2

I know it stretches the guys a little to understand they are a "wife." It is not in the carnal human sense but in the spiritual understanding that we are the "helpmate" that the Father selected for His Son through eternity.

I learn from Jesus how to be a better husband to my wife; and I learn from my wife's example how to be a good helpmate to Jesus. I can't expect something out of her in a manner of which I am not submitting myself to my "husband," Jesus.

Recently I was choosing to read scripture regarding the gal's role in marriage. I had a bad attitude and was accusing my wife in my heart, thinking, *Why can't she read this and see it and want to do what the Bible says? Things would be so great if only…* My juices were just starting to enjoy the stew I was mixing up when I was provoked in my heart to "go ahead and make a list of every area in which you feel she isn't submissive." So I did. I pressed on the pen so hard that I imprinted through several pages at a time in my leather-bound journal. I guess I was enjoying this little exercise until it was mostly done and my fingers were starting to go numb from pressing so hard on that little pen. Then I sensed the Spirit of God say, "Now read over the list real carefully." As soon as I started to reread the dreadful list, I knew my sin was exposed as I realized that everything that I was accusing my beloved were things that I was guilty of myself in my relationship to Jesus Christ. You see, the same things that I was judging her for, I was doing to the one I was to be in submission to. Yes, I repented and realized how difficult a calling God had placed on my wife.

> Likewise, ye wives, be in subjection [to willfully put under another's control, to yield to another's admonition or advice, submission] to your own husbands; that, if any [husbands] obey not the word, they also may without the word [much speaking doesn't change anything] be won by the conversation [manner of conduct, behavior] of the wives; While they behold your chaste [exciting reverence, pure from carnality] conversation coupled with fear.
>
> —1 PETER 3:1–2

Peter is saying, "Women, if your husband is not in obedience to the Word, they will still be influenced by your purity in behavior. They will learn how to be a good husband in subjection to Jesus as you in turn model to them what a good wife looks like."

The flesh will have you point out his inadequacies—what does that accomplish? Peter is giving a spiritual principal; it may go against the carnal wisdom of the day and be distasteful even; but if a wife senses lack and wants change, this is how it is done. Anything else would be a work of the flesh and will only cause a wider rift.

Many Christians love Jesus but are distant from the Father. You are in error if Jesus is greater in your relationship with the Godhead.

> Every good gift and every perfect gift is from above, and cometh down from the Father of lights, with whom is no variableness, neither shadow of turning.
>
> —JAMES 1:17

> And in that day ye shall ask me nothing. Verily, verily, I say unto you, Whatsoever ye shall ask the Father in my name, he will give it you.
>
> —JOHN 16:23

Jesus said, "In that day." What day? The day He goes back to the Father. You shall ask me nothing, but you shall ask the Father in my name and He shall give you whatever you ask. Quit avoiding the Father. Jesus is not going to go over the head of the Father to answer your prayer. Note: we don't tell Jesus or the Father what to do. We ask the Father in the name of Jesus. If you approach prayer differently you ask amiss.

When Jesus taught us how to pray: He said, "Our Father who art in heaven."

- Whose will is to be fulfilled on earth?
- Who supplies our daily bread?

- Who forgives us? (This one has a condition: see below.)
- Who delivers us from evil?

The answer to each of the above questions is our Father in heaven.

> For if ye forgive men their trespasses, your heavenly Father will also for-
> give you. But if ye forgive not men their trespasses, neither will your
> Father forgive your trespasses.
> —MATTHEW 6:14–15

You can't be asking to receive from the Father on one hand and not be willing to give on the other.

Who judges us, the Father or Jesus Christ? (See 2 Timothy 4:1.)

> For the Father judgeth no man, but hath committed all judgment unto
> the Son.
> —JOHN 5:22

> For we must all appear before the judgment seat of Christ; that every one
> may receive the things done in his body, according to that he hath done,
> whether it be good or bad.
> —2 CORINTHIANS 5:10

Jesus is our judge, and at the same time our Savior. Wow!

> Jesus saith unto him, I am the way, the truth, and the life: no man
> cometh unto the Father, but by me.
> —JOHN 14:6

Jesus is the Way, but you are still coming to the Father aren't you?

We say, "If God really loved me I wouldn't be sick or my life wouldn't be in such a mess." That is a voice from another kingdom, the kingdom of the "god of this world," Satan, who is behind all calamities and is blaming your Lord to divert suspicion from himself.

When the Father speaks of His Son, listen to what a loving Father has to say.

> While he yet spake, behold, a bright cloud overshadowed them: and
> behold a voice out of the cloud, which said, This is my beloved Son, in
> whom I am well pleased; hear ye him.
> —MATTHEW 17:5

You should have heard your earthly father speak likewise as though it were your heavenly Father when you were growing up. If you didn't, you've prob-ably had difficulty relating to your heavenly Father because He was misrep-resented to you. If all your father did was punish you, it will be difficult to comprehend a Father of overflowing love.

Even though your earthly father may have neglected you, your Father in heaven has picked you up. He is proud to shout out, "My son, my daughter, I love you!"

> But as many as received him, to them gave he power to become the sons of God, even to them that believe on his name.
>
> —JOHN 1:12

> For as many as are led by the Spirit of God, they are the sons of God. For ye have not received the spirit of bondage again to fear; but ye have received the Spirit of adoption, whereby we cry, Abba, Father. The Spirit itself beareth witness with our spirit, that we are the children of God.
>
> —ROMANS 8:14–16

Your Father in heaven wants to meet you right now to heal the broken heart, the battered heart, the hardened heart, and those that are afraid, feel unclean, or have hurt that goes very deep. God the Father will stretch forth His hand to heal you in the name of Jesus.

Call on the Ancient of Days to restore the breach in the love stream. If your earthly father is unable or unwilling to take back what he has lost, the One who said, "I'll be a Father to the fatherless," will step in and close the gap. He'll repair the breach in the love stream, which will draw you even closer to Him.

> If we have only phileo or eros love toward another we are to be blamed and are not walking in holiness. Phileo or eros don't meet the minimum requirements at judgment.

Jesus Christ came to heal the brokenhearted and to give you liberty, to free you from every bondage. Jesus will be your advocate to restore you completely to our Father.

> The Spirit of the Lord GOD is upon me; because the LORD hath anointed me to preach good tidings unto the meek; he hath sent me to bind up the brokenhearted, to proclaim liberty to the captives, and the opening of the prison to them that are bound.
>
> —ISAIAH 61:1

Our obedience is what qualifies us to receive this agape and the empowering of agape is the work of the Holy Spirit.

The following is a prayer that Paul prayed for the church. He prayed that the agape of the father would increase (exist in abundance) and abound (to be given more than you can possibly contain). It is this agape that is the root cause of the abundant life Christ promises. Verse thirteen states that if we are not streaming this agape, we are to be blamed and we can't be holy before God without it. In other words, if we have only phileo or eros love toward another, we are to be blamed and are not walking in holiness. Phileo or eros do not meet the minimum requirements at judgment.

> And the Lord make you to increase and abound in love [*agape*] one toward another, and toward all men, even as we do toward you: To the end he

may stablish your hearts unblameable in holiness before God, even our Father, at the coming of our Lord Jesus Christ with all his saints.

—1 THESSALONIANS 3:12–13

Now the end of the commandment is charity [*agape*] out of a pure heart, and of a good conscience, and of faith unfeigned.

—1 TIMOTHY 1:5

Pure means cleansed in the Levitical sense and disinfected to kill all the residue and pollutions of sin. *Conscience* refers to spiritual discernment. *Agape* is what makes *faith* sincere and single-minded. Agape requires a work on our part whereby our spirit is cleansed, our discernment is actuated, and our allegiance is unwavering.

Nevertheless I have somewhat against thee, because thou hast left thy first love [*agape*]. Remember therefore from whence thou art fallen, and repent, and do the first works; or else I will come unto thee quickly, and will remove thy candlestick out of his place, except thou repent.

—REVELATION 2:4–5

So we recognize we are missing out big time on agape. Jesus requires us to repent and do first works because without this agape we are fallen or cast off. From where have we fallen? Before the world was formed we were created before Him in agape, and we are required to be restored to that person who is Christlike. Over the next few chapters we will remember from where we have fallen, we will recognize our sin, repent, and do our first works to be fully and painstakingly restored.

HALLOWED BE THY NAME

T HE SECOND SENTENCE of our Lord's Prayer is an easy passage to let slip by without engaging. It was important enough for Jesus to include in this model prayer that He knew would instruct His people for the next twenty or more centuries. Hallowed, as it refers to God, means holy. There is probably no surprise there, as we know God's name is holy.

As God is holy, He cannot set a lower level of spirituality for us to attain to. God doesn't set an impossible standard for His kids, as He created each of us in His image and He knows that once we have been able to stand strong in our wind tunnels, we will be just like Him.

> Be ye therefore perfect, even as your Father which is in heaven is perfect.
> —MATTHEW 5:48

It is God's intention that His messengers would lead the sheep into maturity—the fullness, the holiness, and the agape of Christ.

And he gave some, apostles; and some, prophets; and some, evangelists; and some, pastors and teachers; For the perfecting of the saints, for the work of the ministry, for the edifying of the body of Christ: Till we all come in the unity of the faith, and of the knowledge of the Son of God, unto a perfect man, unto the measure of the stature of the fullness of Christ: That we henceforth be no more children, tossed to and fro, and carried about with every wind of doctrine, by the sleight of men, and cunning craftiness, whereby they lie in wait to deceive; But speaking the truth in love [*agape*], may grow up into him in all things, which is the head, even Christ.
> —EPHESIANS 4:11

> I've tried to be holy how about you? Rather embarrassing when it is discovered how "holely" my act is, especially in my home.

WHY IS THIS SO DIFFICULT FOR ME?

I've tried to be holy. How about you? It's rather embarrassing when it is discovered how "holely" my act is, especially in my home. The Scripture painted a clear picture of how I was to act, so I "acted." The desire of my life was to be pleasing to the Lord and to build my home on the rock with an overflowing love. So how could it fall apart? I had to realize that what I believed and what I practiced got me to the place I found myself in.

I believed Scripture that I wasn't to let the sun go down on my wrath, as that would give the devil an opportunity. So if I perceived an offense, I would badger my beloved until she became reasonable and saw it my way, no matter how late it was at night or how long I had to chase her about the house until my wrath was satisfied and she repented and we made up. The result was that my wife was in fear and shut down. She heard me teach about gentleness and respect, but felt hopeless when I couldn't get what I knew to drop from my poor head down to my heart. It is written that it is the "goodness of the Lord that leadeth to repentance" not the manipulation and force-fulness of the Lord that causes one to blurt out

> God desired to experience our lives more intimately so He needed to move in with those that established a covenant relationship with Him.

words to divert the heat. Jesus said, "If you love Me, *feed* My sheep"; He did not say, "If you love Me, beat My sheep." I knew the scripture said that love is kind, patient, and suffers long, it bears all things, never fails, is not easily provoked, and seeks not its own. I knew a lot of other scripture as well, and yet I found that when it really mattered most, I fell to the depths of unholy passions. I cried out to the Lord often, "Why is this so difficult for me? What part of life do I not understand?"

Thus began a process of relearning the Scriptures from the ground up, as a lot of my understanding was based on the traditions of religious men, which resulted in a weak easy-to-swallow gospel that frankly didn't move any mountains.

I was taught that *sanctify* meant simply "to be set apart." When I was in grade school, I was often set apart in class and that meant I got to sit by myself in the corner of the room and zip the lips. So I tried "to set myself apart" for the Lord and still found I didn't become very holy.

The result of our sanctification is that we become holy, which means we mirror the character of God.

> Sanctify yourselves therefore, and be ye holy: for I am the Lord your God.
> —Leviticus 20:7

God is the same yesterday, today, and forever (Heb. 13:8), thus His requirements of the Old Testament are the same as the requirements of the New Testament. We are to be holy before a holy God; that is not a suggestion.

> But as he which hath called you is holy, so be ye holy in all manner of conversation; Because it is written, Be ye holy; for I am holy.
> —1 Peter 1:15–16

In the Old Testament the Lord required not only the individual to be holy but He also required His house, the temple, to be holy as well.

And the LORD said unto him, I have heard thy prayer and thy supplication, that thou hast made before me: I have hallowed this house, which thou hast built, to put my name there forever; and mine eyes and mine heart shall be there perpetually.

—1 KINGS 9:3

To enter into the holy of holies within the temple, the priests would have to cleanse or sanctify themselves; and if they didn't that meant certain death as they approached a holy God presumptuously and carelessly.

The result of Jesus Christ's ministry is that the temple that used to be a building was moved to a new location—into our very being. God desired to experience our life more intimately so He needed to move in with those that established a covenant relationship with Him.

Know ye not that ye are the temple of God, and that the Spirit of God dwelleth in you?

—1 CORINTHIANS 3:16

Once we move from the kingdom of darkness and into the kingdom of His dear Son, the Certificate of Title for our bodies changes to the new owner as well.

To open their eyes, and to turn them from darkness to light, and from the power of Satan unto God, that they may receive forgiveness of sins, and inheritance among them which are sanctified by faith that is in me.

—ACTS 26:18

POSSESS YOUR TEMPLE IN SANCTIFICATION AND HONOR

We are not our own as we were purchased by Jesus for a price, a great price. Consider the truth that you are a spiritual being that happens to have a body rather than a body that has a spirit. Your body is a tent and is a temporary shelter for your spirit, which is already living for eternity and will soon take on an eternal body.

What? know ye not that your body is the temple of the Holy Ghost which is in you, which ye have of God, and ye are not your own?

—1 CORINTHIANS 6:19

When you purchase a home that was previously owned, you have to renovate it and clean it up so that it is suitable for your family to move into and feel comfortable. In the same manner, prior to the Holy Spirit being able to move in, He has to do a thorough cleansing and renovation so that He'll be comfortable.

That every one of you should know how to possess his vessel in sanctification and honour.

—1 THESSALONIANS 4:4

The best commentary on the Bible is the Bible itself. To properly understand what the Spirit of God means with a particular word, one must search the Scripture to find the word used in similar context and study its meaning. To study the meaning of the word *sanctify*, which occurs over 130 times in Scripture, we'll look at 2 Chronicles 29.

> The priests were to sanctify the temple. How did they do that? They had to first clean out the filthiness, as a place that is holy cannot be full of filth.

The temple of God was all messed up due to years of neglect, such as our bodies were after years of abuse. The priests were to sanctify the temple. How did they do that? They had to first clean out the filthiness, as a place that is holy cannot be full of filth. Filth implies impurity due to immorality and idolatry.

> For our fathers have trespassed, and done that which was evil in the eyes of the LORD our God, and have forsaken him, and have turned away their faces from the habitation of the LORD, and turned their backs.... For, lo, our fathers have fallen by the sword, and our sons and our daughters and our wives are in captivity for this. Now it is in mine heart to make a covenant with the LORD God of Israel, that his fierce wrath may turn away from us. My sons, be not now negligent: for the LORD hath chosen you to stand before him, to serve him, and that ye should minister unto him, and burn incense. Then the Levites arose...and sanctified themselves, and came, according to the commandment of the king, by the words of the LORD, to cleanse the house of the LORD. And the priests went into the inner part of the house of the LORD, to cleanse it, and brought out all the uncleanness that they found in the temple of the LORD into the court of the house of the LORD. And the Levites took it, to carry it out abroad into the brook Kidron.
> —2 CHRONICLES 29:6, 9–12, 15–16

Kidron is a stream that flows between the Mount of Olives and the city of Jerusalem and empties into the Dead Sea. *Kidron* means "dark." The filth of immorality and idolatry had to be dumped into a dark river, which in turn carried it to a "dead" sea.

The temple had become unclean due to the generational sins of their forefathers and their idolatry. *Idolatry* is going to any other place or listening to any voice other than the voice of God. As a result of their sin, they experienced death and their families were in captivity. Our families may be in captivity to addictions, rejection, divorce, abuse, envy, and jealousy or anger, to name a few. In the Old Testament God was very serious about sin and judged accordingly.

> Therefore I will judge you, O house of Israel, every one according to his ways, saith the Lord GOD. Repent, and turn yourselves from all your transgressions; so iniquity shall not be your ruin. Cast away from you all

your transgressions, whereby ye have transgressed; and make you a new heart and a new spirit: for why will ye die, O house of Israel? For I have no pleasure in the death of him that dieth, saith the Lord GOD: wherefore turn yourselves, and live ye.

—EZEKIEL 18:30–32

In the New Testament, what is God's position on sin and the cleansing of the temple, which is now within you and I?

Know ye not that ye are the temple of God, and that the Spirit of God dwelleth in you? If any man defile the temple of God, him shall God destroy; for the temple of God is holy, which temple ye are.

—1 CORINTHIANS 3:16–17

God does not change in His position on sin and His temple. He is a holy God. Does God mean what He says about destroying those who defile His new temple? Yes! I had to rethink my attitude towards sin.

God is good, but at the same time He is severe in His dealings with those who once walked in His ways and then fell into unrepentant sin. He is a holy God, so there is no other option in His approach to sin.

Well; because of unbelief they were broken off, and thou standest by faith. Be not highminded, but fear: For if God spared not the natural branches, take heed lest he also spare not thee. Behold therefore the goodness and severity [sharpness, a cutting off, roughness] of God: on them which fell, severity; but toward thee, goodness, if thou continue in his goodness: otherwise thou also shalt be cut off.

—ROMANS 11:20–22

Jesus teaches that the sin that defiles does not oppress us from outside our bodies but from within our heart our spirit. He makes it clear so there is no mistake—sin comes from our heart and defiles the temple of the Holy Spirit.

There is nothing from without a man, that entering into him can defile him: but the things which come out of him, those are they that defile the man....Do ye not perceive, that whatsoever thing from without entereth into the man, it cannot defile him; Because *it entereth not into his heart,* but into the belly, and goeth out into the draught, purging all meats? And he said, That which cometh out of the man, that defileth the man. For from within, out of the heart of men, proceed evil thoughts, adulteries, fornications, murders, Thefts, covetousness, wickedness, deceit, lasciviousness, an evil eye, blasphemy, pride, foolishness: All these evil things come from within, and defile the man.

—MARK 7:15–23, EMPHASIS ADDED

The will of God, believer, is that you know how to cleanse your temple and to keep it clean and sanctified. We are now the priest of this temple, and as the Levites (priests) had to cleanse themselves and the temple of the Old Testament, so do we have to cleanse ourselves so the temple of God will be

Holy. Addressed to "dearly beloved," the believer is required to cleanse the filth out of the flesh and their spirit.

> Having therefore these promises, dearly beloved, let us cleanse [free from defilement of sin and to pronounce clean in a Levitical sense] ourselves from all filthiness of the flesh and spirit, perfecting holiness in the fear of God.
> —2 Corinthians 7:1

> For this is the will of God, even your sanctification, that ye should abstain from fornication: That every one of you should know how to possess his vessel in sanctification and honour.
> —1 Thessalonians 4:3–4

Before we approach the temple of God within, we have to cleanse our spirits. Not to cleanse our spirits through repentance and sanctification and to approach God is to do so presumptuously.

> The will of God, believer, is that you know how to cleanse your temple and to keep it clean and sanctified.

> And he did evil, because he prepared not his heart to seek the Lord. If any man defile the temple of God, him shall God destroy; for the temple of God is holy.
> —2 Chronicles 12:14

Cleansing or purging is required before our Master can use us and give us credit for our good works.

> But in a great house there are not only vessels of gold and of silver, but also of wood and of earth; and some to honour, and some to dishonour. If a man therefore purge himself from these, he shall be a vessel unto honour, sanctified, and meet for the master's use, and prepared unto every good work.
> —2 Timothy 2:20–21

Our sin puts us on the shelf until we can see where we have fallen short and deal with it so we are not limiting the work God wants to do through His temple.

> Yea, they turned back and tempted God, and limited the Holy One of Israel.
> —Psalm 78:41

Recently I was convicted regarding my approach to cleansing of my temple. I felt unclean after defending myself to a friend, trying to restore my reputation. I was so grieved and worked up in my heart through my actions that I went for a long run, repeating over and over and over:

> *I am Your temple. Fill me. Restore Your temple to its former glory and cleanse it. Give me a zeal for the fear of the Lord. Give me a zeal for holiness. Give me a zeal for the hatred of sin!*

I repented for the uncleanness I brought into the temple. Jesus made Himself of no reputation. I felt I had to preserve reputation and the only way I could do that in my flesh was by judging and uncovering someone I loved deeply.

> And Joshua said unto the people, Sanctify yourselves: for to morrow the LORD will do wonders among you.
>
> —JOSHUA 3:5

My repentance was not done; I realized I was cleansing my temple for my personal benefit, really out of my pride, so I would reap the rewards; whereas God required me to cleanse His temple for His glory. I am not my own—the temple is not my own, but I am my temple's caretaker.

> I am Your temple. Fill me, restore Your temple to its former glory and cleanse it. Give me a zeal for the fear of the Lord. Give me a zeal for holiness. Give me a zeal for the hatred of sin!

The purpose of our lives is for God to experience us. He desires that kind of intimacy with us. A constant joy of my heart was to head out with my beloved wife on long walks to enjoy God's creation of nature. We would take in the beauty together, which would take my experience to a whole different level. I beheld her radiance as she experienced the beauty of a wild flower or a butterfly at such a deeper degree than I was able to. I believe God likes to experience our life through us. He is an intimate loving God.

The kingdom of God is God experiencing you. He does that through those who are sanctified and meet for the Master's use. First works are the activities required to cleanse the temple of God within us so that the glory of the Godhead will be at home in our temple. The temple is not cleansed solely for our benefit, but for the benefit of God who created you, so that He can reside in you; see through you;

> My pride makes me lord of my own life.

use your lips; move your hands; inspire your mind; love upon, within, and through you to be your courage and your boldness.

Pride defiles my temple

God dwells with us in His holy place when and only when we have recognized and dealt with pride. Why is that? Well my pride makes me lord of my own life. The same thing happened to Lucifer, who was in the presence of God then He was lifted up with pride and self-promoting ambition. This ended his relationship with God, as he was now left to his own devices void of God.

> For thus saith the high and lofty One that inhabiteth eternity, whose name is Holy; I dwell in the high and holy place, with him also that is of a contrite and humble spirit, to revive the spirit of the humble, and to revive the heart of the contrite ones.
>
> —ISAIAH 57:15

Sexual sin defiles my temple

Fornication is hidden sexual activity of any sort outside of a covenant marriage bed. Sex makes you one flesh with whoever the activity is with, as that is how God designed it. It is the only sin that forms an unusual tie between your soul, mind, spirit, body, and the object of your sin. Satan knows how fornication defiles the temple, thus expelling the presence of God from His temple, as His vessel is no longer holy. Fornication in this sense also refers to idolatry. Idolatry is misdirected fear, where we obey the thing feared in contrast to godly fear, where we fear God. Satan always has a counterfeit evil to everything that is of God.

> All sin is directed against God, it is rebellion against God. The sin or trespass is always against the government that declares the law.

> What? Know ye not that he which is joined to an harlot is one body? for two, saith he, shall be one flesh. But he that is joined unto the Lord is one spirit. Flee fornication. Every sin that a man doeth is without the body; but he that committeth fornication sinneth against his own body. What? know ye not that your body is the temple of the Holy Ghost which is in you, which ye have of God, and ye are not your own? For ye are bought with a price: therefore glorify God in your body, and in your spirit, which are God's.
> —1 Corinthians 6:16–20

Pride, idolatry, and sexual deviance are singled out in particular in how they defile the temple of God, leaving it unclean and breaking fellowship with a holy God. All sin is directed against God; it is rebellion against God. Sin or trespass is always against the government that declares the law. This is not to say we don't have to go and make each offense right personally; we do. We'll go through in detail your duty regarding offense in another chapter.

> For I acknowledge my transgressions: and my sin is ever before me. Against thee, thee only, have I sinned, and done this evil in thy sight: Behold, I was shapen in iniquity; and in sin did my mother conceive me.
> —Psalm 51:3–5

Hidden sin festers like a wound that won't heal. In a wound, the bright red and purple highlight draws attention to the defect. It is amazing how no matter what I've tried to pull off in secret, it has been exposed, as God loves me and needs me to heal up completely in that defective area.

> But if ye will not do so, behold, ye have sinned against the Lord: and be sure your sin will find you out.
> —Numbers 32:23

All sin defiles the temple leaving it unfit for the Holy Spirit to use.

THY KINGDOM COME

THE KINGDOM THAT the god of this world, Satan, has usurped from Adam is to be replaced with the kingdom of God, one temple at a time. Adam lost the moral majority right to rule the earth through negligence in handling the Master's commands. By becoming a Christian one is immediately enlisted in the Lord's army and must learn to fight with the most advanced and mighty weapons; weapons that are not manmade but mighty in pulling down of massive strongholds (2 Cor. 10:4), weapons that are activated anywhere anytime by voice command.

One thing I've learned is that the Holy Spirit always says what He means and means exactly what He says in the Bible; and if something looks contradictory, it is only because there is something I don't yet understand. There are some incredibly "brave" souls that will pronounce they have discovered error in the Word of God to justify their intermittent allegorizing of Scripture to mold to their fancies, but I am not such a man. To build a solid case in court, an investigator must make no assumptions, even proving the obvious with the evidence of multiple witnesses. I've found most truth in the Bible is missed by the reader assuming that he has a complete understanding of a word or concept, so he doesn't dig deeper.

The main contender for the initial set up of the world's kingdom was not Adam, it was a cherub named Lucifer. The original sin was not Adams either; it occurred long before Adam was formed by the Lord. Consider the five "I wills" of Lucifer that fueled his ambition to be the famous one.

> All of sin and the result thereof have their roots in the same defiance, where we say, "I Will," rather than, "Thy Will."

> How art thou fallen from heaven, O Lucifer, son of the morning! how art thou cut down to the ground, which didst weaken the nations! For thou hast said in thine heart, *I will* ascend into heaven, *I will* exalt my throne above the stars of God: *I will* sit also upon the mount of the congregation, in the sides of the north: *I will* ascend above the heights of the clouds; *I will* be like the most High. Yet thou shalt be brought down to hell, to the sides of the pit.
> —ISAIAH 14:12–15, EMPHASIS ADDED

The root of all sin is pride. Pride is where it is *I will* rather than *Thy will*.

THE EARTH WAS WITHOUT FORM AND VOID. WHY?

We will explore a teaching that may be different from what you may have believed, but I challenge you to explore these ideas from the Word to see if they may be true. Is it possible that a concept that we thought we knew that we knew that we knew may have only been true in part? We will just introduce a concept here and hopefully provoke you to study the precepts on your own. This concept may not be an essential doctrine of the faith, so we will not need to part fellowship should there be differing perspectives on this. There is value in considering some strongly held religious positions by holding them up to the Word to see if they truly line up. If we find that a concept we so strongly believed that we understood is found to be in error through the Scriptures, the question will then need to be asked: "What else have I just accepted as true that may be found to be lacking?"

> In the beginning God created the heaven and the earth. [Here occurs the destruction of Jeremiah 4.] And the earth was without form, and void; and darkness was upon the face of the deep. And the Spirit of God moved upon the face of the waters.
> —GENESIS 1:1–2

There may be a timeframe between Geneses 1:1 and 1:2; and that period of time would be accounted for in Jeremiah 4:23–27.

> I beheld the earth, and, lo, it was without form [*tohuw*], and void [*bohuw*]; and the heavens, and they had no light. I beheld the mountains, and, lo, they trembled, and all the hills moved lightly. I beheld, and, lo, there was no man, and all the birds of the heavens were fled. I beheld, and, lo, the fruitful place was a wilderness, and all the cities thereof were broken down at the presence of the LORD, and by his fierce anger. For thus hath the LORD said, The whole land shall be desolate; yet will I not make a full end.
> —JEREMIAH 4:23–27

Jeremiah is setting the timeframe for this account: it was when the earth was without form and void, which would position it at Genesis 1:2. The heavens were there but gave off no light. The mountains trembled as in the effects of an earthquake. The hills moved slightly. They were experiencing aftershocks of a quake. The cities were broken down and the orchards or plantations were destroyed in an obvious judgment of God. What cities were these? Were there cities on earth prior to Genesis 1:2? Were there men, birds, heavens, and mountains already in existence prior to the seven days of creation recorded in Genesis?

It appears so, as Jeremiah notes mankind was completely wiped out and the birds were chased away. This is definitely not talking about Noah's flood as the heavens still had light then, the earth still had form and was not void, and there were still humans and birds in existence, although few in number. It is apparent that the reason the earth became without form and void was because of God's fierce judgment on a people that lived in cities and kept orchards and plantations for food, a pre-adamic people. The flood of Noah's fame was also because of God's judgment, but the world was only flooded and then dried up again not requiring re-creation.

The writer of Genesis gives a quick summary of what had happened in the first chapter of this book. First he said that God rested from what He made and what He created. God made certain things from the elements that were already there and others were created from nothing.

> And God blessed the seventh day, and sanctified it: because that in it he had rested from all his work which God created [*bara*] and made [*asah*]. These are the generations of the heavens and of the earth when they were created, in the day that the LORD God made the earth and the heavens.
>
> —GENESIS 2:3–4

Secondly, the writer, in reference to the first chapter of Genesis, tells us that it speaks of more than one heaven and earth generation. *Generations* as used here refers to an account of men and their descendants, the course of history of creation. The word *these,* is plural, referring to "generations," which is also plural. The first generation is covered only in verse 1: "In the beginning God created the heaven and the earth." The second generation starts with verse 2: "And the earth was without form, and void."

Upon inspection of the original language in 2 Peter, we have two distinct worldwide floods referred to.

The first passage tells us:

> And spared not the old [*archaios*; a good while ago] world, but saved Noah the eighth person, a preacher of righteousness, bringing in the flood upon the world of the ungodly.
>
> —2 PETER 2:5

To compare the application of the Greek word *archaios* so that we understand what era it refers to, we note that Jesus used the same word to refer to the giving of the law of the Moses era:

> Ye have heard that it was said by them [Moses] of old time [*archaios*]: Thou shalt not commit adultery.
>
> —MATTHEW 5:27

The flood of 2 Peter 2:5 occurred a good while ago during the era of the ancients of the Bible such as Noah and Moses.

Peter then goes on to describe in chapter three what appears to be a different flood of a much older time frame. A different Greek word, *ekpalai*, is used that means of a former age. Furthermore, the Greek word for *beginning* is *arche*, which means the extreme or absolute beginning of all things. Do you think the Holy Spirit is trying to get our attention?

My experience in teaching this is that I usually have scoffers in the audience that just can't believe what is revealed here in the Scripture, as it messes with traditional views. Peter obviously had the same experience, as he too had scoffers who said all things in creation are the same from the beginning. Peter goes on to say these scoffers are willing ignorant of a much older heaven, earth, and flood.

> Knowing this first, that there shall come in the last days scoffers, walking after their own lusts, And saying, Where is the promise of his coming? for since the fathers fell asleep, all things continue as they were from the beginning [*arche*; the extreme or absolute beginning] of the creation. For this they willingly are ignorant of, that by the word of God the heavens were of old [*ekpalai*; of a former age], and the earth standing out of the water and in the water: Whereby the world that then was, being overflowed with water, perished: But the heavens and the earth, which are now, by the same word are kept in store, reserved unto fire against the day of judgment and perdition of ungodly men. But, beloved, be not ignorant of this one thing, that one day is with the Lord as a thousand years, and a thousand years as one day.
> —2 Peter 3:3–8

I don't believe we are ignorant of Noah's Flood. Peter is referring to another time in history when the earth was flooded, causing complete destruction of all flesh. Peter is saying that we are willingly ignorant of the possibilities of an ancient heaven and earth, and we assume that all things are continuing as they were from the beginning of the re-creation that took place in seven days.

The *heavens* is now translated as *universe* and it is very old, of eternity past. Job 22:15–16 reinforces this position: Hast thou marked the old [*owlam*; forever, everlasting or eternity past] way which wicked men have trodden? Which were cut down out of time, whose foundation was overflown with a flood.

This speaks of a very ancient civilization in relation to Jobs life. Job is generally thought to have lived around 1840 B.C., with the flood occurring approximately 500 years prior in 2350 B.C. The Bible would not have used the Hebrew word *owlam* or *eternity past* to describe an event that occurred only five centuries earlier.

Peter is obviously making a distinction between the heaven and earth, which are now and the heavens and earth that were then. The heaven and earth which are now began in Genesis 1:3, not after the flood of Noah's time. After Noah's floodwaters subsided the earth simply reappeared and the heavens were unaltered during the flood (except for the firmament) and neither required re-creation. The first world, "the world that then was," totally perished by floodwaters. The result of the first flood (2 Peter 3:3) was 100 percent annihilation of life; whereas Peter makes the distinction that with the second flood, Noah and his families were preserved. This present world still had men, animals, and birds alive to start over after Noah's flood. After the flood of the ancient world God had to recreate all life forms and turn the lights back on.

There are many interesting arguments to consider. Firstly, crude oil is known to originate from the compression and heating of ancient vegetation and animal life and it is recovered most often from deep underground reservoirs.

We know from Genesis 6:14 that Noah had access to pitch or heavy oil to waterproof the ark before the flood. There is no event between Geneses 1:3 and Noah's flood that would account for vast amounts of vegetation and animal life being suddenly buried at great depth in the earth that would account for the formation of crude oil. However, the concept of the destruction of an earlier inhabited earth offers a much more plausible explanation to the existence of organic crude oil prior to Noah's flood. I wonder what could be found if DNA tests were done on crude oil!

Secondly, when geologists first studied the earth's crustal layers, they were stunned to observe the twists, turns, and breaks. Older rock layers sometimes rested on top of younger layers and pieces of layers were found far from their original position. They were amazed to see the drastic impact of volcanic and tectonic activity from ages past. Geologists were caught off guard at the huge number of extinct species of life evident in the fossil record. In Noah's flood, Genesis chapter seven notes that all beasts and fowls were preserved but that is not true of the ancient flood.

The fossil record provides evidence to a judged earth prior to the flood of Noah, not evolution! Science can now have the older earth they have been so adamant about, but they can't have evolved species. Science can have an old earth, but Christians are still right about the forming of the current generations of man starting about six thousand years ago.

At the beginning of the creation event of Genesis, the earth was already in existence but dark deep down.

> And the earth was without form [*tohuw*], and void [laid waste]; and darkness [place of misery, wickedness, death, wickedness, such as Hades] was upon the face of the deep. And the Spirit of God moved upon the face of the waters.
>
> —GENESIS 1:2

The term *without form* (*tohuw* in Hebrew) refers to something that is laid waste or a place that becomes of chaos. The earth was there in physical form yet void. *Void* (*bohuw*) means emptiness and waste. Destruction or decay has to happen before something becomes waste, and it can't become empty unless it was once filled. *The Lexicon* defines this darkness as an underground prison like Hades.

The scripture provides a second witness to establish this truth in Jeremiah 4:23: "I beheld the earth, and, lo, it was without form, and void; and the heavens, and they had no light."

But God said He did not originally create the earth in such a wasted and desolate condition; and yet in Geneses it is.

> For thus saith the LORD that created the heavens; God himself that formed the earth and made it; he hath established it, he created it not in vain [*tohuw*], he formed it to be inhabited: I am the LORD; and there is none else.
>
> —ISAIAH 45:18

God did not originally create the earth in this state of waste and chaos, so what happened? When God is finished with His work, it is always very good! It is ready to receive and support life. (See Psalm 104:5–7.)

So we have the earth resembling the aftermath of a nuclear war! Isaiah connects the dots as to what happened.

> How art thou fallen from heaven, O Lucifer, son of the morning! how art thou cut down to the ground, which didst weaken the nations!
>
> —ISAIAH 14:12

Man's traditional view of Geneses being the original creation of the earth and heavens cannot provide an answer for how or when Lucifer arrived on earth to weaken the nations, yet he is obviously there to greet Adam and Eve in the Garden of Eden. These mystery nations and their kings were already in existence on earth when Lucifer was cast from heaven to earth.

Lucifer was an anointed cherub of considerable power, influence, beauty, and wisdom until, by his own free will, he allowed the iniquity of pride to grip him and he sinned against God. A third of the angels rebelled with Lucifer (Satan) and were expelled from the presence of God into exile on earth. The time of his fall was surely before the days of Adam, for Satan was already a fallen creature prior to his entrance into Adam and Eve's Garden of Eden.

> Thine heart was lifted up because of thy beauty, thou hast corrupted thy wisdom by reason of thy brightness: I will cast thee to the ground, I will lay thee before kings, that they may behold thee.
>
> —EZEKIEL 28:17

When Lucifer arrived on earth, kings ruled the nations. The first occurrence of a king ruling the nations in the Bible did not happen until Samuel appointed Saul, which would be too late a time period for Satan's fall to occur.

Lucifer is described as an anointed cherub or protector of the earth, and he is stationed in, could it be, another Garden of Eden until iniquity was found in him?

> Thou hast been [past tense] in Eden the garden of God; every precious stone was thy covering, the sardius, topaz, and the diamond, the beryl, the onyx, and the jasper, the sapphire, the emerald, and the carbuncle, and gold: the workmanship of thy tabrets and of thy pipes was prepared in thee in the day that thou wast created. Thou art the anointed cherub

that covereth; and I have set thee so: thou wast upon the holy mountain of God; thou hast walked up and down in the midst of the stones of fire. Thou wast perfect in thy ways from the day that thou wast created, till iniquity was found in thee.

—EZEKIEL 28:13–15

Contrast this description of Lucifer to when he slithers on the scene in Genesis' Garden of Eden; he is anything but a perfect anointed cherub decked out in the riches of the land.

Now the serpent was more subtle than any beast of the field which the LORD God had made. And he said unto the woman, Yea, hath God said, Ye shall not eat of every tree of the garden?

—GENESIS 3:1

Satan was channeling through a serpent in an attempt to destroy the new occupants of the Garden of Eden.

So Eden must have also existed prior to Genesis 1:2. If we do not have a dark gap between Genesis 1:1 and 1:2, when did the account of Satan's fall from heaven occur and when was Lucifer so beautiful in the Garden of Eden? Unexplained gaps are frequent in Scripture.

Consider Jeremiah's words again where he speaks of the fruitful place, which is interpreted as fruit orchard or a cultivated garden, the first Garden of Eden

I beheld the earth, and, lo, it was without form, and void; and the heavens, and they had no light. I beheld the mountains, and, lo, they trembled, and all the hills moved lightly. I beheld, and, lo, there was no man, and all the birds of the heavens were fled. I beheld, and, lo, the fruitful place was a wilderness, and all the cities thereof were broken down at the presence of the LORD, and by his fierce anger.

—JEREMIAH 4:23–26

Could it be that the earth became without form and void as the result of God's judgment of the ancient nations and Satan? Re-creation of the heavens and earth then takes place in seven days. The Spirit of God moves upon the flooded earth, light is restored, and earth is brought to a second habitable state with all its inhabitants and plant life being created along with Adam and Eve. Adam is commanded to "replenish" the earth which means to "fill it up again" or to "restore it" with mankind.

And God blessed them, and God said unto them, Be fruitful, and multiply, and replenish the earth, and subdue it: and have dominion over the fish of the sea, and over the fowl of the air, and over every living thing that moveth upon the earth.

—GENESIS 1:28

Noah was given the same command: "Be fruitful, and multiply, and replenish the earth" (Gen. 9:1). If there were no pre-adamic people, the command to Adam would have been to be fruitful and multiply and fill the earth, rather than fill it up again.

The "darkness" of Genesis 1:2 refers to the temporary realm of Satan and his fallen angels or demons. These demons are in torment because they are seeking a "house" (a warm body) to dwell in. They were not destroyed by the calamity that struck the earth, as they are eternal spirits.

> When the unclean spirit is gone out of a man, he walketh through dry places, seeking rest, and findeth none. Then he saith, I will return into my house [a being] from whence I came out; and when he is come, he findeth it empty, swept, and garnished. Then goeth he, and taketh with himself seven other spirits more wicked than himself, and they enter in and dwell there: and the last state of that man is worse than the first. Even so shall it be also unto this wicked generation.
> —MATTHEW 12:43–45

Back to Satan, now what is his status? He has already been cast from heaven to earth where all living inhabitants were destroyed because of his treachery, so now he must get someone to open the door of their spirit through sin where he can gain entrance into the new world. As a spirit, Satan would have to find a live body to enter into in order to function. The only live body he is able to enter is that of the serpent, which becomes his medium to channel to Eve. Recall that Jesus cast a legion of demons into pigs, so they do inhabit animals.

Through channeling, Satan is able to influence Eve, then Adam, to disobey God by twisting the interpretation of the words of the Lord.

Back in the garden (Genesis 3:8–13), Adam and Eve are hiding from God in the trees. The Lord God calls, "Adam where are you?" Adam says, "I heard your voice and I was afraid, because I was naked, so I hid." The Lord responds, "Who told you that you were naked?"

I'll give you a hint; there are only four in the garden that are capable of speech! Satan told them they were naked. Satan no longer has to channel through the serpent, as once the door was opened by Eve choosing to have faith in Satan over having faith in the Lord, he now has legal access to the spirit of man. Not only does he enter, Matthew 12 tells us that he also holds the door open for seven spirits fiercer than himself: Fear, shame, guilt, pride, accusation, rebellion, and murder.

Satan used those tactics for him and his legions to gain entrance into the entire human spirit. Adam our great, great, ever so great-grandfather made a choice to invite Satan and his enforcers to be a part of all of our lives. The disappointing thing is we have concurred.

> Wherefore, as by one man sin entered into the world, and death by sin; and so death passed upon all men, for that all have sinned.
> —ROMANS 5:12

This is how Satan usurped control of the new kingdom that we live in. Satan said in Genesis 3:5, "In the day you eat thereof, then your eyes shall be opened, and ye shall be as gods [literally devils], knowing good and evil." When they sinned they lost their life and position with God. Satan usurped their role and became the god of this world, a double-crosser. Satan wanted to regain control of the earth at any cost. He does not play fair.

Sin is an open invitation for Satan to usurp control of man. Sin, the greatest of inherited and contagious diseases is how Satan "demon-strates" his total control over his subjects. Sin is the tattoo that states allegiance to the kingdom served.

The Scripture acknowledges Satan's legal right to rule, even though he usurped control by deceiving Adam and Eve. He is called the "god of the world."

> In whom the god of this world hath blinded the minds of them which believe not, lest the light of the glorious gospel of Christ, who is the image of God, should shine unto them.
> —2 Corinthians 4:4

> By the offense of one judgment came upon all men to condemnation; even so by the righteousness of one the free gift came upon all men unto justification of life. For as by one man's disobedience many were made sinners, so by the obedience of one shall many be made righteous.
> —Romans 5:18–19

The question is often asked: "Well, if Christ came to destroy the works of the devil, how come the devil is doing more now than ever?"

> He that committeth sin is of the devil; for the devil sinneth from the beginning. For this purpose the Son of God was manifested, that he might destroy the works of the devil.
> —1 John 3:8

Many say Christ has already bound Satan. If so, he has a very long chain or he made a jail break.

ANOINTED, BUT WAIT!

When God intends on doing a remarkable work in the future, He often gives us a preview acted out in real life to teach us so we will understand what He is doing. Saul, a king anointed to represent God, chose instead to fear the people and obeyed their voice rather than the commandment of the Lord. The Spirit of the Lord then departed from Saul and an evil spirit from the Lord came to torment him. Just prior to the Spirit leaving Saul, Samuel anointed David the shepherd to be the next king of Israel. But even though anointed by God to be king, it would be many years of suffering at the hand of the unstable King Saul before David would actually take his rightful place on the throne. During this wilderness testing experience, David was given many opportunities to kill Saul when Saul was trying to kill him, but David honorably proclaimed, "I shall not touch God's anointed." (See 1 Samuel 26:11.)

Likewise on the cross, Jesus Christ defeated Satan, the "god" of this world; "For this purpose the Son of God was manifested, that he might destroy the works of the devil" (1 John 3:8). Therein lays the key to praying for our loved ones to return to their Lord: pray to remove the blindness placed by the god of this world so that the gospel of Christ would show the path to salvation.

But Jesus won't take His anointed position as King until the earth dwellers' testing period is over at the conclusion of the coming tribulation period. He is holding off allowing all men, which includes all who are reading this book, the opportunity to accept the free ticket out of this mess.

> Therein lays the key to praying for our loved ones to return to their Lord: pray to remove the blindness placed by the god of this world so that the gospel of Christ would show the path to salvation.

> The Lord is not slack concerning his promise, as some men count slackness; but is longsuffering to us-ward, not willing that any should perish, but that all should come to repentance.
> —2 Peter 3:9

Paul said the purpose of the preacher after Christ was crucified was to appropriate what he did on behalf of all men. Paul was writing during the early actions (Acts) of the church, which was subsequent to the Crucifixion and yet His primary role was to free men from the power of Satan.

> To open their eyes, and to turn them from darkness to light, and from the power of Satan unto God, that they may receive forgiveness of sins, and inheritance among them which are sanctified by faith that is in me.
> —Acts 26:18

What Jesus did on the cross was to make the "offer to purchase" to get you back from the kingdom of evil. When you intend to buy a new home, you place an offer to purchase, which once accepted by the seller becomes a legal binding document and outlines the actions you will take prior to assuming possession of the property. One of those actions will be a nonrefundable deposit of something very valuable to indicate how serious you are of closing the deal.

Jesus made the offer on the cross to purchase the world back that Adam abdicated to Satan. The closing date of the transfer would have to be delayed for about two thousand years. So to indicate how serious Jesus was, he left the Holy Spirit (the comforter) in the world as His very valuable deposit.

> Nevertheless I tell you the truth; It is expedient for you that I go away: for if I go not away, the Comforter will not come unto you; but if I depart, I will send him unto you. And when he is come, he will reprove the world

of sin, and of righteousness, and of judgment: Of sin, because they believe not on me; Of righteousness, because I go to my Father, and ye see me no more; Of judgment, because the prince of this world is judged....A little while and ye shall not see me: and again, a little while [approximately 2,000 years], and ye shall see me, because I go to the Father.

—JOHN 16:7–12, 16

Towards the end of this closing period, Satan knows the deal is about up, meaning he is finished so he really starts to "demon-strate."

Therefore rejoice, ye heavens, and ye that dwell in them. Woe to the inhabiters of the earth and of the sea! for the devil is come down unto you, having great wrath, because he knoweth that he hath but a short time.

—REVELATION 12:12

Then we have an awesome heavenly scene on the closing date of the world's purchase. An angel holding up what I believe to be the sealed book containing the title deed to the world shouts, "Who can close the deal?" Only One has paid the price and is qualified to redeem or buy back the world, and that is Jesus Christ the Lion of the tribe of Judah. Here you can read in advance about the largest real estate transfer ever made in the history of the universe.

And I saw a strong angel proclaiming with a loud voice, Who is worthy to open the book, and to loose the seals thereof? And no man in heaven, nor in earth, neither under the earth, was able to open the book, neither to look thereon. And one of the elders saith unto me, Weep not: behold, the Lion of the tribe of Judah, the Root of David, hath prevailed to open the book, and to loose the seven seals thereof...And they sung a new song, saying, Thou art worthy to take the book, and to open the seals thereof: for thou wast slain, and hast redeemed us to God by thy blood out of every kindred, and tongue, and people, and nation; And hast made us unto our God kings and priests: and we shall reign on the earth.

—REVELATION 5:2–10

Friends, most of you will likely be alive to see this transfer of title. What a celebration, what joy, what unimaginable relief, as Jesus Christ takes the kingdom and the usurper, Satan is forcibly exiled to a specially constructed pit! Satan is overcome.

And the great dragon was cast out, that old serpent, called the Devil, and Satan, which deceiveth the whole world: he was cast out into the earth, and his angels were cast out with him. And I heard a loud voice saying in heaven, Now is come salvation, and strength, and the kingdom of our God, and the power of his Christ: for the accuser of our brethren is cast down, which accused them before our God day and night. And they overcame him by the blood of the Lamb, and by the word of their testimony; and they loved not their lives unto the death.

—REVELATION 12:9–11

Now understand this, they overcame Satan but they still faced death. They overcame his attempt to pull them into the pit of eternal separation from God. These Tribulation saints had missed the earlier rapture of the church due to their rebellion; but they now made sure they were found to be faithful to God, as He had provided for them this second chance to get it right.

STOP EVERYTHING AND SEEK THE KINGDOM OF GOD

With this basic understanding of creation and the ongoing battle between light and darkness, I was still perplexed with Christ's command to seek first the kingdom of God. I saw seeking the kingdom of God as a prerequisite for my prayers being answered. Although a believer for decades, I really didn't know what I was to be seeking and probably wouldn't have recognized it if I found it. I saw scripture regarding the "kingdom of heaven" and the "kingdom of God" and by default I just lumped them together as though they meant the same thing; but I wasn't comfortable with that, knowing the Holy Spirit is never careless with the writings of the Word of God.

> But seek ye first the kingdom of God, and his righteousness; and all these things shall be added unto you.
>
> —MATTHEW 6:33

Secondly, in the Lord's Prayer, which is very short, the word *kingdom* is mentioned twice, *heaven* twice, and *earth* once. Why is it necessary to include all this geography in a six-sentence model prayer?

Furthermore, the scriptures teach that the kingdom of God message is hidden from many people, even though in plain view.

> And he said, Unto you it is given to know the mysteries of the kingdom of God: but to others in parables; that seeing they might not see, and hearing they might not understand.
>
> —LUKE 8:10

I was obviously in the category of hearing about the kingdom of God and not being able to see and understand.

Another thing I couldn't understand regarding the other kingdom, the kingdom of heaven, is that the disciples were not to even teach it to the Gentiles; so I'm left out in the dark again.

> These twelve Jesus sent forth, and commanded them, saying, Go not into the way of the Gentiles, and into any city of the Samaritans enter ye not: But go rather to the lost sheep of the house of Israel. And as ye go, preach, saying, The kingdom of heaven is at hand.
>
> —MATTHEW 10:5–7

So I am now challenged, as we have secrets and I'm not in the know. The kingdom of heaven is mentioned thirty-two times, but only in the Book of Matthew. Matthew, like the Book of Hebrews, is primarily a Jewish message and therefore teaches many things that apply specifically to them. The reason the disciples were not to teach the kingdom of heaven to the Gentiles is that it did not concern them. In the New Testament we'll see a Jewish message is woven throughout an otherwise Gentile church document.

As this understanding of these kingdom messages is so important, and more so now at this time of biblical chronology than at any other, we'll examine the twelve kingdom of heaven parables and the seven kingdom of God parables necessary to reveal the mystery.

Jesus provides an interpretation to the meaning of the first two kingdoms of heaven parables that will provide the key to unlocking the intended meaning of the remaining ten.

1. The kingdom of heaven distractions

To help in your understanding of the first two parables, I'll insert into the public version of the parable the interpretation of each phrase that Jesus later interprets in private with His disciples.

> And he spake many things unto them in parables, saying, Behold, a sower [the messenger, in this case Jesus] went forth to sow; And when he sowed, some seeds [the kingdom message itself] fell by the way side [message received into the heart but not understood], and the fowls [devils that pluck out the message that was seeded] came and devoured them up: Some fell upon stony places [uprooted by tribulation and persecution], where they had not much earth: and forthwith they sprung up [an emotional decision], because they had no deepness of earth [easily offended and drops out]: And when the sun was up, they were scorched; and because they had no root, they withered away. And some fell among thorns [the seduction of money and anxiety of life]; and the thorns sprung up, and choked them [falls back into worldly idolatry]: But other fell into good ground [a prepared heart that hears and understands], and brought forth fruit [once taught goes out to teach others], some an hundredfold, some sixtyfold, some thirtyfold. Who hath ears to hear, let him hear.
>
> —Matthew 13:3–9

And the interpretation by Jesus:

> Hear ye therefore the parable of the sower. When any one heareth the word of the kingdom, and understandeth it not, then cometh the wicked one, and catcheth away that which was sown in his heart. This is he which received seed by the way side. But he that received the seed into stony places, the same is he that heareth the word, and anon [immediately] with joy receiveth it; Yet hath he not root in himself, but dureth for a while: for when tribulation or persecution ariseth because of the word, by and by he is offended. He also that received seed among the thorns is he that heareth the word; and the care of this world, and the deceitfulness of riches, choke the word, and he becometh unfruitful. But he that received seed into the good ground is he that heareth the word, and

understandeth it; which also beareth fruit, and bringeth forth, some an hundredfold, some sixty, some thirty.

—MATTHEW 13:18–23

Jesus spoke to prepare the Jewish brethren in advance of the difficulty they would have in accepting the kingdom of heaven message. They would have to be very committed and courageous in their decision to follow Jesus in order to emerge victorious over the devil's constant attempts to wear them down so they would drop the cause. Jesus acknowledges that believing in Him, especially for a Jew, is no walk of leisure but there are those that would stand their ground unmovable in their resolve. This parable anticipates the effect the kingdom of heaven message would have on the Jews; some would accept it, some would accept and turn away, and others would be overcome by workers of iniquity.

2. The kingdom of heaven imposters

Another parable put he forth unto them, saying, The kingdom of heaven is likened unto a man [Jesus Christ] which sowed good seed [children of the kingdom] in his field [the world]: But while men slept, his enemy [demon terrorist organization led by the devil] came and sowed tares [followers of Satan by choice or by default] among the wheat, and went his way. But when the blade was sprung up, and brought forth fruit, then appeared the tares also. So the servants of the householder came and said unto him, Sir, didst not thou sow good seed in thy field? from whence then hath it tares? He said unto them, An enemy hath done this. The servants said unto him, Wilt thou then that we go and gather them up? But he said, Nay; lest while ye gather up the tares, ye root up also the wheat with them. Let both grow together ["saints" and "aints" remain together] until the harvest [Judgment seat of Christ]: and in the time of harvest I will say to the reapers [angels of God], Gather ye together first the tares, and bind them in bundles to burn them [destiny hell]: but gather the wheat into my barn [destiny the kingdom of heaven].

—MATTHEW 13:24–30

Now the interpretation Jesus gave of his own teaching:

Then Jesus sent the multitude away, and went into the house: and his disciples came unto him, saying, Declare unto us the parable of the tares of the field. He answered and said unto them, He that soweth the good seed is the Son of man; The field is the world; the good seed are the children of the kingdom; but the tares are the children of the wicked one; The enemy that sowed them is the devil; the harvest is the end of the world; and the reapers are the angels. As therefore the tares are gathered and burned in the fire; so shall it be in the end of this world. The Son of man shall send forth his angels, and they shall gather out of his kingdom all things that offend, and them which do iniquity; And shall cast them into a furnace of fire: there shall be wailing and gnashing of teeth. Then shall the righteous shine forth as the sun in the kingdom of their Father. Who hath ears to hear, let him hear.

—MATTHEW 13:36–43

"While men slept," the devil was given an opportunity to deceive even the very elect of God. These men may have had a religious experience but were deceived into believing the twisted doctrine of devils. They remained, as Judas did, performing outward works for the kingdom but inwardly were demonized.

He will not pull these false converts, weeds, out until final judgment reveals their chosen secret character. These Judases will believe the lie that since God hadn't stopped them that He approves of what they are doing. The authentic "sold out to the Lord" converts will remain to experience the true riches of the kingdom of the Father commencing with the Millennium.

3. The kingdom of heaven's uninvited guests

The first two parables, "the kingdom of heaven distractions" and "the kingdom of heaven imposters," as interpreted by Jesus, provide the tools needed to interpret the remaining kingdom of heaven parables.

> Another parable put he forth unto them, saying, The kingdom of heaven is like to a grain of mustard seed [a kingdom started with very humble beginnings], which a man [Jesus Christ] took, and sowed in his field [world]: Which indeed is the least of all seeds: but when it is grown, it is the greatest among herbs, and becometh a tree, so that the birds of the air [devils] come and lodge in the branches thereof.
> —MATTHEW 13:31–32

This kingdom of heaven did not start out as the religious leaders of the day expected. They expected a powerful grand entrance of their long-awaited King; but what they got was a King arriving in humility riding on a donkey, a King that came to serve by laying down His life. It seemed that this kingdom was doomed to fail, especially when its leader was crucified and disciples scattered in fear. But look what God has done with man's extremities. The second parable informed that there would be many false converts within the congregation. The third parable paints an unlikely picture of the kingdom, which will be permissive of devils lodging within its framework.

Truly the ways of God are beyond our ability to imagine His purposes.

4. The kingdom of heaven's baker woman

> Another parable spake he unto them; The kingdom of heaven is like unto leaven [misleading doctrine arising from religious man's imagination], which a woman [a deified figurehead of a false gospel] took, and hid in three measures of meal, till the whole was leavened.
> —MATTHEW 13:33

Leaven is applied as a very small substance yet thoroughly pervades an entity by its influence. Leaven is interpreted as follows:

> How is it that ye do not understand that I spake it not to you concerning bread, that ye should beware of the leaven of the Pharisees and of the Sadducees? Then understood they how that he bade them not beware of the leaven of bread, but of the doctrine of the Pharisees and of the Sadducees.
>
> —MATTHEW 16:11–12

The word usage here for *woman* is in the context of indignation. The woman is never the "church" in Scripture but would be the woman described in Revelation as an enemy of the saints of God. Look for a female figure that adds or takes away from the gospel of Jesus Christ; she has worldwide appeal and worship with those that are not familiar enough with the truth of the Scriptures to recognize leaven.

5. The kingdom of heaven is buried treasure

> Again, the kingdom of heaven is like unto treasure hid in a field [world]; the which when a man [Jesus Christ] hath found, he hideth, and for joy thereof goeth and selleth all that he hath, and buyeth that field.
>
> —MATTHEW 13:44

The treasure hidden in the field is the Jewish nation consisting of twelve tribes that have been scattered throughout the world, such that only the Father knows whence they have gone.

> Now therefore, if ye will obey my voice indeed, and keep my covenant, then ye shall be a peculiar treasure unto me above all people: for all the earth is mine.
>
> —EXODUS 19:5

> For the LORD hath chosen Jacob unto himself, and Israel for his peculiar treasure.
>
> —PSALM 135:4

(See also Deuteronomy 4:20, 7:6, 14:21.)

Many teach this treasure is the church, but the Bible only refers to the nation of Israel as a treasure. Furthermore the church is highly visible compared to much of the scattered Jewish nationals. The Old Testament teaches of God's intention to hide Israel among the nations; and we know that to be still true today with only a portion being able to return to their revived homeland.

The treasure is hidden, found, hidden again, and then the field in which the treasure is hidden in is purchased back by Jesus Christ. The nation of Israel has a history of thriving then disappearing in judgment and silence from God only to revive again to favor. The nation of Israel regained its homeland as recently as May 1948 in fulfillment of prophecy. In this treasure parable the field is purchased that contains the treasure, whereas in the next treasure parable, the treasure is not hidden and is purchased openly.

This hidden treasure parable would be representative as how the kingdom of heaven exists during the church age.

6. The kingdom of heaven's irritant treasure

> Again, the kingdom of heaven is like unto a merchant man [Jesus Christ], seeking goodly pearls: Who, when he had found one pearl of great price, went and sold all that he had, and bought it.
> —MATTHEW 13:45–36

Pearls are the only jewels formed in a living organism. Pearls are formed by an oyster secreting a liquid to protect itself from the irritation of a grain of sand inside it. The Jews have been an irritant in the eyes of many nations who hate them, yet they know not why they hate. Nations will be held accountable in God's judgment of the nations as to whether they were a blessing or a curse to the nation of Israel.

The pearl parable would probably represent the kingdom of heaven during the Tribulation period and the preservation of the tribulation saints through their darkest hour.

7. The kingdom of heaven as a catch-all net

> Again, the kingdom of heaven is like a net, that was cast into the sea, and gathered of every kind: Which, when it was full, they drew to shore, and sat down, and gathered the good into vessels, but cast the bad away. So shall it be at the end of the world: the angels shall come forth, and sever the wicked from among the just, And shall cast them into the furnace of fire: there shall be wailing and gnashing of teeth.
> —MATTHEW 13:47–50

I believe this parable is teaching about the kingdom of heaven during the Millennium, where all survivors of the Great Tribulation, or Jacob's trouble, are forced to submit to the iron rule of Christ. Near the end of the Millennium period, the devil is released for a short period for the judgment purposes of God to separate out the hard-hearted and add them to the great furnace.

8. The King of heaven's righteous judgment

> Therefore is the kingdom of heaven likened unto a certain king, which would take account of his servants. And when he had begun to reckon, one was brought unto him, which owed him ten thousand talents. But forasmuch as he had not to pay, his lord commanded him to be sold, and his wife, and children, and all that he had, and payment to be made. The servant therefore fell down, and worshiped him, saying, Lord, have patience with me, and I will pay thee all. Then the lord of that servant was moved with compassion, and loosed him, and forgave him the debt. But the same servant went out, and found one of his fellowservants, which owed him an hundred pence: and he laid hands on him, and took him by the throat, saying, Pay me that thou owest. And his fellowservant fell down at his feet, and besought him, saying, Have patience with me, and I will pay thee all. And he would not: but went and cast him into prison, till he

should pay the debt. So when his fellowservants saw what was done, they were very sorry, and came and told unto their lord all that was done. Then his lord, after that he had called him, said unto him, O thou wicked servant, I forgave thee all that debt, because thou desiredst me: Shouldest not thou also have had compassion on thy fellowservant, even as I had pity on thee? And his lord was wroth, and delivered him to the tormentors, till he should pay all that was due unto him. So likewise shall my heavenly Father do also unto you, if ye from your hearts forgive not every one his brother their trespasses.

—Matthew 18:23–35

The Lord tells in advance how relational practices will be judged when we all stand before Him to give account of how we represented Him to our fellow man.

Paul teaches that when we have the need to judge someone, it would be a signal that we need to inspect our hearts, as we are guilty of the same thing of which we are judging another.

Therefore thou art inexcusable, O man, whosoever thou art that judgest: for wherein thou judgest another, thou condemnest thyself; for thou that judgest doest the same things. But we are sure that the judgment of God is according to truth against them which commit such things. And thinkest thou this, O man, that judgest them which do such things, and doest the same, that thou shalt escape the judgment of God?

—Romans 2:1–3

9. In the kingdom of heaven you don't want to say, "me first"

For the kingdom of heaven is like unto a man [Jesus Christ] that is an householder, which went out early in the morning to hire labourers [kingdom servants] into his vineyard [Israel]. And when he had agreed with the labourers for a penny a day, he sent them into his vineyard. And he went out about the third hour, and saw others standing idle in the marketplace, And said unto them; Go ye also into the vineyard, and whatsoever is right I will give you. And they went their way. Again he went out about the sixth and ninth hour, and did likewise. And about the eleventh hour he went out, and found others standing idle, and saith unto them, Why stand ye here all the day idle? They say unto him, Because no man hath hired us. He saith unto them, Go ye also into the vineyard; and whatsoever is right, that shall ye receive. So when even was come, the lord of the vineyard saith unto his steward, Call the labourers, and give them their hire, beginning from the last unto the first. And when they came that were hired about the eleventh hour, they received every man a penny. But when the first

> Paul teaches that when we have the need to judge someone that would be a signal that we need to inspect our hearts as we are guilty of the same thing of which we are judging another.

came, they supposed that they should have received more; and they likewise received every man a penny. And when they had received it, they
murmured against the goodman of the house, Saying, These last have
wrought but one hour, and thou hast made them equal unto us, which
have borne the burden and heat of the day. But he answered one of them,
and said, Friend, I do thee no wrong: didst not thou agree with me for a
penny? Take that thine is, and go thy way: I will give unto this last, even
as unto thee. Is it not lawful for me to do what I will with mine own? Is
thine eye evil, because I am good? So the last shall be first, and the first
last: for many be called, but few chosen.

—MATTHEW 20:1–16

Who is the vineyard? The best commentary on the Scripture is the Scripture
itself and it tells us who Israel is.

For the vineyard of the LORD of hosts is the house of Israel.

—ISAIAH 5:7

The message is that many laborers will join the kingdom of heaven over time
and the Lord reserves the right to reward them all the same regardless of the
time served. Agape love always wants what is best for the other person; and if we
are troubled by the Lord's judgment, we know we are not matured in our love.

10. The kingdom of heaven's dinner party

And Jesus answered and spake unto them again by parables, and said,
The kingdom of heaven is like unto a certain king [God the Father],
which made a marriage for his son [Jesus Christ], And sent forth his servants to call them that were bidden to the wedding: and they would not
come. Again, he sent forth other servants, saying, Tell them which are
bidden, Behold, I have prepared my dinner: my oxen and my fatlings are
killed, and all things are ready: come unto the marriage. But they made
light of it, and went their ways, one to his farm, another to his merchandise: And the remnant took his servants, and entreated them spitefully,
and slew them. But when the king heard thereof, he was wroth: and he
sent forth his armies [Titus], and destroyed those murderers, and burned
up their city [Jerusalem, A.D. 70]. Then saith he to his servants, The wedding is ready, but they which were bidden were not worthy. Go ye therefore into the highways, and as many as ye shall find, bid to the marriage.
So those servants went out into the highways, and gathered together all as
many as they found, both bad and good: and the wedding was furnished
with guests. And when the king came in to see the guests, he saw there
a man which had not on a wedding garment: And he saith unto him,
Friend, how camest thou in hither not having a wedding garment? And
he was speechless. Then said the king to the servants, Bind him hand and
foot, and take him away, and cast him into outer darkness; there shall be
weeping and gnashing of teeth. For many are called, but few are chosen.

—MATTHEW 22:1–14

The Marriage Supper of the Lamb is the wedding celebration spoken of that will occur at the second coming of Jesus Christ. It will unite the bride of Christ, the church, with the tribulation saints. The servant's guests at the wedding are the Jews. This parable is obviously prophecy with a near and far interpretation. The earlier application is the invitation extended first by John the Baptist and then Jesus Christ for the kingdom of heaven members to be part of the New Testament church. However, most did not accept Jesus as Messiah so they would reject His invitation and their king murdered John the Baptist.

The armies that were sent in A.D. 67–70, led by Titus, laid siege to the city of Jerusalem that culminated in the burning of the city and the temple. The calling of the nation Israel was to be a light to the Gentiles; but when they failed in their calling, the roles were effectively reversed during the era known as the church age.

> I the LORD have called thee in righteousness, and will hold thine hand, and will keep thee, and give thee for a covenant of the people, for a light of the Gentiles; To open the blind eyes, to bring out the prisoners from the prison, and them that sit in darkness out of the prison house.
>
> —ISAIAH 42:6–7

The man that came dressed in his own garment was a man trying to reach God on his own terms. In religion we have men attempting in many goofy ways to reach God, whereas in Christianity we have God reaching down to man to get man's attention. It was God who sent His servants to reach out and invite without hesitation all men to His kingdom celebration.

11. The kingdom of heaven, ready or not

> Then shall the kingdom of heaven be likened unto ten virgins, which took their lamps, and went forth to meet the bridegroom. And five of them were wise, and five were foolish. They that were foolish took their lamps, and took no oil with them: But the wise took oil in their vessels with their lamps. While the bridegroom tarried, they all slumbered [negligent and careless] and slept [slothful]. And at midnight there was a cry made, Behold, the bridegroom cometh; go ye out to meet him. Then all those virgins arose, and trimmed their lamps. And the foolish said unto the wise, Give us of your oil; for our lamps are gone out. But the wise answered, saying, Not so; lest there be not enough for us and you: but go ye rather to them that sell, and buy for yourselves. And while they went to buy, the bridegroom came; and they that were ready went in with him to the marriage: and the door was shut. Afterward came also the other virgins, saying, Lord, Lord, open to us. But he answered and said, Verily I say unto you, I know you not. Watch therefore, for ye know neither the day nor the hour wherein the Son of man cometh.
>
> —MATTHEW 25:1–13

In these two marriage parables, the status of the bride—the church, is never an issue, as it is certain, planned, and the date set. In both parables it is the guest list that is causing the most grief.

The virgins are bridesmaids that accompany the bride. They are Jewish.

> So shall the king greatly desire thy beauty: for he is thy Lord; and worship thou him. The king's daughter is all glorious within: her clothing is of wrought gold. She shall be brought unto the king in raiment of needlework: the virgins her companions that follow her shall be brought unto thee.
>
> —PSALM 45:10–14

Virgins are never used in reference to the church. The term occurs in Matthew three times in reference to the Jewish kingdom of heaven parables and then again in the Revelation chapter fourteen in reference to the 144,000 Jewish eunuchs.

In the parable, which is set at the end of the Tribulation period, some of the companions are ready for their Lord and the others assume they have lots of time to live their lives as they want and are slothful in what matters most—they miss the eternity trip of a lifetime.

12. The kingdom of heaven stewardship and accountability

> For the kingdom of heaven is as a man traveling into a far country, who called his own servants, and delivered unto them his goods. And unto one he gave five talents, to another two, and to another one; to every man according to his several ability; and straightway took his journey. Then he that had received the five talents went and traded with the same, and made them other five talents. And likewise he that had received two, he also gained other two. But he that had received one went and digged in the earth, and hid his lord's money. After a long time the lord of those servants cometh, and reckoneth with them. And so he that had received five talents came and brought other five talents, saying, Lord, thou deliveredst unto me five talents: behold, I have gained beside them five talents more. His lord said unto him, Well done, thou good and faithful servant: thou hast been faithful over a few things, I will make thee ruler over many things: enter thou into the joy of thy lord. He also that had received two talents came and said, Lord, thou deliveredst unto me two talents: behold, I have gained two other talents beside them. His lord said unto him, Well done, good and faithful servant; thou hast been faithful over a few things, I will make thee ruler over many things: enter thou into the joy of thy lord. Then he which had received the one talent came and said, Lord, I knew thee that thou art an hard man, reaping where thou hast not sown, and gathering where thou hast not strawed: And I was afraid, and went and hid thy talent in the earth: lo, there thou hast that is thine. His lord answered and said unto him, Thou wicked and slothful servant, thou knewest that I reap where I sowed not, and gather

where I have not strawed: Thou oughtest therefore to have put my money to the exchangers, and then at my coming I should have received mine own with usury. Take therefore the talent from him, and give it unto him which hath ten talents. For unto every one that hath shall be given, and he shall have abundance: but from him that hath not shall be taken away even that which he hath. And cast ye the unprofitable servant into outer darkness: there shall be weeping and gnashing of teeth.

—MATTHEW 25:14–30

The interpretation of this parable will be difficult if you read it as a stand-alone message; but it is part of a detailed prophecy Jesus gave regarding the tribulation starting in Matthew chapter twenty-four. Matthew chapter twenty-five starts with the words: "then shall the kingdom of heaven" continuing on to the kingdom of heaven, ready-or-not parable of the second coming. Then, the kingdom of heaven stewardship and accountability parables are followed chronologically with the judgment by Christ, entering into the Millennium. Immediately after this parable, Jesus continues:

When the Son of man shall come in his glory, and all the holy angels with him, then shall he sit upon the throne of his glory: And before him shall be gathered all nations: and he shall separate them one from another, as a shepherd divideth his sheep from the goats: And he shall set the sheep on his right hand, but the goats on the left. Then shall the King say unto them on his right hand, Come, ye blessed of my Father, inherit the kingdom prepared for you from the foundation of the world.

—MATTHEW 25:31–34

The word *talent* means a sum of money and is not to be confused with the modern English term of *talent*, which means a gift or special ability.

The man who traveled to a far country is Jesus when He ascended to heaven to sit at the right hand of the father following His resurrection. The Lord made a point that it is "after a long time" that He returns to see what kind of people His servants have become. He is judging them on their compassion for those in need and what they did with the wealth they were entrusted with. Here we have a prophecy of the final courtroom scene at the end of the tribulation.

For I was an hungred, and ye gave me meat: I was thirsty, and ye gave me drink: I was a stranger, and ye took me in: Naked, and ye clothed me: I was sick, and ye visited me: I was in prison, and ye came unto me. Then shall the righteous answer him, saying, Lord, when saw we thee an hungred, and fed thee? or thirsty, and gave thee drink? When saw we thee a stranger, and took thee in? or naked, and clothed thee? Or when saw we thee sick, or in prison, and came unto thee? And the King shall answer and say unto them, Verily I say unto you, Inasmuch as ye have done it unto one of the least of these my brethren, ye have done it unto me. Then shall he say also unto them on the left hand, Depart from me, ye cursed, into everlasting fire, prepared for the devil and his angels: For

> I was an hungred, and ye gave me no meat: I was thirsty, and ye gave me no drink: I was a stranger, and ye took me not in: naked, and ye clothed me not: sick, and in prison, and ye visited me not. Then shall they also answer him, saying, Lord, when saw we thee an hungred, or athirst, or a stranger, or naked, or sick, or in prison, and did not minister unto thee? Then shall he answer them, saying, Verily I say unto you, Inasmuch as ye did it not to one of the least of these, ye did it not to me. And these shall go away into everlasting punishment: but the righteous into life eternal.
> —MATTHEW 25:35–46

The goats were those that were selfish with the resources and wealth they were entrusted with, and the sheep were those that looked after the displaced and suffering Jews that were fleeing the murderous treachery of the Antichrist in the second part of the tribulation period. Jesus taught this parable in similar fashion of a professor who gives a practice exam in preparation for the term final so the students would know in advance what they would be graded on. Jesus will grade the nations on how they respond to the humanitarian crises the Jews will face during the coming Tribulation.

SUMMARY OF THE KINGDOM OF HEAVEN—GOVERNMENT

We will sum up the kingdom of heaven message through the twelve parables drawing highlights from each one. A Jewish believer would have to be very committed and courageous in their decision to follow Jesus in order to emerge victorious over the devil's constant attempts to wear them down. Many of these men may have had a religious experience, but they were deceived into believing the twisted doctrine of devils. They remained as Judas did, performing outward works for the kingdom but inwardly were demonized. The kingdom will be permissive of devils lodging within its framework, as they would have a legal right to be there due to the sin of the people.

A feminine personality who fabricates the gospel of Jesus Christ will be given much acclaim; she has worldwide appeal and worship with those that are not familiar enough with the truth of the Scriptures to recognize leaven. The nation of Israel is as treasure that is hidden, found, hidden again, and then the field in which the treasure is hidden in is purchased back by Jesus Christ.

There will be divine deliverance provided to the tribulation saints to preserve them during their darkest hour. Following the Tribulation we enter the Millennium, where all survivors are forced to submit to the iron rule of Christ. Near the end of the Millennium period, the devil is released for a short period to reveal those who are still double-minded. Man will be judged by how we represented our Lord to our fellow man and on the basis of how we pronounced judgment on our fellow man. Agape love always wants what is best for the other person; and if we are troubled by the Lord's judgment, we know we are not matured in our love.

The calling of the nation Israel was to be a light to the Gentiles; but when they failed in their calling, the roles were effectively reversed during the church age. At the end of the Tribulation period, some of the companions are ready for their Lord and the others assume they have lots of time to live their lives as they want. They are slothful in what matters most and are condemned to eternal judgment in hell. Jesus will grade the nations on how they responded to the humanitarian crises the Jews faced during the Tribulation.

This is part of the kingdom of heaven message that the disciples were to teach to the Jews at the exclusion of the Gentiles and the Samaritans.

The interesting thing about the kingdom of heaven is that it is not spiritual or religious in nature; it is governmental. It is all nations on earth coming under the direct rule of heaven. The twelve apostles will each be given a throne governing one of the twelve tribes of Israel in the Millennium.

> Then answered Peter and said unto him, Behold, we have forsaken all, and followed thee; what shall we have therefore? And Jesus said unto them, Verily I say unto you, That ye which have followed me, in the regeneration when the Son of man shall sit in the throne of his glory, ye also shall sit upon twelve thrones, judging the twelve tribes of Israel. And every one that hath forsaken houses, or brethren, or sisters, or father, or mother, or wife, or children, or lands, for my name's sake, shall receive an hundredfold, and shall inherit everlasting life.
> —MATTHEW 19:27

How did God desire to rule the nations? God desired to rule the nations from the heavens.

> Thy kingdom shall be sure unto thee, after that thou shalt have known that the heavens do rule.
> —DANIEL 4:26

To assist in His kingdom, God choose the prophets and judges to speak and govern on his behalf.

> And all Israel from Dan even to Beersheba knew that Samuel was established to be a prophet of the LORD.
> —1 SAMUEL 3:20

Samuel became the thirteenth judge of Israel. But the people rebelled against God and insisted on having a king set up like the other nations did, so God released them from His kingdom.

> And it came to pass, when Samuel was old, that he made his sons judges over Israel...Then all the elders of Israel gathered themselves together, and came to Samuel unto Ramah, And said unto him, Behold, thou art old, and thy sons walk not in thy ways: now make us a king to judge us like all the nations. But the thing displeased Samuel, when they said, Give us a king to judge us. And Samuel prayed unto the LORD. And the LORD said unto Samuel, Hearken unto the voice of the people in all that

they say unto thee: for they have not rejected thee, but they have rejected me, that I should not reign over them.

—1 Samuel 8:1, 4–7

And Samuel called the people together unto the Lord to Mizpeh; And said unto the children of Israel, Thus saith the Lord God of Israel, I brought up Israel out of Egypt, and delivered you out of the hand of the Egyptians, and out of the hand of all kingdoms, and of them that oppressed you: And ye have this day rejected your God, who himself saved you out of all your adversities and your tribulations; and ye have said unto him, Nay, but set a king over us.

—1 Samuel 10:17–19

Attempt to reestablish the kingdom of heaven fails

A few generations later God would attempt to reestablish the kingdom of heaven with his Son as King. In order for Israel to recognize their King when He came, many prophecies (more than three hundred) were provided in the Scripture, one of which was written by Zechariah. Their King would not enter as other kings did, rather He would choose to ride in on a donkey colt.

Rejoice greatly, O daughter of Zion; shout, O daughter of Jerusalem: behold, thy King cometh unto thee: he is just, and having salvation; lowly, and riding upon an ass, and upon a colt the foal of an ass.

—Zechariah 9:9

This prophecy was fulfilled to the exact date prophesied by Daniel when Jesus Christ came into Jerusalem as King riding on a colt as foretold by Zechariah. Around 600 b.c. Daniel wrote prophetically:

Seventy weeks are determined upon thy people and upon thy holy city, to finish the transgression, and to make an end of sins, and to make reconciliation for iniquity, and to bring in everlasting righteousness, and to seal up the vision and prophecy, and to anoint the most Holy. Know therefore and understand, that from the going forth of the commandment to restore and to build Jerusalem unto the Messiah the Prince shall be seven weeks, and threescore and two weeks: the street shall be built again, and the wall, even in troublous times. And after threescore and two weeks shall Messiah be cut off, but not for himself: and the people of the prince that shall come shall destroy the city and the sanctuary; and the end thereof shall be with a flood, and unto the end of the war desolations are determined.

—Daniel 9:24–26

Below is an excerpt from my upcoming book *Truth or Coincidence*. While it is not in book form yet, you can find my new video series at www.truthorcoincidence .com.

Can we know with mathematical preciseness the exact day Jesus the Messiah is presented as Prince?

The commandment to restore and build Jerusalem was given by King Artaxerxes Longimanus to Nehemiah on March 14, 445 B.C. Using this as the commencement date for the calculation, the Bible says count ahead a total of 69 weeks of years. A week of years is seven years. So with your calculators multiply 69 by 7, which gives you 483 years. At the time of this prophecy the years consisted of 360 days. Now multiply the 483 years you already totaled by 360 days per year to reach 173,880 days. Counting out the days from the command to rebuild Jerusalem, taking into account the leap years, you arrive at April 6, A.D. 32. Or according to the Jewish calendar, it was the 10th of Nisan, just prior to the Passover on the 14th of Nisan, A.D. 32.

Many times during Jesus Christ's ministry the people tried to establish Him as King, to which he replies, "Mine hour is not yet come." Then one day he enters the city on a borrowed donkey and the people roll out the carpet of their garments and branches and Hail Him as Messiah the Prince. The date of this triumphal entry fulfilled Daniels prophecy to the exact day, April 6, A.D. 32, days before the Crucifixion at Passover.

Luke tells how it went down.

> And they brought him to Jesus: and they cast their garments upon the colt, and they set Jesus thereon. And as he went, they spread their clothes in the way. And when he was come nigh, even now at the descent of the mount of Olives, the whole multitude of the disciples began to rejoice and praise God with a loud voice for all the mighty works that they had seen; Saying, Blessed be the King that cometh in the name of the Lord: peace in heaven, and glory in the highest. And some of the Pharisees from among the multitude said unto him, Master, rebuke thy disciples. And he answered and said unto them, I tell you that, if these should hold their peace, the stones would immediately cry out.
>
> —LUKE 19:35–40

So the people didn't reject the Messiah; it was the religious leaders who were asleep at the scrolls and didn't search the Scripture to be able to recognize their King when He arrived. This was the day when Israel rejected the Lord's attempt to set up the kingdom of heaven amongst them. Jesus wept over Jerusalem, as He knew what this would mean for these beloved people. He repeated the prophecy of Jerusalem and the temple to be leveled to the ground.

> And when he was come near, he beheld the city, and wept over it, saying, If thou hadst known, even thou, at least in this thy day, the things which belong unto thy peace! But now they are hid from thine eyes. For the days shall come upon thee, that thine enemies shall cast a trench about thee, and compass thee round, and keep thee in on every side, And shall lay thee even with the ground, and thy children within thee; and they shall not leave in thee one stone upon another; because thou knewest not the time of thy visitation.
>
> —LUKE 19:41–44

Jesus said this happened because they did not know the day of the visitation of their King. They were held responsible to have read and understood God's Word on their own and to have been expecting the establishment of the kingdom of heaven with Jesus as King.

In my book *Truth or Coincidences*, I offer some of the following interesting statistics:

> The Bible is the only holy book that can predict future events with such incredible accuracy to even rival actual eyewitness accounts.
>
> The Old Testament, as we know it today was translated from Hebrew to Greek in 270 B.C. by a group of 72 Hebrew scholars into a book called the Septuagint (meaning *seventy*) of which we have many originals in existence today. In the Septuagint there are well over 300 prophecies concerning the coming Messiah and King that were scribed well over three centuries in advance, so that when He came we would know for certain He was the man we were expecting.
>
> To give you the idea, we'll only talk about eight of these advance descriptions:
>
> 1. Micah predicts the Messiah would be born in Bethlehem. Micah 5:2.
>
> 2. Zechariah notes Messiah would present Himself as King riding on a donkey. Zechariah 9:9.
>
> 3. The same writer said the Messiah would be betrayed for thirty pieces of silver. Zechariah 11:12.
>
> 4. Furthermore, the person that would betray the Messiah was a friend of his, it tells us. Zechariah 13:6.
>
> 5. Zechariah goes on to say that the thirty pieces of silver would be thrown onto the temple floor then used to buy a potter's field. Zechariah 11:13.
>
> 6. Isaiah foretold the Messiah would die in the presence of criminals and yet be buried in the tomb of a rich man. Isaiah 53:9.
>
> 7. The prophet Isaiah predicted that the Messiah—though innocent of His charges—would not open His mouth in defense. Isaiah 53:7.
>
> 8. Psalm 22:16 foresaw the Messiah being put to death by crucifixion even though the Romans did not invent that form of capital punishment for several more centuries in 90 B.C.
>
> The probability of all these predictions happening to one person is the composite probability.
>
> A professor of mathematics and astronomy had 600 students calculate the composite probability and reach a conservative consensus on whether or not Jesus Christ of Nazareth was indeed the man spoken of in advance over three hundred times in the Septuagint or the Old Testament. They agreed that the chances of any one person in history fulfilling all eight precise prophecies was 1 x 10 to the 17th power… How big is that number? If you were to toss one silver dollar in a pile of silver dollars that covered

the entire state of Texas, two feet thick, and then send a blindfolded man in to walk as far as he wants, but to pick up only one coin, the chance of that being the marked coin is 1 x 10 to the 17th power. The Professor went further to say that for any one person to fulfill 48 of the over 300 prophecies would be 1 X 10 to the 157th power. That is the number one with 157 zeros behind it. Physicists say any probability smaller that 1 chance in 10 to the 50th power is an absolute improbability...unless of course you are dealing with divine accuracy and foreknowledge.

To reject the fact that Jesus Christ is indeed who He said he was is to reject a historical occurrence that is authenticated in advance more than any other factual occurrence in the world's history.

The twelve parables of the kingdom of heaven were given by Christ to make sure the nation is ready for Him next time around, but we already know many will not be ready. When Jesus returns at the end of the Tribulation, half of the virgins will have been slothful and are caught with no oil in their lamps and are rejected. History will repeat itself despite two thousand years of warnings given.

Very strong words are reserved for the religious elite. They made a decision to reject their King on behalf of the people they were to be shepherds of. The Pharisees are held responsible by the Lord for the kingdom of heaven being shut up against the nation. That is a heavy indictment.

> But woe unto you, scribes and Pharisees, hypocrites! for ye shut up the kingdom of heaven against men: for ye neither go in yourselves, neither suffer ye them that are entering to go in. Woe unto you, scribes and Pharisees, hypocrites! for ye devour widows' houses, and for a pretence make long prayer: therefore ye shall receive the greater damnation. Woe unto you, scribes and Pharisees, hypocrites! for ye compass sea and land to make one proselyte, and when he is made, ye make him twofold more the child of hell than yourselves.
>
> —MATTHEW 23:13

Those are strong words to say in church. Not only do the religious leaders shut up the kingdom of heaven and not learn from it, they proselytize promising young men in their seminaries to be twice as deceptive as themselves. Have things changed for us amongst the intimidating, multiple-credentialed, and lengthy-titled churchmen? When the Kings of kings came in humility riding on a donkey, He set the example for the rest of His shepherd servants.

Jesus Christ, never one to quit, will return once again (without advance warning) to reestablish the kingdom of heaven and overtaking the kingdoms of this world.

> And the seventh angel sounded; and there were great voices in heaven, saying, The kingdoms of this world are become the kingdoms of our Lord, and of his Christ; and he shall reign forever and ever.
>
> —REVELATION 11:15

The kingdom of heaven is a message woven through Scripture primarily for the Jewish nation, and accordingly, Jesus commanded the apostles to take and teach this message to the Jews.

In the last and eternal stage of this world the kingdom of God and the kingdom of heaven will be as one, with the Lord ruling all nations, Jew and Gentile, from the New Jerusalem.

> And it shall come to pass in the last days, that the mountain of the LORD's house shall be established in the top of the mountains, and shall be exalted above the hills; and all nations shall flow unto it.
>
> —ISAIAH 2:2

Christ followers, let us stand in the gap on behalf of our nations and the church and repent to our Jewish brothers and sisters for a false doctrine being taught in much of the church that God is done with the nation of Israel and that the church has now taken its place. In the Book of Revelation Jesus Christ addresses seven churches regarding what He would commend them for and what they would be judged for. In His address to the Church of Smyrna Jesus says those churches that say they are now Israel and have received all the blessing of the Jews are speaking blasphemy as channeled by Satan himself.

> And unto the angel of the church in Smyrna write; These things saith the first and the last, which was dead, and is alive; I know thy works, and tribulation, and poverty, (but thou art rich) and I know the blasphemy of them which say they are Jews, and are not, but are the synagogue of Satan.
>
> —REVELATION 2:8–9

He says the same thing to the Church of Philadelphia, which is the church most of the evangelical churches feel speaks to them.

> And to the angel of the church in Philadelphia write; These things saith he that is holy, he that is true, he that hath the key of David, he that openeth, and no man shutteth; and shutteth, and no man openeth; I know thy works: behold, I have set before thee an open door, and no man can shut it: for thou hast a little strength, and hast kept my word, and hast not denied my name. Behold, I will make them of the synagogue of Satan, which say they are Jews, and are not, but do lie; behold, I will make them to come and worship before thy feet, and to know that I have loved thee.
>
> —REVELATION 3:7–9

These are strong words because they fit the crime. Satan has been trying to wipe out Israel since their origin, and he will stop at nothing even deceiving the church into cursing them. We perish for lack of knowledge (Hosea 4:6).

A document that the church accepts as divine truth written by the apostle Paul makes that church doctrine heresy:

> What then? Israel hath not obtained that which he seeketh for; but the election hath obtained it, and the rest were blinded...I say then, Have

they stumbled that they should fall? God forbid: but rather through their fall salvation is come unto the Gentiles, for to provoke them to jealousy.
—ROMANS 11:7, 11

The Holy Spirit anticipated the church would be struggling with the role of Israel and wrote to put to rest this conflict. Paul tells us not to be ignorant though our own self-righteous conceits of the fact that God is still in the business of pursuing Israel. The fact of God turning His attention to the Gentile church was to provoke the nation Israel to jealousy, a wake-up shake.

This time of God's silence to Israel caused by the blindness of this beloved nation will last until the "fullness" of the Gentiles comes in. The fullness is a number of believers that the Father has determined will be added to the authentic church of Jesus Christ, and when that number is reached, Satan is bound for a thousand years and Christ sets up His long-awaited kingdom.

> For I would not, brethren, that ye should be ignorant of this mystery, lest ye should be wise in your own conceits; that blindness in part is happened to Israel, until the fulness [a certain number known only by the Father] of the Gentiles be come in. And so all Israel shall be saved: as it is written, There shall come out of Zion the Deliverer, and shall turn away ungodliness from Jacob [Israel].
> —ROMANS 11:25

REVIVAL

The revival that we've been praying for through the Lord's Prayer has now reached Israel.

The Jewish prophet Hosea writes:

> For the children of Israel shall abide many days without a king, and without a prince, and without a sacrifice, and without an image, and without an ephod, and without teraphim: Afterward shall the children of Israel return, and seek the LORD their God, and David their king; and shall fear the LORD and his goodness in the latter days.
> —HOSEA 3:5

King David will be resurrected to complete God's covenant that he would be the prince forever of Israel, and the new temple sanctuary will be in their midst throughout eternity.

> And I will make them one nation in the land upon the mountains of Israel; and one king shall be king to them all: and they shall be no more two nations, neither shall they be divided into two kingdoms any more at all: Neither shall they defile themselves any more with their idols, nor with their detestable things, nor with any of their transgressions: but I will save them out of all their dwelling places, wherein they have sinned, and will cleanse them: so shall they be my people, and I will be their God. And David my servant shall be king over them; and they all shall have one shepherd: they shall also walk in my judgments, and observe my

statutes, and do them. And they shall dwell in the land that I have given unto Jacob my servant, wherein your fathers have dwelt; and they shall dwell therein, even they, and their children, and their children's children for ever: and my servant David shall be their prince forever. Moreover I will make a covenant of peace with them; it shall be an everlasting covenant with them: and I will place them, and multiply them, and will set my sanctuary in the midst of them for evermore.
                                        —EZEKIEL 37:22–26

The kingdom of heaven will result in complete unity, restoration, and sanctification of Israel with King David back in his throne room. Let us celebrate the works of God in advance, as they are beyond what any could think or imagine.

In contrast to the kingdom of heaven parables that are a message primarily to the Jews, we'll look at the subtle differences in the kingdom of God parables that minister to a different group, the Gentile church.

1. Kingdom of God parable of the harvest

(This is similar to the parable of the kingdom of heaven distractions.)

What do you think about Jesus' parables? Are they just stories to apply some spiritual truth? We may have been told not to base our doctrine on parables, and yet Mark said the parables are His doctrine.

And he taught them many things by parables, and said unto them in his doctrine, Hearken; Behold, there went out a sower to sow [the Word of God]: And it came to pass, as he sowed, some fell by the way side, and the fowls of the air [Satan] came and devoured it up [the Word sown in their hearts]. And some fell on stony ground, where it had not much earth; and immediately it sprang up [received Word on emotional high], because it had no depth of earth [appeared to mature quickly but had no solid foundation built] But when the sun was up, it was scorched [by affliction and persecution]; and because it had no root, it withered away [became offended at the difficulty and dropped away]. And some fell among thorns, and the thorns grew up, and choked it [distracted by cares of this world, lusts and deceitfulness of riches], and it yielded no fruit. And other fell on good ground [perceive sense of what is said of God's Word], and did yield fruit that sprang up and increased; and brought forth, some thirty, and some sixty, and some an hundred. And he said unto them, He that hath ears to hear, let him hear. And when he was alone, they that were about him with the twelve asked of him the parable. And he said unto them, Unto you it is given to know the mystery of the kingdom of God: but unto them that are without, all these things are done in parables: That seeing they may see, and not perceive; and hearing they may hear, and not understand; lest at any time they should be converted, and their sins should be forgiven them.
                                        —MARK 4:2–12

This parable speaks of the disservice to new converts that are evangelized by creating an emotional experience for them and then not grounding them in the Word. Jesus speaks directly to the church in Revelation 2:1 and lays out the first steps for a fallen one who is converted:

> Nevertheless I have somewhat against thee, because thou hast left thy first love. Remember therefore from whence thou art fallen, and repent, and do the first works.

When we get to the chapters on lead us not to temptation and deliver us from evil, we'll have an opportunity to go back and do what we were supposed to do when we first believed. This parable speaks of the disservice to new converts that are evangelized by creating an emotional experience for them and then not grounding them in the Word.

This kingdom of God parable is very similar to the kingdom of heaven parable we looked at in Matthew, except for one important phrase: "and their sins should be forgiven them." The concept of "being saved" or "personal forgiveness" never occurs in the kingdom of heaven parables, as it is a kingdom of government and is concerned with national kingdom issues.

Jesus exhorts us to understand this parable of the sower, as it is the key to understanding the doctrine in the rest of the parables.

> And he said unto them, Know ye not this parable? and how then will ye know all parables?
> —Mark 4:13

2. Kingdom of God parable of miraculous harvest

(This is similar to kingdom of heaven imposters.)

The kingdom of God and the kingdom of heaven parables both start out with the seed of the Word being planted followed by the man going to sleep which allows the seed to germinate. In the kingdom of heaven equivalent, the devil comes and sows tares while the man sleeps. However, look closely at what happens in the kingdom of God parable representing the church: a miracle takes place while the man is sleeping.

> And he said, So is the kingdom of God, as if a man should cast seed into the ground; And should sleep, and rise night and day, and the seed should spring and grow up, he knoweth not how. For the earth bringeth forth fruit of herself; first the blade, then the ear, after that the full corn in the ear. But when the fruit is brought forth, immediately he putteth in the sickle, because the harvest is come.
> —Mark 4:26–29

The church is planted by a small group of men known as the twelve apostles, and it takes root and grows miraculously and matures. And then emphasis is on the immediate harvest, which would refer to the rapture of believers. This is, no doubt, evidence of the work of the Holy Spirit in convicting the world of sin and drawing them to the gospel of Christ.

3. Kingdom of God parable of the mustard seed

In this parable the Holy Spirit draws attention to the similarity of the struggles with which the kingdom of God and the kingdom of heaven struggle. Both would be tormented by the presence of Satan and his underlying demons.

> And he said, Whereunto shall we liken the kingdom of God? or with what comparison shall we compare it? It is like a grain of mustard seed, which, when it is sown in the earth, is less than all the seeds that be in the earth: But when it is sown, it groweth up, and becometh greater than all herbs, and shooteth out great branches; so that the fowls of the air [devils] may lodge under the shadow of it.
> —MARK 4:30–32

Jesus has introduced this doctrine here, and we will take a closer look at how to free our lives from the destructive work of the fowl of the air (devils) in chapter seven.

4. Kingdom of God parable of leaven

Another similarity is that both kingdoms would have the leaven of false doctrine, causing them to be inflated. Yeast or leaven causes bread to rise through fermentation, making the bread utilizing the yeast to appear much larger than the bread made without yeast. False doctrine will attract many, many people into the church, as they are told what their itching ears want to hear, which artificially inflates the actual size of the church.

> And again he said, Whereunto shall I liken the kingdom of God? It is like leaven, which a woman took and hid in three measures of meal, till the whole was leavened.
> —LUKE 13:20–21

Leaven, which is really a watered down gospel to make it more attractive to the masses, produces a lukewarm church. Jesus isn't impressed by the size of a church or by its wealth. He judges with a thermometer and only those who are "hot" step forward into the joy of the Lord. At least those who are cold (of the world) are not deceived, as they know where they stand. It is the lukewarm adherents that feel they are safe at indulging in half of what the world has and choosing half of what the kingdom of God has to offer and enjoy both lives. Or can they? The Word says such a person is double-minded and unstable in all their ways; and here Jesus says He can't stomach them and prefers to vomit them out.

> False doctrine will attract many many people into the church, as they are told what their itching ears want to hear, which artificially inflates the actual size of the church.

And unto the angel of the church of the Laodiceans write; These things saith the Amen, the faithful and true witness, the beginning of the creation of God; I know thy works, that thou art neither cold nor hot: I would thou wert cold or hot. So then because thou art lukewarm, and neither cold nor hot, I will spue thee out of my mouth. Because thou sayest, I am rich, and increased with goods, and have need of nothing; and knowest not that thou art wretched, and miserable, and poor, and blind, and naked.

—REVELATION 3:14–16

5. Kingdom of God parable of investment in the future

In the parallel kingdom of heaven parable, the man delivers five talents to one, two to a second, and one to a third. In this parable there are ten servants, each receiving the same portion to invest, and they are to occupy till Jesus returns. Since this is the kingdom of God and not the kingdom of heaven, the slothful servant is not cast into hell, but he loses his promotion into the next stage of the kingdom. Various rewards are offered to the saints based on faithful service during the church age.

And as they heard these things, he added and spake a parable, because he was nigh to Jerusalem, and because they thought that the kingdom of God should immediately appear. He said therefore, A certain nobleman [Jesus Christ] went into a far country to receive for himself a kingdom, and to return. And he called his ten servants, and delivered them ten pounds, and said unto them, Occupy till I come. But his citizens hated him, and sent a message after him, saying, We will not have this man to reign over us. And it came to pass, that when he was returned, having received the kingdom, then he commanded these servants to be called unto him, to whom he had given the money, that he might know how much every man had gained by trading. Then came the first, saying, Lord, thy pound hath gained ten pounds. And he said unto him, Well, thou good servant: because thou hast been faithful in a very little, have thou authority over ten cities. And the second came, saying, Lord, thy pound hath gained five pounds. And he said likewise to him, Be thou also over five cities. And another came, saying, Lord, behold, here is thy pound, which I have kept laid up in a napkin: For I feared thee, because thou art an austere man: thou takest up that thou layedst not down, and reapest that thou didst not sow. And he saith unto him, Out of thine own mouth will I judge thee, thou wicked servant. Thou knewest that I was an austere man, taking up that I laid not down, and reaping that I did not sow: Wherefore then gavest not thou my money into the bank, that at my coming I might have required mine own with usury? And he said unto them that stood by, Take from him the pound, and give it to him that hath ten pounds. (And they said unto him, Lord, he hath ten pounds.) For I say unto you, That unto every one which hath shall be given; and from him that hath not, even that he hath shall be taken away

> from him. But those mine enemies, which would not that I should reign
> over them, bring hither, and slay them before me.
> —LUKE 19:11–27

The Lord, for the most part, deliberately gives us all a small portion to see what our attitude will be towards what we are "blessed" with. Those that are content with what they are given and make the most of their lot in life, have proven their worth as a servant and are given a kingdom of their own to rule in the future physical kingdom of God.

The citizens during the age of the Gentile church who will not have Jesus govern them are not given an investment to make in the kingdom; and because of the decision they made, they are slain. If they don't want to have anything to do with God here on earth, why would they want to spend eternity with Him? The Lord is looking for those who will choose to serve Him out of grateful hearts and after they have shown themselves worthy, He will reward them. Make no mistake about this doctrine.

6. Giving lip service to the kingdom of God

This is a parable of two sons both being of the same Father, God, the first being a Gentile the second being a Jew. Both sons are heirs and are expected to work and make their life count in kingdom productivity.

> But what think ye? A certain man had two sons; and he came to the first, and said, Son, go work to day in my vineyard. He answered and said, I will not: but afterward he repented, and went. And he came to the second, and said likewise. And he answered and said, I go, sir: and went not. Whether of them twain did the will of his father? They say unto him, The first. Jesus saith unto them, Verily I say unto you, That the publicans and the harlots go into the kingdom of God before you. For John came unto you in the way of righteousness, and ye believed him not: but the publicans and the harlots believed him: and ye, when ye had seen it, repented not afterward, that ye might believe him.
> —MATTHEW 21:28–32

When the first son is asked to go work in the vineyard, he responds rudely, "I will not!" He intentionally chose to show little respect to his father, due to his hard-heartedness. This son was not immediately judged for his behavior but was extended grace, as it is the goodness of the Lord that leads us to repentance, and through grace, he eventually repented. The fruit of his repentance from his former resistance is to immediately comply and go to work.

Paul explains the spiritual process of conversion includes not only repentance but also something we'll address later and that is "works congruous with repentance."

> The Gentiles, unto whom now I send thee, To open their eyes, and to turn them from darkness to light, and from the power of Satan unto God, that they may receive forgiveness of sins, and inheritance among

them which are sanctified by faith that is in me…that they should repent and turn to God, and do works meet for repentance.

—Acts 26:17–18, 20

This parable teaches a lesson here in evangelism, which is to never ever give up on people when met with stubborn obstinacy. Those that seemed furthest from the kingdom actually responded quicker than those that were "spiritual." The publican was one who shamelessly traded his reputation and respectability for gain and the harlot that defiled her own body for gain were the first to respond. They had sin, yes, but not the religious pride that blinds even those that appear most zealous.

> Spiritual pride works like an eraser obliterating all the good works a person may have done.

The second son, who was religious and put on a righteous act, said what he thought his father wanted to hear, while in his heart he went the other way.

This parable of Jesus regarding the kingdom of God resembles an Old Testament teaching found in Ezekiel.

But if the wicked will turn from all his sins that he hath committed, and keep all my statutes, and do that which is lawful and right, he shall surely live, he shall not die. All his transgressions that he hath committed, they shall not be mentioned unto him: in his righteousness that he hath done he shall live. Have I any pleasure at all that the wicked should die? saith the Lord God: and not that he should return from his ways, and live? But when the righteous turneth away from his righteousness, and committeth iniquity, and doeth according to all the abominations that the wicked man doeth, shall he live? All his righteousness that he hath done shall not be mentioned: in his trespass that he hath trespassed, and in his sin that he hath sinned, in them shall he die.

—Ezekiel 18:21–24

A religious hypocrite is harder to persuade to see the truth than one who is a worldly sinner, as this "form of godliness" becomes one of Satan's strongholds by which he opposes righteousness. Spiritual pride works like an eraser obliterating all the good works a person may have done.

7. Parable of the kingdom of God leadership exchange

This parable establishes the sin and resulting ruin of the Jewish nation. What is conviction to them is a caution to all that are part of the visible church.

The vineyard is the church, first of the Old Testament then the New. The church is not created but is planted as is a vineyard, thus requiring much nurturing, pruning, and attention by God.

How God persevered is a testament to His grace and unconditional agape love for His people. To reach His people He first sent prophets; they beat Jeremiah, killed Isaiah, stoned Zechariah, and rejected Samuel's sons as judges—to name but a few. God persevered by sending another servant, John the Baptist, whom they beheaded. Finally, never did grace appear more gracious than when the Father, wanting to desperately communicate His love, sent his Son as ambassador. Jesus was sent last; for if nothing else worked, surely this would—surely they would reverence his Son.

Did they hate Jesus that much or was there another stronghold that vexed the priests?

> For he knew that the chief priests had delivered him for envy.
> —MARK 15:10

How could men be so prejudiced against their own best interest and the welfare of their nation? We can never expect to do evil and yet be blessed.

> Hear another parable: There was a certain householder [God], which planted a vineyard [Old and New Testament church], and hedged it round about, and digged a winepress [alter of burnt offerings] in it, and built a tower, and let it out to husbandmen [Jewish religious leaders], and went into a far country: And when the time of the fruit drew near, he sent his servants [Prophets] to the husbandmen, that they might receive the fruits of it. And the husbandmen took his servants, and beat one, and killed another, and stoned another. Again, he sent other servants [such as John the Baptist] more than the first: and they did unto them likewise. But last of all he sent unto them his son [Jesus Christ], saying, They will reverence my son. But when the husbandmen saw the son, they said among themselves, This is the heir; come, let us kill him, and let us seize on his inheritance. And they caught him, and cast him out of the vineyard, and slew him. When the lord therefore of the vineyard cometh, what will he do unto those husbandmen? They say unto him, He will miserably destroy those wicked men, and will let out his vineyard unto other husbandmen [Church Servants], which shall render him the fruits in their seasons. Jesus saith unto them, Did ye never read in the scriptures, The stone [Jesus Christ] which the builders [Jewish leaders] rejected, the same is become the head of the corner: this is the Lord's doing, and it is marvelous in our eyes? Therefore say I unto you, The kingdom of God shall be taken from you, and given to a nation [Gentiles] bringing forth the fruits thereof.
> —MATTHEW 21:33–43

The builders rejecting the stone is the same as the husbandman's killing of the son sent to them. The chief priests and the elders were the builders having the oversight of the Jewish church, the vineyard, which was God's project. So if it were God's project, why would they not allow God a say in placing His Son as chief shepherd to establish doctrine and church practice? God sent His Son so that His will would be done on earth as it was in heaven. God, our super patient Father, still intends on sending His Son yet again to establish His will on Earth; and this time it will take.

It is written, "Seek ye first the kingdom of God, and his righteousness; and all these things shall be added unto you" (Matt. 6:33). The key to unlocking the provision and blessing of the Lord is for us to have our sights locked on to the kingdom of God.

What Will Prevent Me from Entering into the Kingdom of God?

1. The first and most important project for us to do is to repent, thus falling out of agreement with Satan's kingdom of the world and agreeing with the kingdom of God.

> Now after that John was put in prison, Jesus came into Galilee, preaching the gospel of the kingdom of God, And saying, The time is fulfilled, and the kingdom of God is at hand: repent ye, and believe the gospel.
> —Mark 1:14–15

Repentance is required, but repentance from what? In Christ's final letter to the church at Laodicea, He told them:

> As many as I love, I rebuke and chasten: be zealous therefore, and repent.
> —Revelation 3:19

He is speaking to the mature church, admonishing us to be zealous, to leave no stone unturned in our eagerness to be accepted in the kingdom of God. A blanket prayer that we prayed once, God forgive me of all my sins, past present and future, is hardly zealous. *Zealous* means to earnestly desire God's favor, to burn with zeal in discerning and purging our lives of sin. It is to have a perfect hatred towards sin.

2. This chapter is titled, Thy Kingdom Come, which means there must be another kingdom here now that needs to be removed. How is Satan's kingdom removed? One devil at a time. The kingdom of God is evidenced by casting out of devils.

> But if I cast out devils by the Spirit of God, then the kingdom of God is come unto you. Or else how can one enter into a strong man's house, and spoil his goods, except he first bind the strong man? and then he will spoil his house. He that is not with [in agreement with] me is against me; and he that gathereth [united in battle] not with me scattereth [driven by some other impulse] abroad.
> —Matthew 12:28–30

Jesus emphatically states that those that don't join Him in this part of the kingdom battle are really duped and are by default fighting to keep the enemy's kingdom in place. Read this entire passage in context to see what Jesus is saying. We will study this scripture in more detail in chapter seven. (See also Mark 3:20–30 and Luke 11:14–26.)

Many may not be able to receive these words, but please read a passage from the Gospel of Luke where Jesus practices the ministry of the church and describes it as preaching the kingdom of God.

> And they were astonished at his doctrine: for his word was with power. And in the synagogue there was a man, which had a spirit of an unclean devil, and cried out with a loud voice, Saying, Let us alone; what have we to do with thee, thou Jesus of Nazareth? art thou come to destroy us? I know thee who thou art; the Holy One of God. And Jesus rebuked him, saying, Hold thy peace, and come out of him. And when the devil had thrown him in the midst, he came out of him, and hurt him not. And they were all amazed, and spake among themselves, saying, What a word is this! for with authority and power he commandeth the unclean spirits, and they come out. And the fame of him went out into every place of the country round about. And he arose out of the synagogue, and entered into Simon's house. And Simon's wife's mother was taken with a great fever; and they besought him for her. And he stood over her, and rebuked the fever; and it left her: and immediately she arose and ministered unto them. Now when the sun was setting, all they that had any sick with divers diseases brought them unto him; and he laid his hands on every one of them, and healed them. And devils also came out of many, crying out, and saying, Thou art Christ the Son of God. And he rebuking them suffered them not to speak: for they knew that he was Christ. And when it was day, he departed and went into a desert place: and the people sought him, and came unto him, and stayed him, that he should not depart from them. And he said unto them, I must preach the kingdom of God to other cities also: for therefore am I sent.
> —LUKE 4:32–43

Not only did Jesus have this powerful ministry, but He said what He did was just the beginning of what needed to happen. Jesus continues, "When I am back with my Father I will equip my workers to do all that I did and more." (See John 14:11-12.)

> Believe me that I am in the Father, and the Father in me: or else believe me for the very works' sake. Verily, verily, I say unto you, He that believeth on me, the works that I do shall he do also; and greater works than these shall he do; because I go unto my Father.
> —JOHN 14:11–12

If this was the type of kingdom work Christ intended for the church, you should then see Jesus transfer this power and teach accordingly. Well, let's look to the Word and see Jesus first empowering the disciples to purge devils. If they were able to do that, they would also be able to heal diseases.

> Then he called his twelve disciples together, and gave them power and authority over all devils, and to cure diseases. And he sent them to preach the kingdom of God, and to heal the sick.
> —LUKE 9:1

Was this ministry just for the twelve apostles? Well, Jesus took seventy regular folks and empowered them to do as the twelve. Notice their astonishment at the power in the preaching of the kingdom of God.

> After these things the Lord appointed other seventy also, and sent them two and two before his face into every city and place, whither he himself would come. Therefore said he unto them, The harvest truly is great, but the labourers are few. . . . And the seventy returned again with joy, saying, Lord, even the devils are subject unto us through thy name. And he said unto them, I beheld Satan as lightning fall from heaven. Behold, I give unto you power to tread on serpents and scorpions, and over all the power of the enemy: and nothing shall by any means hurt you. Notwithstanding in this rejoice not, that the spirits are subject unto you; but rather rejoice, because your names are written in heaven. In that hour Jesus rejoiced in spirit, and said, I thank thee, O Father, Lord of heaven and earth, that thou hast hid these things from the wise and prudent, and hast revealed them unto babes: even so, Father; for so it seemed good in thy sight.
>
> —LUKE 10:1–9, 17–21

> Why was Jesus rejoicing when he was alone with the Father? It wasn't the smart class, the Scribes, Sadducees, Pharisees or other theologians of the day it was the regular folk who were given the same power as Jesus to defeat the devil.

Why was Jesus rejoicing when He was alone with the Father? It wasn't the smart class, the Scribes, the Sadducees, the Pharisees, or other theologians of the day; it was the regular folk who were given the same power as Jesus to defeat the devil.

After the seventy we see the "complete" Great Commission for the church to continue to preach the kingdom of God as Christ did.

> And he said unto them, Go ye into all the world, and preach the gospel to every creature. He that believeth and is baptized shall be saved; but he that believeth not shall be damned. And these signs shall follow them that believe; In my name shall they cast out devils; they shall speak with new tongues; They shall take up serpents; and if they drink any deadly thing, it shall not hurt them; they shall lay hands on the sick, and they shall recover.
>
> —MARK 16:15–18

If you happen to look this up in your modern version of the gospel, you'll see this passage is removed. There hasn't been a legitimate revival since the plethora of modern adjusted versions of God's Word hit the Bible mega market. I won't take that argument any further here, but I hope I just provoked you to do your homework.

The arguing types would argue that passage was removed, as it wasn't for the church. I think the Holy Spirit anticipated the battle we would be having today to "seek the kingdom of God," so He gave us an example of what happened when Philip the evangelist preached to the new church.

> Then Philip went down to the city of Samaria, and preached Christ unto them. And the people with one accord gave heed unto those things which Philip spake, hearing and seeing the miracles which he did. For unclean spirits, crying with loud voice, came out of many that were possessed with them: and many taken with palsies, and that were lame, were healed. And there was great joy in that city.... But when they believed Philip preaching the things concerning the kingdom of God, and the name of Jesus Christ, they were baptized, both men and women.
> —Acts 8:5–8, 12

The parables of the kingdom of God foresaw that those struggling with spiritual pride in their religious accomplishments would not qualify to be the preachers that ushered in the kingdom of God.

When the power that is to be evident in the kingdom of God is not evident in signs following the preaching of the Word, we must seek the Lord through His whole gospel to see if we are quenching the Spirit through doubt, unbelief, spiritual pride, or other sins that would hinder. One of the main hindrances to the power of the kingdom of God being fully preached is false doctrine propounded by certain of the church hierarchy. This actually brings a curse upon the sheep they are to be protecting and ushering into the kingdom.

> The parables of the kingdom of God foresaw that those struggling with spiritual pride in their religious accomplishments would not qualify to be the preachers that ushered in the kingdom of God.

Now just a thought: if the visible church is not casting out devils now, what are these legions of devils up too? If the sick are not getting healed, what kingdom may still be in place? Is Satan's kingdom given free run, as they have intimidated and infiltrated the churchs' shepherds in the same fashion the mafia may intimidate and infiltrate the police force to be able to do their work without hindrance?

3. A candidate for the kingdom of God cannot go forward by looking in the rearview mirror. Living in the past by keeping a record of wrongs, longing for ungodly pleasures, seeking an ungodly identity role as Eve did, or perhaps by holding onto an offense will be viewed by God as tempting Him; and it limits what He can do.

> And it came to pass, that, as they went in the way, a certain man said unto him, Lord, I will follow thee whithersoever thou goest. And Jesus said unto him, Foxes have holes, and birds of the air have nests; but the Son of man hath not where to lay his head. And he said unto another, Follow me. But he said, Lord, suffer me first to go and bury my father. Jesus said unto him, Let the dead bury their dead: but go thou and preach

the kingdom of God. And another also said, Lord, I will follow thee; but let me first go bid them farewell, which are at home at my house. And Jesus said unto him, No man, having put his hand to the plough, and looking back, is fit for the kingdom of God.

—Luke 9:57–62

How oft did they provoke him in the wilderness, and grieve him in the desert! Yea, they turned back and tempted God, and limited the Holy One of Israel. They remembered not his hand, nor the day when he delivered them from the enemy.

—Psalm 78:40–42

4. The kingdom of God is not encouraged by rituals or religious observances or holidays. During the church age, the kingdom of God is powerful but invisible. The kingdom of God resides within a believer who has cleansed his temple within, so it is suitable for the Master's habitation.

And when he was demanded of the Pharisees, when the kingdom of God should come, he answered them and said, The kingdom of God cometh not with observation [in a visible manner]: Neither shall they say, Lo here! or, lo there! for, behold, the kingdom of God is within you.

—Luke 17:20–21

We don't join the kingdom as a member; we are reborn into it. We are born first by water, which is natural birth, but then we are to be reborn of the Spirit, which is the key to the kingdom of God. The evidence of being born of this Spirit is our pursuit towards being reconciled to the person we were meant to be when we were created in the image of God before the foundation of the world. This person is one who is holy, without blame, and walking before Him in agape love.

Jesus answered and said unto him, Verily, verily, I say unto thee, Except a man be born again, he cannot see the kingdom of God. Nicodemus saith unto him, How can a man be born when he is old? can he enter the second time into his mother's womb, and be born? Jesus answered, Verily, verily, I say unto thee, Except a man be born of water and of the Spirit, he cannot enter into the kingdom of God. That which is born of the flesh is flesh; and that which is born of the Spirit is spirit.

—John 3:3–6

5. A minister of the gospel is responsible to teach the whole counsel of God, which provides balance as the Word is taught in context with the Bible as a whole. The habit of some is to use a scripture verse as a point of departure and then give their own impersonal social gospel. This results in the scattering of the sheep, as they are looking for answers to their problems everywhere else except the church. The pastor will be accountable as to how he prepared his flock to enter into the kingdom of God.

And now, behold, I know that ye all, among whom I have gone preaching the kingdom of God, shall see my face no more. Wherefore I take you to record this day, that I am pure from the blood of all men. For I have not shunned to declare unto you all the counsel of God.
—ACTS 20:25–27

6. A King's kid who is sold out to seeking the kingdom of God will not have to beg the Father for provision. Being anxious about what tomorrow holds or in fear of poverty or lack is actually serving the kingdom we are to be replacing. Provision is the understood inheritance and a God-given right of a kingdom of God saint. I've found that the greatest blessings in my life were not the things I dared pray for. God certainly did more than I could think or imagine. I'm the type of person, I guess, that might take credit for God answering my prayers, so He just loves to surprise me.

Therefore take no thought, saying, What shall we eat? or, What shall we drink? or, Wherewithal shall we be clothed? (For after all these things do the Gentiles seek:) for your heavenly Father knoweth that ye have need of all these things. But seek ye first the kingdom of God, and his righteousness; and all these things shall be added unto you. Take therefore no thought for the morrow: for the morrow shall take thought for the things of itself. Sufficient unto the day is the evil thereof.
—MATTHEW 6:31–34

7. The road to the kingdom is narrow; it is not through the freeway the world travels. Most believers would never think of suing someone in court, especially a fellow believer. Yet, more than fifty percent of Christian couples sue one another through carnal legal proceedings to divide up their households and "children property" in no-fault, no-accountability divorce. This is for a very short-sighted gain, which has eternal consequences for the unrepentant. This will, no doubt, anger many of my brothers and sisters; but as a messenger, I am only presenting the Word to you for your profit and consideration. If I love you, I cannot be silent, knowing the fear of the Lord and His righteous judgments.

But brother goeth to law with brother, and that before the unbelievers. Now therefore there is utterly a fault among you, because ye go to law one with another. Why do ye not rather take wrong? why do ye not rather suffer yourselves to be defrauded? Nay, ye do wrong, and defraud, and that your brethren. Know ye not that the unrighteous shall not inherit the kingdom of God? Be not deceived: neither fornicators, nor idolaters, nor adulterers, nor effeminate, nor abusers of themselves with mankind, Nor thieves, nor covetous, nor drunkards, nor revilers, nor extortioners, shall inherit the kingdom of God. And such were some of you: but ye are washed, but ye are sanctified, but ye are justified in the name of the Lord Jesus, and by the Spirit of our God.
—1 CORINTHIANS 6:6–11

Continual participation with this lengthy list of behaviors is evidence of one who is not prepared for the kingdom of God. If one is still participating with any on this list of offenses, it is evidence that further washing by the Word of God is required to complete sanctification. Are you not quite sure what sanctification is all about? Stay tuned right here, as you'll be given step-by-step ministry in subsequent chapters to set you free from all these bondages, as well as those listed in the two following passages.

> Now the works of the flesh are manifest, which are these; Adultery, fornication, uncleanness, lasciviousness, Idolatry, witchcraft, hatred, variance, emulations, wrath, strife, seditions, heresies, Envyings, murders, drunkenness, revellings, and such like: of the which I tell you before, as I have also told you in time past, that they which do such things [continual practice or habit] shall not inherit the kingdom of God.
> —Galatians 5:19–21

> And walk in love [*agape*], as Christ also hath loved [*agapao*] us, and hath given himself for us an offering and a sacrifice to God for a sweetsmelling savour. But fornication, and all uncleanness, or covetousness, let it not be once named among you, as becometh saints; Neither filthiness, nor foolish talking, nor jesting, which are not convenient: but rather giving of thanks. For this ye know, that no whoremonger, nor unclean person, nor covetous man, who is an idolater, hath any inheritance in the kingdom of Christ and of God.
> —Ephesians 5:2–5

If you have made it this far, you are, no doubt, serious about understanding what you must do regarding the Word to "seek ye first the kingdom of God, and his righteousness; and all these things shall be added unto you" (Matt. 6:33). The primary evidence in your life that you are seeking the kingdom of God is that you'll repent and turn from a lifestyle that enjoys the sin listed in these scriptures, no matter how painful it may be to sever from your uncleanness.

If we are not intentionally seeking the kingdom of God yet demanding God supply our needs and wishes, we are approaching the throne of God presumptuously. We are asking a holy God to grant our requests while we remain in rebellion to His kingdom of God constitution. Since it is our Father's kingdom, He gets to set all the rules; and like it or not, ready or not, He is still coming.

> There is no such thing as luck within the kingdom of God. Luck is the premise for Darwin's theory of evolution involving fortuitous happenstance.

If your prayers seem to hit a brass ceiling, the good news is now you know what you must do to change that. This teaching is too important to rush through, so you may want to go back and review the scriptures in this chapter; and as the Holy Spirit convicts, you get to repent and erase the consequences of habitual sin. You are either "hot," or you are "not" of the kingdom.

If you are still trying to find an easy way to avoid change and repentance, good luck. There is no such thing as luck within the kingdom of God. Luck is the premise for Darwin's theory of evolution involving fortuitous happenstance. OK, I'll tell you what you can say to direct (notice I didn't use the word *wish* either) someone a blessing: the words are "God speed." But there is a responsibility in bidding someone "God speed."

> Whosoever transgresseth, and abideth not in the doctrine of Christ, hath not God. He that abideth in the doctrine of Christ, he hath both the Father and the Son. If there come any unto you, and bring not this doctrine, receive him not into your house, neither bid him God speed: For he that biddeth him God speed is partaker of his evil deeds.
>
> —2 John 1:9–11

THY WILL BE DONE IN EARTH,
AS IT IS IN HEAVEN

IT WAS WELL after midnight; I pulled my patrol car over onto the gravel shoulder of the now desolate street that leads through the light industrial business section of Hinton to talk to a familiar little friend of mine. Looking inquisitively into his brown eyes, I asked, "How's it going Jimmy?" With no hesitation, he stammered, "I'm sorry, but I know you are going to find out anyway, it was me, I just broke into the Turbo gas station!" He proceeded to hand me the booty that was stuffed into the bulging pocket of his hoody. This young man apologized over and over for letting me down. I liked this little fellow. A year or two earlier I had charged him for committing a string of over forty break and enters in town, which put him in jail for a period of time. I asked him to call me when he got out of jail, and he did. I hired him to help out part-time in my little side business manufacturing waterbeds, back when those things were the rage. He was a great little worker. I found out that his dad left years ago, leaving his mom to raise him. To make ends meet, she had a revolving door of hopeless live-in boyfriends who all lent their hand at trying to straighten him out. Jimmy wanted to be anywhere but home. And with no money, no supervision, and lots of time on his hands, he just continued on his juvenile crime spree until I caught him.

Jimmy feared me as a police officer but also had a healthy respect for me, because I believe he knew that I saw the good in him and loved him. When I arrested him late that night, he really couldn't wait to confess his nasty little deed and his disappointment in himself was painfully apparent. Once we experience and receive the much greater agape love our heavenly Father has for us, we reverence Him; but we also fear getting busted by the One who has been so good to us. How could we repay Him with evil after He has extended such mercy?

Abraham's examination

We perhaps are familiar with the unusual story of Abraham, who waited until he was an old man to receive his son Isaac—promised him twenty years earlier by God. Then after all that anticipation and enjoying this youth in his old age, Abraham was asked by God to do the unthinkable, to sacrifice his son upon an alter on the mountain. With a knife in hand raised to slay Isaac:

The angel of the LORD called unto him out of heaven, and said, Abraham, Abraham: and he said, Here am I. And he said, Lay not thine hand upon the lad, neither do thou any thing unto him: for now I know that thou fearest God, seeing thou hast not withheld thy son, thine only son from me. And Abraham lifted up his eyes, and looked, and behold behind him a ram caught in a thicket by his horns: and Abraham went and took the ram, and offered him up for a burnt offering in the stead of his son. And Abraham called the name of that place Jehovahjireh: as it is said to this day, In the mount of the LORD it shall be seen. And the angel of the LORD called unto Abraham out of heaven the second time, And said, By myself have I sworn, saith the LORD, for because thou hast done this thing, and hast not withheld thy son, thine only son: That in blessing I will bless thee, and in multiplying I will multiply thy seed as the stars of the heaven, and as the sand which is upon the sea shore; and thy seed shall possess the gate of his enemies; And in thy seed shall all the nations of the earth be blessed; because thou hast obeyed my voice.

—GENESIS 22:11–18

Abraham is revered through the generations for his great faith in God, knowing that God had promised that through Isaac all the nations would be blessed and so if he were to be slain, God would have a problem and would have to raise him up. That is what we know from Abrahams perspective, but what was God's purpose? Was it to test the faith of Abraham? The purpose of this most difficult test was to determine if Abraham feared God. Abraham was given a command by God to lay down the life of his beloved son; actually God didn't ask Abraham to do something that He wasn't prepared to do with His own Son. This fear isn't the kind of fear where you want to hide, rather it is the kind of fear wherein you want to be obedient to the voice and will of God. Abraham obeyed the voice of God thus receiving a passing grade for fearing God. The graduation present was not something Abraham sought for but something God just wanted to bless Abraham with: a family so large that it would change world history with its influence.

> Did God wave this blessing in front of Abraham first in order to get him to offer up Isaac? "Abraham *if* you offer up Isaac I will bless you big time." No, Abraham had to obey simply because he feared God, and then the Lord poured out His blessing upon him.

Solomon's examination

God also tested a future king in a slightly different fashion but with similar results. God asked Solomon to name whatever he wanted and it would be granted. Would Solomon ask for something that would enrich and enhance his own well-being or would his request give testimony of Solomon's understanding of kingdom of God principles?

> In Gibeon the LORD appeared to Solomon in a dream by night: and God said, Ask what I shall give thee. And Solomon said…Give therefore thy servant an understanding heart to judge thy people, that I may discern between good and bad: for who is able to judge this thy so great a people? And the speech pleased the LORD, that Solomon had asked this thing. And God said unto him, Because thou hast asked this thing, and hast not asked for thyself long life; neither hast asked riches for thyself, nor hast asked the life of thine enemies; but hast asked for thyself understanding to discern judgment; Behold, I have done according to thy words: lo, I have given thee a wise and an understanding heart; so that there was none like thee before thee, neither after thee shall any arise like unto thee. And I have also given thee that which thou hast not asked, both riches, and honour: so that there shall not be any among the kings like unto thee all thy days. And if thou wilt walk in my ways, to keep my statutes and my commandments, as thy father David did walk, then I will lengthen thy days.
>
> —1 KINGS 3:5–6, 9–14

In response to Solomon's unselfish request for discernment to lead God's people in wisdom, God showed His approval by blessing Solomon with many things he did not ask for. The Lord did have a condition on all the blessings, which was to continue in obedience all the days of his life. Unfortunately Solomon rebelled, thus shortening his life to perhaps fifty-eight years, whereas David lived over seventy.

BUT SEEK FIRST THE KINGDOM OF GOD

With the glory of Solomon in mind, Jesus taught this kingdom of God principal with further clarity.

> Therefore I say unto you, Take no thought for your life, what ye shall eat, or what ye shall drink; nor yet for your body, what ye shall put on. Is not the life more than meat, and the body than raiment? Behold the fowls of the air: for they sow not, neither do they reap, nor gather into barns; yet your heavenly Father feedeth them. Are ye not much better than they? Which of you by taking thought can add one cubit unto his stature? And why take ye thought for raiment? Consider the lilies of the field, how they grow; they toil not, neither do they spin: And yet I say unto you, That even Solomon in all his glory was not arrayed like one of these. Wherefore, if God so clothe the grass of the field, which to day is, and to morrow is cast into the oven, shall he not much more clothe you, O ye of little faith? Therefore take no thought, saying, What shall we eat? or, What shall we drink? or, Wherewithal shall we be clothed? (For after all these things do the Gentiles seek:) for your heavenly Father knoweth that ye have need of all these things. But seek ye first the kingdom of God, and his righteousness; and all these things shall be added unto you.
>
> —MATTHEW 6:25–33

Our lustful nature can then inspire us to think, *Well, I see I can't ask for wealth directly; but if I am creative and ask for something to help others then God is bound to do to me what He did for Solomon.*

> Now the end of the commandment is charity [*agape*] out of a pure heart, and of a good conscience, and of faith unfeigned.
> —1 TIMOTHY 1:5

It is impossible to deceive or manipulate the Spirit of God.

> Ye ask, and receive not, because ye ask amiss, that ye may consume it upon your lusts.
> —JAMES 4:3

Don't do anything to receive, but rather do it to please the Father.

Abraham and Solomon sought "first the kingdom of God." They did what was best for others while laying down their own will and ambitions. To seek first the kingdom of God is how "God's will is done on earth as it is in heaven." To seek first the kingdom of God is agape love in action. This kingdom is pursued by fearing God as evidenced by the obedience of one who sees himself as a servant.

Solomon summed up the sole purpose of man in fourteen words:

> Let us hear the conclusion of the whole matter: Fear God, and keep his commandments: for this is the whole duty of man.
> —ECCLESIASTES 12:13

Though the accounts of Solomon and Abraham are very credible in the understanding of the kingdom of God principles, they trifle in comparison to the standard lived out by our Lord Jesus the Christ.

Jesus fully satisfied the will of our Father in heaven, and He fully satisfied the will of our Father on earth. Oh, to be able to say, "I do always those things that please the Father and for the benefit of others."

> Then said Jesus unto them, When ye have lifted up the Son of man, then shall ye know that I am he, and that I do nothing of myself; but as my Father hath taught me, I speak these things. And he that sent me is with me: the Father hath not left me alone; for I do always those things that please him.
> —JOHN 8:28

How do we know what is God's will on earth? It is to do what we observed Jesus accomplish, as He did on earth what He first saw His Father do.

> Then answered Jesus and said unto them, Verily, verily, I say unto you, The Son can do nothing of himself, but what he seeth the Father do: for what things soever he doeth, these also doeth the Son likewise...I can of mine own self do nothing: as I hear, I judge: and my judgment is just; because I seek not mine own will, but the will of the Father which hath sent me.
> —JOHN 5:19, 30

The gospels of Matthew, Mark, Luke, and John are written from varying perspective regarding the acts of Christ so we may understand "sold-out" obedience to the Father, the agape love of the Father in practice, and the fear of God.

Jesus' love was predicated upon obedience to the will of Father God

By Jesus' obedience the agape love of the Father flowed unrestricted to the entire human race. Accordingly, that astounding agape love will flow through us from Christ in response to our obedience.

> If ye abide in me, and my words abide in you, ye shall ask what ye will, and it shall be done unto you. Herein is my Father glorified, that ye bear much fruit; so shall ye be my disciples. As the Father hath loved me, so have I loved you: continue ye in my love. If ye keep my commandments, ye shall abide in my love [*agape*]; even as I have kept my Father's commandments, and abide in his love [*agape*]. These things have I spoken unto you, that my joy might remain in you, and that your joy might be full. This is my commandment, That ye love one another, as I have loved you. Greater love [*agape*] hath no man than this, that a man lay down his life for his friends. Ye are my friends, if ye do whatsoever I command you.
> —JOHN 15:7–14

How do you know what Christ has commanded?

We want to be obedient to the Father; but if you are like me, you've found it difficult. Not long ago one of my sons had a mishap of spilling some oil and gasoline, thus staining our new paved driveway. After I informed him of my displeasure, I slammed the door. My own actions startled me, not to mention what they did to my son. Oh, it didn't take us long to ask forgiveness and forgive each other. He drove off, and I texted him, "Son, I'm so sorry for getting angry. You are so much more important to me than any driveway. Please forgive me." I had no intention of acting so silly, so why did I disobey my Father and misrepresent His love to my son?

I appreciate the honesty of the apostle Paul as he described his battle with his unpredictable humanity:

> For I know that in me (that is, in my flesh,) dwelleth no good thing: for to will is present with me; but how to perform that which is good I find not. For the good that I would I do not: but the evil which I would not, that I do. Now if I do that I would not, it is no more I that do it, but sin that dwelleth in me. I find then a law, that, when I would do good, evil is present with me.
> —ROMANS 7:18–21

How do I know if I've died to self?

There are several precepts introduced by Paul that we'll explore throughout this book. We'll bring forward one concept now regarding the flesh and Paul's complaint that nothing good dwells in it. When my flesh has a brainstorm, I know that in that particular area of my life I haven't died to self. When I die to self, my will takes a back seat and the Father's will prevails.

How do I know if I've die to self? I believe it is when I can be like Christ and offer no comment when someone sets out to maliciously destroy my reputation.

> When my flesh has a brainstorm, I know that in that particular area of my life I haven't died to self. When I die to self, my will takes a back seat and the Father's will prevails.

During a recent time of painful personal crisis, I became aware of some venomous gossip that was taking a swath through a group of my friends. I was all set to go and confront my "friends" and offer the rest of the story. But I couldn't bring myself to go to them, as I knew I was nursing a very bitter spirit. Eventually I was able to inquire of the Lord about the poison in my heart and why was I so anxious. Speaking directly into my heart came the words, "The reason you are so tormented is because you are trying to preserve your reputation; you haven't died to yourself, Dennis." Jesus was able to defend Himself, but He chose silence. He made himself of no reputation when He was maligned, and He is Lord. He was sent to earth to change the world, so you'd think His reputation was the most important thing He had.

> But made himself of no reputation, and took upon him the form of a servant, and was made in the likeness of men.
>
> —PHILIPPIANS 2:7

I knew this was right, and I felt the peaceful correction of conviction shining a light into my troubled heart. But I still was whining to myself. In my business years I took many self-help courses that taught me if I lose my reputation I'm nothing, I'm finished. But God seems to like special project people. Take Paul for example, in his zeal he went about ordering the murders of the very people God would later send him back to minister Christianity.

> We are fools for Christ's sake, but ye are wise in Christ; we are weak, but ye are strong; ye are honourable, but we are despised.
>
> —1 CORINTHIANS 4:10

It is when we are weak that we are strong, and that is another kingdom of God principle.

The disciples were unable to deliver a lad from his insanity, and they inquired of Jesus what they should have done differently.

> Then came the disciples to Jesus apart, and said, Why could not we cast him out? And Jesus said unto them, Because of your unbelief: for verily I say unto you, If ye have faith as a grain of mustard seed, ye shall say unto this mountain, Remove hence to yonder place; and it shall remove; and nothing shall be impossible unto you.
>
> —MATTHEW 17:19–20

The mountain in this story is a destructive evil spirit(s) that we are unable to remove. You have without a doubt heard it said that if you have faith the size of a mustard seed, you could move your mountains. So the poor saint feels that the reason they are not getting healed is because they can't summon up enough faith to even surpass the size of a mustard seed.

> Brother, sister, now hear this; it is not the faith the *size* of a mustard seed, it is faith *as* a mustard seed.

Brother, sister, now hear this; it is not the faith the *size* of a mustard seed, it is faith *as* a mustard seed. A mustard seed sitting in the palm of your hand can do nothing of itself. It isn't until it is buried and it dies to self that it can then germinate, take root, and become the plant it was intended to do. The mustard seed has to have faith that God will do as He said and allow that little seed to be born again once it gives up control of its life and is buried. For our faith to work we have to die to self. Otherwise, if I believe God answered my prayer simply on the basis of the amount of faith that I had, I then have taken the credit for the move of God and that is pride—holding myself in idolatry. The kingdom of God rules are opposite what rules the flesh.

> Verily, verily, I say unto you, Except a corn of wheat fall into the ground and die, it abideth alone: but if it die, it bringeth forth much fruit.
>
> —John 12:24

There is a battle that rages within our spirits as one dies to his own ambitions to take up the enterprise of our Father. Christ opens up His spirit for the believer to understand the battle He fought in being obedient to the desire of His Father to lay down His life for the remission of all sin.

> Saying, Father, if thou be willing, remove this cup from me: nevertheless not my will, but thine, be done. And there appeared an angel unto him from heaven, strengthening him. And being in an agony he prayed more earnestly: and his sweat was as it were great drops of blood falling down to the ground.
>
> —Luke 22:42–44

Jesus Christ wrestled in prayer until gaining victory over His flesh, which wanted to protect itself from death. The flesh dies hard, as it is always inventing a way to protect and preserve itself, thus taking us into the conflict of warring against the will of God.

> Who in the days of his flesh, when he had offered up prayers and supplications with strong crying and tears unto him that was able to save him from death, and was heard in that he feared; Though he were a Son, yet learned he obedience by the things which he suffered.
>
> —Hebrews 5:7–8

Christ, though a sinless man, still had to learn obedience to the Father. How did the Father teach Jesus obedience? Through the things He suffered.

As I contemplated this, I thought, *If Christ had to learn obedience, then who am I to think that I will escape suffering that is required to teach obedience?* I had times on the mountaintop of earthly life, but I didn't start to learn until I was in the deep valley of my wilderness experience. The teaching of this entire book was what God taught me to revive my heart to overcome in victory during a period of prolonged despair in my life. Looking back, when everything was "perfect" in my life, my relationship with the Lord was very shallow and my love for God and man was very fickle. When folks were going through their valleys, I judged them in my heart. But no more; now I understand their pain and I understand the possibility of victory through suffering.

In response to Jesus overcoming the battle of the flesh being obedient to even death, God our Father then lavished Christ with an inheritance totally priceless and eternal.

> As I contemplated this, I thought, if Christ had to learn obedience then who am I to think that I will escape suffering that is required to teach obedience?

> And being found in fashion as a man, he humbled himself, and became obedient unto death, even the death of the cross. Wherefore God also hath highly exalted him, and given him a name which is above every name: That at the name of Jesus every knee should bow, of things in heaven, and things in earth, and things under the earth; And that every tongue should confess that Jesus Christ is Lord, to the glory of God the Father.
> —PHILIPPIANS 2:8–11

Consider again the lives of Abraham, Solomon, and Jesus Christ; would we even be reading about them today if they did not die to self and become obedient to the will of God? Would any of these men have received the vast blessings from the Father if they were following "self-help" principles?

Jesus also did the will of His Father in some other battles He engaged in. Jesus had many teachable moments to expose hypocrisy and false doctrine amongst the churches' elite class. He stood ground against those that profited in the foyer of the temple; He was zealous in protecting the vulnerable while thrashing those that took advantage of them. Jesus' zeal for truth, though, was not self-serving to make Himself "a somebody," but it was for the eternal betterment of others.

WHAT DOES GOD REQUIRE OF ME?

I wanted to know what I would be held accountable for when I have my face-to-face meeting with Jesus, so I searched the Scriptures and compiled a "To-Be List." This is by no means an exhaustive list, but I included those things that I felt the Holy Spirit was highlighting. In a future chapter we'll look at a "What Not to Be List."

I believe many of us live here on earth are in considerable languish about

> I wanted to know what I would be held accountable for when I have my face-to-face meeting with Jesus, so I searched the Scriptures and compiled a "To-Be List."

our lot in life. We believe in eternal life, but act like this trek on earth is all there is. James compares this life with the permanence of vapor. Vapor is what makes up clouds so it is a good idea to get our heads out of there. Compliance to the will of God is impossible if we've made ourselves at home in a place we are only to be living temporarily on our visitor's visa.

Dearly beloved, I beseech you as strangers [a foreigner living in a place without right of citizenship] and pilgrims [from a foreign place living amongst the natives], abstain from fleshly lusts [cravings for what is forbidden], which war against the soul;

—1 Peter 2:11

Peter is persuading the "beloved"—yes, that would be Christians—to watch where they live and be very careful of what turns them on. John goes further telling us that we must choose wisely. Our life is like a coin; we can spend it anyway we want, but we can only spend it once.

> James compares this life with the permanence of vapor. Vapor is what makes up clouds so it is a good idea to get our heads out of there.

Love not the world, neither the things that are in the world. If any man love the world, the love of the Father is not in him. For all that is in the world, the lust of the flesh, and the lust of the eyes, and the pride of life, is not of the Father, but is of the world. And the world passeth away, and the lust thereof: but he that doeth the will of God abideth for ever.

—1 John 2:15–17

Lust of the flesh is everything opposed to seeking the kingdom of God first and His righteousness. It is an unquenchable appetite for feel-good indulgences through such things as entertainment, sports, work, crime, sex, food, gossip, anger, attention, fame, money, collections, hobbies, children, family, or whatever else we think about most of the time. Woven into the fabric of the Christian marriage, for example, are "how-to- score" books, where the couple is encouraged to pursue sex starting first thing in the morning in the kitchen and continuing on that track throughout the day. So what happens in the fella's mind all day long at work as he deals with the constant distractions that pop up on his screen? He is on high alert for things sensual, regardless of the source. I am not a killjoy, as God designed perfect love and intimacy within the confines of marriage. The question is, though, what are we seeking *first*? By seeking first the kingdom of God, the scripture tells us that all the other things we need, will be provided. Whatever is driving you is what you are seeking first.

Lust of the eyes would include one's total fascination with their own appearance and physique and likewise total fixation on the appearance and physique of another's tent. Lust of the eyes is also a metaphor for the "eyes of the mind," which would include the quest to learn but not to see.

The pride of life is gambling our soul on the empty presumption that things on earth are dependable and limited. We may murmur, "Well, we only live once so let's _____"; or, "Life is too short to be unhappy, so I will _____"; or, "I want to experience all this world has to offer," "I am an island onto myself," or "No one else will look after me, so I got to do what I got to do." They love themselves and others at the *eros* level, which is self-service and self-gratification at the expense of other human "objects."

The difficulty occurs when we've invested in the wrong stock our whole life and then the world as we know it closes up shop. Perhaps then they'll coin the phrase, "unholy smoke."

> What doth the LORD thy God require of thee, but to fear the LORD thy God, to walk in all his ways, and to love him, and to serve the LORD thy God with all thy heart and with all thy soul, To keep the commandments of the LORD, and his statutes, which I command thee this day for thy good? Behold, the heaven and the heaven of heavens is the LORD's thy God, the earth also, with all that therein is.
>
> —DEUTERONOMY 10:12–14

1. The Lord requires me to fear Him.

The most aggressive form of cancer within the church is divorce. Folks justify divorce saying, "God wants me to be happy!" A churchman encourages, "God has called you to peace, so if you are unhappy or think you are abused in your marriage get out." He goes on to explain, for example, that abuse would be a woman having to look after the household finances. Proverbs 31 would suggest a woman has an incredible contribution to offer to her family—a contribution that may not be slighted by any man. Really, anytime we misrepresent the love of the Father to those we are supposed to love is abuse. It is called sin, and it is the goodness of the Lord that leads to its recognition and repentance. I'm certainly not advocating any criminal activity within the relationship as being OK, and that is not what we are referring to here.

> What is being said by some is that happiness takes precedence over obedience to the Word of God.

What some are saying is that happiness takes precedence over obedience to the Word of God. "I will divorce and remarry, and if it is wrong I will repent after as God will forgive me," is the taunt. Who would be whispering that in the heart? I know God says He hates divorce, so the whisper is not from Him. To take the premeditated and deliberate steps of rebellion through the lengthy divorce process without repentance is a little different than one who desires to serve the Lord, falls, but gets up, repents and does whatever it takes to avoid falling into sin again. There are sins of passion that occur in the heat of the moment, and then there are the premeditated sins that become a lifestyle. How close can one get to presuming upon the grace of God? I don't know the answer to that as that is between the believer and their Lord, but the question needs to be asked on this side of eternity.

With an international audience a minister pursues a doctrine that devils may have put your marriage together, offering another way of escape from marriage. Those words were to provide an antidote to God's Word, which states, "What God has joined together let not man put asunder." If devils put you together, the justification goes then it would be OK for man to put asunder. But what does the Word say?

> Know ye not that your bodies are the members of Christ? shall I then take the members of Christ, and make them the members of an harlot? God forbid. What? know ye not that he which is joined to an harlot is one body? for two, saith he, shall be one flesh. But he that is joined unto the Lord is one spirit.
> —1 Corinthians 6:15–17

The Word here is that even if you choose to sleep with a prostitute, you become one flesh with her, and God made it that way. Fornicating with a harlot is sin, but the spiritual law is that you are still made one flesh with that person by God, even in your rebellion. This would make the doctrine that devils make married couples one flesh a difficult premise to back up with scripture, not to mention what does one do with all the children born of this union? Are they all illegitimate?

> The rebellious husband will be won over not by words but by the beauty of the chaste behavior of his bride and the converse would be true for a husband to win over a rebellious wife.

Another minister says that a woman only needs to submit to her husband to the degree that he submits to Christ. I suppose that sounds logical if you want to be excused from obedience to the Word. In this case, such doctrine sets up the wife to judge and condemn her husband, as she perceives his spirituality. The converse is that a man need only to love his wife to the degree that she reverences him. Do you see the lie? The Scripture teaches that the rebellious husband will be won over, not by words but by the beauty of the chaste behavior of his bride and the converse would be true for a husband to win over a rebellious wife.

> Likewise, ye wives, be in subjection to your own husbands; that, if any obey not the word, they also may without the word [without one's intervention] be won by the conversation [conduct] of the wives; while they behold your chaste [pure from fault] conversation coupled with fear [reverence for one's husband].
> —1 Peter 3:1–2

I believe anyone who uses Scripture as a point of departure to say what itching ears want to hear may be struggling with the fear of man over his fear of the Lord. The fear of the Lord means I am more dedicated to obedience to the Word of God than I am to the short-lived comfort or lust of my flesh.

Here is a question to provoke: is there any unpardonable sin within a marriage, or any relationship for that matter? The excuse of irreconcilable differences is often cited in court documents as the reason a relationship must end. Is there any relationship anywhere that does not have a number of differences or ideas that are in opposition or oppose each other such that they would never be in total agree-

> The fear of the Lord means I am more dedicated to obedience to the Word of God than I am to the short lived comfort or lust of my flesh.

ment? Usually those differences are what attracted you to that person in the first place, as they provided completion to the person you were not. The focus of irreconcilable differences would reveal the level of love the relationship has fallen to or has been based upon. We say we no longer love each other; actually we don't fall out of love, we fall into sin. The question is not, "Did I marry the right person?" The question is "How do I learn to love (agape) the person I married?" Become as a mustard seed, which must die to self, deal with the sin mountain, and guess what resurfaces?

I've just used the example of disposing of those we vowed to love here through divorce, but all froward and continual sin testifies to fact we do not fear the Lord. Froward and continual sin describes a lifestyle of reckless disregard for what our Father has said.

> A wise man feareth, and departeth [retracts or turns away] from evil: but the fool rageth [alienates], and is confident [folly of careless trust in false peace].
> —PROVERBS 14:16

The *Thayer's Lexicon* expands on the term *rageth*: spiritually, when men move outside the requirements of the covenant by committing sin, to cross the line.

Fear of the Lord is a deterrent to sin. If a person can sin without fear means the conscience is now silent due to fantasy or repetitive sin, and once the conscience is silent, they experience a place of false peace.

> By mercy and truth iniquity is purged: and by the fear of the LORD men depart from evil.
> —PROVERBS 16:6

Continuing shamelessly in our sin is really flaunting our rebellion in the face of a mighty God, and in such rebellion without repentance there is no guarantee our fire insurance is valid. If what you are doing stinks of evil, it is because it is evil. God is the same yesterday, today, and forever (Heb. 13:8), and His hatred of sin has not changed. Society tries to change the laws of morality, but is society going to be there to mount up a victorious defense for its followers in the Day of Judgment?

> The role of the ministry is to reconcile us to the folks we were created before the foundation of the world to be. Reconciliation can only happen through the humility of repentance.

Many readers will be saying, "Well, I have divorced and even remarried once, twice, three times; so now what?" Jesus offered redemption to the woman at the well that had multiple husbands; and that, my friend, is what our Lord still desires to do. And as a messenger I'll show you His way of salvation. But be careful once you have understood the way of knowledge and righteousness you are required to live with it.

2. The Lord requires me to walk in all His ways.

> He wants us to be just like Him—holy. But as he which hath called you is holy, so be ye holy in all manner of conversation [conduct]; because it is written, Be ye holy; for I am holy
>
> —1 PETER 1:15–16

> And all things are of God, who hath reconciled [return to favor] us to himself by Jesus Christ, and hath given to us the ministry of reconciliation [restoration to favor through repentance].
>
> —2 CORINTHIANS 5:18–19

The role of the ministry is to reconcile us to the folks we were created before the foundation of the world to be. Reconciliation can only happen through the humility of repentance.

What was your original prototype like? You were formed holy, faultless, while being effervescent with the agape Father's love. To be reconciled is to restore you to your original condition.

> According as he hath chosen us in him before the foundation of the world, that we should be holy [a living temple sanctified] and without blame [morally faultless] before him in love [*agape*].
>
> —EPHESIANS 1:4

Reconciliation of the believer requires continual cleansing of the flesh and spirit. In other words, our living temple for God must be thoroughly disinfected of all evil and filth so our temple is fit for a King.

> Having therefore these promises, dearly beloved [believers], let us cleanse ourselves from all filthiness of the flesh and spirit, perfecting holiness in the fear of God.
>
> —2 CORINTHIANS 7:1

Now, just how important is this pursuit of holiness and reconciliation?

> Follow [run swiftly to catch it] peace with all men, and holiness [sanctification of heart and life], without which no man shall see the Lord.
>
> —HEBREWS 12:14

3. The Lord requires me to love Him.

Love remains fickle while at the level of the mind (*phileo*) and love is totally selfish at the level of the flesh (*eros*):

> And thou shalt love [*agapeo*] the Lord thy God with all thy heart, and with all thy soul, and with all thy mind, and with all thy strength: this is the first commandment. And the second is like, namely this, Thou shalt love [*agapeo*] thy neighbour as thyself. There is none other commandment greater than these.
>
> —MARK 12:30

Agape love is at the level of the spirit and emanates from there to saturate our soul, mind, and body with the Father's purest form of unselfish love.

4. The Lord requires me to serve Him.

Service in the kingdom of God is not a spectator sport where thousands of people fill the stands in desperate need of exercise observe one or two paid professionals do all the work. The idea of service is to labor with the Lord, as John the Baptist did who understood that he must decrease and the Lord must increase. Another servant, Joshua, proclaimed to the people:

> Now therefore fear [walk in awe before] the LORD, and serve [labor with] him in sincerity and in truth: and put away the gods which your fathers served on the other side of the flood, and in Egypt; and serve ye the LORD. And if it seem evil unto you to serve the LORD, choose you this day whom ye will serve; whether the gods which your fathers served that were on the other side of the flood, or the gods of the Amorites, in whose land ye dwell: but as for me and my house, we will serve the LORD. And the people answered and said, God forbid that we should forsake the LORD, to serve other gods.
>
> —JOSHUA 24:14

Surely most of us don't have these little stone images in our homes that we burn incense to and seek a smoke signal from. What are these other gods? These other gods are those to whom they offered sacrifices—they offered sacrifices to devils.

> And they shall no more offer their sacrifices unto devils, after whom they have gone a whoring. This shall be a statute for ever unto them throughout their generations.
>
> —LEVITICUS 17:7

To sacrifice to devils is to surrender our birthright and suffer loss for the sake of an eight-second ride.

We will explore service further and identify our other gods later in this book.

5. The Lord requires me to keep His commandments.

Obedience is not for the convenience of God but so that we will be able to thrive and experience all that God has for us now and to position us in eternity as ordained by God. Obedience keeps us from pain and frees us from the experience of causing pain to those loved.

> But this thing commanded I them, saying, Obey my voice, and I will be your God, and ye shall be my people: and walk ye in all the ways that I have commanded you, that it may be well unto you. But they hearkened not, nor inclined their ear, but walked in the counsels and in the imagination of their evil heart, and went backward, and not forward.
>
> —JEREMIAH 7:23–24

Jesus taught that once we understood and were immersed in agape love from our Father, we would need no other law. The purpose of law is to govern behavior and provide equitable punishment. The law could only govern our works of the flesh but could not govern our spirits, and that is why things had to change. Now with the temple of the Holy Spirit within us, not only are the works of the flesh governed but also the thoughts and intents of our hearts. If couples agape one another, if friends agape one another, if business partners agape one another, if family members agape one another, there would be no offense requiring the intervention of the law.

> Master, which is the great commandment in the law? Jesus said unto him, Thou shalt love [agape] the Lord thy God with all thy heart, and with all thy soul, and with all thy mind. This is the first and great commandment. And the second is like unto it, Thou shalt love [agape] thy neighbour as thyself. On these two commandments hang all the law and the prophets.
>
> —MATTHEW 22:36–40

The law still applies, except for what parts were replaced by Jesus amending the covenant regarding how sin was to be dealt with, including dietary, sacrifices, and certain of the feasts. Some requirements were specific only to the nation of Israel to set them apart, but Gentiles are not under such a yoke of bondage.

> Think not that I am come to destroy the law, or the prophets: I am not come to destroy, but to fulfil. For verily I say unto you, Till heaven and earth pass, one jot or one tittle shall in no wise pass from the law, till all be fulfilled.
>
> —MATTHEW 5:17–18

I believe I understand correctly that Paul teaches the portion of the Old Testament that particularly applies to the laws and statutes that govern the inward man or his spirit. By governing one's spirit, one would not sin against oneself, others, or God.

> For I delight in the law of God after the inward man.
>
> —ROMANS 7:22

6. The Lord requires me to endure first then comfort others.

Can you see the impurities in gold before it is put into the fire?

The purest form of humility is exhibited in a saint that remains of a beautiful countenance even when subjected to the difficult and cantankerous conduct of one they serve. The scripture says we are not only to take it with grace but we are called and held accountable for our behavior no matter what we are subjected to. Consider what Christ endured. Believers are called to step in His footprints.

> Servants, be subject to your masters [overseer of household or business] with all fear; not only to the good and gentle, but also to the forward [headstrong, depraved, irritable, self willed]. For this is thankworthy, if a man for conscience toward God endure grief, suffering wrongfully. For what glory is it, if, when ye be buffeted for your faults, ye shall take it patiently? but if, when ye do well, and suffer for it, ye take it patiently, this is acceptable with God. For even hereunto were ye called: because Christ also suffered for us, leaving us an example, that ye should follow his steps: Who did no sin, neither was guile found in his mouth: Who, when he was reviled, reviled not again; when he suffered, he threatened not; but committed himself to him that judgeth righteously: Who his own self bare our sins in his own body on the tree, that we, being dead to sins, should live unto righteousness: by whose stripes ye were healed.
>
> —1 Peter 2:18–23

This seems like an impossible requirement. Yes, it is impossible if our flesh is fighting for justice. A mature Christian cannot be offended because they are dead to self and a dead person cannot be offended or hurt.

Further, to that cantankerous despicable individual you have been assigned to; would you like to see the devil have a fit? Counterattack in your heart by declaring, "I'm dead to your sin!" The devil will flee.

If we suffer for mistreatment in doing what is right, we have opened the door to receive blessings of the Father. He sees, He knows, and He loves (*agapes*) you but He also loves (*agapes*) the person who has mistreated you. God separates them from their sin, just as we want Him to separate us from our sin.

> Finally, be ye all of one mind, having compassion one of another, love as brethren, be pitiful, be courteous: Not rendering evil for evil, or railing for railing: but contrariwise blessing; knowing that ye are thereunto called, that ye should inherit a blessing.
>
> —1 Peter 3:8–9

The scripture says we are to agape our enemies. That doesn't mean necessarily we are to be able to go up and give them a big hug, but agape love allows us to be empowered by the Spirit of God to do what is best for them. Peter says the best thing you can do for one who hurt you is to bless them. If you become their judge, then the hands of the Lord are tied and you are left to the fruit of your own devices.

Joseph attracted the jealousy and fury of his brothers who kidnapped him and sold him to the slave traders. He suffered much even having his reputation ruined by a false sexual assault conviction to which he served a lengthy prison term. Can God use a person whose reputation is so tarnished? Doesn't God do a records check to exclude all that are less than perfect from His kingdom? Joseph was later released and given a face-to-face meeting with his brothers who had "destroyed his life." Or did they? Through his suffering Joseph inherited a blessing, just as God promises. Through the school of refinement by suffering, he was chosen to be vice-pharaoh of Egypt and acted as an ambassador to foreign nations to provide much-needed aid during a worldwide drought.

> God monitors our behavior to see how we weather our storms. God doesn't like it when we are treated badly but He loves how we stand unmovable when we are mistreated.

> And Joseph said unto them, Fear not: for [am] I in the place of God? But as for you, *ye* thought evil against me; but God meant it unto good, ... to save much people alive. Now therefore fear ye not: I will nourish you, and your little ones. And he comforted them, and spake kindly unto them.
> —GENESIS 50:19–21, EMPHASIS ADDED

Joseph was "dead to the sins" of his brothers and therefore thrived and didn't allow the blindness of anger, unforgiveness, and retaliation to steal a blessing. As Joseph, his brothers were also in captivity, they had their mobility, sure, but they were in captivity of guilt, shame, envy, jealousy, fear, worry, and lying. They also grew up, turned their lives around and each brother became a ruler of a nation in their own right.

God monitors our behavior to see how we weather our storms. God doesn't like it when we are treated badly, but He loves how we stand unmovable when we are mistreated.

Until we have walked where others are walking, we are unable to be of much comfort to them. Oft times we judge and shred away hope from them rather than bless and encourage, as did those who tried to counsel Job. Once we are in our healing process, our assignment is to apply what we learned in the difficulty to push other saints up to victory.

> Who comforteth [teaches, encourages] us in all our tribulation [that which pressures or burdens our spirit], that we may be able to comfort them which are in any trouble [desperate straits], by the comfort wherewith we ourselves are comforted of God.
> —2 CORINTHIANS 1:4

Please get a good grip of what the apostle Paul learned through his storms, which further qualified him to be of comfort to us:

> For which cause we faint not; but though our outward man perish, yet the inward man is renewed day by day. For our light affliction, which is but for a moment, worketh for us a far more exceeding and eternal

weight of glory; While we look not at the things which are seen, but at the things which are not seen: for the things which are seen are temporal; but the things which are not seen are eternal.

—2 CORINTHIANS 4:16–18

(Please read Isaiah 54:1–17 to see your heritage.)

In kingdom of God terms we can get all perturbed in trying to get back the silver dollar we lost beachcombing and miss the arrival of our ship.

Confirming the souls of the disciples, and exhorting them to continue in the faith, and that we must through much tribulation enter into the kingdom of God.

—ACTS 14:22

This is all a test; it is only a test. Folks that are dead to self can never be failed by an examiner.

7. The Lord requires me to yield much fruit.

Fruit originates at a distance from where it ripens. The source can be traced back from the type of fruit produced. Consider a DNA test that would identify the sperm donor for a child born to a woman.

Is a woman able to create and produce a child in and of herself? Well, except for the miraculous conception of Jesus Christ, of course not. Likewise, with spiritual fruit, it originates from God who through the Holy Spirit "impregnates" us, and we become the passage through which it is born in due season. Our fruit then bears a strong resemblance to our heavenly Father.

Herein is my Father glorified, that ye bear [conveys from conception to birth] much fruit; so shall ye be my disciples.

—JOHN 15:8

Fruit is produced only by surrender to its source. In order for an abundant harvest of fruit to be produced through us, God first takes us through a purging process to cleanse us of impurities. I called in a plumber to fix the drain system of an apartment block. He hooked up a device to the drain that delivers a burst of clean water into the line to purge it of whatever had accumulated to prevent the flow out of wastewater.

In the Old Testament the priests would go in and physically clean the temple and purge or wash it of all impurities. Now that we are the temple of the Holy Spirit, the cleansing is constantly required by the knowledgeable application of the Word of God.

I am the true vine, and my Father is the husbandman [vine dresser]. Every branch in me that beareth [conveys from conception to birth] not fruit he taketh away [remove by force]: and every branch that beareth fruit, he purgeth [cleanse of filth and impurity] it, that it may bring forth more fruit. Now ye are clean [purified as Levitical priests cleansed the temple] through the word [originated From God] which I have spoken unto you.

> Abide [permanent residence] in me, and I in you. As the branch [tender and flexible sprout] cannot bear fruit of itself, except it abide in the vine; no more can ye, except ye abide in me.
>
> —JOHN 15:1–4

Our permanent home is really a branch abiding on the vine; the vine is Jesus Christ and we are the branches. We've talked about being aliens or foreigners on the earth, and now you know where your place of permanent citizenship is—abiding in the kingdom of God. A branch that is severed from the vine is off life support and dies.

> We yield fruit; we do not produce it.

The term *yielding* fruit better describes the role of the branch as the term *beareth* is less in use now. Yield means to surrender to another who has legal right of passage or control. When Jesus is Lord of our life, we've surrendered or yielded to Him so that He can produce fruit through us. We yield fruit; we do not produce it. We are in error if we insist that a branch produces fruit through evangelism. If evangelism isn't happening, it is because the sheep aren't properly fed. Healthy sheep beget sheep. Many step out to evangelize as a work of the flesh under a guilt trip motivated by anxious shepherds. Jesus taught the shepherd through Peter, if you love me feed my sheep (John 21:17). You'll know if they are properly fed, as they will reproduce on their own without any programming.

> Neither yield [place at another's disposal] ye your members as instruments of unrighteousness unto sin: but yield yourselves unto God, as those that are alive from the dead, and your members as instruments of righteousness unto God.
>
> —ROMANS 6:13

Yield your members is a spiritual term meaning criminal intercourse, where the prostitute is the devil. Once we've opened the door to the devil's brothel, we are forced to surrender right of way to the evil one's desire. He has gained legal control until we appropriate the finished work of Jesus Christ to close up shop on the devil.

> It is amazing how much of the believer's ability to be an overcomer requires him to "die to self."

Wolves are only dangerous when they are able to talk their way into the sheepfold, and there are many wolves that are mistaken as shepherds. We are to be fruit inspectors. We inspect fruit by doing our homework through the Word of God. Often we confuse fruit with gifts. A gift may appear to be in operation without the operator abiding in the vine. Much of the work in the church can be done in the flesh, and we can only discern this as good or evil if we, as sheep, abide in the vine.

> Every tree that bringeth not forth good fruit is hewn down, and cast into
> the fire. Wherefore by their fruits ye shall know them. Not every one that
> saith unto me, Lord, Lord, shall enter into the kingdom of heaven; but he
> that doeth the will of my Father which is in heaven. Many will say to me
> in that day, Lord, Lord, have we not prophesied in thy name? and in thy
> name have cast out devils? and in thy name done many wonderful works?
>
> —MATTHEW 7:19–22

It is amazing how much of the believer's ability to be an overcomer requires
him to "die to self." We've seen where we have to die to self to have faith to
move mountains; we have to die to self so we are not offended by the sin of
others; we have to die to our self so we can be obedient to the will of the
Father; we have to die to self so we can agape love; we have to die to self to
walk in humility; and now we have to die again in order to yield a bountiful
spiritual harvest of fruit.

> Verily, verily, I say unto you, Except a corn of wheat fall into the ground
> and die, it abideth alone: but if it die, it bringeth forth much fruit.
>
> —JOHN 12:24

While man may often measure fruit by the number of seats occupying their
pews, the fruit of the Spirit is measured by what our heart yields through our
faces.

> But the fruit of the Spirit is love [*agape*], joy [delight], peace [absence of
> strife between individuals], longsuffering [patience, slowness in avenging
> wrongs], gentleness [grace that pervades entire nature], goodness [putting
> fruit to action], faith [if God said it, that settles it, I'll wait for it], Meekness
> [strength under godly control], temperance [self-control over appetite for
> desires, passions and sensuality] it: against such there is no law. And they
> that are Christ's have crucified the flesh with the affections and lusts.
>
> —GALATIANS 5:22–24

In case you were wondering, to "crucify the flesh" means to "die to self"! A
dead man can't interfere with the work of God.

8. The Lord requires me to be just, merciful, and humble.

> He hath shewed thee, O man, what is good; and what doth the LORD
> require of thee, but to do justly, and to love mercy, and to walk humbly
> with thy God?
>
> —MICAH 6:8

When the kingdom of God comes upon the natives of this world, we'll see
a system of justice that will seem so foreign to our experience.

> For if ye love them which love you, what thank have ye? for sinners also
> love those that love them. And if ye do good to them which do good to
> you, what thank have ye? for sinners also do even the same. And if ye

lend to them of whom ye hope to receive, what thank have ye? for sinners also lend to sinners, to receive as much again. But love [*agapao*] ye your enemies, and do good [do a favor], and lend, hoping for nothing again [no expectations]; and your reward shall be great, and ye shall be the children of the Highest: for he is kind unto the unthankful [unpleasing] and to the evil.

—LUKE 6:32–35

> The kingdom of God concept here is undeniable and that is if you judge, you judge yourself; if you condemn, you condemn yourself; so if you are forgiving, you are forgiven.

Why does God require us to have such a different system of justice? What was God's response to your nasty deviations from the straight and narrow? It is always the goodness of the Lord that leads to repentance.

Then comes mercy which we extend to others by the way we judge them. The kingdom of God concept here is undeniable and that is if you judge, you judge yourself; if you condemn, you condemn yourself; so if you are forgiving, you are forgiven; if you give to others, you receive a return.

> Be ye therefore merciful, as your Father also is merciful. Judge not, and ye shall not be judged: condemn not, and ye shall not be condemned: forgive, and ye shall be forgiven: Give, and it shall be given unto you; good measure, pressed down, and shaken together, and running over, shall men give into your bosom. For with the same measure that ye mete withal it shall be measured to you again.
>
> —LUKE 6:36–38

How do we judge? One way we judge is by receiving gossip, which is one side of a story, and repeating it as truth. We judge by making a decision about a person based on their tent. We judge others to deflect attention from the same sin in ourselves.

> My pride causes God to actually war against me. Pride is not only a block to prayer and healing, but God actually wars against us pushing us back from the position we had gained.

Therefore thou art inexcusable, O man, whosoever thou art that judgest: for wherein thou judgest another, thou condemnest thyself; for thou that judgest doest the same things. But we are sure that the judgment of God is according to truth against them which commit such things...not knowing that the goodness of God leadeth thee to repentance?

—ROMANS 2:1–4

Have you ever noticed that your judgment of another leads to a lockdown rather than repentance?

But he giveth more grace. Wherefore he saith, God resisteth the proud, but giveth grace unto the humble.

—JAMES 4:6

The word *resisteth* means God actually wars against you. Of all vices I think this one tops the list, as I'm not aware of any other sin other than pride that not only blocks the work of God but that He pushes back against you. That is one battle you'll never win.

Exalting ourselves starts with taking the biggest piece of cake. I thought it would be good parenting to train our children to say, "Me last, me last"; but I think I was the first to admit defeat.

> The rarest of godly attributes is humility. Most of us are too proud to admit we have a pride problem. But I noticed I was never too proud to admit someone else had a pride problem.

For whosoever exalteth himself shall be abased; and he that humbleth himself shall be exalted.

—LUKE 14:11

If you toot your own horn, you have a solo act.

9. The Lord requires me to enlist in His army.

The Lord says if you are going to do a sacrificial act you might consider doing it for someone else. In Isaiah 58 it is interesting that the first four of the eight suggestions for getting involved in the lives of others are all in the realm of spiritual warfare. We are to be our brother's keeper. Notice as you read this passage what the return is on your investment of giving through ministry onto others. We all are given the ministry of reconciliation so these blessings are your inheritance.

> Is it such a fast that I have chosen? a day for a man to afflict his soul? is it to bow down his head as a bulrush, and to spread sackcloth and ashes under him? wilt thou call this a fast, and an acceptable day to the LORD? Is not this the fast that I have chosen? [1] to loose the bands of wickedness, [2] to undo the heavy burdens, [3] and to let the oppressed go free, [4] and that ye break every yoke? [5] Is it not to deal thy bread to the hungry, [6] and that thou bring the poor that are cast out to thy house? [7] when thou seest the naked, that thou cover him; [8] and that thou hide not thyself from thine own flesh? Then shall thy light break forth as the morning, and thine health shall spring forth speedily: and thy righteousness shall go before thee; the glory of the LORD shall be thy reward. Then shalt thou call, and the LORD shall answer; thou shalt cry, and he shall say, Here I am. If thou take away from the midst of thee the yoke, the putting forth of the finger, and speaking vanity; And if thou draw out thy soul to the hungry, and satisfy the afflicted soul; then shall thy light rise in obscurity, and thy darkness be as the noonday: And the LORD shall guide thee continually, and satisfy thy soul in drought, and make

fat thy bones: and thou shalt be like a watered garden, and like a spring of water, whose waters fail not. And they that shall be of thee shall build the old waste places: thou shalt raise up the foundations of many generations; and thou shalt be called, The repairer of the breach, The restorer of paths to dwell in.

—ISAIAH 58:5–12

The repairer of the breach is one who repairs the breach in the agape love stream so that the love of the Father restores all those it is intended to reach.

Pure religion and undefiled before God and the Father is this, To visit the fatherless and widows in their affliction, and to keep himself unspotted from the world.

—JAMES 1:27

> The repairer of the breach is one who repairs the breach in the agape love stream so that the love of the Father restores all those it is intended to reach.

The best way to keep unspotted from the world is to not get close enough to let it stain you.

Jesus asked Peter three times if he loved Him, and with each response Jesus exhorted Peter as a shepherd to feed His sheep. To *feed* means to govern and promote health of the entire body, soul, mind, and spirit. Ezekiel lays out the mandate for those who aspire to minister amongst the flocks.

Son of man, prophesy against the shepherds…should not the shepherds feed the flocks?…The diseased have ye not strengthened, neither have ye healed that which was sick, neither have ye bound up that which was broken, neither have ye brought again that which was driven away, neither have ye sought that which was lost; but with force and with cruelty have ye ruled them. And they were scattered, because there is no shepherd: and they became meat to all the beasts of the field, when they were scattered.

—EZEKIEL 34:2, 4–5

The minister is to strengthen and heal the sick, to heal the broken heart, to restore those that are rejected or in fear, and to leave the ninety-nine and seek for the one that goes astray. However, the prophet noted the pastors were not doing as they were assigned, so the sheep, though still in the pews, were scattered. Since they are not getting the help and love they need in the church, they go everywhere else in all the wrong places seeking love and healing.

> A messenger must treat the Word of God the same way God treats His own Word. Never mess with it, never alter it, never soften it and never beat others with it.

10. The Lord requires me to keep my word.

As you approach each new day, ask the Lord, who is counting on you, to keep your word that day. Λ promise is a vow. It is not a sin to refuse to make a promise or a vow, as that is much better than making a vow then having to break it.

> When thou shalt vow a vow unto the LORD thy God, thou shalt not slack to pay it: for the LORD thy God will surely require it of thee; and it would be sin in thee. But if thou shalt forbear [cease or refuse] to vow, it shall be no sin in thee.
>
> —DEUTERONOMY 23:21–22

Every word that proceeds out of the mouth of God is a vow. Because His words are so well chosen and meaningful, He just speaks and nature leaps into existence.

If your words were to be your name, what would your name be?

> I will worship toward thy holy temple, and praise thy name for thy lovingkindness and for thy truth: for thou hast magnified thy word above all thy name.
>
> —PSALM 138:2

Jesus is constantly referred throughout the Bible as the Word.

> And he was clothed with a vesture dipped in blood: and his name is called The Word of God.
>
> —REVELATION 19:13

A messenger must treat the Word of God the same way God treats His own word. Never mess with it, never alter it, never soften it and never beat others with it.

> If there be a messenger [representative of God] with him, an interpreter [ambassador for a king], one among a thousand, to shew unto man his uprightness [what is right].
>
> —JOB 33:23

11. The Lord requires me to know how to wash up.

As our vessel contains the temple of the Holy Ghost, we have to know how to cleanse, to sanctify the entire vessel so it is fit for our King. So do you know how to cleanse your spirit? How about your soul? Your body?

> For this is the will of God, even your sanctification, that ye should abstain from fornication: That every one of you should know how to possess his vessel in sanctification and honour; And the very God of peace sanctify you wholly; and I pray God your whole spirit and soul and body be preserved blameless unto the coming of our Lord Jesus Christ.
>
> —1 THESSALONIANS 4:3–5

In a later chapter we will look at the Word for instruction on this requirement to be sanctified in our entire being: spirit, soul, and body.

12. The Lord requires me to be thankful.

> In every thing give thanks: for this is the will of God in Christ Jesus concerning you.
> —1 Thessalonians 5:18

Redirect all the thanks you receive to the Father. We are required to give thanks to God for the works of service we get to do for Him.

> And whatsoever ye do in word or deed, do all in the name of the Lord Jesus, giving thanks to God and the Father by him.
> —Colossians 3:17

13. The Lord requires me to know how to discern truth.

A person who wants to do the will of God must know doctrine very well. Doctrine is something that has to be searched for, as the beauty of the Word is not skin deep.

> Jesus answered them, and said, My doctrine is not mine, but his that sent me. If any man will do his will, he shall know of the doctrine, whether it be of God, or whether I speak of myself. He that speaketh of himself seeketh his own glory: but he that seeketh his glory that sent him, the same is true, and no unrighteousness is in him.
> —John 7:16–18

14. The Lord requires me to be spiritually ready to move—now.

I haven't counted them myself, but some say there are more than 1,800 prophecies in the Bible accounting for about 8,350 verses or approximately 27 percent of the Bible. What is your attitude toward prophecy? Many church leaders and authors don't seem to think understanding prophecy is a worthwhile endeavor. Which kingdom would profit the most if we were not waiting expectantly for the Lord to return? I think we should ask the Lord what He thinks considering the large portion of the Word that was prophecy at the time it was written.

> But the day [the last day of this present age] of the Lord will come as a thief in the night; in the which the heavens shall pass away with a great noise, and the elements shall melt with fervent heat, the earth also and the works [projects or enterprise] that are therein shall be burned up. Seeing then that all these things shall be dissolved, what manner what sort of persons ought ye to be in all holy conversation [conduct] and godliness [reverence and respect], Looking for and hasting unto the coming of the day of God, wherein the heavens being on fire shall be dissolved, and the elements shall melt with fervent heat?
> —2 Peter 3:10–12

The only book of the Bible that has a blessing attached for the reader who understands is Revelation, which is devoted entirely to prophecy.

> Blessed is he that readeth [to recognize and to know accurately], and they
> that hear the words of this prophesy, and keep those things which are
> written therein: for the time is at hand.
>
> —REVELATION 1:3

I enjoy prophecy and especially those prophecies that have been fulfilled in
the last century or so, as they are strong reminders of who is really in control.
We consider many of these in our work of *Truth or Coincidence*.

The Lord promises that He will open doors which no man will be able to
slam shut for those that are diligent to do what He requires. Furthermore, if
you are up on your prophecy, you'll know that the Lord will remove you from
the time of the Great Tribulation that is coming to try those that have made
the earth their home.

> I know thy works: behold, I have set before thee an open door, and no
> man can shut it: for thou hast a little strength, and hast kept my word,
> and hast not denied my name...Because thou hast kept the word of my
> patience, I also will keep thee from the hour of temptation, which shall
> come upon all the world, to try them that dwell upon the earth.
>
> —REVELATION 3:8, 10

God's Words are His vow.

GIVE US THIS DAY OUR DAILY BREAD

J ESUS' SERMON ON the Mount is transcribed for us in Matthew chapters 5, 6, and 7; and close to the middle of the sermon is the Lord's Prayer. The Lord's Prayer is only six short verses in length, but it perfectly summarizes the entire teaching of the Sermon on the Mount that stretches to 106 verses. This book is written following the context of the sermon in which the prayer is found and accordingly this particular chapter may take on a slightly different flavor than one may taste if the prayer is taught in isolation.

> After this manner therefore pray ye: Our Father which art in heaven, Hallowed be thy name. Thy kingdom come. Thy will be done in earth, as it is in heaven. Give us this day our daily bread. And forgive us our debts, as we forgive our debtors. And lead us not into temptation, but deliver us from evil: For thine is the kingdom, and the power, and the glory, forever. Amen.
>
> —MATTHEW 6:9–13

If the sentence, "Give us this day our daily bread" refers only to praying for food daily, then what Jesus says a few moments later would appear to contradict. I'm not suggesting we are not to pray for our daily needs, and perhaps this passage is like much of the Bible and has a near and far interpretation. What appears on the surface applies to the immediate situation, and what may be somewhat hidden speaks not only of today but also of tomorrow.

I'll spare you the details, but theologians note that the Greek word for *daily* as used in the prayer is not used anywhere else in the Scripture and therefore it is difficult to determine exactly what is meant. The original language suggests we are praying for bread for the day approaching and for the remainder of our lives. Follow this thought as you read what Jesus said shortly after reciting the Lord's Prayer. We are to take no thought for tomorrow nor are we to worry about food or clothing, as our Father knows we have need of before we even pray. The condition of this total freedom about tomorrow's provisions is to seek first the kingdom of God and to seek His righteousness and all our needs will be met.

> Take no thought, saying, What shall we eat? or, What shall we drink? or, Wherewithal shall we be clothed?...For your heavenly Father knoweth that ye have need of all these things. But seek ye first the kingdom of

God, and his righteousness; and all these things shall be added unto you. Take therefore no thought for the morrow: for the morrow shall take thought for the things of itself.

—MATTHEW 6:31–34

There is bread that is required for our flesh or our bodies to live; likewise, there is bread that is required for our spirits to live. Jesus says He is that bread that provides the vitality for our spirit to be redirected from certain death. In our life on earth, traditionally the husband of the home is the sole breadwinner who works to provide natural sustenance for the physical wellbeing of those within his household. But Jesus Christ is the sole breadwinner and intercessor that paid the price of the ransom in full to liberate us from our captivity of doom to abundant eternal life.

> The "Broadway" means you get all the rewards and fame you are entitled to now for immediate but short-enjoyed gratification, and those taking "the road less traveled" means you are entitled to a genuine and vigorous life now and in addition you are sending all your treasure to your Overseer's account as an eternal investment with Jesus Christ as your broker.

Verily, verily, I say unto you, He that believeth on me hath everlasting life. I am that bread of life…This is the bread which cometh down from heaven, that a man may eat thereof, and not die. The Jews therefore strove among themselves, saying, How can this man give us his flesh to eat? Then Jesus said unto them, Verily, verily, I say unto you, Except ye eat the flesh of the Son of man, and drink his blood, ye have no life in you. Whoso eateth my flesh, and drinketh my blood, hath eternal life; and I will raise him up at the last day.

—JOHN 6:47–48

Eternal life is not something that starts when we die. Everyone on earth has eternal life; it is just that most are traveling along Broadway and relatively few have chosen the road less traveled. The "Broadway" means you get all the rewards and fame you are entitled to now for immediate but short-enjoyed gratification, and those taking "the road less traveled" means you are entitled to a genuine and vigorous life now and in addition you are sending all your treasure to your Overseer's account as an eternal investment with Jesus Christ as your broker. The popular saying goes "you can't take it with you when you die" is true for those on the Broadway, whereas those on the road less traveled can send it all on ahead. Is there really a choice?

We are familiar with this next passage being taught when we are about to take communion at church. You may participate with communion once a week, once a month, or once a year, depending on the practice of your local fellowship.

When we eat or appropriate the finished work—the bread—of Jesus Christ on the cross for the remission of our sin, for healing, for sustenance, for mercy, for deliverance, or direction, we are in communion.

> And when he had given thanks, he brake it, and said, Take, eat: this is my body, which is broken for you: this do in remembrance of me. After the same manner also he took the cup, when he had supped, saying, This cup is the new testament in my blood: this do ye, as oft as ye drink it, in remembrance of me. For as often as ye eat this bread, and drink this cup, ye do shew the Lord's death till he come. Wherefore whosoever shall eat this bread, and drink this cup [divine experience] of the Lord, unworthily, shall be guilty [of a crime against] the body and blood of the Lord. But let a man examine [deem worthy] himself, and so let him eat of that bread, and drink [to receive what strengthens onto life eternal] of that cup. For he that eateth and drinketh unworthily, eateth and drinketh damnation [to yield to a hostile spirit] to himself, not discerning the Lord's body.
>
> —1 CORINTHIANS 11:24–29

The warning here is very deliberate and forthright. Yes, Jesus made the most difficult of sacrifices Himself, but He did it in perfect holiness. Therefore, as Christians if we think we can approach the Lord's throne to lobby Him for some change while we are deliberately denying our desperate uncleanness, we bring swift damnation upon ourselves.

Jesus used the same word, *cup*, in the Garden of Gethsemane as He was asking if His Father had another way to save mankind other than going the route of crucifixion. "O my Father, if it be possible, let this cup pass from me: nevertheless not as I will, but as thou wilt" (Matt. 26:39). The word *cup* means more than just a drinking vessel. In the sporting world we have a World Cup or a Stanley Cup to signify the highest of achievements in a particular field of endeavor. The "cup" or, if you will, the "Blood Cup" that Jesus is referring to is the achievement of a lifetime for Christ with all of us being joint heirs of the victory.

The writer of 1 Corinthians, the apostle Paul, advises us that the meat or bread and the drink are indeed spiritual as we partake of the Rock of Jesus Christ. What's really interesting is that the nation of Israel was led by the same Rock throughout the wilderness journey, as recorded in the Book of Exodus. The water and the manna bread provided in the wilderness were both physical and spiritual. It was Jesus Christ that led them in the wilderness, and the Israelites were not even aware of who He was. The Messiah they rejected in the flesh had actually been communing with them for many generations and then knew it not.

> Moreover, brethren, I would not that ye should be ignorant, how that all our fathers were under the cloud, and all passed through the sea; And were all baptized unto Moses in the cloud and in the sea; And did all eat the same spiritual meat; And did all drink the same spiritual drink: for

they drank of that spiritual Rock that followed them: and that Rock was Christ. But with many of them God was not well pleased: for they were overthrown in the wilderness. Now these things were our examples, to the intent we should not lust after evil things, as they also lusted. Neither be ye idolaters, as were some of them; as it is written, The people sat down to eat and drink, and rose up to play. Neither let us commit fornication, as some of them committed, and fell in one day three and twenty thousand. Neither let us tempt Christ, as some of them also tempted, and were destroyed of serpents. Neither murmur ye, as some of them also murmured, and were destroyed of the destroyer. Now all these things happened unto them for exsamples: and they are written for our admonition, upon whom the ends of the world are come. Wherefore let him that thinketh he standeth take heed lest he fall.

—1 Corinthians 10:1–12

Paul said what happened in the wilderness with Israel offers examples to those who will be around for the "End of the World." Brothers and sisters, he is talking to us. They were lusting after evil, in idolatry, committing fornication (sexual sin), partying, murmuring (silent complaining), and tempting Christ (presuming upon His grace). The result of this sin was death for many.

In a second look at the communion passage, we have believers approaching Jesus presumptuously and accordingly many were struck with sickness and many died. God changes not, He judged sin in the Old Testament and He is doing it in the age of the church. The priests of the Old Testament would have to be sanctified or internally cleansed before they could enter the holy of holies to serve God in the temple. If they attended before God unclean, they would be dried up. Now the temple of God has moved, now residing within the believer, but we still have to take the same care as the priests did in approaching the holiest place of their temple. Consider yourself to be in the role of a high priest as seen in the Old Testament who would never allow himself to approach the throne of God without doing his first works of cleansing first.

Wherefore whosoever shall eat this bread, and drink this cup [divine experience] of the Lord, unworthily, shall be guilty [of a crime against] the body and blood of the Lord. But let a man examine himself, and so let him eat of that bread, and drink of that cup. For he that eateth and drinketh unworthily, eateth and drinketh damnation [to yield to a hostile spirit] to himself, not discerning the Lord's body. For this cause many are weak and sickly among you, and many sleep. For if we would judge ourselves [discern good and evil], we should not be judged.

—1 Corinthians 11:27–31

We are to examine and judge our spirit selves in preparation to approaching the Lord of the temple within. Directed at the Christian, the words are strong, actually damning the careless and presumptuous individual who partakes of the ministry, bread and the cup, of the Lord in an unworthy manner without practicing discernment.

We put Christ to open shame when we approach Him deep in unrepentant sin and yet expect a holy God to respond when we snap.

> We put Christ to open shame when we approach Him deep in unrepentant sin and yet expect a holy God to respond when we snap.

The writer of Hebrews indicates that if a person is converted and then falls back to their old ways they crucify the Lord all over again and that it is near impossible for them to be renewed to repentance. I know there is stuff that circulates and re-circulates in theological circles that says "once saved always saved"; I guess I would sooner choose to error on the side of caution with scripture that says a believer that returned to the "Broadway" may be damned. Study for yourself to see if what I'm saying is true. Does it sound like the folks addressed below were once spirit-filled Christians?

> For it is impossible for those who were once enlightened, and have tasted of the heavenly gift, and were made partakers of the Holy Ghost, And have tasted the good word of God, and the powers of the world to come, If they shall fall away, to renew them again unto repentance; seeing they crucify to themselves the Son of God afresh, and put him to an open shame.
> —HEBREWS 6:4–6

A Gentile woman approached Jesus to heal her daughter by casting out an unclean spirit. Jesus calls the ministry of setting a captive free from a devil as children's bread. Jesus, the "Bread of Life," came to destroy the works of the devil.

> For a certain woman, whose young daughter had an unclean spirit, heard of him, and came and fell at his feet: The woman was a Greek, a Syrophenician by nation; and she besought him that he would cast forth the devil out of her daughter. But Jesus said unto her, Let the children first be filled: for it is not meet to take the children's bread, and to cast it unto the dogs. And she answered and said unto him, Yes, Lord: yet the dogs under the table eat of the children's crumbs. And he said unto her, For this saying go thy way; the devil is gone out of thy daughter. And when she was come to her house, she found the devil gone out, and her daughter laid upon the bed.
> —MARK 7:25–30

The woman stood in the gap for the healing of her daughter. The daughter was sanctified by the believing parent. (See 1 Corinthians 7:14.) She knew in order for her daughter to be healed, Jesus would have to command the unclean spirit to depart. In this case Jesus ministered to this little girl at a distance and she was set free.

The calling of a Christian is to replace Satan's "kingdom of this world" with the kingdom of God by learning to fight with the mighty weapons we have.

You may not even know what the enemy in camouflage looks likes. Satan doesn't want you to recognize any of his evil fruit as coming from him. Satan will do whatever is necessary to keep the door open for him to remain active in our lives and to inflict us, and then he tempts us to blame God for what he has done and in so doing remains safe.

SALVATION—DO WE KNOW WHAT IT MEANS?

Salvation is generally assumed to be synonymous with "being saved." It's time to do our homework. In the original languages of the Bible there are at least seven different words that are translated into the single English word *salvation*. In six out of the seven definitions, we find deliverance from evil, saved from moral troubles, and deliverance from the molestation of enemies. The fruit of salvation as seen in these seven words is welfare, prosperity, safety, victory, and being saved.

The best commentary on the Bible is the Bible itself. A Bible study guideline called the "principle of first mention" teaches the student to find the first one or two occurrences of the term in the Bible and study it there in context. A second study guideline is the "principle of biblical constancy" that suggests once a word or phrase is introduced in the Bible its meaning remains constant throughout.

The second occurrence of the word *salvation* in the Bible provides an in-depth look at what it means.

> And Moses said unto the people, Fear ye not, stand still [take your stand], and see the salvation [deliverance, victory over evil] of the LORD, which he will shew to you today: for the Egyptians whom ye have seen today, ye shall see them again no more forever. The LORD shall fight for you, and ye shall hold your peace.
> —EXODUS 14:13–14

Moses was leading the exodus of the nation Israel out of Egypt where they were forced to serve in slavery to the Egyptians for four centuries. Moses had led the people out of Egypt through a mountain pass to the shores of the Red Sea. Now to their horror the Egyptian army had a change of heart and decided to pursue the Israelites. The pursuing army blocked off their only way of escape by land, and the Red Sea, which lay before them, was deep and wide and the Israelites had no boats. The people were exceedingly upset and blamed Moses for their predicament. Then Moses remembered God's Word that He would deliver the nation Israel out of Egypt and take them to a land flowing with milk and honey. God asked Moses, "Why are you crying? I've already given you My word, and that should be enough. Now stretch forth your rod over the sea and stand back and watch it divide." (See Exodus 14:15–16.) Moses then commanded the people to take their stand, to fear not, and see the salvation of the Lord.

Fear is Satan's idea of "faith" that projects doom and despair into the future, whereas faith in God projects hope into the future by reminding us of His spoken promises.

"Fear not" is the most repeated command in the Bible, over sixty-two times, because fear is the opposite of faith.[1]

Then they saw the salvation of the Lord, a way of escape from the enemy was established miraculously by the creating of a dry highway through the Red Sea. As soon as the entire nation of Israel was safe on the other side, the waters returned and destroyed the entire Egyptian army. Salvation as seen here is a miraculous way of escape from the old way of life, "Egypt," and deliverance or victory over the enemy that seeks to destroy us. This deliverance is a work of God that usually includes the human agency, as God in this case used Moses.

Now following this salvation experience, the Israelites expected everything to be different, but they still had to go through a lengthy wilderness experience before they were ready, their faith matured, for the Promised Land, which existed on earth for them. They had to learn not to murmur and complain, to flee from idolatry and fornication, to learn victory over fear and unbelief, and to trust even when they could not see. You see, the work of salvation is not a one-time event; it is a process that often uses the wilderness or valleys of our lives to fully expose the darkness within and to destroy those works. They are exposed so that we are made fit for our Master's use and prepared to enter into the promised land that God has waiting for us while on this earth.

Salvation and the word *saved* both appear in the same verse of Acts 4:12, and they have different meanings.

> Neither is there *salvation* [deliverance from the molestation of enemies] in any other: for there is none other name under heaven given among men, whereby we must be *saved* [delivered from penalty of Messianic judgment and rescued from the fires of hell].
> —ACTS 4:12, EMPHASIS ADDED

The most important healing that any of us can ever experience is to be saved and receive Jesus into our lives as Savior and Lord. I have a definition for *saved* and *salvation* which, I pray, will clarify:

1. *Salvation* refers mainly to our quality of life, present and future. It is deliverance from everything that is evil to reconcile us to the person we were meant to be from the foundation of the world. Salvation includes being saved. We have a fourfold salvation: we are victorious over the penalty, power, presence, and most importantly, the pleasure of sin.

2. *Saved* refers to our destiny, which is eternity with the Lord, as opposed to separation in hell. It is a gift through the grace of God as we appropriate what only Jesus Christ could do in His agape gift of paying the price of sin through the shedding of innocent blood.

> For by grace are ye saved through faith; and that not of yourselves: it is the gift of God: Not of works, lest any man should boast.
> —EPHESIANS 2:8–9

3. *Grace* is a covering while we are growing up. Grace is giving us time to repent and turn away from the kingdom of this world. Grace is not overlooking sin, as that would be against the nature and holiness of God.

We've seen that "being saved" is a gift of God and it is "not of works" and that truth is widely accepted within all of Christianity. But look at the next verse regarding the salvation experience; we have to "work it out" with the fear of God and trembling. If you assume the words *being saved* and *salvation* mean the same, you have a big problem here.

> Wherefore, my beloved [fellow believers], as ye have always obeyed, not as in my presence only, but now much more in my absence, *workout* [to accomplish or achieve] *your own salvation* [deliverance from the molestation of enemies] with fear [reverential fear of God] and trembling [zealous to fulfill this duty].
> —PHILIPPIANS 2:12, EMPHASIS ADDED

Be careful to understand that this passage is addressed to believers, admonishing us that our salvation, our quality of life, our freedom from vexation of evil, requires our active participation to work it out by utilizing the power Jesus Christ has given us to overcome evil and its fruit in our earthly lives.

The professor of the early church in Acts teaches the Christian worker who leads another to Christ has the responsibility to lead them into a process of works befitting repentance.

> To the Gentiles, that they should repent and turn to God, and do works meet [befitting conduct through faith] for repentance [deep sorrow for sin resulting in change of direction].
> —ACTS 26:20

We will teach in a later chapter these "works meet for repentance" or "working out your salvation" in what we call the Steps to Sanctification.

> Nevertheless I have somewhat against thee, because thou hast left thy first love. Remember therefore from whence thou art fallen, and repent, and do the first works; or else I will come unto thee quickly, and will remove thy candlestick out of his place, except thou repent.
> —REVELATION 2:4–5

"First works" are necessary upon our believing in Jesus Christ and again if we participate in sin as the Ephesian Christians did in Revelation 2:4. Sadly, most of us never did this when we were saved, resulting in weakness, illness, powerlessness, and the inability to overcome sin.

From where have we fallen from that we are to bring into remembrance?

> According as he hath chosen us in him before the foundation of the world, that we should be holy [pure in preparation for God] and without blame [without blemish, faultless] before him in love [*agape*].
>
> —EPHESIANS 1:4

We were created in the image of God as Holy, without blame in agape love; and that is where we have fallen from and to which we are commanded to return. Anything that doesn't line up with this description is not who we were created to be, it is not us and we are required to be reconciled to such a person in Christ.

Salvation through sanctification

Our salvation is worked out through a process of sanctification. Sanctification is a spiritual cleansing through the conviction of the Holy Spirit and the understanding of truth through the Word of Truth, which is Jesus Christ.

> But we are bound to give thanks always to God for you, brethren beloved of the Lord, because God hath from the beginning chosen you to salvation [deliverance from molestation of the enemy] through sanctification [purification] of the Spirit and belief of the truth.
>
> —2 THESSALONIANS 2:13

If we were to title the portion of Scripture from Romans to Jude, it would be the "Believer's Sanctification." It is a continual process of shedding the soap scum sticking around from the old man, the world, and from Egypt. It is the lack of sanctification (sin and spiritual problems) that allows the "pains of Egypt" to manifest (show symptoms of a root problem).

> This is God's requirement that we must know how to purify our bodies, minds, and spirits. This is a normal part of daily human living.

This is God's requirement that we must know how to purify our bodies, minds, and spirits. This is a normal part of daily human living.

> For this is the will of God, even your sanctification [purification], that ye should abstain from fornication [illicit sex or idolatry]: That every one of you should know how to possess his vessel [chosen instrument] in sanctification and honour [appreciating the price paid by Christ].
>
> —1 THESSALONIANS 4:3–5

We have a choice to make: either we keep our vessel purified and honorable, or we don't! Of the requirements to sanctify our spirit, soul (mind), and body (flesh), we know the least about the sanctification of our spirit. We may just assume that was all looked after when we first believed. We may spend our entire Christian life trying to sanctify our mind and body and get nowhere through psychology, alternative practices, or self-help programs. Some even give up. For this reason few believers will admit to their pastor or come forward for prayer at church for a problem or difficulty in overcoming sin. All these issues were supposed to have been looked after on the cross. They feel they are alone in

> There are sins we take pleasure in doing and they are difficult to overcome or to even want to overcome.

their inability to overcome. We are frustrated, but we must learn how to sanctify our spirit before we will see any fruit in the mind and body. God said, "My people are destroyed for lack of knowledge" (Hosea 4:6).

If we name the name of Jesus or call ourselves Christians, we must either change our name or develop a perfect hatred of sin in our lives. There are sins we take pleasure in doing, and they are difficult to overcome or to even want to overcome. The bread of Christ is to deliver you from the penalty, presence, power, and pleasure of sin.

> Nevertheless the foundation of God standeth sure, having this seal, The Lord knoweth them that are his. And, Let every one that nameth the name of Christ depart [be revolted and flee from] from iniquity [unrighteousness inside and outside].
> —2 TIMOTHY 2:19

To depart from this iniquity requires a purging of our spirits so we are suitable for our Master's use. If you have wanted desperately to be used by God and the doors haven't opened, the Lord is waiting for you to purge your temple.

> But in a great house [human being] there are not only vessels of gold and of silver, but also of wood and of earth; and some to honour [reverence, or highly valued], and some to dishonor [disgrace or offensive]. If a man therefore purge [cleanse by removal] himself from these, he shall be a vessel unto honour sanctified [separated the profane], and meet [easy to make use of] for the master's use, and prepared [on standby and ready] unto every good work. Flee also youthful lusts: but follow righteousness, faith, charity, peace, with them that call on the Lord out of a pure heart.
> —2 TIMOTHY 2:20–23

If a man purges himself from "these" what?—vessels of dishonor, which are unclean things in our spirit. The "great house" is a believer in Christ that contains or embodies these vessels: of honor (which are good), but also vessels of dishonor (which are disgraceful). Good and evil may co-exist (doesn't mean they are in agreement) together; however, to be useful to our master, the vessels of dishonor have to be purged or cleansed out. This process of purging is called sanctification. We know from Scripture that God will use us in our imperfect state; He just wants us to be in a continual state of "being" sanctified.

THE BLESSINGS OF THE PROMISED LAND

These are exclusive privileges of one who knows what the Lord requires of him or her—and *does* it! God will keep His part of the covenant only with the faithful who love Him and show that love by keeping His commandments.

> The work of agape love through us is conditional on our obedience to God's commands, and at the same time so are blessings conditional on obedience to the commands of God.

> Know therefore that the LORD thy God, he is God, the faithful God, which keepeth covenant and mercy with them that love him and keep his [two] commandments to a thousand generations; [that includes us].
> —DEUTERONOMY 7:9

This verse extends to one thousand generations—there has been less than 150 generations (forty years each) since Adam—so do those that love Him still qualify to receive of God's faithfulness, covenant, and mercy? In the event you are still worried that this writing of the Old Testament still applies consider this:

> And the scripture, foreseeing that God would justify the heathen through faith, preached before the gospel unto Abraham, saying, In thee shall all nations be blessed.
> —GALATIANS 3:8

What was a blessing in the old covenant is still a blessing today in the new covenant!

> And it shall come to pass, if thou shalt hearken diligently unto the voice of the LORD thy God, to observe and to do all his commandments which I command thee this day, that the LORD thy God will set thee on high above all nations of the earth: And all these blessings shall come on thee, and overtake thee, if thou shalt hearken unto the voice of the LORD thy God.
> —DEUTERONOMY 28:1–2

The work of agape love through us is conditional through our obedience to God's commands, and at the same time so are blessings conditional on obedience to the commands of God. So obedience pays off with not only agape but also with blessings beyond what we may think or imagine.

Let's look in Deuteronomy and some other select scriptures to discover what blessings might overtake us:

(Note: as you go through this list, mark the blessings that you are currently receiving.)

1. A full covenant relationship with God
- [ ] **God's mercy, love, and blessing will keep and sustain you (Deut. 7:9–13)**
- [ ] **You'll be established as a holy people onto God (Deut. 28:9)**
- [ ] **Goodness of God will be manifested to you (Deut. 32:9)**

❑ You will have full fellowship with God (Deut. 30:20)
❑ God will hear from heaven and forgive all confessed sin (1 Kings 8:34, 36, 38)
❑ You'll be taught the way you are to walk (1 Kings 8:36)
❑ Your prayers will be answered (1 Kings 8:38, 52)
❑ God will enlighten you (Ps. 34:5)
❑ You'll receive salvation (Ps. 18:35)
❑ You'll live in peace (Ps. 37:37)
❑ You'll experience deliverance (Prov. 11:6)
❑ You'll be God's delight (Prov. 11:20)

2. Favor and prosperity
❑ Multiply the fruit of the womb (Deut. 7:13; 28:4)
❑ You'll harvest of corn, wine, oil, flocks of sheep, and herds of cattle, etc. (Deut. 7:13; 8:4)
❑ The rains will come as required (Deut. 28:12)
❑ You'll possess your promised land (Deut. 8:1; 11:31; 15:4)
❑ You'll lend and not borrow (Deut. 15:6, 28:12)
❑ You'll be given favor before men (Deut. 28:3, 6)
❑ Your baskets and storehouse will have plenty of good things (Deut. 28:5–8)
❑ All the activity of your hands will prosper (Deut. 28:8)
❑ The Lord will open to you all His good treasure (Deut. 28:12)
❑ You'll forget your misery (Job 11:16)
❑ You'll be rewarded according to works (1 Kings 8:39)
❑ God will maintain your cause (1 Kings 8:45, 49)
❑ You'll receive mercy by men (1 Kings 8:50)
❑ You will be satisfied (Ps. 22:26)
❑ Inherit the earth (Ps. 37:11, Matt. 5:5)
❑ Contentment (Prov. 28:6)

3. Health
❑ All the familiar evil diseases of Egypt (see below) will be taken away (Deut. 7:15)
❑ No barrenness (Deut. 7:14)
❑ Extended life for you and your children (Deut. 11:21)
❑ Increased joy (Isa. 29:19)

4. Protection
❑ God will judge those that hate or despise you (Deut. 7:15–18)
❑ You'll be delivered from all your enemies and no man shall be able to stand up against you (Deut. 7:22–29; 11:25; 28:7)
❑ Freedom from former curses (Deut. 30:7, 19)

All blessings without exception are based on obedience. (See Exodus 15:26; 19:5; 20:6; 23:22; Leviticus 26; Deuteronomy 28; 1 Kings 2:3–4; Matthew 10:22; Colossians 1:23; Hebrews 3:6, 14; 6:11.)

That is "abundant life," my friends. We will be partakers of these blessings by choosing a right relationship with our God; or contrariwise, failing to make that choice we by default will anticipate the pain or curses of Egypt. Blessings would be meaningless unless there was an equal and opposite consequence for rebellion against the commandments for which we are blessed.

> Blessings would be meaningless unless there was an equal and opposite consequence for rebellion against the commandments for which we are blessed.

The Pain of Egypt

So if my ancestors or I participate in rebellion against God, what happens? Deuteronomy 28 goes on from the obedience leading to blessings and concludes with the fruits of rebellion that lead to the undoing of our blessings. Rebellion is simply not listening to God's voice and not doing what He says.

> But it shall come to pass, if thou wilt not hearken unto the voice of the Lord thy God, to observe to do all his commandments and his statutes which I command thee this day; that all these curses shall come upon thee, and overtake thee.
> —Deuteronomy 28:15

(Note: as you go through the list, mark the conditions that are currently active in your household.)

1. Mental and emotional
- ❑ **Confusion or bewilderment (Deut. 28:20, 28)**
- ❑ **A despairing, languishing heart or an anxious mind (Deut. 28:65)**
- ❑ **Unable to find rest or sleep (Deut. 28:65)**
- ❑ **Vexation—to be worn down or weakened until you give in and fall (Deut. 28:20)**
- ❑ **Madness—folly from intense anger, insanity, mental illness (Deut. 28:28)**
- ❑ **Oppression—violated or exploited and no man shall save thee (Deut. 28:29)**
- ❑ **Grievous overwhelming distress and inescapable pain (Deut. 28:59)**
- ❑ **Terror and fear (Lev. 26:16)**
- ❑ **Faint of heart (Lev. 26:36)**

2. Repeated or chronic sicknesses (especially if hereditary)
- ❑ **Plagued with diseases causing one to pine or be consumed away (Deut. 28:21)**
- ❑ **Consumption (lung disease) or wasting disease (Deut. 28:22)**
- ❑ **Burning inflammation (Deut. 28:22)**
- ❑ **Incurable boils or inflammations of knees, legs, or feet (Deut. 28:27)**
- ❑ **Severe burning fever (Deut. 28:22)**
- ❑ **Tumors, piles, or hemorrhoids (Deut. 28:27)**
- ❑ **Ulcers (Deut. 28:27)**
- ❑ **Incurable itch (Deut. 28:27)**
- ❑ **Scurvy (Deut. 28:27)**

- ❏ Blindness (Deut. 28:28)
- ❏ Prolonged plagues (Deut. 28:59)
- ❏ Severe and lingering diseases (Deut. 28:59)
- ❏ Every other kind of sickness and plague not described above (Deut. 28:61)
- ❏ Failing eyes (Deut. 28:65)
- ❏ Heart troubles (Deut. 28:65)

3. Child bearing
- ❏ Cursed shall be the fruit of your body or your womb (Deut. 28:18)
- ❏ Infertility (Deut. 28:18)

4. Breakdown of marriage and family alienation
- ❏ Your sons and daughters shall be given unto another people and your eyes shall fail with longing for them and they shall go into captivity—i.e., drugs, sex, satanic music, and the occult (Deut. 28:32, 41)
- ❏ Divorce and adultery (Deut. 28:30)
- ❏ These curses shall be upon thy seed or passed from generation to generation through our genetics (Deut. 28:46)

5. Continuing financial insufficiency
- ❏ Business failures (Deut. 28:17)
- ❏ You will be unsuccessful in everything you do (Deut. 28:29)
- ❏ You shall serve your enemies, whom the Lord will send against you, in hunger, in thirst, in nakedness, and in need of all things, or poverty (Deut. 28:47, 48)
- ❏ Cursed shall be the fruit of thy land and the flocks of sheep (Deut. 28:18)
- ❏ Pestilence or plague destroys livestock (Deut. 28:21)
- ❏ Consumed by the sword, blasting (high winds), and mildew (Deut. 28:22)
- ❏ Drought (Deut. 28:24)
- ❏ Bankruptcy, foreclosure, or lawsuits (Deut. 28:29, 30)
- ❏ Locusts will consume crops (Deut. 28:38)
- ❏ A stranger shall be promoted in your place (Deut. 28:43)
- ❏ A stranger shall lend to you and you not lend to him (Deut. 28:44)
- ❏ Your strength shall be spent in vain (Deut. 28:39; Lev. 26:20)
- ❏ Destruction through natural disasters or wild animals (Lev. 26:22)
- ❏ You shall eat and not be satisfied (Lev. 26:26)
- ❏ Your cities and your sanctuaries will be made waste (Lev. 26:31)

6. Accident prone
- ❏ You shall grope as a blind man gropes in darkness—stumbling (Deut. 28:29)

7. Untimely deaths
- ❏ History of suicides, untimely deaths, or fear of death (Deut. 28:66)

8. Spiritual
- ❏ You will serve other gods (Deut. 28:36)
- ❏ Heaven shall be as brass (thought to be unanswered prayer) (Deut. 28:23)
- ❏ Punished seven times more for sins (Lev. 26:18, 21)

❑ **God will break the pride of your power (Lev. 26:19)**
❑ **God will walk contrary or oppose everything you do with anger (Lev. 26:28)**

What a contrast between the fruits of "agape" and the fruits of "rebellion"!

What are diseases, psychological concerns, business failures, and family break-ups? They are curses! Curses are opposite of blessings.

> But it shall come to pass, if thou wilt not hearken unto the voice of the LORD thy God, to observe to do all his commandments and his statutes which I command thee this day; that all these curses shall come upon thee, and overtake thee.
>
> —DEUTERONOMY 28:15

(Note: Now count what you ticked off and compare the results of the two sections. What is overtaking you, blessings or curses?)

Is there evidence amongst the dear saints and their generations today that curses for rebellion are still producing fruit?

In some of you I've just caused your stomach to do a belly flop. How many saints say that their disease is a blessing from God? I've looked and I can't find sickness and disease listed as a blessing from God that might overtake you.

TO BYPASS DISEASE OR TO BE HEALED AND RESTORED, WHAT MUST I DO?

> If thou wilt diligently hearken to the voice of the LORD thy God, and wilt do that which is right in his sight, and wilt give ear to his commandments, and keep all his statutes, I will put none of these diseases upon thee, which I have brought upon the Egyptians: for I am the LORD that healeth thee.
>
> —EXODUS 15:26

Restoration requires us to do what is right in God's sight and to be zealous to obey Him completely.

Our obedience is far-reaching; the promise is that our obedience or rebellion will also affect our babies and grandbabies.

> Observe and hear all these words which I command thee, that it may go well with thee, and with thy children after thee for ever, when thou doest that which is good and right in the sight of the LORD thy God.
>
> —DEUTERONOMY 12:28

God knew when He placed the tree of the knowledge of good and evil in the garden and commanded His kids, "Now don't touch!" that there would be a chance that they would disobey. God wants meaningful relationships with His kids, and in order for that to happen, His kids must have options and still choose Him. He could have created us all as robots that would strut around saying, "I love you Lord," at the push of a button; but how meaningful would that be to a highly intelligent being?

> But of the tree of the knowledge of good and evil, thou shalt not eat of it:
> for in the day that thou eatest thereof thou shalt surely die.
>
> —Genesis 2:17

On the day that Adam sinned he gave a curse legal right to exist; a curse always requires a cause in order to afflict.

> As the bird by wandering, as the swallow by flying, so the curse causeless
> shall not come.
>
> —Proverbs 26:2

On the day Adam sinned he died spiritually for eternity and allowed death entrance into the human race. This is the beginning of ancestral sins through which the curse is passed down to all generations. Romans 5:12 traces the effect of the curse from Adam to the present day.

> Wherefore, as by one man sin entered [of Satan taking possession] into
> the world, and death by sin; and so death passed [through the generations
> so no one can escape] upon all men, for that all have sinned:…even over
> them that had not sinned after the similitude [likeness] of Adam's trans-
> gression….For if by one man's offense death reigned [highest influence
> or control] by one.
>
> —Romans 5:12, 14, 17

Sin entered into the human race through one couple thus contaminating all future generations with sin and sin's ultimate fruit, death. Even though we may not have committed the same "after the similitude" sin as Adam did, that very sin of Adams is still passed onto us. That is iniquity which flows unde-tected like a computer virus. A virus can enter one computer and be unable to do any harm until it is passed onto another unsuspecting "friendly" computer and the virus manifests there instead.

Before we get feeling a dogmatic sense of superiority which would inspire us to judge one who we feel has a life of many curses in operation, the Word has a caveat.

Sometimes God allows us to be taken into captivity for our good and of course sometimes for evil. Please be careful in judging the reason of the calamity that has fallen upon a brother in the event you take upon yourself a greater sin. I am speaking as much to myself here as I became quite judg-mental of the perceived sin of others in consideration of the affliction that I saw them facing. I would say in my heart, AH HA, surely your sins have found you out by the calamity that has come upon you.

Jeremiah provides the caveat:

> One basket had very good figs, even like the figs that are first ripe: and
> the other basket had very naughty figs, which could not be eaten, they
> were so bad. Then said the Lord unto me, What seest thou, Jeremiah?
> And I said, Figs; the good figs, very good; and the evil, very evil, that

cannot be eaten, they are so evil....Thus saith the LORD , the God of Israel; Like these good figs, so will I acknowledge them that are carried away captive of Judah, whom I have sent out of this place into the land of the Chaldeans for their good [benefit, welfare, prosperity]. For I will set mine eyes upon them for good, and I will bring them again to this land: and I will build them, and not pull them down; and I will plant them, and not pluck them up. And I will give them an heart to know me, that I am the LORD : and they shall be my people, and I will be their God: for they shall return unto me with their whole heart.
—JEREMIAH 24:2–7

The purpose of the captivity of these good people was so that they would be reconciled in wholeness to their God. God placed them into captivity with eternity in mind knowing that it would be hard for his beloved people in the immediate short term. This would be a drastic measure on God's part but He only does it with our eternal interests in mind. It would be like forcing a loved one to go to rehab, they aren't very happy with you are first but when they get out you get a big hug and a kiss.

Then Jeremiah addresses the naughty figs:

And as the evil figs, which cannot be eaten, they are so evil; surely thus saith the LORD , So….. I will deliver them to be removed into all the kingdoms of the earth for their hurt, to be a reproach and a proverb, a taunt and a curse, in all places whither I shall drive them. And I will send the sword, the famine, and the pestilence, among them, till they be consumed from off the land that I gave unto them and to their fathers.
—JEREMIAH 24:8–10

At first glance each of the figs would look similar but inside they were completely opposite; one good one naughty! I have been placed in captivity as a good fig and I admit more often as a naughty fig.

Generational tag
Jungian psychology teaches that the archetypes and dark shadows of our ancestral darkness reside in the collective unconscious and have been flowing as darkness in our generations. This darkness is "iniquity" in the Bible.

The LORD is longsuffering, and of great mercy, forgiving iniquity and transgression, and by no means clearing the guilty, visiting the iniquity of the fathers upon the children unto the third and fourth generation.
—NUMBERS 14:18

Iniquity is participation with the same sin that you, your father, and grandfather have been doing for generations; and it is bearing the same fruit. It shows up in inherited genetic disease and in predisposition to personality characteristics such as molestation, crime, insanity, anger, fear, etc. It also shows up in untimely deaths, poverty, divorce, crime, or addictions that we say very accurately that they "run in the family."

You can't deny genetically inherited diseases. It is a statement of science. Where does it come from?—participation of your ancestors in the same type of sin from generation to generation without repentance.

> And the seed of Israel separated themselves from all strangers, and stood and confessed their sins, and the iniquities of their fathers.
> —NEHEMIAH 9:2

Recorded in Nehemiah we have a six-hour service, three hours reading the book of the law, three hours confessing their sins and the iniquity of their fathers, and capped by worship. This is not about repenting on behalf of another so they are forgiven, as that cannot be done. In this passage confession means that I agree with what God thinks about such sin, and I agree with His verdict on the rebellion of our fathers. You are not guilty of the sin of your ancestors; but because of their sin, you may be vulnerable to Satan's vexation in the same area.

> We acknowledge, O LORD, our wickedness, and the iniquity of our fathers: for we have sinned against thee.
> —JEREMIAH 14:20

Jeremiah is another witness in Scripture as to how the curse of iniquity forwarded, or generational sin, was dealt with.

> Thou shewest lovingkindness unto thousands, and recompensest ["expense it forward" as opposed to "pay it forward"] the iniquity of the fathers into the bosom [soul] of their children after them: the Great, the Mighty God, the LORD of hosts, is his name.
> —JEREMIAH 32:18

Would you like to stop the flow of genetically inherited disease? It can be done. You can change the destiny or captivity of your families if you do the right thing spiritually. You can be healed by Jesus of not only your own sin, but also of the effects your ancestor's sin has on you in regards to genetically inherited diseases, psychological problems, and other curses.

We may think we are "a real stud" in life not realizing that we have "tagged" our children and their children with the fruit of our hidden sin.

Paul reminds Christians that we are sick because of sin and generational iniquity.

> I speak after the manner of men because of the infirmity [weakness or sickness] of your flesh: for as ye have yielded [placed at another's disposal] your members [allowed our bodies to be bonded to another in criminal intercourse] servants [allowed Satan to usurp control] to uncleanness [everything that can be lusted for] and to iniquity unto iniquity; even so now yield your members servants to righteousness unto holiness.
> —ROMANS 6:19

"Iniquity unto iniquity" is the repeating of the iniquity of past generations. The word *unto* means "the end by which a thing is completed" or the iniquity serves in one and its work isn't complete until it is passed to the next generation.

Several of these past New Testament verses are highlighted as there is a kingdom that wants us to believe there is no longer such thing as generational sin so that it can stay in power without being indicted.

> Thou shalt not bow down thyself to them, nor serve them: for I the LORD thy God am a jealous God, visiting the iniquity of the fathers upon the children unto the third and fourth generation of them that hate me; And shewing mercy unto thousands of them that love me, and keep my commandments.
>
> —EXODUS 20:5–6

The guilty are forgiven only with repentance. Generational curses will be broken when we go into ministry of specific sins.

Taken captive and destroyed due to lack of knowledge
There are spiritual laws to follow, as Satan is a legalist. Jesus can't release you from something you don't see; and you can't be forgiven for something from which you don't repent; and He can't forgive you if you are in ignorance.

> Therefore my people are gone into captivity, because they have no knowledge [discernment, perception, skill]: and their honourable men are famished, and their multitude dried up with thirst.
>
> —ISAIAH 5:13

All of us as God's people have been taken into captivity to one degree or another by the devil because we did not have the discernment and tools to be set free. Honorable saints are famished in their quest to be free of their infirmity; they have thirsted for the healing and restoration they read of in the Word but are unable to touch it.

It is possible that some denominations were formed around the rejection of specific knowledge and then a church is developed that grieves the Holy Spirit in certain areas the Lord needs to move in order to reconcile His people. Will God heal or perform a miracle if the folks make a stand that God no longer heals today? Such a stand in the church would be akin to legalizing doubt and unbelief.

> My people are destroyed for lack of knowledge: because thou hast rejected [despised] knowledge [discernment, perception, skill], I will also reject thee, that thou shalt be no priest [occupy minister's office] to me: seeing thou hast forgotten [ceased to care for] the law of thy God, I will also forget thy children.
>
> —HOSEA 4:6

A doctrinal stand that governs the hand of God taken by a minister will limit or even worse, cease the work of God amongst the congregation. The prophet Hosea said the Lord will ignore the children of the pastor who has ceased to take the whole Word of God as the command of God.

After David committed adultery he acknowledged before God the generational iniquity that was part of his human inheritance.

> Behold, I was shapen in iniquity; and in sin did my mother conceive me.
>
> —Psalm 51:5

"Shapen in iniquity" is the inherited curse. You see this in adopted children. Parents brought them up in a wonderful environment—and what happened? They brought inherited iniquity with them that is foreign to the new adoptive family. How is it that a young man displays the character of his father whom he never met?

The battle of the flesh is carried out in the mind and contaminates our spirit if the battle to overcome is lost!

> Take heed to your spirit and let none deal treacherously against the wife of his youth.
>
> —Malachi 2:15

I was taught that the only way the devil could trouble me was by sitting on my shoulder and whispering in my ear, as he had no access to me internally. But the responsibility for following such doctrine was my problem, as I should have gone to the Scripture to see if it was true doctrine. The following words of Jesus make it quite clear where the throne of our defilement rests.

> There is nothing from without a man, that entering into him can defile him: but the things which come out of him, those are they that defile [to make Levitically unclean] the man.
>
> —Mark 7:15

This verse should put to rest the deceptive teaching that good and evil cannot exist in a believer at the same time. Christians have little power over sin because of years of unchallenged teaching.

> But I see another law in my members, warring against the law of my mind, and bringing me into captivity to the law of sin which is in my members.
>
> —Romans 7:23

Paul says there are two laws in his body—one of God and the second of sin. So if you forgive a brother that is the law of God at work. If you practice unforgiveness, you are following the law of sin. Satan administers a kingdom that knows you and your ancestors better than you can imagine. His purpose is to destroy you and your nation.

> Christians have little power over sin because of years of unchallenged teaching.

Further to the curse of death, we also see sorrow, pain, toil, weeds, and hardship entering into the human equation subsequent to "just one little sin" by Adam.

> Unto the woman he said, I will greatly multiply thy sorrow and thy conception; in sorrow thou shalt bring forth children; and thy desire shall be to thy husband, and he shall rule over thee. And unto Adam he said, Because thou hast hearkened unto the voice of thy wife, and hast eaten of the tree, of which I commanded thee, saying, Thou shalt not eat of it: cursed is the ground for thy sake; in sorrow shalt thou eat of it all the days of thy life; Thorns also and thistles shall it bring forth to thee; and thou shalt eat the herb of the field; In the sweat of thy face shalt thou eat bread, till thou return unto the ground; for out of it wast thou taken: for dust thou art, and unto dust shalt thou return.
> —GENESIS 3:16

It should be obvious, that we clearly suffer from these consequences and curses today some six thousand years later; they did not cease to afflict the human race at the cross. I emphasize this, as many teach that the Old Testament is no longer relevant for today and that if you accept Jesus as Savior all effects of the curse are automatically cancelled. Well the curse was dealt with at the cross, but we have to appropriate specifically what Christ did for each curse we see active in our lives. If a curse is active it has a legal right to exist; and as Satan is a legalist we'll have to have it removed according to spiritual principals.

The completion of Christ's work on the cross in destroying Satan and his accompanying works occur at the end of the Millennium.

> And there shall be no more curse: but the throne of God and of the Lamb shall be in it; and his servants shall serve him.
> —REVELATION 22:3

Many say that Christ cancelled the curse on the cross, based on a passage in Galatians and we received that benefit when we accepted Him as Savior. That interpretation is only partly true. The curse that was nullified at the time of the Crucifixion was the "curse of the law," not the curse of Satan or the curse of generational iniquity or the curse of individual sin. The Jewish law was so difficult as to be impossible to obey in order to earn salvation through obedience, so thus the law was a curse to them. The Cross provided an alternative to salvation, thus removing the strict requirements of the law or the curse of the law.

> For as many as are of the works of the law are under the curse: for it is written, Cursed is every one that continueth not in all things which are written in the book of the law to do them. But that no man is justified by the law in the sight of God, it is evident: for, The just shall live by faith. And the law is not of faith: but, The man that doeth them shall live in them. Christ hath redeemed us from the curse of the law, being made a curse for us: for it is written, Cursed is every one that hangeth on a tree.
> —GALATIANS 3:10–13

To show how easily incomplete doctrines can enter the teaching of the church lets expand on a statement I made a couple of paragraphs back. It is often taught that when Christ uttered " It is finished' upon the cross that he was saying that the works of Satan were destroyed. Well if that were true what is going on with the unleashing of all this evil in the world today?

What Christ was saying is that He carried out the commandment of the Father and thus fufilling His assignment as prophesied. It would be a stretch to say that He was referring to destroying the works of Satan in the believer at the time. He did provide a way of escape through His shed blood for the remission of sins thus paving the way for eternal life. He did through the cross provide a way for the Christian to defeat Satan and we'll consider that in depth shortly.

> When Jesus therefore had received the vinegar, he said, It is finished ['*teleo*' to do just as commanded, to perform the last act)]: and he bowed his head, and gave up the ghost.
>
> —JOHN 19:30

Jesus will come on the scene again about three thousand years later to announce that "It is Done" and that is after the Saints have overcome the world and the devil is permanently destroyed at the conclusion of the one thousand year Millenium.

> And he said unto me, It is done. ['ginomai' Christ is the end of the law unto righteousness, Satan is defeated] I am Alpha and Omega, [Jesus Christ] the beginning and the end. I will give unto him that is athirst of the fountain of the water of life freely. He that overcometh shall inherit all things; and I will be his God, and he shall be my son. But the fearful, and unbelieving, and the abominable, and murderers, and whoremongers, and sorcerers, and idolaters, and all liars, shall have their part in the lake which burneth with fire and brimstone: which is the second death.
>
> —REVELATION 21:6

There are no more chances for anyone to alter their eternal destiny. Christ announced the final curtain on man's earthly assignment and now gives the saints their promised inheritance. The 'aints' also get their promised inheritance to the kingdom they pleged their lives to.

Now appropriating the work of Christ upon the cross can break a curse. Jesus will turn the curse into a blessing, and to see that happen, we have some responsibility to consider first.

Religious theory regarding disease and calamities amongst Christians

So how do folks explain the existence of disease or any of the other calamities amongst believers? They say that it is the will of God. Let's consider the logic of such a position.

> 1. If sickness makes us humble and purifies us from carnal ways, we do not need the blood of Christ to cleanse us from sin. This would bring

Christianity to the same level as Hinduism and Buddhism, which teach that the soul is cleansed through suffering.

2. If God intended us for sickness, why would Jesus have taken our sickness and infirmities on himself? (Isa. 53:4–5).

3. If God wanted people sick, then Jesus rebelled by healing those He came in contact with.

4. It is impossible to believe it is God's will for us to be sick and God's will to heal us at the same time. We must give up on one of those beliefs because "a double-minded man is unstable in all his ways." The devil came to steal, kill, and destroy while Christ came to give us abundant life (John 10:10).

5. If sickness is the will of God, then Jesus redeemed us from "God's will" because "He himself took our infirmities and bore our diseases."

Paul, as you know, suffered from his thorn in the flesh. Let's look to see if he calls it a blessing:

> And lest I should be exalted above measure through the abundance of the revelations, there was given to me a thorn in the flesh, the messenger of Satan to buffet [treat violently] me, lest I should be exalted above measure [become haughty].
>
> —2 CORINTHIANS 12:7

Paul identifies Satan as the originator of his "thorn in the flesh." Satan is the "blesser" of our disobedience and he exacts the penalty. The thorn in the flesh was clearly a work of Satan and his underlings. Paul sought the Lord three times to remove this thorn in the flesh and he wasn't set free from its captivity. This would be an example of the captivity regarding the good figs spoken of by Jeremiah that came upon them for their benefit.

It is true that God can and does work out all things for good (Rom. 8:28) and He did so for Paul in 2 Corinthians 12:9, "My grace is sufficient for thee: for my strength is made perfect in weakness."

Jesus healed a man at the Pool of Bethesda who was thirty-eight years diseased; and after He healed the man, Jesus discipled him on how to keep the healing:

> Afterward Jesus findeth him in the temple, and said unto him, Behold, thou art made whole: sin no more, lest a worse thing come unto thee.
>
> —JOHN 5:14

Jesus taught that the calamity was the result of sin, and if he didn't mend his ways it would actually be much worse for him than before the healing.

In order to break the curse, Jesus would have to provide a way to release those that are subjected to bondage and have been taken captive by the devil at the devil's will.

Forasmuch then as the children are partakers of flesh and blood, he also himself likewise took part of the same; that through death he might destroy him that had the power of death, that is, the devil; And deliver them who through fear of death were all their lifetime subject to bondage [slavery to a devil].

—HEBREWS 2:14–15

Just as we have to appropriate the work Jesus Christ did on the cross for the remission—the complete forgiveness of sins, we will see that we will have to appropriate the Cross to cancel any curses that are operative in our lives. We'll lead you through this ministry process shortly.

Satan is amused at the curse he brought upon man, and now he manages to convince most of earth's inhabitants to continue to live under various curses when *Jesus Christ has already provided a way to break us free of our bondages.*

WHEN IS A CURSE ESTABLISHED?

When is a curse established? When we sin and never repent for it. Sin, if dealt with before the sun goes down on our wrath, will never give a curse a foothold.

What would have happened if Adam had repented? Job tells us that Adam never repented but attempted to hide his iniquity.

If I covered my transgressions as Adam, by hiding mine iniquity in my bosom.

—JOB 31:33

I was amused by the efforts of some young lads trying to cover their sin of smoking marijuana in their vehicle. I was following them in my patrol car and could smell the smoke from the pot they were smoking as it sifted in through the fresh air intake of my car's vent system. As I activated the red and blue lights of doom on the police car, the joint could be seen arcing out of their car window as they attempted to destroy the evidence. At the car window they assured me they didn't smoke pot until I inquired about the mat of bluish grey smoke that just wouldn't depart from their car. Marijuana smoke is much heavier than cigarette smoke and lies like a fog rather than dispelling quickly upwards. No matter how clever we think we are at covering our sin, it still stinks to everyone around us.

If we are sick we should rejoice in Isaiah 53. Jesus Christ has purposed in His personal sacrifice to heal us. (See also Isaiah 58:8–14.)

Surely he hath borne our griefs [sickness], and carried our sorrows [pain physical or mental]: yet we did esteem him stricken, smitten of God, and afflicted. But he was wounded for our transgressions, he was bruised for our iniquities: the chastisement of our peace was upon him; and with his stripes we are healed.

—ISAIAH 53:4–5

Jesus was bruised for our iniquities. Iniquities are generational sins that are passed internally from parent to child. Bruising is internal bleeding that Jesus suffered to provide freedom from the curse of generational iniquities.

Indeed, it is the desire of our Lord to heal us; but even more so, His desire for us is that we do not get sick in the first place. I am not saying that every disease will be healed nor do I teach that the reason you may be diseased is because you do not have enough faith.

> God is no respecter of persons.
>
> —Acts 10:34

He will not heal someone else and ignore you. Furthermore, the Lord's desire for us is peace and not evil, which would rule out giving us the curses of Egypt as a blessing to us.

> For I know the thoughts that I think toward you, saith the Lord, thoughts of peace, and not of evil, to give you an expected end.
>
> —Jeremiah 29:11

We will study later the difference our sanctification will make in the answering of our prayers, as there are several sins and stumbling blocks that prevent our prayers from being heard.

Too many good people are like the woman with the issue of blood.

> And a certain woman, which had an issue of blood twelve years, And had suffered many things of many physicians, and had spent all that she had, and was nothing bettered, but rather grew worse.
>
> —Mark 5:25–26

Little has changed; the saints are still exhausting themselves in search for healing and in many cases are worse off in the end than when they first sought out healing.

Why Are the Sheep Scattered?

This is a hard thing, but whom does God hold responsible for the care of the flock? Consider the Lord's requirement for those that minister on His behalf; they are to heal the sick, they are to comfort the broken hearted, and they are to leave the numbers to restore the one who was driven away.

> Son of man, prophesy against the shepherds [pastors] of Israel, prophesy, and say unto them, Thus saith the Lord God unto the shepherds... The diseased have ye not strengthened, neither have ye healed that which was sick, neither have ye bound up that which was broken [wounded], neither have ye brought again that which was driven away, neither have ye sought that which was lost; but with force and with cruelty have ye ruled them. And they were scattered, because there is no shepherd: and they became meat to all the beasts of the field, when they were scattered.
>
> —Ezekiel 34:2, 4–5

Because the shepherds were not doing the work of healing, the sheep were scattered; that means the sheep may be in the pews on Sunday but then are scattered during the week as they go everywhere else but to the church for healing. God wouldn't hold them responsible for not healing the sick if they didn't have the power to do so available to them. God wanted to heal and bind up the sheep through the pastor, but His work was thwarted then just as it is today.

Why are the shepherds unproductive? Because of whom they are looking at.

> Yea, they are greedy dogs which can never have enough, and they are shepherds that cannot understand: they all look to their own way, every one for his gain, from his quarter.
>
> —ISAIAH 56:11

But God said He would seek out those who were abandoned, and were not properly loved to restore them, heal them and strengthen them.

> And Jesus went about all the cities and villages, teaching in their synagogues, and preaching the gospel of the kingdom, and healing every sickness and every disease among the people. But when he saw the multitudes, he was moved with compassion on them, because they fainted, and were scattered abroad, as sheep having no shepherd. Then saith he unto his disciples, The harvest truly is plenteous, but the labourers are few; Pray ye therefore the Lord of the harvest, that he will send forth labourers into his harvest.
>
> —MATTHEW 9:35–38

Jesus did the work of a shepherd, which was healing the sick and diseased; and He noted the reason for the multitude of sick people was because their shepherds weren't doing the work of ministry and the people were scattered (left to own devises to get healed). Jesus noted that there were few laborers for the harvest; He was referring to laborers that would do as He did, as there are an abundance of folks that labor in religious organizations now as there were back then. At the time of Christ there were scores of Pharisees, Sadducees, scribes, high priests, and rabbis; but He still noted the sheep had no shepherd.

> But if I with the finger of God cast out devils, no doubt the kingdom of God is come upon you. When a strong man armed keepeth his palace, his goods are in peace: But when a stronger than he shall come upon him, and overcome him, he taketh from him all his armour wherein he trusted, and divideth his spoils. He that is not with me is against me: and he that gathereth not with me scattereth. When the unclean spirit is gone out of a man, he walketh through dry places, seeking rest; and finding none, he saith, I will return unto my house whence I came out.
>
> —LUKE 11:20–24

When Jesus said, "he that is not with me is against me," He was referring to those who were not with Him in the battle to purge out evil spirits to usher in the kingdom of God. He went further to say that "he that gathereth not with me scattereth." Who is scattered? The sheep are because they are not being set free by the assistance of their spiritual caretakers. "He that gathereth not" references those shepherds and ministers that don't support Jesus in this war against the god of this world.

We are to pray that the Lord of the harvest would send forth His laborers into the harvest; laborers that will gather with Jesus and seek to bring back those that are scattered.

As awesome as the works of Christ were, He says that His laborers will do even greater works than He did because He goes back to join forces with our Father.

> Verily, verily, I say unto you, He that believeth on me, the works that I do shall he do also; and greater works than these shall he do; because I go unto my Father.
>
> —JOHN 14:12

When did Jesus go to the Father?—ten days before the church was baptized in the Holy Spirit, as recorded in Acts 1.

To do as Jesus did we need to study His ministry and we'll have a look at how He ministered to the sick and diseased. To establish the truth of several witnesses, it is necessary to review the evidence of several accounts of Christ's healings.

1. Jesus first deals with the sin in order to heal the palsy. The palsy is thought to be one who is enfeebled by a paralytic stroke.

> And, behold, men brought in a bed a man which was taken with a palsy...And when he saw their faith, he said unto him, Man, thy sins are forgiven thee.
>
> —LUKE 5:18, 20

2. Mary Magdalene was cleansed of seven evil spirits. When the seven evil spirits left, they took the disease with them.

> And certain women, which had been healed [restored to health] of evil spirits and infirmities, Mary called Magdalene, out of whom went seven devils.
>
> —LUKE 8:2

The "accuser of the brethren" would have us believe that we are defiled and second-rate Christians because of our exposure to unclean spirits. But we are not them, we are separate. In fact, the woman out of whom seven devils were purged was the first person Jesus went to see after He rose from the dead. That's huge!

> Now when Jesus was risen early the first day of the week, he appeared first to Mary Magdalene, out of whom he had cast seven devils.
>
> —MARK 16:9

3. Jesus heals the woman with the bowed back by purging her of the spirit of infirmity. Jesus said, "You are loosed from your infirmity."

> There was a woman which had a spirit of infirmity eighteen years, and was bowed together, and could in no wise lift up herself. And when Jesus saw her, he called her to him, and said unto her, Woman, thou art loosed from thine infirmity. And he laid his hands on her: and immediately she was made straight, and glorified God.
>
> —LUKE 13:11–13

After healing this woman Jesus explains that she was bound or chained by a demon; and to break the bond He spoke directly to the demon and commanded it to unhook the chain, be loosed.

> And ought not this woman, being a daughter of Abraham, whom Satan hath bound [legally], lo, these eighteen years, be loosed [deprive Satan of his authority] from this bond on the sabbath day?
>
> —LUKE 13:16

This bond is the term Jesus used to describe the relationship between the person and the unclean spirit. Satan can only deprive a person of their freedom if he has a legal right to their life. The command to be loosed in the name of Jesus Christ would annul the legal precedence.

4. Jesus fulfilled prophecy in using his power to cast out evil spirits. This wasn't done in the Old Testament and was used as one of the signs to identify the Messiah. He did it with His Word only. The devils must obey the words of Jesus.

> When the even was come, they brought unto him many that were possessed with devils: and he cast out the spirits with his word, and healed all that were sick: That it might be fulfilled which was spoken by Esaias the prophet [Isa. 53:4], saying, Himself took our infirmities, and bare our sicknesses.
>
> —MATTHEW 8:16–17

Jesus took our infirmities and sicknesses by casting out the spirits with His Word.

5. No personal sin is mentioned in the next passage. He may have received the deaf and dumb spirit as a generational curse. Nonetheless, what had to be done for the dumb man to speak?

> As they went out, behold, they brought to him a dumb man possessed with a devil. And when the devil was cast out, the dumb spake: and the multitudes marvelled, saying, It was never so seen in Israel.
>
> —MATTHEW 9:32–33

6. How did Jesus know this next fellow had a devil?—by the fruit. The fruit could be anything listed in the list of curses we detailed earlier in this chapter

> Then was brought unto him one possessed with a devil, blind, and dumb: and he healed him, insomuch that the blind and dumb both spake and saw.
>
> —MATTHEW 12:22

7. Now just so that we don't run around thinking we have everyone's problems figured out, the following is recorded for our caution.

And as Jesus passed by, he saw a man which was blind from his birth. And his disciples asked him, saying, Master, who did sin, this man, or his parents, that he was born blind? Jesus answered, Neither hath this man sinned, nor his parents: but that the works of God should be made manifest in him.

—John 9:1–3

Notice Jesus didn't rebuke the disciples for their question of "who sinned?" It was a valid question and certainly from being with Jesus as He healed those we've just looked at they would have reason to ask.

Does it really matter who sinned? The Lord isn't here to apply the guilt trip. The only thing that matters here is that they can be healed by simply discerning the unclean root of the malady and commanding it out in Jesus' name.

8. Discernment is important as seen in the next poor fellow. On the surface it may appear this boy was insane and it would be the spirit of insanity that behaved so harshly; but that would be just the fruit and nothing happens unless the root is loosed. In this case the root was the deaf and dumb spirit.

And one of the multitude answered and said, Master, I have brought unto thee my son, which hath a dumb spirit; And wheresoever he taketh him, he teareth him: and he foameth, and gnasheth with his teeth, and pineth away: And they brought him unto him: and when he saw him, straightway the spirit tare him; and he fell on the ground, and wallowed foaming. And he asked his father, How long is it ago since this came unto him? And he said, Of a child. And ofttimes it hath cast him into the fire, and into the waters, to destroy him: but if thou canst do any thing, have compassion on us, and help us. Jesus said unto him, If thou canst believe, all things are possible to him that believeth. And straightway the father of the child cried out, and said with tears, Lord, I believe; help thou mine unbelief.... He rebuked the foul spirit, saying unto him, Thou dumb and deaf spirit, I charge thee, come out of him, and enter no more into him. And the spirit cried, and rent him sore, and came out of him: and he was as one dead; insomuch that many said, He is dead. But Jesus took him by the hand, and lifted him up; and he arose.

—Mark 9:17–27

The lad suffered since a child, so most likely dealing with generational iniquity. We've seen healings in children as the result of parents standing in the gap and repenting for the generational iniquity that was manifesting. The child, in several cases, wasn't even in the room and no one prayed over the child at the time of healing. Glory be to God!

Some are offended if evangelism and church aren't real pretty. I think sometimes we should come to church in work clothes. Since the church belongs to Jesus Christ, He is the one that charges us with the complete Great Commission of all believers. Many will teach to the word *baptized* and stop, perhaps because they know the rest hasn't happened in their ministry.

> And He said to them, "Go into all the world and preach the gospel to every creature. He who believes and is baptized will be saved; but he who does not believe will be condemned. And these signs will follow those who believe: In My name they will cast out demons; they will speak with new tongues; they will take up serpents; and if they drink anything deadly, it will by no means hurt them; they will lay hands on the sick, and they will recover."
>
> —MARK 16:15–18

When the power of God is not evident in signs following the preaching of the Word, then one needs to seek the Lord to see if they are quenching the spirit through doubt and unbelief or some other sin. Is it ever acceptable to explain away Scripture to match our experiences? Once we start that, where do we stop? God says what He means and means what He says!

Being obedient to the Great Commission that Christ initiated can only be fulfilled through the workings of the entire cast of spiritual gifts within the church.

> But the manifestation of the Spirit is given to each one for the profit of all: for to one is given the word of wisdom through the Spirit, to another the word of knowledge through the same Spirit, to another faith by the same Spirit, to another *gifts of healing* by the same Spirit, to another the *working of miracles*, to another prophecy, to another *discerning of spirits*, to another different kinds of tongues, to another the interpretation of tongues. But one and the same Spirit works all these things, distributing to each one individually as he will.
>
> —1 CORINTHIANS 12:7–11, EMPHASIS ADDED

I highlighted three gifts, not because they are more important, but because they are relevant to this chapter. The gift of healings, miracles, and discerning of spirits are often all required to be in operation for the ministry of healing. With these gifts also comes the power to command the infirmity to go and the evil spirits to be loosed.

One of the foundational practices of the church is to heal the sick and free those vexed with unclean spirits. The church is to be the "Go To" place to be healed. If the church is not doing this, there is no hope for freedom. All we can hope for is that science will come up with some chemical management tools for our many diseases of mind and body.

Lord give us today our daily bread. Amen

FORGIVE US OUR DEBTS, AS
WE FORGIVE OUR DEBTORS

EVERY TIME AN offense occurs between two people, both are forced into debt. This debt requires each one, whether perpetrator or the perceived victim, to pay their personal debt back in full. One has a debt to make amends for his wrong and the second has a debt of forgiveness. The repayment of either debt is not contingent on the repayment of the other first.

The sooner your debt is paid, the less interest or usury is charged. When you charge an item on your credit card, you have a period of time to pay, usually thirty days, to pay debt off in full. If you are unable to pay what is owed in that time frame, the credit card company then charges usury or a high interest rate. However, the grace period for a personal offense debt is much shorter; the grace period completes at the end of the day in which the offense occurs. Satan is a legalist; and as soon as the personal debt goes into arrears, he steps in as the collection agent turning both debtors over to the tormentors to exact a penalty.

> Every time an offense occurs between two people; both are forced into debt. This debt requires each one, whether perpetrator or the perceived victim, to pay their personal debt back in full.

Imposing a penalty or consequence may occur immediately, while the most dangerous is the penalty that is delayed. Satan is a master at delayed time-release and he'll gladly wait until later on in life to demand payment. Now the payment due is not only the original principal amount but has the high unfair price of usury attached. We listed the usury charges in an earlier discussion titled the "Pain of Egypt" or the curses listed in Deuteronomy 28.

As soon as a debt is turned over to the tormentors, we have put a curse in motion. If the debtor does not pay what is due, it then becomes an "inheritance" of the next three to four generations. Partial payments don't work, as the collection agency is ruthless. A partial payment is "I'm sorry but…" or "I'll forgive you once I see a change" or "I can't forgive as I don't believe your apology was genuine" or "Your apology doesn't mean anything as I know you'll just do it again!"

A payment is not considered "paid in full" if any conditions remain unresolved.

An unpaid debt that has gone to collections also affects our credit rating and our access to further credit when we need it. So when we have not forgiven our friend, when the debt is unpaid, our heavenly Father doesn't forgive us and when we pray our words rebound from a brass ceiling as our access to heaven is denied.

Your past beliefs and practices have brought you to the place you find yourself in today. How have they been working for you? Now let's look at Scripture to see if what I said is true.

The Lord's Prayer is recorded twice in Scripture, once in Matthew and a second abbreviated form in Luke. They are both very similar, with Matthew having a Jewish tone to it and Luke using more Gentile wording.

When we sin we not only owe a debt to the person offended but also to God, as we've violated His law, thus sinning against Him. The only way that God will cancel our debts is if we have forgiven the debts for offenses others owe to us.

> And forgive us our debts [to fully pardon what is legally due and owed], as we forgive our debtors [one who has not yet made amends to whom he has injured].
> —MATTHEW 6:12

Notice we are to forgive our "debtors"; that means they have not made amends yet as once they have made amends they are no longer debtors. Jesus said, "Father, forgive them; for they know not what they do" (Luke 23:34).

> And forgive [to abandon the collection of a debt] us our sins [violation of God's law]; for we also forgive [to abandon the collection of a debt] every one that is indebted [an unfulfilled obligation; to have wronged one and have yet to make free from faults] to us.
> —LUKE 11:4

Once we've confessed, the party to whom we have confessed, whether to God or man, has an obligation to cease and abandon the collection of debts; that means the record of wrongs is broken. If you bring up the past again, you simply have not forgiven and cancelled the debt. It is against the character of God to forgive your debts while you are still unable to cancel the debt of someone else:

Not forgiving another no matter what they have done to injure you actually allows what they did to you to injure you over and over and over again.

> For if ye forgive men their trespasses, your heavenly Father will also forgive you: But if ye forgive not men their trespasses, neither will your Father forgive your trespasses.
> —MATTHEW 6:14

This passage follows the Lord's Prayer and just repeats the law of the cancellation of debts; it is all or nothing. Not forgiving another no matter what they have done to injure you actually allows what they did to you to injure you over and over and over again. The best way to get even with one who has hurt you is to freely forgive them and cancel all debts owed. You'll understand once you read on.

> It is against the character of God to forgive your debts while you are still unable to cancel the debt of someone else.

If you are holding onto a debt someone owes you, God is not released to step in and demand payment. As you read this passage it is obvious the kingdom of God runs by a different set of rules than this world does.

> Recompense to no man evil for evil. Provide things honest in the sight of all men. If it be possible, as much as lieth in you, live peaceably with all men. Dearly beloved, avenge not yourselves, but rather give place unto wrath: for it is written, Vengeance is mine; I will repay, saith the Lord. Therefore if thine enemy hunger, feed him; if he thirst, give him drink: for in so doing thou shalt heap coals of fire on his head. Be not overcome of evil, but overcome evil with good.
> —ROMANS 12:17–21

We are "overcome of evil" when we refuse to let go of a personal offense debt. How is God with keeping a record of forgiven debts?

> As far as the east is from the west, so far hath he removed our transgressions from us.
> —PSALM 103:12

If you asked God about past forgiven debts, He would say, "I have no idea what you are talking about."

> We are "overcome of evil" when we refuse to let go of a personal offense debt.

When you've tried to forgive and still have the mind traffic, it could be because we have given mental agreement to forgiveness but our heart doesn't know about the agreement our mind has made.

The cancellation of all debts owed is to reach complete closure the same day in which the offense was brought to light. The last thing you want to do before going to sleep each day is to be able to pray:

> *Father, forgive me for my debts and thank You for giving me the courage and strength to forgive _____ for the debt owed to me. I forgive _____ and I release him/her to You in my total forgiveness from my heart. I release all in Jesus' name.*

> Be ye angry [provoked by the offense of another], and sin not: let not the sun go down [set] upon your wrath: Neither give [surrender control] place [access to your temple] to the devil [slanderer or accuser].
> —EPHESIANS 4:26–27

The word here is that when a debt is carried over until the next morning, the devil has been given legal right of entry to your temple or spirit. When he comes in he is permitted to bring in seven devils more fierce than himself. So what was a little deal yesterday is a mountain today.

Moses also taught the time limit for closure. A vow carelessly made must be broken in the day of utterance. A vow, if negative, becomes a curse; and it also becomes a curse if it is good but is never fulfilled. As the husband is given the spiritual authority, he can cancel the vow thus standing in the gap to sanctify his beloved. Here the debt of a vow is cancelled:

> And if she had at all an husband, when she vowed, or uttered ought [foolish or unrestrained words] out of her lips, wherewith she bound her soul [allow to be taken captive]; And her husband heard it, and held his peace at her in the day that he heard it: then her vows shall stand, and her bonds wherewith she bound her soul shall stand. But if her husband disallowed her on the day that he heard it; then he shall make her vow which she vowed, and that which she uttered with her lips, wherewith she bound her soul, of none effect: and the LORD shall forgive her.
>
> —NUMBERS 30:6–8

What is to be done if we realize we have allowed a vow to stand or are delinquent in forgiving debts of personal offenses? In the next chapter we will provide ministry to break any curses that have been activated and assigned to the tormentors.

Consider how Christ prophesied that Peter would open the door for Satan to sift him as wheat, to work him over, for his boasting in his flesh and for lying about being a disciple of Jesus.

> And the Lord said, Simon, Simon, behold, Satan hath desired to have you, that he may sift [vex to point of overthrow] you as wheat: But I have prayed for thee, that thy faith fail not: and when thou art converted, strengthen thy brethren. And he said unto him, Lord, I am ready to go with thee, both into prison, and to death. And he said, I tell thee, Peter, the cock shall not crow this day, before that thou shalt thrice deny that thou knowest me.
>
> —LUKE 22:31–34

Peter is then questioned by folks as to his connection to Jesus and Peter has a brainstorm:

> Then began he to curse [to call down evils] and to swear [to threaten with an oath], saying, I know not the man. And immediately the cock crew.
>
> —MATTHEW 26:74

This opened the door for Peter to be vexed by Satan. However, within weeks, Peter is reconciled and receives the power of the Holy Spirit upon him in Acts 2. And he preaches adding three thousand souls to the church following his first sermon. The curse was turned into a blessing and very quickly.

This experience qualified Peter to write the following:

> Having eyes full of adultery [breaking alliance with God or having eyes always on the lookout for a sensuous adulterous woman], and that cannot cease from sin; beguiling [catch by bait] unstable [open to seduction] souls: an heart they have exercised with covetous practices [lusts]; cursed [liable to the appointed penalty] children.
>
> —2 Peter 2:14

Peter was teaching New Testament church doctrine. As the result of sin the children are cursed. It is written in the Old Testament the sins of the fathers are visited upon the children to the third and fourth generation. A curse always has to have a trapdoor opened for it to be activated and devils sent on assignment to carry it out. If you see the fruit of a curse, you know there is a cause. Deal with the cause, an unforgiven and overdue debt, and the symptom will go.

> As the bird by wandering, as the swallow by flying, so the curse causeless shall not come.
>
> —Proverbs 26:2

Living out in the country I've learned to make sure dishes with food residue are not left in the kitchen sink overnight, otherwise in the morning not only have flies multiplied, but the occasional mouse will also glean the leftovers in the morning's wee hours. It is quite obvious in the morning who dropped by. These pests do not trouble me unless I've invited them in by leaving bait free for the taking.

A debt is subject to varying usury or interest charges depending on the level of risk. Your credit history investigates how prompt you were at repaying your debts and if you followed the terms of the your loan agreement. Typically, the higher the level of risk the higher the interest rate you are charged. Usury in modern terms is an exorbitant or unlawful rate of interest charged by lenders to people who find themselves in a desperate financial mess.

Bitten by a Serpent

I found it very interesting that when I studied the term *usury, nashak* in Hebrew, in the Bible, it may refer to a high rate of interest or the same word could mean "to be bitten by a serpent" or to be "vexed" or "oppressed." Such an example is found in Numbers where the people were bitten by poisonous serpents as punishment for their complaints and murmuring against God. Their sin opens the trapdoor for the devil to vex them and exact usury upon them as punishment for their unrepentant sin.

> And the people spake against God, and against Moses, Wherefore have ye brought us up out of Egypt to die in the wilderness? for there is no bread, neither is there any water; and our soul loatheth this light bread. And the Lord sent fiery [poisonous] serpents among the people, and they bit [nashak] the people; and much people of Israel died. Therefore the

people came to Moses, and said, We have sinned, for we have spoken against the LORD, and against thee; pray unto the LORD, that he take away the serpents from us. And Moses prayed for the people.
—NUMBERS 21:5–7

It might seem severe to be bitten by poisonous snakes (usury) for being a little anxious and not liking your food; however, such a consequence is just a taste test of what eternal separation from God would be like. It is much better to get a little fiery bite now than to be totally consumed by a raging fire for eternity.

Once the grace period for us to deal with the forgiving of our debtors expires, the devil is then given a lawful opportunity to vex us though the usury that he multiplies to our account. The usury may be addictions, anger, rejection, narcissism, insanity, confusion, fear, poverty, divorce, untimely death, disease, failed eyesight, loss of business, bankruptcy, failed crops, or any other infirmity or plague that is listed as curses resulting from rebellion of either our ancestors or ourselves. Let me ask a couple of questions:

1. When we sin against God; what is the size of the debt to be repaid to God?

For the wages of sin is death; but the gift of God is eternal life through Jesus Christ our Lord.
—ROMANS 6:23

2. When we sin against another person or they cause offense to us; what is the debt to be repaid to the person wronged?

Forbearing [restore] one another, and forgiving [graciously pardon and restore] one another, if any man have a quarrel [a complaint] against any: even as Christ forgave you, so also do ye.
—COLOSSIANS 3:13

I had things so far out of perspective, and my lack of understanding in this area was very painful to my little family. I would commit a nasty sin and go to my heavenly Father and talk to Him about it; and He always forgave and comforted me without the guilt trip. Then with that done I'd go to my beloved and pursued her until I had rung every last ounce of repentance out and then left her drowning in shame. Could you imagine what the angels of the great cloud of witnesses felt about that? Yet I could read this passage in Matthew 18 and not catch on that the Lord was speaking to me. Accordingly, I opened the door to give the tormentors legal access as happened to the unjust servant.

Therefore is the kingdom of heaven likened unto a certain king, which would take account of his servants. And when he had begun to reckon, one was brought unto him, which owed him ten thousand talents. But forasmuch as he had not to pay, his lord commanded him to be sold, and his wife, and children, and all that he had, and payment to be made. The servant therefore fell down, and worshiped him, saying, Lord, have patience with me, and I will pay thee all. Then the lord of that servant was moved with compassion, and loosed [to release a debtor setting a captive free] him, and forgave him the debt. But the same servant went out, and found one of his fellowservants, which owed him an hundred pence: and he laid hands on him [prevailed], and took him by the throat, saying, Pay me that thou owest. And his fellowservant fell down at his feet, and besought him, saying, Have patience with me, and I will pay thee all. And he would not: but went and cast him into prison, till he should pay the debt. So when his fellowservants saw what was done, they were very sorry, and came and told unto their lord all that was done. Then his lord, after that he had called him, said unto him, O thou wicked servant, I forgave thee all that debt, because thou desiredst me: Shouldest not thou also have had compassion [extend help for the consequence of sin as opposed to be hardened] on thy fellowservant, even as I had pity on thee? And his lord was wroth [provoked to anger], and delivered him to the tormentors [to torture with extreme pain until confession obtained], till he should pay all that was due unto him. So likewise shall my heavenly Father do also unto you, if ye from your hearts forgive not [give up a debt, to absolutely give it up] every one his brother their trespasses [nasty deed].

—Matthew 18:23–35

Restoring the One Who Hurt You

Is it OK if I provoke you even a little more when a brother wrongs you? When a brother offends me, I am to have compassion and restore him because of the obvious torment he was subjected to from within his spirit allowing him to do what he did. I appreciate Paul's openness to explain the mixture of good and evil that he was perplexed with, as it gives me an understanding of my own weakness.

For I know that in me (that is, in my flesh), dwelleth no good thing: for to will is present with me; but how to perform that which is good I find not. For the good that I would I do not: but the evil which I would not, that I do. Now if I do that I would not, it is no more I that do it, but sin that dwelleth in me.

—Romans 7:18–20

When we walk in "phileo" love and are offended, we want the offender to recognize how badly they hurt us insisting that they pay for their sin through some form of penalty. Part of that penalty may be silence or sulking, which is evidence of withholding the debt of forgiveness. Whereas in "agape" love we recognize the sin is not them that they have been turned over to the tormentors as captives and are bound to foolish and reckless behavior until they receive the ministry of reconciliation and are loosed. A person walking in agape has died to self and is seeking first the kingdom of God so they know all their needs will receive care from Father God. Agape always does what is best for the other person.

Phileo is a love at the level of the soul or mind and thus fickle and subject to rapid change; whereas agape is love at the level of the heart or spirit, and as it is streamed from the Father, it cannot change. Forgiveness must be from the level of our heart as written by Matthew (18:35): "So likewise shall my heavenly Father do also unto you, if ye from your hearts forgive not every one his brother their trespasses."

> *When a brother offends me I am to have compassion and restore him because of the obvious torment he was subjected to from within his spirit allowing him to do what he did.*

I know that when I've forgiven as an exercise of my mind, the offense keeps recirculating in my mind and bitterness and resentment grows. But I reason, "Well I have forgiven them so I've done my spiritual duty." Forgiveness from the heart through agape results in peace, and you find yourself having compassion for the brother or sister who remains captive.

> This people draweth nigh unto me with their mouth [the thoughts of a man's soul find verbal utterance by his mouth], and honoureth me with their lips [motivated by self-interest]; but their heart [spirit] is far from me.
> —MATTHEW 15:8

Allow God to search and direct your heart so that you are able to pray to forgive in sincerity without fleshly thoughts short-circuiting your works.

> And the Lord direct your hearts [removal of hindrances] into the love of God [*agape*], and into the patient waiting for Christ.
> —2 THESSALONIANS 3:5

Perhaps the best gift we can give to another is forgiveness:

> Withhold not good [a benefit] from them to whom it is due, when it is in the power of thine hand to do it.
> —PROVERBS 3:27

Our sin may be highly visible for all to see; but the Lord beckons us to work it out so that an understanding is reached, and though our sin was nasty, the result is we'd be as a virgin, white, just as though we never sinned.

> *The gift that Father God gave us through His love was forgiveness.*

> Come now, and let us reason together [contend or debate], saith the LORD: though your sins [fault] be as scarlet [bright red cloth die], they shall be as white [cleansed of filthiness] as snow; though they be red like crimson, they shall be as wool.
> —ISAIAH 1:18

The maggot fixes herself permanently to an object and lays her eggs under her body to protect them until they hatch. As the mother dies a scarlet colored fluid is secreted staining her body and covering and protecting her unborn.

Jesus compared himself to this worm in Psalm 22:6: "But I am a worm and no man, a reproach of men and despised of the people." Jesus shed His blood to cover our sin so that we might live through His death. Only agape could do that, to which we are called.

To reason together is in the context of a covenant lawsuit. Judah had been practicing religious festivals, new moons, and appointed feasts of their own design in rebellion against Jehovah. (See Isaiah 1:10–15.) Isaiah calls upon them to repent to remove curses. Curses are the power of unconfessed sin that reaps havoc in our lives. The connotation of reason is to debate our case in court—in the court of the Word of God. To reason is to speak intelligently and to be brought into agreement and understanding with God, self, and others and then make changes, offer restitution, and renounce. Restitution is to make the wrong right.

The benefit of reasoning together is that both parties to an offense have something they can learn and grow from. The scripture says that when I judge another, when I find something they are constantly doing is extremely annoying, the reason I am so choked by their actions is because I have the same problem, though it may be disguised or remote to the situation at hand.

> Therefore thou art inexcusable, O man, whosoever thou art that judgest: for wherein thou judgest another, thou condemnest thyself; for thou that judgest doest the same things.
>
> —ROMANS 2:1

The loudest accusers are always squawking in an attempt to divert attention from something they are trying to keep hidden.

Ginger caught her husband Troy on several occasions indulging in online pornography. She was very incensed by this and would constantly berate him for it, even in front of friends. Troy knew what he was doing was wrong and was ashamed by his weakness; but it seemed the more Ginger chided him, the more difficult it became to overcome.

> The reason I am so choked by their action is because I have the same problem.

Meanwhile in Ginger's closet was seductive clothing that she justified as being fashionable. She would wear these outfits to work, as she enjoyed the flirtatious attention she was getting there. After all, she reasoned, we aren't doing anything so where is the harm? Ginger also enjoyed relaxing evenings indulging in romantic fantasy, chick flicks she called them. Troy never seemed to notice Ginger's behavior as anything to be concerned about. However, romantic fantasy lust was to Ginger what pornography was to Troy. Ginger was aroused by the sensual and emotional escapes while Troy was taking pleasure in the visual and sexual escapes. Both activities erode and harden the respective hearts leading to dissatisfaction and disillusionment, destroying the relationship. With women it is about the journey, whereas with men it is about the destination. Ginger would leave saying she doesn't know who she is and needs to find her real identity that was stolen by her husband. Troy spirals deeper into guilt feeling he alone caused the breakup, thus surrendering complete control to the abyss of bondage. The trips to fantasyland were actually courtesy of a sly tour guide called the devil, and he walks away a free devil, leaving his victims suspicious of each other and tearing the heart out of the one they once loved.

We don't fall out of love; we fall into sin!

Our marriage, the matrimonial church, is used by God to restore us to be wonderfully wholesome. No other spiritual experience works like a marriage, where everything is open and exposed in the home. We act perfect at work or at church; but in the oneness of marriage our uncleanness gets exposed. Because you are one, then everything you do, good or distasteful, affects the other in the deepest level of their spirit. When we are made into one flesh with our mate, our characteristics, good and bad, get mixed up together to make this new entity called a marriage. In a healthy relationship, when something nasty is expressed, they deal with it quickly together as the commitment is to be whole and not to participate with anything that is hurtful or divisive. I say, "Hey, I know I just hurt you and no matter how foolish and insensitive my action appeared, I don't want that between you and me. How can I be returned to favor again in your eyes?"

When our hearts are hardened through pride, we'll deny the obvious nasty deed; in fact we'll get the other so frustrated so that they fall, and then the focus is now switched to the unrighteousness of the one offended. This process adds additional hardening to the proud heart, and the one who is the object of such scorn feels a sense of hopelessness and despair. All they wanted was for it to be a priority for their other half to be courageous enough to rise above their narcissism (a modern term for selfish pride) and shame to repair the breech in the love stream. Satan absolutely gets turned on when we proudly protect his treachery in the marriage by denial and framing another through reversal.

Married couples don't fall out of love; they fall into sin. In their sin they blame each other, the one with whom God made them one flesh. We can never win if we don't recognize the real enemy. The Word addresses Christians, telling us our flesh and blood, our spouse, is not the enemy; the enemy is the well-organized spiritual mafia of demons.

> Put on the whole armour of God, that ye may be able to stand against the wiles [cunning deceit or trickery] of the devil. For we wrestle not against flesh and blood, but against principalities, against powers, against the rulers of the darkness of this world, against spiritual wickedness in high places.
> —Ephesians 6:11–12

Those who try to carnally manage these principalities have taught us, that we need to establish boundaries or walls between those we are supposed to love. It is well past time to thwart the devils entry though the borders of our households, recognizing the real source of marital terrorism. Build all the boundaries you want, as long as you know who the real enemy is and on what side of the wall he belongs.

I believe that if you can't find the procedure you are following to deal with any problem, any sin, any infirmity, or any strife in the Scriptures, you are doing a work of the flesh at best or a dangerous work from the darkness of the popularized occult. We have a very comprehensive owner's manual, the Holy Bible, to guide us, as only our maker knows how He designed us to work body, soul, mind, and spirit in integrated wholeness.

> Build all the boundaries you want as long as you know who the real enemy is and on what side of the wall he belongs.

James provides a summary for dealing with relational concerns that will require an understanding of additional scripture in order to realize all that the Lord has in mind to help you in your healing.

> Confess your faults [reason together] one to another, and pray one for another, that ye may be healed [made whole or sanctified]. The effectual [operating in power] fervent prayer of a righteous man [approved by God] availeth much.
>
> —James 5:16

Very little moves in the kingdom of God unless agape is the moving truck. Agape is the key ingredient as the goal of all confrontation is to bring healing to both parties of the offense particularly to the perpetrator. It is pressing towards the sanctification of each other. For effectual and fervent prayer to be realized, all the blocks for the demonstration of agape love must be removed.

Protocol if someone violates the bond of peace with you

When someone strays from the straight and narrow, in the particular area of the fault, they have given up control to another or their resolve to do good is overtaken through the seduction of evil. The term *overtaken* includes an element of surprise, as often the stuff that comes out of our mouths surprises the one with the mouth more than to the one to which it is spoken.

> Very little moves in the kingdom of God unless agape is the moving truck.

> Brethren, if a man be overtaken in a fault, ye which are spiritual, restore [strengthen; mend to what ought to be] such an one in the spirit of meekness [strength and spirituality under control]; considering thyself, lest thou also be tempted [enticed to sin].
>
> —Galatians 6:1

How you go about restoring one who has fallen will pay eternal dividends. Agape sees this wrong committed from the offender's perspective and is looking for an opportunity to offer the same grace and mercy God extended to them, to pay it forward.

> Brethren, if any of you do err [strays, seduced] from the truth, and one convert [return to true love of God] him; Let him know, that he which converteth the sinner from the error of his way shall save a soul from death, and shall hide a multitude of sins.
>
> —JAMES 5:19–20

And for those that need to keep score:

> And if he trespass against thee seven times in a day, and seven times in a day turn again to thee, saying, I repent; thou shalt forgive him.
>
> ——LUKE 17: 4

Protocol if you offended someone else

In considering whether you offended someone, keep in mind that the offense is as perceived by the one you agape. Matthew says that if he has "ought" (anything) against you, go make it right. Ought can be an obvious slight or sin; it could be something you said that was true, but hurtful. It could be something that made the other feel demeaned or disrespected; or it could be something that is just in their imagination. Go restore them; you'll be the better person for it. If you struggle with this step of humility, you may consider a possibility that pride may be hardening your heart against the expression of agape.

> When approaching one who has been caught "sin-handed," it is best to talk to him while both of you are facing a mirror. Remember you have the debt of forgiveness to pay.

> Therefore if thou bring thy gift to the altar, and there rememberest [a divinely inspired recollection] that thy brother hath ought [anything] against thee; Leave there thy gift before the altar, and go thy way; first be reconciled [renew friendship] to thy brother, and then come and offer thy gift.
>
> —MATTHEW 5:23–24

When you apologize to someone, you own it. If excuses are offered or if you try to pull a slick withdraw, your debt is still outstanding. What is a "slick withdraw"? It is when you apologize but with a slick manipulation of words, you draw the person you are apologizing to as the one really responsible; you reverse the charges.

Protocol for reconciliation if you get stuck

Step one: Cover the one that was overtaken by a fault by going to him privately and discreetly. Prepare his heart for the chat by asking, "Do I have your permission to talk to you about something I am struggling with?" If you go at them too quickly, you will be met with the scorner, and he'll turn on the defense mechanism before he realizes what came out of his lips.

> What is a "slick withdraw"? It is when you apologize but with a slick manipulation of words, you draw the person you are apologizing to as the one really responsible; you reverse the charges.

Moreover if thy brother shall trespass against thee, go and tell him his fault between thee and him alone: if he shall hear thee, thou hast gained thy brother.
—MATTHEW 18:15

Step two: Up to this point you have not talked to a third party about what happened. Now you have spoken to your brother and you were unable to restore him, so you bring along one or two ministers of reconciliation with you and review the matter with the goal of restoration as opposed to accusation. In agape you know that it is "the goodness of the Lord that leadeth to repentance."

> But if he will not hear thee, then take with thee one or two more, that in the mouth of two or three witnesses every word may be established.
> —MATTHEW 18:16

Step three: Take the offender before the church, not to grandstand or draw attention to how you were wronged but with a sincere heart to save a brother from going down to the pit.

> And if he shall neglect to hear them, tell it unto the church: but if he neglect to hear the church, let him be unto thee as an heathen man and a publican.
> —MATTHEW 18:17

Paul instructs the church at Corinth to discipline a fellow that was unrepentant of the sin of incest according to the principle taught by Christ:

> To deliver such an one unto Satan for the destruction of the flesh, that the spirit may be saved in the day of the Lord Jesus.
> —1 CORINTHIANS 5:5

This fellow was a Christian who was taken captive in his sin and released to the tormentors who would afflict his flesh; but note the goal was that his spirit would be saved. The fellow does eventually repent and Paul instructs the church to restore him publicly through the empowering of agape.

> Sufficient to such a man is this punishment, which was inflicted of many. So that contrariwise ye ought rather to forgive him, and comfort him, lest perhaps such a one should be swallowed up with overmuch sorrow. Wherefore I beseech you that ye would confirm [publicly validate] your love [*agape*] toward him.
> —2 CORINTHIANS 2:6–8

We are now going to study the practical ministry of reconciliation; so as workmen for the kingdom of God, we will not have to be ashamed due to lack of knowledge or fear.

AND LEAD US NOT INTO TEMPTATION, BUT DELIVER US FROM EVIL

FOR SATAN TO be most effective in the destruction of mankind, he would want to focus his endeavors on the few things that will ensure his ultimate victory. Satan knows that we are given two great commandments to which we will be held accountable. The first is to agape the Lord our God and the second is to agape our neighbor as we agape ourselves. If we are only able to eros love our sister or brother and, as Peter, only able to phileo love God, we have fallen short of the great commandments.

> Master, which is the great commandment in the law? Jesus said unto him, Thou shalt love [*agape*] the Lord thy God with all thy heart, and with all thy soul, and with all thy mind. This is the first and great commandment. And the second is like unto it, Thou shalt love [*agape*] thy neighbour as thyself. On these two commandments hang all the law and the prophets.
> —MATTHEW 22:36–40

As all the law and the teaching of the prophets hang on these two commandments, I believe all our sin is rooted in our disobedience and rebellion to the same commandments. In this chapter the sin that opposes agape will be exposed so that we can be restored to obedience and right standing with God while we are passing through this wilderness of earth.

In the Scriptures are two or three passages that we have become so familiar with and have memorized so that when we read them we pay no attention to them, as we think we grasp the concepts. However, in reality most of us have only a surface understanding at best. Those passages include the Lord's Prayer, which forms the outline of this book, the great commandments, which form the theme of this book, and now the love chapter of 1 Corinthians 13 that interprets what is meant by the great commandments.

Prayer:

> *In Jesus name we now put aside breaking the grip of all the "know it all" religious spirits, the unloving spirit, and the spirits of blindness, enmity, darkness, rebellion, pride, and confusion. We ask You, heavenly Father, to teach us the truth of Your love and to open our hearts so that we can receive the abundance*

of Your love so that we can in turn return to You, Father, and spread it to those we are to love. We desire to receive all that You have for us. Amen.

Jesus confronted Peter with the most important question that can be asked; "Peter do you agape me?" Peter knew what the question meant and acknowledged, "But Lord you know I have only been able to phileo you!" (John 21:15–17). The Bible says that the only way to know God is through agape, which is the deep love at the spirit level.

> He that loveth [*agapao*] not knoweth not God; for God is love [*agape*].
> —1 John 4:8

We have a debt that will take our entire lifetime to repay and that is the debt of agape. We receive agape from our heavenly Father through Jesus Christ and in turn allow it to stream freely to all. This simple sentence paraphrases the entire law:

> Owe no man anything, but to love [*agapao*] one another: for he that loveth [*agapao*] another hath fulfilled the law.
> —Romans 13:8

Agape is spiritual and cannot be contained or hoarded. Agape flows from within, from our inner spirit, the very place where the Holy Ghost sets up love operations.

> And hope maketh not ashamed; because the love [*agape*] of God is shed abroad [widely distributed] in our hearts [our spirit or temple] by the Holy Ghost which is given unto us.
> —Romans 5:5

The shedding abroad of agape is how God chooses to manifest Himself in you and through you. However, agape is conditional upon our total obedience to the commands of God, as we have studied.

We can know the commands in our mind through learning and memorization, but the keeping of them requires the knowledge to move from the mind down to the heart where knowledge becomes wisdom.

> He that hath [to have in mind] my commandments, and keepeth them [gives respect to from the heart], he it is that loveth [*agapao*] me: and he that loveth [*agapao*] me shall be loved [*agapao*] of my Father, and I will love [*agapao*] him, and will manifest myself [appear, made known] to him.
> —John 14:21

What blocks this knowledge from entering our spirits?—hidden and unconfessed sin. Sin is the filth that defiles our heart; and the Holy Spirit's work will be restricted in a filthy temple. The goal of all the commands of God is that we'll attain to the agape or charity bubbling forth out of sanctified hearts. We'll look at Scripture shortly for insight on the sin that needs to be purged for agape to manifest.

Now the end [the aim] of the commandment is charity [*agape*] out of a pure heart [cleansed temple], and of a good conscience [captivated by the will of God], and of faith unfeigned [unconditional guarantee of fulfillment].

—1 TIMOTHY 1:5

According as he hath chosen us in him before the foundation of the world, that we should be holy and without blame before him in love [*agape*].

—EPHESIANS 1:4

There are two essential requirements in order for agape to manifest in our lives: the first is to be holy, or sanctified, and the second is to be without blame—faultless. That is the truest description about what our heavenly Father created us to be like.

To reconcile us to our original created state, we'll be sanctified through the peace gained through the blood shed by Jesus on the cross. The intention of Jesus is that through His sacrifice we would be restored or reconciled to be holy and without blame once again:

And, having made peace through the blood of his cross, by him to reconcile all things unto himself; by him, I say, whether they be things in earth, or things in heaven. And you, that were sometime alienated and enemies in your mind by wicked works, yet now hath he reconciled In the body of his flesh through death, to present you holy [sanctified], and unblameable [faultless] and unreproveable [absence of any charge] in his sight.

—COLOSSIANS 1:20–22

Restoration to agape requires the eight steps of sanctification that are necessary to remove the presence, power, penalty, and pleasure of sin. Once we've experienced all of this salvation in our spirits it will be so much easier to walk in obedience.

Elect according to the foreknowledge of God the Father, through sanctification of the Spirit, unto obedience and sprinkling of the blood of Jesus Christ: Grace unto you, and peace, be multiplied.

—1 PETER 1:2

Are you ready to see what *Sanctiprize* is all about? Are you ready to fight and take back what is yours of the Lord, your heritage?

In addition to the wonderful benefits already noted consider these three spoils of war that are yours for the receiving:

The first is the eradication of fear. *There is no fear in agape.*

There is no fear in love [*agape*]; but perfect love [*agape*]; casteth out fear: because fear hath torment. He that feareth is not made perfect in love [*agape*].

—1 JOHN 4:18

If agape casts out fear, what else will it remove from our lives? Agape is not an emotion or a character trait but the very empowering of the essence of who God is.

The second spoil of war is that the curse will be broken in our lives and all things will work together for good.

> If agape casts out fear, what else will it remove from our lives? Agape is not an emotion or a character trait but the very empowering of the essence of who God is!

Do you know what *all* means in Greek? It means *all*! This passage is often quoted to comfort all those in distress but its promise is conditional on us loving God at the agape level.

And we know that all things work together for good to them that love [*agapao*] God, to them who are the called according to his purpose.
—ROMANS 8:28

Another result of this war is no evil power or tribulation will be able to separate us from the agape of God. The agape bond once established through obedience and sanctification is inseparable.

Make this scripture your declaration, putting the devil on notice as to where you stand:

> Who shall separate us from the love [*agape*] of Christ? shall tribulation, or distress, or persecution, or famine, or nakedness, or peril, or sword? Nay, in all these things we are more than conquerors through him that loved [*agapao*] us. For I am persuaded, that neither death, nor life, nor angels, nor principalities, nor powers, nor things present, nor things to come, nor height, nor depth, nor any other creature, shall be able to separate us from the love [*agape*] of God, which is in Christ Jesus our Lord.
> —ROMANS 8:35–39

You'll want to declare this scripture out loud whenever you feel you are being vexed.

THE SEVEN STEPS OF "SANCTIPRIZE"

If you were a priest in the Old Testament, how would you approach the holy of holies of the temple? You would sanctify or cleanse yourself and take every precaution to make sure you were right before God; you would know that if you approach the holy of holies presumptuously in your sin, you would precipitate some very unholy smoke. Now that the temple of the Holy Spirit has moved within our tent, we as priests must be on alert twenty-four seven, as we never know when we'll be called to serve. When the call comes it will be too late to scurry about trying to clean it up.

> Know ye not that ye are the temple of God, and that the Spirit of God dwelleth in you? If any man defile [corrupt] the temple of God, him shall God destroy; for the temple of God is holy, which temple ye are.
> —I CORINTHIANS 3:16

Just as you have a workout to exercise your body to keep fit, you have a spiritual workout to keep your temple fit to honor our King—sanctified in order for the Master to use anytime. We are on duty as a uniformed police officer with bulletproof armor, weapons cleaned and loaded, a working flashlight to expose the bad guys, physically fit to meet any challenge, and trained to be one step ahead of the enemy.

> But in a great house there are not only vessels of gold and of silver, but also of wood and of earth; and some to honour, and some to dishonour. If a man therefore purge [thorough cleansing] himself from these, he shall be a vessel [chosen instrument] unto honour, sanctified [pure from sins guilt], and meet [useful] for the master's use, and prepared unto every good work [ready to accomplish anything].
>
> —2 TIMOTHY 2:20–21

Once a temple is defiled it requires purging to loose it from the evil. There is no honor in possessing a messy temple. How much time and money is spent on painting and decorating up our tent? But you know, I've yet to find scripture that says, "You are a chosen instrument of the Lord because you are excessively pretty and good job on the enhancements, enter into the joy of the Lord." Relax, it is OK to take care of ourselves, and most of us know how to clean up real nice on the outside. What would others see if they had a window into your mind and heart making visible your thoughts about them and others? Kind of scary, the stuff of which nightmares are made. Now we understand what God sees and why He offers the solution to clean out the filth.

> Work out your own salvation with fear and trembling. For it is God which worketh in you both to will and to do of his good pleasure.
>
> —PHILIPPIANS 2:12–13

Why would such a workout be done in fear and trembling? This "fear" is a "reverential fear of approaching a holy God" thus giving us the constant challenge to cleanse our temple from what may have corrupted it. We fear that God would not be able to do His will and good pleasure in us, thus separating us from the God we love. Those that fear God can't get to Him fast enough to repent once they realize they have stumbled.

(A reminder: Salvation refers mainly to our quality of life, present and future. It is deliverance from everything that is evil to reconcile us to the person we were meant to be from the foundation of the world. Salvation includes being saved. We have a fourfold salvation: we are victorious over the penalty, power, presence, and, very importantly, the pleasure of sin.)

The Christians at the church of Ephesus were busy performing church but had left their "first agape," Father God. The Ephesus type of church is doing all they can in their own power to make their church relevant to the heathen and the lukewarm Christian, but they have become irrelevant to our Father. The letters to the seven churches in Revelation are to serve as a warning as to what we will be held accountable.

> What would others see if they had a window into your mind and heart making visible your thoughts about them and others? Kind of scary, the stuff of which nightmares are made. Now we understand what God sees and why He offers the solution to clean out the filth.

> Nevertheless I have somewhat against thee, because thou hast left thy first love [*agape*]. Remember therefore from whence thou art fallen, and repent, and do the first works; or else I will come unto thee quickly, and will remove thy candlestick out of his place, except thou repent.
> —REVELATION 2:4–5

Jesus said that the problem with the church was that they left their first agape and that the only way to be restored to the intended relationship with God was by repentance and first works. The mandate of this writing is to lead you in such repentance through first works.

The ministry of reconciliation is to restore each person to whom they were created to be before the commencement of the world. So we have the goal set for us to repent and do first works so we are holy, blameless, and embracing the agape of God.

> According as he hath chosen us in him before the foundation of the world, that we should be holy [saints prepared for God, pure] and without blame [faultless] before him in love [*agape*].
> —EPHESIANS 1:4

Sanctification is a process that appears more than 140 times in the Bible. It is the essence of who a believer is once he has become a Christian: his home, his life, his spirit, soul, and body have all been purged of evil and dedicated to walk in honor and holiness before our Master.

As already noted, King Hezekiah desired to repair the temple, which lay in ruins after years of neglect and attack from invading armies. The process included an interesting process of sanctification during which the priests spent sixteen days removing garbage and debris from the temple so that it would be returned to its original former glory and fit for the Master's occupation. We have to sanctify our temples by getting out the dirt that resulted from years of neglect and invasions from the enemy's legions. Sanctification is a must-have skill for Christians, yet I was a devout Christian for more than three and a half decades and was clueless as to its meaning, never mind how to practice it.

> For this is the will of God, even your sanctification, that ye should abstain from fornication: That every one of you should know how to possess his vessel in sanctification [*hagiasmos*] and honour [recognizing our high value].
> —1 THESSALONIANS 4:3–4

Sanctification is how we honor the sacrifice Jesus Christ paid to allow us a second chance at redemption after the fall of man at the onset of re–creation. Christ endured the shame, humiliation, and pain of the cross because you were worth it; you are highly valued. Our self-rejection and self-hatred would suggest Jesus was wrong about us; now may Satan be exposed for those lies, as Jesus Christ does not sponsor any flops.

> Follow peace [the Messiah's way that leads to salvation] with all men, and holiness [*hagiasmos*; sanctification of spirit and life], without which no man shall see the Lord.
> —HEBREWS 12:14

The Greek word *hagiasmos* is translated in this verse as *holiness*, and whereas in the previous verse, 1 Thessalonians 4:3, it is translated as *sanctification*. Sanctification and holiness are synonymous. This verse tells you how important our sanctification is; you cannot see the Lord without it!

We are one person, but a trinity of spirit, soul, and body that are to be sanctified in unison to bring us into a single-minded purpose of following God in agape.

> And the very God of peace sanctify [purify for temple use] you wholly [completely]; and I pray God your whole spirit and soul and body be preserved blameless unto the coming of our Lord Jesus Christ.
> —1 THESSALONIANS 5:23

I know I've quoted this passage many times as it is so important that we know the truest thing about us. Ephesians 1:4 teaches that in our original portrait we were holy, blameless, and embracing agape; Leviticus 20:7 says we have to be sanctified to be holy; 1 Thessalonians 5:23 states we have to be sanctified to be blameless; and then 1 Timothy 1:5 further states that to have agape love our hearts have to be sanctified or purified.

> Sanctify yourselves therefore, and be ye holy: for I am the LORD your God.
> —LEVITICUS 20:7

> Now the end of the commandment is charity [*agape*] out of a pure [cleansed for temple use] heart [spirit], and of a good conscience, and of faith unfeigned.
> —1 TIMOTHY 1:5

For us to be reconciled back to our original person as intended by God, we need to walk through the sometimes-lengthy process of sanctification.

> Elect [chosen] according to the foreknowledge of God the Father, through sanctification [purified for temple use] of the Spirit, unto obedience [submission] and sprinkling of the blood of Jesus Christ: Grace unto you, and peace, be multiplied.
> —1 PETER 1:2

Peter says that the result of our sanctification is our obedience or submission to the King of kings.

Though Jesus was perfect He still had to learn obedience:

> Though he were a Son, yet learned he obedience by the things which he suffered.
> —HEBREWS 5:8

If Jesus had to learn obedience, how much more would I have to do to learn it; and I would have to learn it by going through much difficulty. The difference with me is that my sin put me into the fixes that led to suffering, whereas Christ had no fault in Him, and His suffering was the consequence of my sin, which manifested in considerable evil against the Son of God. Christ's obedience led to His blood being shed, blood that was not tainted with any sin or iniquity so it qualified as the ultimate disinfectant for purging my sin.

It is written, "For the blood is the life" (Deut. 12:23). The transfusion of the blood of the only begotten Son of the Father reintroduced to the human race pure blood after Adam tainted it for all his future generations.

> And almost all things are by the law purged with blood; and without shedding of blood is no remission.
> —HEBREWS 9:20 26

As sin brings death, blood brings life. Blood is the antidote for sin, as it gives life where death reigned. Shed pure blood is the result of the sacrifice of love and obedience; sin is the result of pride and rebellion. The sacrifice of Jesus trumps the dead works of Satan.

> How much more shall the blood of Christ, who through the eternal Spirit offered himself without spot [blameless] to God, purge [purify for temple use] your conscience [the filter of the mind or soul] from dead works [destitute of meaning] to serve the living God?
> —HEBREWS 9:14

The application of the blood of Christ through the Holy Spirit purges or delivers us from what defiles our temple and it enables us to overcome the accuser, Satan.

> And I heard a loud voice saying in heaven, Now is come salvation, and strength, and the kingdom of our God, and the power of his Christ: for the accuser of our brethren is cast down, which accused them before our God day and night. And they overcame him by the blood of the Lamb, and by the word of their testimony; and they loved not their lives unto the death.
> —REVELATION 12:10

We read back in Philippians 2:12 that we are to work out our salvation with fear and trembling. That "workout" is defined as *sanctification*.

> Brethren beloved of the Lord, because God hath from the beginning chosen
> you to salvation through sanctification of the Spirit and belief of the truth.
> —2 THESSALONIANS 2:13

Working out your salvation involves the purifying process of sanctification that delivers you from the presence, penalty, power, and pleasure of sin. As mentioned earlier, you may have been taught that there is nothing you can do to earn your salvation. It should be taught that there is nothing you can do to earn eternal life, since you can't possibly pay the debt of your sin. Christ paid your debt in full through the shedding of blood. The result of the Cross is the message and hope of the gospel, but the blood shed thereon is the power over sin.

Salvation is not a single event; it is a continual process. Paul lays out the minister's role in the process of salvation, which involves the conviction of the Holy Spirit to open their eyes, their recovery from their captivity and infirmity, and their restoration to the agape of God, blameless and holy through sanctification.

> I have appeared unto thee for this purpose, to make thee a minister [an
> attendant to a King who renders service] and a witness [in legal applica-
> tion] both of these things which thou hast seen,...To open their eyes,
> and to turn [to bring back to the love and obedience of God] them from
> darkness to light [exposure], and from the power of Satan [legal control]
> unto God, that they may receive forgiveness [release from bondage to
> complete pardon] of sins, and inheritance [original purpose] among them
> which are sanctified [purify for temple use] by faith that is in me.
> —ACT 26:16, 18

The sanctification workout is a very powerful, yet simple daily approach to turn your darkness into light and to switch from the power of Satan onto the power of God in every area of your life. These steps will need to be committed to memory. We will practice this with you so that you'll have all the tools you'll need to conquer the enemy as you work out your salvation.

The level of victory you attain depends on you and what you are able to recognize in yourself. If you are using what you learn here to judge another's sin or start designs as to how you'll get a loved one to read this book, you'll see little change in your sanctification. The best witness to another is you being a model for the Lord's countenance. Don't give the devil an opportunity to steal, to kill, and to destroy. This is your time!

The Sanctiprize workout follows the biblical guideline set out by Paul in 2 Timothy. The role of the author is to teach with much Scripture, thus exposing the darkness; and once the darkness is exposed, to demonstrate how to purge your vessels so that you become sanctified. We must be sanctified for the Lord to be able to use us as He sees fit. The Lord gives the repentance, and you are given the weapons to recover yourself from the devil's captivity.

> Nevertheless the foundation of God standeth sure, having this seal, The
> Lord knoweth them that are his. And, Let every one that nameth the name

of Christ depart from iniquity. But in a great house there are not only vessels of gold and of silver, but also of wood and of earth; and some to honour, and some to dishonour. If a man therefore purge himself from these, he shall be a vessel unto honour, sanctified, and meet for the master's use, and prepared unto every good work. Flee also youthful lusts: but follow righteousness, faith, charity, peace, with them that call on the Lord out of a pure heart. But foolish and unlearned questions avoid, knowing that they do gender strifes. And the servant of the Lord must not strive; but be gentle unto all men, apt to teach, patient, In meekness instructing those that oppose themselves; if God peradventure will give them repentance to the acknowledging of the truth; And that they may recover themselves out of the snare of the devil, who are taken captive by him at his will.

—2 Timothy 2:19–26

1. See it. Expose your enemy.

Many of our sins are painfully obvious to us, yet there are other sins of equal importance to get rid of that we are clueless about. The hidden faults are not apparent to the conscience. A man may be suffering from many calamities resulting from an unknown cause that he doesn't know how to escape.

> My pride, unforgiveness, and judgment make it difficult to understand how I could possibly be in sin, but it helps me to see the sin in you!

Who can understand his errors [sin committed through inadvertence or by ignorance]? cleanse [purge out, purify] thou me from secret faults.

—Psalm 19:12

Even though we may be ignorant of the sin, we are still responsible. It is written that we are not to be "ignorant of the devil's devices." Ignorance of the law is no excuse. We are held accountable to know the Word and what the Lord requires of us.

> And if a soul sin, and commit any of these things which are forbidden to be done by the commandments of the Lord; though he wist it not [discerns or recognizes sin], yet is he guilty, and shall bear his iniquity.
> —Leviticus 5:17

The Word of God exposes the evil mind traffic, and it exposes the deeper hidden meditations of the heart or spirit. The Word also makes a distinction between sins that can affect our thoughts or actions and those that may be affecting our bodies. Sin is a created being, a spirit or a creature as stated in Hebrews, which operates in darkness hating the light of the Word.

> For the word of God is quick, and powerful, and sharper than any two edged sword, piercing [penetrating] even to the dividing asunder [separation] of soul and spirit, and of the joints and marrow, and is a discerner [judge] of the thoughts and intents of the heart. Neither is there any

creature [a created fallen spirit being] that is not manifest in his sight: but all things are naked and opened unto the eyes of him with whom we have to do.

—HEBREWS 4:12–13

These creatures are not you, they are unclean spirits, which you must discern or recognize in order to expose. God already knows of their existence, but it is your responsibility to deal with them; there are no shortcuts.

My pride, unforgiveness, and judgment make it difficult to understand how I could possibly be in sin, but it helps me to see the sin in you!

If you do not expose your sin, it will expose itself; and it will be a whole lot more painful with perhaps open shame, a distant God, and/or inflictions such as disease and calamity. Our sin stinks and often only others can smell it.

Behold, ye have sinned against the LORD: and be sure your sin will find you out.

—NUMBERS 32:23

What may be sin to one person may not be sin to another. Each of us has gifts (muscles and resources we manage, we don't possess them) that are to be used as the assignment presents itself. If we don't use our gifts, it is a sin because firstly it is rebellion and secondly it denies the intended recipient of what they are in need of.

Therefore to him that knoweth to do good, and doeth it not, to him it is sin.

—JAMES 4:17

Discernment is the gift that allows us to "see it" and to know what to do with evil once it is recognized. A believer who has matured in discernment will be able to recognize their sin immediately by its affect on others or how they are affected emotionally, spiritually, or physically. They'll say they can't get away with anything anymore; that is a good thing.

Strong meat belongeth to them that are of full age [mature], even those who by reason of use have their senses exercised to discern [judging] both good and evil.

—HEBREWS 5:14

2. Own it. Yes, I did it and I have no excuse for what I did.

To "own it" is to admit your participation with sin without justifying yourself and deflecting accusation towards another. If you have blamed another, you have added sin onto sin, which is what Satan wants.

The very first sin recorded in the Bible exposes this "duck and deflect" weakness. When the Lord approached Adam about his rebellion, he said, "The woman whom thou gavest to be with me, she gave me of the tree, and I did eat" (Gen. 3:12). When the Lord asked the woman, she said, "The serpent beguiled me, and I did eat" (v. 13). Job 31:33 records that Adam never did own up to his sin: "If I covered my transgressions as Adam, by hiding mine iniquity in my bosom." What would have happened with generational sin if Adam and Eve had "owned it"?

One who denies sin has a creature channeling through him to intimidate the one confronting so as to remain hidden in the darkness it needs to survive. Sin concealed with the debt unpaid gives Satan a legal right to place a curse upon us, thus we will not prosper in corresponding areas of our lives. One who confesses sin breaks the stranglehold of that sin; and it must loose us, allowing the curse to be turned into a blessing.

> He that covereth [deny or conceal] his sins shall not prosper [be successful]: but whoso confesseth [to point out, to cast out] and forsaketh [loosed] them shall have mercy [compassion and tender affection].
> —Proverbs 28:13

When we lie we think we are protecting ourselves, but actually we are tricked into working as a double agent for the devil to keep him concealed. Truth busts.

> If we say that we have no sin, we deceive [consent to the seduction of the devil] ourselves, and the truth is not in us....If we say that we have not sinned, we make him a liar, and his word is not in us.
> —1 John 1:8, 10

If we hide our sins we agree with Satan and call God a liar—that's bad! How do we call him a liar? We call God a liar when He calls something a sin and we say, "No, God. That is not a sin anymore."

3. Confess it. Now that you've owned up to it let it go.

> If we confess [deep conviction resulting in admitting guilt] our sins, he is faithful and just to forgive us our sins, and to cleanse [purify for temple use] us from all unrighteousness.
> —1 John 1:9

So it follows that righteousness chases our repentance. Confession is a scrub brush that cleanses our temple.

I had a schoolteacher that would say, "I'll find out who is responsible for this. There are two ways to do this; there is an easy way and there is a hard way. The choice is yours!" The same, of course, goes for dealing with our sin. Every sin incurs a debt that needs to be reconciled.

> As many as I love, I rebuke [convict or use light to expose] and chasten [to mold character by affliction]: be zealous [earnestly pursue good] therefore, and repent.
> —Revelation 3:19

Zealousness is to leave no stone unturned in the pursuit of sanctification. For therapy I built a fishpond in my front yard with an arched bridge and a couple of waterfalls. There is one thing that has tormented me; an elusive water leak somewhere in the thick rubber membrane that lined the pond has allowed about one hundred gallons of water a day to escape. You would think that with that much water draining it would be easy to find the hole, but it wasn't. So to find the holes I eventually resigned myself to the task of individually picking up and removing in excess of three tons of stones that covered the entire membrane, washing it, inspecting for holes, patching them up, and finally gently replacing the rock so as not to puncture the liner again.

> The process of sanctification for me was a drawn-out process for one main reason. I confessed a lot of dirt in my life, but I did much of it as an exercise of the mind just to get through it all.

In my zeal to find the leak, no stone was left unturned. Now as I love God and I fear God, I don't want any nasty hidden sin to drain the power of the Spirit out of me; so I am sure to be very zealous to cleanse my temple of anything that defiles.

The process of sanctification for me was a drawn-out process for one main reason. I confessed a lot of dirt in my life, but I did much of it as an exercise of the mind just to get through it all. What I am aware of now is that genuine repentance occurs at the level of the spirit or heart. My spirit, therefore, has to be opened up to get to the heart of the matter. The Lord admonished in the parable of the unrighteous servant that if we don't forgive from the heart, neither will He forgive us.

Temptation is an invitation to check out the kingdom of this world, and when we fall it is obvious we checked out what Satan was selling. Repentance occurs when we fall out of agreement with Satan's seduction and return home.

> That they should repent and turn to God, and do works meet [corresponding to] for repentance.
>
> —ACTS 26:20

Works meet for repentance must be understood as what God desires to be done to repay the debt, especially if the debt has been turned over to the tormentors and Satan has exacted usury through the placement of a curse.

A curse is often the result of generational iniquity and requires one to stand in the gap to take responsibility so the curse may be broken.

> Keeping mercy for thousands, forgiving iniquity and transgression and sin, and that will by no means clear the guilty; visiting the iniquity of the fathers upon the children, and upon the children's children, unto the third and to the fourth generation.
>
> —EXODUS 34:7

To break a generational curse requires humble confession of our sins and acknowledgement of the iniquity of our bloodline and then applying the finished work of Jesus Christ on the cross to break the legal right of Satan to afflict our sons and daughters.

> If they shall confess their iniquity, and the iniquity of their fathers, with
> their trespass which they trespassed against me, and that also they have
> walked contrary unto me; And that I also have walked contrary unto
> them, and have brought them into the land of their enemies; if then their
> uncircumcised hearts be humbled, and they then accept of the punish-
> ment of their iniquity.
> —LEVITICUS 26:40–41

God joins arms with fellow believers to restore and heal His kids. When praying for the sick, we error if we just demand God heal and are too afraid to deal with the possibility of sin first. God is holy, and we can't expect a holy God to heal us while remaining unrepentant in sin. Not all infirmity is the result of sin, as James points out that while they are ministering *if* he has sinned they will be forgiven during the works of healing. While we are praying we must ask God for discernment of good and evil to expose the works of darkness in order for restoration to wholeness of body, mind, and spirit. Personal fear or lack of knowledge by ministers keeps many people in their pain and suffering need-lessly. If the church body can't minister healing, then the poor saints have no choice but to scatter abroad to seek healing, or rather temporary management, of their disease by seeking the healing modalities out of Egypt.

> Is any sick among you? let him call for the elders of the church; and let
> them pray over him, anointing him with oil in the name of the Lord:
> And the prayer of faith shall save the sick, and the Lord shall raise him
> up; and if he have committed sins, they shall be forgiven him. Confess
> your faults [sin, lapse in good judgment or blunder] one to another, and
> pray one for another, that ye may be healed [freed from sins and cured].
> The effectual fervent prayer of a righteous man availeth much.
> —JAMES 5:14–16

Is it really that simple to confess sins, pray, and be healed? That is called first works and they work.

Once we *see it*, *own it*, and *confess it*—*then* God hears our prayers again, forgives us, and opens the heavens to bless us and to reverse our afflictions.

A Prayer of Repentance

Father God, my sin is exposed and I take responsibility for myself and my ancestors for the iniquities of _____. I confess, I renounce, and I ask forgiveness for this rebellion against You; and I ask that the curse be broken in the name of Jesus Christ of Nazareth.

4. Purge it. Pull it up by the roots and cast it out.

Every sin you can possibly think of has one source, the devil. In the area that we sin or are unrighteous, we are of the devil. The devil doesn't like it when he is singled out, so to some readers he will be whispering these thoughts: "Well, my sin is of the flesh or mine is of the world or I'm a Christian so the devil can't touch me." Test the spirits or the arguments you have with the Word and then you have a decision to make. Yes, there are sins of the flesh or of the world, but the source is still the devil, the god of this world. Yes, you are a Christian, but if you sin, are you of God in that area of your life or of the devil? So once you have fallen out of agreement and confessed sin, the devil has to be purged, as he has no more legal right to vex you. Jesus' purpose was to destroy the works of the devil. Our purpose is the same: to remove one kingdom and to replace it with another.

> God joins arms with fellow believers to restore and heal His kids. When praying for the sick, we error if we just demand God heal and are too afraid to deal with the possibility of sin first. God is holy and we can't expect a holy God to heal us while remaining unrepentant in sin.

> He that committeth sin is of the devil; for the devil sinneth from the beginning. For this purpose the Son of God was manifested, that he might destroy the works of the devil. Whosoever is born of God doth not commit sin; for his seed remaineth in him: and he cannot sin, because he is born of God. In this the children of God are manifest, and the children of the devil: whosoever doeth not righteousness is not of God, neither he that loveth [*agapeo*] not his brother.
> —1 JOHN 3:8–9

As sin and unrighteousness are of the devil, so is the boundary that prevents us from being able to agape our brother or sister as God intended. To agape our neighbor as ourself is a command; to agape God with all are heart, soul, mind, and body is a command. So when we fall short and can't agape as we ought, we are in sin and that sin is of the devil. Guess who doesn't want the true love of God to be spread throughout the world?

We are able to "phileo" or "eros" love (lust) in the flesh, but agape is of the spirit so therefore a purged temple is required for agape to take root. All works of the devil must be purged before we can obey the greatest commandments: to agape God and to agape our neighbor as our self.

> On these two commandments hang all the law and the prophets.
> —MATTHEW 22:40

What is meant by the law and the prophets hang on the two agape commands? It is because in the kingdom of God we have an agape-based government law system. Contrast that to countries that have a history as British colonies, their law is based on the British Common Law system. Accordingly court decisions made in England since the eleventh century are the foundation from which law is interpreted in the United States, Canada, Australia, and other countries of British ancestry.

Satan, the usurper god of this world, has based his laws on his foundational declarations called "The Five I Wills of Lucifer":

> What is meant by the law and the prophets hang on the two agape commands? It is because in the kingdom of God we have an agape-based government law system. Satan the usurper god of this world has based his laws on his foundational declarations called "The Five I Wills of Lucifer."

How art thou fallen from heaven, O Lucifer, son of the morning! how art thou cut down to the ground, which didst weaken the nations! For thou hast said in thine heart, *I will* ascend into heaven, *I will* exalt my throne above the stars of God: *I will* sit also upon the mount of the congregation, in the sides of the north: *I will* ascend above the heights of the clouds; *I will* be like the most High.

—ISAIAH 14:12–14, EMPHASIS ADDED

With the "Five I Wills" as the basis for worldly government, what would be the eventual outcome? I think we would see a world where pride or selfish ambition would be behind every action, every movement, every conflict, every form of pleasure, and every fad. We would have a world where one's own laws usurped the divine laws and were stubbornly in opposition to everything of God, in spite of the reckless disregard for one's own well-being. All roads would eventually lead to destruction, death, and darkness.

As "agape" is the love of God; "pride" is the *love* of Satan!

The purpose of every Christ follower is to replace the hijacked kingdom of this world empowered by pride with the only legitimate kingdom of God empowered by agape. Therefore, fellow messengers, what can be expected when you come up against a principality of pride at every stage of your assignment? Will you be welcomed or rejected? Will you be facing intimidating gates of brass or an open door with the welcome lights on? Will you find love or scorn? Will you be strong? Will you be courageous? Will you do it?

This battle is a fight to the death so it will not be easy. No you can't do it on your own, but:

> The weapons of our warfare are not carnal, but mighty through God to the pulling down of strongholds.
> —2 CORINTHIANS 10:4

Jesus teaches how to pull down strongholds by using His name to do it. He calls it purging or cleansing.

In the Millennium where Christ rules the kingdom of God to govern planet earth, He will introduce a new system of government based on the laws of agape. We are now in agape tactical training camp, where we will learn the rules of engagement with the enemy and the guidelines for restoration recovery, and restoration of those ravaged by conflict. Agape is the only spiritual gift that goes on for eternity; and therefore, eternity's assignments will be based on our agape resume. Our resume can only be developed while at earth school.

When agape gushes forth through us to God, others, and ourselves, we will have reached full maturity and we will be complete, lacking nothing. Consider how could we sin against our neighbor with anger, envy, or theft if we "agaped" him? How could we have self-rejection and addiction or do things that would defile our temple if we "agaped" ourselves? Furthermore, it would be impossible to lack faith or doubt or rebel against our God when we perfect love (agape) Him.

For some of you friends this could be the turning point in your life. Without the tools to work out our salvation, we may face the inevitable as the believers did in the writing of the Hebrews:

> Take heed, brethren, lest there be in any of you an evil heart of unbelief [lack faith], in departing from the living God.
> —HEBREWS 3:12

> Lot was vexed, which is to be constantly bombarded with evil in an attempt to get him to break down through exhaustion to participate with the filth that enveloped him.

Unbelief is sin for the believer, and all sin is of the devil. Unbelief, if not dealt with, pulls the Christian to a point of departure. Unbelief in one area must mean belief in another. If we have unbelief in the kingdom of God, then by default we have belief in the kingdom of this world, so how can we remove what we believe in?

a. Vexed stage door

The Bible says that Lot lived in a city that constantly vexed him. In the Scriptures there are at least twenty-six different Greek and Hebrew words translated to the English terms *vex*, *vexed*, or *vexation*. Lot was vexed (*kataponeo*), which is to be constantly bombarded with evil in an attempt to get him to break down through exhaustion to participate with the filth that enveloped him. Everywhere he looked would be pop-up screens, pictures, advertisements, sensually dressed women, lewd behavior, movies, and songs to get him to soften his stance on sin. That which would have been off limits at one point, he would accept as a way of modern life.

It wasn't that long ago that to live "common law" with a boyfriend or girlfriend was considered total taboo. My first posting with the Royal Canadian Mounted Police was to a small town of about five hundred people in southern Alberta, Canada, in the summer of 1980. In that small town was one young couple that shacked up; what a scandal! In a small rural town where everyone knew your personal business before you did, the verbal tabloids headlined this arrangement for months. But within five years, few would even notice "living in sin," as it was often scorned became the moray of even behind-the-times Canada. Satan knows how to vex us to the breaking point by making something so commonplace that our conscience becomes ineffective to keep us on the straight and narrow.

Lot chose to live in sin city, and was vexed (*kataponeo*) by the depravity, which was very reckless as the devil was like a fly on the front doorframe, waiting for the door to open so he could enter and multiply like crazy. Lot survived the test but his beloved wife was "assaulted" and became a pillar in her community—Sodom. Lot's wife, when given the opportunity to choose between eternal righteousness with God or eternal depravity with the "lusters" of pleasure, chose the pleasure route but was turned into a pillar of salt as an example to those that would look back at their old days of "freedom."

> And turning the cities of Sodom and Gomorrha into ashes condemned [judged] them with an overthrow [destruction], making them an ensample [a warning] unto those that after should live ungodly; And delivered just Lot, vexed [*kataponeō*; to exhaust or break down] with the filthy conversation [*eros*; unbridled selfish lust] of the wicked [one who knows no restraint to gratify his lusts].
>
> —2 PETER 2:6–7

The open, unashamed sensuality of Sodom and Gomorrah are examples of what many cities in North America are exposing, including the city that knows no boundaries—the Internet. Eros in Greek mythology was the primordial god of lust, beauty, love, and intercourse; he was also worshiped as a fertility deity. His Roman counterpart was Cupid, "desire."

So what is vexing you? Fear of poverty; habits or chosen lifestyle of a child; health and well-being of a loved one or yourself; abuse by one who is supposed to love you; false doctrine in your church; gossip and rumors spread to murder your reputation; unfair treatment in the marketplace; the seductive beauty of another's wife; the thoughtfulness and attentiveness of another man; the will of God; pornography; fantasy romance; the loss of a beloved one; lack of sleep; guilt and condemnation over sin and past failure; accounts receivable; constant mind traffic, anxiety, or worry; a friend or family member; retirement; legal or court proceedings; divorce; inability to overcome addictions, anger, or fill in the blank _____; you're not sure.

b. Vexed body

Satan knows the formidable empowerment the Christian has through obedience to the commandment to agape our Lord God with the entirety of each part of our being; body, soul, mind, and spirit. We'll see through Scripture that the devil knows how to separate out each of these areas of our being to entice us into disobedience as all he has to do is get us to open a door of vexation to any or all of our body, soul, mind, or spirit. Once he has won a battle with any part, we are then in rebellion to the one command we were to get right.

> And he answering said, Thou shalt love [*agapeo*] the Lord thy God with all thy heart [spirit], and with all thy soul [higher level of reasoning which

reflects the spirit of man], and with all thy strength [body and physical attributes], and with all thy mind [lower level of understanding and faculty of desire]; and thy neighbour as thyself.

—LUKE 10:27

In the church of Corinth was a believing couple living in open sexual sin. They were excommunicated in order for them to go through a time of sifting by Satan, where their bodies were to be afflicted with the view of their spirits still retaining eternal life in Jesus. Only a believer has a spirit that will spend eternity with Jesus, so this passage is not referring to the heathen.

To deliver [to give custody to Satan for the purposes of being harassed and tormented with devils] such an one unto Satan for the destruction of the flesh [body], that the spirit may be saved in the day of the Lord Jesus.

—1 CORINTHIANS 5:5

Some say that once a Christian, we are untouchable by Satan; but what does the Word teach? It takes a lot of scriptural gymnastics to explain this all away. The real problem is that Satan has used religious authorities to deflect suspicion from himself thus remaining under the radar of discovery and able to continue his covert operations until He has achieved total destruction of his target.

> When we cease to fear how serious God is about obedience and right living we then reap the fruit of apathy.

Ministers with the discernment of vexation will be able to set a tormented person free as Christ did with the grievously pained paralyzed servant.

And saying, Lord, my servant lieth at home sick of the palsy [paralytic], grievously [vehemently, very fearful] tormented [*basanizō*; vexed and tortured with intense pains]...And Jesus said unto the centurion, Go thy way; and as thou hast believed, so be it done unto thee. And his servant was healed in the selfsame hour.

—MATTHEW 8:6, 13

Satan vexes us into disobedience of the Word in order to gain legal right to bring us into slavery. Recall how he tricked Eve to gain entrance into the human race. Eve was a believer who had daily fellowship with God.

If thou wilt not observe to do all the words of this law that are written in this book, that thou mayest fear this glorious and fearful name, THE LORD THY GOD; Then the LORD will make thy plagues wonderful, and the plagues of thy seed, even great plagues, and of long continuance, and sore sicknesses, and of long continuance. Moreover he will bring upon thee all the diseases of Egypt, which thou wast afraid of; and they shall cleave unto thee. Also every sickness, and every plague, which is not written in the book of this law, them will the LORD bring upon thee, until thou be destroyed.

—DEUTERONOMY 28:58–61

When we cease to fear how serious God is about obedience and right living, we then reap the fruit of apathy. The fruits of this apathy are every sickness, plague, disease and infirmity that afflicts the body through a period that seems like eternity. But that is the point to get us to realize that eternal torment is what our options are if we continue in the lie that vexed.

> The LORD shall send upon thee cursing, vexation, and rebuke, in all that thou settest thine hand unto for to do, until thou be destroyed, and until thou perish quickly; because of the wickedness of thy doings [unethical practices], whereby thou hast forsaken me [conned into taking on a lie as not familiar enough with the shepherd].
> —DEUTERONOMY 28:20

An effective intercessory prayer is demonstrated by the woman of Canaan. Her daughter was vexed to the point of total destruction. Regardless of the severity of demonic control the relief is the same through Jesus Christ:

> And, behold, a woman of Canaan came out of the same coasts, and cried unto him, saying, Have mercy on me, O Lord, thou Son of David; my daughter is grievously [destroying, perishing] vexed [*daimonizomai*; to express the mind and character of a particularly violent demon] with a devil....Then Jesus answered and said unto her, O woman, great is thy faith: be it unto thee even as thou wilt. And her daughter was made whole from that very hour.
> —MATTHEW 15:22, 28

The next passage uses the word *possessed* in place of *vexed*, whereas the Greek word is the same. It doesn't matter what you call it, but you must call it!

> Then was brought unto him one possessed [*daimonizomai*] with a devil, blind, and dumb: and he healed him, insomuch that the blind and dumb both spake and saw.
> —MATTHEW 12:22

A vexation by unclean spirits can add disease or take away such things as the senses. Ministry simply demands the devil to go taking his fowl fruit with him.

> As they went out, behold, they brought to him a dumb man possessed [*daimonizomai*] with a devil.
> —MATTHEW 9:32

Our tongue puts into words whatever defilement may be within our heart. Our words become our vows, which set up mountains of regret and injustice against those we have the power to destroy—those who open up their heart to blindly trust us.

> And the tongue is a fire [exercises a destructive power over others], a world of iniquity [false judgment and injustice]: so is the tongue among our members, that it defileth the whole body, and setteth on fire [kindles

the most pernicious evil] the course of nature [origin]; and it is set on fire of hell.

—JAMES 3:6

Those words preheat the oven and cook our birthright.

c. Vexed mind or soul

Workers of iniquity can manifest by seizing the mind either partially or completely. Often it is temporary insanity where the elevator door refuses to open on a couple of floors. Matthew writes that the epileptic fellow was miserably vexed having an apparent death wish by a devil. The devil's vexation was cancelled by the words of Jesus and the boy was cured.

> Lord, have mercy on my son: for he is lunatic [epileptic?], and sore [miserable] vexed [*paschō*; physical suffering as the result of demonic power]: for ofttimes he falleth into the fire, and oft into the water.... And Jesus rebuked the devil; and he departed out of him: and the child was cured from that very hour.
>
> —MATTHEW 17:15, 18

Many people have been set free of food allergies by owning up to sin that would give fear permission to vex our souls. The iniquities are generationally opening the door to afflict the very young. The psalmist teaches that our bodies reject all manner of food because of sin and generational iniquity:

> Fools [despise wisdom] because of their transgression, and because of their iniquities, are afflicted. Their soul abhorreth all manner of meat; and they draw near unto the gates of death.
>
> —PSALM 107:17–18

A foolish person frolics with sin, apparently indifferent to the fear of God, and then is perplexed when afflicted with infirmity coming face-to-face with untimely death.

I find it astounding how many Christians find it difficult to even consider that their problems or diseases may be symptoms of a defiled temple that is in desperate need of a good cleanse. Deuteronomy 28 portrays the variety of curses that molest folks and Proverbs notes that a curse has a cause or a root.

> As the bird by wandering, as the swallow by flying, so the curse causeless shall not come.
>
> —PROVERBS 26:2

Many pray for the symptom to go away, but it won't until it is pulled up with all the roots. What happens when you cut off the visible part of weeds in your lawn? They continue to have a field day, multiplying like crazy unless you discover that you have to get rid of the root.

If I asked you whether the law of God was

> A foolish person frolics with sin, apparently indifferent to the fear of God, and then is perplexed when afflicted with infirmity coming face-to-face with untimely death.

a delight to you or a restriction cramping your lifestyle and intentions, what would be your honest reply?

> And if ye shall despise my statutes, or if your soul abhor [show contempt] my judgments, so that ye will not do all my commandments, but that ye break my covenant: I also will do this unto you; I will even appoint over you terror [trouble, dismay], consumption [wasting disease of the lungs], and the burning ague [high fever], that shall consume the eyes [failing eyesight], and cause sorrow of heart [pine away, broken hearted]: and ye shall sow your seed in vain, for your enemies shall eat it. And I will set my face against you, and ye shall be slain before your enemies: they that hate you shall reign over you; and ye shall flee when none pursueth you. And if ye will not yet for all this hearken unto me, then I will punish you seven times more for your sins.
>
> —LEVITICUS 26:15–18

Our Lord lists the short list here of curses just to get your attention, and if that fails there is more where that came from. We say that isn't fair; then you don't understand the concept of hell that He is trying to divert us from. These afflictions are like warning notifications compared to the life sentence of eternal torment.

> Many pray for the symptom to go away, but it won't until it is pulled up with all the roots.

d. Vexed spirit

You know there are lots of arguments as to how a Christian may or may not be vexed by a devil. It appears that at the time of Christ the same questions were put forward. Jesus said, "Do you not understand, do you not perceive that all evil defilement that we participate with comes out of the heart?" This rules out the flesh, the mind, or the idea of the devil whispering in our ear. I'm OK with what Jesus taught, what about you? He states it so clearly that only a Pharisee could twist it out of context.

> Are ye so without understanding also? Do ye not perceive, that whatsoever thing from without entereth into the man, it cannot defile him; Because it entereth not into his heart, but into the belly, and goeth out into the draught, purging all meats? And he said, That which cometh out of the man, that defileth the man. For from within, out of the heart [spirit] of men, proceed evil thoughts, adulteries, fornications, murders, thefts, covetousness, wickedness, deceit, lasciviousness, an evil eye, blasphemy, pride, foolishness: All these evil things come from within, and defile [temple rendered unclean] the man.
>
> —MARK 7:18–22

> He states it so clear that only a Pharisee could twist it out of context.

First John states that all the sins are of the devil. If we commit any sin, the devil is the source and any sin we commit originates from within our heart or spirit. Therefore, to cleanse the defilement out of our temple, our spirit, we know with whom we are dealing.

> He that committeth sin is of the devil; for the devil sinneth from the beginning. For this purpose the Son of God was manifested, that he might destroy [release the bonds of anyone defiled] the works of the devil.
>
> —1 John 3:8

Paul provides further witness giving testimony of his own battle with overcoming personal sin. He said it is the evil that dwells within him that burps out his nasty activities that he is unable to restrain as it says stuff before he knows what happened. Only a living being or a spirit dwells. If the sin that Paul refers to were not alive but dead, every little thing would be OK, as we would be dead to sin therefore perfect.

> For I know that in me that is, in my flesh, dwelleth [operative in one's heart] no good thing: for to will is present with me; but how to perform that which is good I find not. For the good that I would I do not: but the evil which I would not, that I do. Now if I do that I would not, it is no more I that do it, but sin that dwelleth in me. I find then a law, that, when I would do good, evil is present with me. For I delight in the law of God after the inward man: But I see another law in my members, warring against the law of my mind, and bringing me into captivity to the law of sin which is in my members. O wretched man that I am! who shall deliver me from the body of this death? I thank God through Jesus Christ our Lord. So then with the mind I myself serve the law of God; but with the flesh the law of sin.
>
> —Romans 7:18–25

The result of vexation was captivity or slavery to one Paul did not want to be associated with, the devil. Paul says that even when he is righteous, this evil defilement is still there waiting to strut its dirt. The question is asked, "Who can deliver me?" The answer is Jesus.

A lie just seems to roll off the tongue before I even open my mouth to speak. Ananias, a member of the early church, had a problem with telling lies to make him look better to others. Satan is identified as the originator of the lie that defiled his heart.

> But Peter said, Ananias, why hath Satan filled thine heart to lie to the Holy Ghost, and to keep back part of the price of the land?
>
> —Acts 5:3

The question is asked, "Who can deliver me?" The answer is Jesus.

Anger, exasperation, and indignation are common vexations from the devil that dig their claws into our spirits if we allow ourselves to try to sleep it off. The devil will do whatever he can to put you to sleep in your stuff so you'll wake up the next day with problems that have now grown sevenfold.

Be ye angry [provoked or aroused to anger], and sin not [wander]: let not the sun go down upon your wrath [vexed with indignation or exasperation]: Neither give place [opportunity to act and inhabit] to the devil.
—Ephesians 4:26–27

The writers of the Old Testament also understood that sin rests in our spirits, and like a volcano erupts and then retreats again only to explode when it will do the most damage.

> A lie just seems to roll off the tongue before I even open my mouth to speak.

Be not hasty [*bahal*; compelled with urgent need to explode] in thy spirit to be angry: for anger resteth in the bosom of fools.
—Ecclesiastes 7:9

Serious crimes are the result of being vexed by the devil. David's son Amnon allowed his heart to trip out on his sexual lust for his stepsister Tamar. The devil had total control over Amnon, his slave, forcing him to perform the unthinkable. The scripture states that as soon as Amnon had his way with her, he then hated Tamar with more passion than the lust he had that drove him to rape her in the first place.

And Amnon was so vexed [*yatsar*; to bind or besiege, overtaken], that he fell sick for his sister Tamar; for she was a virgin; and Amnon thought it hard for him to do any thing to her.
—2 Samuel 13:2

Vexation of our spirit doesn't have to result in what we typically think as sin. Solomon said his unquenchable thirst for education and knowledge vexed him. In other writings Solomon said he was also be vexed by excessive work, fantasy, creativity, building, and possessions.

And I gave my heart to know wisdom, and to know madness and folly: I perceived that this also is vexation [*ra`yown*; striving after wind, vain desire] of spirit.
—Ecclesiastes 1:17

We are to beware of the devices of Satan. He may use the desires of a close family member to vex you to do exceedingly evil things. Jezebel introduces some of the most vial wickedness to Israel, firstly through seduction of Ahab the king, and then her treachery defiled her generations. Jezebel's daughter Athaliah vexed her son Ahaziah to be a slave in the hand of the devil to bring great destruction to a once mighty kingdom.

He also walked in the ways of the house of Ahab: for his mother was his counsellor to do wickedly [*rasha*; vexed to act devilishly in ethical, civil and religious relations]. Wherefore he did evil in the sight of the Lord like the house of Ahab: for they were his counsellors after the death of his father to his destruction.
—2 Chronicles 22:3–4

Similarly, in the New Testament, Herod's wife, Herodias, vexes her daughter to demand the murder of John the Baptist at the hand of her father. This clever scheme netted the slavery of the entire royal family, as all were guilty of the unjustified murder.

> And she, being before instructed of her mother, said, Give me here John Baptist's head in a charger.
>
> —MATTHEW 14:8

The stage door to vexation is opened either on purpose or accidently by yourself or one of your ancestors, and then you are vexed from within. Most sin falls into this category when we are troubled by unclean spirits, which are seeking to defile our temple so as to disqualify us from the Master's use. They are seeking to remove the possibility of us realizing agape love.

Confusion is really being double-minded as you waiver between the fruits of the Spirit of God and the corresponding lies of the accuser of the brethren. This ranges from the inability to concentrate in reading the Bible, to infirmity, to conforming to worldly things to doubt, to unbelief, and to fear.

> There came also a multitude out of the cities round about unto Jerusalem, bringing sick folks, and them which were vexed [*ochleo*; confusion, troubled or molested by demons] with unclean spirits [depravity or sin that would defile our temple]: and they were healed [restored] every one.
>
> —ACTS 5:16

The early church grew because that is where the answers were. The unclean spirits that vexed them were purged in the name of Jesus and restoration took place, no therapy.

The recapture of Christians to return them to slavery is the devil's mandate. How many people, do you know that started out well in their walk as Christians only to overcome and fall later in life?

Our conscience is to work as an early warning system that the devil is on the prowl. The devil knows that to be effective he has to vex you slowly over time by breaking down your defense system first so that you change your mind on what you think is evil. Seduction always has an element of mystery and adventure to it. How are doctrines of devils taught? They are taught by seduced preachers and teachers whose sin has unplugged their conscience.

> Now the Spirit speaketh expressly, that in the latter times some shall depart from the faith, giving heed to seducing [to lead astray by a tramp] spirits, and doctrines [misleading teaching and alteration of God's Word] of devils; Speaking lies in hypocrisy; having their conscience seared with a hot iron.
>
> —1 TIMOTHY 4:1–2, AUTHOR'S PARAPHRASE

> **The recapture of Christians to return them to slavery is the devil's mandate.**

Every believer, especially those that are set apart for ministry in the church, parents or community leaders are open season for the fiery darts of the depraved sadistic ones.

Marriage vows are attacked to make a mockery of what God has put together. The vexation promising that liberty, identity, and adventure are really only available outside of the covenant of an existing marriage has little opposition within the self-adjusting doctrine of much of the Christian community. Eve was vexed by a devil promising another path to fulfillment. Now when Eve fell, did the devil come true on his promises? No, of course not. Eve was enticed to slavery through a curse she brought upon herself as did Adam.

> While they promise them liberty [freedom to do as one chooses, no accountability], they themselves are the servants [given over to control of a demon] of corruption [hell]: for of whom a man is overcome [*hēttaomai*; subservient, forced to submit via vexation to one who completely dominates] of the same is he brought in bondage [forced into slavery]. For if after they have escaped [through salvation] the pollutions [defilement of the godly by dabbling too close to depravity] of the world through the knowledge of the Lord and Saviour Jesus Christ, they are again [turned back as Lot's wife] entangled [weave in] therein, and overcome [enticed back to slavery], the latter end is worse with them than the beginning [accountable therefore judged according to knowledge].
> —2 Peter 2:19, author's emphasis and definitions added

An interesting thing I've noted through my kitchen window. The grass is not greener on the other side of the fence; the only place it is greener is on top of my septic tank!

Now a warning to my readers

If you are just reading this book out of curiosity with no intent to walk the way of total righteousness, it is better to shut the book now as we are about to show the way of righteousness and obedience to the holy commandment. It is better to be ignorant of this teaching than to know and return to your old ways. Returning to your vomit is a reference to swallowing up again what was previously cast out. A believer in Christ that asks for forgiveness of sins and then with premeditation follows a path back to the ways of their Egypt are judged much more severely than a nonbeliever. Peter reserves some strong language for those that have experienced cleansing through the blood of Jesus only to return to depravity.

> For it had been better for them not to have known the way of righteousness, than, after they have known it, to turn from the holy commandment delivered unto them. But it is happened unto them according to the true proverb, The dog is turned to his own vomit again; and the sow that was washed to her wallowing in the mire.
> —2 Peter 2:21–22

If a spirit is removed by a work of the Lord and then invited back in for the sake of some vicarious pleasure, the removed spirit is legally able to come back to torment sevenfold.

> When the unclean spirit is gone out [purged or cast out] of a man, he walketh through dry places, seeking rest; and finding none, he saith, I will return unto my house whence I came out. And when he cometh, he findeth it swept and garnished. Then goeth he, and taketh to him seven other spirits more wicked than himself; and they enter in, and dwell there: and the last state of that man is worse than the first.
> —LUKE 11:24–26

At this stage of vexation it is more difficult to find freedom, but there is still much hope for recovery and restoration as there is no mountain too vast that it can't be removed and leveled into the sea.

Purge the temple

Something that dishonors is not worthy to live within a believer's spirit, soul, mind, and body due to the high value Jesus Christ places on one whom He redeemed. To be restored to our original worth, we need to know how to purge our temples to be prepared for the Master's purposes.

> Let every one that nameth the name of Christ depart from iniquity [cease to be vexed]. But in a great house [a believer] there are not only vessels [spirit beings] of gold and of silver, but also of wood and of earth; and some to honour [fit for master's use] and some to dishonour [defiled]. If a man [a great house] therefore purge [thoroughly cleanse] himself from these, he shall be a vessel unto honour, sanctified, and meet [usable, acceptable] for the master's use, and prepared unto every good work.
> —2 TIMOTHY 2:19–21

A minister of restoration is instructed on the approach he is to take on his ministry with an individual in whom he discerns defilement. It is the goodness of the Lord that leads to repentance not the striving and desperation of the minister. Note that the individual recovers themselves through repentance and purging from the vexation of the devil. We don't need to run to a tent meeting every time we need to cleanse our temple. A minister that is dealing with personal uncleanness or hidden, unrepented sin has no business and will be of no effect in conducting this vital work of the ministry of reconciliation with others. The Bible teaches that we can be purged with the care of a sanctified minister or we can be taught to do it ourselves.

> A minister that is dealing with personal uncleanness or hidden unrepented sin has no business and will be of no effect in conducting this vital work of the ministry of reconciliation with others.

> And the servant of the Lord must not strive; but be gentle unto all men, apt to teach,

patient, In meekness instructing those that oppose themselves; if God peradventure will give them repentance to the acknowledging of the truth; And that they may recover themselves [purified for temple use] out of the snare [vexation or seduction] of the devil, who are taken captive by him at his will.

—2 TIMOTHY 2:24

Jesus provides insight into the devil's realm to assist us in the understanding of purging our temple of what has defiled it.

But if I with the finger of God cast out devils, no doubt the kingdom of God is come upon you. When a strong man armed keepeth his palace, his goods are in peace: But when a stronger than he shall come upon him, and overcome him, he taketh from him all his armour wherein he trusted, and divideth his spoils.

—LUKE 11:20–22

It is often said, "My flesh made me do it." Well, beat your flesh all you want to overcome your stuff, but it won't do a bit of good, as you've picked your fight with the wrong guy! And worse yet, the real culprit is getting away with murder. It's like a newspaper that is headlining the outbreak of worldwide war and you pick a fight with the paperboy. Our battle is against an organized squadron that knows no boundaries and consists of a hierarchy as laid out here in Ephesians:

For we wrestle not against flesh and blood, but against principalities [in charge of a dominion], against powers [a strongman of authority], against the rulers of the darkness of this world [the god of this world and his demons], against spiritual wickedness in high places.

—EPHESIANS 6:12

Jesus calls the leader of a devilish squad the strongman. In the next section we will identify several such strongmen. The person he inhabits is called the palace. His goods are in peace as long as he inhabits a being. The "goods" of a particular strongman are the symptom or manifestation by which he is named.

The strongman may be pride. The armor spoken of is the warriors or guards that keep the strongman of pride in power. Each piece of armor is a different destructive spiritual weapon, which distracts or acts as a decoy to prevent the strongman from being exposed. The one stronger than him is the believer that is walking in the authority of Jesus Christ to break apart the kingdom of darkness.

Satan's use of armor is to duplicate the system that God has determined for believers to keep the Holy Spirit producing good fruit in their lives. Good fruit is produced when we put on the armor of God to stand against the wiles of the devil and defeat him. Likewise Satan has armor to keep us in a state of rebellion so that we cannot produce fruit befitting a believer walking in agape. It is this armor of Satan's that must be understood in order to infiltrate and get victory over our addictive captivities. Without this understanding it will be impossible to overcome your addictions, as typically all we know to do is take steps towards governing our flesh and we know what good that will do.

The game of chess is not evil; but the organization of power in chess is similar to that of the kingdom of this world. In chess, the king is the strongman you are dealing with. The strongman has few moves of his own and relies on his armor to protect him and keep him in power within his palace. You may have to eliminate the pawns, knights, bishops, rooks, and the queen—his armor, before the king is exposed in order to check him out. The armor will perform all kinds of sideshows and destructive acts, which are decoys to make it difficult to identify and expose the strongman.

Each piece in a chess game has certain moves to take out or discourage his enemy, as in spiritual warfare. The pawn is like a foot soldier used as a tool by one of higher rank to exact a high rate of usury for unpaid debts by chipping away at many parts of our lives. As there are several pawns in a chess game that can inflict a lot of casualties because of their number, so also in warfare. Jesus removed a group of demons that identified themselves as Legion. A *legion* was the term commonly used for a body of more than four thousand soldiers. The bishop will use his religious rank to dispose scripture, to intimidate, or to twist doctrine so as to protect the strongman with dogma, tradition of men, theology, or spiritual control. The bishop will throw a slant on scripture that seems plausible, but it is off course. A knight is out to flex his intelligence in war with indirect and unperceived moves to vex you with his performance. A rook is a bird similar to a crow. A rook will steal the Word of God as it is planted in your life by causing confusion in the mind of the reader, inability to concentrate, doubt and unbelief, or a distraction to entice. The queen on a chessboard is more powerful, more treacherous, and has more moves than the king does. This is similar to the infamous Bible royal couple, Ahab and Jezebel. Ahab was a weak, apathetic king that was seduced by the sensuality, treachery, intimidation, and ungodly control of a treacherous worldly queen. In spiritual warfare, the king, though a principality, may have soldiers at his command that are much more fierce and treacherous than he.

How do we become a palace for a devil? If we (or our ancestors) allowed him entrance through a trapdoor, he sits on the throne of our life in that area and demands that we be subject to his every demand while exacting a criminal rate of interest on unpaid debts.

Overcoming sin is not a fleshly process of discipline, focus, habit, psychology, or counseling. It requires a mighty power to smash the devil's stronghold or palace and cast him down.

> For though we walk in the flesh, we do not war after the flesh: For the weapons of our warfare are not carnal [given to human weakness and frailty], but mighty through God to the pulling down of strong holds [a strongman fortified within his palace by his defiling armor]; Casting down [to destroy opponents likened to a fortress] imaginations [actions

following the verdict of a seared conscience], and every high thing that exalteth itself against the knowledge of God, and bringing into captivity every thought to the obedience of Christ.

—2 Corinthians 10:3–5

The "imaginations" may refer to hostile Christian doctrine, which stands against your freedom and allows the devil's kingdom to reign. These imaginations are to be cast from your spirit along with the other "high things" (the principalities and powers) that stand against the knowledge of God. The enemy is actively fighting and scheming to keep us from recognizing him as the root of sin and iniquity. He would have us blame our flesh for everything so he will be safe in his palace.

The phrase, "every high thing that exalteth itself against the knowledge of God," is in reference to the devil's ambition to fulfill his "Five I Wills."

For thou [Lucifer] hast said in thine heart, *I will* ascend into heaven, *I will* exalt my throne above the stars of God: *I will* sit also upon the mount of the congregation, in the sides of the north: *I will* ascend above the heights of the clouds; *I will* be like the most High.

—Isaiah 14:13–14, emphasis added

When we use the weapons that are "mighty through God in the pulling down of strongholds" our battle is not over, as we need to keep our temple fortified by the armor of God to prevent further invasion by these terrorists. A spirit that is purged and now outside of a man is in torment, as it needs a being to be its carrier; so it will attempt over and over to return to familiar territory. As soon as the door is opened by us falling into habitual sin, it returns; but he returns with his party crashers, the group of seven, to really thrash the house, as if to retaliate against his eviction.

When the unclean spirit is gone out of a man, he walketh through dry places, seeking rest; and finding none, he saith, I will return unto my house whence I came out. And when he cometh, he findeth it swept and garnished. Then goeth he, and taketh to him seven other spirits more wicked than himself; and they enter in, and dwell there: and the last state of that man is worse than the first.

—Luke 11:24

Many dismiss the possibility that a Christian can be vexed by devils, as they say good and evil can't coexist. That is part of the truth. Paul explains to those that are "worthy of the agape of God" that it doesn't work for a Christian to be double-minded trying to serve two kingdoms. He goes on to say that since it doesn't work, you have a choice to make: purge the evil or allow the wickedness to grieve the Holy Spirit who cannot empower a defiled temple.

And what concord [agreement] hath Christ with Belial [Satan]? or what part hath he that believeth with an infidel [heathen]? And what agreement hath the temple of God with idols [a belief system promoting the devil's

shadow gospel]? for ye are the temple of the living God; as God hath said, I will dwell in them, and walk in them; and I will be their God, and they shall be my people. Wherefore come out [forsake or depart] from among them, and be ye separate, saith the Lord, and touch not [carnal intercourse with heathen practices] the unclean thing [anything that defiles our temple]; and I will receive you, And will be a Father unto you, and ye shall be my sons and daughters, saith the Lord Almighty. Having therefore these promises, dearly beloved [*agapētos*; worthy of God's agape love], let us cleanse [purge, free from defilement of wickedness] ourselves from all filthiness of the flesh and spirit, perfecting holiness in the fear of God.
—2 Corinthians 6:15–7:1, author's paraphrase

How did Jesus teach us to purge our temple of defilement? Jesus simply called the spirit by its manifestation, its appearance, and commanded it to come out and to not return again.

When Jesus saw that the people came running together, he rebuked the foul spirit, saying unto him, Thou dumb and deaf spirit, I charge thee, come out of him, and enter no more into him.
—Mark 9:25

Jesus gave the minister of the church the empowerment to continue doing what He did simply by using His name.

And this did she many days. But Paul, being grieved, turned and said to the spirit, I command thee in the name of Jesus Christ to come out of her. And he came out the same hour.
—Acts 16:18

This ministry of purging is not a prayer. It is a command as you are speaking directly to a vexing spirit removing it from its palace by the authority of Jesus Christ. A believer receives this mighty voice-activated weapon of warfare when he is enlisted in the Lord's army; the pity is few believers are ever taught in basic training, or first works, in how to use it.

Command of Deliverance
(Must be out loud with eyes open. Realize you are speaking directly to the spirit.)

In the name of Jesus Christ of Nazareth and by the power of the Holy Spirit, I take authority over the spirit(s) of _____; I break your power, I cast you out, and command you to return no more.

(Some prefer to say, "In the name of Jesus Christ the Lamb of God who shed His blood for me," in the above prayer.)

You may or may not experience various sensations as your spirit is purged. Such sensations may include belching, yawning, coughing, screaming, dry heaving, abrupt movements, or vomiting. The devil has to go, but he sometimes makes a last ditch effort to remain by digging its hands and feet in and that may result in a sensation that something is caught in the throat, a band tightening, or a choking feeling. Just tell the spirit, "In the name of Jesus, loose me and tear at me no more. You must go in the name of Jesus."

First works are the activities required to cleanse the temple of God within us so that the glory of the Godhead would be at home in it. The temple is not cleansed solely for your benefit but for the benefit of God who created you so that He can reside in you, see though your eyes, speak through your lips, touch through your hands, inspire through your mind, and love through your heart.

> Thus saith the Lord GOD; I do not this for your sakes…but for mine holy name's sake, which ye have profaned [ritually or sexually violated] among the heathen, whither ye went. And I will sanctify my great name, which was profaned among the heathen, which ye have profaned in the midst of them; and the heathen shall know that I am the LORD, saith the Lord GOD, when I shall be sanctified in you before their eyes.
> —EZEKIEL 36:22–23

God's great name is profaned when we irreverently allow His temple to be exposed to the wickedness of Satan through our sin. God desires to bring us to repentance, do first works, and to sanctify our temples so that the heathen will see and believe the great name of the Lord. And, God wants to experience your life through you.

5. Overcome it.

Though the immediate rewards for cleansing our temple and overcoming sin are all the motivation we may need as we realize oneness with the Father, Jesus adds to the importance as in each of the letters to the seven churches in the Book of Revelation 2:7–3:21, He reveals the eternal perspective on overcoming this world's testing.

> He that hath an ear, let him hear what the Spirit saith unto the churches;
>
> [1] To him that overcometh will I give to eat of the tree of life, which is in the midst of the paradise of God.
> —REVELATION 2:7

Paradise sounds like the Garden of Eden as it was intended, but this time the tree of life is something of which we can partake. This tree produces a harvest every month—twelve varieties of fruit. This new kingdom of God has so much for us to experience, but the Scripture doesn't detail it, as we have no vocabulary or ability to understand its magnificence.

> And he shewed me a pure river of water of life, clear as crystal, proceeding out of the throne of God and of the Lamb. In the midst of the street of it, and on either side of the river, was there the tree of life, which bare twelve manner of fruits, and yielded her fruit every month: and the leaves of the tree were for the healing of the nations. And there shall be

no more curse: but the throne of God and of the Lamb shall be in it; and his servants shall serve him.
—REVELATION 22:1–3

[2] He that overcometh shall not be hurt of the second death.
—REVELATION 2:7

Jesus is referring to the church of Smyrna, which it appears will miss the rapture of the rest of the church and will in part be saved as the result of the trial of the Great Tribulation period. They will experience tribulation for a period of "ten days"; I will not speculate as to how long a time period that may be. They are encouraged to be faithful unto martyrdom. Martyrdom is their escape from this tribulation and the key to restoration to God.

> Fear none of those things which thou shalt suffer: behold, the devil shall cast some of you into prison, that ye may be tried; and ye shall have tribulation ten days: be thou faithful unto death, and I will give thee a crown of life.
> —REVELATION 2:10

The Tribulation provides a last opportunity for repentance and overcoming otherwise the future is dark.

> But the fearful, and unbelieving, and the abominable, and murderers, and whoremongers, and sorcerers, and idolaters, and all liars, shall have their part in the lake which burneth with fire and brimstone: which is the second death.
> —REVELATION 21:8

> [3] To him that overcometh will I give to eat of the hidden manna, and will give him a white stone, and in the stone a new name written, which no man knoweth saving he that receiveth it.
> —REVELATION 2:17

Regarding the church at Pergamos Jesus offers little more than eternal life to them due to their dabbling with the false doctrine of the Nicolaitans and Balaam; and furthermore, they were a stumbling block to others and committed fornication.

> But I have a few things against thee, because thou hast there them that hold the doctrine of Balaam, who taught Balac to cast a stumblingblock before the children of Israel, to eat things sacrificed unto idols, and to commit fornication. So hast thou also them that hold the doctrine of the Nicolaitanes, which thing I hate.
> —REVELATION 2:14–15

The deeds of the Nicolaitans are thought to be the ungodly hierarchy of believers.

Jesus Christ is the promised hidden manna that provides eternal life to overcomers.

Your fathers did eat manna in the wilderness, and are dead. This is the bread which cometh down from heaven, that a man may eat thereof, and not die. I am the living bread which came down from heaven: if any man eat of this bread, he shall live for ever: and the bread that I will give is my flesh, which I will give for the life of the world.

—JOHN 6:49–51

[4] And he that overcometh, and keepeth my works unto the end, to him will I give power over the nations

—REVELATION 2:26

In the church of Thyatira the folks had an appetite for the seduction of the spirit of Jezebel of which few repented so they would go directly into the Great Tribulation. In the next section we will have an in-depth look at Jezebel and then it will become apparent why the church folks that are in agreement with her were not spared from the judgment to come upon the earth.

Notwithstanding I have a few things against thee, because thou sufferest that woman Jezebel, which calleth herself a prophetess, to teach and to seduce my servants to commit fornication, and to eat things sacrificed unto idols. And I gave her space to repent of her fornication; and she repented not. Behold, I will cast her into a bed, and them that commit adultery with her into great tribulation, except they repent of their deeds.

—REVELATION 2:20–23

Those that were faithful or that would have repented for participation with the stuff of Jezebel were given a pass to the eternal kingdom of God with assignments to rule nations under the King of kings.

And the kingdom and dominion, and the greatness of the kingdom under the whole heaven, shall be given to the people of the saints of the most High, whose kingdom is an everlasting kingdom, and all dominions shall serve and obey him.

—DANIEL 7:27

The most difficult accomplishment in life has nothing to do with academics, sports, fame, money, or discovery; the most difficult accomplishment is overcoming Satan and finishing our lives well. That is why Jesus Christ rewards the greatest of rewards and future responsibilities.

It can be seen in these passages that it is wrong to assume all believers will receive special assignments or rewards in the kingdom that is to come.

[5] He that overcometh, the same shall be clothed in white raiment; and I will not blot out his name out of the book of life, but I will confess his name before my Father, and before his angels.

—REVELATION 3:5

It seems that only a few people in Sardis were able to hold fast, repent, and be judged worthy of eternal life. Those dressed in white are the bride that accompanies Christ to the Marriage Supper of the Lamb.

Remember therefore how thou hast received and heard, and hold fast, and repent. If therefore thou shalt not watch, I will come on thee as a thief, and thou shalt not know what hour I will come upon thee. Thou hast a few names even in Sardis which have not defiled their garments; and they shall walk with me in white: for they are worthy.

—Revelation 3:3–4

[6] Him that overcometh will I make a pillar in the temple of my God, and he shall go no more out: and I will write upon him the name of my God, and the name of the city of my God, which is new Jerusalem, which cometh down out of heaven from my God: and I will write upon him my new name

—Revelation 3:12

These believers would be assigned a role within the temple of almighty God. The church at Philadelphia was promised that they would escape the trials of the Great Tribulation because they kept the Word of God in fear and obedience. These overcomers will escape the entirety of the Great Tribulation by a supernatural exodus known as the rapture.

> The most difficult accomplishment in life has nothing to do with academics, sports, fame, money, or discovery; the most difficult accomplishment is overcoming Satan and finishing our lives well. That is why Jesus Christ rewards the greatest of rewards and future responsibilities.

Because thou hast kept the word of my patience, I also will keep thee from the hour of temptation [the Great Tribulation], which shall come upon all the world, to try them that dwell upon the earth.

—Revelation 3:10

A final warning is given as to how necessary it is that those that call the Lord Savior must possess their temple in honor unto the living God.

And there shall in no wise enter into it any thing that defileth, neither whatsoever worketh abomination, or maketh a lie: but they which are written in the Lamb's book of life.

—Revelation 21:27

[7] To him that overcometh will I grant to sit with me in my throne, even as I also overcame, and am set down with my Father in his throne.

—Revelation 3:21

The Laodicean churches were large powerful monuments with most people being polite pew sitters with no idea that Jesus referred to them as wretched, miserable, poor, blind, and naked. Their tents attend church but their hearts raced after other things.

> So then because thou art lukewarm, and neither cold nor hot, I will spue thee out of my mouth....As many as I love, I rebuke and chasten: be zealous therefore, and repent.
>
> —REVELATION 3:16, 19

Those of the Laodicean church that were "hot" were especially noted for their ability to overcome within the confines of a church that were Christians only in concept.

> And from Jesus Christ, who is the faithful witness, and the first begotten of the dead, and the prince of the kings of the earth. Unto him that loved us, and washed us from our sins in his own blood, And hath made us kings and priests unto God and his Father; to him be glory and dominion for ever and ever. Amen.
>
> —REVELATION 1:5–6

With each fellowship there are some elements of each of the seven churches within them so no one is singled out as having absolute truth. In a recent conversation with my beloved daughter Breanna, we came to the realization that all the overcomers had something in common. They were all asked to overcome the evil and the apostasy that occurred within their respective churches. They were not necessarily asked to leave where they were but to yield fruit where they were. In the Kingdom of God parables that we studied, the Lord prophesied that within the church there would be weeds and the demonic birds of the air, lodging along with wolves in wool. They would remain until the time of harvest and judgment. The nation Israel was proved within their wilderness church and the gentiles are no different.

The folks of Sodom and Gomorrah no doubt thought that their lifestyle was approved by God because so many were doing it. God was able to reap a harvest of only one man and his two daughters. As God is the same yesterday, in Lot's era, He is the same today, in our era, and He is Holy and righteous tomorrow as well. He alters not with the crazes of planet earth.

> He that overcometh shall inherit all things; and I will be his God, and he shall be my son.
>
> —REVELATION 21:7

A vexing spirit cannot come back if the trapdoors are sealed and your temple is sanctified with the Holy Spirit empowered to do His work. As we have an immune system to protect against germs, we have an overcomer system to protect against evil.

> Casting down arguments and every high thing that exalts itself against the knowledge of God, bringing every thought into captivity to the obedience of Christ.
>
> —2 CORINTHIANS 10:5

Up until a couple of days ago I was really vexed in my thoughts and unable to pen them in. While out enjoying dinner with my brother, he noted my countenance was goofy and challenged me as to why. I conceded that though I felt I had forgiven a pastor for what I perceived were grievous wrongs committed against my family and me, I could not halt the traffic circle in my mind. Being a good brother, he didn't allow me to

> As we have an immune system to protect against germs, we have an overcomer system to protect against evil.

spew for long before challenging, "God is not free to work in your situation as long as you are judging a brother." I was busted, and I couldn't wait to get back home to cleanse the defilement and see if I would be able to gain control over my thoughts. I flipped open my journal. It opened to a page that captivated me because of a verse I had written down only three weeks prior, but at the time I didn't know it applied to me.

> Be ye therefore merciful, as your Father also is merciful. Judge not, and ye shall not be judged: condemn not, and ye shall not be condemned: forgive, and ye shall be forgiven.
> —Luke 6:36–37

I knew the reason I couldn't forgive from my heart was because I had been judging and condemning this individual silently in my mind for many days. When I judge a brother, I pronounce my opinion in my examination of his behavior; and then when I follow up with condemnation, I pronounce him guilty as perceived in my rambling mind.

I did my first works to cleanse the defilement of my judgment, condemnation, and unforgiveness regarding this situation but didn't have the release that I needed in my spirit. I wasn't done yet. I started writing down every situation of recent memory that vexed my thoughts, there were thirty-eight. *No way,* I mused. *I constantly deal with my stuff. How could this much defilement escape my radar?* It was obvious that I was taking pleasure in regurgitating the vomit of past offenses, announcing my judgment and condemnation as each situation would flash over my mind. I repented of it all and suddenly I was refreshed, left with not only a quiet mind but also genuine joy. I was restored.

> Submit yourselves therefore to God. Resist the devil, and he will flee from you. Draw nigh to God, and he will draw nigh to you. Cleanse your hands, ye sinners; and purify your hearts, ye double minded.
> —James 4:7–8

We resist the devil the same way Jesus did; He had scripture committed to memory that He used to rebuke the devil. Choose scriptures that correspond to your area of weakness and memorize them so you can destroy the devil's works.

It is a battle; it is work; but if the evil spirit is unsuccessful in his attempt to return, after a number of attempts he will be gone. Your work is not done at the purging of the enemy.

> Afterward Jesus findeth him in the temple, and said unto him, Behold, thou art made whole: sin no more, lest a worse thing come unto thee.
>
> —John 5:14

It is to be understood that once we have applied the sacrifice of Christ to heal us, we become an actively engaged overcomer for the rest of our lives.

Purging is only one step towards our sanctification; it is not to be the focus. This fellow whom Jesus healed was told to overcome his sin so a worse thing would not happen to him. The "worse thing" is the spirit being able to return through a trapdoor with seven of his evil spirit gang.

A few pages back we looked at the passage of 2 Timothy 2:20–26 that teaches about spiritual warfare; and in that passage is instruction to fill our spirits with righteousness, faith, agape, and peace so there is no room for the devil to return with his house wreckers.

> Flee also youthful lusts [sins we should grow out of]: but follow righteousness [state of being purified and fit for Master's use], faith [fidelity in trust of our godly convictions], charity [*agape*], peace [void of pride which leads to strife], with them that call on the Lord out of a pure heart [purified for temple use]. But foolish and unlearned questions avoid, knowing that they do gender strifes.
>
> —2 Timothy 2:22–23

The greatest of these weapons is the empowering of agape.

> There is no fear in love [*agape*]; but perfect love [*agape*] casteth [purges] out fear: because fear hath torment. He that feareth is not made perfect in love.
>
> —1 John 4:18

If agape delivers us from fear, what else will it rid us of? Could you imagine the look of surprise on a devil's face when he, along with his seven buddies, knocks on the door of our spirit only to have it opened by the spirit of agape? Agape is to fear what light is to rats; they both get terribly uncomfortable and have to flee.

Fasting

Now when the usual ministry did not have effect, the Lord taught the disciples they needed to prepare with prayer and fasting. Fasting removes us as an obstacle to the work of God, as we must die to ourselves and overcome our appetites and lusts. The standard fast is to deprive ourselves of food and drink (except for water) for one meal, a day or perhaps two days to start. Note how the following healing required the dismissal of a devil:

> Lord, have mercy on my son: for he is lunatic [epileptic?], and sore vexed [miserable and antagonized by a devil]: for ofttimes he falleth into the fire, and oft into the water. And I brought him to thy disciples, and they could not cure him….And Jesus rebuked the devil; and he departed out

of him: and the child was cured from that very hour. Then came the disciples to Jesus apart, and said, Why could not we cast him out [expel or deprive of power]? And Jesus said unto them....Howbeit this kind goeth not out but by prayer and fasting.

—MATTHEW 17:15–16, 18–21

Isaiah first prophesied regarding the power and purpose of the "chosen" fast, then Jesus Christ would instruct the disciples of the necessity. Although there were healings in the Old Testament, they were few and far between compared to the ministry Jesus taught and presented to the church.

> Perhaps the greatest move of the Lord over the last two thousand years, apart from the Crucifixion and Resurrection, was ushered in through the fasting and prayer of a Gentile in a Jewish world.

Is not this the fast that I have chosen [approved of]? to loose the bands of wickedness [bands are metaphorical of slavery to sin or addiction], to undo the heavy [oppression] burdens, and to let the oppressed [crushed, broken, discouraged] go free [from slavery or control of a demon who has taken one captive], and that ye break [rip off] every yoke [load not meant to carry]?

—ISAIAH 58:6

Many voices today down play the necessity of fasting, but Jesus seems to teach the opposite; He said that once His earthly ministry is completed and He ascends to the Father, then it will be necessary to fast.

Then came to him the disciples of John, saying, Why do we and the Pharisees fast oft, but thy disciples fast not? And Jesus said unto them, Can the children of the bridechamber mourn, as long as the bridegroom is with them? but the days will come, when the bridegroom [Jesus Christ] shall be taken from them, and then shall they fast.

—MATTHEW 9:14–15

Perhaps the greatest move of the Lord over the last two thousand years, apart from the Crucifixion and Resurrection, was ushered in through the fasting and prayer of a Gentile in a Jewish world. A devout Gentile centurion, Cornelius, who feared God, fasted and prayed and God was moved. Peter, a devout Jew, was summoned to go to the house of Cornelius where several Gentile believers had gathered. Peter ministered unto those gathered and they believed and received the empowering of the Holy Spirit followed by baptism. Thus began the movement of the church as we know today.

And Cornelius said, Four days ago I was fasting until this hour; and at the ninth hour I prayed in my house, and, behold, a man stood before me in bright clothing, And said, Cornelius, thy prayer is heard, and thine alms are had in remembrance in the sight of God.

—ACTS 10:30–31

The example to the church was to also fast and pray for important decisions such as choosing elders and ministers for the fellowship.

> And when they had ordained them elders in every church, and had prayed with fasting, they commended them to the Lord, on whom they believed.
> —ACTS 14:23

> As they ministered to the Lord, and fasted, the Holy Ghost said, Separate me Barnabas and Saul for the work whereunto I have called them.
> —ACTS 13:2

Paul instructs those that are married to abstain from sexual relations while fasting.

> The wife hath not power of her own body, but the husband: and likewise also the husband hath not power of his own body, but the wife. Defraud ye not one the other, except it be with consent for a time, that ye may give yourselves to fasting and prayer; and come together again, that Satan tempt you not for your incontinency.
> —1 CORINTHIANS 7:4-5

To establish something as doctrine in the church, it should be taught and practiced by Christ, it should be continued on in the early church as we see in Acts, and then we should see it further expounded upon by the apostle Paul. So fasting would meet the criteria as doctrine as does communion. Jesus practiced foot washing on the other hand, but we don't see it furthered in the church or mentioned by Paul, so it would not be considered an essential for the church to continue.

6. Worship Him

"Fear not" is the most oft repeated command in the Bible. Fear is perhaps the greatest obstacle we face to overcome. Fear and faith are mutually exclusive, as fear is Satan's faith projecting dread and past failures into the future. In spiritual battle fear must be dealt a deathblow and then we die to self and allow God to fight for us. As long as we are trying to move mountains as a work accomplished by human effort, we tie the hands of God, limiting His salvation.

> Thus saith the LORD unto you, Be not afraid nor dismayed by reason of this great multitude; for the battle is not yours, but God's....Ye shall not need to fight in this battle: set yourselves [take a stand], stand ye still, and see the salvation [deliverance] of the LORD with you, O Judah and Jerusalem: fear not, nor be dismayed; tomorrow go out against them: for the LORD will be with you. And Jehoshaphat bowed his head with his face to the ground: and all Judah and the inhabitants of Jerusalem fell before the LORD, worshiping the LORD.
> —2 CHRONICLES 20:15, 17-18

After hearing the Word and being encouraged by the promise of God, King Jehoshaphat worshiped the Lord. He worshiped after hearing but before receiving.

You may be accustomed to having worship as step number one in your approach to God; but in this writing it is number seven. The reason for this is because of how important worship really is for those who fear God.

> Fear and faith are mutually exclusive, as fear is Satan's faith projecting dread and past failures into the future.

We have a struggle to get the family into the car on schedule; and then once we are all in the car, an argument ensues as tensions are snappy, invariably one family member ends up not feeling very good about himself or herself, and then we arrive in the church parking lot. Frowns transform into smiles through some miraculous make over, and we slide into our seats aware that we are the model family. The music starts to roll with the model parents shooting up their arms to make a wave offering of worship before the Lord. The worship music goes on and on until the leader figures the breathless congregation has now been whipped up into submission with a heart ready to receive the twenty-minute sermonette for the Christianettes.

The point is that worship is a response to the wonderful works of God in our lives; it is not necessarily the purpose of worship to get our hearts sanctified and ready to receive the message. We'll examine the Scripture for what may be a refreshing look at what worship is all about.

God sees our mouth moving and a sound of a familiar song coming from the lips, but it doesn't match the message He is receiving from our spirit. There is no fooling God with this one, as He resides in His temple within us.

> Wherefore the LORD said, Forasmuch as this people draw near me with their mouth, and with their lips do honour me, but have removed their heart [inner spirit] far from me, and their fear toward me is taught by the precept of men.
> —ISAIAH 29:13

The Lord desires us to have a fear towards Him according to a thorough knowledge of His Word. I believe we know what is to come out of our mouths, but if it is different from the stuff in our spirit, we are simply hypocrites with lips. Worship is in vain with uncleanness and rebellion in our hearts.

> Ye hypocrites, well did Esaias prophesy of you, saying, This people draweth nigh unto me with their mouth, and honoureth me with their lips; but their heart is far from me. But in vain they do worship me, teaching for doctrines the commandments of men.
> —MATTHEW 15:7–9

Worship must be from our spirit as our spirit is the source of the fountain of agape, the only love language God can respond to.

> The point is that worship is a response to the wonderful works of God in our lives; it is not necessarily the purpose of worship to get our hearts sanctified and ready to receive the message.

But the hour cometh, and now is, when the true worshipers [real character corresponds to Christian name] shall worship the Father in spirit and in truth: for the Father seeketh such to worship him.

—John 4:23

Truth is narrow—that is why it is truth! When people say to you, "You are so narrow!" Just say, "Thanks!"

When the church of Nehemiah did business with God, the first order of service was to throw out the sundials, as the service lasted twelve hours. The precepts of God were taught directly from the Scriptures for six hours. In response to the teaching of the Word, the people dealt with generational iniquities in order to break the curse upon their people and confessed their personal sin. Now that they were cleansed and freed, they were ready to worship God in spirit and in purity. God was moved.

> And the seed of Israel separated themselves from all strangers, and stood and confessed their sins, and the iniquities of their fathers. And they stood up in their place, and read in the book of the law of the LORD their God one fourth part of the day; and another fourth part they confessed, and worshiped the LORD their God.
>
> —Nehemiah 9:2–3

> I believe we know what is to come out of our mouths, but if it is different from the stuff in our spirit, we are simply hypocrites with lips.

Every word of Scripture is sent from the mouth of God; and once it is received, how can we help but to break out in spontaneous joy and worship?

> So shall my word be that goeth forth out of my mouth: it shall not return unto me void, but it shall accomplish that which I please, and it shall prosper in the thing whereto I sent it. For ye shall go out with joy, and be led forth with peace: the mountains and the hills shall break forth before you into singing, and all the trees of the field shall clap their hands.
>
> —Isaiah 55:11–12

The intended result of receiving the Word of God is joy and peace, ingredients of true worship. How awesome is worship when the mountains and hills join in chorus and the branches of the trees clap.

We worship with the offerings of our substance, which we give in return for the investment God has made in us. When glory is deflected from us unto God, it is received by God as worship.

Our holiness, or sanctification, is a prerequisite in worshiping God. To offer up praises to God from a defiled temple is to approach the holiness of God presumptuously. We are to be holy as He is holy, without such there is no access to fellowship. If our worship seems dry and empty, it probably has to do with our sanctification.

> Truth is narrow—that is why it is truth! When people say to you, "You are so narrow!" Just say, "Thanks."

> Sing unto the LORD, all the earth; shew forth from day to day his salvation. Declare his glory among the heathen; his marvellous works among all nations. For great is the LORD, and greatly to be praised: he also is to be feared above all gods. For all the gods of the people are idols: but the LORD made the heavens. Glory and honour are in his presence; strength and gladness are in his place. Give unto the LORD, ye kindreds of the people, give unto the LORD glory and strength. Give unto the LORD the glory due unto his name: bring an offering, and come before him: worship the LORD in the beauty of holiness [sanctification]. Fear before him, all the earth: the world also shall be stable, that it be not moved.
>
> —I CHRONICLES 16:23–30

With a respectful and healthy fear of God, a saint would be most prepared in their spirit before trying to enter into worship. Most Bible students are familiar with the judgment of God over prideful and rebellious men in the Old Testament. But God changes not. In the time of the early church, Herod received the glory of men unto himself, which rightfully should have been deflected onto the One who spoke through him and put Herod in the position of king. *Glory* is often interchanged with the word *worship* in the New Testament; and no man should usurp the glory that belongs to another, especially God.

> And upon a set day Herod, arrayed in royal apparel, sat upon his throne, and made an oration unto them. And the people gave a shout, saying, It is the voice of a god, and not of a man. And immediately the angel of the Lord smote him, because he gave not God the glory: and he was eaten of worms, and gave up the ghost.
>
> —ACTS 12:21–23

The judgment of Herod's sin was immediate, as the angel of the Lord smoked him. I believe God has extended greater mercy to the later days of the church because of the degree of sin. If he judged now as He did Herod, we would have a lot of worm food. Please do not error in assuming God approves of our sin because He has not passed swift judgment on you; rather

> With a respectful and healthy fear of God a saint would be most prepared in their spirit before trying to enter into worship.

you are seeing His mercy in giving us an extension of life in order to own our sin and deal with it.

> And the times of this ignorance God winked at; but now commandeth
> all men every where to repent.
>
> —ACTS 17:30

God listens in on what we are saying about Him. Our children pick up on our boasting about the incredible acts of God in creation and throughout the world. The blessing to parents is that children grow up in awe of God; and furthermore, God so appreciates how He is taught to His little children that such acts are received as worship.

> Great is the LORD, and greatly to be praised; and his greatness is unsearchable. One generation shall praise thy works to another, and shall declare thy mighty acts. I will speak of the glorious honour of thy majesty, and of thy wondrous works.
>
> —PSALM 145:3–5

Our attempt at worship is foolishness if our religion follows religious ceremony and rites that are extra biblical. We only receive worship points for, and only for, that which closely follows the Word of God. We must worship with a zeal for the holiness and fear of God; to do anything else is really a waste of lip service as the One who is to receive the service of worship sees through to the intents and stuff of the heart.

> Howbeit in vain [fruitless attempt of folly] do they worship me, teaching for doctrines the commandments of men. For laying aside the commandment of God, ye hold the tradition of men, as the washing of pots and cups: and many other such like things ye do. And he said unto them, Full well ye reject the commandment of God, that ye may keep your own tradition.
>
> —MARK 7:7–9

It's really quite simple. If our traditional forms of worship are not rooted in the Word, they are mere entertainment and are in vain. By now one can see there is much more to worship than the singing of songs. We also worship by giving thanks and we worship by "doing good" onto others. God even receives our Christian fellowship as a very pleasing sacrifice.

> By him therefore let us offer the sacrifice of praise to God continually, that is, the fruit of our lips giving thanks to his name. But to do good and to communicate forget not: for with such sacrifices God is well pleased.
>
> —HEBREWS 13:15–16

For those that spend too much time asking the morning mirror to improve their appearance, take heed; we worship by realizing how marvelous God made us and giving Him the glory. God knows we are imperfect, as in earth stage we are still a piece of work in progress. His work isn't finished in us. Consider the wonder of the psalmist as to the multitude of thoughts the Father has towards each of us.

I will praise thee; for I am fearfully and wonderfully made: marvellous are thy works; and that my soul knoweth right well. My substance was not hid from thee, when I was made in secret, and curiously wrought in the lowest parts of the earth. Thine eyes did see my substance, yet being unperfect; and in thy book all my members were written, which in continuance were fashioned, when as yet there was none of them. How precious also are thy thoughts unto me, O God! how great is the sum of them! If I should count them, they are more in number than the sand: when I awake, I am still with thee.

—Psalm 139:14–18

The truest thing about us cannot be reflected by a mirror. The truest thing about us is that we were created before the foundation of the world, holy, without blame, and overflowing with the agape of the Father. Thank God for His intent in reconciling us to our original inner portrait of deep beauty.

We may worship by dancing, singing, and playing instruments. I think the Lord has a special place in His heart for those that break out into spontaneous praise when no one else is around. I especially prefer this as I know that God isn't waiting for me to be pitch and tone perfect and judging my singing ability as to how many worship points I'll get for it.

Praise ye the Lord. Sing unto the Lord a new song, and his praise in the congregation of saints. Let Israel rejoice in him that made him: let the children of Zion be joyful in their King. Let them praise his name in the dance: let them sing praises unto him with the timbrel and harp. For the Lord taketh pleasure in his people: he will beautify the meek with salvation. Let the saints be joyful in glory: let them sing aloud upon their beds.

—Psalm 149:1–5

We may worship while bowing down or kneeling.

O come, let us worship and bow down: let us kneel before the Lord our maker.

—Psalm 95:6

> The truest thing about you cannot be reflected by a mirror.

In the church of Nehemiah it was acceptable to alter their posture from lifting up their hands, to bowing their heads, and finally, lying prone—face down before our Lord.

And Ezra blessed the Lord, the great God. And all the people answered, Amen, Amen, with lifting up their hands: and they bowed their heads, and worshiped the Lord with their faces to the ground.

—Nehemiah 8:6

If you are only able to worship according to the unspoken rigid rules of your denomination, a consideration may be to whom do you surrender? Our lips speak of glory, joy, and an awesome mighty God; while hands thrust firmly to the bottoms of our pockets suggest a hardened heart that is far from what the flesh is doing.

Nonetheless, instead of doing a wave offering in the front pew while mindful of our jewelry and knowing we are being hypocritical with defiled hearts, it would be more honest to stuff our hands into our pockets until we are purged. The hands we lift up are moved by our purified hearts.

> I will therefore that men pray every where, lifting up holy hands [sanctified for temple use], without wrath [agitation of the soul] and doubting [questioning what is true]. In like manner also, that women adorn themselves in modest apparel, with shamefacedness and sobriety; not with braided hair, or gold, or pearls, or costly array.
> —1 TIMOTHY 2:8–9

The order of service includes sharing a song, a teaching, a tongue with an interpretation (in public), or with a prophecy. Many are to be involved, as all have gifts to offer as worship and edification. Isn't something amiss when only paid professionals are offering their "gifts" in "worship services"? That is the hand saying to the foot I have no need of you.

> How is it then, brethren? when ye come together, every one of you hath a psalm, hath a doctrine, hath a tongue, hath a revelation, hath an interpretation. Let all things be done unto edifying….And the spirits of the prophets are subject to the prophets. For God is not the author of confusion, but of peace, as in all churches of the saints.
> —1 CORINTHIANS 14:26, 32–33

> Our lips speak of glory, joy, and an awesome mighty God; while hands thrust firmly to the bottoms of our pockets suggest a hardened heart that is far from what the flesh is doing.

The Bible teaches that all activity of a saint directed to God is received as worship, providing we have cleansed our temples. Worship is service that we get to do in response to what our Father does for us.

7. Serve Him

Without wavering and without doubt I will do it. Praise the Lord for His mercy endureth forever. Call it done! Call it finished! Call it over! Call it made right! Once you've confessed, God holds no sin against you.

The apostle Peter was an ambassador who failed, but his failure is not what defined him. If the disciples dwelt on failures, the work of Jesus would have been in vain. The Lord has a strong hand on you _____ and Satan knows that. May the Lord strengthen you so as not to grieve the Holy Spirit through doubt.

But Peter and John answered and said unto them, Whether it be right in the sight of God to hearken unto you more than unto God, judge ye. For we cannot but speak the things which we have seen and heard.

—Acts 4:19

David did not doubt the recovery and restoration work of the Lord following his sin of adultery and murder. David sought the purging and cleansing of the Lord so that he would again be cleansed and suitable for the Master to use him in teaching others who had fallen as he did.

Purge me with hyssop, and I shall be clean: wash me, and I shall be whiter than snow. Make me to hear joy and gladness; that the bones which thou hast broken may rejoice. Hide thy face from my sins, and blot out all mine iniquities. Create in me a clean heart, O God; and renew a right spirit within me. Cast me not away from thy presence; and take not thy holy spirit from me. Restore unto me the joy of thy salvation; and uphold me with thy free spirit. Then will I teach transgressors [rebels] thy ways; and sinners [exposed to condemnation] shall be converted [restored and brought back] unto thee.

—Psalm 51:7–13

> Overcomers overcome their yesterdays and invest what they've been taught for eternal rewards.

The credentials that qualify for the Master's use are not found listed in any Bible school or seminary's catalogue. Knowledge gained from study remains in the mind only until called upon by human experience, suffering, or tribulation, where it is then transformed by the Spirit of God to soften the heart, thus alerting us to the necessity of purifying our temples.

And not only so, but we glory in tribulations [anything that burdens our spirit regardless of who's at fault] also: knowing that tribulation worketh [achieves] patience [will not fall even with the greatest of trials and suffering]; And patience, experience [tried and proven character]; and experience, hope [confident expectation of good]: And hope maketh not ashamed [disappointed]; because the love [*agape*] *of God is shed abroad in our hearts by the Holy Ghost* which is given unto us.

—Romans 5:3, emphasis added

> Knowledge gained from study remains in the mind only until called upon by human experience, suffering, or tribulation.

The training progression from tribulation, to patience, to experience, to hope achieves the coveted fruit of the agape of God overwhelming our vessels and spilling out to be a covering to others.

Following Peter's great fall wherein he denied knowing Christ and was subsequently sifted by Satan, no doubt following the progression of Romans 5:3, the Lord started to teach Peter what it would require to be a shepherd tending Jesus' lambs and sheep in agape.

For those that have been trained through agape school, they will then be enlisted in service to teach what they have learned to convert others as they were converted. Jesus prayed for Peter, already a believer, to be converted. Converted to what? Peter needed to be converted, which means to be restored to the agape and fear of the Lord.

> And the Lord said, Simon, Simon, behold, Satan hath desired to have you, that he may sift you as wheat: But I have prayed for thee, that thy faith fail not: and when thou art converted [to turn from *phileo* and *eros* love to the *agape* and fear of God], strengthen thy brethren.
>
> —LUKE 22:32–33

After Peter fell to fear and deception in denying he was a disciple of the way of Jesus, Jesus continues on in teaching Peter following His resurrection to encourage Peter to work towards his conversion from the fickle phileo love to the unchanging empowering of agape.

> So when they had dined, Jesus saith to Simon Peter, Simon, son of Jonas, lovest [*agapao*] thou me more than these? He saith unto him, Yea, Lord; thou knowest that I love [*phileo*] thee. He saith unto him, *Feed* [a constant tending and nurturing] my lambs [new converts].
>
> —JOHN 21:15, EMPHASIS ADDED

In verses 15 and 16 two different Greek words are used for *feed*. Firstly Peter was to nurture the tender lambs or the new believers with the milk of the Word; and then Peter was to continue on as a shepherd for the long term, guiding the lambs onto maturity through the meat that would sustain their hearts and boost their immune system to be overcomers.

> He saith to him again the second time, Simon, son of Jonas, lovest [*agapeo*] thou me? He saith unto him, Yea, Lord; thou knowest that I love [*phileo*] thee. He saith unto him, *Feed* [to shepherd, serve, govern, guard] my sheep [those who belong to the Lord].
>
> —JOHN 21:16, EMPHASIS ADDED

Peter was restored to service within two or three months of his sin. The Lord harvested three thousand souls on Peter's first sermon. Peter's message was to repeat what Jesus taught him through his tribulation. Jesus prayed that Peter would be converted, and accordingly Peter preached a message of restoration to the agape of the Father of which we were first created.

> Repent ye therefore, and be converted, that your sins may be blotted out, when the times of refreshing shall come from the presence of the Lord.
>
> —ACTS 3:19

Paul went through considerable tribulation, which God used through Paul's writings to comfort the church over the next two thousand years. If Paul was given a sheltered monastic life where no harm, persecution, or distress could touch him, would he have contributed to the harvest of hearts and the growth of the church as he did?

> Blessed be God, even the Father of our Lord Jesus Christ, the Father of mercies, and the God of all comfort; Who comforteth [come to one's side to strengthen] us in all our tribulation, that we may be able to comfort them which are in any trouble, by the comfort [encourage through our testimony and exhortation] wherewith we ourselves are comforted of God. And our hope of you is stedfast, knowing, that as ye are partakers of the sufferings, so shall ye be also of the consolation [encouragement, refreshment, comfort].
>
> —2 CORINTHIANS 1:3–7

There are many ways to serve the Lord, but the main purpose for all believers is to be able to stand in the gap and engage in warfare on behalf of those entrusted to our care. A minister is not an originator of truth but a subordinate rower, an ambassador who has learned that he can do nothing of his own power; thus he dies to self-ambition and appetites so he can witness without even using words.

The purpose of a ministry is to help free those who are in bondage. Note in the following passage that others were set free or sanctified by the faith that was in Paul; or in other words the minister must be sanctified himself before he can set others free. If one sees little results in their ministry, it would be due to their temple needing cleansing to be available for the Master's use.

> If Paul was given a sheltered monastic life where no harm, persecution, or distress could touch him, would he have contributed to the harvest of hearts and the growth of the church as he did?

> I have appeared unto thee for this purpose, to make thee a minister [a subordinate rower] and a witness [genuineness of their faith proven by character in midst of the storm] both of these things which thou hast seen, and of those things in the which I will appear unto thee;…the Gentiles, unto whom now I send thee, To open their eyes [give entrance to heart and soul], and to turn them from darkness [ignorance of godliness] to light [from pride to agape, from fear to faith, from despair to hope] and from the power of Satan unto God, that they may receive forgiveness [release from bondage or slavery] of sins, and inheritance [eternal Eden] among them which are sanctified [cleansed for temple use] by faith [conviction of truth and fidelity] that is in me.
>
> —ACTS 26:16–18

Service is essential in our own restoration, as we remove our buggy eyes from noticing everything about our own situation and look to the needs of others. The promise therein is that our health will spring forth speedily.

> There are many ways to serve the Lord, but the main purpose for all believers is to be able to stand in the gap and engage in warfare on behalf of those entrusted to their care.

Is not this the fast that I have chosen? to loose the bands of wickedness, to undo the heavy burdens, and to let the oppressed go free, and that ye break every yoke? Is it not to deal thy bread to the hungry, and that thou bring the poor that are cast out to thy house? when thou seest the naked, that thou cover him; and that thou hide not thyself from thine own flesh? Then shall thy light break forth as the morning, and thine health shall spring forth speedily: and thy righteousness shall go before thee; the glory of the LORD shall be thy reward.

—ISAIAH 58:6–8

Meeting the needs of others most often requires no budget or funding at all as the gospel is free; and as we have received of it freely, we are to freely give to others. Some throw money at problem projects hoping they will go away to make up for the lack of the empowering of agape through the Holy Spirit that will really set captives free.

The only "but" you are allowed to say is: "With me this is an impossible situation, *but* with God this is possible!"

> A certain man lame from his mother's womb was carried....to ask alms of them that entered into the temple; Peter said, Silver and gold have I none; but such as I have give I thee: In the name of Jesus Christ of Nazareth rise up and walk. And he took him by the right hand, and lifted him up: and immediately his feet and ankle bones received strength. And he leaping up stood, and walked, and entered with them into the temple, walking, and leaping, and praising God. And all the people saw him walking and praising God.
>
> —ACTS 3:2–9

An ambassador of "good will" knows he is but a servant of God and points all to Jesus taking no glory for himself. In fact if we take any credit that is all the reward we'll receive.

> Take heed that ye do not your alms [deeds of mercy] before men, to be seen of them: otherwise ye have no reward of your Father which is in heaven.
>
> —MATTHEW 6:1

If we are not interested in seeking our own reward, we will be able to minister to those that won't even be able to mutter thanks.

For if ye love [*agapao*] them which love you, what reward have ye? do not even the publicans [those that ruthlessly collect taxes for redistribution] the same?

—Matthew 5:46

These seven steps of "Sanctiprize" will have to be committed to memory. They will become part of your moment-by-moment walk with the Lord. The verses used here give the believer the authority to step out in faith and live a life for the Lord.

> The victory of this war will be reconciliation to the person you were created from the foundation of the world to be: holy, blameless and walking in the love of our Father.

1. See it. Expose your enemy.

2. Own it. Yes, I did it, and I have no excuse for what I did.

3. Confess it. Now that you've owned up to, it let it go.

4. Purge it. Pull it up by the roots and cast it out.

5. Overcome it.

6. Worship Him.

7. Serve Him.

The scripture carefully lays before us in 1 Corinthians 13 what sin we must confront in our lives in order for us to walk in agape or wholeness—a passage most of us just breeze over due to our familiarity with the content; or is it more likely that our eyes and hearts have been blinded by Satan who knows what this empowering of God's love will do to his kingdom?

There are at least sixteen smaller battles you will engage in, in order to win the war. The battlefronts are set out in 1 Corinthians 13. The victory of this war will be reconciliation to the person you were created from the foundation of the world to be: holy, blameless, and walking in the love of our Father.

> Charity [*agape*] suffereth long, and is kind; Charity envieth not; charity vaunteth not itself, is not puffed up, Doth not behave itself unseemly, seeketh not her own, is not easily provoked, thinketh no evil; Rejoiceth not in iniquity, but rejoiceth in the truth; Beareth all things, believeth all things, hopeth all things, endureth all things. Charity never faileth.
>
> —1 Corinthians 13:4

Agape Suffereth Long

Why is "suffering long" or patience first on the list? Is it because of how much trouble we get into by being impatient with ourselves, others, and God. I have been very impatient with the move of God in several areas of my life. I believe He can move mountains, no problem, so it isn't because of lack of faith. My issue is I despised the training that involved the development of my patience. My thinking was flawed; I needed my faith to be strong enough to trust in

God that His timing was perfect. My impatience was a sin that prevented me from the experience of agape in a time when I needed it the most.

> My son, despise not thou the chastening of the Lord, nor faint when thou art rebuked of him: For whom the Lord loveth he chasteneth, and scourgeth every son whom he receiveth. If ye endure [persevere, endure bravely, calmly and trustfully] chastening [training, correction], God dealeth with you as with sons; for what son is he whom the father chasteneth not?...Shall we not much rather be in subjection [submission] unto the Father of spirits, and live?...Now no chastening for the present seemeth to be joyous, but grievous [mourning over loss]: nevertheless afterward it yieldeth the peaceable fruit of righteousness unto them which are exercised thereby [one who strives earnestly to become godly].
> —Hebrews 12:5–11

Once we have declared our faith and confidence in God, our confidence will be tested by a few lessons of patience. The passing of this test of patience is mandatory for kingdom of God subjects. To give us hope through our trials, the Lord promises that He has something very special in mind for us once we overcome.

> I have been very impatient with the move of God in several areas of my life. I believe He can move mountains, no problem, so it isn't because of lack of faith; my issue is I despised the training that involved the development of my patience.

> Cast not away therefore your confidence [fearless and cheerful courage], which hath great recompence of reward [large payout]. For ye have need of patience, that, after ye have done the will of God, ye might receive the promise. For yet a little while, and he that shall come will come, and will not tarry [linger]. Now the just shall live by faith: but if any man draw back [through doubt and fear turn away from what they believed], my soul shall have no pleasure in him. But we are not of them who draw back unto perdition [hell]; but of them that believe to the saving of the soul.
> —Hebrews 10:35–39

> When we are treated badly we do a tough love thing, which is really saying: "If you don't do what I feel is right, then I'll do wrong to teach you!"

There can be no testing of patience when everything in our life is going great. The will of God is the keeping of our patience through whatever trial comes upon us. As stuff happens, remind yourself, "This is only a test! This is only a test!" God monitors our behavior to see how we go through the storm.

> Rejoicing in hope; patient in tribulation [anguish, distress, afflictions or sufferings]; continuing instant in prayer.
> —Romans 12:12

If you are like me, you can see the requirement of being patient in tribulations. But consider the following passage in James where we are to maintain our joy, faith, and patience even during temptations. Wow! James understood that when he was tempted, it allowed whatever sin remaining, hidden in the dark places of his heart, to be exposed; and once it was exposed, he would then purge himself of it. The end result of patience is that we grow up.

> My brethren, count it all joy when ye fall into divers temptations [proving trial, enticement to sin, lapse from the faith or holiness, adversity, tests to prove my character]; Knowing this, that the trying of your faith worketh patience. But let patience have her perfect work, that ye may be perfect and entire, wanting nothing.
>
> —JAMES 1:2–4

There is still one more step to growing up and that is to be patient when we do good things and are still abused or belittled. Our calling isn't to be mistreated, but our calling is to endure with patience when we are mistreated. Any other reaction would be sin. Some help you are if someone messes with you and you retaliate either through a brainstorm, violence, or silence. We are to learn to handle unfair treatment correctly. Our nature, sadly, is often to judge others by their actions and then to judge ourselves by our intent. When we are treated badly we do a tough love thing, which is really saying: "If you don't do what I feel is right, then I'll do wrong to teach you!"

> For what glory is it, if, when ye be buffeted [maltreated] for your faults [mistakes or violations], ye shall take it patiently? but if, when ye do well [something that profits others], and suffer for it, ye take it patiently, this is acceptable with God. For even hereunto were ye called: because Christ also suffered for us, leaving us an example, that ye should follow his steps.
>
> —1 PETER 2:20–21

> *Our nature, sadly, is often to judge others by their action and then to judge ourselves by our intent.*

It is those to whom we are the most vulnerable, those of our own household or family, who can hurt us the most. It is those that are supposed to love us no matter what that can be the source of the most pain in our lives.

> And a man's foes shall be they of his own household.
>
> —MATTHEW 10:36

If Satan wants me to be distant from God, he'll orchestrate injury at the hands of a fellow believer. The closer the relationship the more severe the offense is to us and part of that has to do with our expectations.

> For it was not an enemy that reproached me; then I could have borne it: neither was it he that hated me that did magnify himself against me; then

I would have hid myself from him: But it was thou, a man mine equal,
my guide, and mine acquaintance. We took sweet counsel together, and
walked unto the house of God in company.

—PSALM 55:12–14

Mature Christians don't get offended because they walk in agape. Our Lord
Jesus said, "Father forgive them for they know not what they do" (Luke 23:34).

An offense is a stumbling block that opens the door of distrust or disdain
towards another. An offense entices you to sin. Offense leads to betrayal and
betrayal to hatred.

And then shall many be offended [vexed, provoked or tripped up], and
shall betray [condemn and deliver to judgment] one another, and shall
hate [detest] one another. And many false prophets shall rise, and
shall deceive many. And because iniquity [contempt and violation of law]
shall abound, the love [agape] of many shall wax cold. But he that shall
endure [remain in place rather than run] unto the end, the same shall
be saved.

—MATTHEW 24:10–11

Often the perpetrator of the alleged offense has no intention to cause injury
but the victim condemns the action or words and infers intent. Many offenses
have little to do with the other person but are the fruit of our expectations.
Expectations are premeditated resentments.

For in many things we offend all. If any man offend not in word, the
same is a perfect man, and able also to bridle the whole body.

—JAMES 3:2

> Many offenses have
> little to do with
> the other person
> but are the fruit of
> our expectations.
> Expectations are
> premeditated
> resentments.

If others offend me it is because I have not
died to self. A dead man cannot be offended.
I don't have a choice if and when an offense
will come, but I have a choice in my response.
Furthermore we are often offended by the
number of times a person commits the same
sin. Jesus teaches we have no option but to forgive even if it is seven times in one day for the
same nasty deed.

Then said he unto the disciples, It is impossible
but that offenses will come: but woe unto him, through whom they come!
It were better for him that a millstone were hanged about his neck, and he
cast into the sea, than that he should offend one of these little ones. Take
heed to yourselves: If thy brother trespass against thee, rebuke him; and if
he repent, forgive him. And if he trespass against thee seven times in a day,
and seven times in a day turn again to thee, saying, I repent; thou shalt
forgive him.

—LUKE 17:1–4

Notice the absence of the option of withholding forgiveness. Our self-righteous stand, "I'm not going to accept your apology because I know you are not really serious about your repentance as I know you'll just do it again." What if God were to say that to us when we repent to Him? God asks us to have the same attitude towards repentance of others as He does for us.

This next passage would make a great household motto. To have the ability to cover a transgression you would have to be in a place where you are not offended in the first place. Only one kind of love is able to cover the sin of another, agape, the others, phileo and particularly eros, would think nothing wrong of spreading things around.

> He that covereth a transgression [act of rebellion or sin] seeketh love; but he that repeateth a matter [one who revives unpleasant things which should be forgotten] separateth very friends.
> —Proverbs 17:9

I know of a marriage counselor that without shame states that it is necessary for a spouse to talk over the nasty stuff that occurs in a marriage with others, as they need the support. That policy does the exact opposite of restoring trust in a broken relationship, and furthermore, such advice makes the counselor an accessory to the sin of gossip and separation.

An amorous young man gets married and may not even realize he has any expectations. He comes from a traditional home where his mother performed certain tasks without complaint, then marries a gal only to hear, "I don't do that; that's for you to do," or, "If you don't like the way I do it, you do it!" The difficulty was his expectations, as he assumed that if she really loved him she would want to do these things for him. He is now offended, quickly judges her for what he perceives she has done wrong, and then condemns her as a poor rebellious wife that doesn't love him. Now his mind traffic is spinning out of control through his pain and he is unable to forgive; resentment and retaliation set up camp and set the stage for hatred, anger, and self-pity to join in and have this young man for dinner.

Expectations are a setup—let them go. Rather than take offense, one walking in agape will be able to extend mercy, as that is what the love of our Father does. Outside the realm of God's love, it becomes very difficult to be genuine in extending mercy or a covering of a transgression.

If we take offense it spirals downward very quickly. In order for an offense to take root, we have to judge. Judging pronounces an opinion concerning right and wrong. Following judgment we condemn, which is to declare a guilty verdict. Once we've condemned we have nailed unforgiveness in place and our heart is hardened. The hardened heart then takes pleasure in resentment, retaliation, hatred, anger, and murder. Murder may be physical but is most often destruction of our target's reputation.

Be ye therefore merciful, as your Father also is merciful. Judge not [pronounces an opinion concerning right and wrong], and ye shall not be judged: condemn not [declare a guilty verdict], and ye shall not be condemned: forgive, and ye shall be forgiven.

—Luke 6:36–37

When we are unable to forgive, it is because we have not released our judgment and condemnation on the person. As long as you remain in unforgiveness, you tie the hands of God in His righteous judgment against the one that wronged you and you place a barrier between you and God, preventing any further progress in your spiritual life and your prayers will not be heard.

For if ye forgive men their trespasses, your heavenly Father will also forgive you: But if ye forgive not men their trespasses, neither will your Father forgive your trespasses.

—Matthew 6:14–15

How much time have I spent dancing around the issue rather than just saying I was wrong?

> Failing to forgive may be a sin of greater consequence than that of which you are refusing to forgive another for.

Failing to forgive may be a sin of greater consequence than that of which you are refusing to forgive another for. The fruit of unforgiveness is firstly separation from the love of the person that offended. Secondly, it is separation from God, as you can't receive from a Holy God unless you first release what is unholy. And thirdly, it is retention and assimilation in your temple of the sin you refused to release. The latter is an open door to many diseases and infirmity.

Whose soever sins ye remit [to cast off, release or forgiven], they are remitted unto them; and whose soever sins ye retain [assume possession by refusing to let go], they are retained.

—John 20:23

For those that are the recipients of another's sin, take care of what you do with that defilement. If you do not forgive from your heart, you retain the sin perpetrated upon you along with your own sin of unforgiveness; so you've added sin onto sin—double the original trouble. The best revenge you can take on another is to forgive them.

STEPS TO FREEDOM

If you've been offended for more than a few minutes, it is time to give up the judgment and forgive. Use the list below to remind you who you may have issues with and use the two prayers to gain your freedom.

Forgiveness is a choice, not a feeling!

A Prayer of Repentance for Harboring Bitterness Against Someone

Father God, I recognize that as a result of being hurt, I have allowed myself to hold _____ (i.e., offense, judgment, condemnations, bitterness, unforgiveness, resentment) against _____. I accept responsibility for my sin and I agree with Your verdict on my rebellion. I repent, I renounce, and I ask forgiveness for my participation with these sins. And I ask that their curse be broken in the name of Jesus Christ of Nazareth.

Whose soever sins ye remit, they are remitted unto them; and whose soever sins ye retain, they are retained.

—JOHN 20:23

A Prayer of Forgiveness

Father, as I have been forgiven an exceedingly large debt for my sin, I choose to forgive _____ for _____ me. I ask that You would forgive them as well, and I release them into the freedom of my forgiveness. I pray in the name of Jesus Christ of Nazareth. Amen.

Family

- ❏ Father
- ❏ Mother
- ❏ Sister
- ❏ Brother
- ❏ Son
- ❏ Daughter
- ❏ Stepfather
- ❏ Stepmother
- ❏ Stepsister
- ❏ Stepbrother
- ❏ Husband
- ❏ Wife
- ❏ Ex-husband
- ❏ Ex-wife
- ❏ Mother-in-law
- ❏ Father-in-law
- ❏ Brother-in-Law
- ❏ Sister-in-law
- ❏ Grandfather
- ❏ Grandmother

Health

- ❏ Physician
- ❏ Dentist
- ❏ Nurse
- ❏ Hospital
- ❏ Pharmacist
- ❏ Specialist
- ❏ Alternative health
- ❏ Care Giver

Recreation and Travel

- ❏ Hospitality staff
- ❏ Judges
- ❏ Coaches
- ❏ Referees
- ❏ Teammates
- ❏ Travel

Church

- ❏ Pastors
- ❏ Sunday school teachers

- ❏ Uncle
- ❏ Aunt
- ❏ Cousin
- ❏ Niece
- ❏ Nephew
- ❏ Other relative

Social

- ❏ Friend
- ❏ Neighbor
- ❏ Ex-boyfriend
- ❏ Ex-girlfriend
- ❏ Club or association member

Career

- ❏ Employer
- ❏ Employee
- ❏ Supervisor
- ❏ Co-worker
- ❏ Administration personnel
- ❏ Accounting personnel
- ❏ Other personnel

Business

- ❏ Partner
- ❏ Financial partner
- ❏ Client
- ❏ Competitor
- ❏ Banker
- ❏ Legal matters
- ❏ Supplier
- ❏ Landlord
- ❏ Government official
- ❏ Professional service provider

- ❏ Evangelists
- ❏ Church administrators
- ❏ Elders and deacons
- ❏ Bible study leader or member
- ❏ Counselor
- ❏ Music leader
- ❏ Other church members

Personal Business

- ❏ Insurance agent
- ❏ Real estate agent
- ❏ Banker
- ❏ Investment advisor
- ❏ Government official
- ❏ Politician
- ❏ Legal
- ❏ Service provider
- ❏ Salesman
- ❏ Neighbor
- ❏ Roommate or boarder
- ❏ Landlord
- ❏ Hairdressers, etc.
- ❏ Protection services
- ❏ Criminal
- ❏ Cause of accident
- ❏ Child care

Education

- ❏ Classmate
- ❏ Teacher
- ❏ Principal
- ❏ Bully
- ❏ Institution
- ❏ Professor
- ❏ Adjudicator

Do not let the sun go down tonight on your unforgiveness and wrath. You'll know you have really forgiven them when your mind traffic regarding them stops and the physiological stuff like the lump in the throat or the brain flush is no longer there when you see the person.

Trapdoors (traumas)

God has set up parameters of protection around mankind against the devil. Yet there are legal ways he can get a foothold and we call those trapdoors. Trapdoors exist in our spirit when we unknowingly open a way for evil to take up residence such as when we are subjected to trauma or abuse by others or when faced with unexpected events.

Life events that tear at the heart establish trapdoors. In the event of an unwanted pregnancy, the child could have issues of abandonment and rejection. When parents divorce, children question their own self-worth and may give entry to unloving spirits. Due to sickness, we may engage in alternative therapies that may give entry to occult spirits.

> And that they may recover themselves out of the snare of the devil, who are taken captive by him at his will.
> —2 TIMOTHY 2:26

> Be sober, be vigilant; because your adversary the devil, as a roaring lion, walketh about, seeking whom he may devour.
> —1 PETER 5:8

> Lest Satan should get an advantage of us: for we are not ignorant of his devices.
> —2 CORINTHIANS 2:11

This section is to help you in your discernment of good and evil. It is not necessary for you to go back to the event to relive it and feel its pain and its torment. What is necessary is to look at significant life events only to see if the devil was given an opportunity to take advantage of us either through our personal life or in our generations.

> One thing I do, forgetting those things that are behind and reaching forth unto those things which are before.
> —PHILIPPIANS 3:13

Instructions for ministry regarding trapdoors

Using the following as a guide, check off the experiences in your life that could be trapdoors and include your reactions to those incidences. Your reactions could include: offense, judging, condemnation, bitterness, unforgiveness, resentment, retaliation, anger, hatred, violence, murder (murder with the tongue), fear, rejection, accusation, feelings of abandonment, or self-pity, etc.

This is by no means an exhaustive list but it is helpful in identifying areas that ministry is required. Repent for your wrong reactions using the Prayer of Repentance.

A Prayer of Repentance Regarding Trapdoors

*Father God, I recognize and take responsibility for the sin(s) of
_____, and I ask to be forgiven for my rebellion (and/or the rebel-
lion of my ancestors) that would have given a demon the lawful right of entry
to my spirit through a trapdoor as the result of trauma. I ask that the curse
resulting from this sin be broken in the name of Jesus Christ of Nazareth.*

A Prayer of Resistance

*Father I pray for healing of my pain from the trauma of _____.
I ask to be renewed in my spirit, soul, and body according to who You created me to be from the foundation of the world. Help me to overcome all
areas of temptation so that a trapdoor will not be left accessible by an evil
spirit, as I only have room for your Holy Spirit to reside within me. I pray
in the name of Jesus Christ of Nazareth. Amen*

Trapdoor entry points

1. Conception to Birth

- ❏ Born out of wedlock (bastard's curse) Deut. 23:2
- ❏ Breech or cord around the neck, etc.
- ❏ Conception as result of a crime
- ❏ Conception as result of drunkenness
- ❏ Genetic problems
- ❏ Horrible stories said to pregnant mother
- ❏ Mother's physical or emotional illness
- ❏ Premature birth
- ❏ Rejection
- ❏ Rejection because of gender (boy named Sue)
- ❏ Taken from mother
- ❏ Trauma in birth process
- ❏ Unwanted
- ❏ Use of instruments

2. Illnesses or separation

- ❏ Acne or other disfigurements
- ❏ Death of parent
- ❏ Disease
- ❏ Divorce of parents
- ❏ Emotional Problems
- ❏ Father away at war or because of job
- ❏ Generational or familiar rejection
- ❏ Given up for adoption or abandoned
- ❏ Handicap
- ❏ Hospitalization of self or parents (i.e., being in isolation at birth)
- ❏ Moved to new area
- ❏ Sibling birth

❑ Using sickness to get attention

❑ Working mother

3. Accidents

❑ All other injury or mishap

❑ Near drowning or choking, including being a witness

❑ Sporting accidents

❑ Near accident

❑ Shock

❑ Vehicular accidents

4. Conflicts

❑ A performance-oriented home where love is conditional

❑ Any sexual activity that breaks the marriage covenant

❑ Being in prison

❑ Bosses

❑ Coarse jesting, victimization, or family scapegoat

❑ Doctors (i.e., advised of terminal illness)

❑ False religion or cults

❑ Financial loss or poverty

❑ Incest, molestation, rape, etc.

❑ Neighbors and friends

❑ Peers

❑ Premarital sex or promiscuity

❑ Satanic ritual abuse

❑ Terrorist attacks or war

❑ Victim of verbal, emotional, or physical abuse

❑ Wounding in church

❑ Abortions

❑ Attending military or boarding school

❑ Being the object of lies or gossip

❑ Business relationships

❑ Death of person close to you

❑ Evil words spoken by you, by an ancestor over you, or to you

❑ Family members

❑ Government or legal systems

❑ Loosing virginity outside of protection of godly marriage

❑ Pastors and other church leaders

❑ Persons speaking fear of God or the devil

❑ Robbery or bullying

❑ School or teachers

❑ Victim of racial or cultural prejudice

❑ Vows we've made

5. Witnessing Violence

❑ Graphic violent movies and horror movies

❑ Home

❑ Juvenile homes, foster homes, or orphanages

❑ Military or police service

6. Broken Heart

❑ Broken dreams (Prov. 13:12)

❑ Embarrassment

❑ Loss of promotion or someone else taking recognition

❑ Mistreated by someone that was to love you

❑ Rejection by boyfriend, girl-friend, or fiancé

❑ Slandered

❑ Keeping family secrets

❑ Not feeling safe on ongoing basis

❑ Divorce

❑ Hurt when most vulnerable

❑ Marital separation

❑ Object of cruel joke or remark

❑ Single or childless

❑ Unfulfilled expectations

7. Recorder: it replays events and condemning words

❑ Bitter memories

❑ Traumatic memories

❑ Condemning memories

8. Programming

❑ Being anxious on a daily basis

❑ Shutting down emotionally

❑ Eating out of stress or habit rather than hunger

Declaration to Close Trapdoors

Satan, I hereby renounce you and your kingdom and all your works in my life. I, by an act of my will and in the strength that Jesus Christ of Nazareth gives me, close the trapdoors of my life to all the entry points you have previously gained through my sins and by the injury of others. I speak out, in the name of Jesus Christ, the only begotten of the Father who defeated you at Calvary, that you have no right to trouble me anymore regarding _____, which has now been confessed, repented of, and forgiven, and from which I am now being cleansed by the shed blood of my Lord Jesus Christ.

Impatience and offense workout

Step 1: Prayerfully review the following list and mark each sin you or your generations have participated with. It is important that you are not rushed and that you are in a private place as you go through this.

❑ **Offense:** vexed, provoked, stumbled or tripped up

❑ **Judgment:** pronounces an opinion of an offence concerning right and wrong.

❑ **Condemnation:** declares a guilty verdict against one who allegedly offended you.

❑ **Bitterness:** harboring cruel, biting, harsh, painful, distressing, thoughts toward another; piercing to the feelings or mind

❑ **Unforgiveness:** not willing to excuse or pardon another's fault or wrong-doing, a breach until it is resolved, it stands there waiting to be fulfilled like any debt; holding onto real or perceived offences against you by another

❑ **Resentment:** Bitter indignation at having been treated unfairly; a deep sense of injury, holding on to feelings associated with someone having hurt you (real or imagined hurt)

❑ **Retaliation:** to return evil for evil

❑ **Anger:** a 'brainstorm' excited by a real or supposed injury; usually accompanied with a propensity to take vengeance

❑ **Hatred:** Detest

❑ **Betrayal:** Expose, condemn and deliver to judgment rather than covering a trespass

❑ **Violence:** the threat or infliction of physical force; an act of aggression, verbal, emotional or physical.

❑ **Murder:** to destroy another's reputation with the tongue; to slander; to kill

❑ **Accusation:** an assertion that someone is guilty of a fault or offence; to blame

(Note: If you realize that you've participated with one iniquity part-way down the list to this point, you would also have had to participate with each sin above the one you first recognized.)

❑ **Adultery:** to have unlawful intercourse with another's wife

❑ **Bitterness toward God**

❑ **Bondage:** to become a slave or under the control of an unclean spirit

❑ **Cursing:** uttering obscenities; swearing; using the Lord's name in vain;

❑ **Death:** thoughts of death or dying; accidents; family history of early deaths

❑ **Despising the chastening of the Lord**

❑ **Destroyer:** damage irreparably; to ruin; to devour; to consume; to cause to be wasted either time or money)

❑ **Envy/Jealousy:** spite and resentment at seeing the success of another; antagonism towards someone who has something you want; to desire best/biggest for oneself

❑ **Fear:** a painful emotion or passion excited by the expectation of evil; to feel anxious or apprehensive about a real or imagined event; it is the opposite of faith

❑ **Fornication:** to prostitute one's body to the lust of another; pre-marital sex; illicit sexual intercourse.

❑ **Gossip**

❑ **Hostility:** deep-seated ill will; usually unprovoked aggression

❑ **Impatience:** of others, yourself or the timing of God

❑ **Physical abuse:** physical cruelty, usually on a regular basis and against another's will

- ❑ **Pornography:** any sexually explicit writing, picture, or movie intended to arouse sexual desire
- ❑ **Programming:** automatic performance to a stimuli
- ❑ **Rebellion:** resisting authority, defiance or disobedience to leaders, parents and to God
- ❑ **Record of wrongs:** doing the flashback; playing back the video; record the sayings of another in the heart with purpose of bringing it up to throw in another's face
- ❑ **Rejection:** not being received or acknowledged; cast off; slighted; despised
- ❑ **Self-pity:** a self-indulgent sorrow over your own suffering
- ❑ **Sexual abuse:** incest; forcible sexual acts; verbal abuse of sexual nature; sexual assault; sexual victimization; domination
- ❑ **Shame:** humiliation, disgrace; to dishonor; to treat with contempt in word deed or thought
- ❑ **Slander:** words maliciously spoken that damage the reputation of another; to ridicule; to lessen a person in the esteem of his peers
- ❑ **Strife:** contention for superiority; contention in anger; struggle for victory; love of strife
- ❑ **Suicide:** suicide threats; generational suicide; suicide attempts; thoughts of suicide
- ❑ **Thief:** an embezzler; the name also transferred to false teachers; abuse confidence of others for own gain
- ❑ **Verbal abuse:** a rude expression intended to offend or hurt; put downs; cursing;

Step 2: Go back through the list and pray this prayer inserting the sin in the blank space. You may insert several sins in the blank space at a time if you desire.

Prayer of Repentance
(Preferably out loud)

Father God, I recognize and take responsibility for myself and my ancestors for the sin(s) of _____. I agree with Your verdict on my rebellion. I repent, I renounce, and I ask forgiveness for my participation with these sins, and I ask that their curse be broken in the name of Jesus Christ of Nazareth.

Step 3: Bind the strongman. This is best done by an experienced and trusted ministering friend the first time around.

Prayer to Bind the Strongmen of Bitterness, Offense, and Impatience

In the name of Jesus Christ of Nazareth and by the power of the Holy Spirit, I take authority over the strongmen of bitterness, offense, and impatience. I break your power and bind you and put you on notice that I am destroying your armor in which you trust and I will be coming back to remove you from your palace.

Step 4: Purging the evil. Review the above list again now inserting the sin you have repented of in the blank.

Command of Deliverance
(Must be out loud with eyes open,
realizing you are speaking directly to a spirit)

In the name of Jesus Christ of Nazareth and by the power of the Holy Spirit, I take authority over the spirit(s) of _____. I break your power, I cast you out, and I command you to return no more.

Step 5: Purge the strongman now that you have destroyed his stronghold.

Command of Deliverance
(Must be out loud with eyes open,
realizing you are speaking directly to a spirit)

In the name of Jesus Christ of Nazareth and by the power of the Holy Spirit, I take authority over the strongmen of bitterness, offense, and impatience. I break your power, I cast you out, and I command you to return no more.

Step 6: Pray that God will cause you to increase and abound in His love and that you would be an overcomer in the sins of which you just repented. Ask for a scripture that you will use to resist the devil when he tries to open the trapdoor again to regain entrance to your heart.

Breaking bands of a corrupted covenant
When a relationship has become totally corrupted due to sin, a bond remains uniting the souls whether it be between consenting people, blood relatives, or between a perpetrator and his victim. Really, anything that opened a trapdoor, or with anyone you have been harboring bitterness for a period of time, could establish a band or a soul tie that needs to be severed. After a major breach between Judah and the rest of the Tribes of Israel there were these spiritual bands that needed to be broken to release the brotherhood.

> Then I cut asunder mine other staff, even Bands [to become pledged or bound], that I might break [to void a covenant] the brotherhood between Judah and Israel.
> —ZECHARIAH 11:14

The most common ungodly bonds are established in unlawful sexual unions or severed intimate relationships.

> Know ye not that your bodies are the members of Christ? shall I then take the members of Christ, and make them the members [bound by criminal intercourse] of an harlot [anyone who indulges in unlawful sex whether for gain or for lust]? God forbid. What? know ye not that he which is joined [form intimate connection] to an harlot is one body? for two, saith he, shall be one flesh.
> —1 CORINTHIANS 6:15–16

We find these ties are also formed with those subjected to dominating control, all types of abuse or an excessive need to impress. If you have forgiven but still cannot get the individual out of your mind and they seem to control your every move even though they are nowhere around there would be a band that needs to be severed that unites your souls.

The band or soul tie is broken by first taking responsibility for and repenting of any known sin associated with the person and then using a prayer like this:

PRAYER TO SEVER BANDS

Father God by the power of the Holy Spirit, I ask You to break all ungodly spirit, soul, and body chords and bands that may have been established between _____ and I. I sever the bonds supernaturally and ask You Father to remove from me all influence of _____ and draw me back to Yourself; break the bands of every part of me that is wrongfully tied in bondage to another person. I pray in the name of Jesus Christ of Nazareth. Amen.

AGAPE IS KIND

Peter had very practical training from Jesus regarding his love life, and in his writings he outlines the steps he learned to arrive at the destination of agape. There are nine steps in this progression to maturity in agape. Peter makes a very impassioned plea for us to see this through to the end, calling those who stop partway as blind to eternal matters.

Circle each of the nine steps in 2 Peter that are a must for you to grow up in:

And beside this, giving all [1] *diligence* [zeal, earnestness to achieve] add to your [2] *faith* [conviction of truth consistent with actions] [3] *virtue* [blameless in character]; and to virtue [4] *knowledge* [seeking spiritual truth at level of the intellect] And to knowledge [5] *temperance* [restraint and abstinence of depraved or unrighteous behavior]; and to temperance [6] *patience* [does not surrender or succumb to circumstances and trials] and to patience [7] *godliness* [fear of God manifested in actions]; And to godliness [8] *brotherly kindness* [*phileo* love, affection]; and to brotherly kindness [9] *charity* [*agape*]. For if these things be in you, and abound, they make you that ye shall neither be barren [faith without works] nor unfruitful [destitute] in the knowledge of our Lord Jesus Christ. But he that lacketh these things is blind [mentally], and cannot see afar off [not planning beyond this earthly existence], and hath forgotten that he was purged [cleansed] from his old sins. Wherefore the rather, brethren, give diligence [the only endeavor that matters] to make your calling [invitation] and election [your personal choice to believe] sure: for if ye do these things, ye shall never fall [stumble].

> Truth is not to be celibate, truth is to grab the arm of lovingkindness and walk down the aisle together.

—2 PETER 1:5–10, EMPHASIS ADDED

For step number nine, agape, to abound in your life the Lord will have to be given permission to restore the previous eight virtues in your life. There is a spiritual progression starting at diligence, which is essentially a decision to follow the Lord no matter what, and stepping through faith, virtue, and upward to charity, which we refer to as agape love.

The fruit of the advancement of kindness in your life will be your passion to push all your brothers and sisters up to be all they can be in their relationship with the Lord. Paul became the most effective church leader of all time once obtaining his doctorate in weakness. This is not weakness in moral character but it is dying to self, realizing that nothing happens by our might or power but rather by the spirit of God.

> And he said unto me, my grace is sufficient for thee: for my strength is made perfect in weakness. Most gladly therefore will I rather glory in my infirmities, that the power of Christ may rest upon me.
> —2 Corinthians 12:9

I spent years diligently studying the Scriptures cover to cover to understand truth; and in my immaturity I felt that if I announced this truth everywhere I went, particularly in my home, I would reap a plentiful spiritual harvest. What did I not get? I didn't get the connection of loving-kindness to truth. The acquiring of truth is supposed to change me, and then that truth can only be imparted to others through loving-kindness and mercy. That isn't something you can just determine one day to do differently without going through the growing up process that Peter stepped up for us. Hopefully you folks will grow up quicker than I did, as being in a household of the truth-policeman without love is like being in a thunderstorm trying to guess where the next bolt of lightning will occur.

Truth is not to be celibate, truth is to grab the arm of loving-kindness and walk down the aisle together. Following this pair is righteousness and peace, who are busy kissing. Peace is the pleasant result of our sanctification.

> Mercy [*checech*; loving-kindness] and truth [knowledge resulting in firmness and predictability] are met together; righteousness [intent on straight and narrow] and peace [a satisfied condition where our mind is in agreement with our sanctified spirit] have kissed each other.
> —Psalm 85:10

The psalmist put it so beautifully, "Righteousness and peace have kissed each other!" They belong together as it would be impossible to have peace if living in unrighteousness.

Furthermore, truth of itself doesn't free us from sin until it is coupled with mercy. It is the goodness of the Lord that leads to repentance, not the Lord beating us with truth.

By mercy [*checech*; loving-kindness] and truth [knowledge resulting in
firmness and predictability] iniquity [depravity] is purged [cleansed]: and
by the fear of the Lord men depart [repulsed by] from evil.

—Proverbs 16:6

The Hebrew word *checech* is one of the most important words in the Old
Testament, occurring 241 times. It is most often translated as loving-kindness
or mercy in the Authorized Version. A person exercising this "loving-kindness"
has chosen to treat a stranger as a close family member, extending towards
him the kindness and love normally reserved only for kin. Loving-kindness is
bestowing honor and placing a high value on a person regardless of their personal estate or relationship. Rahab, the harlot in Joshua 2, exercised this mercy
to the Israelite spies, strangers to whom she had nothing in common. In fact
they were there spying on her city in order to attack it. She hid them from her
king's men and helped in their escape.

So wonderful is God's mercy or loving-kindness that He elects to extend it
towards men even when they prove unfaithful to
Him. His loving-kindness towards His beloved
sometimes seems obscured as it did for Noah for
a short time in his life.

> When on one side
> of the mountain,
> it is difficult to see
> what God is doing
> on the other side
> of the mountain.

Many of you who have been obedient to the
Lord and know you are loved of God have gone
through some very deep waters. Noah stands
out in the Scriptures as a man who was bold
in his faith and was obedient to the directions of the Lord, even when many
would say that he was foolish. Noah chose to serve God even if it meant considerable ridicule and losing friends. The prophet Isaiah puts an interesting
perspective on what it was like to be in the ark during the flood. We suppose
that after Noah got into the ark with his family and all the animals that he
heaved a big sigh of relief and said, "Whew, guys, I guess we made it! Let's
enjoy the cruise!"

The ark was like a barge which had no power of its own and no ability to
steer, so during the storm it was "tossed about with tempest" beyond the control of all the humans within. Noah felt forsaken, as though God hid His face
from him, as he was inside the ark with no outside light for over six months.
This paints a picture of what it is like for us as we face the storms. We feel
we are all alone in the darkness of our ship that is sent adrift and unable to
see ahead of us to even prepare for the next wave that will strike us broadside.
The journey seems to go on and on with no light ahead of us, and we have no
strength or ability to alter the course one iota. All efforts to call for help seem
to fall on deaf ears and we may be tempted to wonder, *Does God even know I
am in this mess?* With that sense of abandonment it is difficult to find comfort

and to displace our fears. If the story were to stop there, one would think this is so unfair; but then the next chapter.

Noah opens the window of the ark, the waters are abated, the storm is over and the ark comes to rest miraculously under the obvious guidance of the Spirit of God. The Lord was in total control of the ship all along and never let go.

It is not by might nor by power that our mountains are removed but by the Spirit of the Lord. When on one side of the mountain, it is difficult to see what God is doing on the other side of the mountain until it is removed and the Lord gathers us up in His arms pouring upon us His everlasting loving-kindness.

> For a small moment have I forsaken thee; but with great mercies will I gather thee. In a little wrath I hid my face from thee for a moment; but with everlasting kindness will I have mercy on thee, saith the Lord thy Redeemer. For this is as the waters of Noah unto me: for as I have sworn that the waters of Noah should no more go over the earth; so have I sworn that I would not be wroth with thee, nor rebuke thee. For the mountains shall depart, and the hills be removed; but my kindness shall not depart from thee, neither shall the covenant of my peace be removed, saith the Lord that hath mercy on thee. O thou afflicted, tossed with tempest, and not comforted, behold, I will lay thy stones with fair colors, and lay thy foundations with sapphires.
>
> —Isaiah 54:7–11

During the storm, the peace of God and his mercies may seem disconnected from us but know this: that God didn't depart, but a thief, a destroyer, a liar and an accuser slipped in between to blanket us in darkness in an attempt to separate us from the love of God. The storm test has a purpose to expose the real cause of the tempest so the evil powers that are raging can be purged to keep the ship afloat.

> I know, O Lord, that thy judgments are right, and that thou in faithfulness hast afflicted me. Let, I pray thee, thy merciful kindness be for my comfort, according to thy word unto thy servant. Let thy tender mercies come unto me, that I may live: for thy law is my delight.
>
> —Psalm 119:75–77

I spent much of my life stubbornly chasing wealth and the snares that accompany it, and I learned the hard way that it cost more than it paid. Vanity seekers are the earth dwellers, whereas those that seek mercy have the wisdom and insight valued by those focused towards eternity. We are all living for eternity now, just the destination varies.

> They that observe [treasure, pursue] lying [empty, worthless] vanities [i.e., riches vanish more quickly than a breath] forsake their own mercy [loving-kindness].
>
> —Jonah 2:8

With the ability and power Jesus had, He could have taken over the entire wealth of the world; but He chose the eternal perspective of laying down those ambitions, laying down His life for us. Seems to me that Satan offered the whole world to Jesus as that was valuable to Satan, whereas Jesus knew what would be required for true eternal reward and riches. Jesus obviously sees into eternity, whereas we have to wait for the view. By giving He received. That is the principle of truth married to mercy and kindness.

> Hereby perceive we the love [*agape*] of God, because he laid down his life for us: and we ought to lay down our lives for the brethren. But whoso hath this world's good, and seeth his brother have need, and shutteth up his bowels [like a dark rain cloud that won't release over a drought stricken land] of compassion from him, how dwelleth the love of God in him? My little children, let us not love in word, neither in tongue; but in deed and in truth.
> —1 JOHN 3:16–18

Loving-kindness is authentic when it is dumped upon those that have no intention of even snorting thanks. If we are repaid for our kindness here that is all the reward we will get. The truth is that when you are despised for the good you did, you have reason to be quite happy as you have deferred repayment until eternity.

> But love ye your enemies, and do good, and lend, hoping for nothing again; and your reward shall be great, and ye shall be the children of the Highest: for he is kind unto the unthankful and to the evil.
> —LUKE 6:35

Giving through kindness actually makes the Lord owing to you the debt of love. You cannot outgive the Lord.

> He that hath pity [mercy, loving kindness, show favor] upon the poor lendeth unto the Lord; and that which he hath given [benefited] will he pay him again.
> —PROVERBS 19:17

With the truth of kindness understood, why wouldn't people be lining up to provide of their resources. If you give, it will be given back; if you don't give freely, you lose what ought to have been freely given and open your household up to many curses.

> He that giveth unto the poor shall not lack: but he that hideth his eyes shall have many a curse.
> —PROVERBS 28:27

This area of kindness is a subject that we are graded on by the invisible intent and motive of our hearts. God doesn't need our gifts, as He owns everything. He allows us to give so we can see where our attachments are, whether we've died to self and most importantly to give our ability to agape the shake down.

But this I say, He which soweth sparingly shall reap also sparingly; and he which soweth bountifully shall reap also bountifully. Every man according as he purposeth in his heart, so let him give; not grudgingly [pained, stressed], or of necessity [for one's own advantage]: for God loveth a cheerful [to cause to shine] giver. And God is able to make all grace [merciful kindness] abound toward you; that ye, always having all sufficiency in all things, may abound to every good work.

—2 CORINTHIANS 9:6–8

Unkindness workout

Step 1: Prayerfully review the following list and mark each sin in which you or your generations have participated. It is important that you are not rushed and that you are in a private place as you go through this.

- ❑ Annoyance
- ❑ Carelessness
- ❑ Deceit
- ❑ Heartlessness
- ❑ Inflexibly
- ❑ Intolerance
- ❑ Malice
- ❑ Neglect
- ❑ Resentfulness
- ❑ Shame
- ❑ Stinginess
- ❑ Thoughtlessness
- ❑ Callousness
- ❑ Cruelty
- ❑ Harshness
- ❑ Impulsiveness
- ❑ Insincerity
- ❑ Lying
- ❑ Mercilessness
- ❑ Reluctance
- ❑ Ruthlessness
- ❑ Spite
- ❑ Stubbornness
- ❑ Wickedness

Step 2: Go back through the list and pray this prayer inserting the sin in the blank space. You may insert several sins in the blank space at a time if you desire.

Prayer of Repentance
(Preferably out loud)

Father God, I recognize and take responsibility for myself and my ancestors for the sin(s) of _____. I agree with Your verdict on my rebellion. I repent, I renounce, and I ask forgiveness for my participation with these sins, and I ask that their curse be broken in the name of Jesus Christ of Nazareth.

Step 3: Bind the strongman. This is best done by an experienced and trusted ministering friend the first time around.

Prayer to Bind the Strongman of Unkindness

In the name of Jesus Christ of Nazareth and by the power of the Holy Spirit I take authority over the strongman of unkindness. I break your power and

*bind you and put you on notice that I am destroying your armor in which
you trust and I will be coming back to remove you from your palace.*

Step 4: Purging the evil. Review the above list again now inserting the sin you
have repented of in the blank.

Command of Deliverance
(Must be out loud with eyes open,
realizing you are speaking directly to a spirit)

*In the name of Jesus Christ of Nazareth and by the power of the Holy Spirit,
I take authority over the spirit(s) of _____. I break your
power, I cast you out, and I command you to return no more.*

Step 5: Purge the strongman now that you have destroyed his stronghold.

Command of Deliverance
(Must be out loud with eyes open,
realizing you are speaking directly to a spirit)

*In the name of Jesus Christ of Nazareth and by the power of the Holy Spirit,
I take authority over the strongman of unkindness. I break your power, I
cast you out, and I command you to return no more.*

Step 6: Pray that God will cause you to increase and abound in His love and
that you would be an overcomer in the sins just repented of. Ask for a scripture
that you will use to resist the devil when he tries to open the trapdoor again
to regain entrance to your heart.

AGAPE ENVIETH NOT

It would be most interesting to be able to survey the thoughts of every reader
after glancing at the heading, Agape Envieth Not. How many of you said in
your heart, "Oh, this doesn't apply to me, so I'll skip over it"? When you feel
that repulsion or distraction, start paying attention to what the devil may be
trying to divert you from.

As we look for healing in any area of defect in our lives, we need to be
looking for the root cause and focus our attention there. Many times we
pray and seek deliverance from the symptom but that doesn't do any good.
Someone is struggling with coughing fits, so you medicate the cough, not
realizing the reason the person is coughing is because of lung disease. Did the
cough syrup do anything for the lung disease?

Besides me, do any of you know what it is like to struggle with anger? I
repented of anger more times that I'll ever want to admit and asked God to
remove it; but I couldn't overcome because I still received some sort of intoxi-
cating pleasure in it—so the brainstorms continued. If I had paid more attention to my Bible, I would have seen what the possible root of anger might have
been. Proverbs has this to say:

> Wrath is cruel, and anger is outrageous [downpour, a brainstorm]; but
> who is able to stand [survive, remain] before envy [agitated consumption]?
>
> —PROVERBS 27:4

Envy that goes undetected as anger is so visible and in your face. Anger step aside, it is the envy and jealousy that are the heat source. Envy desires to deprive another of what he has. When we think of envy, we think of some sort of merchandise as being the object of desire; but it just could be something as commonplace as to have your opinion or position heard over that of another.

Jealousy desires to have the same sort of thing for itself. Simply taking the credit for what another did or refusing to recognize the contribution of someone else is the deception of jealousy.

> For jealousy is the rage [poison, anger, hostility] of a man: therefore he
> will not spare in the day of vengeance.
>
> —PROVERBS 6:34

Are there any other possible roots of the symptom of anger? How about scorn? Deal with the scorner and contention and watch as strife and reproach are released from our resume.

> Cast out the scorner, and contention shall go out; yea, strife and reproach
> shall cease.
>
> —PROVERBS 22:10

Again after the scorner is removed, contention must go so that strife has no longer a foothold.

> As coals are to burning coals, and wood to fire; so is a contentious man
> to kindle strife.
>
> —PROVERBS 26:21

There is still another stronghold that manifests anger and that is pride.

> Only by pride cometh contention: but with the well advised is wisdom.
>
> —PROVERBS 13:10

There are many health benefits as well when we deal with envy. Proverbs records that envy is rottenness to the bones. What is in the bones? The marrow is the factory of the white blood cells that are required for a strong immune system. When the white blood cells are not doing their work, there are countless diseases, including all the autoimmune diseases that may have envy and company as the root.

> A sound heart is the life of the flesh: but envy the rottenness of the bones.
>
> —PROVERBS 14:30

The sins in an unhealthy relationship are also a factor in bone disease.

> A virtuous [integrity, fitness, efficiency, worthy] woman is a crown [a dignity, self-respect] to her husband: but she that maketh ashamed [dishonored, humiliated, demeaned] is as rottenness [pervading fear, decay] in his bones.
>
> —PROVERBS 12:4

The good news of all of this is that we now have a track to run on to focus on our healing and the treatment is free. Envy seeks to trouble and diminish the good in others because he does not have what they have.

> For ye are yet carnal [of a sensual deprived nature]: for whereas there is among you envying [fierce indignation, contentiousness], and strife [rivalry, debate], and divisions [boundaries, standing apart], are ye not carnal, and walk as men?
>
> —1 CORINTHIANS 3:3

Envy of the success of another is self-destructive. Rachel gave Jacob the unreasonable ultimatum to give her children or else she'd die, as though he could do much about it. Rachel was given a child, Joseph, and then she died giving birth to her second son, Benjamin. She got what she wanted but her vow and her envy claimed her life so she could not enjoy the fruit of her womb.

> And when Rachel saw that she bare Jacob no children, Rachel envied [burn with zeal against a rival] her sister; and said unto Jacob, Give me children, or else I die.
>
> —GENESIS 30:1

Envy was the root of the treachery the eleven brothers committed against Joseph where they captured him, sold him to slavery, and lied to the father, Jacob, saying Joseph was killed. The brothers were envious of the call God had on Joseph's life:

> And his brethren envied him; but his father observed the saying.
>
> —GENESIS 37:11

> And the patriarchs, moved with envy, sold Joseph into Egypt: but God was with him.
>
> —ACTS 7:9

Similar to the fate that Joseph suffered, Jesus Christ was delivered up for crucifixion (murder) by the chief priests because they were envious of His healing ministry and wanted to eliminate him. Pilate mused in Matthew 27:18, "For he knew that for envy they had delivered him."

Envy is a weapon Satan is adept at using in an attempt to close up shop on the Lord's work. But was he successful with Joseph? Only for a short time, then God turned the curse into a blessing and used Joseph to save the lives of thousands. Was he successful with Jesus? Only for a few hours did he try, then Satan would give up and God turned the curse into a blessing saving millions.

Paul confronted the church at Corinth regarding the stew the believers were constantly heating up:

> For I fear, lest, when I come, I shall not find you [the church] such as I would, and that I shall be found unto you such as ye would not: lest there be debates [power struggle], envying [fierce indignation, contentious] , wraths [hot anger], strifes [seeking to win followers to your faction], backbitings [character assassination], whisperings [secret slandering], swellings [hardness of heart due to activation of pride], tumults [rebellion, usurping authority].
> —2 CORINTHIANS 12:20

I suppose a church that is facing this envy stew has a choice either: it is time to split or it is time to repent and see what God can do to turn the tables on what Satan heated up. James adds that conformity to what the world has stirs up the lustful spirit of envy in Christians. Envy is also a block to answered prayer.

> Ye ask, and receive not, because ye ask amiss, that ye may consume it upon your lusts. Ye adulterers and adulteresses, know ye not that the friendship of the world is enmity [evil opposite of all that is agape] with God? Whosoever therefore will be a friend of the world is the enemy of God. Do ye think that the scripture saith in vain, the spirit that dwelleth in us lusteth to envy?
> —JAMES 4:3–5

So far we've just exposed a little aroma of the stink that this principality and its associates are able to kick up. This study will expose a lengthy list of uninvited guests that are destroying marriages, splitting churches, closing down ministries, causing wars, and pulling down corporations.

> Now the works [occupation] of the flesh are manifest, which are these; Adultery, fornication, uncleanness [impure motives, sensuality, defilement], lasciviousness [carnality, filthy words, indecent body movements, unchaste handling of male or female, wasteful], Idolatry, witchcraft [deception, seductions], hatred [enmity: everything opposed to agape], variance [strife, debate, contention, rivalry], emulations [punitive zeal, envy, jealousy, fierce indignation, diminishes and destroy the good it sees in others], wrath [anger, madness of a drinker], strife [divisive spirit, put self forward], seditions [separation], heresies [dissension arising from diverse opinions and aims], Envyings [deprive another of what he has], murders, drunkenness [intoxication, need not be excessive], revellings [evening drunken parties coupled with impurity, music and obscenely], and such like: of the which I tell you before, as I have also told you in time past, that they which do such things [practice continually] shall not inherit the kingdom of God.
> —GALATIANS 5:19

The Bible has many sin lists and this one in Galatians should have large warning signs placed around its perimeter: "Warning! Must be a heathen who does not care about eternity to lodge herein!" There are those who stumble and participate with the sin included here, but do not feel condemned unless you include these sins as a regular way of life without hesitation, without conscience, and without repentance. Failing to recognize your sins pre-empts you from the kingdom you've been anticipating. So be prepared for much spiritual opposition as you continue with your first works. The opposition may come in the form of distractions, drowsiness, or a desire to do this quickly to get it over with.

There is a powerful family of wickedness that we will be exposing. They are like the mafia that will stop at nothing to protect their interests and to expand their influence. However, for the believer this is but a test to prove whether we will trust in God or be victimized by fear. This is nothing for an equipped believer to fear, as he or she has the tools that are mighty through God in the pulling down of strongholds.

Ahab's father took the throne of Israel by assassinating the king. Ahab then married outside of his people bringing in a very worldly wife, Jezebel, who was fanatical in her devotion to the gods Baal and Ashtoreth. Baal, who uses the male sex organ as his symbol, is a male deity of power and sexuality. Ashtoreth, the female deity, uses the female sex organs for her symbol and is the goddess of fertility, love, and war. The most depraved sexual practices and abominations along with human sacrifice are involved to appease the appetites of these false gods. Jezebel had a herd of 450 prophets of Baal and 400 prophetesses of Ashtoreth to serve her sensual animalistic religious depravity.

The name *Jezebel* means "unhusbanded." Yes, she was married for political purposes but unhusbanded in the sense that she would respect, honor, or submit to no one. She would learn the art of enticing the flesh of others through intimidation, seduction, and domination. If seduction wouldn't serve her purposes, she had no reservation in seeking the death of those in opposition to her. Jezebel sought the death of Elijah and as generational iniquity goes, Jezebel's daughter, Athaliah, murdered her grandsons in order to take the throne for herself. (See 2 Kings 11:1.)

Ahab's power and authority is what attracted his ambitious wife, while he was enticed by the wiles and seduction of this evil, wild, and feisty woman. Ahab represented an accomplished man with a weakness and a dark side.

Jesus warns the church in Revelation about not being able to deal with the most destructive of spirits that He names after this infamous Queen Jezebel. Jesus holds the church responsible to recognize evil within its ranks and to deal with it. Jesus Christ obviously was patient with those vexed by the tendencies and ambitions of Jezebel and gave them space to repent; but pride often prevents one taken captive by this principality to see their way clear to put it to death.

There is a part of the church that believes they will go through the entire Great Tribulation, and they are right. The denomination of Thyatira will go through the tribulation but only because it refused to repent of tolerating the Jezebel spirit. A side note for you students: the church of Smyrna will go through only part of the Tribulation (see Revelation 2:8–10), whereas the church of Philadelphia will escape the entire Tribulation (see Revelation 3:10). So for those that say they are "pre-trib" say "amen," and for those that say they are "mid-trib" say "may you be strong and very courageous," and for those that say they are "post-trib" say "may God be merciful."

> Notwithstanding I have a few things against thee, because thou sufferest that woman Jezebel, which calleth herself a prophetess, to teach and to seduce my servants to commit fornication [desiring anything before its time], and to eat things sacrificed unto idols [belief that Christians are not bound by moral laws of serving only one God]. And I gave her space to repent of her fornication; and she repented not. Behold, I will cast her into a bed, and them that commit adultery with her into great tribulation, except they repent of their deeds. And I will kill her children with death; and all the churches shall know that I am he which searcheth the reins and hearts: and I will give unto every one of you according to your works.
> —REVELATION 2:20–21

> There is a part of the church that believes they will go through the entire Great Tribulation, and they are right regarding themselves.

Because of the great difficulty one taken captive by this stronghold has in repenting and wanting to deal with this spirit, it will often kick up a considerable tempest in trying to intimidate and discourage the minister of reconciliation from trying to expose it.

The church of Thyatira justified the elevation of certain women to leadership roles over the men—a role Paul advised against. But since the church didn't heed the words of Paul, Christ then has to judge the church for their rebellion. The godly order ordained for the church is the same order God ordained for the matrimonial church. This is not male chauvinism; it is how God set it up as He knew what was best for women knowing the men, and he knew what is best for men knowing the women. God seldom explains "why." He just says the "do." Therefore the author will not speculate on God's intention but will just be the messenger that provides commentary on the vital Word of the Lord. The Word will speak for itself. It gives the options for us to choose with the corresponding consequences.

> But I suffer not a woman to teach, nor to usurp authority over the man, but to be in silence.
> —1 TIMOTHY 2:12

There are many women of wisdom and experience that are incredibly gifted as teachers, and Titus recognizes that gift is for the purpose of teaching the younger women so the Word of God is not blasphemed.

> The aged women likewise, that they be in behaviour as becometh holiness, not false accusers, not given to much wine, teachers of good things; That they may teach the young women to be sober, to love their husbands, to love their children, To be discreet, chaste, keepers at home, good, obedient to their own husbands, that the word of God be not blasphemed.
>
> —TITUS 2:3–5

One of the difficulties noted in Revelation 2 regarding Jezebel is that this spirit does not like repentance, as repentance will destroy its stronghold and loose its captives. This principality knows that by refusing to deal with repentance immediately, as Paul teaches in Ephesians, it will be given further place to occupy thus gaining a stranglehold with the parties involved.

> Be ye angry, and sin not: let not the sun go down upon your wrath: Neither give place to the devil.
>
> —EPHESIANS 4:26–27

In any relationship, but particularly in a marriage where husband and wife are one flesh, this tactic of delay of repentance by the devil opens the door to place a curse in the partners' lives, making the struggle now sevenfold more difficult to resolve.

As we study this stronghold, understand that many of the tendencies and vexations of Jezebel and Ahab are not necessarily specific to one sex or the other. Paul reminds us that those who judge another so judge because they are guilty of the same thing. We judge the evil of another to protect the evil we are harboring. (See Romans 2:1–3.)

We only judge to divert

Now, a moment of momentous truth for the author: A few months back, as I was studying this topic, my spirit was vexed and I felt the impulse to write down in my journal all the areas taught in scripture that I thought my beloved wasn't submitting to me. "Yeah, I know what you are thinking." I don't think I ever filled a page so fast. I didn't even have to think; it just came out and I was pressing on my gel pen so hard that it was making an impression through several pages thus defiling them. I was obviously vexed but taking pleasure in the process of my assignment. Then as I reviewed my list, I got a talking to by the Spirit, "Dennis, in each area that you are judging your beloved where she may or may not be submitting to you, you in turn are not submitting in the same areas as a spiritual wife to Jesus Christ!" I muttered, "Come on, that was a set up." But I reviewed the list again, and I knew it was of the Lord. I got to repent of where I wasn't submitting to my husband, my Lord Jesus. We only judge to divert. In my case, my judgment concerning my beloved was just accusation through my vexation.

Ahab goes into a meltdown over his envy for some land that his neighbor has and refuses to sell to him and so Jezebel comes along to fix it. She has

Naboth murdered by enticing two men who were known to have the spirit of lying to condemn Naboth by false testimony.

> But Jezebel [un-husbanded one] his wife came to him, and said unto him [Ahab], Why is thy spirit so sad, that thou eatest no bread? And he said unto her, Because I spake unto Naboth the Jezreelite, and said unto him, Give me thy vineyard for money; or else, if it please thee, I will give thee another vineyard for it: and he answered, I will not give thee my vineyard. And Jezebel his wife said unto him, Dost thou now govern the kingdom of Israel? arise, and eat bread, and let thine heart be merry: I will give thee the vineyard of Naboth the Jezreelite. So she wrote letters in Ahab's name, and sealed them with his seal, and sent the letters unto the elders and to the nobles that were in his city, dwelling with Naboth. And she wrote in the letters, saying, Proclaim a fast, and set Naboth on high among the people And set two men, sons of Belial [lying spirits], before him, to bear witness against him, saying, Thou didst blaspheme God and the king. And then carry him out, and stone him, that he may die.
>
> —1 KINGS 21:5–10

The Jezebel vexation will use manipulation and lies to steal the inheritance and destroy the object of its envy. The dividing of the inheritance through divorce and subsequent death to the household is the work of this kingdom. This is not the work of the beloved spouse, as the battle is not against the flesh and blood but the principalities, and in particular this mafia family of envy.

The Scripture gives insight into the realm of evil: one spirit will pull the trigger of the starting gun setting in motion a relay race of several other unclean spirits that will take the baton and carry it to the finish line, thus completing the assignment of whatever the evil deed may be. The spirit of Jezebel may not actually carry out an evil deed but will provoke in order to instigate someone else to fall.

> But there was none like unto Ahab, which did sell himself to work wickedness in the sight of the LORD, whom Jezebel his wife stirred up.
>
> —1 KINGS 21:25

Elijah the prophet of God sets up a major showdown for the people of Israel so they could see firsthand whether Baal was a god to be feared or whether the Lord his God was the one that should be feared. The test was to see which deity could kindle a fire upon the altar. The 450 prophets of Baal did their song and dance and cut thing and couldn't even get a spark in return from Baal. To make the message clear, Elijah set up an altar and drenched everything, including the wood, with water. God sent fire from heaven and burned up the alter consuming even the water that collected in the trench round about the altar. At this, the prophets of Baal scampered away but were slain by the men of Israel. That was an amazing work of God through the hands of this man Elijah. But look at what happened next: Jezebel didn't take it very well that all her prophets were killed and threatened to kill Elijah. He had just called down fire from heaven to destroy the drenched altar; but then when a bit of fire came from this loudspeaker, Jezebel, he ran, hid, became depressed, and contemplated suicide.

> And Ahab told Jezebel all that Elijah had done, and withal how he had slain all the prophets with the sword. Then Jezebel sent a messenger unto Elijah, saying, so let the gods do to me, and more also, if I make not thy life as the life of one of them by tomorrow about this time. And when he saw that, he arose, and went for his life, and came to Beersheba, which belongeth to Judah, and left his servant there. But he himself went a day's journey into the wilderness, and came and sat down under a juniper tree: and he requested for himself that he might die; and said, It is enough; now, O LORD, take away my life; for I am not better than my fathers.
>
> —1 KINGS 19:1–4

It would seem that Baal and the 450 prophets were so soundly defeated by the God of Elijah that there could be no doubt in anyone's mind as to who was the only true and powerful God. The term *stiff-necked* or *obstinate* would be the word used to describe Jezebel. She was given over to the lie and nothing would persuade her differently. The Scriptures often use the terms *committing adultery* or *fornication* in connection to serving other gods or being in idolatry. When one has committed adultery, they become one flesh with the object of their affections; so a simple change of mind will not break that band. The band or bond (soul tie) must be severed spiritually.

> Because I knew that thou art obstinate [severe, difficult, stiff-necked], and thy neck is an iron sinew, and thy brow brass [brazen forehead, impudent]; I have even from the beginning declared it to thee; before it came to pass I shewed it thee: lest thou shouldest say, Mine idol hath done them, and my graven image, and my molten image, hath commanded them.
>
> —ISAIAH 48:4–5

> Using argument, logic, or counseling to free a person of this lockdown will be met only with scorn.

This is the kingdom that needs to be dealt with when loved ones are swept away by a cult, by a false abusive teacher, or a New Age modality. Spiritual blindness or brainwashing is a condition that can be broken by loosing the bands tying them to the particular spiritual modality, followed by repenting of such involvement and purging. Using argument, logic, or counseling to free a person of this lockdown will be met only with scorn. The Scripture teaches that the weapons of our warfare are not carnal but mighty through God in the pulling down of strongholds.

Be alerted to the manifestations of the Jezebel spirit; this charming person who "loved" you more that life itself will now turn on you. The same person, man or woman, who loved you, is now devoted to destroying you, your reputation, your business, your family, and your ministry and displacing your inheritance. That spirit feels scorned and betrayed and will go to any means to hurt you. Keep in mind that your battle is not with the person, the flesh and blood, but the principalities and powers that are causing the vexation.

> Proud and haughty scorner is his name, who dealeth in proud wrath.
> —PROVERBS 21:24

The Word identifies the root of scorn as being pride; and then Proverbs 22 instructs us to use the believer's choice weapon of warfare and simply cast out the scorner in Jesus' name. This will deal a deathblow to contention, strife, and reproach at the same time.

> Cast out the scorner, and contention shall go out; yea, strife and reproach shall cease.
> —PROVERBS 22:10

Agape is aware, sensitive, strong, predictable, honorable, true, and patient and I could go on and on. There is no love like it.

After Ahab died, Jehu was to be the next king. He was aware of the whoredom and witchcraft of Jezebel, which Jesus Christ would refer to later in the final book of the Bible. So what will he do? Will he tolerate Jezebel, as the church of Thyatira would do later on in history?

> And it came to pass, when Joram saw Jehu, that he said, Is it peace, Jehu? And he answered, what peace, so long as the whoredoms of thy mother Jezebel and her witchcrafts are so many?
> —2 KINGS 9:22–3

The outcome of a discerning life is God will recommend us. He'll choose us to refer the business of those others He loves to.

Now Jezebel wants to be Jehu's queen and dresses up in clothes to seduce in order to get a rise out of him and applies the makeup to complete the whole affair.

> And when Jehu was come to Jezreel, Jezebel heard of it; and she painted her face, and tired her head, and looked out at a window.
> —2 KINGS 9:30

Jehu was not caught in the snare of Jezebel's booby trap; rather the Scripture records that she was cast down at his command and eaten by the dogs of the city. In order for her seduction to have an effect, Jehu would have had to have the corresponding familiar spirit that would drool and fall under its seduction. To defeat this vexing spirit one must have the spirit and sanctification of a Jehu that will deal it the deathblow with no compromise. In case some have forgotten it is not flesh and blood, the person, but rather the principalities and powers that are vexing their muscles through the face of the individual that are to be dealt the deathblow.

If you desire to be an overcomer of evil, your temple cleansing must be ruthless and complete. What I'm getting at is that there are sins we have a disdain for and there are others that we still take pleasure in, as they appeal to our sensual carnal nature while it is still in an unsanctified state. Accordingly, you may try to rid yourself of the stuff you dislike; such as control, envy, strife, and lying; but you desire to retain the evil of seduction, flattery, and sexual immorality, which you take pleasure in. The devil will say, "Well, if you get rid of the sensual pleasures in life, your fun is gone and life will be bland." Thus he instills a fear and a lie regarding the agape walk. The truth that he doesn't want you to experience is that "eros" love leaves one empty, dirty, shamed, and disappointed whereas agape is total fulfillment and peace in body, mind, soul, and heart. Agape is aware, sensitive, strong, predictable, honorable, true, and patient; and I could go on and on. There is no love like it. The outcome of a discerning life is God will recommend us. He'll choose us to refer the business of those others He loves.

In James' written sermon to the believers, he makes it very clear that envy, strife, and bitterness are of the devil (demonic); and when he is allowed access, he holds the door open for a legion of other evil workers.

> But if ye have bitter [harsh, stinky as gall] envying [fierce indignation, contentious], and strife [a desire to put oneself forward while showing disdain for another] in your hearts, glory not [rub it in, gloat], and lie not against the truth. This wisdom descendeth not from above, but is earthly, sensual [private gratification], devilish [demonic]. For where envying and strife is, there is confusion [instability, unpredictable], and every evil work [vexation, workers of iniquity].
> —JAMES 3:14–16

James goes further to contrast this devilish work with the work of the Holy Spirit. These are the main tools of discernment that are to be used to judge every thought and intention we are swishing around in our minds. We must discern the origin of each thought and impulse before we act on it. If we act on a devilish impulse we will have a fair bit of temple work to do.

> But the wisdom that is from above is first pure, then peaceable [a loving peace as contrast to the worlds peace], gentle [fair, transparent], and easy to be intreated [ready to obey, compliant, submissive] full of mercy [kindness extended in allowing others to error] and good fruits [*agathos*; or works of agape that benefit others], without partiality [non-discriminatory], and without hypocrisy [motive and intent are straight up]. And the fruit of righteousness [recommended by God] is sown in peace of them that make peace [nothing to fear from God due to uprightness].
> —JAMES 3:17–18

Here is the deal; if I regard my activity, my ideas, my time, or my possessions as even slightly more significant than that of the person next to me, I'll have strife and envy starting to stink up my life. You know what stink is like; we usually don't smell our own stink, but others sure do.

Our significant others will come up, give us a hug, sniff and sniff again to be sure, and then be repulsed by the stink of our love. If it stinks, they will spit it back in disgust, as it is yucky to them.

> Let nothing be done through strife [a desire to put oneself forward while showing disdain for another] or vainglory [over compensation for what we lack by pretension]; but in lowliness of mind [humility, absence of pride] let each esteem [admire, respect] other better than themselves.
>
> —PHILIPPIANS 2:3

Envy and company workout

Step 1: Prayerfully review the following list and mark each sin you or your generations have participated with. It is important that you are not rushed and that you are in a private place as you go through this.

- ❑ **Abdicating leadership:** fail to undertake responsibility of duty
- ❑ **Abortion:** extermination of a child that is inconvenient or stands in our way
- ❑ **Accusation:** blame, finger pointing
- ❑ **Adultery:** betrayal, falseness, treachery, infidelity, breaking covenant vows
- ❑ **Aggression:** belligerence, violence, hostility
- ❑ **Ahab**
- ❑ **Anger:** irritation, annoyance, rage
- ❑ **Accusation of anger—1 Samuel 17:28**
- ❑ **Anger to compensate for lack of power**
- ❑ **Anger of rejection and rebellion—Esther 1:12**
- ❑ **Anger of frustration—Genesis 30:2, Exodus 32:19**
- ❑ **Blindness of anger—Judges 14:19**
- ❑ **Cruelty of anger**
- ❑ **Curse of anger—Genesis 49:7**
- ❑ **Drivenness of anger—1 Samuel 20:30**
- ❑ **Foolishness of anger—Ecclesiastes 7:9**
- ❑ **Grief of anger—Proverbs 15**
- ❑ **Guilt and shame of anger—1 Samuel 20:34**
- ❑ **Hostility of anger—Psalm 37:8**
- ❑ **Indiscretion of anger—Proverbs 19:11**
- ❑ **Misunderstanding of anger—Numbers 22:17**
- ❑ **Murder of anger—Genesis 49:6**
- ❑ **Pride of anger**
- ❑ **Shame of anger—1 Samuel 20:34**
- ❑ **Vows of anger**
- ❑ **Anti-submissiveness**

- ❑ **Apathy**
- ❑ **Arrogance:** sense of superiority, condescension, conceited, egotism
- ❑ **Attention seeking:** neediness to be "it" all the time, ME ME ME Virus
- ❑ **Backbiting:** spitefulness, viciousness, inflict an injury in exchange for a bump
- ❑ **Bedroom blackmail**
- ❑ **Belittling:** ridicule, scorn, mocking, the opposite of praise
- ❑ **Bitterness:** allows an offence or misfortune to putrefy ones countenance
- ❑ **Brainwashing:** false indoctrination, given over to a lie
- ❑ **Brash, bossy woman:** impatient, vulgar, trashy, arrogant, hasty or pushy
- ❑ **Bullying:** quarrelsome, loudly arrogant and domineering, hounding, harassment, discrimination
- ❑ **Burning passion:** an overwhelming ravenous quest to gratify a lust
- ❑ **Calling evil good or good evil:** given over
- ❑ **Carelessness:** neglect, sloppiness, lack of judgment
- ❑ **Child abuse**
- ❑ **Childish behavior:** infantile reasoning, me first, temper used to control
- ❑ **Chronic dissatisfaction:** feels will lose control or be taken advantage of if they compliment another
- ❑ **Competition:** rivalry, antagonism, struggle for superiority
- ❑ **Compromise:** conformity, lustful appetites are stronger that morals and beliefs
- ❑ **Condemnation:** a biased judge pronouncing a guilty verdict
- ❑ **Conditional love:** fickle, unpredictable, volatile 'phileo or eros' love
- ❑ **Confusion:** bewilderment, uncertainty, misunderstanding, disorder, uncertainty
- ❑ **Considering God's things trivial:** self adjusting righteousness
- ❑ **Contentiousness:** a showdown of who is king/queen of the castle, litigious, touchy
- ❑ **Continuous complaining**
- ❑ **Control:** imposes power, manipulates, oppresses, sidetracks issue to shift blame to confronter
- ❑ **Counterfeit spiritual gifts:** Satan can appear to duplicate all spiritual gifts to the non- discerning
- ❑ **Covetousness:** unjust gain, extortion, greed, unabated lust for more
- ❑ **Critical spirits:** nit-picking, fault-finding, negative, sets standard then stands in judgment
- ❑ **Cruelty:** malice, unashamed callousness or heartlessness, spiteful, maliciousness, evil
- ❑ **Death**
- ❑ **Deception:** cheating, dishonesty, lead astray by cunning or seduction
- ❑ **Defensiveness:** distrustful, shielding evil, deflecting exposure, childish counterattack
- ❑ **Delusion:** false impression, wrong opinion relative to morals or religion, wandering
- ❑ **Demeaning:** humiliating, shameful, undignified

❑ **Depression:** gloominess, misery, dejection, slump
❑ **Despair:** desolation, lose hope, lose heart
❑ **Despising husband/wife:** loathe, scorn, spurn, hold in contempt
❑ **Destruction:** to pull down and destroy house, destroyer, folly
❑ **Destruction of family priesthood:** render ineffective, defiantly oppose
❑ **Dirty stories**
❑ **Discord:** dissension, rebellion, conflict, turmoil
❑ **Discouragement:** crushed spirit, hindered hope, damper, dismay
❑ **Discontentment:** happiness is a moving target, moody, displeasure
❑ **Dishonor:** discredit, disgrace, public disgrace, vindictive, tarnish reputation
❑ **Disobedient:** defiant, insubordinate, wayward
❑ **Disrespect:** brazenness, lip, rudeness, discourteous
❑ **Distrust:** suspicion, doubt, projected deceit
❑ **Divination:** supposed foresight, imaginative
❑ **Divisions or boundaries:** walls to hide fears. Control through spurning. Self-protection
❑ **Divorce** to dismiss, to act treacherously or faithlessly
❑ **Dizziness**
❑ **Dogmatic:** inflexible, doctrinaire, intensely driving your position
❑ **Double-mindedness:** serving kingdom of God and Kingdom of Satan simultaneously
❑ **Doubt:** hesitation, disbelief, reservations, suspicious founded or unfounded
❑ **Doubting manhood**
❑ **Drunkenness:** intoxication, altered or stupefying mental state
❑ **Effeminate:** male who practices unnatural lewdness, soft touch
❑ **Emasculations:** to deprive male of properties of manhood
❑ **Embezzlement:** fraud, stealing, cheating, misappropriation
❑ **Emotional indifference:** unable to sympathize, unresponsive, coldness, indifference
❑ **Emotionalism:** a blown up or unfitting display of strong feelings
❑ **Emulations:** punitive zeal, envy, jealousy, fierce indignation, diminishes and destroys the good it sees in others
❑ **Entitlement of privilege:** demanding favor or right of excessive leisure, diva
❑ **Envyings:** deprive another of what he has
❑ **Exaggeration:** aggrandizement, self enhancement, over compensating
❑ **Exhibitionism (See Ezekiel 23:2-4.):** sexually inspired exposure of part of body to incite, Lady Godiva syndrome
❑ **Excessive appetite:** immoderate consumption of food or vice
❑ **Extortion:** unlawfully obtaining money, property or services through deceit or coercion
❑ **Failure:** collapse, letdown, bankruptcy, malfunction
❑ **False accusation:** malicious innuendo to gain special favor while destroying another
❑ **False pretenses:** misrepresentation or deception of fact that another acts on
❑ **False prophecy:** illegitimately claiming charismatic authority
❑ **False sickness**

❑ **Fantasy:** a sensual, alluring, or emotional trip to escape or incite the appetites

❑ **Fear:** projecting anxiety, terror, failure, panic into future, Satan's faith
    ❑ **Fear of confrontation**
    ❑ **Fear of getting hurt**
    ❑ **Fear of loss of control**
    ❑ **Fear of women**

❑ **Female dominance/control:** governance or authority gained by usurping man's authority

❑ **Female hardness:** without natural affection especially towards children

❑ **Fierce determination:** scheming for tomorrow and squandering today

❑ **Filthy language, obscenity:** expressions that offend usually with sexual connotation

❑ **Flattery:** smooth words that push another down a slippery slope of destruction

❑ **Flirting:** conversation, body language or dress to attract another through sexual arousal

❑ **Fornication:** desiring anything before its time, illicit sexual intercourse, defilement of idolatry

❑ **Forsaking protection:** moving away from spiritual covering of husband or father

❑ **Frigidity**

❑ **Frustration:** exaggerated emotional response to disappointment, exasperation

❑ **Giving place to the devil:** not dealing promptly with all sin or offence

❑ **Gossip:** tale bearer, divulging or receiving personal information that will wound

❑ **Grief:** vexation of a contentious and morose woman

❑ **Gross indecency:** all unnatural sexual activity

❑ **Hardheartedness:** blindness, given over to immorality and addictive behavior, obstinate, proud

❑ **Harlotry:** unfaithful to God, infidelity, transgression against husband

❑ **Hasty marriage**

❑ **Hatred:** enmity: everything opposed to agape
    ❑ **Hatred of men**
    ❑ **Hatred of sons or daughters:**
    ❑ **Hatred of women**

❑ **Heavy spirited:** vexed by oppressive of depressing spirit

❑ **Heresies:** dissension arising from diverse opinions and aims

❑ **Homosexuality**

❑ **Hopelessness:** eaten up by discouragement

❑ **Hot temper**

❑ **Humiliation:** shaming or disgracing through asserting power or control

❑ **Hypnotic control**

❑ **Hypocrisy:** double standards, being less critical of yourself than others, masking truth

❑ **Idolatry:** accepting any teaching, person, or thing ahead of that of a holy and righteous God

❑ **Immorality:** wickedness, depravity

❑ **Impatience:** edginess, anxiety, annoyance, running ahead of the timing of God

❑ **Impulsivity:** inclination to act on impulse rather than thought

❑ **Inability to designate authority**

❑ **Inability to give or receive love**

❑ **Inadequateness:** feeling undeserving, unsuitable, doesn't measure up to _____

❑ **Incessant talking**

❑ **Incest**

❑ **Indecision:** uncertainty, hesitancy

❑ **Infirmity:** frailty, illness

❑ **Ingratitude:** Unthankful, unpleasing

❑ **Insecurity:** aloofness, detachment, timidity

❑ **Intellectualism:** overemphasis on acquiring knowledge but lacking wisdom

❑ **Interference:** meddling, prying, invasion

❑ **Intimidation:** compel to change with force or manipulation or bullying

❑ **Irresponsibility:** waywardness, fickleness, unreliability

❑ **Jealousy:** anger, rage and resentment over losing a relationship or against one who has what you want

❑ **Jezebel**

❑ **Joblessness:** idleness, unemployable, lazy, dependant on others

❑ **Lack of intimacy**

❑ **Lasciviousness:** carnality, filthy words, indecent body movements, unchaste handling of male or females, wasteful

❑ **Lawlessness:** disorder, chaos, anarchy, reckless abandon

❑ **Laziness:** lethargy, slothful

❑ **Leaving things of God to wife**

❑ **Lesbianism**

❑ **Liking sensual women**

❑ **Love of money**

❑ **Lust:** desire or ache for what is forbidden, craving, drivenness

❑ **Lying:** devious, faithless, cheating, dishonest, deceptive, double life

❑ **Macho spirit:** dominating male assertiveness, exaggerated sense of power

❑ **Manipulating women:** influence or control by devious, unfair or ingenious ways

❑ **Masturbation**

❑ **Matrimonial discord:** marriage conflict and dissention

❑ **Mistrust:** doubt, suspicion, paranoia, result of believing a lie

❑ **Misunderstandings:** taking offence at something misinterpreted or confused

❑ **Murder**

❑ **Nagging:** irritating, endless harassment regarding trivial and insignificant things

- ❏ **Narcissism:** excessive self-love and awareness rooted in pride and ego, lack of empathy for others
- ❏ **Negligence of sons or daughters**
- ❏ **Offense:** anger or ire oriented toward some real or supposed grievance
- ❏ **Oppression:** tyranny, conquest, overthrows
- ❏ **Overindulgence:** hedonism, gluttony, greed, self indulgence, self-gratification, high living
- ❏ **Overloading wife**
- ❏ **Overstepping authority:** do more than allowed to do, taking presumptuous advantage
- ❏ **Oversensitivity**
- ❏ **Perversion (sexual & spiritual)**
- ❏ **Pornography**
- ❏ **Possessiveness:** treats another as an object or possession, control fueled by insecurity and jealousy
- ❏ **Pouting:** a charade of despondency to control and gain attention
- ❏ **Poverty**
- ❏ **Preoccupation with self/appearance:** obsession with self yet oblivious to surroundings
- ❏ **Pretentiousness**
- ❏ **Pride:** Satan's counterfeit version of the Father's love
- ❏ **Projected guilt**
- ❏ **Promiscuity:** undiscriminating sexual activity with multiple partner objects
- ❏ **Quick temper**
- ❏ **Rape**
- ❏ **Rationalization:** explaining away or validation of sinful activity
- ❏ **Rebellion:** anything that conflicts with the truth of the Bible
- ❏ **Rebellious children**
- ❏ **Rejection:** says you are a mistake, unacceptable, of no value
- ❏ **Resentment:** harboring ill will against someone for offending you
- ❏ **Retaliation:** getting even, making an offender pay rather than forgive, condemning to your sentence
- ❏ **Revellings:** evening drunken parties coupled with impurity, music and obscenely
- ❏ **Reversal of blame:** rebounding from being confronted with immediate sharp counterattack
- ❏ **Rivalry:** hostile competition
- ❏ **Ruthlessness:** mercilessness, brutality, heartlessness
- ❏ **Sadism:** taking pleasure as result of inflicting pain, abuse or ruin on another
- ❏ **Sarcasm:** remarks that mean the opposite of what they seem to say and are intended to mock or deride
- ❏ **Scheming:** continually devising plots and plans, especially cunning or underhand ones
- ❏ **Scorner:** boasts and mocks simultaneously, arrogant disdain

❑ **Seduction:** enticing sexual attention by means of persuasions, solicitations, promises, flirting or bribes

❑ **Self-defeating:** unwittingly defeat own purpose and well being by words and action of self destruction

❑ **Self-admiration:** unjustified feeling of being pleased with oneself while blind to criticism, narcissism

❑ **Separation:** tearing apart something not meant to be severed through accusation, shame, divorce, violence

❑ **Set up:** to plot an action that will solicit a predictable response to justify or hide ones future intentions

❑ **Sexual abuse**

❑ **Sexual incitement:** vexing to fornication or adultery by flirtation and certain provocation

❑ **Shame:** disgrace or humiliation from sin being brought to light

❑ **Sharp tongue:** speaking in harsh, critical or insulting manner

❑ **Shirking responsibilities:** to avoid or neglect work or duties

❑ **Short temper:** a persisting angry mood looking for excuse to erupt, persons close walk on eggshells

❑ **Sleepiness**

❑ **Sodomy:** fornication through sexual acts that cannot lead to procreation

❑ **Sorcery:** practice of magical arts

❑ **Sorrow:** toil, hardship, pain, languishing, heaviness, grief, torment

❑ **Spirit of religion:** enforce traditions of men over commands of God

❑ **Spiritual blindness:** Hearts hardened due to rebellion and unrighteousness so cannot perceive truth

❑ **Spiritual seduction:** coercing others into following occultic modalities

❑ **Strife:** divisive spirit, put self forward

❑ **Stubbornness:** unreasonably determined to prevail, inflexible, obstinate, perversely unyielding

❑ **Suicide**

❑ **Superiority:** compensating for inferiority by imposing your needs over others

❑ **Thief:** embezzler, pilferer, false teachers who abuse their role for their own gain

❑ **Tragic mistakes**

❑ **Treachery:** betrayal of covenant or vows, treason, sedition

❑ **Turning a blind eye**

❑ **Unbelief that God will provide**

❑ **Uncleanness:** impure motives, sensuality, defilement

❑ **Unforgiveness**

❑ **Ungodly discipline:** disciplining for own pleasure rather than purposes of sanctification

❑ **Unhusbanded:** rebellion against God's order and purpose for marriage habitation

❑ **Unrepentant:** exhibiting no remorse thus highly probable to continue same destructive behavior

❑ **Unteachable:** not interested in truth

- ❑ **Uprooting:** to repeatedly tear up family by the roots
- ❑ **Usurping authority:** to seize and hold the rights of another without biblical authority
- ❑ **Vainglory:** groundless empty pride, vain opinion, error in judging oneself
- ❑ **Variance:** strife, debate, contention, rivalry
- ❑ **Violence**
- ❑ **Wandering:** drifting, unsettled, can't be content or satisfied
- ❑ **Waster of inheritance:** to corrupt, ruin, steal or remove the heritage or legacy of others
- ❑ **Whisperings:** secret slandering, murmuring
- ❑ **Witchcraft:** illegitimate authority, rebellion, extra biblical solutions practices or belief
- ❑ **Withholding love**
- ❑ **Worldliness:** Sacrifice the eternal for temporal pleasures and comforts
- ❑ **Worldly wisdom**
- ❑ **Worship of enterprise**
- ❑ **Wrath:** anger, madness of a drinker

Step 2: Go back through the list and pray this prayer inserting the sin in the blank space. You may insert several sins in the blank space at a time if you desire.

Prayer of Repentance
(Preferably out loud)

Father God, I recognize and take responsibility for myself and my ancestors for the sin(s) of _____. I agree with Your verdict on my rebellion. I repent, I renounce, and I ask forgiveness for my participation with these sins. I ask that their curse be broken in the name of Jesus Christ of Nazareth.

Step 3: Bind the strongman. This is best done by an experienced and trusted ministering friend the first time around.

> For though we walk in the flesh, we do not war after the flesh: For the weapons of our warfare are not carnal, but mighty through God to the pulling down of strongholds; Casting down imaginations, and every high thing that exalteth itself against the knowledge of God, and bringing into captivity every thought to the obedience of Christ; And having in a readiness to revenge all disobedience, when your obedience is fulfilled.
> —2 CORINTHIANS 10:3–6

Prayer to Bind the Strongmen

In the name of Jesus Christ of Nazareth and by the power of the Holy Spirit, I take authority over the strongmen of envy, jealousy, pride, Jezebel, Ahab, Baal, and Ashtoreth. I bind you and I command you to release all the workers of iniquity and unclean spirits that are under your authority.

Step 4: Purging the evil. Review the above list again now inserting the sin you have repented of in the blank. You may list several sins at once in the blank.

Command of Deliverance

(Must be out loud with eyes open,
realizing you are speaking directly to a spirit)

In the name of Jesus Christ of Nazareth and by the power of the Holy Spirit, I take authority over the spirit(s) of _____. I break your power, I cast you out, and I command you to return no more.

Step 5: Purge the strongman now that you have destroyed his stronghold.

Command of Deliverance

(Must be out loud with eyes open,
realizing you are speaking directly to a spirit)

In the name of Jesus Christ of Nazareth and by the power of the Holy Spirit, I take authority over the strongmen of envy, pride, Jezebel, Ahab, Baal, and Ashtoreth. I break your power, I cast you out, and I command you to loose me and return no more.

Step 6: Pray that God will cause you to increase and abound in His love and that you would be an overcomer in the sins just repented of. Ask for a scripture that you will use to resist the devil when he tries to open the trapdoor again to regain entrance to your heart.

Prayer for You, the Overcomer

[Father God,]
    Who can understand his errors? cleanse thou me from secret faults. Keep back thy servant also from presumptuous sins; let them not have dominion over me: then shall I be upright, and I shall be innocent from the great transgression. Let the words of my mouth, and the meditation of my heart, be acceptable in thy sight, O LORD, my strength, and my redeemer. Hear my cry, O God; attend unto my prayer. From the end of the earth will I cry unto thee, when my heart is overwhelmed: lead me to the rock that is higher than I. For thou hast been a shelter for me, and a strong tower from the enemy. I will abide in thy tabernacle for ever: I will trust in the covert of thy wings. Selah. For thou, O God, hast heard my vows: thou hast given me the heritage of those that fear thy name.... [I] shall abide before God for ever: o prepare mercy and truth, which may preserve [me]. So will I sing praise unto thy name for ever, that I may daily perform my vows.
    [In the name of Jesus Christ I pray. Amen]
—PSALMS 19:12–14; 61

AGAPE VAUNTETH NOT ITSELF, AGAPE IS NOT PUFFED UP

I believe we fall into a lifestyle of pride by default, really not knowing what a walk of agape ought to look like, feel like, talk like, and act like. Pride is a kingdom in which all its subjects are easily identified by submission.

In many circles folks refer to the "S word" because of how difficult it is for most to consider the concept of submission. "I won't submit to anyone. I certainly won't submit to a husband. I won't submit to my parents." Is that so! Everyone is in submission to one of two kingdoms; and there are no other options other than a mixture of the two, which makes us double-minded and therefore unstable. Can we say insanity? We choose submission to righteousness in the Father, or by default we choose submission to sin, which is death.

> Know ye not, that to whom ye yield [say I'm available to you] yourselves servants to obey [submit], his servants [bondman, bondmaid] ye are to whom ye obey [step into service when called upon]; whether of sin unto death, or of obedience unto righteousness?
> —Romans 6:16

If the Scriptures say we are to submit to authorities or our husbands, that means we are to submit to righteousness through them to God. Did we hear some "yeah, buts!" from one sex and some "oh, yeahs!" from the other? "Well there is no way I can submit to him. He has such a big head already and by submitting he'll only get worse." So here is the point, and I'm just using the wives here to get a point understood. In the little statement she made, she went into judgment, condemnation, and unforgiveness, and by refusing the direction of the Word to submit to the husband, by default submitted to another kingdom through pride and rebellion. So at this point who has sinned the most?

The Lord understood that as the result of His directive, some men would take advantage and treat those who submit to him very unfairly. God will judge both, and here is how: He'll judge the actions of the one who mistreated his daughter, but He'll also judge his daughter regarding the response—even to unfairness. We don't have a choice as to how we are treated, but we are responsible for what we do in return. Only our Lord can judge this as He passed the same test Himself.

> Servants, be subject to your masters with all fear; not only to the good and gentle, but also to the froward [unfair, headstrong, wicked]. For this is thankworthy, if a man for conscience toward God endure grief, suffering wrongfully. For what glory is it, if, when ye be buffeted for your faults, ye shall take it patiently? But if, when ye do well, and suffer for it, ye take it patiently, this is acceptable with God. For even hereunto were ye called....Likewise, ye wives, be in subjection to your own husbands; that, if any obey not the word, they also may without the word be won by the conversation of the wives.
> —1 Peter 2:18–21; 3:1

I sense that what the Spirit is saying here is that if a person who is wronged retorts in anger and heaps a load of abuse on the bad guy, then that fellow will feel justified in what he did to hurt you in the first place. But if he does something hurtful and you respond in agape, you've just started to soften the hardness of his heart.

OK, I'm not done yet. To the men that said, "Oh yeah, I like this guy!" consider this:

> My brethren, be not many masters, knowing that we shall receive the greater condemnation [much harsher judgment from God as abusing your authority].
>
> —James 3:1

When we behave wickedly, rebel, or judge, we may be deceived into thinking that this stuff is just between the two of us people. In spiritual reality this sin of disregarding Scripture and submitting to the kingdom of this world, we are not doing it to spite the other person but actually we have spited God. If we despise anyone, we have really despised the God who loves that person! God takes the sin against a son or daughter of His personally, and that is *not* something I would recommend you do.

> For God hath not called us unto uncleanness, but unto holiness. He therefore that despiseth [scorns, loathes, spurns, ridicules, belittles], despiseth not man, but God, who hath also given unto us his Holy Spirit.
>
> —1 Thessalonians 4:7–8

There are many voices out there instructing us how to change the behavior of those that are significant in our lives. With "tough love," "establishing boundaries," "profiling," "love languages," "enabling," and other psychological-type approaches, consider the scriptural remedy first. And if it happens to match your psychological methodology, fine; if not, do not submit yourself. For the most part to practice these methods, one would have to judge and then condemn that person to be worthy of such treatment. I know some arms just folded across some chests thinking I've just gone too far. I'm just a brother who knows that being judge and sentencing a loved one to my induced treatment never turned out very well.

> There is a way that seemeth right unto a man, but the end thereof are the ways of death.
>
> —Proverbs 16:25

Fellow and lady saints, we have to know who we are submitting to, putting aside how logical things appear to be or how easy it is to justify. Paul warns of establishing our own righteousness:

> For I bear them record that they have a zeal of God, but not according to knowledge. For they being ignorant of God's righteousness, and going about to establish their own righteousness, have not submitted themselves unto the righteousness of God.
>
> —Romans 10:2–3

By submitting to God the devil resists and has to flee. If we submit to any of the devil's devises, we have told him we are available for him to abuse us in that area and he doesn't have to leave as we've consented.

> Submit yourselves therefore to God. Resist the devil, and he will flee from you. Draw nigh to God, and he will draw nigh to you. Cleanse your hands, ye sinners; and purify your hearts, ye double minded.
>
> —James 4:7–8

God is asking us to live "single-minded" in our submission to Him. To be double-minded is to live "common law," where we draw from both kingdoms in a futile attempt to justify sin as somehow righteous.

> Ye adulterers [faithless towards God] and adulteresses [a breach in relationship to the one we have become one with, to play the harlot], know ye not that the friendship of the world is enmity [the opposite of agape] with God? Whosoever therefore will be a friend of the world is the enemy [hostile adversary] of God.
>
> —James 4:4

We can vow that we'll change: "Yeah, I'll be submissive to God from now on, no matter the cost," but we probably won't be able to stay the "narrow way" very long unless the root system is understood and destroyed. The root is pride.

> The wicked, through the pride of his countenance, will not seek after God: God is not in all his thoughts.
>
> —Psalm 10:4

One day this was my revelation: "I am too proud to admit that I that I have a pride problem!" What must I see in my life to help me to recognize that the nastiest of all creatures has taken up residence within my spirit? Lucifer was created holy, without blame before God in love until he started to transfer what God had given him to do his own side performance.

> It seems the hardest of all God-given attributes to handle in humility is physical beauty, wealth, and intelligence. When we submit to the power of our own attributes, pride, like a maggot infestation, will chew us up.

> Thou wast perfect in thy ways from the day that thou wast created [you and I were also created perfect and watch what happened], till iniquity was found in thee. By the multitude of thy merchandise [trade traffic] they have filled the midst of thee with violence [cruelty, injustice], and thou hast sinned: therefore I will cast thee as profane [defiled his crown] out of the mountain of God: and I will destroy thee, O covering cherub, from the midst of the stones of fire. Thine heart was lifted up [haughty, arrogant, pride] because of thy beauty, thou hast corrupted thy wisdom by reason of thy brightness: I will cast thee to the ground, I will lay thee before kings, that they may behold thee.
>
> —Ezekiel 28:15–17

The first and original sin to take root was pride, so therefore, all sins stem from pride. It seems the hardest of all God-given attributes or blessings to handle in humility is physical beauty, wealth, and intelligence. When we submit to the power of our own attributes, pride, like a maggot infestation, will chew us up.

Looking further at Lucifer's rebellion, what goals did he set for himself? He set five ambitious "I will" goals that elevated himself at the exclusion of God. The "Five I Wills of Lucifer" fueled by pride are the antithesis of submission to God.

> How art thou fallen from heaven, O Lucifer, son of the morning! how art thou cut down to the ground, which didst weaken the nations! For thou hast said in thine heart, *I will* ascend into heaven, *I will* exalt my throne above the stars of God: *I will* sit also upon the mount of the congregation, in the sides of the north: *I will* ascend above the heights of the clouds; *I will* be like the most High. Yet thou shalt be brought down to hell, to the sides of the pit.
> —Isaiah 14:12–15, emphasis added

It is the "I will" that breeds pride, the fertilizer of Satan's kingdom. "Thy will" ushers forward the kingdom of God starting within us.

The "I will" is a sneaky critter; as it comes off our lips, our minds have to catch up to what we just announced. How often have I prayed for God's blessing on a plan of mine and just went ahead and did it? I wasn't asking God, I was simply telling Him. Furthermore, I could tell others that I prayed about it. Such sly rhetoric makes it difficult for others to dispute my intentions, as who can say that God didn't lead?

> Boast [a one man showoff] not thyself of tomorrow; for thou knowest not what a day may bring forth.
> —Proverbs 27:1

An acceptable goal would be to get over the destructive desire to impress.

James, the half-brother of Jesus, uses very strong language for those that trust in their own power and resources presuming upon the stability of the flesh and earthly things. They are insolent and prideful, displaying their destitute emptiness.

The Word is helpful in showing who is really "lord" of your life. Two choices: if we boast of our grandiose goals, we are following the Luciferian dream; or if we walk in agape, our plans would be in submission to the Lord of eternity and He will direct our paths.

> Go to now, ye that say, Today or tomorrow we will go into such a city, and continue there a year, and buy and sell, and get gain: Whereas ye know not what shall be on the morrow. For what is your life? It is even a vapour, that appeareth for a little time, and then vanisheth away. For that ye ought to say, If the Lord will, we shall live, and do this, or that. But now ye rejoice in your boastings: all such rejoicing is evil.
> —James 4:13–16

The chasing of the Luciferian dream will mean we sell our souls to unrealistic deadlines, stress, and mind traffic directed at the next prospect or conquest—to make our children intellectual, artistic, and athletic stars, followed by a self-prescribed intoxicants to help us make sense of it all. There is a right way and a wrong way for us and our households to prosper.

Contrast the Luciferian dream with the markers of a life that submits to the One who knows and holds tomorrow:

How can you tell the difference between agape and pride?—by who is being evaluated.

But the fruit of the Spirit is love, joy, peace, longsuffering, gentleness, goodness, faith, Meekness, temperance: against such there is no law. And they that are Christ's have crucified the flesh with the affections and lusts. If we live in the Spirit, let us also walk in the Spirit. Let us not be desirous of vain glory, provoking one another, envying one another.
—Galatians 5:22–26

"Walking according to the course of this world" and "walking in agape" are mutually exclusive of each other. It is one or the other; they will not combine—not ever. An acceptable goal would be to get over the destructive desire to impress.

The implication in the crucifying of our flesh is that this dying to self is accompanied with intense pain. We don't want to do it; we want to do *self* and have God be OK with that. Have you ever tried to help a child color within the lines by guiding their hands? What happens? You get rebuked, scorned, and set back in your place as one who knows nothing about coloring. When we learn to walk within the lines of the narrow road, that same childish behavior resurfaces. Oh yes, the defiance is more sophisticated, but it is still a childish impudent stronghold.

The gifts are all reconciliation tools to restore us to whom we were created from the foundation of the world to be.

If you have struggled with hearing God's voice in order to have Him direct your paths, it is an indicator that your temple is in need of cleansing. The walk with the Lord in agape is closer than any marriage can be. Here are some of the Lord's rules of engagement:

And whatsoever ye do in word or deed, do all in the name of the Lord Jesus, giving thanks to God and the Father by him.
—Colossians 3:17

Who died for us, that, whether we wake or sleep, we should live together with him.
—1 Thessalonians 5:10

God is the Master builder and has daily instructions for us. If we just indulge Him with a meaningless prayer or a brief appearance at church and then go about and do our own thing, He calls that pride, which He finds as an abomination and that disgusts Him.

> Commit thy works [enterprise, achievement] unto the LORD, and thy thoughts [plan, purpose or invention] shall be established. The LORD hath made all things for himself: yea, even the wicked [hostile to God] for the day of evil. Every one that is proud in heart is an abomination [a disgusting thing] to the LORD.
> —PROVERBS 16:3–5

If I am not praying, it is because I have a proud heart! If I am not laying all my plans at Jesus' feet, it is because I have a proud heart—Thy will vs. my will.

How can you tell the difference between agape and pride?—by who is being elevated. John the Baptist understood this concept, and that is what qualified him to be the front-runner to prepare the way for Jesus to commence His ministry of reconciliation. John said, "He must increase, but I must decrease" (3:30). John had no need to draw attention to himself or his divine calling; he had no desire to make for himself a reputation as "a famous one."

As we allow the Lord to increase, that means we are in submission to Him; our agape will increase and abound. Agape love can ebb and flow, depending on how wide the gate of submission is open in our hearts.

> And the Lord make you to increase and abound in love [*agape*] one toward another, and toward all men, even as we do toward you.
> —1 THESSALONIANS 3:12

As we feel we are increasing in intelligence and knowledge, the tendency is to obtain markers to boast of our intellectual achievement. Since God set only the fruits of the Spirit as markers, man feels the need to confer title. In order for one to give a title to another, he would have to presume the status as of a higher standard in order to be in the position to bestow such an honor. The Lord says that by so doing we are actually proving that we are not wise—the antitheses of what is staged. As concerning the work of the ministry, permit only the Lord God to exalt you in His due time.

> For we dare not make ourselves of the number, or compare ourselves [judge with man as standard] with some that commend themselves [establish themselves as pinnacle of spiritual attainment]: but they measuring themselves by themselves, and comparing themselves among themselves, are not wise. But we will not boast of things without our measure, but according to the measure of the rule which God hath distributed to us, a measure to reach even unto you.
> —2 CORINTHIANS 10:12–15

What may we do with honors that other men have conferred upon us? Cast them at the feet of Jesus, as we will with all our crowns. In the section in this chapter headed Agape Seeketh Not Her Own, we'll have a closer look at this. Isn't God the only one to determine who graduates? After all, who can judge spiritual attainment (actually it's called sanctification) other than God?

> And he said unto them, Ye are they which justify yourselves before men; but God knoweth your hearts: for that which is highly esteemed among men is abomination in the sight of God.
>
> —LUKE 16:15

Pride may have an inroad when a believer is given responsibility before he or she has the spiritual maturity to handle it. Spiritual maturity is not measured by how closely our beliefs and doctrine concur with those of a religious professor or teacher. We have a tradition of men that disguises the gospel; but understand, the Lord only wants what is best for those He called and those He loves.

> Not a novice, lest being lifted up with pride [to blind with conceit, to render foolish or stupid] he fall into the condemnation [a matter to be judicially decided in court] of the devil.
>
> —1 TIMOTHY 3:6

Jesus reserved His biggest shakeups and most direct public admonishing to the men that were positioned in religious service to Him and Father God. He chastised them regarding their motive for having people call them by titles such as father, rabbi, teacher, or master. The titles aren't the real issue; it is what is deep down inside of us that props up these status denotations and badges. We may have different words now to ascribe religious significance and achievement, but the attitude of the heart is what Jesus is talking about. He says the pride and hypocrisy of the shepherds has shut up the doors to the kingdom of heaven for their sheep. I write this with resistance in my heart, as I'm having to deal with the conviction that is spotlighting my pride and need for recognition. My fellow men, let's clean up our business cards and tear down the privileged parking lot signs and only allow Jesus to exalt us. Are you with me? What title does a servant need to have? What title does a servant that has died to self, need to have?

> But all their works they do for to be seen of men: they *make broad their phylacteries* [render themselves conspicuous as more eager than others to keep the law of God], and enlarge the borders of their garments, And love the uppermost rooms at feasts, and the chief seats in the synagogues, And greetings in the markets, and to be called of men, Rabbi, Rabbi. But be not ye called Rabbi: for one is your Master, even Christ; and all *ye are brethren*. And *call no man your father* upon the earth: for one is your Father, which is in heaven. Neither be ye called master [denotes a master teacher]: for one is your Master, even Christ. But *he that is greatest among you shall be your servant*. And whosoever shall exalt himself shall be abased; and he that shall humble himself shall be exalted. But woe unto you, scribes and Pharisees, hypocrites! For ye shut up the kingdom

of heaven against men: for ye neither go in yourselves, neither suffer ye
them that are entering to go in.
—MATTHEW 23:5–13, EMPHASIS ADDED

Jesus says your positioning and hierarchy are goofy as you are all brethren,
which means we are all exalted to the same heavenly place as Christians and
we have the same bloodline through Jesus. That means for the spectators that
are abdicating their responsibility and for the leaders that require man's many
accolades we will need to understand what the Spirit of God is saying to the
churches.

Our gifts are just that, they are gifts. Gifts are not our titles. The gifts aren't
the believer's pursuit, they are just the equipment, which is temporal and for
purposes while restrained to the earth; whereas fruit, in particular agape, is
carried throughout eternity.

> That ye might learn in us not to think of men above that which is written,
> that no one of you be puffed up for one against another. For who maketh
> thee to differ from another? And what hast thou that thou didst not
> receive? Now if thou didst receive it, why dost thou glory, as if thou hadst
> not received it?
> —1 CORINTHIANS 4:6–7

The men God used greatly had similar struggles to what we face. Paul was
vexed by a messenger of Satan, which would be an evil spirit that had legal
right to mess with him due to pride. The pride resulted from how he managed
the revelations he received of the Holy Spirit. The flesh Paul refers to could
be physical, thus the thorn would have been some sort of infirmity; or the
flesh could represent the old nature, thus the thorn would have been spiritual.
Either way the vexing was the result of the sin of pride, and Satan assigned one
from his kingdom to buffet or suppress him. Paul tried three times to purge
the vexing spirit along with its accompanying fruit and was unsuccessful. Paul
describes this spiritual battle in greater detail in his writing of Romans 7:13–25.
The fact that Paul had a spiritual impediment in one area of his life did not
disqualify him or devalue the work he was able to do for God. The essential
thing was to "see it" and "own it," because if he didn't, the outcome of his
ministry would no doubt have been quite different.

> And lest I should be exalted above measure [raise above others in pride]
> through the abundance of the revelations, there was given to me a thorn
> in the flesh, the messenger of Satan to buffet me, lest I should be exalted
> above measure [raise above others in pride]. For this thing I besought the
> Lord thrice, that it might depart from me [cease to vex or oppress].
> —2 CORINTHIANS 12:7

Do you know what the original call to service with Jesus was?

> He said unto them, whosoever will come after me, let him deny himself,
> and take up his cross, and follow me.
>
> —Mark 8:34

The original call has not changed! We are to still deny or die to self, as a dead man can't be proud. Jesus was coming up against a proud religious establishment, and He wasn't interested in starting a new work with just a different group of proud guys.

The gifts are all reconciliation tools to restore us to whom we were created from the foundation of the world to be. Agape does not cause envy in others by boasting about its own achievements. Love is never inspired to impress others with its gifts and achievements.

> Shall the axe boast itself against him that heweth therewith? or shall the saw magnify itself against him that shaketh it? As if the rod should shake itself against them that lift it up, or as if the staff should lift up itself, as if it were no wood.
>
> —Isaiah 10:15

Look at the mess Peter got himself into when he felt spiritual:

> Then saith Jesus unto them, All ye shall be offended because of me this night: for it is written, I will smite the shepherd, and the sheep of the flock shall be scattered abroad....Peter answered and said unto him, Though all men shall be offended because of thee, yet will I never be offended. Jesus said unto him, Verily I say unto thee, That this night, before the cock crow, thou shalt deny me thrice. Peter said unto him, Though I should die with thee, yet will I not deny thee. Likewise also said all the disciples.
>
> —Matthew 26:31, 33–35

Perhaps Peter meant well, but Jesus knew this was Peter's carnal mind speaking so it had to be crushed—human trust in human effort. Peter had to die to self so the Holy Spirit could take over and allow him to return to abide in the vine. God will not share glory with another. Daily reckon as a dead man: a dead man isn't seeking reputation; a dead man can't sin; a dead man can't seek the glorious distraction of the spotlight, so he submits without question.

The wilderness experiences a believer goes through are varied, but the purpose is the same and that is to remove the obstacle of our pride and to purify our spirits. We are humbled only because we were presumptuous and took a seat on comfort row that was not given to us by the Lord.

> And thou shalt remember all the way which the Lord thy God led thee these forty years in the wilderness, to humble thee, and to prove thee [to try by the smell], to know what was in thine heart [spirit], whether thou wouldest keep his commandments, or not.
>
> —Deuteronomy 8:2–3

Jesus puts our intellectual, professional, and creative aptitude into perspective. Really we are quite helpless in and of ourselves, so getting proud about stuff is the dumbest thing ever.

> And which of you with taking thought can add to his stature one cubit? If ye then be not able to do that thing which is least, why take ye thought for the rest?
>
> —LUKE 12:25–26

Paul says that even if we have a great understanding of our little area of specialty, we are still sadly lacking, so I guess we all have to adjust.

> And if any man think that he knoweth any thing, he knoweth nothing yet as he ought to know.
>
> —1 CORINTHIANS 8:2

When we go through our challenges, we are counseled by some to "hold on!" and then by others to "let go!" Those seem opposite to me, so I'm confused. Here is a short little prayer that I've found not only helpful in resisting the devil but released me of having to go into divination in praying for things I really knew nothing about.

Prayer of Submission

I don't know about _____, but I submit it to my heavenly Father in Jesus' name.

Consider filling in the blank with items of business, relationship, planning, sin, addictions, children, infirmity, understandings, finance, or whatever else you have mind traffic over.

Is your life crumbling, messy, increasingly difficult, or perplexing? Stand by for the taproot:

Pride fashions itself in battles of the wits, vain imaginations, debate, envy, strife, slander, gossip, contention, and ungodly gain. Pride is at the root of all disagreements!

> Only by pride [presumptuousness, arrogance] cometh contention [strife, conflict]: but with the well advised [to consult together] is wisdom [skill in war, perception, prudence].
>
> —PROVERBS 13:10

We do things, but do we know why we do things?

Another Proverb places pride as the root of strife and as the antitheses of trust in the Lord.

> He that is of a proud heart stirreth [meddles, excites] up strife [contention, discord]: but he that putteth his trust in the LORD shall be made fat [prosper or to anoint].
>
> —PROVERBS 28:25

With contention or strife it always takes at least two people for it to materialize; so who is the proud one if pride is the root? Both are, even if one is too proud to admit it!

I suppose that folks usually do what their impulsive emotions dictate, and then find the logic to justify what they just did. They find the intellectual reasoning to justify what their emotions have already decided. Pride fueled by fear steps in to save face, but it never does a very good job—ever noticed that?

The Bible teaches there are two forms of pride: outward, which displays arrogance, strife, anger, and such like; and the inward pride, manifesting in shame, self-pity, and feelings like rejection.

Pride is the strongman that holds shame in place. This is where carnal therapeutic management systems may break down, as they don't have the spiritual insight and discernment that can be gained from Scripture to contend with difficulties like shame, guilt, pride, or strife.

> When pride cometh [is introduced], then cometh [enters] shame: but with the lowly is wisdom.
> —PROVERBS 11:2

The psalmist notes that as he judged the proud for their contempt, he became full of contempt and scorn himself. He was so vexed by what this proud dude in his life was doing that he fell into the same pit. He that judges does the same thing as the one he is judging.

> Have mercy upon us, O LORD, have mercy upon us: for we are exceedingly filled with contempt [springing from judgment]. Our soul is exceedingly filled with the scorning of those that are at ease, and with the contempt of the proud.
> —PSALM 123:3-4

Pride is marked by contempt. Contempt is where I feel you are beneath me, so I'll treat you and your ideas with disdain and scorn and I'll be just plain mean to you. Pride causes God to actually war against me. Pride is not only a block to prayer and healing, but God actually wars against us pushing us back from the position we had gained.

> But he giveth more grace. Wherefore he saith, God resisteth [arranging in battle against] the proud but giveth grace unto the humble [lowly in spirit].
> —JAMES 4:6

Grace is not overlooking sin, but it says I'll give you space to repent of your sin.

Jesus explained that the proud religious Pharisee prayed with himself because God wasn't listening. God wasn't listening due to his contemptuous pride and scorn. The Pharisee tried to rub God's face in his good works, sacrifice, and devotion but that wasn't what God was looking for. He was looking for repentance with humility, proof that a person is serious. Our temple is impossible to cleanse if the spirit of pride is standing in the way with its hands planted on its hips in defiance.

> The Pharisee stood and prayed thus with himself [only talking to himself], God, I thank thee, that I am not as other men are, extortioners, unjust, adulterers, or even as this publican. I fast twice in the week, I give tithes of all that I possess. And the publican, standing afar off, would not lift up so much as his eyes unto heaven, but smote upon his breast, saying, God be merciful to me a sinner. I tell you, this man went down to his house justified rather than the other: for every one that exalteth himself shall be abased; and he that humbleth himself shall be exalted.
>
> —LUKE 18:11–14

Pride opens the door for the destroyer to bring us to ruin, pain, calamity, and every evil waste. If one senses they are accident-prone or things just aren't going right, the wrecking ball was put in motion by pride and the haughty spirit.

> Pride [majestic like self-exaltation] goeth before destruction [ruin, a wound, a fracture, shattering], and an haughty spirit [grandeur, lifted up] before a fall [calamity, stumbling].
>
> —PROVERBS 16:18

Divorce and family breakup have pride as the root. We've seen where pride stirs up strife and contention and is a block to prayer, so it is no wonder folks lose hope in marriage restoration—*but God*! The Word shows us the spiritual connection to our mess so we can expose the critter and turn the curse into a blessing. The family of proud folks will be pulled apart with family members being sent into exile, banished from their heritage and those they love.

> The reason my house was troubled was because of two things: greed and pride which would have opened the door to Satan to carry out his curse of destruction and spoiling.

> The LORD will destroy [banish from his house, exiled or pulled down] the house [household, family] of the proud.
>
> —PROVERBS 15:25

Related to pride is greed, which is also a root cause for the destruction of the family and home. One of my biggest regrets in my business life was the obsession with various marketing systems that promised quick and sustained wealth. I would promise whatever needed to be promised to coerce my friends to join in as a fellow distributor. Then once they joined up, I would hassle them to strive for their goals and to make a difference in the lives of their friends by getting them to join as well. This became so obsessive that I could never shut my mind off about who my next big-shot distributor may be, and everyone knew if they came close to me they would get the spiel. I set goals and boasted of my accomplishments in order to entice others to join with me so that I could profit from their drivenness as well. My wife was at home with three babies; and I'd go out and do the business for sixteen to eighteen hours

> God stands for marriages and His will is always in favor of reconcilliation. Reconciliation is never about the other person; it is about you.

a day and couldn't understand why my beloved couldn't get behind it completely. "After all, I'm sacrificing for the family." This mania lasted for about five years as I switched between eight or nine dream companies, all of which ended up in bitter disappointment. Greed coupled with pride blinds, and I couldn't see the destruction I was causing with all my friendships and mostly importantly the one at home, which would eventually face major challenges.

The very thing that I thought would help my young family would eventually lead to tearing it apart. When things went wrong I realized that what I had believed and understood before got me to the place I found myself in so there must be something I didn't comprehend. I found out I didn't get a lot of things and Proverbs 15:25–27 hit me with the fear of God factor. The reason my house was troubled was because of two things: greed and pride, which would have opened the door to Satan to carry out his curse of destruction and spoiling. This may sound strange I'm sure but when I saw the truth in Proverbs 15:25–27, I shouted out "Yes!" Why did I shout out? Because I knew what I needed to do to break Satan's grip on my family, as I was immediately convicted by the Holy Spirit regarding my sin. So I got to repent and allow the Lord to purge me and my household of this evil and break the devils assignment of affliction.

> He that is greedy of gain troubleth [brings evil, affliction and calamity upon] his own house [household, family].
> —Proverbs 15:27

The world of insincere marriage vows says you deserve peace, happiness, and to find your real identity; so go get a divorce and move on, as life is short, your second marriage will be much better, or so the lie goes. However, in the Word there are two choices: be wise and restore, or be foolish and tear it apart.

> Every wise woman buildeth her house [establishes or restores from exile]: but the foolish plucketh [destroys, overthrows, tears down] it down with her hands.
> —Proverbs 14:1

God stands for marriages and His will is always in favor of reconciliation. Reconciliation is never about the other person; it is about you. The Word of God can open up and soften the hardest of hearts. Yes, He can even break through pride and greed and every other evil thing.

Is not my word like as a fire? Saith the LORD; and like a hammer that
breaketh the rock in pieces?
—JEREMIAH 23:29

Has the enemy overwhelmed and torn apart your family? Reconciliation is
never about the other person; it is about you. If you make it about your beloved,
then you entered into judgment and condemnation, which is as far as you'll
get. God won't work within those parameters. There is nothing you can do in
the flesh or on your own to heal a broken family, but the Lord wants in on the
reconstruction. But He does it His way and only if you'll die to self and submit
to only one kingdom. He says to you that if you try to do it on your own, your
labor will be in vain; but if He is allowed to rebuild the family on His foundation, it will happen. The Hebrew word *banah* that is translated into the English
word *build* actually means to rebuild, to restore those exiled, and to establish the
family permanently. How can that be? Because Jesus came not to call the righteous, but sinners to repentance; they that are whole have no need of a physician,
but they that are sick. He restores individuals firstly and then puts them back
into restored families.

Except the LORD build [rebuild, restore,
establish permanently] the house [family],
they labour [toil in weariness] in vain that
build it: except the LORD keep the city, the
watchman [those who watch for iniquity]
waketh but in vain.
—PSALM 127:1

If you can handle all
the pain, cost and
misery of divorce you
can certainly handle
the work of reconciling
your marriage!

An archangel, Lucifer, and two men, King Saul and King Nebuchadnezzar,
were all taken by God and set in a position of power and influence. Beginning
with the example set by Lucifer, all three became exceedingly proud of who
they had become, supposing they had something to do with it. Lucifer was
cast out of heaven to earth with a third of the angels to reign for a limited time
before receiving a daily death sentence for life. Saul died in shame, seeing the
anointing of the Lord removed from him. Only Nebuchadnezzar repented and
was healed and restored to humble greatness.

Many of us blame our families or our spouse's families for the evil we are experiencing. Can any of us honestly blame anyone else for our own pride? Lucifer
was in the family of the heavenly host created by and daily serving the Father
God. Lucifer boasted the "Five I Wills" of his five lifetime achievement pursuits,
the new identity, and incredible happiness that awaited him; and all he had to do
was get past God. Where did this get Lucifer? It got him the pleasure of all the
sin he wanted. It got him a life void of God. If he had any power against God,
the bottomless pit would not be able to contain him, and he could have prevented
the resurrection of Jesus Christ. Satan is a created being with a purpose to flush
out those that would also prefer to live their eternal lives without their Maker.

When you consider the choice they make, the only conclusion you can reach is that pride opens the door to insanity. Pride caused Lucifer to divorce from his family and take a large number of fellow angels with him into exile. Not only did his pride and ambition hurt him, it also destroyed the destiny of those that looked up to him. What did they gain? What did they lose? Where did God set you before pride made you discontented?

> Thou art the anointed cherub that covereth; and I have set thee so: thou wast upon the holy mountain of God; thou hast walked up and down in the midst of the stones of fire. Thou wast perfect in thy ways from the day that thou wast created, till iniquity was found in thee.
> —EZEKIEL 28:14–15

> And the great dragon was cast out, that old serpent, called the Devil, and Satan, which deceiveth the whole world: he was cast out into the earth, and his angels were cast out with him....And his tail drew the third part of the stars of heaven, and did cast them to the earth.
> —REVELATION 12:9, 4

Pride split up the first heavenly family, and so it continues to destroy families today and carry those affected into exile, into ruin, and bewilderment. Bewildered or bewitched, I don't know; but if a person knew the pain, anger, guilt, cost, shame, loss, damage to children, and all the awkwardness they'd experience for the rest of their lives, wouldn't it be easier and less painful to work on their marriage even if they have to put up with some less than desirable idiosyncrasies? The cost of divorce can get the best of ministry and counsel the world over and still have money left over to go on a second honeymoon cruise. If you can handle all the pain, cost, and misery of divorce you can certainly handle the work of reconciling your marriage!

On July 28, 2009, I finished the draft of this section, and I knew the Lord was convicting me as to what was just written. The following is a letter sent out on August 5, 2009, to all my friends and relatives that I had spoken to regarding the details of my separation:

> Greetings,

> While on the plane returning from my daughter's wedding yesterday, I was replaying the vows they wrote and then recited to each other. Those vows were so beautiful, and they were especially meaningful considering their chastity and desire to walk the walk of righteousness together. It will be twenty-five years ago as of Aug. 18th that her parents also recited vows they had written. Something my daughter said convicted me of my treachery over the years towards my beloved wife and especially over the last couple of years.

> I am writing this letter to you to take full responsibility for the pain that I would have caused you and my wife through words that I spoke to you. These were words that I deeply regret saying as they were from the pit

designed to tear down my beloved and lift me up in my pride, as I wanted to cover my shame of marriage failure and protect my reputation. I spoke from my self-serving defensive perspective concerning my take on her state of mind, on her role as a wife, or activity of late. I spoke with disdain in a judging and condemning fashion that is not befitting a man of God as well as a Christian husband and father. I realize that I spread the gall of my bitterness and what I said would have defiled you and hurt you, as I know you to love my wife dearly. My sinful and spiteful words caused division between friends and family and made it awkward to be in fellowship, as that sacred trust was broken. My words were in violation to the vows I made twenty-five years ago and that is evident to all, but for some reason it took me a long time to see the true error of my own ways. Will you forgive me of trying to manipulate you to choose sides by my telling lies, repeating what ought not to be repeated, and making accusations designed to destroy her reputation? Will you forgive me for defiling you with words that should never have been said to you or to anyone else for that matter?

You see, my words are to only be a blessing, but I chose rather to curse and spread my offense. A Proverb came to mind that "The Lord will destroy the house of the proud" and I know that what has come upon my family is the direct result of my pride and the things that a proud person does behind closed doors. Another passage says that "only by pride comes contention or strife" so obviously there would be strife in my home and again my pride would have been the messy root. I take one hundred percent of the responsibility before man and God for the state of my marriage and for all actions and words after its demise. I saw at the wedding how my actions and eventual separation caused me to be a reproach to those that love us as they could see the consequences of my sin played out. I am so sorry for how our marriage separation would have really hurt you...will you forgive me?

I lay no blame, responsibility, or shame upon my wife as whatever I judge she might have done is nothing in comparison to how I hurt her, as I hurt her so much that her heart was no longer safe with me and she saw no option but to seek to escape the pain. I ask you to release her of any attitude or perception you may have held against my beloved due to my wickedness and to hold her blameless.

Through this letter of repentance and personal responsibility I blow out all the fiery darts of the devil and extinguish the fires that he has set ablaze due to my iniquity in Jesus' name.

I will be sending out this letter to many, as I desire to extinguish all that I have set ablaze and to repair the many breaches resulting from my sin. The work of destruction stops right here and now..."Father God I repent for all that I have mentioned here and for the many other sins I have committed that have caused offense to my wife, my children, extended family, friends and all those of our marriage, ministry and business community. And Father I ask that you would remove from the heart and conscience of each person affected the defilement and recollection of the sin that I've committed against you and the wife of my youth. Lord sprinkle your cleansing blood upon my sons and daughter so that their spirits would not carry injury, pain, guilt or offense as the result of this most grievous of sins against your family. I pray in Jesus name amen."

Since my original vow was made before many witnesses, I feel the Lord would have me to deal with my breach of those vows in the same fashion. I implore you to hold my wife faultless regardless of proceedings that may or may not happen concerning our marriage in the future. I ask that you would lay all responsibility firmly where it belongs and that is with her husband, and I in response submit all to my heavenly Father through my Savior who desires to cleanse me and release me of all my past sin and to reconcile us all onto Himself.

This is hard to admit, but I see now that as difficult and heart wrenching as it has been over the last nineteen months, this separation was the only way God could get my undivided attention in order for him to do what He had to do in me. I understand the concept that my wife had no choice but to leave if she ever was to have a better future; a future that belongs to her as her inheritance as a daughter of the most high God; a future of joy, happiness, contentment, peace, prosperity, and safety. She tried everything to communicate her pain to me but I couldn't or wouldn't be able to understand in the state of mind and spirit I was in. To God be the glory of whatever He might yet need to do.

If there is something I missed that was offensive to you or something difficult to understand or needs to be clarified in this letter please let me know so we are all released to our freedom and peace.

Now standing with our Lord in His love,

Dennis

As soon as this letter was sent, I felt a heaviness lifted off of me as the Lord delivered me of the treachery resulting from my pride. There was a freedom that I sought from the Lord for a long time, as I knew there was a block in my spirit that stubbornly remained. At this time, I do not know what the outcome of my marriage will be, but I remain to hope against hope when there is no hope as far as man is concerned.

What is God's view of divorce? He hates it in the strongest of terms. God made man and woman one so that they could pool their incomes and have a nice house—just an observation. God made them one because He wanted to have godly grandchildren in a stable home. Divorce is called treachery or treason and it is violent. How is it violent? Because there is a tearing apart of something that is not meant to be separated, as God made them one. This explains the belligerent anger, lying, cruelty, false accusations, gossip, manipulations, retaliation, jealousy, pride, and every other evil thing that occurs throughout the life of a divorce. Divorce is more painful than death, as this treachery and violence doesn't, or doesn't usually, accompany the passing of a beloved.

And did not he make one?…And wherefore one? That he might seek a godly seed. Therefore take heed to your spirit, and let none deal treacherously against the wife of his youth. For the LORD, the God of Israel, saith that he hateth [to be an adversary, enemy] putting away [divorce]: for one covereth violence [cruelty, damage, unrighteous gain, to spoil, oppression] with his garment, saith the LORD of hosts: therefore take heed to your spirit, that ye deal not treacherously [treason, deceit, falsely, to afflict with ruin].

—MALACHI 2:15–16

Yes, every situation is different, but God wouldn't be so strong in His language if He didn't have the cure for broken hearts in marriage. Is anything too difficult for God? Is your heart so hardened that you want to "move on" no matter what? Moses had difficulty in his marriage and he was separated from his wife, Zipporah, for a season, during which time she lived with her father, Jethro, until she was reconciled with Moses. Even the likes of a man like Moses was not immune to marriage troubles. Moses was a leader to whom God gave the Law and set him up to judge the people, which included the granting of divorce. Moses stood for his own marriage, as he knew God's heart concerning the family. Their separation was a time set aside for healing and restoration at the proper time. (See Exodus 4:25–26; 18:2–5.)

> We have seen that the root of all these things is the deception of pride. The problem in the relationship is not the other person, it is the stronghold of pride and all that goes along with pride to enforce complete ruin.

This marriage passage in Malachi wraps up by saying we tire God out. How is that possible? By repeatedly saying God loves the sinners and sin alike and furthermore by saying God must approve of what we are doing as He hasn't judged us. Saying God is too nice to judge. In this context I believe the prophet is warning about being presumptuous regarding the grace of God and provoking judgment for premeditated rebellion. These are strong words, but wouldn't you sooner hear it on this side of judgment?

Ye have wearied the LORD with your words. Yet ye say, Wherein have we wearied him? When ye say, Every one that doeth evil is good in the sight of the LORD, and he delighteth in them; or, Where is the God of judgment?

—MALACHI 2:17

Is it only the one who petitions divorce that is the proud one? Of course not! Was there strife, contention, judging, accusation, shame, or contempt during the relationship? Can there be strife with only one participating? We have seen that the root of all these things is the deception of pride. The problem in the relationship is not the other person; it is the stronghold of pride and all that goes along with pride to enforce complete ruin. So folks, isn't that good news?

Because if the Scripture is true, it has exposed the real work of treachery so it can be purged. Pack your bags for the second honeymoon.

Back a few paragraphs I made innuendo that the pride that brought a third of the host of heaven down was not logical, it was insanity. Is pride also the root of insanity or mental illness?

What roots out insanity?

Trying to find a concise definition of *insanity* is insane. Some describe it as mental illness of such a severe nature that a person cannot distinguish fantasy from reality, cannot conduct their affairs normally, or is subject to uncontrollable, impulsive behavior. Others add it is a chronic disease, manifested by deviations from the healthy and natural state of the mind, such deviations consisting in a dark and moody perversion of the feelings, affections, and habits. In the case of criminal law insanity is any mental disorder in which the patient cannot be held responsible for their actions.

Some opponents of this insanity defense, including Thomas Szasz, Professor Emeritus of Psychiatry at the State University of New York Health Science Center in Syracuse, New York, believe that psychiatry itself emerged as a way to justify mercy, of making persons "exceptional" and thus not deserving of the harsh punishment we would as a society wish to dole out to people who had extremely selfish or widely shared rationales for their actions. Since extreme selfishness (self-absorption) or broadly shared resentments (i.e., envy of the rich, hatred of another ethnic group) are somewhat infectious behaviors, some argue that schizophrenia and other "mental illness" were defined into existence to protect those whose motives and behaviors were not so infectious, and whose offenses were thus unlikely to be repeated by others. Szasz continues that insanity almost always involves some perversion or distortion of the will.[1]

Perhaps all of us have done things that we are not too proud of that would fit into the insanity slot. What I found interesting is Dr. Szasz's observation after forty-five years of clinical practice: he is saying that insanity is rooted in extreme selfishness, envy and hatred, and I'm sure he was just getting started. Scripture calls those attributes sin, which has pride as the root. Who perverts our logical thinking? Satan does.

Consider the insanity trip of King Nebuchadnezzar. God appointed him in position as king, and yet eventually Nebuchadnezzar had his mind and spirit given over to pride as he wallowed in self-aggrandizement. God moved swiftly to humble him, and He did it through imposing a period of insanity upon this king. The king did repent of pride and his mind was restored, as was his position.

> All this came upon the king Nebuchadnezzar. At the end of twelve months he walked in the palace of the kingdom of Babylon. The king spake, and said, Is not this great Babylon, that I have built for the house

of the kingdom by the might of my power, and for the honour of my majesty?...But when his heart was lifted up, and his mind hardened in pride, he was deposed from his kingly throne, and they took his glory from him. And he was driven from the sons of men; and his heart [mind] was made like the beasts, and his dwelling was with the wild asses: they fed him with grass like oxen, and his body was wet with the dew of heaven; till he knew that the most high God ruled in the kingdom of men, and that he appointeth [established in position] over it whomsoever he will.
—DANIEL 4:28–30; 5:20–21

A similar fate struck King Saul who was "little in his own sight" when first anointed to be king but then he forgot his humble beginnings. Through his pride he rebelled, opening the door to insanity, witchcraft, stubbornness, and idolatry.

Then came the word of the Lord unto Samuel, saying, It repenteth me that I have set up Saul to be king: for he is turned back from following me, and hath not performed my commandments....And Samuel said, When thou wast little in thine own sight, wast thou not made the head of the tribes of Israel, and the Lord anointed thee king over Israel?...For rebellion is as the sin of witchcraft, and stubbornness is as iniquity and idolatry. Because thou hast rejected the word of the Lord, he hath also rejected thee from being king....But the Spirit of the Lord departed from Saul, and an evil spirit from the Lord troubled him. And Saul's servants said unto him, Behold now, an evil spirit from God troubleth thee....And it came to pass, when the evil spirit from God was upon Saul, that David took an harp, and played with his hand: so Saul was refreshed, and was well, and the evil spirit departed from him
—1 SAMUEL 15:10, 17, 23; 16:14–15, 23

As pride had Lucifer deposed, it also had Saul removed from his throne. Pride is the acid of ruin, shame, insanity, and jealousy. Saul's pride continued to manifest in anger, jealousy, and attempted murder. While David was playing the harp in Saul's presence, an evil spirit vexed Saul so that on impulse he threw his spear at David in an attempt to kill him. Psychiatry would call this temporary insanity.

And Saul was very wroth, and the saying displeased him; and he said, They have ascribed unto David ten thousands, and to me they have ascribed but thousands: and what can he have more but the kingdom? And Saul eyed David from that day and forward. And it came to pass on the morrow, that the evil spirit from God came upon Saul, and he prophesied in the midst of the house: and David played with his hand, as at other times: and there was a javelin in Saul's hand.
—1 SAMUEL 18:8–10

Saul repented by blaming the people and didn't take responsibility for his pride as King Nebuchadnezzar had done. Nebuchadnezzar was restored to sanity but Saul was not.

Rebellion is the fruit of pride. All disobedience to the Scripture is rebellion, and rebellion is fueled by pride. Does a curse have a legal right to be destroying your life? Well, if pride is manifesting, the door is open to many a curse and separates us from our Father.

Pride brings with it a curse that will need to be broken in Jesus' name once it is fully repented of. Pride rebels against the Word of the Lord, so rebellion must be exposed and purged along with pride.

> Thou hast rebuked the proud that are cursed, which do err from thy commandments.
> —PSALM 119:21

OK, ducklings, do you know what the only thing is that makes a person ugly? Yep, pride. Each of us has a secret life, and it is silly to pretend that our outward choices are not influenced by who we are on the inside.

Pride is ugly.

We can't make up for what is in our spirits by camouflaging the tent. Real beauty is agape. How many of you know that you can't see pride by staring at yourself in a three-way mirror? Pride is what others may see in you; but they dare not tell you what they see, as proud people contend that they don't have a pride problem.

Pride makes us take the credit for something someone else did. It makes us take the credit for what God gave us and how He made us to look on the outer skin layer. For those of us that are so caught up in our skin and the skin-suit of others, what is the first thing to get eaten by maggots when we die? What part of us is untouchable by maggots? What part is eternal? What were you so proud of again?

Paul works very hard in his letter to the Corinthian Church to get us to understand that our present body is only the seed of our intended bodies we are to inhabit once this earth phase is done.

> But some man will say, How are the dead raised up? And with what body do they come? Thou fool, that which thou sowest is not quickened, except it die: And that which thou sowest, thou sowest not that body that shall be, but bare grain, it may chance of wheat, or of some other grain: But God giveth it a body as it hath pleased him, and to every seed his own body.
> —1 CORINTHIANS 15:35–38

Your body is only a seed and I say that to help us understand how short-lived the lifecycle of a seed is compared to the next stage in its life. You cannot determine how pretty a plant will be judging the outer appearance of the seed. Are not some seeds dry and wrinkly but bare no resemblance to the sweet pea plant it will grow into. Others look cute and fuzzy but grow into thistles or dandelion weeds. Or consider the flamboyant tree (*Delonix regia*), which is known for its spectacular show of colors and yet it comes from one ugly shriveled, contorted seed. Another may be quite the nut or another a bit corny; I am not sure if those are actually to be improved upon though. Isn't it the biggest mistake to question God as to how He made your seed and even greater folly to say to another seed that they will never amount to anything? This is reality, folks.

> So also [is] the resurrection of the dead. It is sown in corruption [decomposing]; it is raised in incorruption: It is sown in dishonor [unseemly, offensive, contempt]; it is raised in glory [splendor]: it is sown in weakness [infirmity, frailty]; it is raised in power. It is sown a natural body; it is raised a spiritual body. There is a natural body, and there is a spiritual body.
> —1 CORINTHIANS 15:42–44

I am about done with the judging of other seeds, how about you? I am sensing that now is a good time to repent of this before we see them face-to-face in glory.

Considering that once our seed is ready, we are raised a spiritual body, what if the splendor and beauty of that body is everything to do with our sanctification and the resulting agape we work out now? What if your seed were to be made ready by tonight? What kind of plant would grow if its only fertilizer were the agape-bearing fruit today?

The need for approval

One of the greatest driving forces in a man's life is the need for approval. Who are you seeking it from? To answer that question, who is the first person you want to show or share your accomplishments with? My rejection puts my acceptance from man on a higher plane than my acceptance by God.

Rejection communicates that a person is unacceptable, was a mistake, is of no value, doesn't belong, is unwanted, can't fit in, or is unloved. This message is communicated through a disgusted look, disdain, an impatient answer, a snub, neglect, abandonment, or silence.

We all know that sting, that deep hurt, because we were all born with an innate longing for love and acceptance. By experiencing the full force of rejection in all of its torment and brutality, Jesus knows your pain. He will be there so you don't have to suffer the lonely torment He did. Jesus was totally abandoned when His spirit was the most vulnerable.

> Reproach [scorn, contempt] hath broken my heart; and I am full of heaviness: and I looked for some to take pity [show compassion], but there was none; and for comforters, but I found none.
> —PSALM 69:20

He has been through rejection and He knows what we need. Jesus pleads, "Here, take My hand."

When my father and my mother forsake me, then the LORD will take me up.

—PSALM 27:10

Jesus anticipated the potential that wounded people who become parents would have to reject those they were supposed to love.

Can a woman forget her sucking child, that she should not have compassion on the son of her womb? yea, they may forget, yet will I not forget thee.

—ISAIAH 49:15

The schoolyard chant, "Sticks and stones may break my bones, but words will never hurt me," is an incredible untruth. The wound from a stick heals and is forgotten, but the sting of words can ring in our ears for life. These words repeat the same shock to our heart every time the memory of them recirculates in our mind.

The devil loves to bring back to our memory the shameful and vile things that we were victimized by or how we victimized others in order for those vile acts to become our identity and shape our future. Read this passage over and over until you understand your Lord's desire for you from today onwards:

Fear not; for thou shalt not be ashamed: neither be thou confounded [humiliated, dishonored]; for thou shalt not be put to shame: for thou shalt forget the shame [confusion, vile thing] of thy youth, and shalt not remember the reproach [scorn, stigma] of thy widowhood [living in exile] any more. For thy Maker is thine husband; the LORD of hosts is his name; and thy Redeemer the Holy One of Israel; The God of the whole earth shall he be called. For the LORD hath called thee as a woman forsaken [abandoned, neglected] and grieved in spirit [tortured, vexed, sorrowful], and a wife of youth, when thou wast refused [rejected, become loathsome, despised], saith thy God. For a small moment have I forsaken thee; but with great mercies will I gather thee.

—ISAIAH 54:4–7

Rejection is a very sensitive spirit that picks apart words, scrambles intentions, judges facial expressions, looks at every action through a microscope, yet is very self-centered. Self-centeredness is pride, and pride is behind rejection, as strange as that may seem.

When we know the area of another's vulnerability, it is easy to push their buttons to cause them pain and torment.

For in many things we offend all [cause misery, cause to stumble]. If any man offend not in word, the same is a perfect man, and able also to bridle [hold in check, restrain] the whole body.

—JAMES 3:2

Pride workout

Step 1: Prayerfully review the following list and mark each sin you or your generations have participated with. It is important that you are not rushed and that you are in a private place as you go through this.

- ❑ **Abandonment**
- ❑ **Accusation**
- ❑ **Adultery:** immorality, infidelity, double minded, betrayal of spouse and God
- ❑ **Anti-social behavior**
- ❑ **Arrogance:** pompous, disdainful, pretension, vanity, audacity
- ❑ **Blasphemy:** irreverence, abuse, slander, railing, injurious speech, heresy
- ❑ **Boasting:** braggart, empty pretender, grandstander, know-it-all, show-off, crowd pleaser
- ❑ **Condemnation:** pronounce judgment, disparage, criticize, depreciate, damn
- ❑ **Contempt:** intense disrespect regarding one you feel is inferior, willful disobedience
- ❑ **Contention:** discord, strife in debate, striving in rivalry
- ❑ **Control:** need to have everything done your way; people need permission from you to breath!
- ❑ **Covetousness:** to desire wrongfully without regard for rights of others
- ❑ **Deceit:** misleading others for own benefit, cunning, fraud, hypocrisy
- ❑ **Depression:** severe despondency typically felt over a period of time and accompanied by feelings of hopelessness and inadequacy.
- ❑ **Despisers of God:** regard as unworthy of consideration, dismiss
- ❑ **Despisers of man:** opposed to goodness in men, suspect, shun, repudiate
- ❑ **Destruction (home/family/enterprise)**
- ❑ **Discontentment:** never able to find anything to fill the void; constantly dissatisfied with the situation and place you find yourself in
- ❑ **Disobedient:** defiant, contrary, insubordinate, perverse, wayward, not compliant
- ❑ **Domination:** despotism, oppression, supremacy
- ❑ **Double-mindedness:** wants best of both worlds – God's and Satan's. Unstable in all his ways
- ❑ **Doubt and unbelief**
- ❑ **Elitist:** snobbish, belief that certain classes of people deserve favored treatment
- ❑ **Enmity:** everything opposite and opposing agape
- ❑ **Entitlement:** lives in narcissistic fantasy world needy of leisure, attention, excessive admiration, advancement, center of everyone's attention, power
- ❑ **Envy:** spite, begrudge, crave, desire, lust, yearn, to burn with zeal, stingy
- ❑ **Evil eye:** glance intended to cause harm, curse, hostile
- ❑ **Evil surmising:** attribute some selfish or evil motive behind every good deed
- ❑ **Evil thoughts:** uncontrollable mind traffic, troublesome, injurious, pernicious
- ❑ **Excessive need for:**
  - ❑ acceptance

- ❑ approval
- ❑ identity
- ❑ love
- ❑ **Exploitive**
- ❑ **Fabricated personality:** what you have created for yourself to hide insecurity, insincerity and to hide the unloving spirit
- ❑ **False accusers:** lying allegations out of scorn and malicious intent to destroy
- ❑ **False burden-bearing:** carrying the weight of other people's problems
- ❑ **False responsibility:** one who assumes the blame for a problem or situation they had nothing to do with in a pitiful attention getting way
- ❑ **Fantasy lust:** to greatly desire things of ones creative fantasy; to believe with an unrealistic faith that you will receive the object of your lustful passion.
- ❑ **Fear:**
  - ❑ **Fear of abandonment**
  - ❑ **Fear of failure**
  - ❑ **Fear of God**
  - ❑ **Fear of man**
  - ❑ **Fear of rejection**
  - ❑ **Fear of vulnerability**
- ❑ **Flattering lips:** corrupt and deceitful words to incite pride in others
- ❑ **Foolishness:** stupidity combined with stubbornness, ridiculous explanations, indiscretion
- ❑ **Fornication:** remarriage after unbiblical divorce, all sex apart from covenant spouse, lust
- ❑ **Froward heart:** habitually disposed to opposition and disobedience, crooked, perverted
- ❑ **Fury:** goaded by anger, heat, rage, hot displeasure, indignation, venom
- ❑ **Grandiosity:** exaggerated sense of self-importance, as if nobody else in picture
- ❑ **Haughtiness:** scornfully and condescendingly proud, showing arrogant superiority
- ❑ **Heaviness:** anxious care, a dark pain, dejection, gloom, a weighted heart
- ❑ **Humiliation:** degradation, dishonor, embarrassment, disgrace
- ❑ **Luciferian spirit:**
  - ❑ **I will ascend above the heights of the clouds**
  - ❑ **I will ascend into heaven**
  - ❑ **I will be like the most High.**
  - ❑ **I will exalt my throne above the stars**
  - ❑ **I will sit also upon the mount of the congregation**
- ❑ **Idolatry**
- ❑ **Imaginations:** a judgment, decision, a reasoning such as is hostile to the Christian faith
- ❑ **Incontinent:** without self-control, intemperate
- ❑ **Insanity**

❑ **Insecurity:** lack of confidence and assurance that who they really are measures up
❑ **Judgment**
❑ **Lack of empathy:** unable to identify with feelings of others, tune out as soon as others talk, no concern for others distress, emotional numbness
❑ **Lack of trust in God, self, and others**
❑ **Lasciviousness:** unbridled lust, excess, outrageousness, shamelessness
❑ **Lovers of their own selves:** too intent on one's interest, selfish
❑ **Lust:** depraved or corrupt passion for things forbidden
❑ **Lying**
❑ **Manipulation:** to cleverly or unscrupulously (i.e. pouting, anger, avoidance, etc) control or influence those around you
❑ **Martyrdom:** a display of feigned or exaggerated suffering to obtain sympathy or admiration
❑ **Murders**
❑ **Muttering and complaining**
❑ **Narcissism:** abnormal love for oneself, one's own body and sexual characteristics, absurd vanity, feel they have to take care of everything as everyone else is unreliable and unfit
❑ **Neediness**
❑ **Oppression**
❑ **Perverse disputing:** constant contention, incessant wrangling, empty business
❑ **Proud:** focus on self, pre-eminent, to blind with conceit
❑ **Racism**
❑ **Rebellion:** resisting authority, defiance or disobedience to government, police officers, church leaders, employer, parents and to God
❑ **Rejection**
❑ **Religious superiority**
❑ **Self-accusation**
❑ **Self-anger**
❑ **Self-bitterness**
❑ **Self-condemnation**
❑ **Self-hatred**
❑ **Selfishness**
❑ **Self-pity**
❑ **Self-rejection**
❑ **Self-resentment**
❑ **Self-retaliation**
❑ **Self-unforgiveness**
❑ **Shame**
❑ **Spirit of blindness**
❑ **Spiritual pride**
❑ **Strife:** electioneering for office, a desire to put one's self forward, self-promoting

- ❑ **Strifes of words:** to contend about words, to wrangle about empty and trifling matters
- ❑ **Stumbling:** accident prone
- ❑ **Superficial:** shallow, phony, insincere
- ❑ **Theft**
- ❑ **Tongue that speaks proud:** great, large in magnitude in intensity, loud in sound
- ❑ **Trucebreakers:** that cannot be persuaded to enter into a covenant, implacable
- ❑ **Unforgiveness**
- ❑ **Unholy**
- ❑ **Unsubmissive:** rebellion against order of God in family, church, government
- ❑ **Unthankful:** ungracious, unpleasing, unthankful
- ❑ **Vainglory:** groundless, self esteem, empty pride, a vain opinion, error
- ❑ **Violence:** aggression, ferocity, vehemence, intensity
- ❑ **Wickedness:** depravity, iniquity
- ❑ **Witchcraft**
- ❑ **Without natural affection:** unsociable, inhuman, unloving

This is only a partial list. Ask the Lord if He sees something else that needs to be purged here.

Step 2: Go back through the list and pray this prayer inserting the sin in the blank space. You may insert several sins in the blank space at a time if you desire.

Prayer of Repentance
(Preferably out loud)

Father God, I recognize and take responsibility for myself and my ancestors for the sin(s) of _____. I agree with Your verdict on my rebellion. I repent, I renounce, and I ask forgiveness for my participation with these sins, and I ask that their curse be broken in the name of Jesus Christ of Nazareth.

Step 3: Bind the strongman. This is best done by an experienced and trusted ministering friend the first time around.

Prayer to Bind the Strongmen of Pride and Rejection
(Out loud)

In the name of Jesus Christ of Nazareth and by the power of the Holy Spirit, I take authority over the strongmen of pride and rejection. I break your power and bind you and put you on notice that I am destroying your armor in which you trust and I will be coming back to remove you from your palace.

Step 4: Purging the evil. Review the above list again now inserting the sin you have repented of in the blank.

Command of Deliverance
(Must be out loud with eyes open,
realizing you are speaking directly to a spirit)

*In the name of Jesus Christ of Nazareth and by the power of the Holy Spirit,
I take authority over the spirit(s) of _____. I break your
power, I cast you out, and I command you to return no more.*

Step 5: Purge the strongman now that you have destroyed his stronghold.

Command of Deliverance
(Must be out loud with eyes open,
realizing you are speaking directly to a spirit)

*In the name of Jesus Christ of Nazareth and by the power of the Holy Spirit,
I take authority over the strongmen of pride and rejection. I break your
power, I cast you out, and I command you to return no more.*

Step 6: Pray that God will cause you to increase and abound in His love and
that you would be an overcomer in the sins just repented of. Ask for a scripture
that you will use to resist the devil when he tries to open the trapdoor again
to regain entrance to your heart.

AGAPE DOES NOT BEHAVE ITSELF UNSEEMLY

The room was abuzz with final preparations for the wedding. A small group of
ladies were huddled around a table applying their artistic flare to the wedding
decorations. A group of amorous young men arrived to check out the progress
when they appeared to become frozen in a trance. They had made their way
to a section of the room that would afford them the best view of one of the
gals at the table. She was voluptuous and adorned with a fitted blouse with
a plunging neckline revealing a portion of her bust. She seemed totally unin-
terested and apparently oblivious to the silent clamor of the men. They stood
there unashamedly with all their eyes locked simultaneously onto this woman's display for what seemed like several minutes. The movement and expression of their eyes told a story of what they were reading into this very awkward
situation. This was unseemly behavior.

Unseemly behavior feeds the preoccupation with bodily and sexual pleasures
that would create sexual heat. In this most familiar of scenes, the woman's attire
was intended to excite lust or sexual desire in a coy demurring and not-so-inno-
cent fashion. The men were aroused and in such a state showed no restraint and
were without shame of their immodesty. The most accepted definitions of the
words of the original language for *unseemly* mean the nakedness of the woman's
genitals without shame; a man preparing in his heart disgrace for his virgin; and
indecency as determined by the Word of God and not the morays of society.

If there is a topic I wish I did not have to address in this book this would be
it. When we observe the display of behavior as I just described, the tendency

is one of two things depending on your stuff: to lust after what you see or secondly to judge the woman as being loose.

It is time to expose the creature that has destroyed the most powerful nations in the past and has a stranglehold on much of the world now. This creature is identified by Hosea as the spirit of whoredoms.

This spirit attacks covenant beginning with sensuality, seduction, unfaithfulness, adultery, and fornication to break the two most vital of relationships: the relationship between man and God and between a man and his wife. This principality is also behind the extraordinary attraction, lust, exposure, and focus on the woman's breasts.

> And they committed whoredoms [to commit adultery with a husband while she has a husband] in Egypt; they committed whoredoms in their youth: there were their breasts pressed [immodestly pressing or pushing], and there they bruised [to immodestly fashion, ply, produce] the teats [breasts] of their virginity [maiden].
> —Ezekiel 23:2–10

The spirit of whoredoms sweeps through generations without much opposition as it appeals to the pleasurable lust of sin so accordingly there is little motivation to halt the behavior. Participants are held in captivity and the consequences of this sin are for life if not eternity, as rebellion leads to drunkenness to lust to fornication to bastard children (including abortion) to further adultery to idolatry to the occult to spiritual blindness and to destruction. It has no boundaries and knows no shame in its primarily sexual deviant behavior.

> Whoredom and wine and new wine take away the heart…for the spirit of whoredoms [adultery, fornication and resulting bastard children] hath caused them to err [to wander astray mentally, morally and physically], and they have gone a whoring [commit fornication with man and against God] from under their God. They sacrifice upon the tops of the mountains, and burn incense upon the hills, under oaks and poplars and elms [occultic worship], because the shadow thereof [is] good: therefore your daughters shall commit whoredom, and your spouses shall commit adultery.
> —Hosea 4:11–13

Hosea continues his teaching on this principality to expose the rebellion and pride that blinds the minds of men concerning the truth of God. Satan starts, for example, with just a little "cute rebellion" in the dress of a teenage girl with the long-term plan to blind the hearts of men and women from God.

> They will not frame their doings [exchange behavior and lifestyle] to turn unto their God: for the spirit of whoredoms [adultery, fornication and resulting bastard children] is in the midst of them, and they have not known the LORD. And the pride of Israel doth testify to his face: therefore shall Israel and Ephraim fall in their iniquity; Judah also shall fall with them.
> —Hosea 5:4–5

Here is the really, really good news at the end of this difficult study. Once the creature is exposed, all the curses brought upon us can be reversed. The bastard's curse and the curse of fornication, adultery, pride, and rebellion stop here. For those countless thousands bound to the captivity of being conceived out of wedlock, this is where your healing begins. Furthermore, now we know how to minister to a prodigal who is running from the Lord. Are you with me?

Paul was the author of the "love chapter" in Corinthians that we are studying, and he also wrote the Book of Romans. Romans chapter one expounds on this teaching of unseemliness and is very blunt regarding God's position on such behavior.

Romans one is referring to "men who hold the truth in unrighteousness." Those are Christians who have accepted the truth of the Gospel of Christ but, as we will see, walk in unbridled lust and are addicted to repulsive and vulgar sin. The chapter concludes by saying men "who knowing the judgment of God, that they which commit such things are worthy of death" (v. 32). It is emphasizing that these Christian men know this sin is rebellion against God but have made it a way of life thus placing their eternity in the balances.

> For the wrath of God is revealed from heaven against all ungodliness [lack of reverence and fear of God] and unrighteousness [falling short of holiness of God] of men, who hold the truth in unrighteousness [contradicting their profession of faith by their sinful conduct].
>
> —ROMANS 1:18

The prevailing wind of doctrine explains away our sin and makes it of no consequence once we have taken our hell insurance policy by investing only in a short prayer of salvation. If you've held such a doctrine, I challenge you to now study to see if it is true. Verse twenty-one continues that the men to be addressed knew God. But that is as far as it went, and they soon came up with a designer religion to legalize whatever was their fantasy. This is not good.

> Because that, when they knew God, they glorified him not as God, neither were thankful [grateful of all God's blessings]; but became vain [empty and foolish] in their imaginations [think they are wise in their perverse and reprehensible principles], and their foolish [lost sight of what makes for salvation] heart [spirit] was darkened [light is extinguished].
>
> —ROMANS 1:21

In their pursuits the light that once burned within them is extinguished, and they become fools losing their destiny purpose.

> Professing themselves to be wise, they became fools [as salt that has lost strength and flavor].
>
> —ROMANS 1:22

Once the door is opened to this proliferation of sin and a child of God walks through the door, the door slams shut behind him and it cannot be reopened from the side of sin except through sanctification. God is the doorman and there is no sneaking past while still stinky with defilement. The battle is much more difficult now to be released, as the believer finds himself surrounded by all the traffic of wickedness, which is enticing through lust to draw him several steps further back with every single step he takes to get out. Discouragement is the arrow shot constantly at the heart of the unsanctified saint.

> Wherefore God also gave them up [excommunicated to demonic captivity] to uncleanness [sensual defilement] through the lusts [craving for evil] of their own hearts [spirit], to dishonor [treat with contempt by molestation] their own bodies between themselves.
> —ROMANS 1:24

> We may fear genetics as something that is unchangeable, a messenger of doom, when it is just a record of what traits are to be left to future generations. These records are meant to be reversed back to good just as easily as they were contaminated with the virus of evil way back.

The abundance of sin we are dealing with in the rest of the chapters affects us in the area of the soul and spirit, whereas this one targets our bodies, especially through the enticement for sexual sensations and emptiness. Thus begins the addictive cycle, as the desire is there to satisfy the craving, immediately one crashes in to a pit of emptiness with the only temporary relief being another dopamine rush derived from feeding the addictive demons.

> Flee fornication. Every sin that a man doeth is without the body; but he that committeth fornication sinneth against his own body.
> —1 CORINTHIANS 6:18

The door to this captivity is opened by the sin of idolatry, which is the glorification and adulation of people and objects of our "eros" lusts:

> Who changed the truth of God into a lie, and worshiped [adoration and idolization] and served the creature [what God created] more than the Creator, who is blessed for ever.
> —ROMANS 1:25

A believer will know God gave them up when they have the experience of Samson. Samson gave into the sensual excitement of the seductive Delilah; and in so doing, the Spirit of God left him. The Bible says he knew not that the Spirit left him until he needed the power to escape his temptation and the power wasn't there. What a sad situation—to have God leave us and we are not even aware of it. Like Samson, we will be offered redemption but there may be a high price to be paid as our sin is exposed through marriage breakup, addictions, sexually transmitted diseases, destruction, waste, and behavioral lockdowns.

For this cause God gave them up [excommunicated to demonic captivity] unto vile [humiliating disgrace] affections [wounding from satisfying a devilish desire]: for even their women did change the natural use into that which is against nature [contrary to created purpose].

—Romans 1:26

There is a way of escape and recovery from this captivity, as was demonstrated with Peter; he was given up to the power of Satan. His captivity lasted until his heart was converted and purged of his fickle love, carnality, and boasting.

And the Lord said, Simon, Simon, behold, Satan hath desired to have you [as Job to be tried by afflictions], that he may sift you as wheat: But I have prayed for thee, that thy faith fail not: and when thou art converted, strengthen thy brethren.

—Luke 22:31

After Satan released Peter, he went and preached an impromptu sermon where three thousand people were added to the church. God does not despise one who goes through this vexation.

I believe that to be "given up" and to "do that which is against nature" is spiritual, but it also involves a spiritual genetic predisposition that science has shown to exist in generational alcoholism and homosexuality. How

> The Lord will swiftly remove us from this captivity once our heart has proclaimed the fear and reverence of the Lord evidenced by our repentance and cleansing through sanctification.

are genetics changed? Through ministry including breaking the generational curses. We may fear genetics as something that is unchangeable, a messenger of doom, when it is just a record of what traits are to be left to future generations. These records are meant to be reversed back to good just as easily as they were contaminated with the virus of evil way back.

For I the Lord thy God am a jealous God, visiting the iniquity [through genetics] of the fathers upon the children unto the third and fourth generation of them that hate me; And shewing mercy unto thousands of them that love me, and keep my commandments.

—Exodus 20:5

The message here is that the generational iniquity is passed down to the generations, but the Lord is desirous to show mercy so that those that love Him may have a way of escape.

And likewise also the men, leaving [divorcing or swapping] the natural [contrary to instincts] use of the woman, burned in their lust one toward another; men with men working that which is unseemly [shameful use of genitals], and receiving in themselves that recompence [internal consequence, i.e., disease] of their error [straying] which was meet [necessity by divine decree].

—Romans 1:27

We are deceived into thinking we are getting away with our defiance, as we can't perceive the judgment of God in the manner we might expect. What happens is our mind that is created holy and blameless in the image of God is short-circuited to follow our lusts and runs on a nasty virus software created by the devil to which we are oblivious, as our conscience is now ineffective. We will then be doing things that we believe to be normal but are in fact reprehensible.

> If we take pleasure or are entertained by these sins carried out by others, we are guilty of the same sin: God is not amused.

And even as they did not like to retain God in their knowledge [wanted benefits without responsibility and accountability], God gave them over [excommunicated to demonic captivity] to a reprobate mind [not functioning as intended], to do those things which are not convenient [forbidden and shameful].

—ROMANS 1:28

Once the door is opened the enemy comes in with a flood of depravity.

So shall they fear the name of the LORD from the west, and his glory from the rising of the sun. When the enemy shall come in like a flood, the Spirit of the LORD shall lift up a standard [demanding a swift departure] against him.

—ISAIAH 59:19

The Lord will swiftly remove us from this captivity once our heart has proclaimed the fear and reverence of the Lord evidenced by our repentance and cleansing through sanctification.

Being filled with all unrighteousness [holiness displaced by sensual lusts], fornication [forbidden sexual activity] wickedness [bent on destroying happiness of others], covetousness [painfully pursuing another's advantages], maliciousness [cruelty out of spite]; full of envy, murder [elimination of opponent] , debate [strife, contention], deceit [to lure and trap], malignity [taking everything with an evil connotation]; whisperers [secret slander, smear] Backbiters [murders the reputation of the absent], haters of God [actions show exceptional depravity to things of God] , despiteful [insulting, arrogant and rude], proud [self-preeminent while others treated with contempt], boasters [a fraudulent empty pretender], inventors of evil things [vicious schemes] disobedient to parents [deliberately obstinate], Without understanding [foolishly abolishing God to their demise], covenantbreakers [rationalize right to breach vows and agreements], without natural affection [without instinctive family love], implacable [cannot be persuaded to enter into covenant], unmerciful [hard-hearted cruelty and spitefulness].

—ROMANS 1:29–31

Entertained by the sin of others

Some of you will go through this list and say, "I think I'm doing pretty well. I'm not involved in a secret life of such sin." Consider this: Do you ever watch shows where couples are participating in premarital sex or a movie where a fight between actors ends up in murder? Or have you read the news tabloids about the destructive antics of celebrities? Perhaps someone downloaded to you a private inside look into the sin of their husband or wife that you are swishing around in the recesses of your mind. We may not have actually done the sins listed in Romans one, *but* if we take pleasure or are entertained by these sins carried out by others, we are guilty of the same sin: God is not amused.

> Who knowing the judgment of God, that they which commit such things are worthy of death, not only do the same, but have pleasure in them that do them.
>
> —Romans 1:32

My son took the list from Romans 1 and placed it on a card he carries in his wallet as a reminder to filter out the entertainment that would defile his spirit.

Covenant breaker

What would a covenant breaker look like within the covenant of marriage? The husband and wife have mutually exclusive rights over each other's sexuality. The power of absolutely all sexual experiences is in control of one's husband or wife.

> Perhaps we could also use the term *captivity*, which would add the spiritual dimension to addictions. In this captivity one is forced into a lifestyle completely devoted to satisfy the cravings of darkness or a usurping spiritual entity.

> The wife hath not power of her own body, but the husband: and likewise also the husband hath not power [authority to activate] of his own body, but the wife.
>
> —1 Corinthians 7:4

Those outside of covenant are to have no sexual experiences. Those in covenant are not to have any private sexual experiences. That defiles the marriage bed. I'm aware of society's expression of sexuality, but society doesn't govern the Word of God; the Word of God governs society and that doesn't change. If society bends from the divine law, it is in error and invites payment according to its deeds. If you don't believe me, just wait and see; but I won't be around to say I told you so. The rules of sexual engagement are simple: all sexual encounters are to be linking one lawful husband and his only lawful wife together. The second option? Well there isn't one!

Any sexual encounter that is not in the open for both to see being consensual is fraud.

> Defraud ye not one the other, except it be with consent for a time, that ye may give yourselves to fasting and prayer; and come together again, that Satan tempt you not for your incontinency [lack of self-control].
>
> —1 Corinthians 7:5

Defrauding your spouse with any private sexual experience or withholding sex is a trapdoor that would allow the devil an opportunity. Marital oneness is two separate people with one intimacy, one heart, and of one flesh.

Fantasy and pornography cause strife in the marriage bed, as the desire to experience what is acted out on the screen becomes a requirement for fulfillment. One then demands and the other goes into shame and guilt. Refusing to do such acts is not defrauding the other. The one insisting on the new level of performance has probably broken the marital covenant, has given the power of their body over to the harlot of pornography or the amour of fantasy.

When a portion of the marital covenant is breached, the answer isn't divorce, it is reconciliation. This is modeled after our relationship with our Lord. When we breach covenant with God, does He divorce us? If you think so you don't know Him. Jesus compares the life of the matrimonial church with the relationship He has with the ecclesiastical church.

The term *addiction* doesn't appear in the Scriptures, but the concept is there. In Romans 1 Paul uses the phrases "gave them up" or "gave them over"; and in other writings Paul uses the term *delivered*. More accurately I should say the Greek word in all these references is *paradidōmi*, which the translators interpret as "gave them up/over" or "delivered." One isn't abandoned to an empty space but one is turned over to the control of another or, as already defined, excommunicated to demonic captivity. Perhaps we could also use the term *captivity*, which would add the spiritual dimension to addictions. In this captivity one is forced into a lifestyle completely devoted to satisfy the cravings of darkness or a usurping spiritual entity.

> You are captive to anything you cannot lay down by an act of your will.

Your poor head may be screaming at you to throw away this book about now; but before you do, consider the witness of Jesus and Paul to see if what I am saying can be verified. In his counsel to the church of Corinth regarding a fellow believer that was involved in fornication and incest, he said the following:

> Deliver such an one unto Satan for the destruction of the flesh, that the spirit may be saved in the day of the Lord Jesus.
>
> —1 Corinthians 5:5

This fellow was delivered to the control of Satan who would give him a good scrubbing down so that he would hopefully come to repentance so that he wouldn't lose his soul. In 2 Corinthians 2:5–11 this fellow showed considerable remorse, repented, and was rejoined to the church—so mission was accomplished.

On another occasion Paul spoke to Timothy regarding two ungodly folks in the church that were spreading false doctrine, and they also were delivered to Satan in order that they may learn not to blaspheme.

> Of whom is Hymenaeus and Alexander; whom I have delivered unto Satan, that they may learn not to blaspheme.
>
> —1 TIMOTHY 1:20

Jesus taught that a man who wouldn't forgive a brother would also be delivered to the tormentors.

> And his lord was wroth, and delivered him to the tormentors [torturers], till he should pay all that was due unto him. So likewise shall my heavenly Father do also unto you, if ye from your hearts forgive not every one his brother their trespasses.
>
> —MATTHEW 18:34

Accordingly, if we have a repetitive or addictive behavior, no amount of chemical alteration or psychological therapy will heal the defect. It will manage it until the patient mismanages his treatment. You cannot deliver one from a spiritual captivity unless you follow the prescription of the divine healer Jesus who is available to us to destroy the works of the devil and set the captive free.

You are captive to anything you cannot lay down by an act of your will. It might be TV, video games, gambling, pornography, work, education, prescription drugs, illegal drugs, alcohol, soap operas, romance novels, entertainment, intellectual pursuits, foul language, gossip, sweets, coffee, or ungodly soulties; in fact, you can be captive to just about anything.

> The eyes of the mind will be on constant duty to scan every horizon to locate the next appetizer that will fuel the sensual system as we strive for the entrée of ultimate desire.

Rather than condemn a person for drinking in excess or participating in any other form of addictive behavior, seek out why they need to have the half dozen drinks in a sitting. What is the cause of their misery; what are they trying to escape from?

Peter says that whatever sin we bow down to or participate with that spirit then has the right to take us captive.

> While they promise them liberty [to do as one pleases], they themselves are the servants [serving another in disregard to one's own best interest] of corruption [misery or moral decay]: for of whom a man is overcome [weakened due to a spiritual defect], of the same is he brought in bondage [taken captive or involuntary servitude].
>
> —2 PETER 2:19

The devil promises us liberty to do whatever we please, but he doesn't tell us what the next chapter of his charade will hold for us. Paul contradicts the devil's message that we can sin because after all we are under grace. Paul says when you sin you sell yourself into involuntary servitude to a very evil master that pays with the death sentence. Through sin we submit to darkness until the light is turned on, thus renouncing the darkness. It works that way every time.

> What then? shall we sin, because we are not under the law, but under grace? God forbid. Know ye not, that to whom ye yield yourselves servants [serving another in disregard to one's own best interest] to obey, his servants ye are to whom ye obey; whether of sin unto death, or of obedience unto righteousness?
>
> —Romans 6:15–16

What a pity to live a life in submission to and to fulfill the appetite or urges of an unclean spirit. The demands of an addictive spirit are so unreasonable that one will give everything to satisfy it in total disregard for their own interests, family, and even eternity.

Two millennia ago Peter lays out the advance of addictive behavior that would become the great plague of the world and, disappointedly, the church as well. He speaks of the eyes being full of adultery. The usage of the Greek word here for *eyes* is not eyesight but the "eyes of the mind." The eyes of the mind will be on constant duty to scan every horizon to locate the next appetizer that will fuel the sensual system as we strive for the entrée of ultimate desire. The eye of the mind is very ingenious at finding an immediate solution to have what one may think is an innocent and discreet little fix. That little fix could be derived from secretly stalking someone for a moment or two just to get a better look at their tent. The eyes are designed to be a filter for what enters our spirit but when vexed it is no longer a "filter" but a "filther." The "h" identifies where the author of the vexation comes from—hell.

For instance, this driven tendency cannot be cured by trying to train your eyes not to look lustfully at a voluptuous trap. The reason is the eyes are the instrument of the desire but not the handler. The handler is the evil spirit that was given entrance and has overtaken the controls of the senses and associated faculties.

Peter teaches that this vexation of unseemly addictive behavior curses our children, which, unless stopped, dooms them to the wrath of the penalty of sin. This is referring to generational iniquity.

> Having eyes [of the mind, instrument of evil desire] full [locked on] of adultery [unclean, eyes always on the watch for an adulteress] and that cannot cease from sin [cannot be quieted, unable to stop]; beguiling [catch by bait, entice] unstable souls [the personality or character that expresses the spirit]: an heart [spirit] they have exercised with covetous practices [greedy appetite for sensual pleasures or trip outs]; cursed children [generational iniquity]:

> Which have forsaken the right way, and are gone astray, following the way
> of Balaam the son of Bosor, who loved the wages of unrighteousness.
>
> —2 PETER 2:14–15

Verse 18 says the door to addictions is through an enticement of the flesh to fulfill the lust of your dreams. The flesh is always the weakest and most base part of our being, so hence the focus on the flesh. Quickly then the eyes of the mind make preparations for the big sin event opening up the spirit to say, "Oh, why not?" The bait is eaten, the trap snaps, and the addictive unseemly behavior becomes part of the soul or character and emotions of the person. Now the original enticement will no longer work as bait, so a nastier, bigger, bolder, dirtier trap is laid before the now unstable soul.

> For when they speak great swelling words of vanity, they allure [entice,
> deceive, bait] through the lusts [expectancy of arousal] of the flesh,
> through much wantonness [whatever is disgraceful], those that were clean
> escaped from them who live in error.
>
> —2 PETER 2:18

Did you catch what type of person was enticed to participate in these disgraceful lusts? The person referred to is one that was "clean escaped," a convert to Christianity but now has chosen to live in error.

What about all the other sins; do they have the same captivating affect as the unseemly and addictive sins? Jesus says that whatever sin you participate with you serve that sin as you are given over to it. All sin takes into captivity, or, if you will, all sin is addictive because you serve it until you fall out of agreement with it.

> Jesus answered them, Verily, verily, I say unto you, Whosoever com-
> mitteth sin is the servant [serving another in disregard to one's own best
> interest] of sin.
>
> —JOHN 8:34

Some people taken hostage have been known to fall in love with their captors. How bizarre is that? Members of the Symbionese Liberation Army (SLA) took hostage, Patty Hearst, granddaughter of Randolph Hearst, the publisher. Within months of her capture, she was seen robbing a bank with the SLA and then on video she renounced her parents, fiancé, friends, and heritage. Yes, perhaps brainwashed, she had a relationship with one of her captors and eluded police for almost two years. Initially sentenced to twenty years in prison, it was later reduced to about seven years; then she received a presidential pardon twenty years later.

The spirits of bondage will take a hostage, brainwash him, and convert him to commit acts that were totally incomprehensible to him just a short time previous. She becomes one with her new captors and gives up her heritage to satisfy their ideals.

Just as Patty eventually renounced her involvement with her captors, we, too, can and will receive a full pardon from the King of kings.

> If the Son therefore shall make you free, ye shall be free indeed.
> —John 8:36

Ministry to free the captives of addiction must deal with all that has become unclean: the body, soul, mind, and spirit. We'll need to recognize what opened the door to such lust so it can be closed and the curse broken. We don't go back and relive the pain of such event, just recognize that something happened at such and such. Going to great detail about a past hurtful event will only give the devil further opportunity to injure us again and again. He loves the replay because replay stirs up even more evil than the first occurrence; as now you have self-pity, condemnation, judgment, bitterness, resentment, revenge, hatred, and much more added after the door was opened to injury. Some call Jesus into the painful event, but that is not scriptural. Where is Jesus now? He is in heaven seated at the right hand of God. When Stephen was stoned by the mob, he looked up and saw Jesus standing for him. Jesus objects to your injury, and He stands up for you.

> If we decide to engage anyway in the wicked behavior, the still small voice of conscience is hushed and the devil deceives the individual into justifying their dark path as being OK with God as they are now at peace, howbeit a false peace.

Have you ever pondered why no one ever contracts sexually transmitted diseases within the confines of a godly marriage?

Resulting from David's adulterous affair with Bathsheba, he contracted a loathsome venereal disease that kept him doubled over in a burning pain resembling the piercing of arrows. In addition to the disease, David was ostracized by his friends; and his detractors gossiped about him—quite a price to pay for an eight-second ride. He was promised liberty but dealt captivity to the devil's vexation. David makes the direct connection between his adultery and his disease:

> For thine arrows stick fast in me, and thy hand presseth me sore. There is no soundness in my flesh because of thine anger; neither is there any rest in my bones because of my sin. For mine iniquities are gone over mine head: as an heavy burden they are too heavy for me. My wounds stink and are corrupt because of my foolishness. I am troubled; I am bowed down greatly; I go mourning all the day long. For my loins are filled with a loathsome disease: and there is no soundness in my flesh. I am feeble and sore broken: I have roared by reason of the disquietness of my heart.
> —Psalm 38:2–8

David's plight was discerned by a prophet to be the result of adultery. The prophet approached David and led him to take responsibility and repent for his sin. This is David's testimony regarding his healing and deliverance from his captivity:

> I waited patiently for the Lord; and he inclined unto me, and heard my cry. He brought me up also out of an horrible pit, out of the miry clay, and set my feet upon a rock, and established my goings. And he hath put a new song in my mouth, even praise unto our God: many shall see it, and fear, and shall trust in the Lord. Blessed is that man that maketh the Lord his trust, and respecteth not the proud, nor such as turn aside to lies.
>
> —Psalm 40:1–4

David's addiction was cured and he was released as a free man.

When one is given over to captivity, the work of the conscience is put on hold, as we are past feeling. When a person first experiments with a new exciting sin, his conscience, the still small voice, warns him to turn and run. If we decide to engage anyway in the wicked behavior, the still small voice of conscience is hushed and the devil deceives the individual into justifying their dark path as being OK with God as they are now at peace.

> Having the understanding darkened, being alienated from the life of God through the ignorance that is in them, because of the blindness of their heart: Who being past feeling have given themselves over unto lasciviousness [knows no restraint in pursuing the object of his lust], to work all uncleanness with greediness [consequences of sin don't matter when serving the master of sin].
>
> —Ephesians 4:18

He can purify us so that we become as a virgin without any condemnation.

> Come now, and let us reason together, saith the Lord: though your sins be as scarlet, they shall be as white as snow; though they be red like crimson, they shall be as wool.
>
> —Isaiah 1:18

Consider this prayer of David's in Psalm 51 and personalize it. This prayer of David concerned his adultery and murder.

> *Have mercy upon me, O God, according to thy lovingkindness: according to the multitude of thy tender mercies blot out my transgressions. Wash me thoroughly from mine iniquity, and cleanse me from my sin. For I acknowledge my transgressions: and my sin is ever before me. Against thee, thee only, have I sinned, and done [this evil] in thy sight: that thou mightest be justified when thou speakest, and be clear when thou judgest. Behold, I was shapen in iniquity; and in sin did my mother conceive me. Behold, thou desirest truth in the inward parts: and in the hidden part thou shalt make me to know wisdom. Purge me with hyssop, and I shall be clean: wash me, and I shall be whiter than snow. Make me to hear joy and gladness; that the bones which thou hast broken may rejoice. Hide thy face from my sins, and blot out all mine iniquities. Create in me a clean heart, O God; and renew a right spirit within me. Cast me not*

away from thy presence; and take not thy holy spirit from me. Restore unto me the joy of thy salvation; and uphold me with thy free spirit. Then will I teach transgressors thy ways; and sinners shall be converted unto thee. Deliver me bloodguiltiness [all that is unseemly], O God, thou God of my salvation: and my tongue shall sing aloud of thy righteousness. O Lord, open thou my lips; and my mouth shall shew forth thy praise. For thou desirest not sacrifice; else would I give it. ... The sacrifices of God are a broken spirit: a broken and a contrite heart, O God, thou wilt not despise. Do good in thy good pleasure unto [_____]: [re]build [_____]. Then shalt thou be pleased with the sacrifices of righteousness.

[I pray in the name of Jesus my Lord, Amen.]

Unseemliness workout

Step 1: Prayerfully review the following list and mark each sin you or your generations have participated with. It is important that you are not rushed and that you are in a private place as you go through this.

- ❑ **Abortion**
- ❑ **Adultery**
- ❑ **Alcoholism**
- ❑ **Anger**
- ❑ **Anorexia**
- ❑ **Arrogance**
- ❑ **Backbiters:** murders the reputation of the absent
- ❑ **Bastard Children**
- ❑ **Bestiality**
- ❑ **Blasphemy**
- ❑ **Boasters:** a fraudulent empty pretender
- ❑ **Bulimia**
- ❑ **Conceived in drunkenness/lust**
- ❑ **Covenant breaking:** rationalize right to breach vows and agreements
- ❑ **Covetousness:** painfully pursuing another's advantages
- ❑ **Cruelty**
- ❑ **Debate:** strife, contention
- ❑ **Deceit:** to lure and trap
- ❑ **Despitefulness:** insulting, arrogant and rude
- ❑ **Destruction**
- ❑ **Dishonor**
- ❑ **Disobedience to parents:** deliberately obstinate
- ❑ **Distortion, lying, deception**
- ❑ **Drug addictions**
- ❑ **Drunkenness**
- ❑ **Envy**
- ❑ **Fantasy**
- ❑ **Foolishness:** without understanding, foolishly abolishing God to their demise

- ❏ **Fornication**
- ❏ **Gluttony**
- ❏ **Haters of God:** actions show exceptional depravity to things of God
- ❏ **Homosexuality**
- ❏ **Hostility**
- ❏ **Idolatry**
- ❏ **Immodesty**
- ❏ **Immorality**
- ❏ **Implacable:** cannot be persuaded to enter into covenant, (i.e. marriage)
- ❏ **Incest**
- ❏ **Inordinate affection:** the ungodly bonding of members of the same sex
- ❏ **Inventors of evil things:** vicious schemes
- ❏ **Irresponsibility**
- ❏ **Lesbianism**
- ❏ **Licentiousness:** promiscuous and unprincipled in sexual matters
- ❏ **Loss of virginity**
- ❏ **Lust:** craving for evil
- ❏ **Maliciousness:** cruelty out of spite
- ❏ **Malignity:** taking everything with an evil connotation
- ❏ **Masturbation**
- ❏ **Materialism**
- ❏ **Murder:** elimination of opponent
- ❏ **Occultic worship**
- ❏ **Pornography**
- ❏ **Pride:** self pre-eminent while others treated with contempt
- ❏ **Profanity:** blasphemous or obscene language
- ❏ **Rage**
- ❏ **Rebellion**
- ❏ **Reprobate mind:** not functioning as God intended
- ❏ **Risk-taking:** Gambling, Financial Risk Taking, extreme sporting
- ❏ **Self-centeredness**
- ❏ **Self-injury**
- ❏ **Sexually deviant behavior**
- ❏ **Smoking**
- ❏ **Sodomy**
- ❏ **Spiritual Blindness**
- ❏ **Uncleanness:** recklessly immoral and impure, lustful wasteful living
- ❏ **Ungodliness**
- ❏ **Unmerciful:** hard hearted cruelty and spitefulness
- ❏ **Unreliability**
- ❏ **Unthankfulness**
- ❏ **Verbal and physical threatening**
- ❏ **Voyeurism:** deriving sexual pleasure from observing unsuspecting individuals
- ❏ **Whisperers:** secret slander, smear
- ❏ **Whoredoms**

❑ **Wickedness**
❑ **Without natural affection:** without instinctive family love

This is a partial list. Ask the Lord to show you what else He wants you to be released from.

Step 2: Ask and wait.

> *Lord, is there any other sin that I have been unable to lay down on my own that You want me to deal with?* _____

Step 3: Since many of these sins are against our bodies, which contain the "temple of the Holy Spirit," you'll want to repent for defiling your temple by participation with these sins.

Step 4: Go back through the list and pray this prayer inserting the sin in the blank space. You may insert several sins in the blank space at a time if you desire.

Prayer of Repentance
(Preferably out loud)

> *Father God, I recognize and take responsibility for myself and my ancestors for the sin(s) _____. I agree with Your verdict on my rebellion. I repent, I renounce, and I ask forgiveness for my participation with these sins, and I ask that their curse be broken in the name of Jesus Christ of Nazareth.*

Step 5: Bind the strongmen. This is best done by an experienced and trusted ministering friend the first time around.

Prayer to Bind the Strongmen of Addictions and Unseemliness

> *In the name of Jesus Christ of Nazareth and by the power of the Holy Spirit, I take authority over the strongmen of addictions, whoredoms and unseemliness. I break your power and bind you and put you on notice that I am destroying your armor in which you trust. I will be coming back to remove you from your palace.*

Step 6: Purging the evil. Review the above list again now inserting the sin you have repented of in the blank.

Command of Deliverance
(Must be out loud with eyes open,
realizing you are speaking directly to a spirit)

> *In the name of Jesus Christ of Nazareth and by the power of the Holy Spirit, I take authority over the spirit(s) of _____. I break your power, I cast you out, and I command you to return no more.*

Step 7: Purge the strongman now that you have destroyed his stronghold.

Command of Deliverance
(Must be out loud with eyes open,
realizing you are speaking directly to a spirit)

In the name of Jesus Christ of Nazareth and by the power of the Holy Spirit, I take authority over the strongmen of addictions, whoredoms, and unseemliness. I break your power, I cast you out, and I command you to return no more.

Step 8: Pray that God will cause you to increase and abound in His love and that you would be an overcomer in the sins just repented of. Ask for a scripture that you will use to resist the devil when he tries to open the trapdoor again to regain entrance to your heart.

Pray Daniel's Prayer

O Lord, to me belongs confusion of face, to [_____], and to our fathers, because we have sinned against thee. To the Lord our God belong mercies and forgivenesses, though we have rebelled against him; neither have we obeyed the voice of the LORD our God, to walk in his laws, which he set before us by his servants the prophets. Yea, [_____]have transgressed thy law, even by departing, that [_____] might not obey thy voice; therefore the curse is poured upon us, and the oath that is written in the law of Moses the servant of God, because we have sinned against him. And he hath confirmed his words, which he spake against us, and against our judges that judged us, by bringing upon us a great evil.... As it is written in the law of Moses, all this evil is come upon us: yet made we not our prayer before the LORD our God, that we might turn from our iniquities, and understand thy truth. Therefore hath the LORD watched upon the evil, and brought it upon us: for the LORD our God is righteous in all his works which he doeth: for we obeyed not his voice. And now, O LORD our God, that hast brought thy people forth out of the land of Egypt with a mighty hand, and hast gotten thee renown, as at this day; we have sinned, we have done wickedly. O LORD, according to all thy righteousness, I beseech thee, let thine anger and thy fury be turned away from thy [_____]: because for our sins, and for the iniquities of our fathers, [_____] are become a reproach to all that are about us. Now therefore, O our God, hear the prayer of thy servant, and his [her] supplications, and cause thy face to shine upon thy sanctuary that is desolate, for the LORD's sake. O my God, incline thine ear, and hear; open thine eyes, and behold our desolations, and [_____] which is called by thy name: for we do not present our supplications before thee for our righteousnesses, but for thy great mercies. O LORD, hear; O LORD, forgive; O LORD, hearken and do; defer not, for thine own sake, O my God: for [_____] are called by thy name. [According to the peace given to us by Jesus through His blood shed on the cross for us we pray. Amen]

—DANIEL 9:8–19, AUTHOR'S ADAPTATION

AGAPE SEEKETH NOT HER OWN

Agape streams from the Father, through Jesus, to the husband, the wife, and then to the children. But what flows upstream back to the source?

He that speaketh of himself seeketh his own glory: but he that seeketh his glory that sent him, the same is true, and no unrighteousness is in him.

—JOHN 7:18

> The most interesting thing is Jesus was a servant to men, women, and children everywhere, but only wanted His work of service to be known by the Father.

Agape, of course, flows back upstream, as we are to agape God through everything we are. However, cloaking agape as it flows back upstream is the glory due The Father resulting from the ministry of His holiness, righteousness, and love.

What are we? Are we creators of the good news of the gospel? No. We are messengers, reporters, and recipients for the grace and mercy of the Lord; and accordingly, no such servant can claim ownership or take credit for the words, the works, and decrees of his king. As messengers, all we can do is pass along all glory and gratefulness to the originator of the message.

A man's wife and children are his glory; however, the man does not hold onto this glory but deflects it to the Father. This glory is the fruit of agape rather than adulation for his position. If the glory would be from the wife and children to the man due to adulation or basically idolatry, it would be the works of eros, the self-serving love.

For a man indeed ought not to cover his head, forasmuch as he is the image [likeness of His divine nature] and glory [dignity, grace] of God: but the woman is the glory of the man.

—1 CORINTHIANS 11:7

Whatever God creates, Satan is following close behind with lies and deception to pervert His love and to discourage the saints so the empowering of agape is hushed in the family. Once agape is breached, the glory of the family is tarnished.

Children's children [grandchildren] are the crown of old men; and the glory of children are their fathers.

—PROVERBS 17:6

Jesus Christ was worthy of glory and honor because of His sacrificial servant heart; but even though He was worthy, He still deflected all glory to His Father. He sought not to do the will of man, to please man, but He chose to please the Father. So it was fitting that He only received approval from whom He was trying to please. The most interesting thing is Jesus was a servant to men, women, and children everywhere, but only wanted His work of service to be known by the Father.

> And I seek not mine own glory [deflects all to the Father]: there is one that seeketh and judgeth [approves, esteems]...Jesus answered, If I honour myself, my honour is nothing: it is my Father that honoureth me; of whom ye say, that he is your God.
>
> —JOHN 8:50, 54

Jesus did not seek honor from men nor did he accept honor from men. He knew and practiced something we find difficult to do. "I receive not honour from men" (John 5:41).

Had Jesus received glory from man he would have missed out on this:

> For he received from God the Father honour and glory, when there came such a voice to him from the excellent glory, This is my beloved Son, in whom I am well pleased.
>
> —2 PETER 1:17

As Jesus lived, and He knew how to really live, we are to model Him. Paul also sought no profit or honor in return for his ministry.

> Even as I please all men in all things, not seeking [striving, demanding] mine own profit [benefit, promotion], but the profit of many, that they may be saved.
>
> —1 CORINTHIANS 10:33

He made sure he was free from the trappings of being a hireling so he could save the lost. He paid his own way so man couldn't be his master and so hinder the power of freedom and authority in his ministry. Money is one way of receiving honor from men if it is expected out of the wrong heart. Paul erred on the side of caution, working as a tent maker so he would be able to minister without charging the people.

> What is my reward then? Verily that, when I preach the gospel, I may make the gospel of Christ without charge [without expense], that I abuse not my power [authority, strength] in the gospel.
>
> —1 CORINTHIANS 9:18

When Paul wrote to the Philippian church regarding Timothy, he noted how rare it was indeed to have a servant of the gospel that did not seek his own profit, honor, attention, and well-being. Timothy was a man that was focused on what was Jesus Christ's. The work of the ministry of reconciliation belongs to Jesus not to any man; no man may usurp the glory of God and later expect God to reward him.

> But I trust in the Lord Jesus to send Timotheus shortly unto you....For I have no man likeminded, who will naturally care for your state. For all seek their own, not the things which are Jesus Christ's.
>
> —PHILIPPIANS 2:19–21

God in His grace has made the work of ministry a mystery to the religious elite, the professionals. As long as they are seeking their own, they will really be clueless of the things of God that they profess to be so knowledgeable in. He will erase all the good works of man if they seek their own glory.

> But God hath chosen the foolish things of the world to confound the wise; and God hath chosen the weak things of the world to confound the things which are mighty; And base things of the world, and things which are despised, hath God chosen, yea, and things which are not, to bring to nought [erase, destroy] things that are: That no flesh should glory in his presence.
> —1 Corinthians 1:27–29

In writing this section I had no intention at all of going in the direction that it has. These scriptures have convicted me, realizing that most if not all of my works of ministry were self-serving in many respects. I sought to do the work of God, but I was the first to see what accolades I would get from man. And it was especially meaningful if in addition to their accolade was some sort of reward. Oh, but for the grace of God! The question may be: if we receive the glory, are we really doing the work in the name of Jesus or is it in our own name but just adding Jesus' name in the post script?

> Not every one that saith unto me, Lord, Lord, shall enter into the kingdom of heaven; but he that doeth the will of my Father which is in heaven. Many will say to me in that day, Lord, Lord, have we not prophesied in thy name? and in thy name have cast out devils? and in thy name done many wonderful works? And then will I profess unto them, I never knew you: depart from me, ye that work iniquity.
> —Matthew 7:21–23

If we receive the honor and glory, we are in big trouble! God recognizes us when we agape Him and that agape is accompanied with the glory and honor due His name. I believe scripture teaches that if any man receives the honor for the work of ministry he accomplishes, then he better enjoy that honor because that is all he'll ever get.

> Take heed that ye do not your alms before men, to be seen of them: otherwise ye have no reward of your Father which is in heaven.
> —Matthew 6:1

True evidence that we are not "seeking our own" is where people see and receive our ministry given to them and respond by giving glory to God and not to the vessel.

> Let your light so shine before men, that they may see your good works, and glorify your Father which is in heaven.
> —Matthew 5:16

So when Jesus taught that whoever wanted to accomplish great things for the Lord must do so by being a lowly servant, He knew the judgment of God and didn't want His ministers to disqualify themselves.

When my children were young there were many battles as to who would be first, so I thought I'd try a little experiment and train them to say, "Me last, me last!" I recall all that happened is they were silenced for a moment or two. Yet I can hardly blame them, as I struggle with being last in anything unless there is really no cost to being so nice. What I find interesting is how many Christian fellowships have the word *First* in their name but how few if any have the words *Second* or *Third* or *Last*. Since I am in so much trouble now, why stop? I think that by saying they are first, they really desire to be first at being last, as any man that desires to be first shall be last of all.

> Agape is doing what is best for the person loved, it is giving and not holding; it is ministering with glory, honor, and position all deflected to our Father.

> And he sat down, and called the twelve, and saith unto them, If any man desire to be first, the same shall be last of all, and servant of all.... But so shall it not be among you: but whosoever will be great among you, shall be your minister: And whosoever of you will be the chiefest, shall be servant of all. For even the Son of man came not to be ministered unto, but to minister, and to give his life a ransom for many.
>
> —MARK 9:35, 10:43–45

Agape is doing what is best for the person loved, it is giving and not holding; it is ministering with glory, honor, and position all deflected to our Father.

Jesus made himself of no reputation; that is really hard to do when you think about it. I've fought fiercely to protect my reputation against gossip, lies, and such like. Get this, I've also fought to protect my reputation against the truth; even if that means I lie and accuse another to deflect the shame.

I have a lot of reverence for Jesus who made Himself of no reputation as He didn't seek His own comfort or His own rights. With that spirit of humility and agape, Jesus was able to defeat the devil on every test.

> Fulfill ye my joy, that ye be likeminded, having the same love [*agape*], being of one accord, of one mind. Let nothing be done through strife [pride, rivalry] or vainglory [glories when another is provoked]; but in lowliness of mind [humble opinion of oneself] let each esteem [place first] other better [on top] than themselves. Look not every man on his own things, but every man also on the things of others. Let this mind be in you, which was also in Christ Jesus: Who, being in the form of God, thought it not robbery to be equal with God: But made himself of no reputation, and took upon him the form of a servant, and was made in

the likeness of men: And being found in fashion as a man, he humbled himself, and became obedient unto death, even the death of the cross.

—PHILIPPIANS 2:1–8

Jesus did not seek the reputation of being the High Priest; it was given to Him by his Father who recognized His faithfulness in overcoming the worldly lusts and wanted to honor Him.

> He is loving us into eternity. That is why we can't despise the chastening of the Lord.

Jesus was God and perfect in all His ways, but He had to learn. He had to learn to be obedient, and the only way Father God could teach Jesus that was by allowing His most beloved Son to suffer many things.

> So also Christ glorified not himself to be made an high priest; but he that said unto him, Thou art my Son, to day have I begotten thee.... Though he were a Son, yet learned he obedience by the things which he suffered.
> —HEBREWS 5:5, 8

I've cried out to God many times to maintain a very high standard of comfort; and now I'm trying to learn that I am not to despise the chastening of the Lord because that shows He loves me as a son. This love is agape, and you need to know and understand what is said here. If the Word said He chastens those whom He "phileo" loves, be very afraid, as that is a fickle love that will grow very weary of your stuff. But, no, this love

> Equals are equals, but submission is still a struggle as we have to defer our rights to the prosperity of another.

that He chastens us through is agape, which is the only love that is eternal—He is loving us into eternity. That is why we can't despise the chastening of the Lord. Agape can only do what is best for the person permanently loved. You see, God is at work to train us not for this temporary visit to earth but for our role and purpose for eternity. After this earthly passage He will have no need to further chasten, mold, and train us, as we will then be completely restored to His image, therefore without character flaws.

> Ye have not yet resisted unto blood, striving against sin. And ye have forgotten the exhortation which speaketh unto you as unto children, My son, despise not thou the chastening [the cultivation of the soul to correct mistakes and to curb passions] of the Lord, nor faint [become feeble through exhaustion] when thou art rebuked [convicted, to expose to light] of him: For whom the Lord loveth [*agapao*] he chasteneth [to mold by the afflictions of evils and calamities], and scourgeth [punishment that results in physical discomfort] every son whom he receiveth [redeems as His own].
> —HEBREWS 12:4–6

Through the obedience that Jesus learned, He was able to resist temptation even to the point of resisting in anguish with blood weeping out of His pores; that is intense battle and He had the blood sweat to prove His courage and obedience. He asked, "God, please save these earth dwellers by some other way; there must be another way." Nevertheless, Jesus said, "I only want to do your will." He submitted to the Father completely. Now if the story ended right there, we could complain, "Lord, that wasn't fair for Jesus to have to die." But the next chapter shows that through dying to self, He submitted to the will of the Father and all of history is measured from His sacrifice and deliverance from the power of death.

> The person you are submitting through has an even greater responsibility before God as he is closely monitored by the Father as to how he receives the submission of another.

> And he went a little further, and fell on his face, and prayed, saying, O my Father, if it be possible, let this cup pass from me: nevertheless not as I will, but as thou wilt.
>
> —MATTHEW 26:39

Was it difficult for Jesus to submit? Yes, it was; but He submitted despite His reservations and personal discomfort. It was OK for Him to ask the Father if there was another way; and God understood, as it wasn't in defiance but He was just struggling with the difficulty of the assignment. Even in His questioning He still had every intention of submitting to His Father no matter what the cost. He was not seeking His own will, He was always seeking the Father's will. He just wondered if there was another way for the Father to accomplish that will rather than by way of the Cross. That is divine teamwork modeled for man.

Ephesians 5 instructs us that submission works differently depending on the relationship of the other person to us. As we are to agape our neighbor as ourselves, we are to submit to each other as we are equals before God. Equals are equals but submission is still a struggle, as we have to defer our rights to the prosperity of another:

> Let no man seek his own, but every man another's wealth.
>
> —1 CORINTHIANS 10:24

Here is the tough part; submission to God is usually through another person then upward to Jesus Christ and then the Father. In the family the submission flows up the love stream. A wife submits because she fears God and reverences her husband. This way pride can have no part as submission can only happen with humility; and if submission is revolting then the good news is, as we'll see in 1 Peter 5, one knows that pride is standing in the way of the agape experience. Why do I say good news? Because pride was just exposed so it can be dealt the death blow.

> Submitting [a voluntary attitude of giving in, cooperating and assuming responsibility] yourselves one to another in the fear [reverence] of God. Wives, submit yourselves unto your own husbands, as unto the Lord. For the husband is the head of the wife, even as Christ is the head of the church: and he is the saviour of the body.... Nevertheless let every one of you in particular so love [*agapao*] his wife even as himself; and the wife see that she reverence her husband.
>
> —EPHESIANS 5:21–23, 33

Is it ever possible to voluntarily submit when pride is manifesting in us? The person you are submitting through has an even greater responsibility before God, as the Father closely monitors him as to how he receives the submission of another. Does he receive it through pride or does he receive it in even greater humility than the person that submitted to him? How another receives the submission of another though is none of our business. God is the only judge of that. We can't submit to a person and at the same time be their judge. Our need to judge is rooted in pride, which of course is the antithesis of submission.

> Likewise, ye younger, submit [a voluntary attitude of giving in, cooperating and assuming responsibility] yourselves unto the elder. Yea, all of you be subject [submit] one to another, and be clothed with humility: for God resisteth the proud, and giveth grace to the humble. Humble yourselves therefore under the mighty hand of God, that he may exalt you in due time: Casting all your care upon him; for he careth for you.
>
> —1 PETER 5:5–7

Agape submits; pride resists. Pride is Satan's version of his perverted love. Another block to submission is our fear, so fear will have to be dealt the death-blow as well. Perfect agape casts out fear.

God giveth grace to the humble, because He knows how difficult submission can be if the one you are submitting to may not be acting very loving. He offers grace to those who submit—even to the froward. If you choose to submit in such a situation, you have the Lord's backing; if you don't submit, you are on your own. This is, of course, assuming you are not asked to do anything that is contrary to the Word and unclean to you.

How does Christ repay the sins of those who offend and injure me? He dies for them; He pays the price for their sin.

In your house of worship the Lord has appointed a shepherd to watch over your soul; and for your own profit you are to submit to your shepherd. Submission to your pastor doesn't include judging him, as he has to give account on his own to the Lord.

> Obey them that have the rule over you, and submit yourselves: for they
> watch for your souls, as they that must give account, that they may do it
> with joy, and not with grief: for that is unprofitable for you.
>
> —HEBREWS 13:17

God has placed our civil leaders in place as well, and we are to submit to
them. What about if you disagree with a government policy? Are we to unite
in civil disobedience? Well, Peter knew about this one as he lopped off the ear
of one of the local leaders in an act of defiance. Jesus didn't agree with what
Peter did, and He healed the ear. So later in life Peter learned that the godly
way to demonstrate is to do the will of God, which is to do well and in so
doing you'll silence the ignorant policies of the foolish.

> Submit yourselves to every ordinance of man for the Lord's sake: whether
> it be to the king, as supreme; Or unto governors, as unto them that are
> sent by him for the punishment of evildoers, and for the praise of them
> that do well. For so is the will of God, that with well doing ye may put
> to silence the ignorance of foolish men.
>
> —I PETER 2:13–15

If a person you submit to has authority over you and treats you bad, whose
problem is that? It is his, as he must give account to God sooner or later, and
that's his journey. Know what your journey is and don't get pulled off course by
someone else's pride. If you do retort in anger, strife, or by refusing to submit,
what is the root of your sin? It is pride as well. How foolish is it to fight pride with
pride? Yeah, pretty dumb. And you are now guilty of the same sin and perhaps
a few others and may now be in worse shape than the one you were bitter with.

> Submit yourselves therefore to God. Resist the devil, and he will flee
> from you.
>
> —JAMES 4:7

Everyone submits. We all submit to one kingdom or the other. If we choose
to submit to God, the devil runs out of fuel.

Now in addition to glory and honor, we have submission and reverence
flowing upwards in the love stream; and that is the will of God and that is the
glory due His name.

Glory seekers' workout

Step 1: Prayerfully review the following list and mark each sin you or your
generations have participated with. It is important that you are not rushed and
that you are in a private place as you go through this.

- ❑ **Abusing power**
- ❑ **Despising the chastening of the Lord**
- ❑ **Disobedient to authority**
- ❑ **Disobedient to the law**
- ❑ **Doing alms before men**

- ❑ **Exaggerating talents**
- ❑ **Gender dominance**
- ❑ **Identity consumed with reputation**
- ❑ **Irreverence to God**
- ❑ **Irreverent to husband**
- ❑ **Lies in self-promotion**
- ❑ **Need to prove superiority over another's achievement**
- ❑ **No fear of God**
- ❑ **Preoccupation with appearance**
- ❑ **Pride**
- ❑ **Ruthlessly competitive**
- ❑ **Seeking honor from men**
- ❑ **Seeking own profit**
- ❑ **Self-idolatry**
- ❑ **Self-martyrdom to gain attention**
- ❑ **Self-sabotage**
- ❑ **Striving for control**
- ❑ **Taking glory for work of God**
- ❑ **Unable to celebrate another's success**
- ❑ **Unable to submit: a voluntary attitude of giving in**
- ❑ **Ungodly order in home**
- ❑ **Ungodly order in the church**
- ❑ **Vain glory when another is provoked**

Step 2: Ask and wait.

> *Lord, is there any other sin that I have been unable to lay down on my own that You want me to deal with?* _____

Step 3: Go back through the list and pray this prayer inserting the sin in the blank space. You may insert several sins in the blank space at a time if you desire.

Prayer of Repentance
(Preferably out loud)

> *Father God, I recognize and take responsibility for myself and my ancestors for the sin(s) of _____. I agree with Your verdict on my rebellion. I repent, I renounce, and I ask forgiveness for my participation with these sins, and I ask that their curse be broken in the name of Jesus Christ of Nazareth.*

Step 4: Purging the evil. This is best done by an experienced and trusted ministering friend the first time around. Review the above list again now inserting the sin you have repented of in the blank.

Command of Deliverance
(Must be out loud with eyes open,
realizing you are speaking directly to a spirit)

> *In the name of Jesus Christ of Nazareth and by the power of the Holy Spirit,*
> *I take authority over the spirit(s) of _____. I break your power,*
> *I cast you out, and I command you to return no more.*

Step 5: Pray that God will cause you to increase and abound in His love and that you would be an overcomer in the sins just repented of. Ask for a scripture that you will use to resist the devil when he tries to open the trapdoor again to regain entrance to your heart.

AGAPE IS NOT EASILY PROVOKED

A believer taking a stable walk in agape is going to face the treachery of Satan from time to time, as he'll attempt to provoke us to rebel against God through discouragement, anger, or perhaps our lack of physical needs. Such testing usually happens at the peak of our life's work when we think we are doing just fine.

Moses, even though God spoke to him in the burning bush and upon a burning mountain, still fell for the provoking of his spirit to burn with anger by Satan.

God told Moses to speak to the rock and it would yield water to satisfy the thirst of the traveling nation of Israel. But Moses was vexed by the constant complaining of the people and misrepresented God to the people, as though God were mad at them. Moses took a swing at the rock with his rod while scolding the people. God was watching as always to see how He would be represented to the sheep that He loved:

> And Moses and Aaron gathered the congregation together before the rock, and he said unto them, Hear now, ye rebels; must we fetch you water out of this rock? And Moses lifted up his hand, and with his rod he smote the rock twice: and the water came out abundantly, and the congregation drank, and their beasts also. And the LORD spake unto Moses and Aaron, Because ye believed me not, to sanctify me in the eyes of the children of Israel, therefore ye shall not bring this congregation into the land which I have given them.
> —NUMBERS 20:10–12

The psalmist tells us that Moses was provoked to anger. He was provoked to be angry in his spirit, not in his mind. Thus the battle was one in the spiritual realm.

> They angered him also at the waters of strife, so that it went ill with Moses for their sakes: Because they provoked his spirit, so that he spake unadvisedly with his lips.
> —PSALM 106:32–33

To be placed in the love stream is to be placed in a position of trust and responsibility to be an ambassador for the kingdom of God to which there is no such thing as being off-duty. We are all stationed as an ambassador that heads a permanent mission assignment from God our Father. Ambassadors are entrusted with extensive power; power to love, build up, and heal, or power to curse and destroy when that power is abused. In the world system an ambassador has what is called diplomatic immunity to guard him against his own folly; but in the kingdom of God an ambassador is held to a higher level of responsibility than any unbeliever. In case you haven't connected with what I am saying, we are ambassadors of the mightiest of kingdoms sent to represent the only King of kings to an earthly kingdom bent on rebellion.

If we then rebel against the King of kings ourselves, as ambassadors we misrepresent His love, mercy, and grace; thus those that the Father is trying to reach through us are confused and bewildered. God has extended His grace to you now to complete the work of reconciliation in you, His saint, first so that once you are fully converted you'll go out as a new person that will turn your world "upside up" for Him.

> We are ambassadors of the mightiest of kingdoms, sent to represent the only King of kings to an earthly kingdom bent on rebellion.

Our purpose as ambassadors for Christ is to be ministers of reconciliation and ministers of restoration.

> If any man be in Christ, he is a new creature: old things are passed away; behold, all things are become new. And all things are of God, who hath reconciled us to himself by Jesus Christ, and hath given to us the ministry [ambassador who executes the commands of God] of reconciliation [restoration of sinners to their Father]; To wit, that God was in Christ, reconciling the world unto himself, not imputing their trespasses unto them; and hath committed unto us the word of reconciliation. Now then we are ambassadors for Christ, as though God did beseech you by us: we pray you in Christ's stead, be ye reconciled [returned to favor and status within the family] to God. For he hath made him to be sin for us, who knew no sin; that we might be made the righteousness of God in him.
> —2 CORINTHIANS 5:17–21

Another leader, perhaps equal to Moses in stature amongst the people of Israel, was King David. He was also provoked to sin; and this time Scripture names the originator of the incitement to rebellion: why it was the originator of rebellion himself, Satan.

> And Satan stood up against Israel, and provoked [*cuwth*; incited] David to number Israel.
> —1 CHRONICLES 21:1

So when we see what Satan was able to do to Moses and David, I believe we can have much more mercy towards our leaders who fall: mercy and not judgment.

After Moses and David, who was the next God-ordained leader to be placed on earth? It was Jesus; and Satan even attempted to provoke Him to rebel in order to disqualify the Son of God.

> And when the tempter [Satan] came to him, he said, If thou be the Son of God, command that these stones be made bread.
>
> —MATTHEW 4:3

Moses and David represented the law and the law's inability to conquer sin; Jesus represented the agape of the Father, and it was strong enough to conquer sin and the father of lies, Satan. That is the message and purpose of the gospel. Agape is an empowering of the essence of God that needs to destroy all the enemies that stand in the way of its total victory in our spirits.

> Pride is the developer, with strife as its architect that constructs the barrier of mountains between people who love.

Did Satan admit defeat when he could not tempt Jesus face-to-face? No he just waited for the opportunity to use the lips of the beloved disciple Peter. Again Jesus recognizes where the shot from the snipers crossbow came from, and He stops the flaming arrow and counterattacks.

> But he turned, and said unto Peter, Get thee behind me, Satan: thou art an offense unto me: for thou savourest not the things that be of God, but those that be of men.
>
> —MATTHEW 16:23

Satan can provoke directly, and we see he often provokes us through the people we love dearly. King Ahab was provoked through his wife, Queen Jezebel. The Hebrew word *cuwth* was translated as *provoked* in 1 Chronicles 21:1 and in the next passage in 1 Kings it is translated as "stirred up." Satan is the only instigator of rebellion and needs to be recognized as such, regardless of where the shot comes from.

> But there was none like unto Ahab, which did sell himself to work wickedness in the sight of the LORD, whom Jezebel his wife stirred up [*cuwth*, provoked].
>
> —1 KINGS 21:25

As parent ambassadors when we misrepresent the kingdom of God to our house, our children will suffer with anger.

> And, ye fathers, provoke not your children to wrath: but bring them up in the nurture and admonition of the Lord.
>
> —EPHESIANS 6:4

Satan uses the element of surprise; he'll strike when our guard is down and through the person from whom we least expect it—usually a family member or one of the household of faith. So if he can instigate a cheap shot through one person to another who in turn defends the shot by anger, he has created a shoot-out or better known as strife. So a door is crashed open in both people for him to return with seven devils fiercer than himself. The door crasher was rebellion, and once inside rebellion tags his team of offense, judgment, condemnation, anger, unforgiveness, resentment, retaliation, and hatred—oops that's eight. These uninvited party crashers mix it up in a mixture called strife. Strife is the architect that constructs the barrier of mountains between people who love.

Pray for discretion, as it is the split-second time delay machine that gives us the ability to recognize the shot as coming from beyond the face in front of us.

Patience is the grace that allows us to recognize that Satan has just seriously abused a close friend of mine in order to get a clear shot at me. So who are you going to be mad at? It is really dumb to be mad at the human shield Satan hides behind, isn't it?

> The discretion [recognition of a cunning craft] of a man deferreth [defers to patience] his anger; and it is his glory [honor, splendor] to pass over [look beyond] a transgression [act of rebellion].
>
> —PROVERBS 19:11

Do you have need to apologize to someone right now? Be of good courage and go do it. Get in the car or pick up the phone and get it done now, please! This book can wait.

For those of us that still have a need to provoke others in order to be fulfilled, here is our license to do so:

> And let us consider one another to provoke unto love [agape] and to good works.
>
> —HEBREWS 10:24

Provoked workout

Step 1: Prayerfully review the following list and mark each sin you or your generations have participated with. It is important that you are not rushed and that you are in a private place as you go through this.

- ❑ **Bazaar exaggeration of normal behavior**
- ❑ **Carnally minded**
- ❑ **Consistently inconsistent**
- ❑ **Covering inadequacies with caustic responses**
- ❑ **Deflecting exposure by reversal**
- ❑ **Impulsiveness**
- ❑ **Inability to empathize with effects of my behavior on others**
- ❑ **Indifferent locked heart**
- ❑ **Irritated easily**
- ❑ **Loose lips**
- ❑ **Misrepresenting the love of God to others**
- ❑ **Overreaction**
- ❑ **Provoked to anger by actions of others**
- ❑ **React to criticism with rage and resentment**

❑ **Rebellion against God**
❑ **Sharp-tongued**
❑ **Short-sighted**
❑ **Speaking without thinking**
❑ **Unable to express genuine compassion**
❑ **Unable to overlook a fault or offense**

Step 2: Ask and wait.

> *Lord, is there any other sin that I have been unable to lay down on my own that You want me to deal with?* _____

Step 3: Go back through the list and pray this prayer inserting the sin in the blank space. You may insert several sins in the blank space at a time if you desire.

Prayer of Repentance
(Preferably out loud)

> *Father God, I recognize and take responsibility for myself and my ancestors for the sin(s) of _____. I agree with Your verdict on my rebellion. I repent, I renounce, and I ask forgiveness for my participation with these sins, and I ask that their curse be broken in the name of Jesus Christ of Nazareth.*

Step 4: Purging the evil. This is best done by an experienced and trusted ministering friend the first time around. Review the above list again now inserting the sin you have repented of in the blank.

Command of Deliverance
(Must be out loud with eyes open,
realizing you are speaking directly to a spirit)

> *In the name of Jesus Christ of Nazareth and by the power of the Holy Spirit, I take authority over the spirit(s) of _____. I break your power, I cast you out, and I command you to return no more.*

Step 5: Pray that God will cause you to increase and abound in His love and that you would be an overcomer in the sins just repented of. Ask for a scripture that you will use to resist the devil when he tries to open the trapdoor again to regain entrance to your heart.

AGAPE THINKETH NO EVIL

It is evil to think that God will not do what He said He will do. When God speaks, worlds leap into existence; when He breaths, dust gets up and walks around; when He promises to make a way for you, even the waters will part and wave you through. God's words are not feeble musings; each word orders heaven and earth to adjust accordingly.

Agape cannot fear nor can it doubt as those are not available options; agape comes standard with the belief that if God said it or wrote it down the deal is finished, just wait to see.

It is evil to think that God will not do what He said He will do.

Do you know what sin the Israelites, who were delivered from the slavery in Egypt, committed that resulted in them being destroyed in the wilderness short of the Promised Land? Was it rebellion, or maybe because they didn't have enough faith, or was it the worship of the golden calf, or could it been because of their complaining about the dining hall food?

The Lord heard the prayer of the people and responded with a promise to deliver them from their captors and take them to the land of promise flowing with milk and honey—Canaan. The Word of God proclaimed that He came down to free them from Egypt and move them to the good land; I think that was quite clear.

> And the LORD said, I have surely seen the affliction of my people which are in Egypt, and have heard their cry by reason of their taskmasters; for I know their sorrows; And I am come down to deliver them out of the hand of the Egyptians, and to bring them up out of that land unto a good land...unto a land flowing with milk and honey.
> —EXODUS 3:7–8

After a lengthy battle involving many signs and wonders, the nation Israel is gathered up and takes a path towards the Red Sea. At the shores they feel they are trapped, for the Egyptians have broken their word and are now pursuing from behind with their army. Ahead of them is the Red Sea but it is vast and impassable and they have no boats.

The lesson Moses will now teach is about not falling to fear, but rather to embrace the promise of the Lord. The Lord came down to deliver them all the way from Egypt to Canaan; so is deliverance going to happen or will the Lord have miscalculated the enemy? Will the Lord have to throw in the flag and say this was tougher than He thought? If you think our Lord even hesitated, you don't know Him.

> And Moses said unto the people, Fear ye not, stand still, and see the salvation of the LORD, which he will shew to you to day: for the Egyptians whom ye have seen to day, ye shall see them again no more for ever. The LORD shall fight for you, and ye shall hold your peace.
> —EXODUS 14:13–14

Isn't that a fantastic practical lesson on overcoming obstacles? The concept we are to grasp is to hold our peace and allow our Lord to fight for us.

Armed with this powerful faith lesson, Israel crossed the wilderness and sent spies to access the land God promised to them. Two of the spies, Caleb and Joshua, come back just stoked regarding the bountiful land the Lord had set before them, and said, "What are we waiting for, this is fantastic!"

> And Caleb stilled the people before Moses, and said, Let us go up at once, and possess it; for we are well able to overcome it.
>
> —NUMBERS 13:30

However, there was doubt in the camp. The other ten spies were freaking out in fear. "Maaaaan, do you want to diiiiiiiie? These guys are huge and muscle-bound; and look at us pipsqueaks." These spies refused to acknowledge the promise and deliverance of the Lord because they were overcome by fear. They brought to Moses an evil report because it was now mingled with fear, doubt, and unbelief.

> Fear is Satan's faith, which cancels out faith in God and gushes forth in unbelief, discouragement, and despair.

> But the men that went up with him said, We be not able to go up against the people; for they are stronger than we. And they brought up an evil report [Why evil? it contradicted God's Word] of the land which they had searched unto the children of Israel, saying, The land, through which we have gone to search it, is a land that eateth up the inhabitants thereof; and all the people that we saw in it are men of a great stature. And there we saw the giants, the sons of Anak, which come of the giants: and we were in our own sight as grasshoppers, and so we were in their sight.
>
> —NUMBERS 13:31–33

Our giants may include cancer, heart disease, financial issues, relationships, kids, marriage, adultery, addictions, problems at church, or a tough decision to be made. Can you turn the tables and regard those as mere grasshoppers before a mighty awesome God?

> And all the children of Israel murmured [protested, complained bitterly] against Moses and against Aaron: and the whole congregation said unto them, Would God that we had died in the land of Egypt! or would God we had died in this wilderness! And wherefore hath the LORD brought us unto this land, to fall by the sword, that our wives and our children should be a prey? were it not better for us to return into Egypt? And they said one to another, Let us make a captain, and let us return into Egypt.
>
> —NUMBERS 14:2–4

Oh no! What just happened? In their fear they cursed themselves in a prayer by saying God should have just left us in Egypt to die rather than to bring us all this way to destroy us in the middle of nowhere. His Word said, "I have come to deliver you from the Egyptians and take you into this Promised Land." But by doubting Him, they opened up a trapdoor as big as the wilderness that would eventually swallow all but Caleb and Joshua.

> And the LORD said unto Moses, How long will this people provoke [spurn, despise] me? and how long will it be ere they believe [confirm trust by faith] me, for all the signs [proof, miracles] which I have shewed [accomplished] among them?
>
> —NUMBERS 14:11

What sin provoked the Lord? Their belief in the promise of God was overcome by fear. Fear is the sin that resulted in the nation of Israel perishing in the desert. Fear is Satan's faith, which cancels out faith in God and gushes forth in unbelief, discouragement, and despair. We may think, "Well, isn't God stronger than Satan and can overcome whatever is thrown at us?" The question isn't about strength, it is about infidelity. If we accept Satan's word over God's, that is like committing adultery against God. Satan projects fear and dread into the future, so he should be easy to recognize. God projects faith, hope, and peace into our future. Whose report will you act on?

Satan's grip of death was broken by Jesus Christ who conquered death when He rose again. So what gives Satan back his power of death? Fear does. Fear is like living on death row not knowing which sound you hear down the hall is the executioners coming to take you from your cell and escort you to your final torture chambers and death gallows.

What is the difference between a criminal serving time in prison and a Christian in bondage to fear? The criminal knows he is in prison and the Christian doesn't.

> I will put my trust in him.... Forasmuch then as the children are partakers of flesh and blood, he also himself likewise took part of the same; that through death he might destroy him that had the power of death, that is, the devil; And deliver [set free, purge] them who through fear [terror, dread] of death were all their lifetime subject [under obligation and unable to escape] to bondage [languishing in conditions of slavery].
>
> —HEBREWS 2:13–15

Contrast the slavery to the bondage of fear to what is available to all sheep that belong in the kingdom of God:

> For I know the thoughts that I think toward you, saith the LORD, thoughts of peace, and not of evil, to give you an expected end.
>
> —JEREMIAH 29:11

Worry and anxiety

The hardships that are the most difficult to endure are those that never happen. God has designed fear to protect us from harm and to preserve life. However Satan often takes what God designs for good and alters it for his purposes. Fear, as it is designed, is for very short periods of time, whereas an ungodly fear puts us in a continuous fight-or-flight mode. This causes the body to constantly release chemicals that were only designed to be released for very limited amounts of time, thus the body wears out from being in a pro-longed hyper-state. Stress is the modern-day term for the spirit of fear.

> Be careful for nothing [fear, stress, anxiety]; but in everything by prayer and supplication with thanksgiving let your requests be made known unto God. And the peace of God, which passeth all understanding, shall keep your hearts and minds through Christ Jesus.
>
> —PHILIPPIANS 4:6–7

What condition suits you best; a bondage to fear or an indescribable liberty of peace?

The existence of any fear, stress, or anxiety in one's life is evidence that agape is not fully released in your life. However, as the agape of the Father increases in your life, fear won't stand a chance at gaining a foothold within your heart.

> The hardships that are the most difficult to endure are those that never happen.

> There is no fear in love [*agape*]; but perfect love [*agape*] casteth out [purges] fear: because fear hath torment [a penalty, punishment]. He that feareth is not made perfect [complete or accomplished] in love [*agape*].
>
> —I JOHN 4:18

Pride was at the root of man's first sin, but what was the manifestation of man's first sin?—*fear.*

Can a proud person struggle with self-esteem or identity issues? He sure can. With Adam and Eve's first sin, they suddenly became very aware of their bodies and were ashamed of them. With the door opened to one little sin, the devil will come in like a flood.

Who caused Adam and Eve to sin? Satan. Following their sin they obviously felt very guilty, but it was fear that caused Adam and Eve to change their behavior and hide. So who is the author of fear? Satan.

> And he said, I heard thy voice in the garden, and I was afraid, because I was naked; and I hid myself. And he said, Who told thee that thou wast naked?
>
> —GENESIS 3:10–11

Who told them they were naked? There were only three people there: God, Adam, and Eve, and that suggestion wouldn't have come from any of them. So where was Satan? He no longer had to channel through the serpent, as he had now gained entrance into the human race and was able to make suggestions regarding sin from within the spirit of Adam and Eve, as well as all their descendants.

Let's deal with this now

Allow me to ask a personal question. Are you hiding your body because you are ashamed of it? Are you disguising, adjusting, or covering up parts of your body because of fear of how others will see you? Will you repent now for your fear and shame regarding some attribute of your body? If Satan has placed fear in your heart, it becomes your faith; and your body will hear that message and make your body respond accordingly. Autoimmune diseases are the result of the body attacking itself, as it has believed an evil report; that evil report could be passed along as a secret through your generations. What effect do you think your fear, self-rejection, and shame will have on your metabolism? Could such vexations be causing your metabolism to slow down preventing the proper burning of certain foods allowing them to stick around? Are all your efforts to lose weight by diet and exercise being totally frustrated? Ask the Lord to show you what sin may be holding you captive thus directing your hypothalamus to modify the involuntary functions in your body in a way that would slowly lead to the demise of your system.

Lets look at another common root of weight gain and that is over eating. I believe the Bible provides additional consideration to weight gain and that is over eating is the symptom of at least three root causes; gluttony, unjust business practices or continued dabbling in new age or occultic healing and religious practices. Before these are dismissed as not applying to your situation you need to ask; do I see these things in my generations and secondly have I been the victim of fraud, theft or cheating that would open a trap door allowing the devil an opportunity?

The result of the iniquity spoken of by Micah was not necessarily that they didn't have enough food but rather that they would eat and never feel satisfied or satiated so the tendency would be to over eat. Our satiation system works as an early limit switch to warn us when we have enough food to avoid over eating. It is similar to becoming rich but not being satisfied by it.

> Shall I count them pure with the wicked balances, and with the bag of deceitful weights? For the rich men thereof are full of violence, and the inhabitants thereof have spoken lies, and their tongue is deceitful in their mouth. Therefore also will I make thee sick in smiting thee, in making thee desolate because of thy sins. Thou shalt eat, but not be satisfied [unable to feel satisfied or satiated]; . . . Thou shalt sow, but thou shalt not reap; . . . For the statutes of Omri are kept, and all the works of the house of Ahab [occultic worship, theft, swindling, jealousy and murder brought on by Jezebel], and ye walk in their counsels; that I should make thee a desolation, and the inhabitants thereof an hissing: therefore ye shall bear the reproach of my people.
>
> —MICAH 6:11–16

Paul in his letter to his Philippian friends warns about those who are given over to gluttony or have made their belly their god. To be given over is a term for addictions in which we are living solely to satisfy the cravings of another creature in that area of our life. It controls us and even rewrites our genetics to keep it that way. Jesus came to set the captive free so victory is yours through the salvation of the Lord.

(For many walk, of whom I have told you often, and now tell you even weeping, that they are the enemies of the cross of Christ Whose end is destruction, whose God is their belly [to be given up to the pleasures of the palate, to gluttony], and whose glory is in their shame [what was enjoyable at the time is now our shame], who mind earthly things.)

—Philippians 3:18

Since our body is the temple of the Holy Spirit and we have participated with its injury by overeating it would be necessary to repent for causing injury and bringing uncleanness to the temple.

Weight problems are a sensitive issue and may no one run with this brief teaching to condemn others. There are many other possible roots to weight gain, but I trust this brief study will be used by God to pave the way to your freedom. Remember weight gain is the symptom of a root problem that God wants to expose in your life, and there is no shame in the Kingdom of God work of sanctification.

Pause to take as much time as possible in dealing with these matters. I would suggest writing out a very personal prayer of repentance and restoration in your journal or the back cover of your Bible. If anything mentioned in the above paragraphs struck you, it is probably in places that you have been struggling with most of your life. Go ahead take your time; after all, you are worth it! May you recover yourself from the snares of the devil in the name of Jesus.

Now back to the garden with our ancestors. From here on man will have to struggle against fear before any work with the Lord can be accomplished. What were the two words uttered prior to every major announcement in the New Testament? *Fear not!* These were the first words the angels said to Joseph, Mary, Zacharias, and the shepherds. They were the first words Jesus said to the disciples when they were called to Jairus' household when their daughter died, and to John prior to being given Revelation. "Fear not" is the shortest command and the most repeated command of God—at about sixty-two times.

> Fear is putting our faith in Satan that he will give us those destructive heart's desires. Fear is Satan's faith and it works, just never in a good way.

The spirit of fear is not from God; it is designed to make you withdraw, lose your courage, and imagine hardship and calamity at every turn. It projects a thought impulse backed up by a chemical enforcement to make us experience a nonevent in three dimensions. Fear is an abusive control tactic used by the devil to provide us torment in every area of our lives.

For God hath not given us the spirit of fear [also shyness, introversion, cowardice], but of power, and of love, and of a sound mind.

—2 Timothy 1:7

Fear produces the opposite of power, love, and a sound mind: Fear produces weakness, hatred, and insanity. Choose this day, blessing or cursing, life or death, health or sickness, success or failure, peace or hostility.

> I have set before you life and death, blessing and cursing: therefore choose life, that both thou and thy seed may live: That thou mayest love the LORD thy God, and that thou mayest obey his voice, and that thou mayest cleave unto him: for he is thy life, and the length of thy days: that thou mayest dwell in the land which the LORD sware unto thy fathers, to Abraham, to Isaac, and to Jacob, to give them.
> —DEUTERONOMY 30:19–20

We cannot be in fear and serve God at the same time. We cannot serve fear and agape God. So fear is a major block to an abundant Christian walk.

Fear is at the root of many allergies, eating disorders, gastrointestinal disorders, asthmas, and various illnesses where we have the fear of food, chemicals, pets, allergens, death, destruction, and many other things.

> So that his life abhorreth bread, and his soul dainty meat.
> —JOB 33:20

As a person fears in his heart, that will be truth for him. Our unabated fear gives Satan the legal grounds to put the kingdom of darkness in motion to precipitate the evil we anticipate through our fear.

Medical science will tell you that the root of heart disease is fear, stress, and anxiety. Did you know that the greatest physician stated that two thousand years ago? Here is what Jesus said:

> Men's hearts failing them for fear.
> —LUKE 21:26

Fear is putting our faith in Satan that he will give us those destructive heart's desires. Fear is Satan's faith and it works, just never in a good way.

> For as he thinketh in his heart, so is he: Eat and drink, saith he to thee; but his heart is not with thee. The morsel which thou hast eaten shalt thou vomit up, and lose thy sweet words.
> —PROVERBS 23:7–8

How about those eating disorders? What causes one to vomit up their food? What lie are you thinking and believing about yourself?

Dear friend, how often have you shrunk back from approaching someone because of your anticipation of the look of disappointment, contempt, or scorn on their face. Do you know that the Lord desires to set you free so you can be bold and confident in your walk?

> Be not afraid of their faces: for I am with thee to deliver thee, saith the LORD.
> —JEREMIAH 1:8

Sleep disturbances and nightmares are rooted in fear. The Lord desires that your sleep would be sweet (pleasant); and in order for you to enjoy that, fear will have to go.

> When thou liest down, thou shalt not be afraid: yea, thou shalt lie down, and thy sleep shall be sweet.
>
> —Proverbs 3:24

> I will say of the LORD, He is my refuge and my fortress: my God; in him will I trust. Surely he shall deliver thee from the snare of the fowler, and from the noisome pestilence. He shall cover thee with his feathers, and under his wings shalt thou trust: his truth shall be thy shield and buckler. Thou shalt not be afraid for the terror by night; nor for the arrow that flieth by day.
>
> —Psalm 91:2–5

Jesus corrected Martha because she took so much on herself that she couldn't handle it and became anxious. One anxious person in the room upsets everything, like a coyote slinking past a dog kennel.

> But Martha was cumbered about much serving, and came to him, and said, Lord, dost thou not care that my sister hath left me to serve alone? bid her therefore that she help me. And Jesus answered and said unto her, Martha, Martha, thou art careful [anxious, stressed out] and troubled [disturbed, disquieted] about many things: But one thing is needful: and Mary hath chosen that good part, which shall not be taken away from her.
>
> —Luke 10:40–42

Jesus Christ gave a thought-provoking sermon on anxiety and how useless and counterproductive fear and anxiety are. Jesus points out that we can't even cause our height to increase by giving thought to it; and if you can't even do that, why are you trying to change so many other issues that you have absolutely no control over?

> And he said unto his disciples, ...Take no thought for your life, what ye shall eat; neither for the body, what ye shall put on. The life is more than meat, and the body is more than raiment. Consider the ravens: for they neither sow nor reap; which neither have storehouse nor barn; and God feedeth them: how much more are ye better than the fowls? And which of you with taking thought can add to his stature one cubit? If ye then be not able to do that thing which is least, why take ye thought for the rest? Consider the lilies how they grow: they toil not, they spin not; and yet I say unto you, that Solomon in all his glory was not arrayed like one of these. If then God so clothe the grass, which is to day in the field, and to morrow is cast into the oven; how much more will he clothe you, O ye of little faith? And seek not ye what ye shall eat, or what ye shall drink, neither be ye of doubtful mind. For all these things do the nations of the world seek after: and your Father knoweth that ye have need of these things. But rather seek ye the kingdom of God; and all these things shall

be added unto you. Fear not, little flock; for it is your Father's good pleasure to give you the kingdom.

—Luke 12:22–32

Here is the reminder again that our only assignment is to seek the kingdom
of God, as the benefits of belonging to that kingdom is that our needs are a
privilege of membership. Membership does have its privileges, especially when
you are speaking about a kingdom that really has unlimited resources with the
staff to take care of you.

No matter how much thought you put into your pet project, even thoughts
intensified by anxiety, you cannot cause even the slightest change for the better.

If we go into sin while about daily things, God will withdraw His blessings.
He will not be provoked. We were taught to pray, "Give us this day our daily
bread." Once you've done that, drop the subject and go on to bigger things;
such as seeking the kingdom of God.

If you are like me, I used to carry my stress around like a badge of honor.
I took it as a complement when folks would say, "You have so much on your
plate, I don't know how one person could handle that all. I'd be so stressed
out." But then I found out that stress was not a good thing, it's bad. Not only
is it bad for the health, but stress, which is anxiety which is fear, is a sin as I
am to fear not. If I am in fear that means I am double-minded and unstable
in all my ways, as I am trying to serve fear and faith at the same time

David returned from a tour of duty with his army back home to Ziklag to
find out the Amalekites had burned it to the ground and all the women and
children were taken captive, including two of David's wives. This was prior
to David becoming king. On top of David's personal grief, his countrymen
wanted to lynch him as they blamed him for the loss of the city. This was an
extremely stressful situation! But David kept his peace and encouraged himself
in the Lord. If David had not sought the Lord, it would have been a sin for
him, and no doubt the outcome would have been very different.

What method do you use to handle your stress?

> And David was greatly distressed [to be in exceedingly narrow straights];
> for the people spake of stoning him, because the soul of all the people
> was grieved [bitter, enraged], every man for his sons and for his daugh-
> ters: but David encouraged [strengthened, obtained support] himself in
> the Lord his God.
>
> —1 Samuel 30:6

David prayed for direction and asked the Lord specific questions: should I
pursue these armies, and if I do, will I be given victory?

> And David enquired at the Lord, saying, Shall I pursue after this troop?
> shall I overtake them? And he answered him, Pursue: for thou shalt surely
> overtake them, and without fail recover all.
>
> —1 Samuel 30:8

The Amalekites are associated with ruthlessness, trickery, and tyranny. You may have had a loved one carried away into captivity by the Amalekites through their lies and treachery. That is very difficult to face, but take the courage of David and inquire of the Lord what route you should take in discerning and destroying the Amalekites (the devil and his mob) and whether the Lord will give you victory. Such an inquiry led the author to writing of this work.

Once receiving confidence and direction from the Lord, all David had to do was go clean up. He pursued the Amalekites, thrashed them, and retrieved all the women and children unharmed, plus he took a large spoil!

Fear workout

Step 1: Prayerfully review the following list and mark each sin you or your generations have participated with. It is important that you are not rushed and that you are in a private place as you go through this.

> I sought the LORD, and he heard me, and delivered me from all my fears.
> —PSALM 34:4

> And deliver them who through fear of death were all their lifetime subject to bondage.
> —HEBREWS 2:15

- ❑ Fear of abandonment
- ❑ Fear of affliction or misery
- ❑ Fear of animals—snakes, spiders, etc.
- ❑ Fear of another's bitterness
- ❑ Fear of another's sexuality
- ❑ Fear of another's words
- ❑ Fear of authority
- ❑ Fear of being a poor host/hostess
- ❑ Fear of being cursed
- ❑ Fear of being robbed or injured
- ❑ Fear of betrayal
- ❑ Fear of bondage to sin
- ❑ Fear of chemicals
- ❑ Fear of children rejecting God
- ❑ Fear of criticism
- ❑ Fear of death
- ❑ Fear of deliverance
- ❑ Fear of disability
- ❑ Fear of disease
- ❑ Fear of divorce
- ❑ Fear of addictions and addictive behavior
- ❑ Fear of allergic reactions
- ❑ Fear of an evil report
- ❑ Fear of another's facial expressions
- ❑ Fear of another's silence
- ❑ Fear of antigens
- ❑ Fear of being alone
- ❑ Fear of being controlled
- ❑ Fear of being deceived
- ❑ Fear of being shamed
- ❑ Fear of blood
- ❑ Fear of change
- ❑ Fear of children
- ❑ Fear of commitment
- ❑ Fear of dark
- ❑ Fear of death in sleep
- ❑ Fear of dependency
- ❑ Fear of disapproval
- ❑ Fear of disfiguration
- ❑ Fear of doctors and hospitals

- ❑ Fear of drowning
- ❑ Fear of evil spirits
- ❑ Fear of father or mother
- ❑ Fear of fire
- ❑ Fear of God—negative, due to lack of knowledge
- ❑ Fear of humiliation
- ❑ Fear of insanity
- ❑ Fear of losing appearance with age
- ❑ Fear of losing salvation
- ❑ Fear of loss of relationship
- ❑ Fear of loss of spouse
- ❑ Fear of menopause
- ❑ Fear of needles
- ❑ Fear of not getting deliverance
- ❑ Fear of own nakedness
- ❑ Fear of pain
- ❑ Fear of pregnancy
- ❑ Fear of punishment
- ❑ Fear of rejection
- ❑ Fear of responsibility
- ❑ Fear of some secret sin or iniquity preventing God's work in my life
- ❑ Fear of success
- ❑ Fear of suffocation
- ❑ Fear of the enemy
- ❑ Fear of unknown
- ❑ Fear of war, conflict
- ❑ Fear of water
- ❑ Fear of weapons
- ❑ Fear others won't do it right or will let you down
- ❑ Fear that _____ will never change
- ❑ Fearful dreams, nightmares
- ❑ Inferiority
- ❑ Perfectionism
- ❑ Fear of environment
- ❑ Fear of failure
- ❑ Fear of financial ruin or loss
- ❑ Fear of food, drink, clothes, housing, chemicals, insect bites, germs
- ❑ Fear of harassment
- ❑ Fear of inadequacy
- ❑ Fear of judgment or condemnation
- ❑ Fear of losing children
- ❑ Fear of loss of confidence
- ❑ Fear of loss of reputation
- ❑ Fear of man
- ❑ Fear of natural disasters and storms
- ❑ Fear of noises
- ❑ Fear of my opponent
- ❑ Fear of own sexuality
- ❑ Fear of poverty
- ❑ Fear of public speaking, performance
- ❑ Fear of races, cultures—bigotry
- ❑ Fear of reproof
- ❑ Fear of sex or loss of it
- ❑ Fear of spouse
- ❑ Fear of suffering
- ❑ Fear of the dying process
- ❑ Fear of tomorrow
- ❑ Fear of vomiting
- ❑ Fear of wasted years
- ❑ Fear of weakness
- ❑ Fear of women
- ❑ Fear that God will not come through for me
- ❑ Fear you've committed unpardonable sin
- ❑ Horror
- ❑ Panic attacks
- ❑ Phobias—i.e., claustrophobia

❑ **Self-consciousness**   ❑ **Shyness**
❑ **Speculative fear**   ❑ **Superstitions**
❑ **Suspicion**   ❑ **Worry and anxiety**

This is a partial list. Ask the Lord to show you what additional bondage He wants you to be released from.

Step 2: Ask and wait.

*Lord, is there any other sin or any other fear that I have been unable to lay down on my own that You want me to deal with?*_____

Step 3: Go back through the list and pray this prayer inserting the sin in the blank space. You may insert several sins in the blank space at a time if you desire.

Prayer of Repentance
(Preferably out loud)

Father God, I recognize and take responsibility for myself and my ancestors for the sin(s) of _____. I agree with Your verdict on my rebellion. I repent, I renounce, and I ask forgiveness for my participation with these sins, and I ask that their curse be broken in the name of Jesus Christ of Nazareth.

Step 4: Bind the strongman. This is best done by an experienced and trusted ministering friend the first time around.

Prayer to Bind the Strongmen of Fear and Pride
(Out loud)

In the name of Jesus Christ of Nazareth and by the power of the Holy Spirit, I take authority over the strongmen of fear and pride I break your power and bind you and put you on notice that I am destroying your armor in which you trust. I will be coming back to remove you from your palace.

Step 5: Purging the evil. Review the above list again now inserting the sin you have repented of in the blank.

Command of Deliverance
(Must be out loud with eyes open, realizing you are speaking directly to a spirit)

In the name of Jesus Christ of Nazareth and by the power of the Holy Spirit, I take authority over the spirit(s) of _____. I break your power, I cast you out, and I command you to return no more.

Step 6: Purge the strongman now that you have destroyed his stronghold.

Command of Deliverance
(Must be out loud with eyes open, realizing you are speaking directly to a spirit)

In the name of Jesus Christ of Nazareth and by the power of the Holy Spirit, I take authority over the strongmen of fear and pride; I break your power, I cast you out, and I command you to take all residue of evil spirits with you. I command you to return no more.

Step 7: Pray that God will cause you to increase and abound in His love and that you would be an overcomer in the sins just repented of. Ask for a scripture that you will use to resist the devil when he tries to open the trapdoor again to regain entrance to your heart.

> Deception isn't obvious; that is why it is deceptive.

AGAPE REJOICETH NOT IN INIQUITY, BUT REJOICETH IN THE TRUTH

Rejoiceth [thrives] not in iniquity [violating standard of God's truth], but rejoiceth [takes part in another's joy, congratulates] in the truth.
—1 CORINTHIANS 13:6

This chapter contains a hard message where we realize that many things we don't even think to question and yet participate in are actually lies. Deception isn't obvious; that is why it is deceptive.

Jesus reserved the strongest of words for religious people who, though spiritual, had their minds already made up concerning their truth and were too set in their ways to learn anything new, much less to consider the accuracy of their established viewpoints. When He saw this stubborn peculiarity surface, Jesus identified the source as the devil, as all lies and their accompanying death wish come from the devil.

> God calls Jesus the Word so everything that opposes His Scriptures recorded in the Holy Bible is antichrist and a lie.

Ye are of your father the devil [slanderer, false accuser, opposed to God], and the lusts [desire for what is forbidden] of your father ye will do. He was a murderer from the beginning, and abode not in the truth, because there is no truth in him. When he speaketh a lie, he speaketh of his own: for he is a liar, and the father of it. And because I tell you the truth, ye believe me not.
—JOHN 8:44–45

No matter how obvious the truth is, the father of lies will endeavor to spin it into a lie. He doesn't lie just for the sake of lying, everything he twists is calculated to affect you in the most strategic and vulnerable parts of your spirit to bring about your eternal death.

Who is a liar but he that denieth that Jesus is the Christ? He is antichrist [adversary of the Messiah], that denieth [rejects] the Father and the Son.
—1 JOHN 2:22

And every spirit that confesseth not that Jesus Christ is come in the flesh is not of God: and this is that spirit of antichrist, whereof ye have heard that it should come; and even now already is it in the world.

—1 JOHN 4:3

The spirit of antichrist is identified as the power that is behind the attempts to eliminate the power of God in our lives by spreading the lie.

The devil represents everything that is opposite to the image and nature of God. A diversion is put up in an attempt to block the flow of the love stream that originates from the Father and to create a false image of who the Father is.

Hereby know we the spirit of truth, and the spirit of error. Beloved, let us love [*agape*] one another: for love [*agape*] is of God; and every one that loveth [*agapao*] is born of God, and knoweth God. He that loveth not knoweth not God; for God is love [*agape*].

—1 JOHN 4:6–8

He will lie about the existence of God, the love of God, the fairness of God, the ability of God to heal and restore, the call of God, the way to worship God, our worthiness to be loved, and the worthiness of others to be loved. Actually he has a lie for everything pertaining to our relationship with God.

For the time will come when they will not endure sound doctrine; but after their own lusts shall they heap to themselves teachers, having itching ears; And they shall turn away their ears from the truth, and shall be turned unto fables.

—2 TIMOTHY 4:3–4

Many Christian watchdog ministries exist to expose a plethora of false teachers in an attempt to free the poor people from them. These people searched to find such a teacher to follow; they were not interested in sound doctrine. False teachers only exist because people are attracted to their message. All of us are without excuse when we have the Scriptures preserved through the ages, as the Word was intended to be proclaimed. The responsibility lies with shepherd and sheep to discern truth. God, of course, will judge righteously between the two. That is His job.

The New Age religion was started by Cain who invented his own approach to God and angrily demanded that God would respect his alternative worship.

Everything that violates the Word is antichrist, as it defies the nature of God. God calls Jesus the Word, so everything that opposes His Scriptures recorded in the Holy Bible is antichrist and a lie.

Who changed the truth of God into a lie.

—ROMANS 1:25

A lying antichrist spirit will not allow you to agape God, yourself, or your neighbor. Why? Because God's greatest command will be the main criteria on how one will be judged at the end of the age.

> Jesus said unto him, Thou shalt love the Lord thy God with all thy heart [spirit], and with all thy soul, and with all thy mind. This is the first and great commandment. And the second is like unto it, Thou shalt love thy neighbour as thyself. On these two commandments hang all the law and the prophets.
> —MATTHEW 22:37–40

> If Satan can entice us to sin and then get us to think we dealt with the sin by sinning further, he has caused a major breach in the love stream.

With every truth Satan has a lie. He'll lie to you about yourself, he'll lie to you about others, and he'll lie to you about God. We'll need to recognize what the lie looks like in each of these three areas so we can apply the truth serum to it and turn all the curses into multiplied blessings.

1. Exposing the devil's lies about God

This lie resulted in the first murder in the Bible. Cain, who invented his own approach to God and angrily demanded that God respect his alternative worship, started the New Age religion. Abel was obedient and offered one of his choice animals as a sacrifice onto God; but Cain listened to Satan's lie that God would accept burnt corn. God always has and always will require the shedding of blood for the remission of sin.

> And almost all things are by the law purged with blood; and without shedding of blood is no remission.
> —HEBREWS 9:22

Since this sacrifice required the shedding of blood, it would have been a sin offering. Understand how brazen Satan is. The offering was to deal with sin, and yet Satan enticed Cain to sin in his method of dealing with sin. So he sinned and then added more sin on top of it, as though that would somehow fix the problem and God would be OK with such rebellion and mockery. God gently approached Cain and said that He would forgive him if he just went out and made the proper offering as Able did. The logical response for Cain would be to say, "Sorry Lord, I don't know what got into me. And thanks for being patient with me. I'll gladly redo the offering." But Cain snapped, obviously vexed by the devil to respond to God by killing a righteous man.

> And in process of time it came to pass, that Cain brought of the fruit of the ground an offering unto the LORD. And Abel, he also brought of the firstlings of his flock and of the fat thereof. And the LORD had respect unto Abel and to his offering: But unto Cain and to his offering he had not respect. And Cain was very wroth, and his countenance fell. And the

LORD said unto Cain, Why art thou wroth? and why is thy countenance fallen? If thou doest well, shalt thou not be accepted? and if thou doest not well, sin lieth at the door. And unto thee shall be his desire, and thou shalt rule over him. And Cain talked with Abel his brother: and it came to pass, when they were in the field, that Cain rose up against Abel his brother, and slew him.

—GENESIS 4:3–8

Satan gives an alternative remedy to deal with sin

Does Satan continue to lie to us about how we are to deal with our sin? Of course, if he can entice us to sin and then get us to think we dealt with the sin by sinning further, he has caused a breach in the love stream. For example, we may have been taught "once saved, always saved," so no matter what you do it's covered by the prayer you prayed twenty-seven years ago; and there's no need to repent again as that one prayer covered all your sins—past, present, and future. Perhaps you still have an Old Testament belief where you must confess or petition the aid of a "go-between," rather than approach the throne of God boldly for the forgiveness of sins. Some will confess some of their obvious sins to God but choose not to forgive a friend who has offended them and hold onto the bitterness, judgment, and condemnation against that person for years. Some will sin and then atone for their sin by doing good; all that does is give the sin a chocolate coating but inside it is still bitter. Then there is a more deceptive condition of conformity, where we will live and sin under the umbrella of one ancient religious, scientific, occultic, or psychological quasi-spiritual modality and then come to Father God expecting Him to help us, though we have no intention of letting go of the former deceptive practice. What I'm trying to say will become clear once we start looking at some specifics in Scripture.

Jude uses the example of three wicked religious deceivers—Cain, Balaam, and Core—to expose some methods used by Satan to divert worship to himself. Cain is the father of the occultic religious and spiritual system that we call New Age. Cain used anger, jealousy, intimidation, and elimination of his opponents to further his evangelism. Balaam is a deceiver that concocted a subtle plan to place a stumbling block to entice the people to be seduced into sexual immorality and bondage. Core (Korah) set himself up as judge and religious critic who led the rebellion against the orthodox leadership methods of Moses.

But these speak evil [disregard, discredit] of those things which they know not: but what they know naturally [surmise, guess], as brute [destitute of reason, absurd] beasts [ignorant hellish bound], in those things they corrupt themselves [destroy or perish]. Woe unto them! for they have gone in the way of Cain [the fabricator], and ran greedily after the error [fell astray ,unrestrained, a stumbling block, prodigal] of Balaam [most abandoned deceiver] for reward, and perished [exchanged eternal life for] in the gainsaying [rebellion] of Core [one who rebelled against Moses].

—JUDE 1:10–11

How does Satan divert worship to himself?

Satan knows exactly what he needs to do to divert all religious worship to himself without his victim being any the wiser. He superimposes his kingdom over top of the kingdom of God wherever he has the invitation. Isaiah uses the term "cover with a covering," which refers to the creation of precious metal gods where a thin layer of molten metal is poured over a mold to create the image. It is a system that mirrors godly spirituality but it is a mask or an imposter that usurps the worship of God.

Isaiah speaks of "adding sin to sin," which is Satan's method of operation where he causes an affliction or infirmity through enticement to sin and then comes around with his own special medicine to treat it; thus he receives the worship and idolatry he is envious of. He doesn't heal the malady, but he covers it over or masks it so it remains but you are no longer consciously aware of it. So we are in double jeopardy where we have sinned and suffered for it and then in our search for healing we find a false peace through the "shadow of Egypt" remedy, which is really only fighting sin with sin. If we seek advice and healing from anyplace other than God first, that is rebellion. He doesn't say He won't use the skill of a physician, but what God is saying is that He will do the referral if necessary.

> Woe to the rebellious children, saith the Lord, that take counsel [sought advise], but not of me; and that cover with a covering [one kingdom [Satan's] poured over the top of another], but not of my spirit, that they may add sin to sin: That walk to go down into Egypt, and have not asked at my mouth; to strengthen themselves in the strength of Pharaoh [human protection and healing], and to trust in the shadow of Egypt[occultism]! Therefore shall the strength of Pharaoh be your shame [to be duped, disgraced and worse off], and the trust in the shadow of Egypt [occultism] your confusion.
>
> —ISAIAH 30:1–3

Paul makes no mistake in stating that men suffer from infirmity due to their bondage to sin and that they make it worse by adding "iniquity unto iniquity," or as Isaiah said, "sin unto sin." I believe adding "iniquity unto iniquity" not only deals with personal sins but also refers to repeating generational sins, so thus you have certain diseases and addictions that travel through the family tree.

> I speak after the manner of men because of the infirmity of your flesh: for as ye have yielded your members servants to uncleanness [slaves to immorality, lust, and impurity] and to iniquity unto iniquity; even so now yield your members servants to righteousness unto holiness.
>
> —ROMANS 6:19

Few would contend with the statement that Egypt was the founding nation of the studies of magic, witchcraft, alchemy, and other supernatural phenomena we group together as occultism. The occult deals with the magic science of energy flow and energy relationships. Occultic meditation is a means of intentionally and persistently directing these energies from a power source to accomplish some desired spiritual or physical outcome. This ancient magic is a corrupted form of religion designed to coerce a particular evil stronghold into action. Those that practice in the occult know how to open a trapdoor to allow entrance to an evil spirit so they can benefit from its manifestation, which may be a false peace, euphoria, a relief in one area of struggle, and, as we'll soon see, even the appearance of miracles.

> For the idols have spoken vanity [empty and vain], and the diviners [a parallel practice to biblical prophecy] have seen a lie [false tongue or prophecy, deception], and have told false [worthless] dreams; they comfort in vain [false peace or healing]: therefore they went their way as a flock [followed the multitude of goats], they were troubled [afflicted, humiliated, depressed], because there was no shepherd.
> —ZECHARIAH 10:2

God anticipated that people would suffer sickness, disease, or loss and desired to empower His shepherds to minister restoration. Zechariah states the reason the folks went to worldly counselors and healers is because there were no shepherds that were fit for the Master's use. Ezekiel bluntly reprimands the pastors for not healing and strengthening the sick, for not restoring the broken hearts, and for not rescuing those that the enemy had carried away. Ezekiel would not have reprimanded these men so harshly if it had been nearly impossible for them to carry out these tasks of ministry. A God-fearing physician or surgeon is actually a shepherd to the people to minister not only to the physical but to the spiritual destiny. Today the roles of a medical practitioner are highly specialized with severe time restraints; nonetheless, there is still the responsibility to perhaps tag-team with another who will be a shepherd to complete the healing.

If TV is the opiate of the masses, the "shadow of Egypt" is the opiate of the Gentile church.

> Son of man, prophesy against the shepherds [pastors] of Israel, prophesy, and say unto them, Thus saith the Lord GOD unto the shepherds; Woe be to the shepherds of Israel that do feed themselves! should not the shepherds feed the flocks?...The diseased [wounded, grieved, sick, faint] have ye not strengthened [such as wrapping a wound or sore joint], neither have ye healed [fully restored] that which was sick, neither have ye bound up [correct a broken bone or stop the trickle] that which was broken, neither have ye brought again [turned back, restore, refresh] that which was driven away [banished, outcast, gone astray], neither have ye sought that which was lost [to fall into danger of divine judgment]; but with force [strength] and with cruelty [harsh, without understanding, impatient] have ye ruled [dominated, tread down] them. And they were scattered, because there is no shepherd: and they became meat to all the beasts of

the field, when they were scattered. My sheep wandered through all the mountains, and upon every high hill: yea, my flock was scattered upon all the face of the earth, and none did search or seek after them.

—Ezekiel 34:2, 4–6

If TV is the opiate of the masses, the "shadow of Egypt" is the opiate of the Gentile church.

Often in churches the pews may be full for .05 percent of a person's week but the rest of the time the people are scattered as they go everywhere else but to the shepherd to pursue healing of their minds, bodies, and relationships.

King Asa was a God-fearing king who did much to restore his nation to righteousness before God, but he did leave some of Egypt's healing modalities in place just in case God didn't come through for him. The sad commentary on Asa's life was that he suffered for two years with a disease of his feet and he sought the care of the physicians of Egypt rather than seeking God first, and so he died. The obvious innuendo is that if he had sought the Lord first, he would have been healed.

> Jesus spoke a stern warning for us today to watch for these diviners or false prophets that will seduce even the smart class with various signs and wonders.

> And Asa in the thirty and ninth year of his reign was diseased in his feet, until his disease was exceeding great: yet in his disease he sought not to the Lord, but to the physicians. And Asa slept with his fathers, and died in the one and fortieth year of his reign.
>
> —2 Chronicles 16:12–13

What would seeking the Lord look like? Perhaps, first of all, in order that a person is not approaching God presumptuously, he would want to cleanse his temple and that may be enough to be healed. If not, go and ask the Lord as to what may be the root or the open door individually or generationally that needs to be exposed so that the symptom of the hidden rotten fruit can be exposed.

Exposing the bad boy of divination

We hear the term divination and we shut down to it, thinking that we are innocent of that bad boy as we may believe that it just refers to the astrologers and palm readers and such like. *Divination* is any word given that one presumes God has spoken when He hasn't. A divination is a lie where we misquote or misrepresent the will and position of God on a matter. A lying divination, for example, would be reading from a Bible translation that has been altered to reflect the beliefs of the authors who subscribe to the "shadow of Egypt" and we are not aware of it.

> They have seen vanity and lying divination, saying, The Lord saith: and the Lord hath not sent them: and they have made others to hope that they would confirm the word. Have ye not seen a vain vision, and have

ye not spoken a lying divination, whereas ye say, The LORD saith it; albeit I have not spoken?

—EZEKIEL 13:6–7

Jesus spoke a stern warning for us today to watch for these diviners or false prophets that will seduce even the smart class with various signs and wonders. Be watchful of the little deceptions, as the big ones are too obvious. If what you see happening amongst Christians is not found in your Bible, it is a lie. You may be told, "Well, God is doing a new thing or this is new revelation." Believe them not! The Lord said there will be nothing new, as He foretold us all things and He did that knowing we'd have to discern even what takes place in our pulpits.

> The one in idolatry is the patient, student, or admirer; and the one in witchcraft is the authority, the teacher, or the superstar.

For false Christs and false prophets shall rise, and shall shew signs and wonders, to seduce, if it were possible, even the elect. But take ye heed: behold, I have foretold you all things.

—MARK 13:22–23

Two other terms, *witchcraft* and *idolatry*, also cause us to zone out. We think of a witch in a black gown and hat mixing up a potion and casting spells and an idol as a ceramic form that we set on our shelf at home to talk at. Satan also lies about definitions and understanding what God is referring to; and he is able to make evil occultic things so acceptable and adorable that we will tell our children about them at bedtime and then we will buy their paraphernalia for our kids to play with and their outfits to dress up in. What are we thinking?

I believe that witchcraft refers to a practitioner or trafficker of any "shadow of Egypt," extra-biblical craft, doctrine, medicine, exercise, meditation, healing form, or any manipulator of energies. One practicing witchcraft establishes themselves as "one who knows" and as "one who has arrived"; and furthermore, they are the person who through their own lifestyle and enticement lead others into rebellion.

Accordingly, the one who is guilty of idolatry would seek the counsel and healing of a witchcraft practitioner. The one in idolatry is the patient, student or admirer; and the one in witchcraft is the authority, the teacher, or the superstar. Stubbornness is the most accurate description of one who is in idolatry, as they will react in anger, resentment, and many other evil things to anyone who dares question them. They will seldom be receptive to altering the lie they bought into. It is very common for children to just accept the religion they were born into without studying on their own to see if the single most important decision in their life is factually based.

And Samuel said, Hath the LORD as great delight in burnt offerings and sacrifices, as in obeying the voice of the LORD? Behold, to obey is better than sacrifice, and to hearken than the fat of rams. For rebellion is as the sin of witchcraft, and stubbornness is as iniquity and idolatry. Because thou hast rejected the word of the LORD, he hath also rejected thee from being king.

—1 Samuel 15:22–23

Switchcraft

Perhaps it would make sense to add an "s" to witchcraft making it "switch-craft," as it is a method Satan uses to switch worship from God unto himself.

Similar to the term *divination*, as used in the Old Testament, we have false prophets and sorcerers in the New Testament church. As with all deceivers, they channel their teachings from an evil spirit as they change the truth of God into a lie. Their hidden agenda is to prevent those who are seeking the Lord from hearing the whole truth of the gospel or to twist what God has said. A false prophet is often one who says, "God told me." And what they were told is found out later to be lacking. It is easy for some to use a phrase not realizing the implications if they are found out to be wrong. They may be used to saying, "God told me such and such," in order to be heard and to shut down any opposition. That is a form of spiritual control and manipulation or as noted in Acts, It could be sorcery or false prophecy.

> Whether a person has the truth is not measured by their zeal but is commended to those who are only interested in submitting to God's perspective and righteousness.

> They found a certain sorcerer [powers channeled from an evil spirit], a false prophet [lies under oath of being divinely inspired], a Jew, whose name was Barjesus: Which was with the deputy of the country, Sergius Paulus, a prudent man; who called for Barnabas and Saul, and desired to hear the word of God. But Elymas the sorcerer [certain scholars and priests, teachers, astrologers, magicians] for so is his name by interpretation withstood [opposed, resisted] them, seeking to turn away the deputy from the faith. Then Saul, [who also is called Paul,] filled with the Holy Ghost, set his eyes on him, And said, O full of all subtilty [deceit] and all mischief [unscrupulous, reckless], thou child of the devil, thou enemy of all righteousness, wilt thou not cease to pervert the right ways of the Lord? And now, behold, the hand of the Lord is upon thee, and thou shalt be blind, not seeing the sun for a season. And immediately there fell on him a mist and a darkness; and he went about seeking some to lead him by the hand.
>
> —Acts 13:6–11

In this particular case the root of blindness was participating with sorcery to cause others not to see the truth.

Satan directs many undercover ministers, pastors, prophets, and apostles in the church who are his servants taught through our seminaries and seldom exposed through their resumes. The responsibility to recognize the fruit lies with the sheep, who will know the voice of their Master spoken through the lips of a true servant. Many won't and will remain in the church as tares or birds of the air until the final judgment.

> For such are false apostles, deceitful workers [teachers who promote a carnal Christianity], transforming themselves into the apostles of Christ [messengers]. And no marvel; for Satan himself is transformed into an angel of light. Therefore it is no great thing if his ministers [servants] also be transformed as the ministers of righteousness; whose end shall be according to their works.
> —2 Corinthians 11:13–15

> There are few things that would cause the Lord to drive anyone away from him but one thing that will get you gone from his presence is submitting to the heathen abominations of spiritual practices.

The question may be: how can Satan perform miracles? If an evil spirit is behind blindness, insanity, or infirmity, all Satan has to do is direct the spirit to quit manifesting and he comes around looking like the hero and a miracle worker.

> For they are the spirits of devils, working miracles, which go forth unto the kings of the earth and of the whole world, to gather them to the battle of that great day of God Almighty
> —Revelation 16:14

> And deceiveth them that dwell on the earth by the means of those miracles which he had power to do in the sight of the beast; saying to them that dwell on the earth, that they should make an image to the beast, which had the wound by a sword, and did live.
> —Revelation 13:14

Whether a person has the truth is not measured by their zeal but is commended to those who are only interested in submitting to God's perspective and righteousness. Everything they are taught or that they read is carefully filtered through the Word of God. That can never be accomplished by the casual reader of the Bible.

> For I bear them record that they have a zeal of God, but not according to knowledge. For they being ignorant of God's righteousness, and going about to establish their own righteousness, have not submitted themselves unto the righteousness of God. For Christ is the end of the law for righteousness to every one that believeth.
> —Romans 10:2–3

Many folks remain in darkness by default and ignorance as they establish their own righteousness. They assume they are good people so therefore what they are doing must be OK with God. The most interesting occurrence is their claim to know what the Bible says or does not say; but they have never read it, never, and it is a big book to presume we know all of its contents.

Conformity

In an unregenerate state we will have difficulty in discerning many truths from the lies of a devil. As we sanctify our bodies, minds, and spirits, we will be better able to scrutinize and separate the truth from the deception. Prove your religion, prove your holiday, prove your tradition, prove what is taught, prove what you read, prove your thoughts; and in so doing, the will of God will be established in you.

> I beseech you therefore, brethren, by the mercies of God, that ye present your bodies a living sacrifice, holy, acceptable unto God, which is your reasonable service. And be not conformed to this world [fashioned after one who is lost]: but be ye transformed [complete alteration in character and conduct] by the renewing of your mind, that ye may prove [examine to determine if genuine] what is that good [profitable to the benefit of others], and acceptable, and perfect [consummate human integrity and virtue], will of God.
> —Romans 12:1–2

Conformity to the world is evidence of to whom we have submitted our souls. There are few things that would cause the Lord to drive anyone away from Him; but one thing that will get you gone from His presence is submitting to the heathen abominations of spiritual practices. These spiritual practices are generally cloaked in something that provides some perception of benefit, as the spiritual deception would be obvious if presented alone. An example would be Hinduism's evangelism through the very popular yoga.

> When thou art come into the land which the Lord thy God giveth thee, thou shalt not learn to do after the abominations of those nations. There shall not be found among you any one that maketh his son or his daughter to pass through the fire [sacrifice their life], or that useth divination, or an observer of times [fortuneteller, spiritism], or an enchanter [take as an omen, to divine], or a witch [summons evil through incantations or chanting], Or a charmer [bind to evil], or a consulter with familiar spirits [demands favors from the spirits of the dead], or a wizard [consults the python spirit, a false prophet], or a necromancer [to enquire or pray to anyone dead or alive apart from Jehovah]. For all that do these things are an abomination unto the Lord: and because of these abominations the Lord thy God doth drive them out from before thee. Thou shalt be perfect with the Lord thy God.
> —Deuteronomy 18:9–13

Some of these practices may not be recognizable as they morph quickly into different forms and combinations, but the roots remain the same. Labyrinths, mazes, sacred geometry, sacred spaces, contemplative prayer, meditation through emptying the mind or repetitive chants, yoga, Halloween, or worship of the sun and moon would be examples of the "shadow of Egypt" that diviners have attempted to Christianize.

Are the things of God, things that He has already confirmed in the Word, sufficient for you or are you keeping the doors open for something else?

> Beware lest any man spoil you through philosophy [speculative science or branch of knowledge] and vain deceit [resulting in emptiness and devoid of truth], after the tradition of men, after the rudiments of the world [delusive grandiose and cultic speculations], and not after Christ.
> —Colossians 2:8

In fact a person can be completely broke and have a greater sin towards the love of money than a very wealthy person does.

Lest we have mutiny, I will give no comment on what this next verse may be speaking to:

> Thus saith the LORD, Learn not the way of the heathen, and be not dismayed at the signs of heaven; for the heathen are dismayed at them. For the customs of the people are vain: for one cutteth a tree out of the forest, the work of the hands of the workman, with the axe. They deck it with silver and with gold; they fasten it with nails and with hammers, that it move not.
> —Jeremiah 10:2–4

If you are still reading, I guess I must be a scrooge you can still love.

Our Father, in love, asks that we reconsider every generational and spiritual tradition in our lives to see if they have their roots on the right foundation.

The precepts of God, especially the origins of things in the spiritual realm, are only confusing and foolishness to anyone who has the zeal for knowledge but won't submit to the lordship of Jesus. This blindness is how the Spirit of God hides the precious Word from the ministers of Satan that have infiltrated the church. Indeed, to a believer surrendered to the walk of agape, the lies of Satan's servants are immediately exposed for the folly and wickedness that they are, even with their desperate striving to authenticate themselves. So the best they can do is give the wisdom of man, which receives its empowering from one who is disguised as an angel of light and who will misuse scriptural laws and twist to accomplish his end.

> Which things also we speak, not in the words which man's wisdom teacheth, but which the Holy Ghost teacheth; comparing [interpreting, judging] spiritual things with spiritual. But the natural man [governed by sensuous appetites and passions] receiveth not the things of the Spirit of God: for they are foolishness unto him: neither can he know them, because they are spiritually discerned. But he that is spiritual judgeth all things, yet he himself is judged of no man.
> —1 Corinthians 2:13–15

In the motivational self-improvement world and in its corresponding religious counterparts, you'll hear references to the "power within." Yes, there are two possible powers that are available from within our spirits, and we can only submit to one of them.

> Walk not as other Gentiles walk, in the vanity [emptiness] of their mind, Having the understanding [ability to think through] darkened [to be covered over with a covering], being alienated [shut off to intimacy] from the life of God through the ignorance [willful blindness especially of things divine] that is in them, because of the blindness [stupidity due to dulled perceptions and discernment] of their heart [spirit]: Who being past feeling [apathetic, insensitive to honor and shame] have given themselves over unto lasciviousness [gluttony, filthy words, indecent bodily movements, unchaste handling of males or females], to work [gain by performance and pain] all uncleanness [impure motives regarding personal consumption] with greediness [to achieve no matter what even by extortion].
> —Ephesians 4:17–19

Jesus taught that it is difficult for those who trust in riches to enter into the kingdom of God. Now Satan would agree with that statement and will have his ministers teach his methods of pursuing or accumulating wealth to see who he can persuade to switch destinies. Jesus teaches one thing and the spirit of antichrist will scorn it and offer an alternative deception. Wealth in and of itself is not the problem; the problem is all in the spirit of the beholder. In fact a person can be completely broke and have a greater sin towards the love of money than a very wealthy person does.

> Perverse disputing [useless occupation and endless strife] of men of corrupt [infestation resulting in destruction] minds, and destitute [defrauded, deprived] of the truth, supposing that gain [to procure for oneself] is godliness [denotes piety and favor]: from such withdraw thyself. But godliness [reverential fear] with contentment [a perfect condition of life with the mind at peace] is great gain.
> —1 Timothy 6:5

I want to carefully draw particular attention to the word *witchcraft* in Galatians 5, which is translated from the Greek word *pharmakeia*. The meaning here is somewhat narrower in scope from the translated word *witchcraft* that we considered back in 1 Samuel 15. *Pharmakeia* and *pharmakeus* are the words from which *pharmacy* or *pharmacist* are respectively derived. *Pharmakeus* is translated in Revelations 21:8 as sorcerers or one who prepares or uses magical remedies.

There is an important place for doctors. There is a place for medication. They provide immediate care to bind up a wound or a give valuable diagnosis or give you comfort until you reach your healing. A physician that deals primarily with the physical and emotional will seldom say he cures disease; rather they help to manage it. When you take a drug, it is an attempt to bypass the penalty of the curse of rebellion and stubbornness artificially without taking responsibility for the sin that causes the physiological problem. The drug "covers with a covering" because it is a counterfeit cure; it simply masks the real problem and doesn't deal with the root, which is spiritual.

Medication gives you an altered state of soul or biological consciousness. The old enemy goes undealt with while you are chemically managed and altered—that is why it is sin. In many cases you still have the pain you just can't feel it.

> Now the works of the flesh are manifest, which are these; adultery, fornication, uncleanness, lasciviousness [disgraceful, shameless conduct and speech] Idolatry, witchcraft [pharmakeia: use of medicine, drugs, spells, poisoning], hatred [enmity: everything opposed to agape], variance [contention, strife], emulations [jealous and contentious rivalry], wrath [anger, indignation], strife [self-seeking, seeking to win followers], seditions [divisions, dissension], heresies [self-serving erroneous opinions], envyings, murders, drunkenness [intoxication], revellings [drunken outdoor party and march], and such like: of the which I tell you before, as I have also told you in time past, that they which do such things [continuous and habitual actions] shall not inherit the kingdom of God.
> —GALATIANS 5:19–22

The passage concludes with strong words saying those "which do such things shall not inherit the kingdom of God." The phrase "do such things" is referring to one who makes the seventeen sins listed as a way of life, seeing no need to repent and turn from their participation with such evils. A person who is ill should seek God first, and with God's referral take the treatment as prescribed while you seek the Lord for thorough healing of mind, body, soul, and spirit.

Initially this all sounds difficult if not impossible as we relate it to our spiritual experiences to date. It is strong meat for sure; perhaps even tough, difficult to chew meat.

> But strong meat belongeth to them that are of full age, even those who by reason of use have their senses [perceiving, understanding, judging] exercised [as one who strives earnestly to become godly] to discern both good and evil.
> —HEBREWS 5:14

I have found I can rely on the symptom to expose the sin that I am most susceptible to, and for me the root cause is always the same. When I have a nosebleed I'm usually harboring hostility toward someone and usually I don't have to think very long to recall who I'm bitter with. I deal with my stuff and the bleeding stops without fail. I seldom get headaches anymore, but when I do it is usually because I'm in a state of confusion, as I know what is the right thing to do but I am in conflict with myself as to whether I'll choose to do what I know to be right. I avoided surgery for carpal tunnel syndrome and tennis elbow by dealing with things like self-hatred and self-rejection along with drivenness, performance, and perfectionism. If the tingling sensation comes back now in my wrists or elbows, I would discern from my past experience that I've opened the door and entertained some iniquity; and I deal with it. My eyesight will go blurry when I'm in judgment and condemnation of someone, and the symptoms won't go away until I repent and forgive the object of my mind traffic. If I'm worried and stressed out, I tend to sigh a lot; or if I'm in fear or unwilling to forgive, I may experience a lump in my throat. With lower back pain, for which I used to seek regular chiropractic care, I now know from experience than that pain indicates I'm carrying a burden I'm not meant to carry. My stiff neck is from, you guessed it—stubbornness.

I may try to get away with my sin, as there are certain ones (I know it is goofy) that I take some kind of pleasure in and I won't want to repent. However, when my sin manifests in discomfort, then I can't wait to get before my Father and do a purging of my uncleanness.

I owe a debt of gratitude to Henry Wright for his book, *A More Excellent Way,* written from his deep understanding into the spiritual roots of our infirmities and calamities. My health has never been better than it is now, as many things from childhood troubled me. The glory goes to God who does what He said He would do.

From the beginning, starting with Eve, Satan has enticed people into his kingdom by daring man and woman to rebel against a command of God by saying, "Ye shall not surely die! Go ahead and do it, you'll actually be enlightened like me." And folks listen to him. Consider the directive of God concerning religious paraphernalia, pictures, ornaments, and statues in our homes and churches.

> In God's mind anyone who disobeys Him in this area of imagery and idolatry hates Him.

> Lest ye corrupt yourselves, and make you a graven image [a figure or statue cast, carved, or molten] the similitude [image, representation] of any figure [image, statue, idol], the likeness of male or female, The likeness of any beast [cattle, beast of burden, wild animal], that is on the earth, the likeness of any winged fowl [birds] that flieth in the air, The likeness of any thing that creepeth [reptiles, rodents] on the ground, the likeness of any fish that is in the waters beneath the earth: And lest thou lift up thine eyes unto heaven, and when thou seest the sun, and the moon, and the stars, even all the host of heaven, shouldest be driven to worship them [hold in idolatry and seek insight, bow down to], and serve them [place in bondage or servitude], which the LORD thy God hath divided [distributed] unto all nations under the whole heaven.
> —DEUTERONOMY 4:16–19

We may be innocent of servitude to any image now, but the Bible says not to have any lest you or anyone else in your house be driven or tempted to bow to them in the future. To serve them is to be placed in bondage to them; and guess which kingdom would want you to be in servitude and bondage to a lie?

What kingdom would want our kids to plaster the walls of their room with images of the plethora of American idols and images of creatures involved in the prohibited arts reflecting the "shadow of Egypt"?

Who is in heaven now? The Lord knowing what is best for you, commands you not to have any image, picture, statue, or form of any

> God has a reason for what He commands. Your initial time on earth is to prepare you for what God has for you forever onward.

heavenly body or any heavenly being displayed before you. Furthermore, we are prohibited from worshiping anything that could represent anything in the earth beneath; so that would rule out the images of the devil and his demons and other gods of folklore, religious tradition, or imagination.

> Thou shalt have no other gods before me. Thou shalt not make unto thee any graven image, or any likeness [representation, picture, form] of any thing that is in heaven above, or that is in the earth beneath [includes the earth surface and below including hell], or that is in the water under the earth: Thou shalt not bow down [treat as superior to yourself] thyself to them, nor serve them: for I the LORD thy God am a jealous [will not stand for any rival usurping His position] God, visiting [appointing or assigning] the iniquity of the fathers upon the children unto the third and fourth generation of them that hate me
>
> —EXODUS 20:3–5

Do you get the feeling as you read this last passage that God is very serious about this particular sin? In God's mind anyone who disobeys Him in this area of imagery and idolatry hates Him. The consequences of these sins affect not only us but our generations; as well as Satan is given the license he lusts for to bring your whole family into bondage and servitude to him.

Paul makes a point that men will produce images of heavenly beings, such as those cute little angels, that they have never seen and can only imagine in their fleshly mind. Their fleshly mind is carnal and cannot see the things of God. God doesn't want these images made in the first place, so He'd never inspire their creation.

> Let no man beguile you of your reward in a voluntary humility and worshiping of angels, intruding into those things which he hath not seen, vainly puffed up by his fleshly mind
>
> —COLOSSIANS 2:18

A judge must be impartial, otherwise he would be removed from his position. Would you be impartial in the future if you worshiped and adored an angel's imagined beauty now?

> Know ye not that we shall judge angels?
>
> —1 CORINTHIANS 6:3

I know this is hard especially for those whose generations are steeped in tradition and many of these items have been passed down to them. I guess the question is how have they been working for you so far; and based on what you have just seen in Scripture, how will they benefit you in the future? In the new covenant there isn't a single private or corporate religious symbol, image, or ornament of any description that is authorized for divine purposes.

God has a reason for what He commands. The purpose for your initial time on earth is to prepare you for what God has for you forever onward. The great difficulty would be that if you were beholding and in bondage to inept images of certain beings now, what would happen then when you were given your inheritance, which includes reigning over the real version of what you had the idol of? How can you be trusted to rule over something that you once worshiped?

> And the kingdom and dominion, and the greatness of the kingdom under the whole heaven, shall be given to the people of the saints of the most High, whose kingdom is an everlasting kingdom, and all dominions shall serve and obey him.
> —Daniel 7:27

These words that Daniel spoke—were they a new revelation? A new direction that God was considering for His people? No, not at all! In the very beginning God positioned man just under the Godhead, having charge over the fish, the foul, the animals, and every creeping thing with all the plants and trees for his consumption. But then men listened to the lie, and rather than rule over these creatures, they started to worship them even placing the creatures higher than themselves. Hence, in the Book of the Law, God commanded that men created in His image were not to worship the fish, the foul, the animal, or the creeping animals.

> Lest ye corrupt yourselves, and make you a graven image, the similitude of any figure, the likeness of male or female, The likeness of any beast that is on the earth, the likeness of any winged fowl that flieth in the air, The likeness of any thing that creepeth on the ground, the likeness of any fish that is in the waters beneath the earth: And lest thou lift up thine eyes unto heaven, and when thou seest the sun, and the moon, and the stars, even all the host of heaven, shouldest be driven to worship them, and serve them, which the Lord thy God hath divided unto all nations under the whole heaven.
> —Deuteronomy 4:16-19

Nothing but nothing material can represent God or His Son Jesus. God purposefully made sure we didn't know what He looked like knowing our tendency to need to look at something and then point at it and say that is our God.

God doesn't want us to have any images of Him, either. First of all Jesus said, "No man has seen God at any time"; that includes all the artists. Secondly, the prophet Isaiah said this of Jesus:

> For he shall grow up before him as a tender plant, and as a root out of a dry ground: he hath neither form [beautiful appearance and figure] nor comeliness [splendor and majesty]; and when we shall see him, there is no beauty [great looks] that we should desire him [have his body in idolatry].
> —ISAIAH 53:2

Jesus doesn't want to be a poster boy or be reduced to the rendering of an artist or sculptor. Nothing but nothing material can represent God or His Son Jesus. God purposefully made sure we didn't know what He looked like, knowing our tendency to need to look at something and then point at it and say that is our God. When we see Jesus we won't recognize Him from the pictures and forms that have proliferated the planet, as the Scripture says there is nothing beautiful or attractive or handsome about His tent.

We are made in God's image. The word *image* is as a shadow. A shadow isn't something material but it moves with Him as a spirit. Jesus said to the woman of Samaria that she worshiped something but wasn't quite sure what that was. Then Jesus clarifies and narrows it down for us that the only way to worship God is in spirit and in truth. If it is worshiping Him as graven image or through a picture, that would be in a dreamed-up physical form, so it would be in the flesh not in spirit. And since we don't know what God and His Son look like, the portrayal cannot be in truth.

> Ye worship ye know not what: we know what we worship: for salvation is of the Jews. But the hour cometh, and now is, when the true worshipers shall worship the Father in spirit and in truth: for the Father seeketh such to worship him. God is a Spirit: and they that worship him must worship him in spirit and in truth.
> —JOHN 4:22–24

Jesus is seated on the right hand of the Father in heaven now. Can I ask a difficult personal question? Is it worshiping Him in spirit and in truth if we are still seeing an image with Him upon the cross? The cross is the instrument of His death, but He is far beyond that now. The only symbol Jesus authorized us to commemorate His sacrifice was by communion with the bread and the wine in remembrance of Him.

Your destiny is so great that you cannot even perceive what it may be like, as we have no words or pictures of what to anticipate. Is it worth it for you to clean house and church? You do have to choose! You are created in the image of God and so be you!

> And hast made us unto our God kings and priests: and we shall reign on the earth.
> —REVELATION 5:10

Are you serious about removing anything that may be holding you back from the revived abundant life the Lord has in mind for you? What if God wanted you to be totally sold out to the truth and go through your house to consider your games, videos, books, magazines, ornaments, jewelry, pictures, and clothing and bring them to His light? Would you?

> But he that doeth truth cometh to the light, that his deeds may be made manifest, that they are wrought in God.
> —John 3:21

Satan does not like to be exposed especially in the area of lying and deceit and you need to be forewarned that you could be facing the wrath of Cain from religious zealots.

The kind of zeal God is calling for was modeled by the early church. They did not celebrate with a garage sale, they had a bonfire.

> And many that believed came, and confessed, and shewed their deeds. Many of them also which used [practiced, exercised], curious [taken up with trifles and superfluous activity] arts brought their books together, and burned them before all men: and they counted the price of them, and found it fifty thousand pieces of silver. So mightily grew the word of God and prevailed [shown by extraordinary power to overcome and wondrous deeds].
> —Acts 19:18–20

Did you note what the result was of these believers giving over their costly occultic wares? Revival came to town.

Often for revival God has to start a fresh work as it is difficult for old wineskins to hold new wine. Many dear saints pray for revival for years and don't see anything as revival is the result of action in purging our lives of everything that is unclean and repenting. For extra points I would suggest reading 2 Kings 23:1–25 regarding the revival of King Josiah.

What we are doing here is fighting a long battle for freedom from various types of bondage as we were born into captivity due to generational iniquity going back to Adam and Eve. Remember this; where the battle is intense the victory will be great.

> For the time is come that judgment must begin at the house of God: and if it first begin at us, what shall the end be of them that obey not the gospel of God? And if the righteous scarcely [with difficulty] be saved, where shall the ungodly [destitute of reverential fear of God] and the sinner appear?
> —Peter 4:17

From the very beginning of the church age, believers had to make a stand, they had to be bold and unusually courageous in face of the opposition and scorn the devil would throw at them, usually using the lips of the ones they loved the most. You will have to stand on your own, and the Lord will receive you as a son and daughter.

Satan does not like to be exposed especially in the area of lying and deceit and you need to be forewarned that you could be facing the wrath of Cain from religious zealots.

> Be ye not unequally yoked together with unbelievers: for what fellowship hath righteousness with unrighteousness? and what communion hath light with darkness? And what concord hath Christ with Belial? or what part hath he that believeth with an infidel? And what agreement hath the temple of God with idols? for ye are the temple of the living God; as God hath said, I will dwell in them, and walk in them; and I will be their God, and they shall be my people. Wherefore come out from among them, and be ye separate, saith the Lord, and touch not the unclean thing; and I will receive you, And will be a Father unto you, and ye shall be my sons and daughters, saith the Lord Almighty.
> —2 CORINTHIANS 6:14–18

The world offers a temporary peace similar to the calm before a catastrophic storm; but then after the calm comes the storm of judgment and separation for eternity. This false peace is from ignorance, and ignorance, as the saying should go, is not bliss. If you are living in rebellion with open or hidden sin and you feel at peace with it, your peace is a sedative from the devil who only wants you to be distracted in the pleasure of sin until the race is over. When it is too late for repentance, who will be your comforter?

> Peace I leave with you, my peace I give unto you: not as the world giveth, give I unto you. Let not your heart be troubled, neither let it be afraid.
> —JOHN 14:27

There are two shadows for us to walk in; the shadow of Egypt or the shadow of your Father. Satan's ministers seek to cover you in the shadow of Egypt, selling peace and prosperity when there is no peace and no prosperity. These ministers know no shame in their deception. They could be the professors, the teachers, the doctors, the priests, the presidents, the psychologists, the pastors, the personalities, the parents, the friends, the authors, the movie producers, the song writers, the artists, the counselors, the entertainers, the merchants, or even the miracle workers. They will teach peace and prosperity, but what is lacking are recognition, repentance, and restoration through the only One that paid the price to destroy the works of the devil.

> For from the least of them even unto the greatest of them every one is given to covetousness; and from the prophet even unto the priest every one dealeth falsely. They have healed also the hurt of the daughter of my people slightly, saying, Peace, peace; when there is no peace. Were they ashamed when they had committed abomination? nay, they were not at all ashamed, neither could they blush.
> —JEREMIAH 6:13–15

Conformity to the world through occultism

The occult is often a very subtle deception that offers an enticement or a shortcut to God's plan to facilitate Satan's desire to superimpose his kingdom over top of the kingdom of God. Deception is not obvious, that's why it is deceptive.

Methods of Discernment:

1. Who was the founder of this modality?
2. What was their spirituality?
3. What culture did it come out of?
4. What were their beliefs?
5. Who is their God or gods?

If in doubt or unable to answer any of the above questions, err on the side of wisdom and caution until you know that you know that you know that it aligns up with Scripture and you've tested the spirits to determine their origin.

Wherever this new modality doesn't line up with the Word, you'll receive a line of reason: "Never mind all that. You are a Christian and that alone sanctifies it. After all, isn't the curse broken?" You cannot change or separate the practice from the spirituality. A Christian practitioner of an occultic modality does not change the modality to a Christian one. For instance, having a Christian play with an Ouija Board does not change it into a righteous game.

Conformity workout

Step 1: Prayerfully review the following list and mark each sin you or your generations have participated with.

This list is by no means exhaustive, but hopefully as you go through it you'll be reminded by the Spirit of God of that other uncleanness that also must go. I'll caution each reader that this section can be very difficult for many. If you see something you like or make a living from listed here, a diversion of anger, accusation, and condemnation will manifest toward the messenger. It is important that you are not rushed and that you are in a private place as you go through this. (For further study on the items in the following list, please visit our website: www.sanctiprize.com.)

❑ Acupressure

    ❑ Myotherapy   ❑ Orgonomy
    ❑ Reflexology   ❑ Rolfing
    ❑ Zone Therapy

❑ Acupuncture   ❑ Aliens, ETs, and UFOs
                              (extraterrestrials)

❑ Angels   ❑ Animal worship
❑ Apparitions   ❑ Applied Kinesiology
❑ Ascended masters   ❑ Astral projection

- ❑ Astrology
- ❑ Automatic writing or journaling
- ❑ Biofeedback
- ❑ Black magic
- ❑ Chanting
- ❑ Clairaudience
- ❑ Colorology
- ❑ A Course in Miracles, by professor Helen Schucman
- ❑ Crystals/New Age
- ❑ Cursing/guttural swearing

- ❑ Déjà vu

- ❑ Dream work, Jungian, or Senoi Dream Theory
- ❑ Dungeons and Dragons/role-playing games
- ❑ Emiagrams
- ❑ False prophets
- ❑ Feminism/goddess worship/ Wicca (female witch)
- ❑ Fetishes
- ❑ Fire walking

- ❑ Halloween

  - ❑ trick or treat
  - ❑ costumes

- ❑ Aura reading
- ❑ Baha'ism
- ❑ Birthstones
- ❑ Bloody Mary (game)
- ❑ Charms
- ❑ Clairvoyance
- ❑ Conjuration
- ❑ Crystal ball/eight ball (crystallomancy)
- ❑ Pagan ceremonies
- ❑ Death or dying movement (see also Elizabeth Kublar-Ross, *Tibetan Book of the Dead*, and *Into the Light*)
- ❑ Divination (see Deuteronomy 28:10–12.)
- ❑ Drug trips/recreational drugs
- ❑ Eckankar
- ❑ ESP
- ❑ Familiar spirit (see Leviticus 20:6)
- ❑ Feng shui
- ❑ Financial bondage
- ❑ Geomancy
- ❑ Ghosts/spirits/haunted houses

  - ❑ Jack O' Lantern
  - ❑ black cat

When thou art come into the land which the LORD thy God giveth thee, thou shalt not learn to do after the abominations of those nations. There shall not be found among you any one that maketh his son or his daughter to pass through the fire, or that useth divination, or an observer of times, or an enchanter, or a witch. Or a charmer, or a consulter with familiar spirits, or a wizard, or a necromancer.

—DEUTERONOMY 18:9–11

- ❑ Healing visualization
- ❑ Homeopathy
- ❑ Idolatry/idol worship
- ❑ Heavy metal
- ❑ Hypnotism

Thou shalt not make unto thee any graven image, or any likeness of any thing that is in heaven above, or that is in the earth beneath, or that is in the water under the earth. Thou shalt not bow down thyself to them, nor serve them: for I the Lord thy God am a jealous God, visiting the iniquity of the fathers upon the children unto the third and fourth generation of them that hate me.

—Exodus 20:4–5

- ❑ Incense
- ❑ Iridology
- ❑ Jungian Psychology
- ❑ Labyrinths/maze
- ❑ Magic (white/black/stage)
- ❑ Mediums
- ❑ Mind Dynamics
- ❑ Moxibustion (vital energy/KI)
- ❑ Nature worshipers (see Ezekiel 8:16)
- ❑ New Age
- ❑ Occult (see Acts 19:19)
  - ❑ Occultic books
  - ❑ Occultic music
  - ❑ Ouija board
  - ❑ Parapsychology
  - ❑ Pilates
  - ❑ Prosperity movement
  - ❑ Rebirthing (prana yoga)
  - ❑ Rosicrucianism
  - ❑ Sacred geometry/space
  - ❑ Science fiction
  - ❑ Secret brotherhoods/sisterhoods/fraternities/sororities/blood oaths
  - ❑ Self-realization
  - ❑ Silva Mind Control/Mind Dynamics
  - ❑ Stonehenge

- ❑ The Inner Peace Movement
- ❑ Jewelry/talismans/peace sign/yin and yang
- ❑ KKK/white power movements
- ❑ "Light as a feather" game
- ❑ Martial arts
- ❑ Metaphysics
- ❑ Movies
- ❑ Mythology (use the supernatural to interpret natural events)
- ❑ Necromancy (see 1 Chronicles 10:13; 1 Samuel 28; Deuteronomy 18:11, 28:10; Isaiah 8:19)
- ❑ NLP (Neuro-linguistic programming)
- ❑ Numerology
- ❑ Occultic characters (elves/genies/fairies/cherubs/leprechauns/Mother Earth/Gaia)
- ❑ Occultic themes/statues
- ❑ Palm reading
- ❑ Personality profiling
- ❑ Poltergeist
- ❑ Psychic reading/portraits
- ❑ Reincarnation
- ❑ Rune stones
- ❑ Satanism
- ❑ Séances
- ❑ Self-motivation
- ❑ Shamanism
- ❑ Sorcery/pharmakeia
- ❑ Strange fire

> Now the Spirit speaketh expressly, that in the latter times some shall depart
> from the faith, giving heed to seducing spirits, and doctrines of devils
>
> —1 TIMOTHY 4:1

(See Leviticus 10:1, 20:6; Exodus 30:9; Deuteronomy 4:2, 13:1–4, 17:3; Jeremiah 5:31, 32:35, 44:19, 51:38–40; Isaiah 8:16–20; Matthew 16:4, 24:5; Acts 19:13; 1 Corinthians 14:15, 32; Titus 2:1; 1 Thessalonians 5:19–22; 2 Thessalonians 2:9–10; 1 Timothy 4:1; 2 Timothy 3:12–4:4.) You can't go wrong or be judged by God by sticking stubbornly close to the Word.

- ❑ **Superstition**
- ❑ **Taoism**
- ❑ **Telekinesis**
- ❑ **Therapeutic Touch**
- ❑ **Transcendental Meditation**
- ❑ **Urantia**
- ❑ **Voodoo/Vodun**
- ❑ **Water witching/divining**
- ❑ **Yin and Yang**
- ❑ **Tea leaf reading**
- ❑ **Theosophy**
- ❑ **Third Eye**
- ❑ **Unification Church/Moonies**
- ❑ **Vampirism/role-playing/Gothic/ Goth**
- ❑ **Warlocks**
- ❑ **Witchcraft divination (see Deuteronomy 18:10–12)**
- ❑ **Yoga**

This is only a partial list. This principality morphs into a new form as soon as the light is shed on the existing spiritual/healing modality. Ask the Lord to show you what additional conformity or bondage He wants you to be released from.

Step 2: Ask and wait.

> *Lord, is there any other sin that I have been unable to lay down on my own that You want me to deal with?* _____

Step 3: Go back through the list and pray this prayer inserting the sin in the blank space. You may insert several sins in the blank space at a time if you desire.

Prayer of Repentance
(Preferably out loud)

> *Father God, I recognize and take responsibility for myself and my ancestors for the sin(s) of* _____. *I agree with Your verdict on my rebellion. I repent, I renounce, and I ask forgiveness for my participation with these sins, and I ask that their curse be broken in the name of Jesus Christ of Nazareth.*

Step 4: Bind the strongman. This is best done by an experienced and trusted ministering friend the first time around.

Prayer to Bind the Strongman
(Out loud)

> *In the name of Jesus Christ of Nazareth and by the power of the Holy Spirit, I take authority over the strongmen of conformity and the occult. I break your*

power, I bind you, and I put you on notice that I am destroying your armor in which you trust. I will be coming back to remove you from your palace.

Step 5: Purging the evil. Review the above list again now inserting the sin you have repented of in the blank.

Command of Deliverance
(Must be out loud with eyes open,
realizing you are speaking directly to a spirit)

In the name of Jesus Christ of Nazareth and by the power of the Holy Spirit, I take authority over the spirit(s) of _____. I break your power, I cast you out, and I command you to return no more.

Step 6: Purge the strongman now that you have destroyed his stronghold.

Command of Deliverance
(Must be out loud with eyes open,
realizing you are speaking directly to a spirit)

In the name of Jesus Christ of Nazareth and by the power of the Holy Spirit, I take authority over the strongmen of conformity and the occult. I break your power, I cast you out, and I command you to take all residues of evil spirits with you. I command you to return no more.

Step 7: Pray that God will cause you to increase and abound in His love and that you would be an overcomer in the sins just repented of. Ask for a scripture that you will use to resist the devil when he tries to open the trapdoor again to regain entrance to your heart.

2. Exposing the devil's lies about you

The second stage of Satan's lies is to lie about you. The lie may be about how God made you, why He made you, that He made you worthless, that you are unclean and shameful, that you can't be forgiven, that it is all your fault, that you have a little flaw, that you were a mistake, that the world would be better off without you, that you aren't lovable; or maybe he tells you that God hears everybody else but not you. He may open the door to abuse you by an accusation resembling a personal assault by amplifying a flaw or a judgment placed in your mind. Once your mind runs with such an accusation, you'll start to believe it and then you open the second door to accept his condemnation. Once we've bought into the condemnation of the devil, the third door opens to separation from God due to our shame, fear, or guilt.

> How can Satan mess with you if you are dead to all his stuff and are not moved at all; you just stand there and shrug your shoulders?

Those three steps are laid out by Paul in Romans. Paul offers the antidote for each step of Satan's lies for you to quote back to the lies.

1. Respond to the lying spirit of accusation by reminding Satan that you are the elect of God and you are justified in Christ.

2. Respond to the lying spirit of condemnation by declaring to Satan that Jesus died for you and most definitely He rose again and is seated by the Father in heaven interceding on your behalf.

3. Respond to the lying spirit that would separate you from the agape of God by claiming your absolute victory over all tribulation, all distress, all persecution, all famines, all nakedness, all peril, and the destruction, as you've died to yourself and are fully alive in Jesus Christ.

> [1] Who shall lay any thing to the charge [to bring a judgment, personal assault, complaint or any other accusation against] of God's elect? It is God that justifieth. [2] Who is he that condemneth [pronounce sentence]? It is Christ that died, yea rather, that is risen again, who is even at the right hand of God, who also maketh intercession for us. [3] Who shall separate us from the love [*agape*] of Christ? shall tribulation [pressure, affliction, oppression, burden], or distress [extreme anguish and worry], or persecution, or famine [scarcity of provisions], or nakedness [lack of clothing], or peril [danger], or sword [as instrument of judgment]? As it is written [in Psalm 44], For thy sake we are killed [to die to self regarding something] all the day long; we are accounted [as factual] as sheep for the slaughter [unconscious of what lies ahead next]. Nay [nevertheless], in all these things we are more than conquerors [surpassing victory, no contest], through him that loved [*agapao*] us.
>
> —ROMANS 8:33–37

Paul figured out the most profoundly effective weapon against the devil's frequent attacks: to be in such a place that you really could not care less about all the heat. How can he mess with you if you are dead to all his stuff and are not moved at all; you just stand there and shrug your shoulders? It would be like someone thinking they hurt you by ripping you off of five dollars when you know you have nine million dollars in the vault at the bank. That is how great your victory is in any contest you may face with the devil when the Lord is playing on your side. Knowing your victory prior to going into battle will make it impossible for you to lose your peace separating you from the love of God.

Your demeanor would be as playful as the carefree sheep in the corral having neither idea nor concern regarding their impending butchering. Paul isn't telling us we are all going to be butchered, he is referring to the peace the sheep has prior to impending calamity.

Moses was no different than most men in that he believed he did not measure up to the requirements of a task and therefore wanted to be passed by. He believed a lie about himself that he had a speaking problem and wasn't as gifted and eloquent as other men. He believed he was flawed and was ashamed. God reminded Moses that he did not make a mistake in forming Moses' mouth and speech and nor was He about to make a mistake in setting Moses up as leader of Israel. Still Moses didn't believe God's choosing but rather chose to believe the accusation or flaw that was planted in his mind by a lie. God was then angered at Moses because of whom he believed as opposed to God.

> And Moses said unto the LORD, O my LORD, I am not eloquent, neither heretofore, nor since thou hast spoken unto thy servant: but I am slow of speech [heavy and dull], and of a slow tongue. And the LORD said unto him, Who hath made man's mouth? or who maketh the dumb, or deaf, or the seeing, or the blind? have not I the LORD? Now therefore go, and I will be with thy mouth, and teach thee what thou shalt say. And he said, O my LORD, send, I pray thee, by the hand of him whom thou wilt send. And the anger of the LORD was kindled against Moses.
>
> —EXODUS 4:10–14

The Spirit of God wanted us to understand the truth about Moses in the New Testament Book of Acts. Moses was a gifted leader able to direct and influence through his communication and his actions, and that was very apparent through the forty years of his assignment. Satan would have wanted Moses to disqualify himself by believing the lie he cleverly implanted in Moses' mind, and what a lie it proved to be.

> The decoration on the outside does not make up for living a lie within one's spirit. God doesn't applaud or even notice how good you look today unless it is of an inner radiance.

> And Moses was learned in all the wisdom of the Egyptians, and was mighty [powerful and influential] in words and in deeds.
>
> —ACTS 7:22

Jeremiah also contended with the Lord when he was called, stating that he couldn't speak eloquently either, and besides that he was too young and didn't have enough experience. The Lord said, "Vow not, I am a child," as he needed Jeremiah to understand that every word he would speak must not be flippant, belittling, or unconstructive. Furthermore, there is power in the words and thoughts of the heart, so we must not allow lies to be repeated, as it tells us in Proverbs 23:7: "For as he thinketh in his heart, so is he."

Then the Lord roots out another barrier, and that was fear. Fear, which manifests often as shyness or as introversion, must not be something we agree with, thus allowing it to become part of our identity.

> Before I formed thee in the belly I knew thee; and before thou camest forth out of the womb I sanctified thee, and I ordained thee a prophet unto the nations. Then said I, Ah, Lord GOD! behold, I cannot speak: for I am a child. But the LORD said unto me, Say not [avow], I am a child [youth]: for thou shalt go to all that I shall send thee, and whatsoever I command thee thou shalt speak. Be not afraid of their faces: for I am with thee to deliver thee, saith the LORD.
>
> —JEREMIAH 1:5–8

The psalmist understood how he was to think about how he was fashioned by his creator. He gave God glory for every part of his being and was at peace without any fear because he knew where he stood.

> For thou hast possessed my reins: thou hast covered me in my mother's womb. I will praise thee; for I am fearfully and wonderfully made: marvellous are thy works; and that my soul knoweth right well. My substance was not hid from thee, when I was made in secret, and curiously wrought in the lowest parts of the earth. Thine eyes did see my substance, yet being unperfect; and in thy book all my members were written, which in continuance were fashioned, when as yet there was none of them. How precious also are thy thoughts unto me, O God! how great is the sum of them! If I should count them, they are more in number than the sand: when I awake, I am still with thee.
>
> —Psalm 139:13–18

To put yourself down, to complain about your appearance, to hate your body, to despise the color of your skin, or envy the stature of another is to dispute and contradict the will of God in your design. Despise not the work of the potter, as that would be a sin unto you and your generations.

> O man, who art thou that repliest against [contradicts, disputes] God? Shall the thing formed say to him that formed it, Why hast thou made me thus [appointed or fashioned]? Hath not the potter power over the clay, of the same lump to make one vessel unto honour, and another unto dishonour?
>
> —Romans 9:20–21

The Lord gave Samuel a lesson on how to judge a man for the usefulness of God's service. Man tends to worship the temporary, the tent, while God only sees the heart of our matter.

> But the Lord said unto Samuel, Look not on his countenance [*mareh*; physical appearance], or on the height of his stature; because I have refused him: for the Lord seeth not as man seeth; for man looketh on the outward appearance [the temporary physical tent], but the Lord looketh on the heart [the spirit part of us that lasts for eternity].
>
> —1 Samuel 16:7

Tent makeovers are the unreal craze now in North America, where every part of the body is open for alterations, eliminations, or additions. With such an extreme interest in the human sensual body, it has become a real vexation of spirit to the believer. Our appearance is to be a reflection of what is inside our hearts. The decoration on the outside does not make up for living a lie within one's spirit. God doesn't applaud or even notice how good you look today unless it is of an inner radiance. That chaste inner radiance, gentleness, and humility are very rare. That would be of a character that is totally OK with how God made the tent and considers the sanctification of the spirit and soul one's daily offering unto the Lord.

> Whose adorning [decoration] let it not be that outward adorning of
> plaiting [elaborate gathering] the hair, and of wearing of gold, or of put-
> ting on of apparel; But let it be the hidden [secret] man of the heart, in
> that which is not corruptible [immortal], even the ornament of a meek
> and quiet spirit [not occupied with self], which is in the sight of God of
> great price [surpassing value due to rarity].
>
> —1 PETER 3:3–4

Meek does not mean *weak*; it is strength under submission. Our spirit is
quiet when it is at peace; peace in turn is the fruit of one who has learned to
"die to self."

The word translated as *countenance* in Psalms 43 describes a true makeover.
The health of our countenance is emanating from the face or spirit of God
from within. How can one have a nasty countenance if He is walking in agape
and in truth?

> Why art thou cast down [despairing], O my soul? and why art thou dis-
> quieted [murmuring, troubled] within me? hope in God: for I shall yet
> praise him, who is the health [deliverance, victory] of my countenance
> [*paniym*; the face of God from within], and my God.
>
> —PSALM 43:5

In the last section we spoke of how Satan lies in superimposing his kingdom
over that of God's. So, too, with us he has us put on a mask, a brave face
that says peace, peace, when inwardly things are numb, hurting, bewildering,
vanity, and fast-tracked to death. Our Maker is a master at original creation
but He also specializes in restoration.

The Book of Job describes a man in considerable pain that can't eat; his
body is thin and frail with a premature date with death and destruction waiting at the door. What Job knows is that this fellow is being reproved, but he doesn't know why; so an interpreter is sent from God to reconcile this man to wholeness. The special gift this interpreter had is now advanced in the church through the gift of discernment of spirits.

> Paul commended those who would hear the word then go and search and study the Scriptures to see if what he was saying was true.

> He is chastened [reproved, corrected] also with pain [physical or mental]
> upon his bed, and the multitude of his bones with strong pain [entire body
> in constant pain]: So that his life abhorreth bread, and his soul dainty
> meat. His flesh is consumed away, that it cannot be seen; and his bones
> that were not seen stick out. Yea, his soul draweth near unto the grave [pit
> of hell] and his life to the destroyers [to die prematurely by punishment or
> misconduct]. If there be a messenger [an ambassador] with him, an inter-
> preter, one among a thousand, to shew [to bring to light] unto man his
> uprightness [what is right and what is ought to be done]: Then he is gra-
> cious unto him, and saith, Deliver [set free] him from going down to the

pit: I have found a ransom [price of redemption]. His flesh shall be fresher [revived or restored] than a child's: he shall return [reverse] to the days of his youth [youthful vigor]: He shall pray unto God, and he will be favourable unto him: and he shall see his face with joy: for he will render [turn back, restore] unto man his righteousness.

—Job 33:19–26

The side effect of our Lord's healing through sanctification is that our flesh will receive a makeover and revitalization from the only One who can reverse aging. Did I just save you a bunch on reconstructive surgery? When I first began the process of cleansing my temple of all its defilement, I was constantly rubbing my cheeks and facial muscles, as they were hurting. Then it dawned on me that the pain was from the muscles that allow me to smile, I guess they hadn't been exercised for a long time and were droopy; and God was in the process of changing my countenance.

There are doctrines of men that bring a heresy, saying that the gifts that are required for the ambassador and interpreter to restore one taken captive by the devil are not for the church; thereby the sheep are left to scatter, with no hope and only able to pursue the stuff of the shadow of Egypt for healing. They deny the very Lord they profess to represent. They are liars and wolves in sheep's clothing. Many will point to the extremes of "charismania" for their position and others will explain away the Word based on what is not happening in their following rather than ask God what would it take for us to be an "Acts of God" church. In the last chapter we'll explore the power and the glory of God in greater detail.

> Agape love will care for the body and always do what is best for it and not place it purposefully in harm's way or expose it to uncleanness.

> But there were false prophets also among the people, even as there shall be false teachers among you, who privily shall bring in damnable heresies [result in eternal misery in hell], even denying the Lord that bought them, and bring upon themselves swift destruction.
>
> —2 Peter 2:1

Paul commended those who would hear the word then go and search and study the scriptures to see if what he was saying was true. The scriptures are final authority and they confirm or deny that the minister represents the heart of the Father. Resulting from truth the body of believers grew on a solid foundation.

> And the brethren immediately sent away Paul and Silas by night unto Berea: who coming thither went into the synagogue of the Jews. These were more noble than those in Thessalonica, in that they received the word with all readiness of mind, and searched the scriptures daily, whether those things were so. Therefore many of them believed.
>
> —Acts 17:10–12

The lies we believe make us hostile to the word of God in our minds. Indeed, some of the most hostile folks are those that profess godliness but hold doctrines that deny the power of God and ignorantly recommend people to the power of Satan through the "Shadow of Egypt" deception.

> And, having made peace through the blood of his cross, by him to reconcile all things unto himself; by him, I say, whether they be things in earth, or things in heaven. And you, that were sometime alienated [separated from God] and enemies [hostile to doctrine of God as seen by their sin] in your mind [faculty of understanding] by wicked [work of the evil one himself] works, yet now hath he reconciled In the body of his flesh through death, to present you holy and unblameable and unreproveable in his sight.
>
> —Colossians 1:20–22

You were chosen before the foundation of the world that you would be holy and without blame before Him in love and that is the truest thing about you. Do you believe? Agape love will care for the body and always do what is best for it and not place it purposefully in harm's way or expose it to uncleanness.

Are you unblameable and unreproveable in your love for yourself? Do you see the reflection of the face of God through your countenance or are you preoccupied with the reflection of your tent in the mirror? To love yourself in truth is by agape, which is a love at the spirit level. Eros love is the one that gets turned on or off at the flesh level when in front of the mirror. Paul teaches that a man who agapes his wife will agape himself and it has to be that way because they are one flesh. Contrariwise, if a man does not agape himself he is not capable of "agape loving" his wife. This special love one has for oneself is not festering in pride, as pride is Satan's perverted brand of self-love.

> So ought men to love [*agapao*] their wives as their own bodies. He that loveth [*agapao*] his wife loveth [*agapao*] himself. For no man ever yet hated his own flesh; but nourisheth and cherisheth it, even as the Lord the church...Nevertheless let every one of you in particular so love [*agapao*] his wife even as himself; and the wife see that she reverence her husband.
>
> —Ephesians 5:28–33

The test for your agape walk is your unconditional love for others even when they are unloving in return. God agapes us when we are yet in sin and rebellion. Having this kind of love does not guarantee it will be reciprocated. Even with the perfection and the intensity of God's love; does everyone respond in kind back to God? Jesus had agape love towards Judas and yet Judas betrayed him. As you are increasing in the agape of God, you may be tested in a way you never thought possible, as your life is refined in the fire as was Jesus. I say this so we don't believe the lie that we are unlovable when we are rejected.

The command is to agape our neighbor just as we are to agape ourselves. Knowing the type of love you are to have for yourself, have you believed and repeated a lie about yourself? Is God preparing your heart for you to be reconciled to the purity of agape towards yourself?

> For all the law is fulfilled in one word, even in this; Thou shalt love [*agapao*] thy neighbour as thyself.
> —GALATIANS 5:14

Do you know who is pouring out their heart to the Father in the following prayer?

> And hide not thy face from thy servant; for I am in trouble: hear me speedily. Draw nigh unto my soul, and redeem it: deliver me because of mine enemies. Thou hast known my reproach, and my shame, and my dishonour: mine adversaries are all before thee. Reproach hath broken my heart; and I am full of heaviness: and I looked for some to take pity, but there was none; and for comforters, but I found none.
> —PSALM 69:17–20

The author of this prayer was our Lord Jesus. He knows the pain of what rejection and abandonment feels like, so He is qualified to be your comforter and very help in your greatest time of need. He is also practiced up to teach us by example of what agape is capable of.

I appreciate the honesty of the apostle Paul in describing his struggle as a believer with indwelling sin. He describes a sin being that has a mind of its own that would manifest through him contrariwise to his own conviction and discipline. Paul determined in his mind not to do certain things he hated, but yet he found himself, to his dismay, doing them anyway. Then he said it wasn't him doing it but the sin that resided within his spirit. He was able to separate himself from sin but still take responsibility for it. This is how we can struggle with sin but still agape ourselves while we are seeking deliverance. If Paul believed this sin was who he was, he would not be seeking to purge himself from his sin through Jesus Christ.

> For that which I do I allow not: for what I would, that do I not; but what I hate, that do I. If then I do that which I would not, I consent unto the law that it is good. Now then it is no more I that do it, but sin that dwelleth in me. For I know that in me (that is, in my flesh) dwelleth no good thing: for to will is present with me; but how to perform that which is good I find not.... For I delight in the law of God after the inward man: But I see another law in my members, warring against the law of my mind, and bringing me into captivity to the law of sin which is in my members. O wretched man that I am! who shall deliver me from the body of this death? I thank God through Jesus Christ our Lord. So then with the mind I myself serve the law of God; but with the flesh the law of sin.
> —ROMANS 7:15–18, 22–25

This is a key point—if you do not accept yourself unconditionally, you cannot defeat any of the "self" spirits because they are there to reinforce themselves and explain to you why you are failing.

Workout of rejection

Step 1: Prayerfully review the following list and mark each sin you or your generations have participated with. It is important that you are not rushed and that you are in a private place as you go through this.

☐ **Attention getting:** thirsts for attention through jesting, sulking, bravado or bullying.

☐ **Competition:** tells you that you are not a whole person unless you win.

☐ **Division (See 1 Corinthians 12:2.):** Will not allow you to flow with other people

☐ **Excessive talking:** deeply rooted in insecurity, which is fear

☐ **Fabricated personality:** What you have created for yourself to hide insecurity and to hide the unloving spirit.

☐ **False piety:** doing religion to be seen of men. All acts of love seem to be over-done

☐ **Fear**

☐ **Guilt:** form of condemnation regarding excessive, self-indulgent or unfounded introspection

☐ **Insecurity**

☐ **Isolation:** can't stand to be around people. Will tend to idolize animals

☐ **Lack of confidence**

☐ **Need for approval:** If they can see the changed person I am then they will love me. If they were spiritual they would never have distanced themselves in the first place. You have to accept yourself as God accepts you.

☐ **Perfectionism:** Not permitting yourself to be anything less than what you perceive to be perfect; is rooted in insecurity.

☐ **Programming:** Automatic performance or response without thought or consideration of the consequences

☐ **Self-abasement:** Belittling or degrading yourself. Your thinking of yourself must line up with the thoughts your heavenly Father has towards you.

☐ **Self-anger or wrath:** Triggered by self-accusation, self-condemnation and perfectionism; will make someone else the victim also, not just you.

☐ **Self-annihilation:** Lost union with God; eliminating your worth

☐ **Self-assertion:** removes God and insists on your own rights no matter who you trample on

☐ **Self-bitterness:** hate yourself

☐ **Self-comparison:** Makes the person you are comparing yourself to a god – that is idolatry. This happens in business networking where we hang around with successful people. Why do you feel inferior to those of a particular arena? If you are not careful you will end up as an extension of that person, not God's image.

☐ **Self-condemnation:** To choose hell

❏ **Self-consciousness:** lack of self-approval. Element of fear of man and fear failure.

❏ **Self-deception:** MCI people are positive they have no fear but when you ask them to tell you about their mother they respond with, "I hate Her, I'm afraid she'll put me down." Or take lust and love, which have different spirits behind them. Lust always takes, where love never does.

❏ **Self-doubt:** Tied to fear and lack of conviction.

❏ **Self-exaltation:** used to tempt Eve, " You shall be as gods!" But he didn't say the "gods" were actually demons. Demons know good and evil.

❏ **Self-hatred:** autoimmune disease where body attacks itself. It responds to feelings.

❏ **Self-idolatry:** Self-worship or extreme admiration of self

❏ **Selfishness or self-centeredness:** revolves around self-preservation, always wants to be served

❏ **Self-murder:** suicide or words spoken about oneself such as, "I'd be better off dead."

❏ **Self-mutilation:** one of the fastest growing realities among teens; from piercing, to scaring, to tattoos, to bulimia, to anorexia, to sado masochism, to fetishes

❏ **Self-pity:** Massive amounts of psychogenic pain. Psycho means soul. No organic reason for pain in spine, muscles, ligaments and tendons. (i.e. fibromyalgia). Gives reasons why you can't be healed; amplifies every thought; unable to even imagine reaching beyond oneself to freely reach out to others with no regard for self; promotes kingdom of self.

❏ **Self-pride:** Self-enthronement. You are enshrined in yourself and all you think about is your reality – what is going on in your life.

❏ **Self-questioning:** second-guess yourself so much you never accomplish anything

❏ **Self-rejection:** Produces the deepest pain known to man

❏ **Self-resentment:** bitter indignation towards yourself

❏ **Self-retaliation:** Includes over eating and mutilation. This is the spirit that causes women to seek after an abusive relationship. She'll go eye to eye with the one who will reject her.

❏ **Self-righteousness:** living by own set of rules as Cain

❏ **Self-sabotage:** fruit of rejection. You need love and someone comes along to love you and you push them away.

❏ **Self-torment:** this is a fear. If you have ever been a victim of anybody with an unloving spirit, there has been an immediate transference of those spirits into you, like it or not. Everything you've been exposed to is capable of influencing you and becoming part of you.

❏ **Self-unbelief:** Tied to fear and you don't see yourself the way the Word talks about you

❏ **Self-unforgiveness:** keeping a record of wrongs against yourself and not letting go

❏ **Self-violence:** such as slam dancing to get an adrenaline rush

- ❑ **Suppression:** is a form of bondage. I don't want to think about it or talk about it
- ❑ **Unloving spirit:** (Strongman) produces the deepest breaking of the human heart.
- ❑ **Victimization:** Glorifies and indulges in being a victim

This is a partial list. Ask the Lord to show you what additional bondage He wants you to be released from.

Step 2: Ask and wait.

Lord, is there any other sin that I have been unable to lay down on my own that You want me to deal with? _____

Step 3: Go back through the list and pray this prayer inserting the sin in the blank space. You may insert several sins in the blank space at a time if you desire.

Prayer of Repentance
(Preferably out loud)

Father God, I recognize and take responsibility for myself and my ancestors for the sin(s) of _____. *I agree with Your verdict on my rebellion. I repent, I renounce, and I ask forgiveness for my participation with these sins, and I ask that their curse be broken in the name of Jesus Christ of Nazareth.*

Step 4: Purging the evil. This is best done by an experienced and trusted ministering friend the first time around. Review the above list again now inserting the sin you have repented of in the blank.

Command of Deliverance
(Must be out loud with eyes open,
realizing you are speaking directly to a spirit)

In the name of Jesus Christ of Nazareth and by the power of the Holy Spirit, I take authority over the spirit(s) of _____. *I break your power, I cast you out, and I command you to return no more.*

Step 5: Pray that God will cause you to increase and abound in His love and that you would be an overcomer in the sins just repented of. Ask for a scripture that you will use to resist the devil when he tries to open the trapdoor again to regain entrance to your heart.

3. Exposing the devil's lies to you about others

Jesus had a group of men drag a woman they say they caught committing adultery to Him so that He would condemn her to death. Jesus—man He's cool—knelt down and wrote some notes in the ground so that this gal's smart accusers could read them. These notes penetrated the hearts of each accuser and they left swiftly with their cloaks in a knot. Perhaps he reminded each of these men of their own shortcomings that would earn them the same sentence. Such is the way with accusation.

> When Jesus had lifted up himself, and saw none but the woman, he said unto her, Woman, where are those thine accusers [an oppressor on assignment from Satan]? hath no man condemned thee? She said, No man, Lord. And Jesus said unto her, Neither do I condemn thee: go, and sin no more.
> —JOHN 8:10–11

People act as though Jesus would commend them for bringing a bad guy they busted to His attention so they can clean up the streets. That is where we don't understand Jesus, as He came to heal, to save, and to make the crooked walk straight. If repentance is required, He does convict through His gentleness. Satan keeps himself very busy enticing a person to sin and then comes around to shamelessly expose them. Satan is the author of all accusation. An accusation may have an element of truth, but it is still a lie.

> And I heard a loud voice saying in heaven, Now is come salvation, and strength, and the kingdom of our God, and the power of his Christ: for the accuser of our brethren is cast down, which accused them before our God day and night.
> —REVELATION 12:10

Satan knows he can only use certain people to accuse another person. Do you know who that might be? The only people he can channel his condemning message through are those who are chargeable of the exact thing of which they are going to accuse another. Paul knows this principal is so accurate that he is able to state that in whatever I judge a brother or sister of, I expose myself identifying my own sin as the same.

> Satan keeps himself very busy enticing a person to sin and then comes around to shamelessly expose them.

> Therefore thou art inexcusable, O man, whosoever thou art that judgest: for wherein thou judgest another, thou condemnest thyself; for thou that judgest doest the same things.
> —ROMANS 2:1

There is no good thing that can come out of accusation. It is the primary weapon used by Satan to separate friends who take offense to the accusation and then get into a tiff; and Satan walks away because we didn't recognize his skills as a ventriloquist using our friend as the dummy. Hopefully I can now catch myself before I agree to accuse another and say, "Uuh huh! Since I was just provoked to say that stuff that means I have the same nasty critter inside of me; and he just exposed himself so I can catch him in his own trap and purge it from within me." Isn't that fun?

I would go so far as to say that I notice in myself that even when I am angry in my heart against another for something they allegedly did, I am guilty of the same thing that I am angry at them over. It is so predictable in me that I can use the object of my anger to discern, or detect, an unclean thing in me, I repent of that issue in my own life and guess what? I am no longer angry at the other person for whatever they did. This is a great way to beat an anger problem, better than any pill and cheaper than therapy.

Sometimes a person we love may do some-thing that seems so awful and out of character for them and it causes a lot of damage and pain. Such a thing happened to Joseph when his brothers, because of jealousy, sold him into slavery in Egypt to get rid of him. Read what Joseph said when God brought those treacherous brothers before him a few years later:

> I would go so far as to say that I notice in myself that even when I am angry in my heart against another for something they allegedly did I am guilty of the same thing I am angry at them over.

And Joseph said unto his brethren, Come near to me, I pray you. And they came near. And he said, I am Joseph your brother, whom ye sold into Egypt. Now therefore be not grieved, nor angry with yourselves, that ye sold me hither: for God did send me before you to preserve life. For these two years hath the famine been in the land: and yet there are five years, in the which there shall neither be earing nor harvest. And God sent me before you to preserve you a posterity in the earth, and to save your lives by a great deliverance. So now it was not you that sent me hither, but God: and he hath made me a father to Pharaoh, and lord of all his house, and a ruler throughout all the land of Egypt....But as for you, ye thought evil against me; but God meant it unto good, to bring to pass, as it is this day, to save much people alive.
> —GENESIS 45:4–8; 50:20

The devil's deeds are often used by God to accomplish the most important and ambitious undertakings in the world. Was Judas' plot to betray Jesus directly out of the pit of evil? Yes. But what was the result? As Joseph preserved his own people, Jesus also preserved His own people; just the numbers were different.

> And supper being ended, the devil having now put into the heart of Judas Iscariot, Simon's son, to betray him.
> —JOHN 13:2

What can often seem like an awful thing that wrecks everything may actually be the very thing that God uses to accomplish His plan. When the unpredictable happens between husband and wife, between friends, between ministry associates, or between those engaged in business or work together, don't be too surprised if a mountain isn't being adjusted lower to allow the will of God to be done on earth. So rather than take the offense against the one who seemed to cause the big upset, find out what you have not been understanding. That is why Paul can say:

> And we know that all things work together for good to them that love
> God, to them who are the called according to his purpose.
> —ROMANS 8:28

Not all things are good in and of themselves, but the end result is. Balaam wanted to make some money, so he intended to use his position as prophet to curse the nation of Israel. A bad thing? Yes. But God turned the curse into a blessing instead. That's our God!

> Because they met not the children of Israel with bread and with water, but hired Balaam against them, that he should curse them: howbeit our God turned the curse into a blessing.
> —NEHEMIAH 13:2

What constitutes an offense or stumbling block is not from your perspective but from the viewpoint of the one you agape.

I find the following one of the most sobering events in the Bible. It was a judgment of death resulting from a man and wife telling a lie in the early church. The lie was unnecessary but only self-serving in making the couple appear more generous than they were. This passage gives a clear teaching on how sin takes hold in a believer. We know they were believers because they were in the church; and only a believer can lie to the Holy Spirit, as a nonbeliever doesn't have the kind of relationship to do so at this level. Firstly, Satan seeded the thought in their spirit to lie. Secondly, the couple thought they were just telling the lie to men but they weren't they were actually lying directly to the Father and the Holy Spirit. Thirdly, the couple was held responsible for participating with the sin, even though someone other being, Satan, clearly prompted them do it.

> But a certain man named Ananias, with Sapphira his wife, sold a possession, And kept back part of the price, his wife also being privy to it, and brought a certain part, and laid it at the apostles' feet. But Peter said, Ananias, why hath Satan filled thine heart to lie to the Holy Ghost, and to keep back part of the price of the land? Whiles it remained, was it not thine own? and after it was sold, was it not in thine own power? why hast thou conceived this thing in thine heart? thou hast not lied unto men, but unto God....Then Peter said unto her, How is it that ye have agreed together to tempt the Spirit of the Lord? behold, the feet of them which have buried thy husband are at the door, and shall carry thee out. Then fell she down straightway at his feet, and yielded up the ghost: and the young men came in, and found her dead, and, carrying her forth, buried her by her husband. And great fear came upon all the church, and upon as many as heard these things.
> —ACTS 5:1–4, 8–11

God is still a God of judgment, make no mistake; and only by grace is He not pronouncing immediate judgment of sin against the believer but is giving us a measure of time to get it corrected through sanctification. The church as it is could not stand to that level of holiness and have any saints remain. We are still accountable; we are just given grace or the space to do first works according to repentance.

Paul checked his heart daily to see if there was anything between him and God and between himself and others. There are secret faults that can really hurt someone, crushing their soft hearts causing offense. Paul strived to correct those sorts of things, not explain them away. A perfect conscience void of offense is what allowed Paul to do so many things for God.

> And herein do I exercise [take pains or strive] myself, to have always a conscience void of offense toward God [blameless and holy], and toward men.
> —ACTS 24:16

What constitutes an offense or stumbling block is not from your perspective but from the viewpoint of the one you agape. The offense is as experienced from the eye of the beholder. Paul would say it doesn't matter what you intended, just do what needs to be done, suck it up, and set your brother or sister free from what is trying to take them captive.

> Let us not therefore judge one another any more: but judge this rather, that no man put a stumblingblock or an occasion to fall in his brother's way.
> —ROMANS 14:13

Workout of accusation

Step 1: Prayerfully review the following list and mark each sin you or your generations have participated with. It is important that you are not rushed and that you are in a private place as you go through this.

- ❏ **Accusation:** towards God/self/others; to charge with a fault; to blame
- ❏ **Bitterness**
- ❏ **Comparing myself to others:** feelings that you don't measure up or elevating yourself above others
- ❏ **Competition:** striving against others to achieve dominance; rivalry to acquire attention, love, acceptance etc
- ❏ **Control:** the need to have everything done your way; not allowing anyone the freedom to make mistakes; bossy;
- ❏ **Deceit:** to lead another to act on one's false misrepresentation as though it were true; treachery
- ❏ **Destroyer:** if things seem to be falling to ruin or loss or separation around you—the destroyer may be at work
- ❏ **Division:** dissension; broken friendships; alienation; separation
- ❏ **Envy or Jealousy**

- ❑ **Fear:** a painful emotion or passion excited by the expectation of evil; to feel anxious or apprehensive about a real or imagined event; it is the opposite of faith
- ❑ **Guilt:** feelings of remorse or responsibility for real or imagined misdeeds or from sense of inadequacy
- ❑ **Isolation:** detached; often shy or lacking social skills; loneliness
- ❑ **Judging others:** to pronounce a verdict on someone's intent based on your perception of another's actions; tendency is to condemn another for what you do yourself
- ❑ **Lying**
- ❑ **Manipulation:** to cleverly or unscrupulously control or influence those around you
- ❑ **Misunderstanding:** wrong interpretations; assuming you know when you don't
- ❑ **Need for approval**
- ❑ **Offense:** insult, an occasion of stumbling or causing another to stumble
- ❑ **Perfectionism:** motivated by a belief that one is worthless in the eyes of others unless on can present oneself and one's work perfectly; no allowance for error;
- ❑ **Prefabricated personality:** changing your personality to adapt to different environments i.e. a tough guy at work, a teddy bear at church and a couch potato at home; you feel people will not accept you for who you really are.
- ❑ **Programming:** automatic reaction or performance to a stimulus
- ❑ **Racism:** superiority or inferiority; prejudice
- ❑ **Rebellion:** resisting authority, defiance or disobedience to leaders, parents and to God
- ❑ **Replay:** repeating a matter over and over in your head as if you could somehow change it, fix it or figure it out; reliving the pain every time you rehearse it
- ❑ **Scapegoat:** one made to bear the blame for the rest of the family problems
- ❑ **Self-pity:** the self-indulgent belief that your life is harder and sadder than everyone else's; dwelling on one's own sorrows or misfortunes
- ❑ **Shame:** a painful sensation excited by the consciousness of guilt: dishonoured; disgraced
- ❑ **Suspicion:** the imagination of the existence of something without proof;
- ❑ **Torment:** to be harassed or distressed in ones own mind
- ❑ **Unworthiness:** feelings of having no value

This is a partial list. Ask the Lord to show you what additional bondage He wants you to be released from.

Step 2: Ask and wait.

> *Lord, is there any other sin that I have been unable to lay down on my own that You want me to deal with?* _____

Step 3: Go back through the list and pray this prayer inserting the sin in the blank space. You may insert several sins in the blank space at a time if you desire.

Prayer of Repentance
(Preferably out loud)

Father God, I recognize and take responsibility for myself and my ancestors for the sin(s) of _____. I agree with Your verdict on my rebellion. I repent, I renounce, and I ask forgiveness for my participation with these sins, and I ask that their curse be broken in the name of Jesus Christ of Nazareth.

Step 4: Purging the evil. This is best done by an experienced and trusted ministering friend the first time around. Review the above list again now inserting the sin you have repented of in the blank.

Command of Deliverance
(Must be out loud with eyes open,
realizing you are speaking directly to a spirit)

In the name of Jesus Christ of Nazareth and by the power of the Holy Spirit, I take authority over the spirit(s) of _____. I break your power, I cast you out, and I command you to return no more.

Step 5: Pray that God will cause you to increase and abound in His love and that you would be an overcomer in the sins just repented of. Ask for a scripture that you will use to resist the devil when he tries to open the trapdoor again to regain entrance to your heart.

Agape Beareth All Things

The assertion that "agape beareth all things" is a little obscure in its meaning. What it means is that I love you and I've got your back. In combat, when one soldier cuts out from behind a protected area exposing himself to enemy fire, his buddy vows, "I've got your back." He is saying you can trust me with your life; and whatever comes your way, you can count on me to be there and cover you to see you through.

> It is too easy to share all someone may be doing in too much detail. In so doing not only do you destroy the reputation of the one referred to but also your sin becomes worse with greater consequences than whatever they did, because you've breached a very important assignment of trust.

Thou art my servant [bondman, person of covenant]; I have chosen thee, and not cast thee away [reject, despise]. Fear thou not; for I am with thee: be not dismayed; for I am thy God: I will strengthen thee; yea, I will help thee; yea, I will uphold [sustain, support] thee with the right hand of my righteousness [Jesus Christ]. Behold, all they that were incensed against thee [vexed, furious] shall be ashamed and confounded [humiliated, dishonored]: they shall be as nothing; and they that strive [dispute at law, contend] with thee shall perish [divine judgment]. Thou shalt seek them, and shalt not find them, even them that contended with thee: they that war [battle] against thee shall be as nothing, and as a thing of nought. For I the LORD thy God will hold thy right hand, saying unto thee, Fear not; I will help thee.

—ISAIAH 41:9–13

You have just read the covenant of agape from the very mouth of God where He declares how He has your back covered forever.

Walk backwards

Walk backwards to cover the nakedness of your spouse, walk backwards to cover the nakedness of those you love, as in order to thrive everyone needs to have that special someone with whom they feel very secure and freely able to trust. It is too easy to share all someone may be doing in too much detail. In so doing not only do you destroy the reputation of the one referred to but also your sin becomes worse with greater consequences than whatever they did, because you've breached a very important assignment of trust. This breach of trust becomes a curse. Gossip is treachery regardless of how cleverly you try to disguise it as concern, as a prayer request, or as a show of vulnerability to open up to a new confidante. Gossip and exposure cursed Canaan to a life in involuntary servitude.

> And Noah began to be an husbandman, and he planted a vineyard: And he drank of the wine, and was drunken; and he was uncovered within his tent. And Ham, the father of Canaan, saw the nakedness of his father, and told his two brethren without. And Shem and Japheth took a garment, and laid it upon both their shoulders, and went backward, and covered the nakedness of their father; and their faces were backward, and they saw not their father's nakedness. And Noah awoke from his wine, and knew what his younger son had done unto him. And he said, Cursed be Canaan; a servant of servants shall he be unto his brethren. And he said, Blessed be the LORD God of Shem; and Canaan shall be his servant.
>
> —GENESIS 9:20–26

When you've discovered a brother or sister in a compromising place, did you go in to take pictures to publish and note every detail with intent to replay it over and over and over again to others? If so, make haste to repent and restore. To do so you will have to die to self; you'll be broken but you will live. You'll find forgiveness with repentance, which will be of necessity to break the ill repayment of the curse. Such a curse left unchallenged will create greater devastation with you than to the one you uncovered the nakedness of.

> By mercy and truth iniquity is purged: and by the fear of the LORD men depart from evil.
>
> —PROVERBS 16:6

Our agape is to cover and protect a person who has sinned. Why? Is the Lord impressed when we go to Him accusing another of sin? Well, no. Is the Lord impressed when we expose the nakedness of one who fell? No again. Does it do any good if I retain their sin and replay it back to them from time to time so they learn from their mistakes? I guess not. So then, which kingdom would want the sins of a brother or sister exploited? How has it made you feel when you have exposed the iniquity of someone through an energetic gossip conference? Empty? Dirty? Defiled? Those are rotten fruits and are not from God but from Satan, as he was successful in sucking you into even greater sin than your target. Now in the event you are able to participate in gossip and not have your conscience try to tweak your lips, it is because you have done it too much and you are given over to the sin and your heart is hardened. If so, this section is especially for you.

> And above all things have fervent [willing to be stretched to the limit] charity [*agape*] among yourselves: for charity [*agape*] shall cover [conceal, offer protection] the multitude of sins.
> —1 PETER 4:8

> So then which kingdom would want the sins of a brother or sister exploited?

Bearing another in agape can be a long-term assignment that will stretch, discourage, and drain you on one hand; but on the other hand, by not giving in you may have saved one soul from going into the pit. Agape shows who the source is, especially when it takes you through an extended wilderness journey with another.

> With all lowliness [having nothing but receiving all things from God] and meekness [strength under submission], with longsuffering [enduring patient hope], forbearing [encouraging and supporting their stand] one another in love [*agape*]; Endeavouring to keep the unity of the Spirit in the bond of peace.
> —EPHESIANS 4:2

Agape is a supernatural love that will stand no matter how long it takes for the one loved to return home to the Lord. This may be for a special friend, a family member, or perhaps a prodigal child or spouse that has been taken captive by the devil. The goodness, patience, and gentleness of agape will bring them back, not unzipped lips.

> Or despisest thou the riches of his goodness [more than a quality it is action] and forbearance [delaying of punishment, overlooking for a time] and longsuffering [slowness in avenging wrongs]; not knowing that the goodness of God leadeth thee to repentance [begin to abhor their misdeeds]?
> —ROMANS 2:4

Covering by love may involve one who has not only lied to you but stolen from you as well. Many are the stories of those who have lent a helping hand only to have their kindness rewarded with violence, robbery, or slander. Jesus said concerning those in the act of murdering Him, "Forgive them, Father, for they know not what they do." Jesus learned to die to self; and from that vantage point His only concern was the lost state of man. And that included even the most treacherous and those with the biggest mouths. Jesus zipped His lips and washed them in grace and forgiveness, as agape bears all things.

> Jesus Christ came with a radical message to redeem the world and I find His doctrine regarding love the most revolutionary, almost militant in kindness and far-reaching in extreme efforts to redeem those held captive by evil.

> But brother goeth to law with brother, and that before the unbelievers. Now therefore there is utterly a fault among you, because ye go to law one with another. Why do ye not rather take wrong [unjust or wicked violation]? Why do ye not rather suffer yourselves to be defrauded [robbed, deprived]? Nay, ye do wrong, and defraud, and that your brethren.
>
> —1 CORINTHIANS 6:6–8

Jesus Christ came with a radical message to redeem the world; and I find His doctrine regarding love the most revolutionary, almost militant, in kindness and far-reaching in extreme efforts to redeem those held captive by evil.

> I say unto you which hear, Love [*agapao*] your enemies, do good to them which hate you, Bless them that curse you, and pray for them which despitefully use you. And unto him that smiteth thee on the one cheek offer also the other; and him that taketh away thy cloke forbid not to take thy coat also. Give to every man that asketh of thee; and of him that taketh away thy goods ask them not again. And as ye would that men should do to you, do ye also to them likewise. For if ye love them which love you, what thank have ye? for sinners also love those that love them. And if ye do good to them which do good to you, what thank have ye? for sinners also do even the same. And if ye lend to them of whom ye hope to receive, what thank have ye? for sinners also lend to sinners, to receive as much again. But love ye your enemies, and do good, and lend, hoping for nothing again; and your reward shall be great, and ye shall be the children of the Highest: for he is kind unto the unthankful and to the evil. Be ye therefore merciful, as your Father also is merciful.
>
> —LUKE 6:27–36

Ever noticed that God doesn't ask us to do anything that He doesn't always do?

Workout of the hardened heart

Step 1: Prayerfully review the following list and mark each sin you or your generations have participated with. It is important that you are not rushed and that you are in a private place as you go through this.

- ❑ **Cursing a brother**
- ❑ **Despitefully using**
- ❑ **Failure to permit another to wrong you**
- ❑ **Gossip**
- ❑ **Hardened heart**
- ❑ **Incensed against a brother**
- ❑ **Not fearing the Lord**
- ❑ **Pride**
- ❑ **Replaying sin**
- ❑ **Retaining another's sin**
- ❑ **Rewarding kindness with treachery**
- ❑ **Stubbornness**
- ❑ **Taking a dispute with a brother to court**
- ❑ **Taking pleasure in another's misfortune**
- ❑ **Taking pleasure in another's sin**
- ❑ **Uncovering the nakedness of another**

This is a partial list. Ask the Lord to show you what additional bondage He wants you to be released from.

Step 2: Ask and wait.

> *Lord, is there any other sin that I have been unable to lay down on my own that You want me to deal with?* _____

Step 3: Go back through the list and pray this prayer inserting the sin in the blank space. You may insert several sins in the blank space at a time if you desire.

Prayer of Repentance
(Preferably out loud)

> *Father God, I recognize and take responsibility for myself and my ancestors for the sin(s) of* _____. *I agree with Your verdict on my rebellion. I repent, I renounce, and I ask forgiveness for my participation with these sins, and I ask that their curse be broken in the name of Jesus Christ of Nazareth.*

Step 4: Purging the evil. This is best done by an experienced and trusted ministering friend the first time around. Review the above list again now inserting the sin you have repented of in the blank.

Command of Deliverance
(Must be out loud with eyes open,
realizing you are speaking directly to a spirit)

*In the name of Jesus Christ of Nazareth and by the power of the Holy Spirit,
I take authority over the spirit(s) of _____. I break your
power, I cast you out, and I command you to return no more.*

Step 5: Pray that God will cause you to increase and abound in His love and
that you would be an overcomer in the sins just repented of. Ask for a scripture
that you will use to resist the devil when he tries to open the trapdoor again
to regain entrance to your heart.

AGAPE BELIEVETH ALL THINGS

God gives His Word and then fully expects his family to take His direction
and run with it, not looking back, never doubting, but anticipating the accomplishment of every little thing proclaimed. To doubt what God said is sin, and
it results in His great displeasure towards us. This displeasure is something
to take very seriously as it sorts out those that say they believe in God versus
those whose belief stands up under fire.

The Israelites were treated to the miracle of
the parting of the Red Sea and the destruction
of their enemies followed by manna food falling
from the sky and water coming from the rock—
all this serving as an introduction to what God
would continue to do for them. Then comes the
test to see what was learned; and it comes in the
form of a wilderness where God is quiet for a
season. In our minds we may think God has

> God creates us and
> then continues to
> shape us throughout
> our lives using whatever
> method will accomplish
> that which is best for
> us with our eternal
> calling in perspective.

deserted us. What will we do now? Will we now turn to our own imaginations
or will we stay the course of belief, not wavering?

> But with whom was he grieved [very displeased, angry] forty years? was
> it not with them that had sinned, whose carcases fell in the wilderness?
> And to whom sware he that they should not enter into his rest [eternal
> promised blessings with God], but to them that believed not? So we see
> that they could not enter in because of unbelief.
> —HEBREWS 3:17–19

Many say they believe *in* God. How many just believe God?

The testing may come after we have crossed a major milestone in our faith
walk. Such was the experience of Noah. He built the ark amidst considerable ridicule then escaped the coming judgment on earth after he was secured
inside the ark. Then came an interesting paradox. Up to this time, Noah was
able to work and achieve much with his hands, as he was really energized to
fulfill the strange assignment he was given in building the boat in the middle

of the prairie. Once Noah was inside the ark, he lost all control, as the ship was without power and steering thus being adrift. Furthermore, with no windows he could not see what obstacle would lie in his path. For this brief time, God was silent, as far as Noah was concerned; though God was still guiding the ark, it didn't feel like that to Noah. Noah was tossed about by the first major storm in history and found no comfort within the dark confines of this craft. The testing was now all within the confines of Noah's mind. Would he still be able to believe when he could do nothing about the circumstance he was in? Could he keep his peace in the storm?

> For a small moment have I forsaken thee; but with great mercies will I gather thee. In a little wrath I hid my face from thee for a moment; but with everlasting kindness will I have mercy on thee, saith the LORD thy Redeemer. For this is as the waters of Noah unto me: for as I have sworn that the waters of Noah should no more go over the earth; so have I sworn that I would not be wroth with thee, nor rebuke thee. For the mountains shall depart, and the hills be removed; but my kindness shall not depart from thee, neither shall the covenant of my peace be removed, saith the Lord that hath mercy on thee. O thou afflicted, tossed with tempest [a raging storm], and not comforted behold, I will lay thy stones with fair colors, and lay thy foundations with sapphires.
>
> —Isaiah 54:7–11

> Unbelief is the result of evil in our spirits; it is sin that, if left undetected, will lead to our departing the faith, hence the necessity of an early detection.

We can be floundering around in a storm for some time before we accept that we have no ability to alter the course we are on and are powerless to effect any change. Finally we are placed where God can say, "Now that you are finished your reckless blind driving, do you mind if I take the wheel?" Paul was radical in his belief, as he knew that when he was helpless in trials he could not control, then the power of Jesus Christ would be able to work in him. He actually was excited about the situations he could not manage, as then he got to see real power work. We are not strong when we presume to be strong. Really we are just using different words to describe, once again, the foundational necessity of dying to self.

> And he said unto me, My grace is sufficient for thee: for my strength is made perfect in weakness. Most gladly therefore will I rather glory in my infirmities, that the power of Christ may rest upon me. Therefore I take pleasure in infirmities, in reproaches, in necessities, in persecutions, in distresses for Christ's sake: for when I am weak, then am I strong.
>
> —2 Corinthians 12:9–10

If the wilderness trip you are on is to test your patience, as most of them are, how are you doing with it? It is very possible that many will fall away from their faith when they are tested, and in particular when the test is to develop patience.

God creates us and then continues to shape us throughout our lives using whatever method will accomplish that which is best for us with our eternal calling in perspective.

> Cast not away therefore your confidence [bold assurance no fear], which hath great recompence [mega payment] of reward. For ye have need of patience, that, after ye have done the will of God, ye might receive the promise. For yet a little while, and he that shall come will come, and will not tarry. Now the just shall live by faith: but if any man draw back, my soul shall have no pleasure in him. But we are not of them who draw back unto perdition; but of them that believe to the saving of the soul.
>
> —HEBREWS 10:35–39

The belief test is difficult to pass, so it is no wonder the incredible reward offered to those examined thereby. The same Greek word translated as *believe* is also translated as *faith* in the Book of Hebrews. Our Father watches intently as you face the belief challenge and is greatly pleased with you when you get it, even though you've had many false starts.

> But without faith it is impossible to please him: for he that cometh to God must believe that he is, and that he is a rewarder of them that diligently seek him.
>
> —HEBREWS 11:6

Unbelief is a spiritual defect, which is separated from you through developmental processes that our heavenly Father engineers to purify you. Unbelief is the result of evil in our spirits; it is sin that, if left undetected, will lead to our departing the faith, hence the necessity of an early detection.

> Take heed, brethren, lest there be in any of you an evil heart of unbelief, in departing from the living God.
>
> —HEBREWS 3:12

What are works that justify us? They are proper conduct through difficulties traversed by one who follows the precepts of God. Abraham's belief in God was tested like no other man. And when Abraham triumphed over fear, doubt, and unbelief, he was declared righteous and accepted as a friend of God. Abraham had false starts in understanding his own weakness in his belief and faith, but he learned and eventually became strong and unmovable. There is no man more formidable against the enemy than one fortified with an unshakable belief in his Father.

> Was not Abraham our father justified by works, when he had offered Isaac his son upon the altar? Seest thou how faith wrought with his works, and by works was faith made perfect? And the scripture was fulfilled which

saith, Abraham believed God, and it was imputed unto him for righteousness: and he was called the Friend of God. Ye see then how that by
works a man is justified, and not by faith only.

—JAMES 2:21–24

The belief that will move our mountains will first go through a maturing
process such as developed Abraham, Paul, and Christ. Our faith will be of no
effect if we are requesting a move of God on our behalf while we are holding
any offense against a brother or sister. So the first question to ask when our
faith isn't working is: Is there anyone whom I haven't forgiven from my heart;
is the debt of forgiveness fully paid?

> For verily I say unto you, That whosoever shall say unto this mountain,
> Be thou removed, and be thou cast into the sea; and shall not doubt in
> his heart, but shall believe that those things which he saith shall come to
> pass; he shall have whatsoever he saith. Therefore I say unto you, what
> things soever ye desire, when ye pray, believe that ye receive them, and
> ye shall have them. And when ye stand praying, forgive, if ye have ought
> against any: that your Father also which is in heaven may forgive you
> your trespasses.
>
> —MARK 11:23–25

The second question to ask when faith is weak is: Do I fear anything; am I
in fear that God won't provide?

> But when Jesus heard it, he answered him, saying, Fear not: believe only,
> and she shall be made whole.
>
> —LUKE 8:50

God intends for us to do wondrous things through our belief in Him;
works as powerful as demonstrated daily through Jesus Christ.

> Verily, verily, I say unto you, He that believeth on me, the works that I
> do shall he do also; and greater works than these shall he do; because I
> go unto my Father.
>
> —JOHN 14:12

Can you see now why God is so desirous to work patiently with us to fully
develop our steadfast belief?

The basis of our belief is whatever the Scripture has said, as opposed to
what religion and tradition of man expounds. We can have many beliefs about
God, but if they are not scripturally enforced, we will not receive the empowering of the Spirit of God.

> He that believeth on me, as the scripture hath said, out of his belly shall
> flow rivers of living water. (But this spake he of the Spirit, which they
> that believe on him should receive: for the Holy Ghost was not yet given;
> because that Jesus was not yet glorified.)
>
> —JOHN 7:38–39

(On a side note: the parentheses in this verse were placed there by John as commentary on the words of Jesus, as when he wrote this, John had the benefit of hindsight.)

What empowers our faith? Our faith is empowered by agape, the love of the Father; hence the necessity to be converted, as Peter was, from the unstable and fickle phileo love to the agape love which doesn't fail. Peter had to go through a wilderness experience and be sifted by Satan in order for his love to be purified.

> God intends for us to do wondrous things through our belief in Him; works as powerful as demonstrated daily through Jesus Christ.

Following that testing Peter was blessed with an unshakable faith in his Lord.

> But faith which worketh [is empowered] by love [*agape*].
> —GALATIANS 5:6

Hebrews reiterates that our assignment is to restore our true heart, which is holy and without blame before God in agape. This restoration results from a sanctified heart, soul, and body, giving us the full assurance of faith necessary to do the works we saw Jesus do.

> Let us draw near with a true [as created from foundation of the world righteous without blame] heart in full assurance of faith, having our hearts sprinkled [spirit purified through blood sacrificed by Christ] from an evil conscience [soul], and our bodies washed with pure water [purified of uncleanness].
> —HEBREWS 10:22

The scriptures contain a vast amount of prophecy of which God holds us accountable to be aware. I believe of particular importance are the prophecies that have been fulfilled in our generations. There are many concerning the reestablishment of Israel as a nation; current world events; political, technological, and religious phenomena; to name a few. It is beyond the scope of this writing to indulge in the excitement of the unfolding of events the only wise God foretold. There were more than three hundred prophecies fulfilled perfectly in the birth, ministry, and sacrifice of Jesus. So that we should know without doubt that Jesus was the long-anticipated Messiah. As God's Word has been without error in recording ahead of time what has recently happened, it has also prerecorded all the significant events yet to happen regarding the peoples of earth. Understanding prophecy is another key element in building our unshakeable belief that we serve the one true God. All will come to pass, so let's prepare so that none of us or our loved ones are caught in darkness.

> There failed not ought of any good thing which the LORD had spoken unto the house of Israel; all came to pass.
> —JOSHUA 21:45

Daniel's friends were young men with unsinkable faith. They were able to declare to the king, "Go ahead and do what you will with us, as you are no contest to our God." Now that is a good attitude!

> If it be so, our God whom we serve is able to deliver us from the burning fiery furnace, and he will deliver us out of thine hand, O king.
>
> —Daniel 3:17

Daniel lived his whole life with the same belief, and God protected him from the lions when he was thrown into their den.

Workout of doubt and unbelief

Step 1: Prayerfully review the following list and mark each sin you or your generations have participated with. It is important that you are not rushed and that you are in a private place as you go through this.

- ❑ **Carnality or relying on my own strength to do work of God**
- ❑ **Cowardess**
- ❑ **Doubt**
- ❑ **Evil conscience**
- ❑ **Fear that God won't provide**
- ❑ **Grieving God**
- ❑ **Impatience regarding work of God**
- ❑ **Lack of faith**
- ❑ **Looking back, especially when things get difficult**
- ❑ **Not seeking God**
- ❑ **Unbelief promise of God will be fulfilled for me**

This is a partial list. Ask the Lord to show you what additional bondage He wants you to be released from.

Step 2: Ask and wait.

> *Lord, is there any other sin that I have been unable to lay down on my own that You want me to deal with?* _____

> Faith is substance; it is a magnet, and hope is the magnetism of which we observe its effect, but it can't be seen. So the object of our faith is established first and then we are drawn towards it by hope.

Step 3: Go back through the list and pray this prayer inserting the sin in the blank space. You may insert several sins in the blank space at a time if you desire.

Prayer of Repentance
(Preferably out loud)

Father God, I recognize and take responsibility for myself and my ancestors for the sin(s) of _____. I agree with Your verdict on my rebellion. I repent, I renounce, and I ask forgiveness for my participation with these sins, and I ask that their curse be broken in the name of Jesus Christ of Nazareth.

Step 4: Purging the evil. This is best done by an experienced and trusted ministering friend the first time around. Review the above list again now inserting the sin you have repented of in the blank.

Command of Deliverance
(Must be out loud with eyes open,
realizing you are speaking directly to a spirit)

In the name of Jesus Christ of Nazareth and by the power of the Holy Spirit, I take authority over the spirit(s) of _____. I break your power, I cast you out, and I command you to return no more.

Step 5: Pray that God will cause you to increase and abound in His love and that you would be an overcomer in the sins just repented of. Ask for a scripture that you will use to resist the devil when he tries to open the trapdoor again to regain entrance to your heart.

AGAPE HOPETH ALL THINGS

We've looked at the scriptures relating to faith and belief, so how does hope fit in? Isn't hope the same as faith? Definitions abound for both *faith* and *hope*, but they just seemed to add to my confusion. One thing I've learned is that if it is important enough to understand, the scriptures will reveal it, as the best commentary on the Scriptures is always the Scripture itself. Faith is substance; it is similar to a magnet. Hope is the magnetism of which we observe its effect, but it can't be seen. So the object of our faith is established first, the magnet, and then we are drawn towards it by hope, the magnetism.

> Now faith [conviction of truth, the confidence of what we believe in] is the substance [the assurance of a title deed, guarantee] of things hoped for [trust focused], the evidence of things not seen.
> —HEBREWS 11:1

Agape hopes all things and to have hope for all things we have to be broken: to die to self. If we haven't died to self then our flesh will come up with desperate shortcut survival measures to solve our problems.

Hope is like stamina that takes us through or around our obstacles to reach the object of our hope, which is the substance of faith. Stamina is the staying power, determination, and resilience that gives us the ability to recover quickly from setbacks and spring back into shape after being stretched to a place beyond comfort.

> Why art thou cast down [despairing, depressed], O my soul? and why art thou disquieted [murmuring, troubled] in me? Hope thou in God: for I shall yet praise him for the help [deliverance, salvation, victory] of his countenance [the face of God].
> —PSALM 42:5

Do you know what virtue is coupled with hope and at the same time is a prerequisite for hope? If I become impatient in waiting for the Lord's deliverance, I immediately lose my hope and my peace becomes despair. We have need of the development of patience in our lives so that we can have hope. Patience is nurtured into maturity by only one thing: tribulation, which means to break or to have pressure applied through desperate straits. Experience speaks of repeating the trials over and over until we learn to stop trying to help God out in our own strength and eventually wait and trust in the work of the Lord. It is this progression that develops an unsinkable hope. Thus refined, we'll experience the things hoped for, as we are now standing with the empowering of agape.

> Therefore being justified by faith, we have peace with God through our Lord Jesus Christ: By whom also we have access by faith into this grace wherein we stand, and rejoice in hope of the glory of God. And not only so, but we glory in tribulations also: knowing that tribulation worketh patience; And patience, experience; and experience, hope: And hope maketh not ashamed [disgraced or dishonored]; because the love [*agape*] of God is shed abroad in our hearts by the Holy Ghost which is given unto us.
>
> —Romans 5:1–5

> Being broken doesn't mean being destroyed and badly hurt it means we have died to our stubborn flesh and are now willing to be guided by the love of our Father.

I must admit that I moaned a little here wishing that there must be an easier way to learn hope rather than through the experiences of tribulation. After all, aren't we studying the Word regarding agape, the love of the Father? Agape hopes all things, and to have hope for all things, we have to be broken; to die to self. If we haven't died to self, then our flesh will come up with desperate shortcut survival measures to solve our problems. Satan tempted Jesus to accept his shortcut in immediately obtaining the kingdom of earth by bowing to him rather than take the broken way of the cross.

Broken

A wild horse has to be broken before it can be of service to its master. Breaking in a horse is a process used by man to remove the horse's fear of being ridden and replacing it with trust and understanding. A horse properly trained may turn with just a gentle nudge of the rider's knee with no force on the bit even required. In a sense, we are like the wild horse that needs to be broken to be suitable for our Master's use, able to follow His lead with just a gentle nudge. Being broken doesn't mean being destroyed and badly hurt, it means we have died to our stubborn flesh and are now willing to be guided by the love of our Father.

> The sacrifices of God are a broken spirit: a broken and a contrite heart, O God, thou wilt not despise.
>
> —PSALM 51:17

The biographies of many men are written in the Scriptures for us to learn from their struggles and experience the result of what they hoped for. I like the story of Joseph, as he was victimized, falsely accused, and forgotten in prison for many of the most productive years of his life, which makes it seem that God is unfair—that is until we read the final chapter. Then we see the tribulations of Joseph were worth it, as they prepared him to be an ambassador of the Father to deliver his household and his nation.

> For even Christ pleased not himself; but, as it is written, The reproaches of them that reproached thee fell on me. For whatsoever things were written aforetime were written for our learning, that we through patience and comfort of the scriptures might have hope.
>
> —ROMANS 15:2–3

One of the attributes of God is patience, and He wants us to be just like Him. Once we have repeatedly experienced the fulfillment of what we hope for, it will then pull us through our next tribulation with expectations, as we can't wait to see what God is going to do next. Nothing can compare with getting to be a part of God's deliverance where captives are set free, the broken hearted are bound up, and the diseased are healed.

> Rejoicing in hope; patient in tribulation; continuing instant in prayer.
>
> —ROMANS 12:12

Hope is to focus beyond what we can see.

Hope will get you through the labor pains.

> It is good that a man should both hope and quietly wait for the salvation of the LORD.
>
> —LAMENTATIONS 3:26

> And the Lord direct your hearts into the love of God, and into the patient waiting for Christ.
>
> —2 THESSALONIANS 3:5

> I wait for the LORD, my soul doth wait, and in his word do I hope. My soul waiteth for the LORD more than they that watch for the morning.
>
> —PSALM 130:5–6

There will be certain events which we may wait for years before we see our prayers answered; but when it does come to pass, it is amazing how quickly you'll forget the long wait and just revel in the joy of what you now recognize as God's perfect timing and amazing deliverance.

> Hope deferred [prolonged] maketh the heart sick [sad or grieved]: but when the desire [hope] cometh, it is a tree of life.
>
> —PROVERBS 13:12

God doesn't hope, rather He purposes in His heart what He has in store for you. And look what He says about you; He says He wants to give you what you are hoping for:

> For I know the thoughts that I think toward you [purposed or imputed], saith the Lord, thoughts of peace [completeness, harmony, fulfillment], and not of evil, to give you an expected end [things hoped for].
> —Jeremiah 29:11

When we mature in our stand of agape, we'll see that what we hope for is also what God purposes in His heart for us to receive. The reason is that when we fully understand and walk in His ways, our hearts will already be aligned with His will. So when we ask, we ask with pure unselfish motive; and God delights in that. Do you believe that?

> Delight thyself also in the Lord; and he shall give thee the desires of thine heart. Commit thy way unto the Lord; trust also in him; and he shall bring it to pass.
> —Psalm 37:4–5

It is one thing to place your hope in something that is commonplace and easily accomplished, and it is quite something else to place your hope in something that would require supernatural intervention or a miracle to see the fulfillment. Abraham had hope that God would break the laws of nature and give him a son, even though he was nearly a hundred and his wife ninety.

> Who against hope believed in hope, that he might become the father of many nations, according to that which was spoken, So shall thy seed be.
> —Romans 4:18

When God leads you to a place of trusting in Him for the supernatural, He will generally speak directly to you in advance either through His Word, by a vision, through a dream, or through prophecy. Following the receipt of God's advance proclamation is most often a period of time where patience is tested and hope is stretched to see if you will allow anyone to steal your hope. Satan knows of God's promise to you; and he'll attempt to counterattack with weapons, such as discouragement or by inspiring us to opt to carnal efforts where we try to "help God out" as He is taking too long.

Hope is to focus beyond what we can see. The hope we are saved by is the hope of the gospel.

> For we are saved by hope: but hope that is seen is not hope: for what a man seeth, why doth he yet hope for? But if we hope for that we see not, then do we with patience wait for it.
> —Romans 8:24–25

The gospel teaches us to have hope in many things that are to come, which are essential to have in mind, as they are the magnet that pulls us through life, particularly the tough times. Furthermore, the scripture says, "*agape*…hopes all things"; so the question then ought to be, what things are we to hope in? We've looked at hope as it pertains to the believer's unique and personal experiences of life, and now we'll look at hope as it applies to things all believers have in common—the hope of the gospel.

1. The hope of being forgiven. The hope of righteousness. The pursuit of the believer is righteous as we walk and grow up before God to be holy, without blame before Him in agape. The faith is the truth or substance of what our hope draws us toward.

For we through the Spirit wait for the hope of righteousness by faith.

—GALATIANS 5:5

2. The hope of heaven.

For the hope which is laid up for you in heaven, whereof ye heard before in the word of the truth of the gospel.

—COLOSSIANS 1:5

3. The hope of Christ living within us His temple.

To whom God would make known what is the riches of the glory of this mystery among the Gentiles; which is Christ in you, the hope of glory.

—COLOSSIANS 1:27

4. The hope of the Resurrection of all those who passed on ahead of us and the hope of the return of Jesus.

And have hope toward God, which they themselves also allow, that there shall be a resurrection of the dead, both of the just and unjust.

—ACTS 24:15

5. The hope of the second coming of Jesus Christ to this earth to set up the kingdom of heaven.

Looking for that blessed hope, and the glorious appearing of the great God and our Saviour Jesus Christ.

—TITUS 2:13

6. The hope of eternal life.

That being justified by his grace, we should be made heirs according to the hope of eternal life.

—TITUS 3:7

7. The hope of the fathers, which are the promises laid out in the Old and New Testaments. We are the recipients of these promises even though they were made to our forefathers.

And now I stand and am judged for the hope of the promise made of God unto our fathers.

—ACTS 26:6

8. The hope of realizing all that God has called us to do and also to receive what is the heritage of the servants of the Lord. (See Isaiah 54.)

The empowering and stand of agape through our sanctification is the riches of His glory, the believer's inheritance.

The eyes of your understanding being enlightened; that ye may know what is the hope of his calling, and what the riches of the glory of his inheritance in the saints, And what is the exceeding greatness of his power to us-ward who believe, according to the working of his mighty power.

—Ephesians 1:18–19

9. Winning lost souls by the hope within.

But sanctify the Lord God in your hearts: and be ready always to give an answer to every man that asketh you a reason of the hope that is in you with meekness and fear.

—1 Peter 3:15

10. The hope of not having to place our trust in man and the doctrine of man but rather our hope is with the one God who is and was and is to come. Our hope is in the One that can actually do something!

Put not your trust in princes, nor in the son of man, in whom there is no help. His breath goeth forth, he returneth to his earth; in that very day his thoughts perish. Happy is he that hath the God of Jacob for his help, whose hope is in the Lord his God.

—Psalm 146:3–5

11. The hope of our new glorified bodies that will be just like the one Jesus now has.

Beloved, now are we the sons of God, and it doth not yet appear what we shall be: but we know that, when he shall appear, we shall be like him; for we shall see him as he is. And every man that hath this hope [expectation] in him purifieth himself, even as he is pure.

—1 John 3:2–3

Now the God of hope fill you with all joy and peace in believing, that ye may abound in hope, through the power of the Holy Ghost.

—Romans 15:13

Workout of hopelessness

Step 1: Prayerfully review the following list and mark each sin you or your generations have participated with. It is important that you are not rushed and that you are in a private place as you go through this.

❑ Depression
❑ Murmuring
❑ Pessimism
❑ Shame
❑ Trust in man
❑ Unteachable

❑ Hopelessness
❑ Negativity
❑ Proud heart
❑ Troubled
❑ Trust in the doctrine of men

This is a partial list. Ask the Lord to show you what additional bondage He wants you to be released from.

Step 2: Ask and wait.

Lord, is there any other sin that I have been unable to lay down on my own that You want me to deal with? _____

Step 3: Go back through the list and pray this prayer inserting the sin in the blank space. You may insert several sins in the blank space at a time if you desire.

Prayer of Repentance
(Preferably out loud)

Father God, I recognize and take responsibility for myself and my ancestors for the sin(s) of _____. I agree with Your verdict on my rebellion. I repent, I renounce, and I ask forgiveness for my participation with these sins, and I ask that their curse be broken in the name of Jesus Christ of Nazareth.

Step 4: Purging the evil. This is best done by an experienced and trusted ministering friend the first time around. Review the above list again now inserting the sin you have repented of in the blank.

Command of Deliverance
(Must be out loud with eyes open,
realizing you are speaking directly to a spirit)

In the name of Jesus Christ of Nazareth and by the power of the Holy Spirit, I take authority over the spirit(s) of _____. I break your power, I cast you out, and I command you to return no more.

Step 5: Pray that God will cause you to increase and abound in His love and that you would be an overcomer in the sins just repented of. Ask for a scripture that you will use to resist the devil when he tries to open the trapdoor again to regain entrance to your heart.

Step 6: Examine the ten things we are to have our hope in and pray that God would increase your hope through the Holy Spirit in each area. Repent wherever you've harbored doubt and unbelief, thus destroying your hope.

AGAPE ENDURETH ALL THINGS

I'm now considering the potential for grievous error certain strongly held beliefs of mine opened me up to. I held the principal for myself and taught others likewise that we'd know we were in the will of God if we were at peace. Secondly, I believed and taught that God wanted more than anything for me to be happy. I know I need to explain myself. These noble pursuits are, indeed, what God wants for us, but it may not be so simple to determine the will of God. What I've learned is that if I am given over to certain sins, my conscience is dulled, resulting in me having peace while enjoying the pleasure of my sin. Pleasure of sin also has a measure of excitement associated with it. Many things done in secret cause the heart to beat a little faster, thus appearing to come across to us as joy. However, are we accepting a shortcut to peace and joy from the same evil one that offered Jesus a shortcut to obtaining the kingdom of the world? God offers the kingdom of heaven and the kingdom of God, whereas Satan offers the kingdom of world.

> Jesus answered, My kingdom is not of this world: if my kingdom were of this world, then would my servants fight, that I should not be delivered to the Jews: but now is my kingdom not from hence.
> —JOHN 18:36

Jesus said this is a battle that is not even worth fighting. He was before Pilate who had earthly power to condemn Him to death and was looking for an excuse to not have to. And Jesus responds, "If My kingdom were of this world I'd take you on, but I offer no defense" (author's paraphrase). That is really something. While I am in the kingdom of the world, I get testy about someone that found a way to get past me in a waiting line, whereas Jesus was faced with someone who received false accusations and wanted His life and He lets them take it. I get riled up and have little power to change the smallest of things, but Jesus is completely calm and yet could have levelled the courtroom and blinded all the guards and silenced the tongue of the judge and sent His accusers into orbit and He does nothing. To have power to make a wrong right and to choose not to use it is what the kingdom of God is like when its servants are visiting the kingdom of this world.

> However, are we accepting a shortcut to peace and joy from the same evil one that offered Jesus a shortcut to obtaining the kingdom of the world?

How much of our anxiety, worry, and anger is due to fighting for the wrong kingdom, the kingdom of the world? We are then actually fighting for the god of this world, Satan, to preserve his kingdom. (See 2 Corinthians 4:4.) This is why we have spent so much space in this book showing you the kingdoms so you can recognize which kingdom you want to fight for.

I'm not a "killjoy." Rather, I am for "real joy" and "genuine peace."

> Peace I leave with you, my peace I give unto you: not as the world giveth, give I unto you. Let not your heart be troubled, neither let it be afraid.
> —JOHN 14:27

The world cannot offer the peace any of us are so longing for. Get over your love affair with the world because this chapter of eternity is so exceedingly short and so much depends on our attachments.

Jesus had peace in the most desperate times of His life because He understood and served only the kingdom of God. Until Jesus returns to take back the world from the devil, we are aliens in hostile territory. Jesus warned us ahead of time that we will have considerable difficulties in the meanwhile.

> Behold, the hour cometh, yea, is now come, that ye shall be scattered, every man to his own, and shall leave me alone: and yet I am not alone, because the Father is with me. These things I have spoken unto you, that in me ye might have peace. In the world ye shall have tribulation: but be of good cheer; I have overcome the world.
>
> —JOHN 16:32–33

How do I know which kingdom I'm really supporting? Well, it is whether or not I have a deep sense of peace in my heart, even in the midst of the burning fiery furnace. When Peter was still trying to figure out this concept, he lopped off a guy's ear with his sword, which Jesus patiently replaced. Then to preserve his behind, Peter denied being a follower of Jesus; he did that three times.

Jesus approached God our Father on three occasions about an alternative to going the route of the cross, as He wasn't at peace about it. The gospels record that Christ was "sorrowful and very heavy," which means to be in great distress and troubled regarding His purpose.

> And he took with him Peter and the two sons of Zebedee, and began to be sorrowful [inward grief and overwhelming sadness], and very heavy [anguish, distressed, troubled]. Then saith he unto them, My soul is exceeding sorrowful even unto death: tarry ye here, and watch with me.
>
> —MATTHEW 26:37–38

What would have happened if, after praying the first time, He said, "You know I'm not at peace about being a sin offering for the people of the earth, so this can't be God's will. I am done with this nasty assignment, Father"?

Finally, after pleading with God for the third time, Jesus was strengthened and was at peace. Soon after the Judas group came to arrest Him. The One that wrote the book regarding our faith, first walked in the sandals of a human being facing the most difficult of assignments. His faith, once refreshed, took Him joyfully to the cross because He believed His Father had only the best in mind for His only Son and also for the human race.

> Looking unto Jesus the author [a pioneer that sets the standard] and finisher [set highest standard of perfection] of our faith; who for the joy that was set before him [destined] endured [face bravely and calmly] the cross, despising the shame [disgrace], and is set down at the right hand of the throne of God.
>
> —HEBREWS 12:2

> The Father did not even spare His only Son from difficulties that would cultivate a virtue in Him, such as obedience.

Jesus had an assignment that required unimaginable endurance. Agape endures all things, as agape always does what is best for the person loved; it always does what is best for the person that agapes himself as well. Every believer has an assignment given to them that requires varying degrees of endurance. The author of the Book of Hebrews relates the very difficult agape journey of Christ, comparing to that with which the believer would inevitably come face-to-face.

> For consider him that endured such contradiction [object of much dispute and opposition] of sinners against himself, lest ye be wearied [made sick] and faint [depressed and give up] in your minds. Ye have not yet resisted [stood in front lines in battle] unto blood, striving [fighting] against sin. And ye have forgotten the exhortation which speaketh unto you as unto children, My son, despise [hate, detest, dismiss] not thou the chastening [cultivation of the soul to increase virtue] of the Lord, nor faint when thou art rebuked [convicted, punished] of him: For whom the Lord loveth he chasteneth, and scourgeth every son whom he receiveth... If ye endure chastening, God dealeth with you as with sons; for what son is he whom the father chasteneth not?
> —HEBREWS 12:3–7

You may be enduring the intense pain of a prodigal spouse or child, loneliness, the death or illness of one very dear to you, the perplexity of financial straits, the exposure of your sin, or being exposed to the abuse of another's sin. How do you endure? I believe there are two paths. The first path is that of a victim taking matters into our hands to correct the situation or the other person involved while preserving our own reputation. The second approach is to say, "Lord, what do you need to teach me through this? What do I need to understand? What is lying hidden within me that must be exposed? I know the situation I'm facing is not about anybody else but about how I'll walk before You through this valley."

However, that being said, the Scripture does not advocate us enduring crimes committed against our person or our property without involving local church and/or the laws of the land. God placed the authorities there for that purpose. Assuming we have the authorities involved with the perpetrator of our pain, how are we to treat the person that hurt us? Jesus taught that we are to agape even our enemies, even those who despitefully use us and persecute us. This kind of love is supernatural and cannot be done in the flesh and can't be accomplished if we hold one in condemnation and judgment.

The Word asks us to consider how Jesus dealt with the intensity of the sin and injustice that surrounded Him; He dealt with it all through the empowering of agape; the same love He streamed to us.

So how long do we have to endure? We are to endure to the end, whenever that may be. To stop short of that is to be wearied and faint thus falling short of the glory of God.

> And ye shall be hated of all men for my name's sake: but he that endureth to the end shall be saved.
> —MATTHEW 10:22

The Father did not even spare His only Son from difficulties that would cultivate a virtue in Him, such as obedience. Those difficulties included being on the receiving end of the sins of those He loved, of false accusations in courts, and for the first time experiencing the Father's silence.

> Who in the days of his flesh, when he had offered up prayers and supplications with strong crying and tears unto him that was able to save him from death, and was heard in that he feared; Though he were a Son, yet learned [strengthened and increased by exercise] he obedience [submission] by the things which he suffered [vexed by desperations or evils]; And being made perfect [complete, or to be proved worthy of state], he became the author [source, the only way] of eternal salvation unto all them that obey him.
> —HEBREWS 5:7–9

The kingdom of the world serves only as a place to do our endurance training in preparation for our role in the kingdom of God.

Tempered

Jesus was greatly strengthened through the fiery trials He went through. Glass that is required in demanding environments, such as the automobile windshield or a shower door, has to be strengthened. Glass is immensely strengthened when placed in a furnace and heating it up to about 720 degrees Celsius. This glass is now tempered; it will withstand incredible pressure to break it, is heat resistant, and is tough enough to take the rough usage demanded by carafes in coffee makers. Ordinary glass is easily shattered when exposed to rough usage because it has not been through the fire.

The first significant testing Jesus faced was right at the beginning of His public ministry when Satan tempted Him on three occasions to try to solicit Him to sin. The first area of testing was in the area of personal sins and temptations.

It is with this knowledge that we can glory in our temptations and testings, knowing that God is not punishing us for our past but tempering us so we'll be strong enough to handle the demands of what lies ahead of us so we won't shatter under the pressure.

Secondly, Jesus would be facing a variety of afflictions at the hands of His countryman including rejection, weariness, accusation, doubt, mourning, weeping, scorn, unbelief, lying, violence, hatred, cursing, jealousy, entrapment, and gossip during the bulk of His ministry time. So perhaps the second area of testing would involve the correct response to the maltreatment and sin of others.

The third area and most difficult time of our Lord's testing came right near the end of His ministry regarding His faith, trust, and endurance. This was when all He had to go on were words previously spoken of by the Father who at this point became silent to Jesus' prayer and strong crying. So the third area of testing was to prove His love, submission, and complete trust in Father God, even when God was silent for a season.

To mature into agape our love must be proved through fire in these three levels: relationships with others, ourselves, and with God. As Jesus experienced, so will the believer. The trials will get more and more difficult as God is preparing His ambassadors for the next level of assignment. The last testings of Christ were necessary to develop the endurance and obedience He would need for the final assignments of His arrest, condemnation, torture, and crucifixion.

When the temptation comes from God, it is for the purpose of proving, perfecting, and preparing someone; it is never for the purpose of causing one to fall. When the temptation is from Satan, it is to open the door so he can steal, kill, and destroy. Temptations from God push us forward and up, whereas the temptations from Satan pressure us backwards and down.

> Blessed is the man that endureth [face bravely and calmly] temptation [*peirasmos*; to test or prove agape and virtue]: for when he is tried [approved, genuine], he shall receive the crown of life, which the Lord hath promised to them that love him.
> —JAMES 1:12

It is with this knowledge that we can glory in our temptations and testings, knowing that God is not punishing us for our past but tempering us so we'll be strong enough to handle the demands of what lies ahead of us so we won't shatter under the pressure. Satan was involved in sifting Peter, after Peter stepped backwards, but God turned the curse into a blessing and the result was that thousands and thousands of people would be saved directly through his ministry and his writings. This is what Peter wrote when he "grew up":

> Beloved, think it not strange concerning the fiery trial which is to try you, as though some strange thing happened unto you: But rejoice, inasmuch as ye are partakers of Christ's sufferings; that, when his glory shall be revealed, ye may be glad also with exceeding joy. If ye be reproached for the name of Christ, happy are ye; for the spirit of glory and of God resteth upon you: on their part he is evil spoken of, but on your part he is glorified. But let none of you suffer as a murderer, or as a thief, or as an evildoer, or as a busybody in other men's matters. Yet if any man suffer as a Christian, let him not be ashamed; but let him glorify God on this behalf. For the time is come that judgment must begin at the house of God: and if it first begin at us, what shall the end be of them that obey not the gospel of God? And if the righteous scarcely be saved, where shall the ungodly and the sinner appear? Wherefore let them that suffer according to the will of God commit the keeping of their souls to him in well doing, as unto a faithful Creator.
> —1 PETER 4:12–19

Even if the stuff that happens to us is dished out by the devil, we know that all things work together for good—for those that "agape" God. That oft quoted passage in Romans 8:28 has a caveat: all things will work together for good to them that love (*agape*) God and to them who are the called according to His purpose.

So when God puts us through the fire, is that a good thing or a bad thing?

There is a passage that should be considered as it relates to temptation. James 1:13 says, "Let no man say when he is tempted that he is tempted of God." This would seem to contradict James 1:12 that we just looked at where it says, "Blessed is the man that endureth temptation." The problem is that James 1:12–13 was written originally with three different Greek words: *peirazo, apeirastos,* and *peirasmos,* to which we have only one English term, *temptation*, or its derivative, *tempted*. I trust that if you review these two passages along with the inserted notes in the brackets that the intent will become evident.

> I wonder how many times we win a convert only for them to end up worse than before as they have a part of the truth but not enough to keep away discouragement and they fall away.

> Let no man say when he is tempted [*peirazo*; entangled or solicited to sin], I am tempted [*peirazo*; entangled or solicited to sin], of God: for God cannot be tempted [*apeirastos*; not temptable] with evil, neither tempteth [*peirazo*; entangled or solicited to sin], he any man.
>
> —JAMES 1:13

God is known to try and strengthen men by adversity in order to prove their faith. But men on the other hand test and prove God when they doubt His power and deliverance.

> Ye shall not tempt [test or prove] the LORD your God, as ye tempted him in Massah.
>
> —DEUTERONOMY 6:16

A good way to qualify us for an extended wilderness trip is to deal with our affliction by hardening our hearts towards our own sin and questioning God by demanding He deal bountifully with us while we remain in our sin.

> O come, let us worship and bow down: let us kneel before the LORD our maker. For he is our God; and we are the people of his pasture, and the sheep of his hand. To day if ye will hear his voice, Harden not your heart, as in the provocation, and as in the day of temptation in the wilderness: When your fathers tempted me, proved me, and saw my work. Forty years long was I grieved with this generation, and said, It is a people that do err in their heart, and they have not known my ways: Unto whom I sware in my wrath that they should not enter into my rest.
>
> —PSALM 95:6–11

The adversities of our wilderness desolations are used by God to determine our level of commitment as followers. Our reaction to difficulties exposes what has been trying to hide in our heart. At that point the choice becomes whether we will we chose to entertain the evil desires that surface or whether we will we have the fortitude to overcome the temptation.

> And thou shalt remember all the way which the LORD thy God led thee these forty years in the wilderness, to humble [to afflict or exercise] thee, and to prove [test by adversity to try their faith, tempt] thee, to know what was in thine heart, whether thou wouldest keep his commandments, or no.
> —DEUTERONOMY 8:2

Many will vow to follow the Lord but give up as their commitment is tested during their journey through their wilderness. When a new convert is introduced to the kingdom of God, it is of utmost priority to prepare them to endure temptations and afflictions that must come to give their newfound faith foundation and to continue to purge their spirits of any uncleanness. I wonder how many times we win a convert only for them to end up worse than before, as they have a part of the truth but not enough to keep away discouragement and they fall away.

> When the unclean spirit is gone out of a man, he walketh through dry places, seeking rest, and findeth none. Then he saith, I will return into my house from whence I came out; and when he is come, he findeth it empty, swept, and garnished. Then goeth he, and taketh with himself seven other spirits more wicked than himself, and they enter in and dwell there: and the last state of that man is worse than the first. Even so shall it be also unto this wicked generation.
> —MATTHEW 12:43–45

When the Lord comes we want Him to see all the good works that we have done in His name. Yes, the works are noble, but there is something of equal importance that may be overlooked to our detriment: the trial of our faith and agape. It is often easier to perform works and to give than it is to endure the temptations and testings that also work to establish our faith.

Trial by temptation—really?

Jesus became exceedingly sorrowful and very heavy as the Father was preparing His Son for victory through what lie ahead for Him. Peter tells us to rejoice when we see such preparations being set before us and to endure the season of heaviness where we undergo severe stress testing.

Our faith, to be worth anything, has to go through the trial by temptation. This is not the temptation of enticement to sin but high-heat testing to strengthen faith, love, and character. What we may think are our failures are actually part of the purification process, as each stumble reveals weakness of doubt and unbelief or fear, which we can then be delivered from. Now with fear doubt and unbelief exposed, our faith will become much more stable and predictably unmovable.

> Wherein ye greatly rejoice, though now for a season, if need be, ye are in heaviness [sorrowful, grieved] through manifold [various] temptations [serving to test one's faith, holiness and character]: That the trial [approval] of your faith, being much more precious than of gold that perisheth, though it be tried with fire, might be found unto praise and honour and glory at the appearing of Jesus Christ.
> —1 Peter 1:6–7

Paul understood that when his road became very rough, it was because he had been relying on his own strength again and the difficulty was God's way of showing Paul that he got lost and found himself off-roading. Without an all-terrain vehicle to get him out of the bog, he became weighed down.

On a crisp fall night I was driving a police four-wheel-drive SUV in search of a lost hunter and his young son in a wooded area, not far from the Rocky Mountains. This fellow's wife insisted on coming along as an extra set of eyes to look out for her family. We left the gravel logging road and headed up a trail that we thought would take us up to a higher vantage point, where we would have a better chance of spotting a campfire in the surrounding valley. I had my eyes fixed on a fallen tree that jutted out into the path and was steering to the left to avoid it, totally unaware that the tall grass I was driving through was extra tall for a reason; it was a swampy patch resulting from a spring that flowed through the peat moss. The police truck suddenly tilted sharply and high centered with the four wheels spinning but going nowhere. I was stuck and bad and with a unit that did not have a winch or any equipment to dig my way out. I radioed for the local forest warden to come and tow me out, as he had much better equipment than we did. But the only problem was I had no idea how to give him instructions to where we were. The sun was setting and he would have a difficult time seeing my tracks, as I had turned off the remote logging road. So now the search team was in need of rescue.

I was in a narrow strait now, as the RCMP would frown on me for placing this civilian at risk and question my decision to have her join me. I decided to walk out to the main road and wait for the warden. I left the lady in the truck, where she would be safe, and headed out on foot. Within minutes I heard, or at least I thought I heard, the sound of a nasty bear or something, and I started to feel very vulnerable. The narrow trail I was walking down was cut through a tall stand of lodge pole pine trees by the seismic crews who make a path just wide enough for their trucks to pass through. I knew the way out, I was well trained as a policeman (but not necessarily as a woodsman), and I had a weapon, but I was terrified. I felt so small and alone, and I was so sure that whatever was following me could see me but I couldn't

see them. I started running all the while thinking how little effect my little
.38 caliber police issue revolver would have against a black bear unless I hit it
just right. I ran through the darkness with my heart racing and rehearsing in
my mind every prayer I could think of while flipping back to what I would
do if I were approached by a drooling bear. I felt I was running for ages, and
I guess it was over an hour until I reached the main road where I was soon
able to flag down the warden.

I was never so happy to get into a vehicle and slam the door shut on the
terrifying darkness. I took the warden more than five miles back into the
woods where he stopped a considerable distance from my truck, as he had a
much heavier truck and didn't want to sink in the damp peat moss as I did.
I stretched out his winch cable and fastened it to a tow hook on my unit.
Within a short time he had pulled me back to solid ground. Then I received a
little scolding from this much older and weathered forest warden for driving
where I did. My passenger was doing her best to be brave; but had become
increasingly alarmed for me and her husband, as she heard a warning over the
radio about a bear problem in the area while I was running to the road. The
hunter and his boy turned up in a few hours at daybreak after they found their
way back to where they had left their vehicle.

I was so confident and assured of myself until I got bogged down in the
wilderness. It was then that I realized that the only strength and hope that I
had was apart from myself.

> And he said unto me, My grace is sufficient for thee: for my strength
> [miracle working power] is made perfect [most effective] in weakness.
> Most gladly therefore will I rather glory in my infirmities, that the power
> of Christ may rest upon me. Therefore I take pleasure in infirmities [sick-
> ness, trials, troubles, emotional turmoil], in reproaches [insult, mental
> injury], in necessities [anguish, squeezed into narrow strait] in persecu-
> tions, in distresses [extreme affliction, tribulation] for Christ's sake: for
> when I am weak, then am I strong.
> —2 CORINTHIANS 12:9–10

Had Joseph despised
his brothers and
became bitter against
them, he would not
have proved himself
to be worthy of the
assignment God was
preparing him for.

When I put my uniform on, fastened up the
bulletproof vest, and attached the gun belt, I
felt invincible. But now you know that when
a little distress came, my carnal armor fell
off and I was just as frail as any man. For a
moment, that little trek in the bush seemed difficult, but it was over so fast that little endurance was required.

Now, as many of you have experienced, I
understand the deep feeling of intense pain, rejection, and emptiness, since
my beloved announced she no longer wanted to be married to me and she left

with my youngest son. Divorce papers arrived soon after to slip me into the deepest of pits I have ever been in. A bankruptcy and many infirmities did not compare to the pain of the broken heart I now realized along with the shame and anger that a marriage separation puts a person through.

Satan intended the separation to steal, kill, and destroy; but it was through this affliction that God became very real to me. He gently and patiently began to show me the uncleanness that needed to be exposed so that my love would work as God intended.

> Before I was afflicted I went astray: but now have I kept thy word.
> —PSALM 119:67

Joseph was kidnapped and sold as a slave by his brothers. While working as a slave he was falsely accused of rape for which he spent several years in an Egyptian prison. The deed of the brothers caused Joseph to suffer incredible pain, separation, imprisonment, loneliness, maltreatment, false accusation, rejection, and anguish, for which many would say they couldn't blame him for being bitter and wanting to get even with his brothers when he got the chance. However, when the tables turned and Joseph was in a position to make things very miserable for his brothers, he couldn't, as he knew for certain that God used their treachery to prepare him for his assignment. God dealt with the brothers, and they were brought to a place of repentance where God could now use them to be the leaders of the twelve tribes of Israel that He had in mind to establish. Had Joseph despised his brothers and became bitter against them, he would not have proved himself to be worthy of the assignment God was preparing him for.

If your beloved dealt treacherously with you and cast you into the pit of divorce, you can't blame your spouse anymore than Joseph could blame his brothers. If a church leader cheated you in business or you were wrongfully dismissed from a job, is it possible you are about to receive a Joseph assignment? How could Joseph judge his brothers, especially after he had seen the next chapter? How can we judge someone who has dealt us a fatal blow to some area of our life, when God may be watching very closely to see if we qualify for kingdom of God work?

> And Joseph said unto them, Fear not: for am I in the place of God? But as for you, ye thought evil against me; but God meant it unto good, to bring to pass, as it is this day, to save much people alive.
> —GENESIS 50:19–20

We've looked at the following passage already, but read it again to allow the Spirit of God to show you the purpose of the affliction you have been subjected to. It's time to make a decision about what you are going to do with all of those that dealt treacherously against you. Are you ready?

> Servants, be subject to your masters with all fear; not only to the good and gentle, but also to the froward. For this is thankworthy, if a man for conscience toward God endure grief, suffering wrongfully. For what glory

is it, if, when ye be buffeted for your faults, ye shall take it patiently? but if, when ye do well, and suffer for it, ye take it patiently, this is acceptable with God. For even hereunto were ye called: because Christ also suffered for us, leaving us an example, that ye should follow his steps: Who did no sin, neither was guile found in his mouth: Who, when he was reviled, reviled not again; when he suffered, he threatened not; but committed himself to him that judgeth righteously: Who his own self bare our sins in his own body on the tree, that we, being dead to sins, should live unto righteousness: by whose stripes ye were healed. For ye were as sheep going astray; but are now returned unto the Shepherd and Bishop of your soul.

—1 PETER 2:18–24

Now a moment of truth, are we seeking to be cleansed and sanctified for the benefit we'll receive, or are we pursuing sanctification for the glory of the kingdom of God? Walking in "phileo" will have us seeking spiritual benefit for selfish motive, whereas in "agape" we'll be seeking spiritual benefit for our brothers and sisters. Timothy learned, as an understudy of Paul, to endure all things for the sake of others; and he was able to do that by dying to self. The benefit of dying to self is beyond comprehension to one still walking in fleshly desires.

> It's time to make a decision about what you are going to do with all of those that dealt treacherously against you.

Wherein I suffer trouble, as an evil doer, even unto bonds; but the word of God is not bound. Therefore I endure all things for the elect's sakes, that they may also obtain the salvation which is in Christ Jesus with eternal glory. It is a faithful saying: For if we be dead with him, we shall also live with him: If we suffer, we shall also reign with him: if we deny him, he also will deny us.

—2 TIMOTHY 2:9–12

This is agape when we are able to endure all things for the sake of others; that is what Jesus would do!

But watch [be calm, circumspect] thou in all things, endure afflictions [suffer hardships and troubles], do the work of an evangelist, make full proof [fully accomplish] of thy ministry.

—2 TIMOTHY 4:5

Workout of despising the chastening of the Lord

Step 1: Prayerfully review the following list and mark each sin you or your generations have participated with. It is important that you are not rushed and that you are in a private place as you go through this.

❑ **Accepting the false peace of the world**   ❑ **Accusation**

❑ Carnality: resorting to own power to help God out

❑ Depression

❑ Despising the chastening of the Lord in the life of a beloved one

❑ Dulled conscience due to flagrant sin

❑ Entrapment

❑ Gossip

❑ Heaviness

❑ Jealousy

❑ Prodigal: rebellion and reckless waste

❑ Scorn

❑ Servitude to the kingdom of the world

❑ Thinking evil upon another

❑ Violence

❑ Cursing

❑ Despising the chastening of the Lord in my life

❑ Doubt

❑ Enacting evil upon another

❑ Giving up when road became too rough

❑ Hatred

❑ Impatience

❑ Lying

❑ Rejection

❑ Seeking sanctification with wrong motive

❑ Testing God

❑ Unbelief

❑ Weariness

This is a partial list. Ask the Lord to show you what additional bondage He wants you to be released from.

Step 2: Ask and wait.

> *Lord, is there any other sin that I have been unable to lay down on my own that You want me to deal with?* _____

With the exception of agape, all the spiritual gifts are temporarily designed only for the church era.

Step 3: Go back through the list and pray this prayer inserting the sin in the blank space. You may insert several sins in the blank space at a time if you desire.

Prayer of Repentance
(Preferably out loud)

> *Father God, I recognize and take responsibility for myself and my ancestors for the sin(s) of _____. I agree with Your verdict on my rebellion. I repent, I renounce, and I ask forgiveness for my participation with these sins, and I ask that their curse be broken in the name of Jesus Christ of Nazareth.*

Step 4: Purging the evil. This is best done by an experienced and trusted ministering friend the first time around. Review the above list again now inserting the sin you have repented of in the blank.

Command of Deliverance
(Must be out loud with eyes open,
realizing you are speaking directly to a spirit)

In the name of Jesus Christ of Nazareth and by the power of the Holy Spirit, I take authority over the spirit(s) of _____. I break your power, I cast you out, and I command you to return no more.

Step 5: Pray that God will cause you to increase and abound in His love and that you would be an overcomer in the sins just repented of. Ask for a scripture that you will use to resist the devil when he tries to open the trapdoor again to regain entrance to your heart.

Agape Never Fails

Agape is likened to the relationship of the sun to the moon and the moon to the earth. The sun is the agape source, which is the Father. We are the moon, which has no light of its own; so when we are apart from agape, we are in darkness, desolate, and cold. When the agape rays hit our moon, we reflect it to others throughout our world; and a portion of the light is absorbed by the moon for its own benefit. Perfect agape would be as a full moon, where all the love that is intended for the earth arrives as it is fully reflected by the moon. When we are in sin we may only reflect a quarter, half, or three-quarters of the agape we are intended to stream to those we are to love. Or we could be a new moon, a new convert from phileo to agape love; who doesn't reflect any light yet at all to the world but is receiving the love of the Father and will soon be able to pass that along. If we are taken into captivity with sin, it is likened to the eclipse, partial or total, where the agape love is blocked out by an object that is standing in the path.

With the exception of agape, all the spiritual gifts are temporarily designed only for the church era. The gifts are to minister to a needy, sinful people; but once this chapter is over, the only gift that remains for eternity is the more excellent way, agape.

> Charity [*agape*] never faileth: but whether there be prophecies, they shall fail; whether there be tongues, they shall cease; whether there be knowledge, it shall vanish away. For we know in part, and we prophesy in part. But when that which is perfect is come, then that which is in part shall be done away.
> —1 Corinthians 13:8–10

If you were like me going through this study of 1 Corinthians 13, you soon realized that agape is so much more than an emotional warm and wacky love. Agape becomes our entirety; it defines us. And it is through agape that we can become God-like, as our actions and reactions become predictable and righteous no matter what broadsides us. Agape behaves very differently than one who buys into the worldly, fleshly philosophy of what "normal" behavior should be. Agape is not given to any carnal appetites and actions. Agape is the motivation for us to cleanse our temple to be suitable for the Master's purposes and companionship. We don't know what kind of body we'll have, but we do know what kind of character we'll have.

> Behold, what manner of love [*agape*] the Father hath bestowed upon us, that we should be called the sons of God: therefore the world knoweth us not, because it knew him not. Beloved, now are we the sons of God, and it doth not yet appear what we shall be: but we know that, when he shall appear, we shall be like him; for we shall see him as he is. And every man that hath this hope [confident expectation] in him purifieth [temple cleansed for divine presence] himself, even as he is pure [referring to God: sacred, pure from carnality, immaculate].
> —1 JOHN 3:1–3

The time God chose for us to grow up in agape is here and now in preparation for our next assignment, which will be to reign with Jesus throughout the Millennium and beyond. If you were to accomplish only one thing here on earth, this would be it. Agape is the only attribute that we take with us into eternity; and the only time allotted for its development, as far as we know, is here and now. There is no scripture that teaches that if we fail and ignore agape, no worries, we'll all just be granted a full portion of it anyway when we meet Jesus. Agape is not measured by the size of the ministry or the quantity and quality of good things we have done. It is measured by the judging criteria set out in 1 Corinthians 13. The only commandments we will be judged on have to do with our agape for the Godhead, our fellow man, and ourselves.

What is the one thing that will give us confidence in approaching our day of judgment? It would be to use our time in this world to be reconciled to the person we were created from the foundation of the world to be; holy, without blame in agape. In other words, if we are walking in agape, we would be holy and without blame; and in that place of maturity we would fear nothing.

> Herein is our love [*agape*] made perfect [complete or accomplished], that we may have boldness [free and fearless confidence] in the day of judgment: because as he is, so are we in this world. There is no fear [terror, dread] in love [*agape*]; but perfect [mature, complete] love [*agape*] casteth out fear: because fear hath torment. He that feareth is not made perfect in love. We love him, because he first loved us.
> —1 JOHN 4:17–19

First-degree afflictions

Many of you have experienced the most difficult of afflictions, and I don't want to make light of your pain. But to use the words of Paul who knew pain and suffering as well as just about anyone, consider a partial list of some of the afflictions he endured:

Are they ministers of Christ? (I speak as a fool) I am more; in labours more abundant, in stripes [a blow to wound, heavy affliction, and public calamity] above measure, in prisons more frequent, in deaths oft [mortal perils]. Of the Jews five times received I forty stripes [whipped] save one. Thrice was I beaten with rods [bludgeoned with batons] , once was I stoned [capital punishment by pelting with stones], thrice I suffered shipwreck, a night and a day I have been in the deep [the deep sea]; In journeyings often, in perils [dangers] of waters, in perils of robbers, in perils by mine own countrymen, in perils by the heathen, in perils in the city, in perils in the wilderness, in perils in the sea, in perils among false brethren; In weariness [intense grief coupled with sorrow and trouble] and painfulness [hardship, distress], in watchings [sleeplessness] often, in hunger and thirst, in fastings often, in cold and nakedness.... If I must needs glory, I will glory of the things which concern mine infirmities [disease, weakness].

—2 CORINTHIANS 11:23–27, 30

No doubt that is a lot for one man to endure, but look what Paul says previously in the same letter to the Corinthians regarding these afflictions:

The torment in the second half of the tribulation will be so nasty that men will try to kill themselves, but will not be able to escape by death.

For which cause we faint not; but though our outward man perish, yet the inward man is renewed day by day. For our light affliction [easy to bear], which is but for a moment, worketh [accomplishes] for us a far more exceeding and eternal weight of glory; While we look not at the things which are seen, but at the things which are not seen: for the things which are seen are temporal; but the things which are not seen are eternal.

—2 CORINTHIANS 4:16–18

For Paul to say these are "light afflictions," he must be aware of a much greater affliction that men will endure. Is it possible that there are much heavier afflictions? Yes, there are. We've seen that there are afflictions that are for the purpose of testing us in preparation for our future assignments and our eternal destiny. There are afflictions that are the result of the curse of sin. I'll call these first-degree afflictions.

Second-degree afflictions

But an even greater affliction awaits those that are found to be lukewarm or cold in their relationship to Jesus Christ at the time of His surprise inspection and graduation, the Rapture. The affliction will be so great during the second half of the tribulation period that men will desire death as the only way to escape, as death would be a comfort from their pain. These are the second-degree afflictions.

> And the kings of the earth, and the great men, and the rich men, and the chief captains, and the mighty men, and every bondman, and every free man, hid themselves in the dens and in the rocks of the mountains; And said to the mountains and rocks, Fall on us, and hide us from the face of him that sitteth on the throne, and from the wrath of the Lamb: For the great day of his wrath is come; and who shall be able to stand?
>
> —REVELATION 6:15–17

The torment in the second half of the tribulation will be so nasty that men will try to kill themselves, but will not be able to escape by death. No matter how severe their injury, they will not find death to release them.

> Hell is torment that is not escapable through the relief of death.

> And to them it was given that they should not kill them, but that they should be tormented five months: and their torment was as the torment of a scorpion, when he striketh a man. And in those days shall men seek death, and shall not find it; and shall desire to die, and death shall flee from them.
>
> —REVELATION 9:5–6

No matter what our body goes through this side of tribulation and eternal judgment, it is light affliction in comparison. Eternity in hell is the third-degree affliction.

Third-degree afflictions

Hell is eternal torment that is not escapable through the relief of death. Think about that. Folks that are in a lot of inescapable pain in the later stages of disease welcome death, and the family comforts themselves by saying that at least they are no longer suffering and the pain is gone. That is only a true statement for a believer and servant of Jesus Christ. We cannot fathom affliction that knows no escape. But imagine if that loved one who was in so much pain due to their illness just kept living and living and living, in fact never could die and their condition remained unchanged. You've now had an introduction to hell.

> So shall it be at the end of the world: the angels shall come forth, and sever the wicked from among the just, And shall cast them into the furnace of fire: there shall be wailing and gnashing of teeth.
>
> —MATTHEW 13:49–50

> And the beast was taken, and with him the false prophet that wrought miracles before him, with which he deceived them that had received the mark of the beast, and them that worshiped his image. These both were cast alive into a lake of fire burning with brimstone [sulfur, as used in manufacture of black gunpowder].
>
> —REVELATION 19:20

The beast is the world leader that is empowered by Satan who rises to world domination during the seven-year tribulation period. Among many things, he will bring in a one-world currency and identification system. The identification system is referred to as the mark of the beast and without it people will not be able to buy and sell or travel; so there will be tremendous pressure to take the mark. It is thought this mark could be an embedded microchip that carries our financial, health, personal, and affiliation data. The system will have obvious benefits, as it will kill the drug trade and money laundering activities as the world switches to a cashless society and into a system that all transactions are monitored. It will provide data on earnings and tax evasion, for instance. Satan knows that Jesus is coming to set up His kingdom on earth, and he will attempt to beat Christ to it and will deceive many. If you are reading this book after this leader has gained control, the rapture would have removed many believers from the world. You have a decision to make that will cost you your life. Do not take the mark of the antichrist leader; choose martyrdom instead through which by faith you will escape the second and third degree afflictions spoken of here. And partway through the tribulation you'll be delivered, catching up to those believers that were prepared to meet their Lord prior to the tribulation.

> And when he had opened the fifth seal, I saw under the altar the souls of them that were slain for the word of God, and for the testimony which they held: And they cried with a loud voice, saying, How long, O Lord, holy and true, dost thou not judge and avenge our blood on them that dwell on the earth? And white robes were given unto every one of them; and it was said unto them, that they should rest yet for a little season, until their fellowservants also and their brethren, that should be killed as they were, should be fulfilled....And one of the elders answered, saying unto me, What are these which are arrayed in white robes? and whence came they? And I said unto him, Sir, thou knowest. And he said to me, These are they which came out of great tribulation, and have washed their robes, and made them white in the blood of the Lamb. Therefore are they before the throne of God, and serve him day and night in his temple: and he that sitteth on the throne shall dwell among them. They shall hunger no more, neither thirst any more; neither shall the sun light on them, nor any heat.
> —REVELATION 6:9–11; 7:13–16

To whom do you still have an outstanding debt of love to be repaid? What is stopping you from paying your debt right now?

8

FOR THINE IS THE KINGDOM

The Lord's Prayer, as short as it is, refers to the "kingdom" twice, and I believe that is not by accident. The first reference to the kingdom is that it will come—future tense. The second reference speaks as though the kingdom were here—present tense. So there is something very important between the two references of the kingdom that charges us to usher in the kingdom of God. The calling of the Christian is to replace one kingdom with another, and that happens individually first and foremost before we can change the world. We all want to change the world; but God's priority for us is to change ourselves, then He can change the world through us. Pay close attention to the four sentences between the two kingdom references.

> After this manner therefore pray ye: Our Father which art in heaven, Hallowed be thy name. *Thy kingdom come.* Thy will be done in earth, as it is in heaven. Give us this day our daily bread. And forgive us our debts, as we forgive our debtors. And lead us not into temptation, but deliver us from evil: For *thine is the kingdom*, and the power, and the glory, for ever. Amen.
> —Matthew 6:9–13, emphasis added

It is for this reason that Jesus warns us ahead of time that stuff will get stirred up, particularly within a family. Why within a family? Because of the generational iniquity they have in common. Satan doesn't want to lose the inroads he made into the destruction of those residing in the family tree.

The personal pronouns, *us, we,* and *our,* occur collectively eight times, whereas *them, you,* and *your* just don't happen. The reference to *others* only happens once the kingdom of God is in place in our spirits and the kingdom of the devil is purged.

> But if I with the finger of God cast out devils, no doubt the kingdom of God is come upon you.
> —Luke 11:20

While the kingdom of darkness is in place within one's heart, they may well be living in relative peace. They may even comment, "Why do I need God? I have everything I want and things are going very well."

When a strong man armed keepeth his palace, his goods are in peace.
—Luke 11:21

Strife isn't stirred up until this kingdom of darkness is exposed, and then it fights for its life cursing the one who is attempting to remove it from its palace, which is our spirit. The devil kicks up such a stink so as to get us to think it is us who are wrong and to intimidate us, the ministers of righteousness, so that we will abandon our mission of ushering in the kingdom of God.

It is for this reason that Jesus warns us ahead of time that stuff will get stirred up, particularly within a family. Why within a family? Because of the generational iniquity they have in common. Satan doesn't want to lose the inroads he made into the destruction of those residing in the family tree.

> Think not that I am come to send peace on earth: I came not to send peace, but a sword. For I am come to set a man at variance against his father, and the daughter against her mother, and the daughter in law against her mother in law. And a man's foes shall be they of his own household. He that loveth father or mother more than me is not worthy of me: and he that loveth son or daughter more than me is not worthy of me. And he that taketh not his cross, and followeth after me, is not worthy of me. He that findeth his life shall lose it: and he that loseth his life for my sake shall find it.
> —Matthew 10:34–39

It is necessary to warn a believer, especially after going to the level of sanctification through first works, that there will be conflict in relationships, as the devil wants to keeps his goods in place. He keeps his goods in place by striking out like a snake to intimidate you so you'll back off. He doesn't want to have to leave the body he has usurped control of or partial control of. So when you see the manifestation through others, realize that it is not the flesh and blood that you see and love that is causing the problem, but it is the principalities and powers that are using their faces.

Now you may be murmuring that this is more than I signed up for; but hold your peace, there is more: for things to be rebuilt they have to die first; they must pass away. And then God will use you through the ministry of reconciliation to restore all things new, better than they ever were.

> Therefore if any man be in Christ, he is a new creature: old things are passed away; behold, all things are become new. And all things are of God, who hath reconciled us to himself by Jesus Christ, and hath given to us the ministry of reconciliation; To wit, that God was in Christ, reconciling the world unto himself, not imputing their trespasses unto them; and hath committed unto us the word of reconciliation.
> —2 Corinthians 5:17–19

Are you prepared to be a kingdom builder? Or, by default, would you choose to leave the kingdom of Satan at peace within the hearts of those you love?

Ignoring the kingdom of darkness doesn't make it go away; it makes you party to its offense and separates you from God. It makes you an enemy of God.

> Ye adulterers and adulteresses, know ye not that the friendship of the world is enmity [opposes the agape of the Father] with God? whosoever therefore will be a friend of the world is the enemy of God. Do ye think that the scripture saith in vain, The spirit that dwelleth in us lusteth to envy? But he giveth more grace. Wherefore he saith, God resisteth the proud, but giveth grace unto the humble. Submit yourselves therefore to God. Resist the devil, and he will flee from you.
>
> —JAMES 4:4–7

The four sentences sandwiched between the references to the kingdom of God in the Lord's prayer relate to our dying to self, to cleansing the impurity from our temples, to forgiving all offense, to overcoming and replacing the pride of the devil with the agape of the Father. You may have gone through the chapters in this book doing the workout of ministry and are still struggling; perhaps you are as the blind man who needed a second touch from Jesus.

> And he cometh to Bethsaida; and they bring a blind man unto him, and besought him to touch him. And he took the blind man by the hand, and led him out of the town; and when he had spit on his eyes, and put his hands upon him, he asked him if he saw ought. And he looked up, and said, I see men as trees, walking. After that he put his hands again upon his eyes, and made him look up: and he was restored, and saw every man clearly.
>
> —MARK 8:22–25

For the second touch, I would suggest working through the ministry lists again, as what was holding you in captivity to iniquity addressed first may be held in place in your hearts by something you dealt with much later; therefore you'll have to go back. Sanctification is like pealing the layers off of an onion; there is an order to it, as everyone's layers are formed in differently. When I'm in a particular battle, I review the applicable battle plan daily and engage in the warfare. There is never a day that I don't go through at least part of the eight steps to sanctification.

What is the one thing that will give us confidence in approaching our day of judgment? It would be to use our time in this world to be reconciled to the person we were created from the foundation of the world to be; holy, without blame in agape. In other words, if we are walking in agape, we would be holy and without blame. In that place of maturity we would fear nothing.

> We are bound to thank God always for you, brethren, as it is meet, because that your faith groweth exceedingly, and the charity *[agape]* of every one of you all toward each other aboundeth; So that we ourselves glory in you in the churches of God for your patience and faith in all your persecutions and tribulations that ye endure: Which is a manifest token of the righteous judgment of God, that ye may be counted worthy

of the kingdom of God, for which ye also suffer: Seeing it is a righteous thing with God to recompense tribulation to them that trouble you.

—2 Thessalonians 1:3–6

> God will generally require our obedience and not tell us what He is preparing us for.

Paul continues in this letter teaching that the key to eternal life is in knowing God and submitting to the gospel. What is the gospel? The *gospel* is a broad term for the kingdom of God, which we gain eternal membership into with salvation through sanctification made possible only because of the finished work of the Messiah, Jesus Christ. This salvation is not only a belief but also it is a daily process of submission to Christ and a corresponding deliverance from the vexation of the devil. Whichever kingdom is submitted to through our pursuits, love (eros, phileo, or agape), and focus now, is the kingdom that gets to claim us for everlasting.

> And to you who are troubled rest with us, when the Lord Jesus shall be revealed from heaven with his mighty angels, In flaming fire taking vengeance on them that know [to experience through observation and discovery] not God, and that obey [submit to] not the gospel [the good news of the kingdom of God and salvation or deliverance through Christ] of our Lord Jesus Christ: Who shall be punished with everlasting [lasts as long as eternal life!] destruction from the presence of the Lord, and from the glory of his power.
>
> —2 Thessalonians 1:7–9

Believers are to pick up their cross with courage and follow; that is to submit to Jesus Christ. Before Jesus was able to pick up His cross, recall the preparation the Father put Him through to prepare Him for that assignment. Your cross is whatever your individual assignment is, and the training for such will of necessity be tough and costly. This cross can only be picked up by agape and humility just as Jesus did. Jesus Christ had to die to His own will and desires and do the will of the Father.

> And whosoever doth not bear his cross, and come after me, cannot be my disciple. For which of you, intending to build a tower, sitteth not down first, and counteth the cost, whether he have sufficient to finish it? Lest haply, after he hath laid the foundation, and is not able to finish it, all that behold it begin to mock him. Saying, This man began to build, and was not able to finish. Or what king, going to make war against another king, sitteth not down first, and consulteth whether he be able with ten thousand to meet him that cometh against him with twenty thousand? Or else, while the other is yet a great way off, he sendeth an ambassage, and desireth conditions of peace. So likewise, whosoever he be of you that forsaketh not all that he hath, he cannot be my disciple.
>
> —Luke 14:27–33

God will generally require our obedience and not tell us what He is preparing us for. We find out what He has in mind after we prove to Him which kingdom we will serve through our darkness and wilderness.

Jesus glorified the Father on earth. Let's be like Jesus and glorify God our Father and without compromise finish the work He is preparing us for.

> I have glorified thee on the earth: I have finished the work which thou gavest me to do.
> —John 17:4

Agape, the character of God, will not allow Him to fail to keep His covenant or rescind His mercy once it is granted to those in submission to Him. God is a covenant keeper, and His followers will be known because they do as their Father does.

> Know therefore that the LORD thy God, he is God, the faithful God, which keepeth covenant and mercy with them that love him and keep his commandments to a thousand generations.
> —Deuteronomy 7:9

The thousand generations of God's covenant includes you, as we are only around the one hundred and fifty count now.

JESUS' PRAYER FOR US TELLS US OUR PRIORITY

Jesus prays very earnestly to Father God on our behalf. Would you like to listen in on what Jesus considers as the most important things for us to grasp while we are in preparation? Read this passage first and then review, thanking God for where you have been obedient and repenting for where you have fallen short. Then rewrite this as a personal prayer in your journal and refer to it often.

> These words spake Jesus, and lifted up his eyes to heaven, and said, Father, the hour is come; glorify thy Son, that thy Son also may glorify thee: As thou hast given him power over all flesh, that he should give eternal life to as many as thou hast given him. And this is life eternal, that they might know thee the only true God, and Jesus Christ, whom thou hast sent. I have glorified thee on the earth: I have finished the work which thou gavest me to do. And now, O Father, glorify thou me with thine own self with the glory which I had with thee before the world was. I have manifested thy name unto the men which thou gavest me out of the world: thine they were, and thou gavest them me; and they have kept thy word. Now they have known that all things whatsoever thou hast given me are of thee. For I have given unto them the words which thou gavest me; and they have received them, and have known surely that I came out from thee, and they have believed that thou didst send me.
>
> I pray for them: I pray not for the world, but for them which thou hast given me; for they are thine And all mine are thine, and thine are mine; and I am glorified in them. And now I am no more in the world, but these are in the world, and I come to thee. Holy Father, keep through

thine own name those whom thou hast given me, that they may be one, as we are. While I was with them in the world, I kept them in thy name: those that thou gavest me I have kept, and none of them is lost, but the son of perdition; that the scripture might be fulfilled. And now come I to thee; and these things I speak in the world, that they might have my joy fulfilled in themselves. I have given them thy word; and the world hath hated them, because they are not of the world, even as I am not of the world. I pray not that thou shouldest take them out of the world, but that thou shouldest keep them from the evil. They are not of the world, even as I am not of the world. Sanctify them through thy truth: thy word is truth. As thou hast sent me into the world, even so have I also sent them into the world. And for their sakes I sanctify myself, that they also might be sanctified through the truth. Neither pray I for these alone, but for them also which shall believe on me through their word; That they all may be one; as thou, Father, art in me, and I in thee, that they also may be one in us: that the world may believe that thou hast sent me. And the glory which thou gavest me I have given them; that they may be one, even as we are one: I in them, and thou in me, that they may be made perfect in one; and that the world may know that thou hast sent me, and hast loved them, as thou hast loved me. Father, I will that they also, whom thou hast given me, be with me where I am; that they may behold my glory, which thou hast given me: for thou lovedst me before the foundation of the world. O righteous Father, the world hath not known thee: but I have known thee, and these have known that thou hast sent me. And I have declared unto them thy name, and will declare it: that the love wherewith thou hast loved me may be in them, and I in them.

—JOHN 17, EMPHASIS ADDED

THE POWER AND THE
GLORY FOREVER. AMEN

W HY DO I feel that some of my brethren skipped all the hard stuff in the middle of this book, going directly to this chapter on power? No shortcuts, honey. There is a very good reason I believe that the Lord placed this section at the end of His prayer, and that is because we have a lot of stuff to deal with first before the fullness of His power will become evident.

God has intended for us to enjoy the fruits of His power, His agape, and of a sound mind in the total absence of fear. We've explored in depth that pride is at the top of the list as to what hinders the agape love, and it is also pride that is behind the unsoundness of mind or insanity.

> For God hath not given us the spirit of fear; but of power [*dynamis*; as to perform miracles], and of love [*agape*], and of a sound mind.
> —2 TIMOTHY 1:7

Accordingly, what might be the main hindrance to the work of the power of God?

> But if ye will not hearken unto me, and will not do all these commandments; And if ye shall despise my statutes, or if your soul abhor my judgments, so that ye will not do all my commandments, but that ye break my covenant: I also will do this unto you; I will even appoint over you terror, consumption, and the burning ague, that shall consume the eyes, and cause sorrow of heart: and ye shall sow your seed in vain, for your enemies shall eat it. And I will set my face against you, and ye shall be slain before your enemies: they that hate you shall reign over you; and ye shall flee when none pursueth you. And if ye will not yet for all this hearken unto me, then I will punish you seven times more for your sins. And I will break the pride of your power; and I will make your heaven as iron, and your earth as brass: And your strength shall be spent in vain: for your land shall not yield her increase, neither shall the trees of the land yield their fruits.
> —LEVITICUS 26:14–20

In the Book of Leviticus we see that the Lord had considerable difficulty coaching His people to live a worthy life of righteousness. So, as the result of their continued state of rebellion, the consequences included disease, loss of eyesight, broken hearts, financial loss, withdrawal of protection from evil, and all efforts for gain were vain. With heaven as iron, their prayers were not heard and the silence from the Lord would be bewildering. The root cause of their rebellion was the "pride of their own power." They had become self-sufficient; for their daily direction and supply they would look no farther than themselves, not inquiring from the only One who had the true perspective on their matters. It is interesting that this entire affliction came upon them, and there still was no repentance and no remorse but only stubborn defiance.

I Will or Thy Will?

All of sin and the results thereof have their roots in the same defiance, where we say, "I Will," rather than, "Thy Will." Lucifer had the same struggle with rebellion. He chose to boldly proclaim in his life's mission statement: I will, I will, I will, I will, and I will! The result was not what Lucifer expected. He expected all this power, influence, and fame; and he did get that for a short season, but he will be evicted from his mansion and stripped of his freedom and power and exchange it for a shanty town where he will be detained for eternity in downtown hell.

> How art thou fallen from heaven, O Lucifer....For thou hast said in thine heart, I will ascend into heaven, I will exalt my throne above the stars of God: I will sit also upon the mount of the congregation, in the sides of the north: I will ascend above the heights of the clouds; I will be like the most High. Yet thou shalt be brought down to hell, to the sides of the pit.
>
> —Isaiah 14:12–15

Lucifer's mistake was thinking that the power he had was his own. God has equipped all living beings with a measure of power. All this power is spiritual in nature and substance. This power from God is an ability to do certain things, but the operation and control of this power is entrusted to the recipient. The recipient can choose to use this power for his own pleasures, or he can give it away for the greater good in agape. All power is of God, and the portion that is assigned to the living is our responsibility as to whether we will use it for good or evil.

> We have the power to have a secret life, to gossip, to speak perverse things, to murmur and complain, but only for a limited time. Satan has also abused his power, but it is only for a limited time; then everything Satan has done will be exposed.

> Let every soul be subject unto the higher powers [exousia]. For there is no power [exousia] but of God: the powers [exousia] that be are ordained of God.
>
> —Romans 13:1

A son that is left a large inheritance has a choice as to how he uses it. He can use it to buy pleasure craft and vices to satisfy his own lusts. Or, he can set up a foundation to bless those who have not been blessed as he was. He did not create the inheritance, but he was simply entrusted with it and given the freedom do with it as he chooses. The power we receive is like an inheritance, and it is transferable.

Jesus Christ was ordained with holy power from on high; then along comes Satan who offers Christ an impressive power, howbeit an unclean, perverted, and destined to soon fail, power. Jesus was able to immediately discern the aberration because of His familiarity with the true.

Lucifer was given considerable power prior to his fall because of the position he held, and then pride redirected this power to everything unclean and self-serving.

> And the devil, taking him up into an high mountain, shewed unto him all the kingdoms of the world in a moment of time. And the devil said unto him, All this power [authority over government of mankind] will I give thee, and the glory of them: for that is delivered unto me; and to whomsoever I will I give it. If thou therefore wilt worship me, all shall be thine. And Jesus answered and said unto him, Get thee behind me, Satan: for it is written, Thou shalt worship the Lord thy God, and him only shalt thou serve.
> —LUKE 4:5–8

What would have happened if Jesus had accepted the power Satan offered to Him? What power have you tapped into that is a digression and not of God?

Perverted spiritual power spreads like leaven or yeast but it will be exposed for what it is. We have the power to have a secret life, to gossip, to speak perverse things, to murmur and complain, but only for a limited time. Satan has also abused his power, but it is only for a limited time; then everything Satan has done will be exposed and dealt with in severity.

> Beware ye of the leaven [moral failure, false doctrine, hypocrisy] of the Pharisees [outwardly pious but inwardly cesspools], which is hypocrisy. For there is nothing covered [concealed or covered up] that shall not be revealed [uncovered]; neither hid [secret life], that shall not be known. Therefore whatsoever ye have spoken in darkness [in your sin or backslidden state] shall be heard [attended to] in the light [exposed to spiritual truth] and that which ye have spoken in the ear in closets [private conversation with those of familiar folly] shall be proclaimed upon the housetops. And I say unto you my friends, Be not afraid of them that kill the body, and after that have no more that they can do. But I will forewarn you whom ye shall fear: Fear him, which after he hath killed hath power [*exousia*] to cast into hell; yea, I say unto you, Fear him.
> —LUKE 12:1–5

Only God has the power to evaluate our lives and exercise judgment determining the destiny of all living and dead. How we use the power entrusted to us will determine if we will be among the relative few accepted at the gates to the kingdom of God. There is nothing more painful than to be thrust out of the kingdom of God. We are used to having hope and choices of pleasure now; but when we find ourselves on the wrong side of the gates leading to the kingdom of God, even weeping and gnashing our teeth together won't ever change the situation. It is the reverential fear of God that will allow us to crush rebellion and its pride so we aren't mislead to the path downtown to hell.

> Then said one unto him, Lord, are there few that be saved? And he said unto them, Strive to enter in at the strait gate: for many, I say unto you, will seek to enter in, and shall not be able. When once the master of the house is risen up, and hath shut to the door, and ye begin to stand without, and to knock at the door, saying, Lord, Lord, open unto us; and he shall answer and say unto you, I know you not whence ye are: Then shall ye begin to say, We have eaten and drunk in thy presence, and thou hast taught in our streets. But he shall say, I tell you, I know you not whence ye are; depart from me, all ye workers of iniquity. There shall be weeping and gnashing of teeth [extreme anguish and utter despair of men consigned to hell], when ye shall see Abraham, and Isaac, and Jacob, and all the prophets, in the kingdom of God, and you yourselves thrust out.
>
> —LUKE 13:23–28

Paul expounds on the Lord's teaching to instruct those that suffer affliction now at the hands of vain and unrighteous persons. As God desires that everyone repent, He will extend His grace to those difficult folks. But don't take His grace and patience as His approval of sin or that He has turned a blind eye to it.

> So that we ourselves glory in you in the churches of God for your patience and faith in all your persecutions and tribulations that ye endure: Which is a manifest token of the righteous judgment of God, that ye may be counted worthy of the kingdom of God, for which ye also suffer: Seeing it is a righteous thing with God to recompense tribulation to them that trouble you; And to you who are troubled rest with us, when the Lord Jesus shall be revealed from heaven with his mighty angels, In flaming fire taking vengeance on them that know not God, and that obey not the gospel of our Lord Jesus Christ: Who shall be punished with everlasting destruction from the presence of the Lord, and from the glory of his power.
>
> —2 THESSALONIANS 1:4–9

Many are so attached to the kingdom of the world; but what a pity that is for that is all they'll get. What's here is nothing compared to the kingdom of God where the glory of God's power will be unleashed and uninhibited by evil and destruction. This is our hope, and it is this hope that will pull us through anything. The glory of the power is of our heavenly Father only; isn't it great to be His kids?

It is of the will of the Father to give us a glimpse of what He has in store for us now through the Holy Spirit.

> Now unto him that is able to do exceeding abundantly above all that we ask or think, according to the *power* [*dynamis*; ability to perform mighty works] that worketh in us.
> —EPHESIANS 3:20, EMPHASIS ADDED

The same Spirit that conquered death and raised Jesus up occupies your temple and not because He is seeking a place to sleep! The Spirit of the power of God is bursting at the seams of the temple desiring to set up a command center to oversee operations pertaining to your role in the kingdom of God.

> But if the Spirit of him that raised up Jesus from the dead dwell in you, he that raised up Christ from the dead shall also quicken [endue with power to restore and invigorate] your mortal bodies by his Spirit that dwelleth in you.
> —ROMANS 8:11

You have the Spirit of the living God within you, but what hinders the power?

HINDRANCES TO THE POWER

Here again we will see the limitations of the English language in the word *power*, which is translated from several different Greek words. Back in Ephesians 3:20, we find the word *dynamis*, which is the ability to perform miracles or the mighty works of God. We know the ability is there because the Bible says so; but does it need to be unleashed? I believe the mystery lies in an understanding of the next Greek word, *exousia*, which has also been translated as *power*.

> You have the Spirit of the living God within you, but what hinders the power?

> Therefore doth my Father love me, because I lay down my life, that I might take it again. No man taketh it from me, but I lay it down of myself. I have power [*exousia*] to lay it down, and I have *power* [*exousia*] to take it again. This commandment have I received of my Father.
> —JOHN 10:17–18, EMPHASIS ADDED

The Greek word *exousia* is interesting, as it speaks of being justified, thus denying the presence of any hindrance, combined with authority, power, and capability to perform a certain action.

Jesus had the power to lay His life down and raise it up again, as there would be nothing that could hinder the power of God. It is interesting that to Jesus every word from His Father was a commandment, a call to arms, even more than a promise or a suggestion. I believe that is a vital component of faith—that we realize every word of the Holy Bible is God's commandment as it came forth from His spirit. There will be portions of the Scripture that we don't understand, that even appear to contradict, but all that means is we don't have a complete understanding yet. And, no doubt, some truth remains hidden as a mystery until we are ready to receive it. God will often hide truth from religious wolves and reveal it instead to babes whose only desire is to fear God and walk before Him in obedience.

> Money in the hands of the wrong minister gives him power to do the works of God in the flesh. Much of the work of the church can be accomplished with wealth which may blind the hearts of the saints to their own wretchedness.

For a believer it is very important to understand what may hinder the work of God through us. Many obstructions were removed subsequent to the working out of your sanctification which you have already gone through, but there remain a few considerations.

Satan will hinder or distort the truth to get us to take many exits from the narrow road of purity in an attempt to steer us back unto the broad road that leads to destruction. Seeds are planted in the fellowship of disobedience and rebellion that will soon infect the entire body and prevent the power of God from being able to work in their midst.

> Ye did run well; who did hinder [beat you back, construct an obstruction] you that ye should not obey the truth? This persuasion [deception] cometh not of him that calleth you. A little leaven leaveneth the whole lump.
> —GALATIANS 5:7–9

Money hinders

Paul chose to minister without charge to the people so he would not abuse the power of the gospel. The exchange of money often changes things, not only from the perspective of the person paid but from those that pay as well. Money can cause the message of the gospel to be weakened to please those with the fattest money bags.

> If we have sown unto you spiritual things, is it a great thing if we shall reap your carnal things? If others be partakers of this power over you, are not we rather? Nevertheless we have not used this power; but suffer all things, lest we should hinder the gospel of Christ…What is my reward then? Verily that, when I preach the gospel, I may make the gospel of Christ without charge, that I abuse not my power in the gospel.
> —1 CORINTHIANS 9:11–12, 18

Money in the hands of the wrong minister gives him power to do the works of God in the flesh. Much of the work of the church can be accomplished with wealth, which blinds the hearts of the saints to their own wretchedness. What a sad state it is for many church folks to get involved in campaigns to raise money and goods for various projects but have neglected their salvation.

I know thy works, that thou art neither cold nor hot: I would thou wert cold or hot. So then because thou art lukewarm, and neither cold nor hot, I will spue thee out of my mouth. Because thou sayest, I am rich, and increased with goods, and have need of nothing; and knowest not that thou art wretched, and miserable, and poor, and blind, and naked.

—REVELATION 3:15–17

Peter faced an incident that to our shame is very prevalent today; the church acts like a sorcerer if it tries to sell the power of God in lieu of sanctification. The power received in such a state of presumption may not originate from whence one thinks.

> And he did not many mighty works there because of their unbelief.

And when Simon saw that through laying on of the apostles' hands the Holy Ghost was given, he offered them money, Saying, Give me also this power, that on whomsoever I lay hands, he may receive the Holy Ghost. But Peter said unto him, Thy money perish with thee, because thou hast thought that the gift of God may be purchased with money.

—ACTS 8:18–20

Sin and iniquity hinder

Satan is greedy for those who aren't discerning and just looking for the signs and wonders, which he can also perform to deceive even those that seem quite bright.

Even him, whose coming is after the working of Satan with all power and signs and lying wonders.

—2 THESSALONIANS 2:9

Our sin and iniquities will hinder the work of God and prevent the good things He wants to do for us to happen.

Your iniquities have turned away these things, and your sins have withholden [denied, hindered] good things from you.

—JEREMIAH 5:25

Doubt hinders

Doubt and unbelief that God is a God of miracles and healing will hinder the healing power of our Lord and cause Him to pass over us in favor of true believers. So for those who don't believe God is a God of the miraculous, that will be truth for them in their lives.

And he did not many mighty works there because of their unbelief.

—MATTHEW 13:58

Offense hinders

We cannot remain in our sin and somehow think the Spirit of God is OK with doing His work in such an unclean temple. Those of a religious spirit will say you cannot earn your salvation and that the power of God as it is a gift. The jargon used means little; the fact is that God—whether yesterday, today, or tomorrow—hates sin and is not comfortable in working in its mess; so sanctification is required as we daily workout our salvation with fear and trembling.

> And grieve [offend] not the holy Spirit of God, whereby ye are sealed unto the day of redemption. Let all bitterness, and wrath, and anger, and clamor, and evil speaking, be put away from you, with all malice: And be ye kind one to another, tenderhearted, forgiving one another, even as God for Christ's sake hath forgiven you.
> —Ephesians 4:30–32

Despising certain gifts hinders

The next verse adds to what was just read, that our sin smothers the power of God. Another thing that extinguishes God's work is teachings from the pulpit that approve selections of the gifts of the Spirit that are not miraculous in nature and reject the others as not being relevant.

> Quench [extinguish the fire and suppress the power] not the Spirit. Despise [dismiss as irrelevant for today] not prophesying [inspired declaration of past, present or future truths of God]. Prove [discern if worthy to be received] of all things; hold fast that which is good. Abstain from all appearance of evil. And the very God of peace sanctify you wholly; and I pray God your whole spirit and soul and body be preserved blameless unto the coming of our Lord Jesus Christ.
> —1 Thessalonians 5:19–23

Coupled with the work of the Spirit of God is the exhortation to sanctify or cleanse wholly our body, soul, mind, and spirit.

It seems such a waste to spend all this time doing church without even knowing who we really serve and what He requires of us.

The church was never meant to be a place where we go hear a few words, sing a few words, say a few words, and leave with a few words. The church is to not only hear the words, but to then see the demonstration of the Spirit which would authenticate the message given. The power of the Spirit is seen in many, many ways, so we will only be able to show you a few, as books would be required to teach fully.

> And my speech and my preaching was not with enticing words of man's wisdom, but in demonstration of the Spirit and of power: That your faith should not stand in the wisdom of men, but in the power of God.
> —1 Corinthians 2:4–5

Our faith is not established so much in the sermon but what follows the sermon. The reason is because a sermon can follow all the homiletic essentials taught in our seminaries through proclamation of the Word but still be completely devoid of any power. The power isn't seen in enticing intelligent words, as then the preacher man would tend to take the glory.

Works of the flesh hinder

Paul calls the church of the Galatians foolish because they were led into error regarding the work of the power of God and didn't even know it. The Galatian church would have begun seeing mighty things through the ministry of Paul but became content to reminisce about what happened years ago not realizing the candle was smothered in their midst.

> O foolish Galatians, who hath bewitched [lead away in error] you, that ye should not obey the truth, before whose eyes Jesus Christ hath been evidently set forth, crucified among you?...Are ye so foolish? having begun in the Spirit, are ye now made perfect by the flesh? Have ye suffered so many things in vain? if it be yet in vain. He therefore that ministereth to you the Spirit, and worketh miracles among you, doeth he it by the works of the law, or by the hearing of faith?
> —GALATIANS 3:1, 3–5

Paul feels so strong about this lack of the power of God in the church that he admonishes the people that if it isn't demonstrated, they are to move on.

> Having a form of godliness, but denying the power thereof: from such turn away.
> —2 TIMOTHY 3:5

Simply looking at numbers does not tell the story of the presence of the power of God; if it did we could just go be spectators at a football stadium. It seems such a waste to spend all this time doing church without even knowing who we really serve and what He requires of us.

The message is thus: do not grieve, do not quench, and do not despise the work of the Holy Spirit amongst believers. But as with all teachings in the church, we are to prove their authenticity by comparing the instruction and activity with the Word. Be aware of the potential of churches that are not seeing a manifestation of the move of God to accept strange fire and present it as a new authentic move of God.

Winking at sexual immorality hinders

The Corinthian church prided themselves in how relevant they were with the changing times and how accepting they were to include those that were living in open sexual immorality. Paul said this is not good, as allowing just one couple to continue on in their sin will infect the entire body. A church that winks at sin will be operating completely devoid of the power of God but may continue carrying on as a work of the flesh and carnality. What a tragedy to have the Spirit of God leave and not even be aware of it.

It is reported commonly that there is fornication among you, and such fornication as is not so much as named among the Gentiles, that one should have his father's wife. And ye are puffed up, and have not rather mourned, that he that hath done this deed might be taken away from among you…In the name of our Lord Jesus Christ, when ye are gathered together, and my spirit, with the power of our Lord Jesus Christ, To deliver such an one unto Satan for the destruction of the flesh, that the spirit may be saved in the day of the Lord Jesus. Your glorying is not good. Know ye not that a little leaven leaveneth the whole lump? Purge out therefore the old leaven, that ye may be a new lump, as ye are unleavened. For even Christ our passover is sacrificed for us.

—1 CORINTHIANS 5:1–2, 4–7

An open door of toleration of known sexual sin within a church will allow entrance to a proliferation of uncleanness, thus defiling the entire body. In our desire to be relevant which kingdom are we now fighting for?

> A church that winks at sin will be operating completely devoid of the power of God but may continue carrying on as a work of the flesh and carnality. What a tragedy to have the Spirit of God leave and not even be aware of it.

Jezebel hinders

Not only did sexual immorality hinder the work of God but so does mixing the pagan practices in with the holy. The spirit of Jezebel with all its sensualities and false doctrines, which we've devoted considerable attention to elsewhere in this work, will not only prevent the work of God but it will also lead to the destruction of the body and to judgment.

Notwithstanding I have a few things against thee, because thou sufferest that woman Jezebel, which calleth herself a prophetess, to teach and to seduce my servants to commit fornication, and to eat things sacrificed unto idols. And I gave her space to repent of her fornication; and she repented not. Behold, I will cast her into a bed, and them that commit adultery with her into great tribulation, except they repent of their deeds. And I will kill her children with death; and all the churches shall know that I am he which searcheth the reins and hearts: and I will give unto every one of you according to your works.

—REVELATION 2:20–23

The door to repentance was open for a period of time; but repentance can be nearly impossible with the heart hardened, as the power and pleasure of notoriety will seduce a captive to give up anything to feed the compulsions.

> The power of God is not a call to mediocrity but to the level of purity that Christ walked.

Sceva, the chief priest, had seven sons who presumed that because they were religious and well-known, they could also do the ministry that Paul did through the power of God. They became quite the sideshow in the church, but note what happened after.

> Then certain of the vagabond Jews, exorcists, took upon them to call over them which had evil spirits the name of the Lord Jesus, saying, We adjure you by Jesus whom Paul preacheth.…And the evil spirit answered and said, Jesus I know, and Paul I know; but who are ye? And the man in whom the evil spirit was leaped on them, and overcame them, and prevailed against them, so that they fled out of that house naked and wounded. And this was known to all the Jews and Greeks also dwelling at Ephesus; and fear fell on them all, and the name of the Lord Jesus was magnified. And many that believed came, and confessed, and shewed their deeds. Many of them also which used curious arts brought their books together, and burned them before all men: and they counted the price of them, and found it fifty thousand pieces of silver. So mightily grew the word of God and prevailed.
> —ACTS 19:13, 15–20

The people sought the Lord in fear for their own skins and got serious about falling out of agreement with their sin. The result was a revival that swept the land. Revival is precipitated from repentance, brokenness, and renouncing sin individually so that the power of God can work corporately.

There is consequence for presuming upon the power of God in our approaching His throne in our carnality and uncleanness.

WORK OF REVIVAL

To complete the work of revival, God has provided everything necessary for us to be restored to the person we were created from the foundation of the world to be—holy, without blame in agape. The power of God is not a call to mediocrity but to the level of purity that Christ walked.

> According as his divine power hath given unto us all things [complete set of tools] that pertain unto life [life in the absolute sense of what God designed it to be] and godliness [reverence, moral chastity] through the knowledge of him that hath called us to glory [exalted state of splendor] and virtue [excellence in purity, thought and feeling].
> —2 PETER 1:3

God has called us to His glory and virtue, a high calling—so high that it cannot be reached if God didn't also provide us the means or the tools required to do so. His divine power is given for the purpose of completely restoring us to be the person we were created to be from the foundation of the world.

The first area of restoration we will consider is that of healing. The ministry of Jesus will be briefly reviewed and then we'll follow how Jesus transferred His healing ministry to the twelve, then to the seventy, and finally to the church onward to today. At the conclusion of this section, you'll need to make a decision regarding the question: "Does God still heal today?" Once that question is out of the way so the Spirit is not grieved, then God will be able to complete the work He desires to do in your midst.

What was the primary motive behind Jesus Christ's mission to this world? It was simply to destroy the works of the devil. These works were enticements to mankind to sin resulting in their captivity, infirmity, and afflictions. With this as a premise, it will make more sense as to why most of the power encounters with the Holy Spirit, including many of the spiritual gifts given to the church, have to do with warfare and destroying the works of the devil.

> He that committeth sin is of the devil; for the devil sinneth from the beginning. For this purpose the Son of God was manifested, that he might destroy the works of the devil.
>
> —1 JOHN 3:8

The battle against the works of the devil will continue until the end of the tribulation. At the end of the Millennium where there will be a short uprising again by the devil and then he is cast into the bottomless pit and the battle will be done. In the mean time we are in warfare along with Jesus, the army General, providing the weapons of our warfare to destroy the devil's strongholds. These weapons are spiritual, and they were established, thanks to the work of Jesus Christ on the cross and His victory over death.

Jesus demonstrates the purging of evil spirits in order to heal disease. He heals the woman with the bowed back by purging her of the spirit of infirmity by which Satan had bound her for eighteen years.

> Behold, there was a woman which had a spirit of infirmity eighteen years, and was bowed together, and could in no wise lift up herself. And when Jesus saw her, he called her to him, and said unto her, Woman, thou art loosed from thine infirmity. And he laid his hands on her: and immediately she was made straight, and glorified God.... Ought not this woman, being a daughter of Abraham, whom Satan hath bound, lo, these eighteen years, be loosed from this bond on the sabbath day?
>
> —LUKE 13:11–13, 16

To be *bound* is the term Jesus used to describe the relationship between the person and the unclean spirit that resulted in the debilitating disease. If Satan bound a person to an infirmity, Jesus would break the captive free by commanding her to be loosed.

Jesus fulfilled prophecy in using His power to cast out evil spirits. That work wasn't available in the Old Testament times and was used as one of the signs to identify the Messiah when He came. He did it with His Word only. The devils must obey the words of Jesus.

> They brought unto him many that were possessed with devils: and he cast out the spirits with his word, and healed all that were sick: That it might

be fulfilled which was spoken by Esaias the prophet, saying, Himself took
our infirmities, and bare our sicknesses.

—MATTHEW 8:16–17

As this was a fulfillment of prophecy, it is pivotal to consider just how Jesus
took our infirmities and bare our sicknesses. He did so very simply by using
His word to cast out the spirits that manifested in the disease.

In Jesus' healing ministry to a dumb man, what did He do to bring about
the healing? He cast out the spirit so the fellow was free to speak again.

> As they went out, behold, they brought to him a dumb man possessed
> with a devil. And when the devil was cast out, the dumb spake: and the
> multitudes marvelled, saying, It was never so seen in Israel.
>
> —MATTHEW 9:32–33

The early church understood the oppression of the devil and knew it resulted
in sickness—physically, mentally, and spiritually. The healing required the
power of the Holy Spirit to recover and restore people who were taken captive
by the enemy in war.

> How God anointed Jesus of Nazareth with the Holy Ghost and with
> power: who went about doing good, and healing [restore physically, men-
> tally and spiritually] all that were oppressed [controlled or taken captive]
> of the devil; for God was with him.
>
> —ACTS 10:38

After a period of time Jesus equipped the
twelve disciples to heal the sick, and they did
so in the same manner He did, except for one
difference—they would have to do so not in
their name but in the name of Jesus Christ.
When a believer is empowered to heal the sick

> Revival will happen
> once judgment and
> repentance begins at
> the house of the Lord.

and raise the dead, he'll have to know how to use the weapon of such warfare and that is to purge unclean spirits.

> And when he had called unto him his twelve disciples, he gave them power
> against unclean spirits, to cast them out, and to heal all manner of sickness
> and all manner of disease....And as ye go, preach, saying, The kingdom
> of heaven is at hand. Heal the sick, cleanse the lepers, raise the dead, cast
> out devils: freely [granted without obligation] ye have received, freely give.
>
> —MATTHEW 10:1, 7–8

It is interesting that Jesus told them to give in the same manner they
received, and that was without paying for it and without obligation.

When the extent of Christ's ministry had expanded, He then sent out
a group of seventy believers equipping them to heal the sick. The seventy
reported back that through their ministry of healing the devils were subject to
the name of Jesus as well.

> After these things the Lord appointed other seventy also, and sent them two and two before his face into every city and place, whither he himself would come....Heal the sick that are therein, and say unto them, The kingdom of God is come nigh unto you....And the seventy returned again with joy, saying, Lord, even the devils are subject unto us through thy name.
>
> —Luke 10:1, 9, 17

Then towards the end of the earthly ministry, Jesus laid out His commission for the church, which was to preach the gospel and that will be accompanied by purging of evil spirits, healing, and divine protection.

The Great Commission is usually abbreviated to include only the first two of the five verses of the proclamation in Mark 16. Why may the last three verses, 17–20, be left out? Well firstly there is a kingdom that doesn't want this to happen and a comparison of modern scripture will show that even the Bibles used in some churches omit the complete charge given by Christ. These modern translations will excuse the omission stating that the manuscripts they used didn't have it. Secondly, I think a lot of preaching reflects only the experience of the leaders and doesn't necessarily compare their experience to what the Word says will happen. Once again the first two verses can be accomplished without the miraculous power of God; and where the miraculous works of God occur to give witness to the veracity of the ministry, they are strangely, but not surprisingly, omitted.

God is not a respecter of persons; He desires to heal everyone. You qualify as an "everyone"!

> And he said unto them, Go ye into all the world, and preach the gospel to every creature. He that believeth and is baptized shall be saved; but he that believeth not shall be damned. *And these signs shall follow them that believe*; In my name shall they cast out devils; they shall speak with new tongues; They shall take up serpents; and if they drink any deadly thing, it shall not hurt them; they shall lay hands on the sick, and they shall recover....And they went forth, and preached every where, the Lord working with them, and confirming the word with signs following. Amen.
>
> —Mark 16:15–18, 20

Revival will happen once judgment and repentance begins at the house of the Lord. If the author is in error, you will not see such signs and wonders performed through the disciples and the church subsequent to the delivery of the Great Commission. If there is no further evidence then the author is a liar and a false teacher, but if there is more evidence and teaching concerning such, we have reason to examine why. Are you with me? This is not a condemnation to the church but only a call to recognition and repentance so that God can work through a body that does not grieve the work of the Spirit.

In the letter to the church at Corinth, Paul lists out how God would equip the church through the Holy Spirit to do its work.

> And God hath set some in the church, first apostles, secondarily prophets, thirdly teachers, after that miracles, then gifts of healings, helps, governments, diversities of tongues.
>
> —1 CORINTHIANS 12:28

One of the foundational practices of the church is to heal the sick and free those vexed with unclean spirits. The church is to be the "go to" place to be healed. If the church is not doing this, there is no hope for freedom. All we can hope for is that science will come up with some chemical management tools for our many diseases of mind and body.

As the symptom of infirmity in our lives gives testimony that we may have a spiritual root problem, accordingly the existence of as many diseases in the church as in the "unchurched" tells us that many of our churches have a spiritual problem.

The writer of the Hebrews didn't want the church to forget to teach and rejoice over the great salvation we have; it is a salvation that not only saves but also delivers and performs miracles. Moses needed a rod to perform miracles, but we have the Holy Ghost within to do even greater wonders—something not to be neglected or forgotten.

> How shall we escape, if we neglect so great salvation; which at the first began to be spoken by the Lord, and was confirmed unto us by them that heard him; God also bearing them witness, both with signs and wonders, and with divers miracles, and gifts of the Holy Ghost, according to his own will?
>
> —HEBREWS 2:3–4

Who are "them that heard him"? They are the ministers of the early church that were carrying out the Great Commission. Their authenticity was sealed by the Lord's touch of miraculous works that these gospel workers could not possibly do in their own strength. I am not putting down teaching or preaching whatsoever, but rather saying that the Lord authenticates them as originating from Him through works of power.

The Lord says, "I change not," and, "I am always in the great business of salvation, which includes healing and deliverance." God is not a respecter of persons; He desires to heal everyone. You qualify as an "everyone"!

> There came also a multitude out of the cities round about unto Jerusalem, bringing sick folks, and them which were vexed with unclean spirits: and they were healed every one.
>
> —ACTS 5:16

Philip had credibility and much fruit as an evangelist as he taught the Scriptures first, then signs followed the teaching of the Word, just as Jesus said in His commissioning in Mark 16:15–20.

The Book of Acts is the seminary for kingdom workers with instruction through example and word of how the church is to be built and maintained.

> Then Philip went down to the city of Samaria, and preached Christ unto them. And the people with one accord gave heed unto those things which Philip spake, hearing and seeing the miracles, which he did. For unclean spirits, crying with loud voice, came out of many that were possessed with them: and many taken with palsies, and that were lame, were healed. And there was great joy in that city.
>
> —Acts 8:5–8

If any are still skeptical, the next verse will be even harder to take. We know the work that Jesus did in His short tour of ministry and that many miracles evidenced the One who commissioned Him. Jesus proclaimed that not only would believers do as He did, but they would do even greater works. The Holy Spirit of God will perform these greater works through us.

> Verily, verily, I say unto you, He that believeth on me, the works that I do shall he do also; and greater works than these shall he do; because I go unto my Father. And whatsoever ye shall ask in my name, that will I do, that the Father may be glorified in the Son. If ye shall ask any thing in my name, I will do it.
>
> —John 14:12–14

When did Jesus go to the Father? Ten days before the church was baptized in the Holy Spirit. Believe the Word! He says, "Not only will you do what I did but you'll do greater works!" We know His Word is good. Do we believe on Him? Do we receive the Word as the commandment of God?

I'll stop here for a second and remind you of the decision you need to make. Answer the question posed earlier: "Does God still heal today?"

Power to be witnesses

> But ye shall receive power, after that the Holy Ghost is come upon you: and ye shall be witnesses unto me both in Jerusalem, and in all Judaea, and in Samaria, and unto the uttermost part of the earth.
>
> —Acts 1:8

Power to hope

It is interesting that we cannot even hope if the Holy Spirit did not empower us to believe.

> Now the God of hope fill you with all joy and peace in believing, that ye may abound in hope, through the power of the Holy Ghost.
>
> —Romans 15:13

Power to love

As I set out to write this chapter, I thought this would be the easiest to do, as I had already studied the gifts at length and ministered around the filling of the Holy Spirit. I thought all I would need to do is just summarize each gift with corresponding scripture and I'd wrap this book up. But for many weeks I was restrained in my heart, and I began to realize that though all the gifts are so very important for the work of the ministry, there is something even more important to seek the Lord for. My tendency was to study the gifts and then to count them as though they were spiritual inventory. I found in my heart of hearts that I was comparing myself with others and would be puffed up if I felt I had a greater inventory than another believer. Or if I felt someone else had more, I would have a jealous thing come over me where I would secretly glory in their eventual demise. I'm sure you're saying, "You mean we read this long book all this way only to find out at this late stage just how nasty the author can be?" Spiritual gifts are just *that*—they are gifts given freely of the Holy Spirit as He determines the need in the church. So why would I glory in them as though I did something to earn them?

Howbeit, we'll need to look briefly at 1 Corinthians 12 to show how the gifts pertain to the warfare we, as soldiers, are engaged in. The gifts are spiritual weapons that either aid in the recovery of those taken captive by the devil, restore those afflicted by the devil, or help us to be overcomers in resisting the devil and living an abundant life as we look forward to the coming of the kingdom of God.

> For to one is given by the Spirit the word of wisdom; to another the word of knowledge by the same Spirit; To another faith by the same Spirit; to another the gifts of healing by the same Spirit; To another the working of miracles; to another prophecy; to another discerning of spirits; to another divers kinds of tongues; to another the interpretation of tongues: But all these worketh that one and the selfsame Spirit, dividing to every man severally as he will....And God hath set some in the church, first apostles, secondarily prophets, thirdly teachers, after that miracles, then gifts of healings, helps, governments, diversities of tongues.
> —1 CORINTHIANS 12:8–11, 28

Paul then asks the question, are all apostles? Are all teachers? And so on, to illustrate the point that obviously not all have those gifts but they may have some of them.

> Are all apostles? are all prophets? are all teachers? are all workers of miracles? Have all the gifts of healing? do all speak with tongues? do all interpret?
> —1 CORINTHIANS 12:29–30

But Paul is trying to lead us somewhere beyond the gifts listed above to something so much more that is available to every sanctified, single-minded believer. The next phrase in verse 31, "But covet earnestly the best gifts," is often thought to refer back to what was previously said, and so we strive for which one of the many gifts we feel is somehow more highly regarded by God. Part of the problem is where the chapter break was placed. You see, the Bible was originally written without chapter and verse. They were later added by theologians simply to help us find a particular passage easier; but they are not necessarily inspired of the Spirit.

I believe Paul is telling us that these gifts are important but for us not to focus on them as though they are the most important and most necessary for the church because they are not. The Spirit of God gives those gifts as He wills, but the next gift is the one we all were created with and it is the truest thing about us even though it may be currently hindered due to sin. Because it can be hindered, the next verse accurately tells us to pursue the greatest gift with wholehearted zeal. Paul tells us with all he has said up to that point, he now wants us to realize the more excellent way—the purpose for which you need to be devoted to above all else.

> But covet earnestly [pursue with zeal] the best [more profitable, benevo-lently good] gifts [extraordinary powers that are beyond human abili-ties]: and yet [so now consider this] shew [expose to your eyes and heart] I unto you [accordingly] a more excellent [exceedingly beyond measure] way [course of conduct].
> —1 CORINTHIANS 12:31

In the event your are wondering what the "more excellent way" that he has yet to talk about, all you have to do is keep on reading. Paul tells us that we can have the special gifts listed above like tongues, prophecy, knowledge, understanding, interpretations, faith, helps, and even martyrdom; but if we don't have "agape," the rest mean nothing.

> Though I speak with the tongues of men and of angels, and have not charity [agape], I am become as sounding brass, or a tinkling cymbal. And though I have the gift of prophecy, and understand all mysteries, and all knowledge; and though I have all faith, so that I could remove mountains, and have not charity [agape], I am nothing. And though I bestow all my goods to feed the poor, and though I give my body to be burned, and have not charity [agape], it profiteth me nothing.
> —1 CORINTHIANS 13:1–3

Jesus did great things for the kingdom; and He makes a most outrageous statement that once He goes to the Father, the Holy Spirit will do even greater works through His beloved followers of the Way.

It is clear we can even perform miraculous things and yet be in rebellion to the only com-mands we are to get right—to agape God and to agape our neighbor as our self.

All the gifts, except for one, will cease, as they are essentially for the sanctification of the believer in the church and will no longer be required once God draws the curtain closed on the church age.

> Charity [*agape*] never faileth: but whether there be prophecies, they shall fail; whether there be tongues, they shall cease; whether there be knowledge, it shall vanish away.
> —1 CORINTHIANS 13:8

Even faith and hope will cease, as once we are in the kingdom of God, the object of our hope and substance of our faith has materialized, leaving only one gift that we need for eternity—agape.

> And now abideth faith, hope, charity [agape], these three; but the greatest of these is charity [*agape*].
> —1 CORINTHIANS 13:13

I believe we need to know what is the most important thing for us to accomplish in our dusty lives; and to make sure that, even if we only get that one thing right, it is so we are found to be in favor with God at judgment. Agape opens the gates of the kingdom of God.

> When we are walking in agape, our prayers will be aligned with the will and heart of God already so that our prayers will be answered and the Son will be glorified.

What one thing distinguishes us as Jesus' disciples? Is it the miracles? Is it the three point sermons? Is it the prophecy? Is it the veracity of tongues, or perhaps even gifts to the poor? The only gift Satan cannot duplicate or make counterfeit is "agape." Such divine love emanating through the life of a believer is how the Son and the Father are glorified in us.

> Jesus said, Now is the Son of man glorified [true identity and purpose revealed] and God is glorified [the love of God is revealed through the works He would do through His son to recover and restore man] in him. If God be glorified in him, God shall also glorify him in himself, and shall straightway glorify him. Little children, yet a little while I am with you. Ye shall seek me: and as I said unto the Jews, Whither I go, ye cannot come; so now I say to you. A new commandment I give unto you, That ye love [*agapao*] one another; as I have loved [*agapao*] you, that ye also love [*agapao*] one another. By this shall all men know that ye are my disciples, if ye have love [*agape*] one to another.
> —JOHN 13:31–35

At the conclusion of His ministry, Christ gave the Great Commission and, even of greater importance, at the same time He reinforced again to us the great commandment as His strongest desire for us. Both the Great Commission and the great commandment require considerable power beyond us to fulfill. They are not easy assignments that we can "just fake it until we make it" through carnal efforts.

Jesus did great things for the kingdom; and He makes a most outrageous statement that once He goes to the Father, the Holy Spirit will do even greater works through His beloved followers of the Way. There are, however, two conditions for the work of God to manifest in such a great way. Firstly, when we pray we ask the Father in Jesus' name. Secondly, we keep His commandments. Our prayers are not directed to the Holy Spirit or to Jesus, but to our Father in the name of Jesus. In that manner the Father is glorified in His Son. Now you know Jesus' commandments to agape, and if you are in rebellion to them and ask anyway, you may be presuming upon the grace of God.

> If perfect love [agape] casts out fear what else will it do?

> Verily, verily, I say unto you, He that believeth on me, the works that I do shall he do also; and greater works than these shall he do; because I go unto my Father. And whatsoever ye shall ask in my name, that will I do, that the Father may be glorified in the Son. If ye shall ask any thing in my name, I will do it. If ye love [*agapao*] me, keep my commandments. And I will pray the Father, and he shall give you another Comforter [the Holy Spirit], that he may abide with you for ever; Even the Spirit of truth.
> —JOHN 14:12–17

Hence is the emphasis on the obedience to the debt of love as we've considered in Corinthians 13. Many believers use the term frequently that they "walk in the Spirit," which is a true statement. But we must be aware that the Spirit of God can depart from us and we perceive it not, as Samson experienced once the Philistines cut his hair and the basis of his strength was now gone. Consider using the phrase, "I walk in agape," or, "I walk in my Father's love." The interesting thing about that is as soon as our love becomes fickle and unpredictable, we know we have strayed from Him. As soon as we repent and do first works, His love will increase and abound once again. I believe that the terms "walk in the Spirit" and "walk in agape" are synonymous; but one term is over used in religious culture and is seldom challenged. When I profess my desire to walk in agape, I am accountable to a very high standard of godliness. It is interesting that people know immediately what such a stand should look like. When we are walking in agape, our prayers will be aligned with the will and heart of God already so that our prayers will be answered and the Son will be glorified.

Is our self still alive?

The apostle John, who no doubt understood the love of our Father very well, further specifies that if we do not die to self and are not merciful, we don't have the agape of the Father expressed in us; and then when we pray our heart will restrain us until the unclearness is purged. I find that when I recognize and deal with the unclearness within me, my subsequent prayer usually changes, as my impure and selfish motives have now been exposed so I can approach my Father with a pure heart.

> Hereby perceive we the love [*agape*] of God, because he laid down his life for us: and we ought to lay down our lives for the brethren. But whoso hath this world's good, and seeth his brother have need, and shutteth up his bowels of compassion from him, how dwelleth the love [*agape*] of God in him? My little children, let us not love in word, neither in tongue; but in deed and in truth. And hereby we know that we are of the truth, and shall assure our hearts before him. For if our heart condemn [finds fault or uncleanness] us, God is greater than our heart, and knoweth all things. Beloved, if our heart condemn us not, then have we confidence toward God. And whatsoever we ask, we receive of him, because we keep his commandments, and do those things that are pleasing in his sight. And this is his commandment, That we should believe on the name of his Son Jesus Christ, and love one another, as he gave us commandment. And he that keepeth his commandments dwelleth in him, and he in him. And hereby we know that he abideth in us, by the Spirit which he hath given us.
> —1 JOHN 3:16–24

Is there any question that we receive whatever we ask if we keep His commandment of agape? This is the more excellent way and this is the best gift, which we are to covet. After all, if perfect love [*agape*] casts out fear, what else will it do? It is in the walk of agape that we'll see the promise of Jesus fulfilled where we'll do even greater works than He did on earth.

If we are walking about or ministering under the umbrella of our own name, man glorifies himself; and God would that no man would glory in his presence. A man that has died to self cannot receive the glory, and a dead man cannot be proud. "Jesus must increase and we must decrease," John the Baptist proclaimed. The Lord delights to heal and restore when it is known that the messenger, the ambassador, will not accept the credit and the glory for the mighty work the King of kings did.

> When Jesus heard that, he said, This sickness is not unto death, but for the glory of God, that the Son of God might be glorified thereby.
> —JOHN 11:4

Our purified temple ushers in the empowering of the Holy Ghost to do the mighty works of God, thus glorifying our maker and our owner.

> What? know ye not that your body is the temple of the Holy Ghost which is in you, which ye have of God, and ye are not your own? For ye are bought with a price: therefore glorify God in your body, and in your spirit, which are God's.
> —1 CORINTHIANS 6:19–20

If God is withholding good fruit, it is only as a drastic measure to get our attention so we will yield to the vine, Jesus, in reverential submission. Our sin and rebellion cause a breach in the love stream so fruit cannot be yielded as God purposes and instead Satan's kingdom receives a growth spurt.

> Herein is my Father glorified, that ye bear much fruit; so shall ye be my disciples.
>
> —John 15:8

THREE STAGES IN OUR RELATIONSHIP WITH THE HOLY SPIRIT

I believe the Word teaches three stages in the relationship a person has with the Holy Spirit. These three stages are highlighted by the use of three different prepositions in the original language. The first passage considered contains the first two prepositions, *in* and *with*.

> Even the Spirit of truth; whom the world cannot receive, because it seeth him not, neither knoweth him: but ye know him; for he dwelleth *with* [*para*; alongside] you, and shall be *in* [*en*; within, as to be pregnant] you.
>
> —John 14:17, emphasis Added

The Holy Spirit was *with* (*para*) us prior to our conversion, walking alongside convicting us of sin and pointing us to Jesus.

> It is expedient for you that I go away: for if I go not away, the Comforter will not come unto you; but if I depart, I will send him unto you. And when he is come, he will reprove the world of sin, and of righteousness, and of judgment of sin, because they believe not on me.
>
> —John 16:7–9

At the moment we accepted Jesus into our lives the Holy Spirit moved *in* (*en*). He is a gentleman and will not force His way until the door is opened and He is welcomed.

This was the same relationship that Jesus had with the Holy Spirit when He was still a child. With the Holy Spirit "*en*" Him, Jesus grew strong in spirit and in wisdom and grace. Perhaps today much of devout Christianity is at this level of relationship with the Holy Spirit.

> And the child grew, and waxed strong *in* [*en*] spirit, filled with wisdom: and the grace of God was upon him.
>
> —Luke 2:40, emphasis added

God has something more—the beautiful empowering through the *epi* or *upon* relationship. This special relationship with the Holy Spirit was required even for Jesus before He could start His public ministry. Note that Jesus already had the Spirit of God *in* Him since a child; but now at the age of thirty, a deeper level of the relationship was required and from here on Jesus performed many miracles.

> And John bare record, saying, I saw the Spirit descending from heaven like a dove, and it abode *upon* [*epi*] him. And I knew him not: but he that sent me to baptize with water, the same said unto me, *Upon* [*epi*]

whom thou shalt see the Spirit descending, and remaining *on* [*epi*] him, the same is he which baptizeth [overflow in abundance, to identify with] with the Holy Ghost.

—JOHN 1:32–33, EMPHASIS ADDED

Now a word in preparation of what may come your way after this further work of the Holy Spirit: we spoke of infirmity, afflictions, tribulation, and temptations used of God to expose any uncleanness so that they may be identified and purged in order for the temple of the Holy Spirit to be restored and fit for the Master's use. Such chastening happens in a wilderness experience, such as what happened to Jesus after He had this incredible baptism of the Holy Spirit and He heard the voice of His Father for the first time. Immediately Jesus was driven into the wilderness to be tempted for forty days by Satan. I believe because Jesus stood strong against the devil, His testing was limited to only forty days.

> And it came to pass in those days, that Jesus came from Nazareth of Galilee, and was baptized of John in Jordan. And straightway coming up out of the water, he saw the heavens opened, and the Spirit like a dove descending upon him: And there came a voice from heaven, saying, Thou art my beloved Son, in whom I am well pleased. And immediately the Spirit driveth him into the wilderness. And he was there in the wilderness forty days, tempted of Satan; and was with the wild beasts; and the angels ministered unto him.
>
> —MARK 1:9–13

After briefly considering the relationship of Jesus Christ with the Holy Spirit, how did that compare with the disciples of Jesus? Well, first we see Jesus giving the disciples the Holy Ghost, which gave them the initial power to minister to people bringing them to repentance and forgiveness of their sins, but nothing further.

> Then said Jesus to them again, Peace be unto you: as my Father hath sent me, even so send I you. And when he had said this, he breathed on them, and saith unto them, Receive ye the Holy Ghost: Whose soever sins ye remit, they are remitted unto them; and whose soever sins ye retain, they are retained.
>
> —JOHN 20:21–23

The ministry of the disciples to this point would be similar to that of John the Baptist, where he preached repentance and confession of sin followed by baptism. We have no record of John the Baptist healing or doing works of miracles, and neither did the disciples until later.

> John did baptize in the wilderness, and preach the baptism of repentance for the remission of sins. And there went out unto him all the land of Judaea, and they of Jerusalem, and were all baptized of him in the river of Jordan, confessing their sins.
>
> —MARK 1:4–5

The Gospel of Luke records that John had the Spirit *in* (*en*) him, but he would not go beyond that in his lifetime.

> And the child grew, and waxed strong *in* [*en*] spirit, and was in the deserts till the day of his shewing unto Israel.
> —LUKE 1:80, EMPHASIS ADDED

Back to the disciples: Jesus blew on them to receive the Holy Ghost, but now tells them to go to Jerusalem and wait for the Spirit to come *upon* (*epi*) them so they could fulfil the Great Commission.

> And, behold, I send the promise of my Father upon you: but tarry ye in the city of Jerusalem, until ye be endued [clothed] with power from on high.
> —LUKE 24:49

Mark refers also to Christ prophesying over the disciples, and he includes the miraculous signs and wonders that would now follow their ministry once they receive the Holy Spirit upon them.

They are still following John the Baptist with "repent and be baptized," but the remainder of the Great Commission will be left undone; so people will be saved but may remain captive to disease and iniquity.

> And he said unto them, Go ye into all the world, and preach the gospel to every creature. He that believeth and is baptized shall be saved; but he that believeth not shall be damned. And these signs shall follow them that believe; In my name shall they cast out devils; they shall speak with new tongues; They shall take up serpents; and if they drink any deadly thing, it shall not hurt them; they shall lay hands on the sick, and they shall recover.
> —MARK 16:15–18

In Acts 2, according to the prophecy of Jesus Christ, the disciples now receive the Holy Spirit *upon* them and a miraculous sign provides evidence of what happened.

> And when the day of Pentecost was fully come, they were all with one accord in one place. And suddenly there came a sound from heaven as of a rushing mighty wind, and it filled all the house where they were sitting. And there appeared unto them cloven tongues like as of fire, and it sat *upon* [*epi*] each of them. And they were all filled with the Holy Ghost, and began to speak with other tongues, as the Spirit gave them utterance.
> —ACTS 2:1–4, EMPHASIS ADDED

Validate

Once we see a work of the Spirit in the church, we are to verify and support it in the word, which Peter does as he validates the signs and wonders by prophesy from the prophet Joel.

But this is that which was spoken by the prophet Joel [2:28–32] And it shall come to pass in the last days, saith God, I will pour out of my Spirit upon all flesh: and your sons and your daughters shall prophesy, and your young men shall see visions, and your old men shall dream dreams: And on my servants and on my handmaidens I will pour out in those days of my Spirit; and they shall prophesy: And I will shew wonders in heaven above, and signs in the earth beneath; blood, and fire, and vapour of smoke: The sun shall be turned into darkness, and the moon into blood, before that great and notable day of the Lord come: And it shall come to pass, that whosoever shall call on the name of the Lord shall be saved.

—ACTS 2:16–21

> The weapons of our warfare are mighty through God in pulling down strongholds and reconciling men to the person they were created from the foundation of the world to be.

There is a movement in the church that claims that the gifts of the Holy Spirit are not for today but were only to kick-start the early church. Well, rather than weigh into their experience-based doctrine, how about we just consider what the Word says? The books of Acts and Joel both say that God will pour out His spirit in "the last days." What "days" are they referring to? Well, I'm glad you asked. The particular signs we are to look for, which would identify the days of this work of the Holy Spirit are that the sun will be turned to darkness and the moon to blood. So the gifts of the Holy Spirit are required and in effect until these signs take place. The only time these signs occur in the Scripture since the start of the church is in Revelation 6, which places us towards the end of the Tribulation period and just prior to the second coming of Jesus Christ. The sixth seal unleashes a major earthquake, which darkens the sun, and the moon becomes as blood.

> And I beheld when he had opened the sixth seal, and, lo, there was a great earthquake; and the sun became black as sackcloth of hair, and the moon became as blood.
>
> —REVELATION 6:12

The Holy Spirit, knowing that there would be much controversy today about the work of the gifts, prompts Peter to repeat that the gifts of the Holy Ghost will continue to the "children that are afar off." These children are all those who God calls and are saved, that would be us today. If the gifts were soon to cease, Peter would not have used the term "afar off," which is translated from the Greek word *makran*, meaning "a great way" or "far hence."

> Then Peter said unto them, Repent, and be baptized every one of you in the name of Jesus Christ for the remission of sins, and ye shall receive the

gift of the Holy Ghost. For the promise is unto you, and to your children, and to all that are afar off, even as many as the Lord our God shall call.

—Acts 2:38–39

Whose disciple are you?

If we grieve the Holy Spirit, He will not do the miraculous work in our midst due to doubt and unbelief. Where does that leave those that do not believe in the continued work of the Holy Spirit, including healing, miracles, prophecy, and such like? Would they not be likened to the disciples, including John the Baptist, prior to the commencement of the church where they have the Holy Spirit *in* (*en*) them? They are still following John the Baptist with "repent and be baptized," but the remainder of the Great Commission will be left undone; so people will be saved but may remain captive to disease and iniquity. Whose disciple do we want to be; John the Baptist's or Christ's?

> I indeed baptize you with water unto repentance: but he that cometh after me is mightier than I, whose shoes I am not worthy to bear: he shall baptize you with the Holy Ghost, and with fire: Whose fan is in his hand, and he will throughly purge his floor, and gather his wheat into the garner; but he will burn up the chaff with unquenchable fire.
>
> —Matthew 3:11–12

Jesus needed the baptism of the Holy Spirit prior to starting His ministry, and He said the same is true for us. "After the Holy Spirit is come upon (*epi*) you, then you'll have power to go out and be witnesses." (See Acts 1:8.) We are mistaken when we think of witnessing as something that we *do*, when in reality it is something that we *are*. It is living the life fully empowered to be overcomers and great lovers.

The disciples had to wait in the upper room for several days until they were empowered before they went out to represent the Father. What would happen in our land if all ministers of the gospel had to hold off from their ministries until there was evidence that they were baptized with the Holy Spirit of power, truth, and the more excellent way of agape?

> This I say then, Walk in the Spirit, and ye shall not fulfil the lust of the flesh.
>
> —Galatians 5:16

What does a ministry look like that fulfills the Great Commission Christ initiated? Following Philip's preaching the captives were set free, the sick were healed through "first works," and revival hit the city.

> Then Philip went down to the city of Samaria, and preached Christ unto them. And the people with one accord gave heed unto those things which Philip spake, hearing and seeing the miracles which he did. For unclean spirits, crying with loud voice, came out of many that were pos-

sessed with them: and many taken with palsies, and that were lame, were
healed. And there was great joy in that city.

—Acts 8:5–8

The weapons of our warfare are mighty through God in pulling down
strongholds and reconciling men to the person they were created from the
foundation of the world to be.

At some point after the conversion of these Samaritans through Philip's
ministry, Peter and John came and prayed that these new believers would go
deeper in receiving the Holy Spirit *upon* (*epi*) them. This is clearly a subsequent work of the Holy Spirit in addition to what happened at the time of
conversion.

> Now when the apostles which were at Jerusalem heard that Samaria had
> received the word of God, they sent unto them Peter and John: Who,
> when they were come down, prayed for them, that they might receive the
> Holy Ghost: (For as yet he was fallen upon none of them: only they were
> baptized in the name of the Lord Jesus.) Then laid they their hands on
> them, and they received the Holy Ghost.
>
> —Acts 8:14–17

The parentheses in verse 16 were placed there by the writer of Acts to give
commentary on what happened to these believers of Samaria. They were converted and baptized in the name of the Lord
Jesus, which would be similar to John the
Baptist's ministry, but didn't enter into the
third stage of the relationship with the Holy
Spirit.

A similar event happened in Ephesus' and it
is important to have more than one example so
we can be sure of our doctrine. These people
had repented and were converted by disciples of John the Baptist. When Paul
came along he knew to ask about their relationship with the Holy Spirit. These
new believers didn't even know what he was talking about, so Paul taught
them and prayed with them and through the laying on of hands they received
the Holy Spirit "upon" them.

> Paul is very serious
> about this and he can't
> understand why folks
> would have such a
> resistance to the work
> of the Holy Spirit.

> Paul having passed through the upper coasts came to Ephesus: and
> finding certain disciples, He said unto them, Have ye received the Holy
> Ghost since ye believed? And they said unto him, We have not so much
> as heard whether there be any Holy Ghost. And he said unto them, Unto
> what then were ye baptized? And they said, Unto John's baptism. Then
> said Paul, John verily baptized with the baptism of repentance, saying
> unto the people, that they should believe on him which should come
> after him, that is, on Christ Jesus. When they heard this, they were baptized in the name of the Lord Jesus. And when Paul had laid his hands

upon them, the Holy Ghost came *on* [*epi*] them; and they spake with
tongues, and prophesied.

—ACTS 19:1–6

Paul asked these believers if they had received the Holy Spirit since their
conversion. They replied, "We didn't know there was such a thing." In a little
while, I'll be asking you the same question. Friends, have you received the
empowering of the Holy Spirit since you became Christians? Are you experiencing torrents of living water bursting forth from your life, or just a trickle?

> He that believeth on me, as the scripture hath said, out of his belly shall
> flow rivers of living water. (But this spake he of the Spirit, which they
> that believe on him should receive: for the Holy Ghost was not yet given;
> because that Jesus was not yet glorified.)
>
> —JOHN 7:38–39

John wrote this book several years after the fact and had the advantage of
hindsight to explain what Jesus said; and thus verse 39 is in parentheses, as it is
his commentary. John explained that Jesus was talking about the empowering
of the believer's life by the Holy Spirit.

Beswitched?

Paul, who was never one to dance around an important topic, said to the
believers in Galatia that they were foolish in believing the false doctrine of
some dude over the truth of the written Word. He went on to tell them that
they had it so good at the beginning, as the Spirit of God was with them; but
now they wanted to do church in the flesh, leaving the Spirit outside.

> O foolish Galatians, who hath bewitched [brought evil upon] you, that
> ye should not obey the truth, before whose eyes Jesus Christ hath been
> evidently set forth, crucified among you? This only would I learn of you,
> Received ye the Spirit by the works of the law, or by the hearing of faith?
> Are ye so foolish? having begun in the Spirit, are ye now made perfect
> by the flesh?
>
> —GALATIANS 3:1–3

It is foolish to "do church," denying the full power of the Holy Spirit! I
have another rant from Paul to show you.

> Ye stiffnecked and uncircumcised in heart and ears, ye do always resist
> the Holy Ghost: as your fathers did, so do ye.
>
> —ACTS 7:51

Do you get the idea that the early church had the same difficulty as we do
today in accepting the empowering of the Spirit of God? Paul is very serious
about this and he can't understand why folks would have such a resistance to
the work of the Holy Spirit. Paul isn't done yet; in fact he says we are to part
company with religious performing folks who block the power of our God.

Having a form of godliness [reverence], but denying [rejecting even to one's own detriment] the power thereof: from such turn away.

—2 TIMOTHY 3:5

Have you received all that God has in mind for you?

My question is, friends: "Have you received the gift of the Holy Spirit since you have become a Christ follower?"

The Scripture gives us a couple ways to receive the gift of the Holy Spirit and the first is simply to ask:

If ye then, being evil, know how to give good gifts unto your children: how much more shall your heavenly Father give the Holy Spirit to them that ask him?

—LUKE 11:13

Friends, have you received the empowering of the Holy Spirit since you became Christians? Are you experiencing torrents of living water bursting forth from your life—or just a trickle?

A Prayer to Help You in Your Quest to Receive the Holy Spirit

Father, thank You for saving me. Thank You for salvation. Thank You for forgiving me. Forgive me for grieving Your Holy Spirit through doubt, unbelief, and dead works. I'm born again, and I want to be a helpmeet for Jesus. I want to be available to the Holy Spirit and I want to do the work of the Father. Father, You said in Your Word that if I ask for the Holy Spirit that You will give Him to me. Father, I am asking in the name of Jesus, give me the Holy Spirit, anoint me to do the good works You have for me, provide the gifts I'll need to do my part in Your kingdom, and, Father, empower me with faith and hope and, most importantly, a full measure of Your agape love.

In addition to praying yourself to receive the Holy Spirit upon you, may also ask those in the body of Christ to lay their hands on you in prayer to receive the Holy Ghost.

Who, when they were come down, prayed for them, that they might receive the Holy Ghost: (For as yet he was fallen upon none of them: only they were baptized in the name of the Lord Jesus.) Then laid they their hands on them, and they received the Holy Ghost.

—ACTS 8:15–17

A Prayer to Pray for Another to Receive This Gift of the Holy Spirit

Father, I bless _____ in the name of the Lord Jesus Christ. If we ask You to give us the Holy Spirit, You will. We are crying out right now for the Holy Ghost to come upon us, in the name of Jesus. Receive the Holy Spirit and be baptized in the Holy Spirit in the name of Jesus. If you believe, you will receive. "God has not given you a spirit of fear, but of power and of love and of a sound mind." Therefore, be not ashamed of the testimony of our Lord!

Perhaps you have already received the outpouring of the Holy Spirit upon you, but through sin or neglect the gifts are no longer working through you. Paul told Timothy to stir them up:

> Wherefore I put thee in remembrance that thou stir up the gift of God, which is in thee by the putting on of my hands.
>
> —2 Timothy 1:6

A Prayer to Stir Up Gifts

In the name of Jesus, be renewed in the power of His might. Any gifts that are in there, in the name of Jesus be stirred up!

If Paul were with you now I believe this would be his closing prayer for you. Rewrite it in first person to be a personal intimate prayer to your Father who delights to hear from you.

> I bow my knees unto the Father of our Lord Jesus Christ, Of whom the whole family in heaven and earth is named, That he would grant you, according to the riches of his glory, to be strengthened with might by his Spirit in the inner man; That Christ may dwell in your hearts by faith; that ye, being rooted and grounded in love, May be able to comprehend with all saints what is the breadth, and length, and depth, and height; And to know the love of Christ, which passeth knowledge, that ye might be filled with all the fulness of God. Now unto him that is able to do exceeding abundantly above all that we ask or think, according to the power that worketh in us, Unto him be glory in the church by Christ Jesus throughout all ages, world without end. Amen.
>
> —Ephesians 3:14–21

NOTES

CHAPTER **5**

GIVE **U**S **T**HIS **D**AY **O**UR **D**AILY **B**READ

1. From website: http://blueletterbible.org/ (accessed January 26, 2011).

CHAPTER **7**

AND **L**EAD **U**S **N**OT INTO **T**EMPTATION, BUT **D**ELIVER **U**S FROM **E**VIL

1. Psychology Wiki, "Thomas Szasz," http://psychology.wikia.com/wiki/Thomas_Szasz (accessed December 10, 2010).

ABOUT THE AUTHOR

Dennis Bank has been teaching the Word of God for thirty years. His teaching is enriched by his experience as a police investigator, a businessman, and a Bible student, along with the successes and failures as a husband and father of three. He has uncovered truths seldom spoken of in church; truths he feels have been long ignored and yet are absolutely essential in order for us to be reconciled to the person we were created from the foundation of the world to be. He is passionate to see the church take back its role as the sole God-ordained destination to recovery, restoration, reconciliation, and healing of the saints.

As a byproduct of his Bible study, Dennis has founded Truth or Coincidence, a media company that produces short, captivating video reports on a variety of topics across the body of Christ. He believes that in addition to faith, we can know that God is who He said He is and will do what He says He will do as the Holy Bible validates archeology, medicine, prophecy, oceanography, biology, astronomy, and mathematics. There is room for the logical and critical thinking minds to know the Bible is the Word of God apart from just being told they have to believe by faith.

Dennis is an engaging speaker for conferences and is currently rewriting his five-day ministry manual for The Strong Tower summit meetings.

CONTACT THE AUTHOR

SHARE@SANCTIPRIZE.COM

TO SEE WHAT ELSE WE ARE DOING, CHECK OUT:

WWW.TRUTHORCOINCIDENCE.COM

PERSONAL NOTES

Personal Notes